Scrimshaw *and* Provenance

Stuart M. Frank

MYSTIC SEAPORT®

The Museum of America and the Sea®

Mystic Seaport is the nation's leading maritime museum. Located along the banks of the historic Mystic River in Mystic, Connecticut, the Museum houses extensive collections representing the material culture of maritime America, and offers educational programs from preschool to postgraduate.

For more information, call us at 888-973-2767 or visit us online at www.mysticseaport.org

Scrimshaw *and* Provenance

A Third Dictionary of Scrimshaw Artists

Stuart M. Frank
Senior Curator, New Bedford Whaling Museum
Director Emeritus, Kendall Whaling Museum

For Mary,
with the love of many years

Mystic Seaport
75 Greenmanville Ave.
Mystic, Connecticut 06355
860-572-0711
www.mysticseaport.org

First edition
Printed in the United States of America

Designed by Bonnie Goff
Morrill, Maine

Printed by Thomson Shore
Dexter, Michigan

ISBN 978-0-939511-36-5

Cataloging-in-Publication Data

Frank, Stuart M.
Scrimshaw and provenance: a third dictionary of scrimshaw artists / Stuart M. Frank — Mystic, Connecticut : Mystic Seaport, ©2013.
380 p. : ill. ; cm. Includes bibliographical references and indexes.

ISBN 978-0-939511-36-5

1. Scrimshaw –Biography- Dictionaries. 1. Title.

NK6022 .F737 2013

TABLE OF CONTENTS

ACKNOWLEDGEMENTS

Grateful acknowledgement is made to the following individuals whose generous help made this volume possible, by submitting scrimshaw for examination, by participating in the national consortium of scrimshaw collectors and scrimshaw historians, by assisting with the research, by providing the names of scrimshaw artists, photographs or descriptions of attributed scrimshaw, biographical and provenance data, bibliographic citations, and other useful information: Joshua Basseches (Harvard Museum of Natural History and Peabody Essex Museum of Salem), Dr. Donald Boger and Mary Boger, Ronald Bourgeault (Northeast Auctions, Portsmouth, New Hampshire), the late William J. Boylhart, Ken Brown (Frank's Fisherman, San Francisco), Craig Bruns (Independence Seaport, Philadelphia), Fred Calabretta (Mystic Seaport), Rod and Becky Cardoza (West Sea Company, San Diego), Dr. Jack H.T. Chang, Tom and Barbara Conley, Ryan M. Cooper, Carl Crossman, Paul Cyr (New Bedford Free Public Library), Dr. Angelo DeFalco, the late H. Richard Dietrich, Jr. (Dietrich American Foundation), Dr. Daniel R. Finamore (Peabody Essex Museum of Salem), Dr. Suzanne Finney, Stephen Fletcher (Skinner's, Marlborough and Boston, Massachusetts), Michael Gerstein, João A. Gomes Vieira, Alan Granby and Janice Hyland (Hyland Granby Antiques, Hyannisport, Massachusetts), Louis Hammond, Ernest Helides, Robert and Nina Hellman (Nina Hellman Antiques, Nantucket), David R. Hillier (Antiques Associates at West Townsend, Massachusetts), Henry Hornblower III, Llewellyn Howland III, Gregg Hurwitz, Andrew Jacobson, Dr. Brock Jobe (Winterthur Museum), Paula E. Johnson and Dr. Paul F. Johnston (National Museum of American History, Smithsonian Institution), Dr. Susan A. Lebo, Judith Navas Lund, Rider McDowell, Sam McDowell, the late Paul Madden, Charles A. Manghis, Dr. Kenneth R. Martin, Frederick Mitchell (Whalemen's Shipping List, New Bedford), Hope Morrill (Cape Cod National Seashore), Niles Parker (Nantucket Historical Association and Penobscot Marine Museum), William N. Peterson (Mystic Seaport), John F. Rinaldi (Kennebunkport, Maine), Dr. Rick Schafer, Gordon and Pamela Stanley, John Sylvia, Joseph Vallejo, Dr. Pieter van der Merwe (National Maritime Museum, Greenwich), Dr. Walter Van Horn (Anchorage Museum of History and Art), Hon. Paul E. Vardeman, and Rodi York (Mystic Seaport); also Bill Baccus, Robert Ballintine, Susan Barnett, Max Berry and the late Heidi Berry, Bradford Bickley, Lorna Boulanger, Peter Bump, Dr. Charles Burden, Brian Culity, the late Professor Curtis Dahl, Winifred Durfee Dimock, Nancy Druckman (Sotheby's New York), Tony Dumitru (Nantucket Historical Association), Gary Eckstine, Lewis K. Eisenberg, Michael Gill, Georgia Gosnell and the late Thomas Gosnell, William E. Hughes, the late Arthur Kobacker and Sara Jo Kobacker, Dr. Norman Krasnagor and Rebecca Krasnagor, Captain Alvin Mandly, Adam Moniz, Rafael Osona (Nantucket), Michael Porlides, Fred and Beverly Rosenquist, Michael P. Scorey, Anne Savours Shirley, Dawn Blake Souza, Edward Stecewicz, Tim Sylvia, Lawrence Tatro, Tom Watlington, Professor Donald Warrin, Michael Yates, and Andrew Zarauskas. The many courtesies extended to me by the folks at several other institutions are also much appreciated, notably the American Antiquarian Society, the Bostonian Society, the Bristol, Newport, and Warren Historical Societies in Rhode Island, the Farnsworth Art Museum in Rockland, Maine, and the reference and special collections departments at the public libraries in New Bedford, Boston, and Middleborough, Massachusetts.

My colleagues at the New Bedford Whaling Museum, notably including Jean Banker, Mary Jean Blasdale, Robert Hauser, Michael Lapides, Kate Mello, and Laura Pereira, were ever helpful and generous with their time and expertise. Michael P. Dyer's astute textual citations were very numerous and especially valuable. The insightful contributions of "my" volunteer Scrimshaw Forensics® team — the late Donald E. Ridley, Richard Donnelly, Michael Gerstein, Dr. Vasant Gideon, Judith Navas Lund, Dr. Sanford Moss, and James Vaccarino — were indispensable at every juncture. Several years' worth of "my" Curatorial Interns at the Whaling Museum added pleasure, energy, and useful contributions throughout the process, notably by Antony Adler, Jordan Berson, Christine Choi, Morgan Fryer, Veronica Garrett, Betsey Golden, Thomas Hardy, Catlin Hayes, Michael Ide, Catherine Labelle, Cathryn Lamontaigne, Christopher Louvar, Megan MacGregor, Dayna Meehan, Jonathan Olly, Sarah Parks, and Evander Price.

I am flattered and honored by the friendship and encouragement of Michael Stone, Ellen Cohn, and Catherine Reynolds, and an indispensable partnership with Paul O'Pecko and Stephen White at Mystic Seaport to produce this volume. On the production side, I am grateful to Mary Anne Stets, who shepherded the book to press; Bonnie Goff, who did the design; and Thomson Shore, who did their customary fine and efficient job of printing and binding.

I am particularly grateful to my friends Jonathan Blum and Gregg Hurwitz, whose generous philanthropy made publication of the book possible; and to Dr. Mary Malloy, who has been putting up with all this for years, patiently and uncomplainingly and always immensely helpfully.

Stuart M. Frank

Foxborough, Massachusetts

ABBREVIATIONS FOR REPOSITORIES AND SOURCES REFERRED TO IN THE TEXT

AMHA	Anchorage Museum of History and Art, Alaska
AMNZ	Auckland Museum, New Zealand
ANMM	Australian National Maritime Museum, Sydney
ASM	Alaska State Museum, Juneau
BUW	Burke Museum, University of Washington, Seattle
CCC	Commander Chr. Christensen's Whaling Museum, Sandefjord, Norway
CMC	Canadian Museum of Civilization, Ottawa
DAF	Dietrich American Foundation, Chester Springs, Pennsylvania
DCHS	Dukes County Historical Society / Martha's Vineyard Museum, Edgartown, Massachusetts
FSM	Flensburg (Germany) Schiffahrtsmuseum and Städtisches Museum.
HLC	Huntington Library, Pasadena, California.
HMM	Hull Maritime Museum (former Town Docks Museum), Hull, UK
KNB	Kendall Collection, New Bedford Whaling Museum
KWM	Kendall Whaling Museum, Sharon, Massachusetts (the collection merged into the New Bedford Whaling Museum in October 2001)
MFA	Museum of Fine Arts, Boston, Massachusetts
MSM	Mystic Seaport Museum, Mystic, Connecticut
NBFPL	New Bedford Free Public Library, New Bedford, Massachusetts
NBPS	New Bedford Port Society papers (on deposit at the Research Library of the New Bedford Whaling Museum)
NBWM	New Bedford Whaling Museum, New Bedford, Massachusetts
NCP	Nicholson Collection, Providence Public Library, Providence, Rhode Island
NHA	Nantucket Historical Association, Nantucket, Massachusetts
NHS	Newport [Rhode Island] Historical Society
NMM	National Maritime Museum, Greenwich (London), UK
PEM	Peabody Essex Museum, Salem, Massachusetts
PLSR	Point Lobos State Reserve, Carmel, California
PMM	Penobscot Marine Museum, Searsport, Maine

PMS	Peabody Museum of Salem, Massachusetts (founded as the East India Marine Society in 1799; now merged with the Essex Institute, hence the new designation PEM in this edition)
QVM	Queen Victoria Museum and Art Gallery, Hobart, Tasmania
SFL	Scrimshaw Forensics Laboratory®: located at KWM (1987-2001) and NBWM (since October 2001)
SIW	Smithsonian Institution, Washington, D.C.
SJM	Sheldon Jackson Museum, Sitka, Alaska
UAM	University of Alaska Museum, Fairbanks
USNH	U.S. Naval Historical Center, Washington, D.C.
WAM	Western Australian Museum, Perth, Western Australia
WHS	Warren Historical Society, Warren, Rhode Island

ABBREVIATIONS FOR AUCTION HOUSES AND DEALERS REFERRED TO IN THE TEXT

BJ: 1-4	Barbara Johnson Whaling Collection, Sotheby Parke Bernet, New York. [Offered in four separate auction sales, catalogued in 4 vols.: (1) 11-12 Dec. 1981; (2) 24-25 Sept. 1982; (3) 29-30 Apr. 1983; (4) 16-17 Dec. 1983.]
Bourne	Richard A. Bourne Co., Hynannis, Massachusetts.
Cowan	Cowan's Auctions, Inc., Cincinnati, Ohio
DeLuca	Maritime Antiques, Inc. (Chuck DeLuca, proprietor), York, Maine
Granby	Hyland-Granby Antiques, Hyannisport, Massachusetts
Hellman	Nina Hellman Antiques, Nantucket, Massachusetts
Julia	James A. Julia Auctions, Fairfield, Maine
Madden	Paul Madden Antiques, Sandwich, Massachusetts
McInnis	Paul McInnis, North Hampton, New Hampshire
Northeast	Northeast Auctions, Portsmouth, New Hampshire
Osona	Rafael Osona Auctions, Nantucket, Massachusetts
Rinaldi	John F. Rinaldi, Kennebunkport, Maine (catalogues)
Skinner	Skinner, Inc., Boston, Bolton, and Marlborough, Massachusetts
Sotheby's	Sotheby's, New York and London
West Sea	West Sea Company, Old Town, San Diego, California

SCRIMSHAW AND PROVENANCE

The *Dictionary of Scrimshaw Artists,* published in 1991, was the first attempt to do for the elusive field of scrimshaw what others had already done for various other art historical genres – to provide a basic biographical reference to identify individual artists and the contexts of their artistic endeavors. This was not so much to establish a canon as it was to explore the specifics of the divergent circumstances and careers of the men (mostly) and women who made scrimshaw on shipboard in the nineteenth century — with some significant attention to precursors in earlier times, and to occupational scrimshanders (as distinct from revival practitioners) in the twentieth century. *More Scrimshaw Artists* expanded upon the first volume and increased the inventory of known and suspected practitioners. For the present volume, institutional and family provenance records, a vigorous auction market, and increasing awareness among increasingly sophisticated collectors have provided access to the names of more than three hundred artists who were hitherto unidentified. Meanwhile, in the years since the first two volumes were published the availability of historical and genealogical resources has been greatly improved. These, together with the newly-examined provenance records, have enhanced our knowledge and understanding of scores of scrimshaw artists whose biographical sketches appear in the previous volumes and are expanded or corrected here.

It is worthy of note that a large proportion of the scrimshaw makers who appear as such for the first time in this volume are directly connected with the New Bedford Port District, primarily for the simple reason that the greatest hoard of hitherto unexplored, uncatalogued, and undocumented scrimshaw was concentrated in the large collection of the New Bedford Whaling Museum. Ever since it was founded in 1903 the Museum has been accumulating — primarily by gift and bequest, but also through occasional purchases — scrimshaw of virtually every sort, mostly from local sources and from descendants of local families. While the Kendall Collection was largely researched and catalogued prior to its merger into the New Bedford Whaling Museum in 2001 — in fact, most of it prior to the publication of the *Dictionary of Scrimshaw Artists* in 1991 and *More Scrimshaw Artists* in 1998 — the scrimshaw at New Bedford for the most part lay fallow for its first hundred years while the resources of the Museum were devoted to other pursuits. The merger itself was a motive cause for the massive recataloguing and documentation of which this book, as well as several lesser publications, several exhibition vignettes, and a projected major "permanent" exhibition and catalogue, are the partial results. The Museum's holdings are in fact so voluminous and its exhibitions, public programs, and other professional activities so extensive, that it was not until the merger that proper attention could be turned to the vast holdings of scrimshaw — with the additional dividend that, with the even larger Kendall Collection immediately at hand, and with the participation of an increasingly sophisticated community of astute collectors and dealers, a truly monumental number of pieces could be examined and compared side-by-side.

The collection turned out to be uncommonly rich in basic provenance materials — or, more accurately, rudimentary provenance *clues* and documentary *leads* that had never been properly followed up. Therefore, much of the research for this volume consisted of tracing the provenance, connecting the donors historically and genealogically to their whaling forebears, and seeking to establish the context and authorship of the increasing number of pieces — still a minority — that can be reasonably attributed on the basis of empirical evidence, rather than mere speculation.

The same principles apply also to the scrimshaw artists whose names and works were generously submitted by friends, colleagues, collectors, and families all over the country. Their names appear in the Acknowledgements section.

It is significant that among Native Alaskan artists both the age-old tradition of ivory carving and the century-old tradition of decorative scrimshaw remain strong. There are nowadays whole dynasties of Inupiaq, Yup'ik, and Yupik carvers; also Chukchi on the Siberian side of the Bering Strait, and Inuit artists in Canada and Greenland. However, as this is an historical compilation, only those born prior to 1918 and working prior to 1940 are eligible to appear here — that is, only those whose careers were contemporaneous with the Yankee whaling era, in which so many Native people participated and which inspired some of their own scrimshaw-making.

Analogously, the same criteria apply to the still-vibrant scrimshaw-making activities of the Azores Islands and Madeira, whose continuing traditions are represented only by those artists born prior to 1918 and working prior to 1940.

This compendium also includes a handful of Continental European artisans who are known or suspected to have worked in whale or walrus ivory; a few whose criteria for inclusion can best be described as miscellaneous (though not random); and a few who, though they were not actually scrimshaw-makers themselves, were influential or instrumental in enabling scrimshaw to happen. More than a handful of British and Australian whalemen-artists are represented, but the overwhelming majority of the men and women presented here are Americans and adoptive Americans, most of them active aboard American whaling vessels between the 1820s and 1920s. As such, they exemplify the grassroots mainstream of New England's deepwater whaling trade, a unique, remarkably diverse, remarkably egalitarian, and remarkably upwardly-mobile community of specialist laborers and officers who earned their livelihoods on the heaving decks of ships far at sea, for years at a time, thousands of miles from home, and thousands of miles from anything for which their previous lives had prepared them.

This is as it should be, as it was these adventurous Americans who dominated the whaling trade in the nineteenth century, who accordingly produced the overwhelming majority of scrimshaw, and whose legacy is the splendid and engaging diversity of artworks, practical implements, and workaday utensils and tools that grace today's maritime museums and private collections, providing thereby a unique window into the texture of life at sea in the Age of Sail; and, not incidentally, a panorama of the ingenuity, optimism, generous-heartedness, and aesthetic contours of mostly young Americans when the Repubic itself was still young.

ALL HANDS EMPLOYED SCRIMSHONTING

In his shipboard journal aboard the bark *Zone* of Fairhaven, Massachusetts, writing in 1857, boat-steerer John Harlow corroborates the purported whalers' rule of thumb that, at least on some vessels, scrimshawing was prohibited until after the first thousand barrels of oil were stowed down, and that thereafter scrimshaw-making could threaten to get out of hand: "We have got a thousand barrels of Oil now, 'scrimshonting' has commenced! Where will it end?"

The original context of *scrimshaw*, rather than referring to the sailors' recreational handcrafts for their own amusement, was to produce tools, fittings, gear, and other objects for the ship: fids, seam rubbers, thole pins, belaying pins, sheave blocks, snatch blocks, tool handles, and so on. The original raw material, sperm whale skeletal bone, was readily available and had no other commercial application; moreover, assigned scrimshandering had the added advantage of providing useful work for potentially idle hands. Many captains recognized that this was productive and cost effective, and the word *employment* often figures into mention of scrimshaw on shipboard, especially in the first half of the nineteenth century. John Coggeshall mentions "all hands employed scrimshonting" aboard the brig *By Chance* of Dartmouth, Massachusetts, in 1826; Michael Cumiskey testifies to several occasions on which the crew of the ship *Abigal* of New Bedford were "employe[d] schrimshonen" during 1835-38; John T. Hogle reports "all hands employed in scrimshorning" aboard the New Bedford bark *London Packet* in 1843; and on the New Bedford ship *Janus* in July 1846, the third mate, Richard C. Reynolds, says of the crew, "Employment is scrimshoning." Though *employment* is somewhat equivocal as to whether it be meant literally or figuratively — that is, whether the crew were put to work by the captain or the mate to make things for the ship, or were merely indulging in an optional pastime in their leisure hours — allusions to assigned ship's work and scrimshaw are occasionally conjoined, as in Benjamin W. Golden's remark aboard the Fairhaven ship *Sharon* in October 1839, when the crew were "employed in fitting rigging and turning bone fids."

As a leisure-time recreational activity among whalemen, by the 1830s and '40s scrimshandering appears to have become virtually universal on the homeward-bound passage. There are many indications of official sanction from the aftercabin, not only owing to the principle of busywork for idle hands (a balm in the increasingly disorderly and undisciplined atmosphere of being homeward-bound at last), but also owing to the officers' and captains' own scrimshandering activities, which, if the testimony of their juniors be believed, sometimes approached a level of obsessive fixation. For Archelaus Baker, Jr., captain of the Fairhaven bark *John A. Robb* in the late 1850s, "squimshaw" was clearly a means of relaxation to which he resorted only occasionally. The crew must have had official sanction for scrimshawing when, according to John B. Wade on the New Bedford ship *George and Susan* in 1864, they "Lashed the Wheel and all hands [were] schrimshoning." The preliminaries were certainly organized group activities. As the prolific scrimshaw-maker William H. Chappell (q.v.) describes it aboard the New Bedford bark *Wade* in October 1842, after the cutting-in, trying-out, coopering, and stowing-down were completed, "All hands [were] out working most laboriously on the jaw bone of a whale," undoubtedly preparing it for scrimshaw (as there was not really any other reason to bother with whale jawbones or teeth).

Lyman Healy, in the New Bedford ship *William Thompson* (1835-38), Marshall Keith, first mate of the bark *Cape Horn Pigeon* of Dartmouth (1866-67) and schooner *Edith May* of Wellfleet (1867-69), John S. Coquin aboard the New Bedford barks *Globe* (1869-72) and Merlin (1872-76), Thomas F. Pease in the New Bedford bark *Alaska* (1880-84), and many others, refer to cleaning whale teeth, presumably for scrimshandering — though possibly some of them were intended for bartering in the Pacific or for the limited wholesale market back home. In either case, all of these whalemen (qq.v. here and in *More Scrimshaw Artists*) are known to have made scrimshaw themselves. Willie E. Burbank, a fifteen-year-old cabin boy in the bark *Tamerlane* under Captain Barnabas Alvin Briggs (q.v. in the *Dictionary*) is a bit more specific: in January 1880 he reports a "Barrel of teeth shared" and "sculptors at work." James Holly Bartlett, remarking on his experiences in the steam-bark *William Baylies* of New Bedford during 1886-87, mentions scrimshaw as a matter of course: "The jaw [of the sperm whale] has no value, except for the teeth, which are pure ivory and the jaw itself, a solid white bone of which the members of the crew may carve handsome canes or other articles which they etch [sic] with various figures or sketches of vessels, whales or other things pertaining to the business" (*Patriot Ledger*, Quincy, Massachusetts, n.d., 1964; NBWM archive).

On many vessels scrimshaw-making could involve a whole watch or even the entire ship's company simultaneously. Third mate John L. Decker's comments aboard the New Bedford bark *Mars* are typical. In February 1857 he writes, "The watch was scrimshoning," and in August, "The watch engaged scrimshoning." Jason L. Braley, one of the mates in the ship *Stephania* and bark *Louisa* during 1847-50, reports, "watch employed in scrimshonting." A few years later, as captain of the bark *Falcon* during 1859-62, Braley uses the same phrasing, except that his spelling had deteriorated in the meantime: "watch imployed [sic] in scrimshonting." Remarks about scrimshaw often refer to the entire crew. William Gifford, third mate of the bark *Benjamin Cummings* of Dartmouth, has "all hands scrimshoning" in January 1858. Third mate John S. Coquin, a dedicated scrimshaw-maker himself, reports the same thing on several occasions aboard the New Bedford bark *Globe* during 1869-72. Sereno Edwards Bishop, a young passenger on the homeward passage of the whaleship *William Lee* of Newport, Rhode Island, during 1839-40, describes several occasions on which not only the captain and mates, but even some of the passengers, himself included, were making scrimshaw of various different types (see Appendix IV).

The practice persisted well into the declining days of whaling in the twentieth century. Charlotte E. Church, the captain's wife aboard the San Francisco bark *Andrew Hicks* in 1907, writes, "Men employed scrimsawing." On the same vessel in 1915, first mate William H. Griffith reports in his journal, "nothing doing except sawing up bone, men trying to make canes." In Robert Cushman Murphy's superb published narrative of the brig *Daisy* during 1912-13 (*Logbook for Grace*, 1947), it appears that just about everybody in the mostly African-American and Cape Verdean crew did some scrimshawing at some point or another. This and a tooth in NBWM that was engraved by Jayme Fortes (q.v.) in 1917 are testimony not only to the latter-day persistence of the genre, but also to its continuing polyglot, universal appeal among whalemen of every incoming nationality.

Unfortunately, only a few whaler-diarists are specific about what "the watch" or "all hands" were making during these sometimes frenzied scrimshandering episodes. In the case of Hiram R. King aboard the New Bedford bark *Fortune* in February 1856, it was finger rings. Frederick Howland Smith, a dedicated scrimshaw-maker and master of the New Bedford bark *Petrel*, reports in December 1873 an even more trivial pursuit: "all hands employed making sleeve buttons." However, by far the mainstream interest was making more substantial souvenirs and gifts for the folks back home. On the ship *Gazelle* in 1864 Frederick H. Lawrence proclaims, "Scrimshoning is the order of the day" and "Butter knives and canes are being manufactured by wholesale." On the ship *Mary Frazier* in 1865,

Nathan T. Cottle reports "all hands at work making canes." Likewise, more than thirty years later, in 1896 aboard the San Francisco bark *Horatio,* William F. Joseph, himself an inveterate scrimshaw artist, twice observes, "Everybody Making Canes." Homeward-bound in the ship *Lucy Ann* of Wilmington, Delaware, in 1844, seaman John F. Martin quips, "Scrimshawing. There are enough canes in this ship to supply all the old men in Wilmington." Sereno Edwards Bishop, a young passenger on the *William Lee* during 1839-40, describes one of the passengers, a Mr. Vanderzee (q.v.), making, buying, and swapping for scrimshaw among the crew, evidently in order to assemble a stockpile of mementos, curios, and gifts to carry home.

People often wonder how a sailor on the heaving and pitching deck of a ship at sea could possibly create the meticulous engraving, precise joinery, delicate inlay, and subtle ornamentation that characterize the best scrimshaw; and some have speculated — erroneously, as it turns out — that whalemen-artists must have waited for a calm, or for the shelter of a port, or plied their skills ashore, lest their work be ruined by a rolling sea. Far from it. It is eminently clear from literally hundreds of whalemen's remarks in their journals that scrimshandering was primarily a shipboard pursuit in leisure hours at sea, foul weather notwithstanding except perhaps in the most extreme circumstances. The authoritative testimony of Josiah E. Chase, captain of the New Bedford bark *Hunter,* may confidently be taken to typify many sailors' attitudes, that in heavy weather, once the sails were reefed and hatches battened down, there was little else to do, providing the perfect opportunity for recreational scrimshawing: "Aug 31, 1870. Commenced with half a Gale. Empl[oyed] myself making Julia's swifts." On the other hand, we have the testimony of Sereno Edwards Bishop's aboard the *William Lee* (1839-40) to corroborate the reasonable expectation that at least some sailors brought ivory and bone home to be worked ashore (see the articles on Sereno Edwards Bishop and —— Anderson).

The implication in some whalemen's journals is sometimes that scrimshawing was practiced to the exclusion of all other activities. An anonymous journal of the ship *L.C. Richmond* reports on March 12, 1857, "Employed in scrimshoning &c.," and on March 14, "Employed in doing nothing but scrimshoning &c." According to Nathan T. Cottle, on a day or two in July 1865 there was "Nothing going on but scrimshorning" aboard the ship *Mary Frazier,* and Frederick Lawrence says much the same of the *Gazelle.* His journal entry for May 28, 1864 is "Nothing a doing but scrimshonting and many busily engaged in that," and on Feb. 18, 1865, "Scrimshoning is the order of the day." In August 1865 he exempts himself: "Most everybody is scrimshoning but me," and adds on another occasion, "Not anything a going on but Scrimshoning." Moses H. Wilcox likewise excludes himself from the scrimshawing frenzy. On the only three occasions he mentions scrimshaw aboard the New Bedford bark *Osceola* (1870-72), he has the "officers scrimshoning," but of himself reports only things like "I made 2 scrap tubs and other ship dut[i]es," followed immediately by "officers scrimshoning." There were in fact more than a few common foremast hands and junior officers who took a dim view of the scrimshandering activities of their superiors, such as William W. Manchester, second mate of the New Bedford bark *Palmetto* during 1880-83, who is impatient with the voyage and with the senior officers: "Nothing in sight and no sign of [there] ever being any spirm [sic] whales around here[.] the old man and the mate devote there [sic] time at Schrimshorning[;] that is all they think of." When Frederick Lawrence's shipmates aboard the *Gazelle* in 1864 characterize "scrimshoning" as "the only thing uppermost here," Lawrence's reply is, "There was never anything said more true." Perhaps William H. Poole said it best in his journal of the New Bedford bark *Platina* in July 1874: "Scrimshorn. Scrimshorn."

Scrimshaw and Provenance

A Third Dictionary of Scrimshaw Artists

An asterisk (*) indicates an artist whose biography appears in one of the previous volumes and is expanded, updated, or corrected here.

* **Abbott, George R.** (fl. circa 1857-61). The George R. Abbott who made the panbone fid that is inscribed, signed, and dated "Ship / Oregon / Fairhaven / May 27th / 1858 / G.R. Abbott" (noted in the *Dictionary*; in DAF, from Bourne 22 Aug 1972, #28), is presumed to have been at sea in the *Oregon* of Fairhaven for the duration of the voyage (1857-61). Thus, he was almost certainly not the same George R. Abbott who sailed in the New Bedford bark *Dominga* in October 1858 and likely remained with that vessel until she was condemned at Paita in January 1862. Moreover, the namesake on the *Dominga* was a green hand — a lowly berth unlikely to attract anyone to transfer who was already rated Ordinary Seaman on the *Oregon*. Thus, for both reasons, the two were almost certainly not the same man, and there is no reason to connect either one with a large wooden box (in KNB) inlaid with whale ivory stars and tetraskeles (pinwheel-like devices with four blades), labeled on the bottom in pencil holograph, "Bark Deminga [sic] 1862." See Henri Zinke.

Akin, Warren [Aiken] (fl. circa 1822-57). A New Bedford whaleman and descendant of whalemen, he made an inlaid sewing box for his daughter; in NBWM. The wooden box with hinged lid is inlaid and trimmed on the top and sides with whale ivory, tortoise shell, baleen, and wood, and has the initials "MEA" inlaid on the front panel, carved whale ivory feet, and an interior divided into eleven sections and drawers with whale ivory knobs. The provenance is "made by Captain Warren Aiken for his daughter, Maria Ellis Aiken." There is also, pasted inside the lid, an engraving entitled "Apollo and the Shepherds" by the English-born American illustrator Stephen H. Gimber (1810-1862), but it is not clear whether it was put there by the maker or the daughter.

Maria Ellis Aiken, for whom the sewing box was made, was born in 1829, the eldest of the seven children of Warren Akin and Joanna Bolles Akin of Rochester, Massachusetts. One suspects that Warren may have made three such boxes, one for each of the daughters: the next two, Lydia and Mary Bolles, were only two and three years younger than Maria, respectively. On the other hand, the eldest sister was not only a stay-at-home (Lydia evidently married and moved out of the house by age 19, and Mary may soon have followed), but Maria was clearly someone with domestic skills. She became a dressmaker (and advertised as such in the New Bedford City Directory), never married, lived with her parents in Rochester throughout their lives, then moved to New Bedford, where she was still living and working in 1901.

Warren Akin (born 1804) and Warren Aiken, Jr. (born 1835) were father-and-son whalemen (the father spelled the name *Akin*, the son *Aiken*, while the public records and whaling annals vary). Each of them had an early start at making a career of whaling and each of them rose to first mate but no higher. Warren Sr. was born at Dartmouth, Massachusetts, the son of John Akin and the former Huldah Forster. He likely served a youthful apprenticeship as a cooper and may even have made some of his early voyages as a ship's cooper — which appears to be the case because after he retired from seafaring at age 53, and well into his seventies, he worked as a cooper in Rochester/Mattapoisett, Massachusetts. He married Joanna Bolles in 1828 and moved to her hometown of Rochester, where they raised their children. After eight or ten voyages that began at age 17 — the known ones are the New Bedford brig *Dragon* (1822-23), of which his kinsman Benjamin Akin was captain; two in the ship *Canton* (1826-28), one in the ship *Eagle* (1829-32), and two or three in the bark *Dryade* of Rochester (1833-38), probably winding up as second mate — he finally made it to first mate at age 37, in the bark *Hope* of New Bedford (1841-42). But something evidently went wrong and there was no promotion to captain and no other voyage as first mate for quite a while. His next four voyages were as second mate, in the ship *St. George* (sailed 1843), from which he transferred to the *Minerva* (1845-48), then the *Sarah* of Mattapoisett (1848-51) and the *Orozimbo* of New Bedford (sailed 1851). At the advanced age of 49 he was evidently able to transfer from the *Orozimbo* to a first mate's berth for the 24th lay in the bark *A.R. Tucker* of Dartmouth (1853-57). This voyage was his last. His namesake son followed his father's footsteps in the whale fishery as a kind of professional mate, but never a captain. In fact, Warren Junior was second mate in the ship *Brewster* of Mattapoisett (1857-60) and then made his final voyage as first mate in the very same vessel in which his father had made his final voyage as first mate a decade earlier, the bark *A.R. Tucker* (1861-64), which in the interim had been transferred from Dartmouth to New Bedford.

Akin, William (fl. circa 1819-33). A walking stick with a whale ivory tip, silver ferrule, and plain, L-shaped handle of whale ivory, has a lightweight shaft comprised of 119 shark vertebrae "strung" on a wooden core — an unusual feature, as shark vertebrae canes normally have a steel core. It was donated to NBWM in 1905 by Emma Cornelia Ricketson with a provenance stating that it came from the Akin family and was made by William Akin. The donor was born in 1838 at Dartmouth, Massachusetts, the daughter of "Captain" Joseph Ricketson 2d and the former Sophia Kirby; she was a lifelong resident of New Bedford and never married. Her father and grandfather were commission merchants in New Bedford who, as such, were owners, managing agents, and brokers of whaleships. Of the several men named William Akin who went whaling, only one is known to have served in a Ricketson vessel. This William Akin, born circa 1803, gave his residence as New Bedford when he made his maiden voyage in the ship *Midas* (1819-20). He likely made a second voyage in an unidentified vessel (1820-22), then a third in the ship *Mercury* (1822-25), followed by another unknown voyage or two (1825-29), after which he was in the ship *Frances Henrietta* (1829-33), which was one of the Ricketson's ships at least by 1834. At this time Akin was living in Dartmouth (the Ricketsons' hometown) and was probably an officer on the *Francis Henrietta*. In any case, this voyage, and the fact that they were both living in the village of Dartmouth, are the only known connections between any whaleman named William Akin and the Ricketson family, though there were several other men named William Akin living in Dartmouth.

* **Albatross Artisan** (fl, circa the 1830s-40s). One account of the sea birds prominently featured on the few known works by this hand, the unidentified whaleman-artist was awarded an ornithological sobriquet after the largest and grandest species of pelagic bird. His pictorial sperm whale teeth were previously thought to be by the same hand as those of the so-called Pagoda Artisan, whose actual name (based on an apparent signature on an oversize powder horn) was evidently S. Baker. Improved research resources and closer scrutiny of the powder horn have now enabled

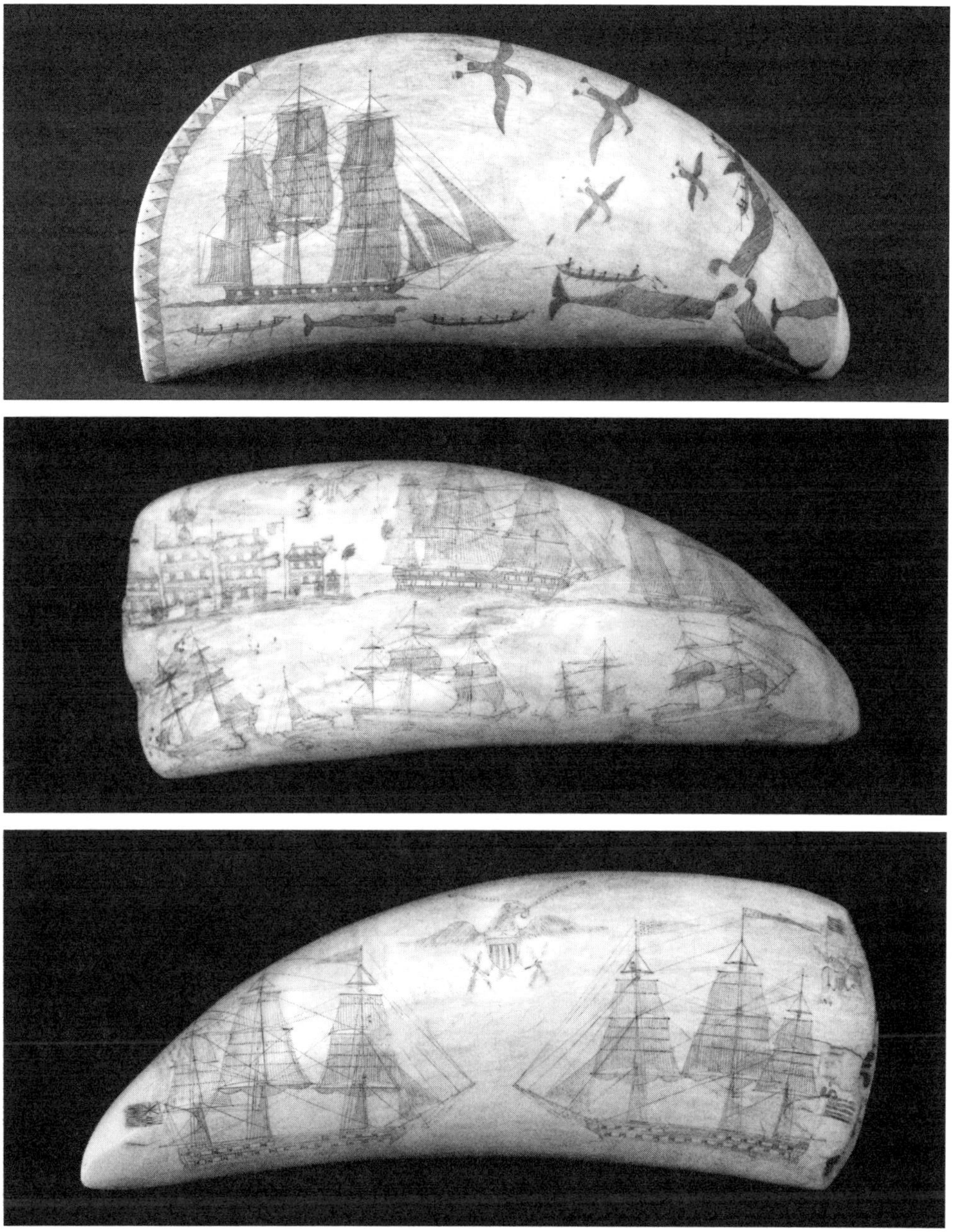

Fig. 1. **Teeth by the Albatross Artisan** (top) **and the Pagoda Artisan,** the latter now identified as Silvanus Baker. Until recently only one example of the Albatross Artisan's work was known, and the Pagoda and Albatross scrimshaw were thought to have been by the same hand. However, with the discovery of a second Albatross tooth it became clear that the Albatross scrimshaw (still known in only two or possibly three examples) is much finer and has a much higher polish. By comparison, the Pagoda Artisan's work is sketchy, the patina tends to be dull, and the teeth and two attributed powder horns typically feature various forms of his curious, pagoda-like buildings and, often, lofty sailing vessels with spidery rigging. The Albatross Artisan photo is courtesy of Northeast Auctions, Portsmouth, N.H. (21 Aug. 2005, lot #757). The Pagoda Tooth is one of several in the New Bedford Whaling Museum (photos by Richard Donnelly).

identification of the maker as Silvanus Baker (q.v.) and the recipient as John Rook (q.v.), which in turn occasioned further study of all of the pieces that had hitherto been attributed to the same hand. Combined with the recent appearance at auction of a masterpiece tooth by the Albatross Artisan, this facilitated more exacting comparisons, resulting in the conclusion that two different artists were responsible for their creation. The powder horn, eight teeth, and a clamp for a swift are now credited to Silvanus Baker, AKA the Pagoda Artisan, while two very superior teeth are attributed to the Albatross Artisan, clearly the more accomplished of the two, who still remains anonymous. The distinguishing feature of the Pagoda Artisan's iconography is the peculiar, Chinatown-like character of the architecture in his seaport scenes, as described in the *Dictionary*, hence the Pagoda moniker. Any similar stylistic eccentricities in the Albatross Artisan's work are minor features and are much less extreme. By contrast, the Albatross Artisan's scrimshaw is distinguished by the appreciably larger size and graceful shapes of the teeth themselves, greater clarity of engraving, a more open style with substantially more negative space interspersed within the component pictures, extremely high polish, and a deep and lustrous patina, and especially, of course, a profusion of pelagic birds in flight. (As these birds are not anatomically correct with respect to any particular species, some writers have described them as seagulls or eagles; but in standpoint of size they seem more like albatrosses, with a prodigious wingspan and all the dignity attributed to the species by Samuel Taylor Coleridge.) Only two examples of the Albatross Artisan's work have been conclusively identified, both in private collections. At different times, both of them set new records for auction prices realized. The one illustrated in Flayderman (107 and 73, top), from the Barbara Johnson Collection, appeared as color a vignette on the title page of the *Time-Life* book, *The Whalers* (1979), and was later sold at auction (Osona, 14 Aug. 1993). The other, an even better example, surfaced in 2006, prompted the renewed assessment reflected here, and later made headlines at auction (Northeast, 19-20 Aug. 2006).

* **Albro, Caleb J.** (fl. circa 1835-47). One of his famous engraved teeth commemorating the 1835-39 voyage of the ship *John Coggeshall* of Newport, Rhode Island, went to his shipmate and fellow scrimshaw maker J.N. Sherman (q.v.) of Foxborough, Massachusetts, who became a lifelong friend on the voyage. The tooth has a monochrome sperm whaling scene and spouting sperm whale on the front, with a polychrome standing female figure on verso (believed to be an actual portrait of an unidentified family member), and is elaborately ascribed to the John Coggeshall voyage in Albro's characteristically proficient graver's hand. Two other Albro masterpieces engraved to an equivalently high standard were identified in recent years and are now in private collections (reported by John Rinaldi and Rod Cardoza). A third (reported by Alan Granby) is unsigned and not specifically ascribed to the *John Coggeshall*; in standpoint of style alone it could have been made by Caleb or his brother and shipmate Thomas (q.v. in the *Dictionary*), either on the *John Coggeshall* or some other vessel; however, it is in many significant respects so similar to the one in NBWM that Caleb engraved and passed along to J.N. Sherman, that it leaves little doubt that this one is also by Caleb's able hand, likely made at about the same time on the *John Coggeshall*. It also has a monochrome sperm whaling scene and spouting sperm whale on the back (in this case stipple engraved), but the gracefully wrought text refers to the scene rather than to the *John Coggeshall*, and the scene is surmounted by a delicate, claret-colored clouds-and-sunburst device.

Caleb Albro was born in Portsmouth, Rhode Island, probably in 1816, the son of Peleg and Ann Albro. After returning from his one whaling voyage, he married Martha Stedman Taylor in 1839, started a family at Jamestown, Massachusetts, meanwhile continuing to work as a mariner and, for a few years, as a merchant sea captain. By 1850 he had evidently left off seafaring entirely and taken up farming full time with the help of Martha's father and brother, both named Benjamin Taylor and both of them living on the Albro farm in Jamestown. A few years later Caleb and Martha moved the family to a farm in nearby Portsmouth, Massachusetts, where they raised a total of ten children, nine of whom survived to adulthood. In the late 1850s Albro hired James Stowell Sherman, the eldest son of his former shipmate and fellow-scrimshaw maker J.N. Sherman. The boy was still in his teens at the time; but in 1863 the farmhand apprentice, by then 24, married Albro's daughter, Mary Taylor Albro, age about 17. Caleb J. Albro died in 1893. A namesake grandson, Caleb J. Albro, Jr., inherited at least one of the teeth. He lived for a while in Norwich, Connecticut, and was later a candy maker in Hartford. Mary Taylor Albro Sherman's grandson, Everett B. Sherman — who was the great-grandson of both Caleb Albro and J.N. Sherman — bequeathed to NBWM the tooth by Caleb Albro that Caleb had given his shipmate J.N. Sherman on the *John Coggeshall*, together with an inlaid walking stick that Sherman himself made on that same voyage.

Allen, Thomas F. (fl. circa 1850-63). A massive crimper that has a curl-ornamented foreshaft with a pierced-work shield motif and knife-type handle carved from a single tooth, a two-tine fork mortised onto the foreshaft, a fluted whale ivory jagging wheel, and wooden trim, was given to NBWM by Stephen H. Taylor in memory of Carolyn R. Taylor in 1948. Mr. Taylor (b. 1874) had been Superintendent of the New Bedford Water Works; Carolyn, better known as Carrie, was his older sister (b. 1867). Neither Stephen nor his Taylor forebears made any whaling voyages; they simply were not a whaling family. His grandfather, William H. Taylor, originally from Newport, Rhode Island, was a merchant in New Bedford, and their father, John Pitman Taylor (b. circa 1830), was a druggist. But beginning around 1850 they had boarding with them in New Bedford a young sailor from Rhode Island named Thomas F. Allen, who may have been a relation from back in Newport. He was born circa 1835 and at age 15 got his Seaman's Passport (Protection Paper) at New Bedford, where he shipped as a green hand in the ship *William Hamilton* (1850-54). It appears likely that Tom Allen made the crimper on this or one of his subsequent voyages and presented it to some member of the Taylor family when he returned. (It being a kitchen implement, the most likely recipient would have been his surrogate mother, Elizabeth Ann Pitman Taylor, who had married William H. Taylor in 1821.) The captain of the *William Hamilton*, Humphrey Shockley, came home sick before the voyage was over. Thomas Allen also left the voyage early, perhaps accompanying Captain Shockley back to New Bedford. There he obtained another passport, now stating his residence as Falmouth, Massachusetts, on Cape Cod, and shipped out as boatsteerer in the ship *Montreal* under Captain S.L. Gray (1853-57). This turned out to be an enormously successful voyage, yielding an astonishing total of 14,377 barrels of whale oil and 51,899 pounds of "bone" (baleen), in addition to 100 barrels of sperm oil sent home (Starbuck, 505). His next voyage was a more conventional success, in the ship *George and Susan* as a third mate (1857-61). By the time he returned in April 1861 the Civil War was newly underway, and he appears to be the same Thomas F. Allen who served for a while as a private in Company B, 3rd Massachusetts House Artillery Regiment of the Union Army. Beginning in 1863 he made a few merchant voyages, but evidently did not go whaling again and his subsequent activities have not been discovered.

Allen, William Alfred (fl. 1841-45). Michael P. Dyer suggests that, judging from an illustration in Allen's two-volume journal of his one and only whaling voyage (in NBWM), Allen may have tried his hand at scrimshaw on at least one tooth (in KNB). As a green hand in the New Bedford ship *Samuel Robertson* (1841-46) he incorporated into one of his journal-page headings, dated June 17, 1843, an ink vignette measuring only about ¾ x ½ inch (19 x 12.7 mm) consisting of a double-flue harpoon crossed with a lance, a bone spade, and a whaleboat hatchet, in the manner of a Whalemen's Coat-of-Arms. This particular device is unlike any of the several analogous examples that have occasionally appeared in print, but is remarkably similar to one on the tooth, a larger version of almost the same arrangement: it reverses the positions of harpoon and lance, is of course far more detailed (if only because of its much larger size), and lacks the hatchet. The journal is otherwise so festooned with title pages, fancy headings, usually careful handwriting, and ornate calligraphy (in many places) — in addition to poems, song texts, and dedications — and is so obviously intended to b shown to the folks back home, as to characterize the author as a chronic ornament-maker. It would be remarkable if during his whaling days he did not try his hand at scrimshaw, even if the vaguely similar tooth is not a specimen of his efforts.

Little is known of the man himself except what can be gleaned from the journal. He was born in 1821 in Westbrook, Maine, just outside Portland, had a brother named Charles E. Allen (to whom a portion of the journal is dedicated), evidently got a very good education (judging from his perceptive observations and articulate prose), was 20 years old when he shipped out (according to his Protection Paper), made only the one voyage (likely having become disenchanted of whaling from the many floggings that took place on the *Samuel Robertson*, which Allen notes disparagingly in his narrative and lists chronologically in the back of the journal), and had a namesake kinsman (a nephew or cousin?), born at Falmouth, Maine, in 1849, the son of Alfred R. Allen and Salome Libby, who became proprietor of a wood-planing mill and dealer in tiles in Portland.

Almy, Christopher (fl. circa the 1790s). On a whaling and sealing voyage to the South Pacific in the ship *Barclay* of New Bedford under Captain Griffin Barney during 1797-99, two decades before the word scrimshaw was in general use — in fact, likely before it was even invented, and some twenty years before the advent of pictorial *scrimshaw* on shipboard, Almy wrote in his journal (in LC) that the crew were making *gimcracks* (reported by Daniel R. Finamore). He specifically mentions a backscratcher and a pie crimper:

> *23 Dec. 1798. All of us employed in scraping and packing whale bone. Most of the men employed in making gimcracks out of whale bone and whale teeth. I am making a back scratcher, a long handle of whale bone carved like a twisted rope, and a little white hand of whale tooth on the end for a scratching the back. Jacob is making a sea horse holding wheel for crimping the edges of pies. We have more fleas than pies on this vessel.*

Christopher Almy has not been identified. There were several men of that name from Dartmouth, Massachusetts, adjacent to New Bedford, but none of them seems to have been of an appropriate age to have been in a whaling crew in the late 1790s. The author of the *Barclay* journal was likely one of the several men named Christopher Almy who were born in the late 1760s and early 1770s in Tiverton and Portsmouth, Rhode Island.

Almy, John C., Jr. (fl. circa 1850-54). Retired New Bedford whaling master associated with a controversial bone object. Catalogued as "John Almy's carved whalebone watch hutch," it is not actually a hutch at all but a box: essentially an eight-sided bone casket, pictorially engraved on the top and sides, with a brass hasp, hinges, and edging, trim; screwed onto a pierced-work bone backboard with a swan motif; and stipple-engraved on the back "John Almy's Watch Case 1882" (Northeast, 19 Aug. 2007, #227). There have been serious reservations about its authenticity, it was passed at auction (demonstrating a certain lack of confidence), and absent any provenance it will always remain in doubt. The inscription could only refer to John C. Almy, Jr. (1826-1909), who in 1882 was long retired and living in Dartmouth, Massachusetts. The implication is that he may have done the scrimshaw himself. He was the son and namesake of Captain John C. Almy, Sr., master of four whaling voyages in New Bedford vessels (1843-54). John Jr. was born in Rhode Island, married Mary Wheeler in 1844 (a union that evidently produced no issue), was the captain of only one whaling voyage, in the bark *Harvest* of New Bedford (1850-54), and in the mid 1880s moved with his wife to Ashland, Massachusetts, where he died in 1909.

Almy, William H. (fl. circa 1820s-1860). New Bedford whaling master credited with a panbone busk, polychrome engraved with hearts and flowers flanking the oversize inscription in bold capitals, "ALMIRA ALMY"; in NBWM. A career whaleman born in South Dartmouth, Massachusetts, William H. Almy (1814-1860) married Almira D. Brownell (c1822-1891) of South Dartmouth in 1839, and brought her with him on two whaling voyages of which he was captain, in the bark *Cape Horn Pigeon* of Dartmouth (1854-58) and the bark *Roscoe* of New Bedford (1859-60). Also on both voyages was their only son George, who was a green hand in the *Cape Horn Pigeon* and an able seaman in the *Roscoe*; and their daughter Minerva (or Myra Ann), who was about seven years old when she embarked the first time. Captain Almy's early voyages are not known. His first command was the bark *Fortune of Plymouth* (1840-44), just after he was married. George was born in 1841 while William was away at sea, and Minerva was born in 1845 when he was ashore for a year or two without a ship. Almy next took a job as first mate of the New Bedford ship *Charles Drew* (1846-49), and was afterwards given command of the ship *St. Peter* (1849-52). John C. Shaw (q.v.) appears to have been one of Almy's boatsteerers on the *St. Peter*. Then came the two voyages already mentioned, in the *Cape Horn Pigeon* and the *Roscoe*, with Almira, George, and Minerva on board. The *Cape Horn Pigeon* was quite a plum, a brand new vessel, constructed at Dartmouth by the great African-American shipbuilder John Mashow, financed in part by Captain William Howland (q.v.) and Captain Almy himself: Almy held a permanent 2/32nds ownership interest. But the *Cape Horn Pigeon* was to be the family's swan song. Sadly, on February 3, 1860, early in the *Roscoe* voyage, both father and son perished when "Captain Almy and 7 men (part of two boats' crews) [were] killed by a whale 1859 [sic]" (Starbuck, 571). After her heartbreaking loss, Almira and Minerva went to live in South Dartmouth with Almira's parents: Stephen Brownell, a carpenter, shipwright, and farmer; and his wife Phebe.

Alves, José Vieira (fl. circa 1860s-'70s). A "deep-sea whaler" from Pico, in the Azores Islands, he went whaling in American ships but continued to live on Pico. He was "known for the ivory and bone pieces he made on board during his long voyages" (Gomes Vieira, 2003, 103), but if any of his scrimshaw survives it has not been identified as such. Born circa 1851, his only known voyage

— which could not have been his only voyage — was as boatsteerer in the Fairhaven bark *Lydia* (1874-77). One of his grandsons, Dimas José Alves Soares (1929-1996), is well regarded as a latter-day scrimshaw artist whose work is represented in private collections in Portugal.

Amos, Matthias (fl. circa 1830s-60s). One of several fine whale ivory and skeletal bone swifts in the collection of the Cape Cod National Seashore — but it is no longer known which one — came with a provenance attributing it by tradition to Matthias Amos, a Wampanoag Indian from Mashpee, Cape Cod (reported by Hope Morrill, Curator). Born in 1816, he was the son of career mariner Israel Amos (circa 1786-) and Mary "Polly" née Robbins (1789-1865), and is reputed to have been a descendant of the great Native chief, Metacom, known as King Philip (F. Mitchell, "Cape Cod," *Century Magazine*, 26:5, Sept. 1883, 643-658). He went to sea at an early age and was still whaling in his forties, in the course of several deepwater voyages working his way up the shipboard hierarchy to first mate, mostly on vessels sailing from Provincetown but also in the bark *Pamela* of New Bedford (1855-58). Around 1850 he married a Mashpee Wampanoag woman named Clarissa, who "before her marriage, taught school near Mercy's wigwam" (loc. cit.), and with her raised five children. Matthias is said to have been a proficient raconteur and among his best-known yarns was about how he first heard of the Civil War when, in the spring of 1861, the whaling schooner of which he was first mate was captured by the Confederate Navy cruiser *John C. Calhoun*, of which the sequel was a "romantic escape with his crew from New Orleans, by the connivance of a domesticated Southerner from Cape Cod" (*loc cit.*) (in fact, three Provincetown whaling vessels were taken by the *Calhoun* in the first months of the war). When Amos left off seafaring he took up farming in Mashpee and became one of the community's most prominent and prosperous citizens — an influential landowner, an incorporator of the town, selectman, town treasurer, and a deacon of his church (*Journal of the House of Representatives of the Commonwealth of Massachusetts*, Boston, 1886; Rosemary H. Burns, "Popponesset by the Sea," *Mashpee Commons Courier*, 2004). When he died in 1885, he left "a snug property for his widow and children" (Simeon L. Deyo, *History of Barnstable County*, Massachusetts, New York, 1890, 707-719). The youngest of his three sons, Lysander, born in 1858, followed his father into a career of farming and public service: he was made collector of taxes at age 22, married Flora E. Bearse, and served on the school committee and as town treasurer, town clerk, justice of the peace, and treasurer and clerk of his church. The middle son, Horatio, followed his father and grandfather to sea at age 14 and was a career mariner up to age about 35. He married Ellen F. Gardiner, served as a selectman and town treasurer, and from 1886 into the twentieth century "operated a successful shellfish business from his oyster shack on the south shore of Daniels Island" in Mashpee (Burns, *Ibid*).

Anderson, — (fl. circa 1836-40). He was in the crew of the Newport, Rhode Island, whaleship *William Lee* (1836-40) when a young passenger, Sereno Edwards Bishop (q.v.), kept a journal (in KNB) that describes various scrimshaw activities. Bishop's remarks about Anderson are particularly significant because they inadvertently corroborate three aspects of shipboard scrimshaw practices that, while perhaps obvious, have hitherto seldom if ever been confirmed by firsthand testimony: first, that whale teeth and other raw materials were sometimes traded or sold among the whalemen themselves (see the article on Mr. Vanderzee); second, that some practitioners cut off the bottoms of teeth "so that they will stand up straight"; and third, that some whalemen took raw materials home, to be scrimshandered ashore. On Feb. 22, 1840 Bishop wrote, "MrV[anderzee] Bought of Anderson today a pair of whale's teeth[;] they are the largest that I ever saw. Anderson has a number of them which he has scraped off clean and cut of[f] the bottoms so that they will stand up straight[.] he is going to carry them home to be carved." Unfortunately, Anderson is not identified further.

* **Archer, James** (fl. circa 1839-56). He is the attributed maker of an exceptionally large, elaborate dressing stand, with drawers and a tilting mirror, inlaid with 1900 individual pieces carved out of eight different materials, including ebony, whale ivory, and baleen (in NHA; cited in Winslow 1955, 10; illustrated in color in Carpenter 1987, Pl. XIX; and noted in the *Dictionary*). A swift has since come to light with the same attribution and original recipient, acquired at a local antiques show at St. Mary's Church in Carmel, California (reported by Sam McDowell). The shaft, ribs, collar, and struts are panbone, with a cup surmount, gasket, and fittings turned from whale ivory and inlaid with red sealing wax. An unusual, perhaps even unique feature is that, rather than having a turnbuckle or thumbscrew to hold the cage in place by pressure against the shaft, the expansion mechanism here is a series of three holes, spaced at regular intervals like the holes in a belt, and in place of a thumbscrew there is a turned whale ivory handle with a steel post that can be inserted in any of the holes to secure the turned ivory collar that supports the cage. The swift is mounted on a wooden, two-tier sewing box, of which the top (through which the shaft penetrates to a mount inside) is semicircular and inlaid with seven mother-of-pearl diamonds, each with a rose incised and painted on it. The top lifts off to provide access to nine posts that accommodate nine spools, from each of which the thread is to be drawn through one of nine wooden nozzles arranged along the semicircular vertical wall of the upper tier. The lower tier has a drawer with two wooden mushroom pulls, inlaid with a diamond bearing the initials "MA" engraved in an ornate script with a border of red sealing wax. The whole box ensemble is supported by four carved-and-turned wooden legs, the front two overlaid with oblong vertical strips of bone on each of which a flowering vine echoes the rose-and-vine motif on the inlay above. A pencil holograph on the bottom of the drawer, presumed to be in the maker's own hand, reads: "James Archer / Captain, Ship Afton / For my wife Mary. / 1854." There is also a handwritten paper insert in another hand: "Captain James Archer of Nantucket for wife Mary on bark Afton between 1853 and 1856."

The *Dictionary* notes that Archer built the dressing table "while master of the bark *Afton* of New Bedford, 1853-56... as a gift for his wife Mary"; that he was born on Nantucket in 1810, served as an officer and captain on New Bedford vessels, was thrice married, and died in Providence in 1869. However, the sequence of wives was not then known in detail. It is now clear from genealogical and census records that what was originally reported in the NHA files, and hence in the *Dictionary*, is erroneous. Archer married Sarah Higgins (1813-1842) on Nantucket in 1831; their daughter was Emeline C. Archer, born in 1831, who married Phineas Peckham of Fairhaven in 1853. Sarah's died in 1842, and in 1843 Archer married Harriet Louisa Stall of New Bedford, about whom nothing else is known and who appears nowhere as Mrs. Archer in the census data or the available genealogical records. Louisa, as she was evidently called, died sometime before 1853, when Archer married a Nantucket dressmaker, Mary C. Ray (born 1819). So he must have made the swift and dressing stand for his new bride on the voyage in the *Afton* that commenced a few weeks after their wedding. The 1860 census reports James, mariner, and Mary, dressmaker, living on Nantucket with three children, among them George, mariner, age 16, who must have been Louisa's son. In 1880, eleven years after James's death, his widow was living in Providence, Rhode Island, with three adult children and a nephew.

Arey, Walter (fl. late 19th century). A double-cage swift of whale ivory and bone, "mounted on a sailor-made box decorated with inlaid compass rose and stars" is reportedly "signed by Walter S. Arey, Hallowell, Maine"; on the wooden box, a hinged lid opens "to two covered sections, the underside inscribed and stamped with the maker's name in several places, the whole raised on small [whale skeletal] bone feet" (Northeast Auctions, 20-21 August, 2005, #768). The description goes on to report erroneously that "Walter S. Arey... was a Master of vessels of Washington Mill Co." However, this is in confusion with the *father* of the *wrong* Walter S. Arey. The actual sea captain in the coastwise lumber trade was Theodore R. Arey (circa 1845-1915), who was born somewhere in Maine but lived most of his adult life in the Washington Territory and Washington State. During the Civil War he was a private in Company M of the Maine Horse Artillery (1863-65), mustering at Franklin, Maine, and suffered from a deformed wrist from a battlefield sabre cut. He went into the coasting trade in 1865, lived for many years at Port Hadlock, Washington, and was master of the coastal barkentine *J.M. Griffith*. According to the Washington Territorial Census, he was living at Port Hadlock, aged 43 in 1889; his obituary in a Port Townsend newspaper, dated 24 July 1915, reports that he was 71 at the time of his death. He married Frances Boyd and had two sons, one of whom was named Walter. This Walter was born in Washington Territory, not in Maine; he never lived in Maine, and was no sea captain, but rather a machinist at Hadlock, Washington.

Of the several other men named Walter Arey (Walter was a common name in the Arey clan, especially among Areys born in the late 1860s), Walter Arey of Hallowell, Maine, whose name and residence appear on the swift, was born circa 1867. The 1920 U.S. Census lists him as 53 years old at that time, married to a woman named Sarah, but gives no occupation and names no children. The elegant swift with his name on it seems rather too early a model to have been made by a man born as late as 1867: it could conceivably have been made by someone else, earlier, perhaps a namesake forebear at Hallowell. However, it seems more likely that the Walter Arey of Hallowell who was born circa 1867 was an *heir* to the swift, rather than the *maker*, and that his name on it is one of ownership rather than authorship. In any case, no whaling voyages have been identified.

Ashley, Edward R. (fl. circa 1841-67). New Bedford whaling master. By implication from the scrimshaw itself, but in the absence of any direct testimony, he is credited with a 10 ½-inch (27 mm) wooden chest, dovetail joined, with a hinged lid, one drawer with a turned wooden pull, the sides inlaid with hearts, diamonds, arrows, and geometrical designs in whale ivory and tropical woods, and a rectangular whale ivory plaque with chamfered corners, centered on the stepped lid, polychrome engraved with a spread eagle, crossed American flags, and two anchors, surmounted by the name in bold serifed capitals "E.R. ASHLEY" (Rinaldi Catalogue #35, 2004, item #39). John Rinaldi commented in 2004 that when the box was sold at auction 30+ years before (Bourne, August 1973, lot #80), the description noted that there was also "an important affidavit document signed by Edward R. Ashley giving his brother power of attorney while he was away on a whaling voyage aboard the ship '*Reindeer*,'" but that "sometime since the 1973 sale the document has been lost or separated from the box." Ashley was a career whaleman, born circa 1822; his younger brothers

George and Thomas were also mariners, the sons of William Ashley and his wife Delania, farmers in Fairhaven, Massachusetts. It was Edward who made the greatest success of whaling. He embarked on his maiden voyage by 1841 and ascended rapidly through the ranks — especially rapidly when his progress was accelerated by Captain Seth Blackmer. Ashley was Blackmer's third mate in the ship *Roman 2d* (1847-50) and he was able to skip the next step in his career when Blackmer — evidently pleased with Ashley's abilities — signed him as first mate on his next command, the Fairhaven ship *Erie* (1850-53). Ashley was then poised for command. Immediately after the *Erie* voyage he became captain of the *William Wirt* (1853-56), followed by the *Reindeer* (1856-60) and the *Governor Troupe* (1862-67), all New Bedford ships. His wife, the former Adra C. Braley (born circa 1835), accompanied him on at least two voyages, and their two sons were both born at Hilo, Hawaii — Edward W. circa 1855, during the *William Wirt* voyage, and Granville in 1865, when Captain Ashley had the *Governor Troupe*. By the time their daughter Lucy Delana came along their voyaging was over and they were living on a farm in Acushnet, where Lucy was born in 1867. The implication about the box, of course, is that it was either from the *Reindeer* voyage itself, or from the voyage immediately preceding it, when the power of attorney might have been deposited therein and the box left with Ashley's brother while the captain was at sea in the *Reindeer*. The brother would have been William, the youngest, the one who was not a sailor. On the other hand, without a specific provenance based upon documentary evidence or at least on family testimony, any such circumstances are merely speculative.

Ashley, Marcus M. (fl. 1862-64). The plain sperm whale panbone shaft of an unfinished cane, lacking any pommel, handle, or ferrule, found in the walls of a house in Lakeville (formerly part of Middleborough), Massachusetts, leads to a sad story. From the provenance of the house it is possible to attribute the scrimshaw to its only known whaleman occupant, a farmer's son who went on three whaling voyages in schooners out of Sippican. Marcus Ashley was born in 1841 at Middleborough, the son of David and Lavinia Ashley. In youth he worked as a farmhand on the family place, but possibly because his brother John, older by five years, was set to inherit the farm, or perhaps in order to escape conscription into the Union Army, at age 21 he went whaling, first in the *Admiral Blake* (1862), then in the *James* (1863). But like the unfinished scrimshaw, Marcus's life and career ended unfinished. In May 1864 he sailed in the schooner *Emerald*, but the schooner soon foundered with all hands.

Atkins, James (fl. circa 1848-81). He was master of eight whaling voyages in schooners out of Provincetown (1866-81), and at one point in his journal he alludes to what was likely scrimshaw-making. Backscratchers were one of the earliest forms of whalemen's scrimshaw: known makers include Christopher Almy in the 1790s and Thomas Smith Taylor in the 1870s (qq.v.); and it is evidently to a backscratcher that Captain Atkins refers in his entry for May 27, 1869 aboard the schooner *Agate*, though he provides no particulars: "This day squally. Saw one sail (a schooner) bound to the Southward. Worked on the cutting stage, and grannie scratcher. So ends this day." Captain Atkins was born at Provincetown in 1833, the second son of Rual Atkins, mariner, and Rebecca Atkins; he married a woman named Hannah, who bore him a daughter, and he lived more than a decade into the 20th century.

Austin, Andrew (fl. circa 1830-'60s). Azorean-American whaleman: a tooth inscribed "1849 Andrew Austin of Platina, Rochester, Massachusetts," in a private collection, is the only piece attributed. He was born in 1812 on the island of Graciosa and emigrated to New England in the crew of an unidentified whaleship. So too his brother Joseph, two years younger. They settled in Chilmark, Martha's Vineyard, they both made careers as professional deck officers on New Bedford whaleships, and they wed sisters. Andrew's wife, whom he married in 1837, was Augusta M. Tilton, a local woman from one of the Island's oldest and most numerous families. Joseph married her kid sister Evalina. In his whaling career, Austin appears to have been a kind of perpetual second mate. While his early voyages are not known, on the four that are known he was second mate, in the ship *Hercules* of New Bedford (1845-47), barks *Platina* of Westport (1847-50) and *Elizabeth* of Mattapoisett (1850-52), and ship *Canton* of New Bedford (1855-58). Joseph and Evalina remained on Martha's Vineyard, where they raised a family, but by 1860 Andrew, Augusta, and their only son, James — born in 1838 and also a career whaleman — moved to Westport, Massachusetts; they also lived for a while in New Bedford. The inscription on the tooth is something of an anomaly, as neither the ship nor the man was from Rochester, with which Austin's only documented connection was the bark *Elizabeth*, registered in the adjacent Sippican town of Mattapoisett.

Baker, Amos C., Sr. (fl. circa 1830-80). New Bedford whaling master and lighthouse keeper who produced a variety of utilitarian scrimshaw: a panbone fid engraved with the initials "ACB"; a small sheave block of sperm whale ivory with brass rivet fastenings, crudely incised "Made by Capt. A.C. BAKER aboard the SHIP MESSENGER 1852"; various small woodworking-type tools for making scrimshaw that are themselves scrimshaw (i.e., that have whale ivory or panbone handles), including a handsaw, screwdriver, claw hammer, rasp, auger, gouge, etc.; and a whale ivory crimper with fluted jagging wheel, dated 1853. He may also have made ornamental items that are indistinguishable from the generally more decorative work of his son and namesake (q.v. below). The scrimshaw of father and son are in a family legacy collection that also includes logbooks, journals, letters, and assorted whaling and Lighthouse Service memorabilia, which in the twentieth century had somehow come into the possession of the family attorney and descended to the attorney's heirs, who donated them to NBWM in 2005 and 2006.

Amos Crowell Baker, Sr., was born in 1811, the son of one Sylvanus Baker and the former Bethiah Crowell, who had come to Dartmouth, Massachusetts, from Yarmouth on Cape Cod. Amos went to sea at an early age and rose to command seven whaling voyages out of New Bedford and Fairhaven: two in the ship *George Washington* (1845-48, 1848-51), the one in the *Messenger* (1851-55) with which his scrimshaw is most closely associated, then the barks *John Dawson* (1855-59), *Union* (1863-64), and *Sarah* (1865-67), and the brig *Oxford* of Fairhaven (1867-68). He retired from whaling in 1868, worked for a while as a supervisor in one of New Bedford's burgeoning cotton mills, and became Keeper of the Clark's Point Lighthouse in New Bedford in 1872, succeeding his uncle, Henry M. Smith, a carver of wooden figureheads and billetheads for the whaling fleet, who was the first keeper of Clark's Point Light (1842-72). As it turned out, Smith was the first and Baker the second of four generations of the same family to serve as keepers of New Bedford's principal lighthouses (Clark's Point and its successor), spanning 100 years, from 1842 to 1941. In 1836 Amos had married Amy Briggs, who bore him three children, of whom the oldest was Amos Crowell Baker, Jr. (q.v.), who succeeded his namesake father first as a whaling master and then as lighthouse keeper. The senior Baker also held an ownership interest in the Dartmouth schooner *Hope in Delight,* in which his partners included (in addition to his infant son) his father, Sylvanus Baker; his uncle, Ensign Baker, who served as captain; and the famous whaling merchant-financiers Ivory H. Bartlett, Alexander H. Seabury, and William O. Brownell, who were among the leading figures of Dartmouth. Amos Baker died in 1881.

Baker, Amos C., Jr. (fl. circa 1851-80). New Bedford whaling master and lighthouse keeper who made a variety of utilitarian and ornamental scrimshaw items. Definitely by his hand are two whale ivory crimpers with fluted jagging wheels and pistol-grip handles that have floral patterns and initials inlaid in tortoise shell and abalone — one has "EFB," indicating Emily F. Baker (née Durfee), his wife; the other, "AB," for Amy Baker (née Briggs), his mother. There is also a similarly decorated whale ivory paper knife, similarly inlaid "EFB." Attributions include three polychrome teeth, one with a standing female figure, and a pair with floral motifs; and an elegant, full-scale, double-cage swift with panbone shaft and ribs, and whale ivory sprockets, clamp, and finial. He probably made several other pieces that came with the Baker family collection, some of which may be the work of his father, Amos C. Baker, Sr. (q.v.): a pair of bud vases, each made from a hollowed-out whale tooth mounted on a column of turned whale ivory in the form of stemmed goblets with fluted rims; a coconut-shell dipper with whale ivory fittings and finial on the wooden handle; a spatulate spreader of sperm whale ivory with a handle that has tortoise shell "cheeks"; a cow horn serving spoon; a turned whale ivory napkin ring; three whale ivory bodkins; and a whale ivory tatting shuttle. It was also probably Amos Jr. (but possibly his father) who brought home some larger-than-average raw teeth and a whole section of gum from a juvenile sperm whale with the teeth still embedded. All of these are part of a family legacy collection that includes logbooks, journals, letters, and assorted whaling and Lighthouse Service memorabilia, donated to NBWM by heirs of the Baker family attorney.

Amos Crowell Baker, Jr., was born at Dartmouth, Massachusetts, in 1839, the oldest of three children of Captain Amos Crowell Baker and the former Amy Briggs. He undertook his maiden voyage at age 12 as ship's boy under his father in the New Bedford ship *Messenger* (1851-55), and did a watercolor portrait of the ship and several other drawings in his journal of the voyage (NBWM). He served under his father again as seaman in the bark *John Dawson* (1855-59), made a second voyage in that vessel as a boatsteerer under Captain John W. Cornell (1859-62), and on his next voyage, as third mate in the bark *Awashonks* (1862-65), he was seriously injured by a whale and "lay for 80 days on his back while a leg bone broken in two places was knitting. He was gone 38 months, and on his return stayed ashore until his injured leg was as strong as the other" (Obit., 1911). Maybe sooner than he really should have, he sailed as second mate in the bark *Stafford* (1865-67), and "again met with misfortune, and was disabled in a fight with a whale" (loc.cit.). He was back at sea soon afterwards as first mate of the bark *Atlantic* (1868-72), but was not appointed as captain immediately following that voyage, which was the usual expectation. Perhaps he failed to get a favorable recommendation from Captain Henry R. Craw of the *Atlantic;* perhaps he did not get an offer he liked; or perhaps he had suffered enough battering for a while and chose to remain on hiatus ashore. Or perhaps he merely wanted to spend some time with his bride: he had married Hattie Holmes Jones in 1867 but had been away at sea for most of the time since. In any case, during 1872-74 he was Overseer in the Cloth Room of New Bedford's Potomska textile mill.

Hattie bore him a son in February 1874 but, sadly, she died of complications from childbirth two weeks later (the poor child, James, lived only seven years). Amos went back to sea the same year. In November 1874 he was given command of the bark *A.R. Tucker* (the famous little vessel in which Daniel Lake Ricketson had recently completed the celebrated voyage chronicled by his wife), in which he made two fairly successful Atlantic Ocean sperm whaling voyages. It is worth noting that the future scrimshaw artist and whaling captain J.T. Edwards (q.v.) joined the crew of the *A.R. Tucker* at Flores, in the Azores Islands, in 1874; and that Captain Baker held two ownership interests in the vessel: a 2⁄32nds share in the profits from each of his own voyages, and 1⁄32nd from the voyage following. Between voyages in 1876 he was married for the second time, to Emma F. Durfee, who bore him another son in August 1877; but by the time Charles Amos Baker was born Captain Baker was already at sea again in the *A.R. Tucker*. He could have continued whaling for many more years, but in 1880 he was appointed to succeed his father as Keeper of Clark's Point Light, strategically located on a point of land projecting into Buzzards Bay at the mouth of the Acushnet River south of New Bedford. This remained his occupation for the remainder of his life. In 1898 Clark's Point Light was replaced by Butler Flats Light, a tower built like as island in the middle of the estuary itself. Baker moved out there as its first Keeper, with son Charles as Assistant. He also had a daughter, Amy Frances, born in 1889, to whom he would become very close. He was widowed for a second time in 1902, then married a woman named Susan, from whom he was separated not very long afterwards. It is not clear whether the couple were formally divorced (though divorce proceedings were certainly in progress by 1910), but, oddly, in 1910 U.S. Census reports Amos twice, at two different addresses: one living with his son at Butler Flats Light, the other at his estranged wife's address in town. He died in 1911, exactly 100 years after his father's birth. He was succeeded as Lighthouse Keeper by his son and assistant, Charles Amos Baker, who continued for the next 30 years to 1941, 100 years after his great-great uncle Henry Smith first started at Clark's Point Light.

Baker, Archelaus, Jr. (fl. circa 1830s-75). His remarks about scrimshaw when he was captain of the Fairhaven bark *John A. Robb* serve, if nothing else, to corroborate the obvious notion that scrimshawing on shipboard was so common that it usually passed without comment in seamen's letters and journals. On January 1, 1861, Baker wrote in his journal, "I feel the best that I have for the last 8 Months[;] commenced Squimshoning the first I have dun for the last 6 months." He was evidently a regular "squimshoner" until six months before, when he started feeling ill; and it was only when his return to scrimshaw became a symptom of his recovery that it seemed to him worthy of mention. Six or eight months previous, when, according to his own later testimony, he was actively working at scrimshaw, he was silent on the subject; and he did not mention any of the many other times he must have been making scrimshaw on this and previous voyages. From what little documentation there is, it appears that most of the whalers who worked at scrimshaw did so fairly often and fairly regularly, conditions permitting. It is clear from Baker's remarks, and from testimony about him, that under normal circumstances he, for one, was a more regular and frequent scrimshaw-maker than his day-to-day journal entries indicate.

Remarkably, in the 18th century and throughout the 19th there were many mariners, farmers, and tradesmen in southeastern Massachusetts named Archelaus Baker, including two whaling masters. The popularity then of what today would be an unusual name results in a hopeless tangle of census data, vital records, and shipping papers, compounded by the corrupting influences of amateur genealogists who have frequently re-jumbled what was already a difficult process of separating one Archelaus Baker from another. Thus, while the whaling careers may be fairly discernable, the family backgrounds and shoreside activities are not. There was a slightly earlier Captain Archelaus Baker, Jr., who was master of the New Bedford bark *Cora* in the 1840s; but the man who was captain of the *John A. Robb* was younger, from Dartmouth, Massachusetts, served as first mate of the New Bedford ship *Hibernia* (1846-49), which was also his first command (1849-53), and was master of five other voyages. One of these, in fact the next after *Hibernia*, turned out to be one of the most harrowing ordeals in the annals of whaling. He sailed for the Indian Ocean in the Dartmouth bark *Henry H. Crapo* in June 1854, and 30 months later, towards the end of what had been shaping up as an excellent voyage, the vessel was "Lost at sea January 19, 1857, with a full cargo of sperm oil." Almost all hands were lost: "the captain and one man — the sole survivors — were rescued by the English steamer *England*" (Starbuck, 519). Baker's next voyage was the one in the *John A. Robb* (1857-61), after which he finished out his career in three New Bedford vessels, the ship *Canton 2d* (1862-66), bark *Vigilant* (1867-70), and bark *Hercules* (1871-75).

Baker, George W. (fl. circa 1887-1907). San Francisco whaleman credited with an ensemble of six "half-hull" models of whales carved out of sperm whale ivory, each 3-5 inches (76-13 mm) in length, each labeled below on its individual ivory plaque, "HUMPBACK," "PIKED OR LESSER" [i.e., minke], "SPERM," "RIGHT," "ARCTIC RIGHT," and "NARWHAL" (the latter with a spiral tusk separately carved out of whale ivory), mounted on a crest-like wooden backboard approximately 11 x 11 inches (28 x 28 cm) in size, with curled and perfled edges, surmounted by an openwork bone filigree ornament; in a private collection. A small whale ivory plaque bears the engraved title, "The GREAT WHALES of the OCEAN / Made by / Geo. W. Baker of the / Bk LANCER." The provenance is undocumented and the attribution is puzzling, because while the whale effigies are carved out of sperm whale ivory, the only voyages associated with the *Lancer* on which it could have been made were purely right- and bowhead-whaling expeditions to the Western Arctic on which no sperm whales were taken, thus one would expect such a piece to have been carved out of walrus ivory, which was plentiful in San Francisco and in the Western Arctic.

The *Lancer*, constructed as a ship at Newburyport, Massachusetts, in 1852, was converted to a bark in 1869, and afterwards made five whaling voyages out of New Bedford (1869-86) and three out of San Francisco to the North Pacific and Western Arctic (1887-90). The vessel was condemned at Vladivostok in 1890 and taken out of service. Of several American whalemen named George W. Baker, only one was active contemporaneously with the whaling career of the *Lancer* and the Western Arctic bowhead fishery. He must have made some earlier voyages as a green hand and seaman, of which the records have not been discovered: at least one of these could have been in the *Lancer*, perhaps during 1887-89 out of San Francisco (for, according to the crew lists for the New Bedford voyages, Geroge W. Baker was surely not in the *Lancer* at any earlier time). His documented voyages were as boatsteerer in the steamer *Beluga* (1900-01), fourth mate in the *Beluga* and steamer *Karluk* (1901-03), third mate in the *Karluk* (1904-06), and second mate in the ship *Jeanette* (1907). Nothing else is known about him. Regardless of authorship, the piece in any case typifies the latter-day genre of half-hull whale specimen boards, produced more often by shoreside souvenir-makers in the 1910s, '20s, and '30s (and later by Azorean carvers) than by deepwater whalemen on shipboard.

* **Baker, John.** The *Dictionary* cites a "Wooden medicine cabinet with whale bone inlay, found on Nantucket and attributed in BJ:2 (#356): 'According to tradition, the cabinet was made by John Baker aboard the bark *Osprey*, which was converted to the whaling trade in 1851 and made at least ten whaling voyages.'" There were many men named John Baker in the 19th-century New Bedford whaling trade, in connection with which it is worth noting that crew lists survive from nine of the ten voyages of the bark *Ospray* (not *Osprey*). No one with the surname Baker appears on any of them. If anyone named Baker ever embarked on a whaling voyage in the *Ospray* it must have been the 1857-62 outing, the one for which the outward manifest is absent in the rolls of the New Bedford Port Society; and without the crew list for corroboration, there is no evidence that anyone named Baker ever served aboard the *Ospray* in any capacity.

* **Baker, S.** This artist was formerly known as the Pagoda Artisan owing to his curious treatment of architectural features in his harbor scenes, which resemble stereotypical Chinese examples, and his work was associated with that of the Albatross Artisan, which was believed possibly to be by the same hand. However, recent comparisons by the SFL, employing improved methods that only lately became available as applied to scrimshaw, indicate conclusively that the Pagoda and Albatross Artisans (qq.v.) were two different artists and not one, as previously conjectured. An oversize powder horn signed "S. Baker" (in KNB), together with eight teeth and a panbone C-clamp (in various museum and private collections), are now attributed to S. Baker, who is confidently identified as Silvanus Baker (q.v.).

Baker, Silvanus (fl. circa 1831-36). An unusually large, profusely ornamented, and elaborately inscribed powder horn (in KNB) bears the date 1836 and the names John Rook and S. Baker (qq.v. in the *Dictionary*). The identity of John Rook (q.v.), for whom the piece was evidently engraved, has since become incontrovertibly clear. That Rook did not engrave it himself is indicated by a cryptographic inscription that appears to be a dedication *to* John Rook, and the apparent signature "S. Baker." Circumstantial evidence indicates that the maker was Silvanus Baker, a former whaleman who became a master mariner in the coastwise trade but who was likely not yet a captain in 1836 when the powder horn was engraved.

The horn is S-curved, about 18-inches (46 cm) long, with a turned wooden base inserted in the broad end, fastened with three wooden pins, with the center drilled and threaded to accommodate a screw-on wooden finial stopper. A leather band at the narrow end is for attaching a shoulder strap. The main body of the horn is ornately engraved over almost the entire surface. There are four broadside portraits of warships under sail: a full-rigged ship of 58 guns flying a commission pennant at the main and square house-flag-like pennants at the fore and mizzen; a full brig and a hermaphrodite brig (or half brig), each carrying 22 guns and flying similar square pennants; and a so-called brigantine with 22 gunports, flying the same square pennants. There are also two American spread-eagles, several buildings rendered in the distinctive manner of the Pagoda Artisan, and an accurate depiction of a whaleboat in pursuit, with the harpooner wielding a large double-flue iron. These are interspersed with various landscape vignettes, foliage, trees, fish, stars, geometric shapes, etc., all haphazardly arranged, surmounted at the narrow end by a harlequin diamond pattern and cryptic inscriptions, arranged circumferentially. One of these can be fairly readily deciphered and provides essential clues to the authorship and original ownership:

"1836 ST[ATE] OF MAIN[E] / PHIPSBURG MAIN[E]." The other is a crude and more enigmatic cryptogram: "yyURyyUBICURyyFORME" ["Too wise you are, too wise you be; I see you are too wise for me"]. Boldly inscribed on the main body are "JOHN ROOK HIS HORN," "PANDIES," and "SHIP BOSTON." In 1836 John Rook, who is presumed to have been the recipient of the piece rather than its maker, was a 30-year-old fisherman and former deepwater sailor living in Phippsburg. Whether he or Silvanus Baker ever served in a ship named *Boston* has not been ascertained. The American ship-of-the-line can only be the USS *Superior*, an oversize, heavily armed frigate of 58 guns (though naval ordnance varied), launched in 1814 at Sacketts Harbor, New York, for War of 1812 service on the Great Lakes. The significance of *pandies* here is unclear. A *pandy* is a *fulling mill* (for *fulling* or *felting* wool in textile manufacture), and Pandy is accordingly said to be a common place-name in Wales. To *pandy* is also British slang, meaning to strike someone on the open palm of the hand with a cane, ruler, or strap, a kind of punishment encountered in old style English public schools. A scholar is thus *pandied*, and in the course of time might receive several *pandies*. However, in the context of a Down East powder horn the meaning is obscure, even to the extent of whether the word is intended as a noun or verb. Perhaps it is a private signal referring to some now-forgotten occurrence between maker and recipient.

As far as can be determined from extant records, of all the men named S. Baker in the State of Maine who were old enough conceivably to have engraved a powder horn in 1836, Silvanus was the only professional mariner, the only whaleman, and in fact the only one with significant experience as a deepwater sailor. His only known whaling voyage was in the ship *Lancaster* of New Bedford (1831-34), where his name appears as S. Baker and his age is incorrectly given as 25 (he was actually a few months short of his twentieth birthday at the outset of the voyage). His firsthand knowledge of whaling is reflected in the technically competent whaling scene on the powder horn; so, too, on the eight sperm whale teeth engraved with ships, broadside portraits of sperm whales, whaling scenes, and harborscapes that are attributed to the same hand. Whether he made any other whaling voyages is not known, but he may be the same man who appears later in the maritime records only as "Captain S. Baker," just as his name is rendered on the *Lancaster* shipping papers and and the signature on the powder horn. He was master of the merchant brig *Yucatan*, 177 tons, in the Commercial Line out of Boston on the Baltimore run in 1843, and the same vessel in the reconstituted so-called New Line, running between Philadelphia and Mobile beginning in 1845. That would have been before his one other whaling voyage in the *John Dawson*.

Silvanus Baker was born in 1811 in Dennis, Massachusetts, on Cape Cod, where the Baker clan is enormous and the name Sylvanus or Silvanus occurred often in each generation from the 17th century into the 20th. This Silvanus was the second son of Nathaniel Baker and the former Thankful Covil of Dennis. It is not known whether he went to sea at an early age, which he probably did; nor how he came to settle in Maine, just outside Portland, unless it were to take advantage of the manifold opportunities for seafarers and mechanics occasioned by Maine's burgeoning shipbuilding industry and robust seaborne economy (Baker was a mere ten years old when Maine became a state); nor how he was associated with John Rook, to whom the powder horn is inscribed. In any case, throughout his adult life he was a resident of Yarmouth, Maine, and earned his living by the sea. Around the time of the date on the powder horn (when he may still have been living in Massachusetts and working as a whaleman), or shortly thereafter, he married a woman named Mary, who was also from Massachusetts. They had four sons and two daughters, all born in Maine.

At least two of the sons followed their father to sea and settled with their families on adjacent farms in Yarmouth. The family had a hired hand named Edward Thompson who was around the same age as the Bakers's older children and lived with them for decades to tend to the farming while the other menfolk were at sea. To what extent Captain Baker may have held shares in the vessels and cargoes he managed is unknown, but the family's circumstances appear to have been comfortable. He died sometime before 1880.

Superficial similarities in the layout and iconography of engraved teeth by the Pagoda Artisan (now identified as Silvanus Baker) and the Albatross Artisan (still anonymous), combined with the scarcity and inaccessibility of works by the Albatross Artisan, which precluded any side-by-side comparison, led some observers to group them all together as the work of the same hand (an erroneous position reflected in the *Dictionary* and *More Scrimshaw Artists*). The recent appearance of a masterpiece tooth by the Albatross Artisan (Northeast Auctions, 19-20 August 2006) enabled direct and more exacting scrutiny, resulting in the conclusion that the two hands are decidedly not the same. The curious, Chinatown-like architecture of the buildings in the Pagoda Artisan's seaport scenes, as described in the *Dictionary,* remain the principal distinguishing features of this artist's work, hence the moniker. However, such pagoda-like eccentricities are only vaguely approximated in the work of the Albatross Artisan, where the appreciably larger size, more spacious format, and graceful shapes of the teeth themselves, the much greater clarity and open style of the engraving, the extremely high polish with a deep and lustrous patina, and especially the large birds in flight, are characteristic and distinctive. In addition to the powder horn signed *S. Baker,* currently eight teeth and a panbone clamp are confidently attributed to Silvanus Baker, AKA the Pagoda Artisan: two in NBWM, one in KNB, two others quite similar to the KNB tooth in private collections (reported by Edward Stecewicz, Jonathan Blum, and Paul Vardeman), one in NCP (reported by Judith N. Lund), one in SSS (Hellman & Brouwer, pp. 36f), and two from the Barbara Johnson Collection (one in Sotheby's New York, BJ1:11-12; and one that passed through the Johnson, Wehle, and Cohen collections and was thrice sold by Bourne: 31 July 1989, #80; 2 Aug. 1983, #345; 30 May 1990 #178). The simple panbone C-clamp (reported by William J. Boylhart) was presumably intended for a swift and is lathe-turned out of sperm whale panbone, with a baluster-shaped, threaded panbone turnbuckle; it has a characteristic, monochrome-engraved, pagoda-type building with a tower and a weathervane in the form of a whale on one side, and a full brig under sail on the other side, with features of the sails, hull, and flags that strongly resemble the ships and brigs on the powder horn and the various Pagoda teeth. Scrimshaw by the Albatross Artisan is far scarcer (only two teeth are known for sure), ranks with the best pictorial works ever produced by a whaleman, and has consistently set records for prices realized at auction (Flayderman, 107 and 73, top; *Time-Life, The Whalers,* 1979. title page; Osona, 14 Aug. 1993; and Northeast, 19-20 Aug. 2006). See the articles on John Rook and the Albatross Artisan. (Silvanus Baker of Yarmouth, Maine, is not to be confused with Sylvanus Baker of Dartmouth, Massachusetts, a career whaleman born circa 1818: he was the eldest son and namesake of a resident of Harwich, on Cape Cod, who was originally from Dartmouth; one of his sons was Amos C. Baker, Sr. [q.v.]; Amos C. Baker, Jr. [q.v.] was his grandson.)

Balch, John W. (fl. circa 1850s-'80s). Descendants have provided a convincing provenance and family history that names John W. Balch as having engraved a pair of walrus tusks "during his long voyages at sea" (reported by Joanne Balch Coser). On the tusks are figures of scantily-clad show-girls, four sitting and one standing; and a classical nude, with cherub hovering nearby. The show-girls have not been identified but the other figures, copied after a contemporaneous engraved illustration, certainly represent Cupid and Psyche. All of them, as well as the ensemble itself, are reminiscent of tusks with multiple figures engraved by N.S. Finney (q.v.).

John William Balch was born in 1834 in Trescott, Maine, the eldest of eleven children of ship-builder, merchant, and sea captain John Balch and the former Mary Elizabeth Chaloner. The son's early career is not documented and it is unknown whether he ever went whaling, but by the time he joined the Union Navy at age 28 in 1861 he had accumulated sufficient sea experience to qualify him for an immediate command. This was partly a result of family connections having given him a jumpstart on his career. In 1857, when he was only 23, he was installed as captain of the ship *Troy*, 712 tons, in the Hurlbut Line on the New York to Antwerp run: the ship had been built by his father in 1854. Balch served to the end of the Civil War and a few months after: from September 1861 to November 1862 as Acting Master of the USS *Florida*, then as commander of the *Houquah*. He suffered capture and imprisonment by the Confederacy at Salisbury, South Carolina, then at the infamous Libby Prison in Richmond, where "family tradition mentions him carving small bones"— likely bones from the soup salt beef served to the inmates, analogously to the prisoner-of-war carvings by French mariners held in British prison hulks during the Napoleonic Wars. In the meantime, in November 1862, during a brief hiatus between his stints in the *Florida* and the *Houquah*, he married Mary E. Turner. After his discharge in October 1865 Balch had a long second career as a merchant sea captain on the Pacific coast, living and working out of San Francisco. There was no issue from the marriage, but Mary accompanied him on several voyages. In fact, she died at sea near Rio de Janeiro in 1889, and family lore reports, "there was almost a mutiny by his men because [the captain] refused to bury her at sea. The sailors felt it was bad luck to have a dead woman's body on board." After Balch died in 1911, the tusks passed to his niece, Mary Elizabeth "Molly" (née Balch) Noble, then through two more generations to the current collateral descendants.

* **Bangs, Eli [Jr.]** (fl. circa 1856-61). Ship's cooper credited with two substantial, well engraved works of scrimshaw that descended in the Bangs family along with associated whaling materials. The *Dictionary* notes a mantle ornament consisting of a pair of walrus tusks, each engraved on one side with sealing-wax highlights, depicting the standing figure of a Renaissance navigator with a globe, in the manner of latter-day portraits of Columbus; and a standing female symbolic figure in Classical toga, with nautical paraphernalia including large sheave blocks. They are mounted together vertically on a flat, rectangular wooden stand, with walrus ivory pilasters on the front cornices, the skirt inlaid with circles, triangles, and diamonds of marine ivory, mother of pearl, and assorted woods, surmounted by a smaller wooden platform with carved wooden legs, supporting a pair of plain, polished sperm whale teeth, each on its own chamfered wooden base; the gift of Idella M. Mandley, granddaughter of Eli Bangs, in 1977. The other is a pair of teeth, each with both sides densely polychrome engraved: one with a standing figure of Liberty holding a wreath and an equestrian portrait after the French painter David's "Bonaparte Crossing the Alps"; the other with a figure of Liberty, a Union shield, and an eagle on one side, and on the other side a starboard broadside view of a full-rigged ship under plain sail, flying signal flags, an owners' pennant, and a U.S. ensign, off a rocky coast with a lighthouse. The latter pair was purchased from a Bangs descendant in 2003 with a shipboard whaling journal in two volumes, kept by the artist as ship's

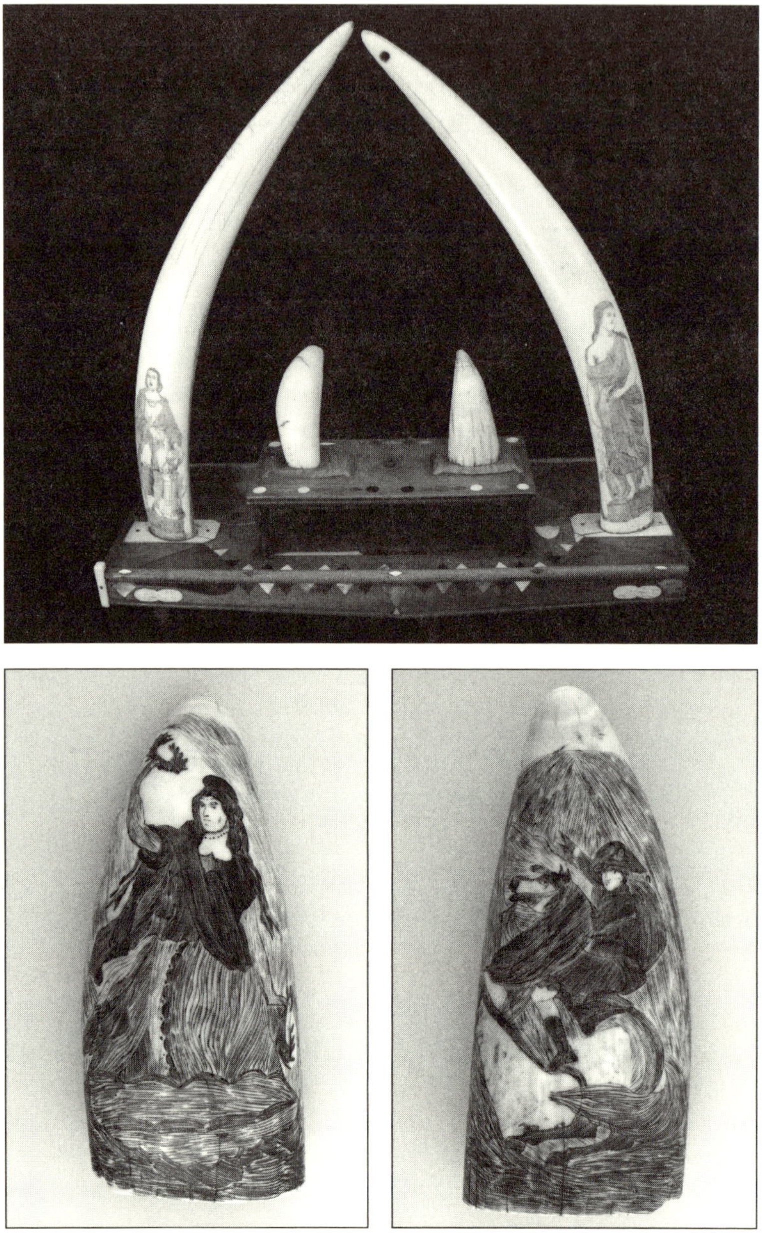

Fig. 2. **Scrimshaw by Eli Bangs.** A mantle stand featuring a pair of scrimshawed walrus tusks set into a whale ivory base, two undecorated sperm whale teeth, whale ivory corner posts, walrus ivory pilasters, and a skirt and platforms inlaid with geometrical ornaments of marine ivory, mother of pearl, and assorted woods. The tusks are engraved with the standing figure of a navigator in Renaissance garb with a globe, in the manner of latter-day portraits of Columbus (left); and a standing female figure in Classical toga, with nautical paraphernalia including large sheave blocks and cordage. Below: A pair of densely polychrome-engraved teeth featuring an equestrian portrait of Napoleon Crossing the Alps, after Jacques-Louis David circa 1801-05, and a figure of Columbus holding a wreath. (The other sides have a figure of Liberty with a Union shield; and a broadside view of a full-rigged ship, flying signal flags, owners' pennant, and American ensign, off a rocky coast with a lighthouse.) Collection of the New Bedford Whaling Museum.

cooper on the maiden voyage of the New Bedford whaling bark *Helen Mar* (1856-61); also his military discharge papers, a photograph of him as a Union Army officer (circa 1862), and another from later years (circa 1910-20). The whaling records, and hence the *Dictionary*, report his birthplace as Bridgeton, New York, but it was actually Bridgeton, New Jersey, where he was born in January 1836, the son of Eli A. Bangs, originally from Philadelphia, and the former Mary Schuek, who died soon after. Thus young Eli was raised by his father and two subsequent wives. (Unaccountably, the 1900 U.S. Census erroneously reports him as having been born in Virginia). His one documented voyage was the one in the *Helen Mar* (1856-61), where the great whaleman-artist Robert W. Weir, Jr., was one of his shipmates. He served as a lieutenant in the 5th Delaware Union Army Volunteers during the Civil War, worked as a cooper and carpenter in Wilmington until circa 1875, then was proprietor of his own cooperage in Baltimore, where at least two of his four sons worked as apprentices. While the U.S. Census consistently lists him as a cooper, the family genealogy identifies his occupation as mariner. His wife's name was Esther, he was a lifelong member of the Grand Army of the Republic, he fathered two daughters as well as the four sons, he was widowed in 1885, and he died in 1923.

* **Banknote Engraver** — see William T. Lavare

Barrett, Thomas Jefferson (fl. circa 1846-47). Officer on a Mystic, Connecticut whaleship credited with being the co-maker of a piece of scrimshaw furniture. Captain George Bailey, in his logbook of the bark *Vermont* during 1846-47, reports that the mate designed a desk that was built by the ship's carpenter. Thomas Jefferson Barrett was the mate, but the identity of the carpenter has not surfaced, the desk surely perished before the voyage ended, and nothing further is known about Mr. Barrett. The *Vermont* was built in 1831 at Kennebunk, Maine, made five whaling voyages from Poughkeepsie, New York (1832-43), and was sold to a consortium of new owners for whom she made two additional voyages from Mystic. The first, commanded by Jonathan Nash, Jr. (1843-46), was essentially uneventful except for a few injuries. The second, with Bailey as captain and Barrett as mate, fared badly and ended worse. Six men died from "African fever," another drowned, and the vessel itself was wrecked in the Indian Ocean on either St. Paul Island or Amsterdam Island (reports differ), a total loss. The survivors were brought home in the Fairhaven ships *Calumet* and *Friendship* and the New Bedford ship *Cicero*. As Barrett's name does not appear on any casualty list he was almost certainly among the rescued, but in all likelihood the desk went down with the *Vermont*. Though there were several men named Thomas Barrett whaling at around this time, this particular one has not been definitively identified in any subsequent whaling crew.

Bartlett, A.L. (fl. circa 1851-58). A cane (walking stick) "made by A.L. Bartlett" was donated to NBWM by his granddaughter in 1992, along with his letters home written at sea. The cane has a panbone shaft carved with a double-spiral rope motif that carries over onto the whale ivory shank, with a large whale ivory pommel carved in the form of a turk's head (monkey's fist) knot. Alanson L. Bartlett was born at Bristol, Vermont, circa 1837, the son of Charles and Mehitable Bartlett. He and his brother Charles, elder by one year, grew up on the family farm at Croydon, New Hampshire, and each went whaling at age 14. In October 1851, when Charles was already several months at sea as a green hand and "second cooper" in the bark *Favorite* of Fairhaven (1850-53), Alanson got his first Protection Paper (seaman's passport) at New Bedford and sailed as a green hand for the

150th lay in the ship *Natchez*, Captain Worthen Hall (1851-55). It turned out to be an immensely successful voyage, returning in total 251 barrels of sperm oil, 3,431 barrels of whale oil, and 38,450 pounds of whalebone (baleen). He was issued a second Protection Paper in October 1855 immediately prior to embarking on his second voyage. In fact, he got a new passport for each of his three voyages, in each case with his legal name properly listed as Alanson Bartlett and updating his age correctly; but he evidently did not like the name, and on the ship's articles it consistently appears in shortened form as *Lanson* Bartlett (which has been mis-transcribed as *Samson* and *Lawson* in various tabular records); also, for reasons not explained, this second passport gives his residence as Augusta, Maine, while his third passport, issued in 1860, reverts to naming his birthplace instead (Bristol, Vermont). His second voyage was as a boatsteerer for the 90th lay in the ship *Good Return*, Captain Benjamin F. Wing (1855-58), which vessel proved even better than her name and produced a truly splendid return, amounting to 221 barrels of sperm, 3,443 barrels of whale, and 19,400 pounds of bone. After the *Good Return* Alanson left off whaling for a while: the 1860 census has both brothers as living in back in Croydon with their parents; Charles was still listed a sailor, but Alanson was working as a peddler at that time. His 30-month hiatus from whaling precisely coincided with Captain Wing's hiatus; and when Benjamin Wing went to sea again, "Lanson" went with him, this time as third mate (carrying yet a third Protection Paper) in the ship *Young Phenix* (1860-63). The voyage was a more modest success and proved to be Alanson's last. The 1870 census reports him as head of household on a farm at Croydon, married to Julia Ann Haines (born in 1840 or '41), whose parents, Hazen and Lucinda Haines, were living with them. He and Julia and their two children were still living on the farm in 1880, after which the record becomes equivocal. A census report of 1900 implies that Julia may be the "aunt" Julia A. Bartlett, born circa 1841, who in was living in Brooklyn, New York, with nephews Walter and Arthur Lincoln, and a flawed family genealogy that claims she lived until 1904, it also appears that she may have died in childbirth in 1883, as the 1900 U.S. Census records Alanson Bartlett, born in Vermont circa 1837, living on a farm in Plainfield, New Hampshire, with a wife of fifteen years named Mary, indicating that they were married around 1885. In any case, it was Alanson and Julia Ann's namesake daughter, Julia Ann Bartlett (1883-1966), born in Croydon, who married Thomas Waterman Woodward (1882-1936) in 1901, inherited the scrimshaw, and passed it along to her grandchildren.

Bartlett, David H. (fl. circa 1825-65). As captain of the ship *Grand Turk* of New Bedford he had a lathe on board, and an entry in his journal dated October 26 1835 reports, "schrimshonting [with] the turning lathe gowing [sic]"; in November he notes simply on three or four occasions, "Schrimshonting &c." (NBWM). Typically, he does not specify what he was making, and none of his scrimshaw has come to light. Born in 1806 at Dartmouth, Massachusetts, he was the son of Sylvanus and Mary Bartlett, went whaling in his teens, and spent his entire active career of forty years in New Bedford ships. His first vessel is not known, but from his second or third voyage until he became a captain at age about 30 all of his voyages were to the Brazil Banks and South Atlantic grounds: two outings in the *Mercator* (1828-29 and 1829-30), followed by the *Hydaspe* (1830-32), *Ceres* (1832-34), and *Grand Turk* (1834-36). As a captain, all of his voyages were to the Indian Ocean and Pacific grounds: two in the *Roman 2d* (1836-38 and 1838-40), three outstanding successes in the *Orozimbo* (1840-43, 1843-45, and 1848-51), and one voyage each in the *James Arnold* (1862-63) and *Henry Taber* (1864-65). Meanwhile, he was married to Eliza M. Russell (1807-1870), who bore him three sons, of whom the eldest, James Nye Bartlett (1835-1872), was a whaleman in the 1850s, including a voyage as mate of the *Callao* (1858-62). Captain Bartlett died in 1875.

Bartlett, Gideon Nye (fl. circa 1874-78). As a clerk-apprentice for his grandfather, one of New Bedford's most prominent whaling merchants, Gideon represented the owners aboard whaleships on at least two occasions, where he may or may not have tried his hand at scrimshaw and made the eagle-head cane (walking stick) that he is said to have carried afterwards, which otherwise must have been made for or presented to him (donated to NBWM by his granddaughter in 1965). It is a fairly standard type, with a wooden shaft, brass tip, and curved (crook) handle consisting of seven segments of whale ivory with seven tortoise shell disc separators, with the outermost segment full-round carved in the form of the head of an eagle, the eyes formed by two brass round-headed nails, clutching a ball in its open beak, with the tongue visible. Bartlett, born circa 1855, was the son of George F. Bartlett, Sr. and Clara G. Nye Bartlett, and a grandson of Ivory H. Bartlett, whaling merchant, proprietor of the house of I. H. Bartlett & Sons. Gideon entered the family business early as a clerk and, beginning at age 18, evidently sometimes represented its interests in the field while "learning the ropes" at first hand. He was aboard the bark *Ocean* for six weeks in 1874 and a series of whaling barks for two months in 1878 (the *Rainbow, John Howland,* and *Progress* of New Bedford, and the *Coral* of San Francisco). He was a merchant on his own account.

Bartley, Theodore D. (fl. circa 1851-54). He made only one deepwater voyage, as a green hand in the whaleship *California* of New Bedford (1851-54), and was afterwards a canal boat captain and merchant trader in upstate New York. No scrimshaw by his hand is known. But he was originally a gunsmith by trade — the son of a gunsmith, a gunsmith's apprentice in youth, and in later life a gunsmith again. He had thus been trained (by his father) in the use of tools, metal engraving, and woodworking, crafts he mastered well enough to provide him a livelihood. This, combined with the fact that on his whaling voyage he produced a journal and numerous monochrome pencil and ink drawings (in KNB), some of them quite competent, makes it difficult to believe that he did not also make scrimshaw, or at least try his hand at scrimshandering. In his seafaring days he was an artsy fellow. In addition to the drawings his journals contain faithful transcriptions of a handful of sentimental poems as well as nine song texts, among them such popular numbers as "The Mistletoe Bough" by Thomas Haynes Bayly and Henry Rowley Bishop, the pseudo-pirate song "I'm Afloat, I'm Afloat" ("The Rover of the Sea") by Eliza Cook and Henry Russell, the famous hymns "The Ocean Burial" (which became the model for the even more famous cowboy song that begins "O bury me not on the lone prairie") and "From Greenland's Icy Mountains," and two important folk ballads on nautical themes. These are a rare North American manifestation of "The Loss of the *Ramillies,*" a naval epic of 1760, and the universally popular nineteenth-century shipboard hit, "The Dark-Eyed Sailor" (all ten of Bartley's song transcriptions are printed in my *Ballads and Songs of the Whale-Hunters* and are anthologized in my *Jolly Sailors Bold*). Bartley's scrimshaw may simply not have been identified as such; perhaps some of it will surface someday.

Theodore Declarmont Bartley was born in 1830 at Granby, Oswego County, New York, the son of Robert A. Bartley (1806-1880), gunsmith, and the former Sophronia Meacham (1806-1878). The family lived for a while in Pennsylvania in the 1830s and moved to East Norwalk, Ohio, where in the 1840s Theodore apprenticed under his father. For reasons unexplained, in October 1851, at age 21, he signed for the 1/200ths lay in the *California* and spent the next 31 months hunting sperm whales, right whales, and bowheads on the Pacific and North Pacific grounds. After he returned from whaling in May 1854 he stayed a few days at the Boston Mariners' Home, then shipped in the merchant brig *Matanzas*, bound from Boston to Charleston, South Carolina, with a cargo of ice. He remained with that vessel for several months and may have made additional saltwater merchant voyages, but by 1856 he was back to Ohio working in his father's gun shop. That was the year he married Mary Eliza Felton (1835-1892). The couple settled in her native Dresden, N.Y., where Theodore built a sailing canal boat and earned his living for the next three decades carrying cargoes on Lake Champlain, the Hudson River, the Erie Canal, and the St. Lawrence, most of the time with his wife and family on board. (Nowadays, the Bartleys may be the best known canal boat family in America, since publication of the book *Life on a Canal Boat: The Journals of Theodore D. Bartley, 1861-1889,* edited by Russell P. Bellico, in 2004). In 1889 or thereabouts Bartley retired from canal boating, became a gunsmith in Dresden again, and held at least one patent for gun parts. He was widowed in 1892 and died in 1914.

Baptista, José Francisco Fidalgo—see Fidalgo Baptista, José Francisco

Beane, Joshua F. (fl. circa 1864-69). This sometime whaleman from Maine wrote a narrative of his whaling experiences, entitled *From Forecastle to Cabin,* subtitled *The Story of a cruise in many seas, taken from a journal kept each day, wherein was recorded the happenings of a voyage around the world in pursuit of whales.* It was published in 1905 in New York under his full name, Joshua Fillebrown Beane, and is actually an account of two sequential voyages in the New Bedford bark *Java* in the 1860s, which for literary reasons Beane conflates into a single voyage. In a mere six paragraphs devoted to scrimshaw he presents a respectable catalogue of the principal types and materials, remarks on the seeming compulsion of some whalemen to sell their scrimshaw "at the first port entered" (see the article on William Martin), and implies (though he never says directly) that he did some "scrimshoning" himself, of a type or types unspecified. The narrative, though it dissembles and obfuscates in places, is a rousing good one, but it and the author's biography have remained obscure. Meanwhile, none of Beane's scrimshaw has come to light, while that of his captain, Manuel Enos (q.v. in the *Dictionary*), has become famous and is widely regarded as among the best figural scrimshaw ever rendered by a whaleman.

In the book Beane claims to have risen from green hand to seaman, boatsteerer, third mate, and second mate, all in the course of the one voyage, which would have been a remarkable, if not unprecedented achievement. However, this was poetic license; it actually took him two voyages, which is impressive enough. He was born somewhere in Maine in 1842, the son of a man named Shepard Beane, whom Joshua claims was a graduate of the China [Maine] Academy and had been a district school teacher in "the wilds of the Pine Tree State"; but whatever he may have been before, by 1850 he was farming in Lee Township in Penobscot County and raising two children with his wife Paulina. Joshua claims that the main impetus for his shipping out in his youth was his boyhood romantic vision of seafaring, but avoidance of service in the Union Army may have been an additional motive, and was in any case a convenient byproduct, as it was for many New England lads. He worked in a lumber yard in Lee before he went whaling, evidently lied about his age when he got his Protection Paper (passport) in 1860 — it states his age as 22 but he was only

18 at the time — and shortly after he returned from back-to-back voyages in the *Java* in 1869 he married a woman from Canada named Lydia who was a year or two older, and took up farming and raising a family of their own in Lee. A few years later they moved to Machias, way Down East in Washington County, where he was sales representative and local agent for a sewing machine manufacturer. By 1900 he was Deputy Sheriff of Washington County, with his wife, two adult daughters (both of them music teachers), and a twenty-year-old son living at home, along with a servant to do the housework. This is the period in which Beane wrote his whaling narrative; and the trail ends there. (See the article on Edward B. Phinney.)

* **Bertonccini, John** (fl. circa 1890-after 1931). As noted in the *Dictionary*, this Swedish-born whaleman and sea captain of Italian ancestry is credited with a whale ivory ring, dated 1913 (BJ:2 #439) and possibly two ivory wedding bands (BJ:4 #328). It is very likely that there was other scrimshaw, not yet discovered. But an interesting variation on scrimshaw by his hand (produced early in his career, long before he was given his first command) surfaced in a private collection in 2008. Bertonccini first went whaling out of New Bedford around 1890 and embarked on his first Arctic voyage circa 1892. According to John Bockstoce, he wintered over with the whaling fleet for the first time during 1893-94, and from then "until the 1930's he was in the Arctic nearly continuously on whalers and trading vessels" (Bockstoce 1977, 45). He is accordingly best known for his oil paintings and watercolors of the whaling fleet in the Western Arctic, especially panoramic wintering scenes of the crews playing soccer and baseball on the pack ice, surrounded by banked whaleships, with the wooden sheds of Herschel Island visible in the background (KNB, NBWM, and private collections). However, he also produced the same type of wintering scene, complete with soccer game, the entire Arctic whaling fleet, and the Herschel Island background vignette, painted in oils in miniature on the concave "spoon" of a ladle carved by Natives out of musk ox horn (reported by Kerry Grund and examined at SFL).

A native of Stockholm born in 1872, Bertonccini served in the crew of various New Bedford and San Francisco whaling vessels from circa 1890 to 1914. Though he made several voyages as boatsteerer and mate, and was made captain of the steamer *Jeannette* circa 1914, no whaling voyages are recorded for the *Jeannette* under his command. He went whaling again in 1923, when he was appointed captain of the San Francisco motor schooner *Arctic*, which was wrecked on his second voyage five miles south of Cape Smyth in the Chukchi Sea (Alaska) on 10 August 1924 — exactly two weeks before the bark *Wanderer*, the last American square-rigged whaler, was wrecked on Cuttyhunk Island, outward-bound from New Bedford. After this, Bertonccini continued in various senior capacities (but never as captain) in the motor ships *Charles Brower* (1926) and *Patterson* (1928), the schooner *Emma* (1929), and as mate of the *Patterson* (1931). He died in 1947. There are biographical sketches in the *Dictionary*; "Johnny the Painter," in *The Bulletin from Johnny Cake Hill*, NBWM, Spring 1974, 14-16; Dorothy E.R. Brewington, *Dictionary of Marine Artists*, 1982.

Biley, A. (fl. circa 1852). A tooth engraved with a broadside portrait of a full-rigged ship flying an American flag, surmounted by a spread eagle clutching a riband inscribed "A. BILEY 1852"; on the back, a full-length standing figure of a sailor in striped shirt, neckerchief, short jacket, and bell-bottom trousers, holding a broad-brimmed hat aloft in his left hand, a cutlass in his right, with palm trees is the background (Rinaldi, Cat. 35, 2004). The identity of the artist is unknown. The surname is usually Irish, and there were many immigrants from Ireland named Biley in various parts of the country by the 1850s, however almost no male Bileys in the northeastern United States with the initial A. An Alfred Biley, born in Maine circa 1838, was just about the only one, and his occupation and geography a few years after the date on the scrimshaw is suggestive. A fisherman by trade, he was living in a boarding house in Gloucester, Massachusetts, in 1860. In 1852, at approximately 14 years of age, he would have been younger than average but not necessarily *too* young to have gone whaling and made the scrimshaw. However, no record of any voyages has been found for this or any other A. Biley.

Bishop, Sereno Edwards (1827-1909). At twelve years old he was a passenger on the 1839-40 homeward passage of the whaleship *William Lee* of Newport, Rhode Island. His journal (in KNB) makes several astute and quite valuable comments about scrimshaw (see Appendix IV). He also experimented with scrimshaw himself. In November 1839 he made "a small paper cutter of white whalebone [panbone]," in February 1840 he was making a ship model (presumably with fittings of ivory or panbone), and in March 1840 writes, "I had a bone cane given to me." The son of missionaries Artemas and Elizabeth (née Edwards) Bishop, he was born at Kealakeakua, Hawaiian Islands, in 1827, and was aboard the *William Lee* on his way to the USA for the first time, to attend the Collegiate Institute at Rochester, New York. He later graduated from Amherst College (1843-46) and the Auburn Theological Seminary (1848-51), was ordained in 1852, married Cornelia A. Sessions, the daughter of a minister in Albany, New York, and after briefly occupying a couple of pulpits in New York State he returned to the Hawaiian Islands to serve as a seamen's chaplain at Lahaina (1853-62). He was afterwards a missionary in Hawaii (1862-65), principal of the Lahainaluna Seminary on Maui (1865-77), and editor of *The Friend* (1887-1902), the famous magazine for seamen published by the Oahu Bethel Church in Honolulu, where he resided from 1877 until his death in 1909. He was awarded an honorary Doctor of Divinity degree by Amherst College in 1896.

* **Blanchard, George** (fl. circa 1839-42). His remarks about scrimshaw in his shipboard journal as a green hand in the ship America of Hudson, New York, 1839-42 (in NWBW), are quoted in *More Scrimshaw Artists*: "all hands * 'skrimshoning'. (There's a puzzler for a landsman)... * Skrimshoning: Working White and Black Bone into Canes, Corset Boards, Paste Cutters, knitting sheathes, Thimbles [etc.]." " White and Black Bone" are whalemen's terms for skeletal bone and baleen, respectively. By "Corset Boards" he means *corset busks* or (in British lingo) *staybusks*. By "Paste Cutters" he means *pastry* cutters, i.e., *pie crimpers*, the scrimshaw examples usually bring the kind with jagging wheels. A *knitting sheath*, also known as a *knitting stick*, is a device that attaches to the knitter's clothing to hold one of the knitting needles steady, freeing a hand to manage the yarn. They were commonly made out of boxwood but were often fancy-carved out of ivory or other materials. None of Blanchard's scrimshaw has been discovered, but several good pieces by his shipmate, John Marble (q.v. in the *Dictionary*), who was an officer on this same voyage and appears to have been quite a prodigious scrimshaw-maker, are in a Marble Family legacy collection in KNB. George Blanchard was born circa 1823 in Cairo, New York, and after his voyage in the *America* evidently served part of a voyage as an ordinary seaman in the New Bedford ship *Governor Troup* (1841-44). He was then in the bark *Solomon Saltus* of Fall River, Massachusetts (1845-48), where he is reported (probably erroneously) to have been second mate. (A 22-year-old son of a farmer from upstate New York, lacking in expe-

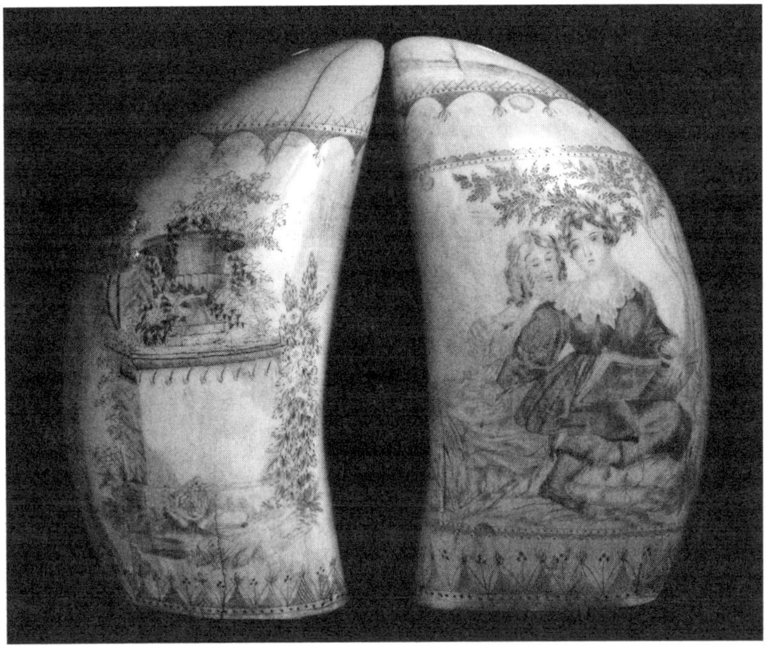

Fig. 3. **Tooth by the anonymous Banknote Engraver.** The two sides of this superlative specimen exhibits most of this artist's identifying characteristics, including exceptionally fine engraving and filigree borders that Norman Flayderman called banknote-like. Private collection.

Fig. 4. **Tooth by Benjamin Blossom.** The cherub or *putti* figure on one side is copied after a detail of "An Allegorical Representation of May" in *Gleason's Pictorial Drawing-Room Companion* of May 13, 1854. The image on the other side was extracted from an engraving of a child alongside a standing figure of a woman (the latter absent on the scrimshaw) in the March 1858 issue of *Harper's New Monthly Magazine*. Kendall Collection, New Bedford Whaling Museum (photos by Richard Donnelly).

rience, would hardly have been suited for so senior a berth. Blanchard was a veteran of only the one voyage and a half, and there is no evidence that he had ever served as a boatsteerer or junior mate, which was the usual prerequisite.)

* **Blossom, Benjamin C.** (fl. circa 1857-89). New Bedford whaling master credited with several well crafted works of engraved and "built" scrimshaw. In addition to the items listed in the *Dictionary* — an inlaid wooden box reportedly inscribed "C.B. Blossom" (in PEM) and a polychrome floral vase made from a small tooth engraved with an image described as Cupid (Eldred, 21 Oct. 1989, #500) — a polychrome tooth depicting a cherub is signed in stipple-engraved uppercase letters below the picture, "B.C. BLOSSOM" (KNB; illustrated in the KWM Newsletter, 17:3, 1999, 5). Several polychrome teeth in private collections have also been identified by James Vaccarino on the basis of iconographic, stylistic, calligraphic, and palette resemblances to the "Cupid" vase and cherub tooth. Some of these have similar images of cherubs in flight, others have pictures of children at play, drawn freehand and pinprick-transferred from printed illustrations. Additional biographical data has also emerged. Benjamin C. Blossom was born in 1839 (not 1840) at Dartmouth, Massachusetts. (not at Hicksville, New York, as one transcription of ship's articles seems to indicate), the son of farmer Benjamin B. Blossom and the descendant and namesake of a soldier who served with George Washington at Valley Forge. In the 1860s and '70s he was still a bachelor living on his parents' farm and was closely associated with two fellow whalemen scrimshaw-makers who became his brothers-in-law, John C. Haskins and John L. Reed (q.v.), who were also living there with their wives (Benjamin's two sisters). His mother, the former Sarah Poole, was seven years older than his father, who married rather late in life. Benjamin also married late in life, his wife was also named Sarah and was ten years his senior. There is no record of children, nor any provenance to explain the descent of Blossom's evidently prodigious output of superior scrimshaw.

Booth, A.V. — see Booth Family

Booth, Amasa A. (fl, circa 1854-55). Born in 1835, he was the youngest of six brothers named from Middleborough, Massachusetts, five of whom went whaling and at least one of whom made scrimshaw. However, owing to shortfalls in the vital records, Amasa's parentage has not been definitively established, nor is it not known whether or not he was the maker or the recipient of some of the Booth family scrimshaw (a large tooth, several panbone busks, and a C-clamp for a swift are attributed). His documented whaling voyages were as ship's boy in the *Alexander* of New Bedford (1848-51) and a brief stint in the crew of the Fairhaven ship *Mary Ann* (1854-55) before deserting ship in Peru. See the article on the Booth Family.

Booth, Charles Weaver (fl. circa 1841-45). Born in 1824, he was the third of six brothers from Middleborough, Massachusetts, five of whom went whaling — Charles as a green hand in the New Bedford bark *Mars* (1841-45). See the article on the Booth Family.

Booth, Francis M. (fl. circa 1842-47). Born in 1826, he was the fourth of six brothers from Middleborough, Massachusetts, one of whom engraved several panbone busks (including one naming the ship *Fenelon*) and a tooth inscribed "A.V. Booth." Of the five brothers who went whaling, Francis was the only one to have been in the ship *Fenelon* of New Bedford — on two voyages, in fact, as a green hand (1842-44) and able seaman (1844-47). See the article on the Booth Family.

Booth, Henry Brightman (fl. circa 1844-53). Born in 1819, he was the eldest of the six Booth brothers from Middleborough, Massachusetts, five of whom went whaling and at least one of whom was a scrimshaw maker. His whaling career is not fully documented, but he made at least three or four voyages — perhaps more — including a stint on the bark *Emma* (sailed 1844), from which he transferred to the ship *St. George*, where he was a seaman and then boatsteerer on two successive voyages (returned 1853). He died in 1880. See the article on the Booth Family.

* **Booth, J.V.** Misidentified as such in the *Dictionary*. See the articles on the Booth Family and the Fenelon Engraver.

Booth, Philander Gates (fl. circa 1839-48). A career whaleman born in 1822, he was the second of six brothers from Middleborough, Massachusetts, five of whom went whaling and one of whom engraved several panbone busks (including one that names the ship *Fenelon*) as well as a tooth inscribed "A.V. Booth." His maiden voyage was in the Wareham brig *Inga* (1839-40), he was then an able seaman in the New Bedford brig *Peri* (1840-41), and boatsteerer in the ship *Lucas* of New Bedford (1842-43). On what vessel or vessels he voyaged next is not known, but he died at sea in 1848, "killed by a whale." See the article on the Booth Family.

Booth Family (fl. circa 1839-57). Six polychrome panbone busks and a polychrome tooth have been identified (by Donald Boger, Rod Cardoza, and the KNB/NBWM staff) as being by the same hand. One of the busks (of three in KNB) is inscribed "Fenelon"; the tooth and another busk are inscribed with the name "A.V. Booth"; and the tooth and a third busk are respectively inscribed "M[ary] Ann" and "Ship Mary Ann". Naturally enough, "A.V. Booth" has been taken as a signature — mistakenly, as it turns out — and hitherto the scrimshaw has accordingly been attributed to an anonymous artist, the so-called *Fenelon* Engraver (q.v.) and an unidentified sailor-artist named A.V. Booth. Once the seven pieces were identified as being by a single hand, it followed that A.V. Booth and the *Fenelon* Engraver were perceived as one and the same artist. However, it turns out that "A.V. Booth" is not a signature, A.V. Booth was not the artist, and the chain of attribution in this case is rather complex.

It begins with Francis M. Booth, the only man of that surname who was ever in the crew of the whaler *Fenelon*; and Amasa A. Booth, the only Booth who ever served in the *Mary Ann*. They were part of a fairly large clan of Booths from Middleborough, Massachusetts, among whom more of the young males in their generation went whaling than did not — in this case five brothers out of six: Henry Brightman Booth (1819-1880); Philander Gates Booth (1822-1848), who died at sea ("killed by a whale"); Charles Weaver Booth (1824-); Francis M. Booth (1826-), who made two voyages in *Fenelon* (1824-47); and Amasa A. Booth (1835-), who was briefly in the crew of the Fairhaven ship *Mary Ann* (1854-55). "A.V. Booth" refers to a woman with the sonorous moniker Ariadne Victory Booth, born in 1818, the older sister of the five Booth brothers. It was almost certainly one of the brothers — though it is not known which — who produced the seven works of engraved scrimshaw.

Amasa's parentage presents a bit of a mystery. There were at least seven men from Middleborough named Booth who went whaling in the 1840s and '50s. However, as the vital records of Middleborough trail off after 1832, some kinships remain unclear. The four older Booth brothers were all born between 1819 and 1826, the sons of Abiel Peirce Booth and Betsy Brightman Weaver Booth. They each went whaling sometime during 1838-49, though no two ever served together on the same vessel. A fifth brother, Lucius Carey Booth, never went whaling, but his birth in 1829 is duly recorded; so too that of their kid sister, Sarah Jane, born in 1832. Amasa, born in 1835, *may* have been their youngest brother (the sixth), but owing to the shortfall in the records his name is absent from genealogical compilations. They were all also somehow related to another clan of Booths in Middleborough. Wilder Perry Booth, son of Gilbert Booth and Nancy Wilde Wiles Booth, was born in 1823 and was whaling during 1844-46. Amasa could possibly have been *his* younger brother, and in fact it was with Wilder's uncle Alden Booth (born 1803), a widower farmer in Middleborough, that Amasa was living in 1850 — though whether in the capacity of apprentice, cousin, nephew, or son is not known. A younger whaleman from Middleborough who was also named Alden Booth (born 1836) was either Amasa's cousin or his kid brother.

Apart from Alden, Amasa, born in 1835, was the youngest and his career the most controversial. His first outing, as cabin boy in the whaleship *Alexander* of New Bedford, was undertaken at the tender age of 14. They sailed in May 1848, but according to New Bedford Port Society records Amasa deserted not long after (it is not clear exactly when, as no logbook or journal of the voyage is known to survive). His means of returning home and his activities during the next several years are not known, but the 1850 U.S. Census (the only census in which he appears at all) identifies him as age 15 at the time, occupation mariner, living on a farm in Middleborough with Alden Booth, age 47, kinship not specified. In September 1854, Amasa (giving his age as 18) obtained a new Protection Paper (passport) and went as a seaman in the ship *Mary Ann* of Fairhaven. However, on the indisputable testimony of both the second and fourth mates, each of whom kept journals of the voyage (in NBWM), Amasa deserted ship again, this time at Paita (Peru) in March 1855. And with that, he disappears from the historical record.

So of all the Middleborough Booths who went whaling, Amasa seems at first to be the least likely to have made the scrimshaw. He was a mere child when Francis was in the *Fenelon*, had no connection with the *Fenelon* himself, was certainly not aboard the *Mary Ann* long enough — nor was he whaleman enough — for attribution of the *Mary Ann* scrimshaw to be readily convincing. He was a chronic runaway and never completed a voyage, deserting both times long before they could have taken enough whales to warrant scrimshawing. Nevertheless, the tooth bears the name of his sister (A.V. Booth) and *his* ship (*Mary Ann*). If he made the *Fenelon* busk, it may have been long after his older brother Francis's actual *Fenelon* voyages (which took place when Amasa was only between the ages of nine and twelve). Though Amasa was an utterly failed whaleman, he could nevertheless have been an avid artist-practitioner. Otherwise, it would seem more likely (but still remains a matter of speculation) that an older kinsman who had been whaling before made the *Mary Ann* scrimshaw as a gift for Amasa in anticipation of his forthcoming voyage in the *Mary Ann*, just as the same older brother might have made the "A.V. Booth" scrimshaw for Ariadne.

Another plausible candidate for scrimshaw artist is Francis M. Booth, the fourth oldest brother. Born in 1826, he was two voyages in the New Bedford ship *Fenelon*, as a green hand (1842-44) and ordinary seaman (1844-47) — his only whaling voyages. He was afterwards a farmer in Middleborough. However, the *Fenelon* connection is the only factor that suggests Francis as the scrimshaw artist in preference to his three older brothers (why would anyone *else* put the name of Francis's ship on a busk?). But he may well have been far away and out of reach by the time Amasa was in the *Mary Ann*. Francis left off whaling and took up farming in 1847, but in 1849 he obtained a new Protection Paper at New Bedford, indicating that he intended to go to sea again, likely as a member of a Gold Rush company heading around Cape Horn to go prospecting in California. Francis may be the F.M. Booth, laborer, whom the U.S. Census lists living among miners at Shasta, California, in 1860 — after which he disappears from view. Francis was not likely in Middleborough in 1854, when Amasa was preparing to go in the *Mary Ann*.

The fifth oldest brother, Lucius Carey Booth (1829-1907), was a carpenter who never went whaling. He eventually married Ellen Maria Peirce in 1856 and moved to Santa Rosa, California, where he raised a family and continued in the carpentry trade. He was a skilled artisan, but it is unlikely that he made any scrimshaw.

This leaves three brothers. The oldest was Henry Brightman Booth, born in 1819. He was a green hand in the New Bedford bark *Emma* in 1844, and during the course of the voyage he transferred to the ship *St. George*, in which he was evidently promoted to boatsteerer, returning to New Bedford in 1853. He then left off whaling and took up farming. There is no evidence that he ever married, or that he ever did any scrimshaw — mostly because there simply is little evidence of anything about his life and affairs. He died of paralysis in New Bedford in 1880.

The third brother was Charles Weaver Booth, born in 1824. He made only one voyage, as a green hand in the bark *Mars* of New Bedford (1841-45), then went whaling no more. His subsequent activities are unknown.

The second brother, Philander Gates Booth, born in 1822, was the only career whaleman in the clan. Presuming that all seven pieces of Booth scrimshaw are by the same hand, Philander's chronology presents a bit of an impasse. Because he was the only one of the brothers to go whaling before Ariadne married in 1839 and thereby changed her name, Philander would seem to be the most likely maker of the "A.V. Booth" pieces; but he perished too early to have scrimshawed the *Mary Ann* pieces with Amasa's forthcoming voyage in mind. The year he died at sea, "killed by a whale" in 1848, was the same year that young Amasa went to sea for the first time in the *Alexander* and fully six years before Amasa went in the *Mary Ann*.

The intended recipient of the "A.V. Booth" scrimshaw was Ariadne Victory Booth, born at Middleborough in 1818, the first child of Abiel and Betsy Booth, and the older sister of the whaling brothers. She is reported to have been thrice married, first in 1839 to a man named Jorden, a union that evidently produced no issue. If this be the case, her surname would have changed at that time, leading to the assumption that the "A.V. Booth" scrimshaw was probably made before 1839, before Ariadne became Mrs. Jorden. However, reports of this marriage are vague and documentation is sketchy: it may be apocryphal. In 1845 she married Jacob Tomson (or Thompson) at Lakeville, Massachusetts, and two years later bore a son, named Francis. She was later widowed again and married Elijah W. Barrows of Middleborough in 1853.

Unfortunately, no definitive clue has yet come to light to indicate definitively which of the affectionate brothers made the scrimshaw for their oldest and youngest siblings, Ariadne and Amasa, and the other pieces by this distinctive hand.

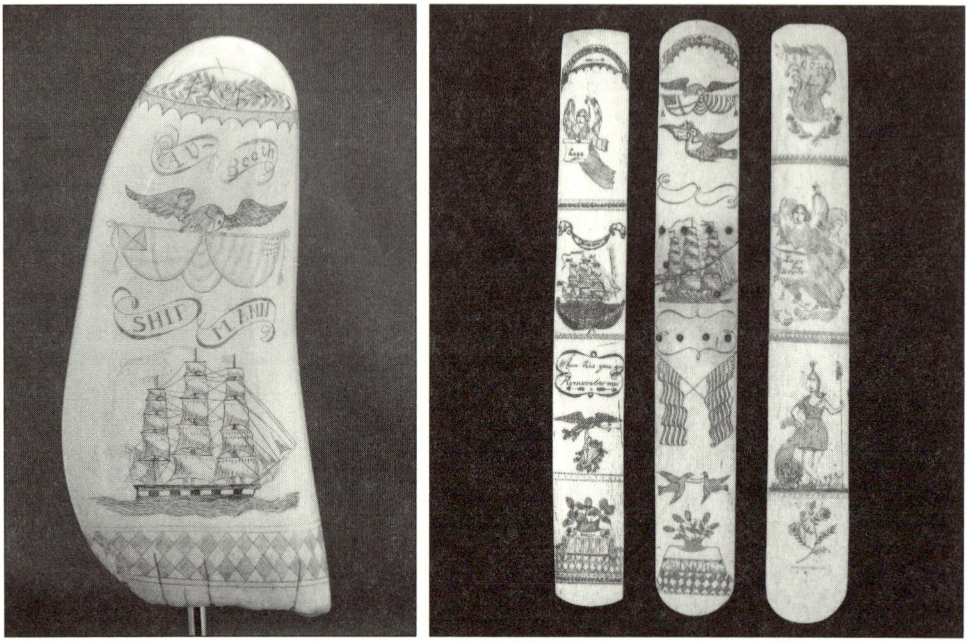

Fig. 5. **One of the five Booth brothers of Middleborough, Massachusetts,** engraved this tooth (in a private collection) and three panbone busks (Kendall Collection, New Bedford Whaling Museum). Photos by Donald C. Boger and Richard Donnelly.

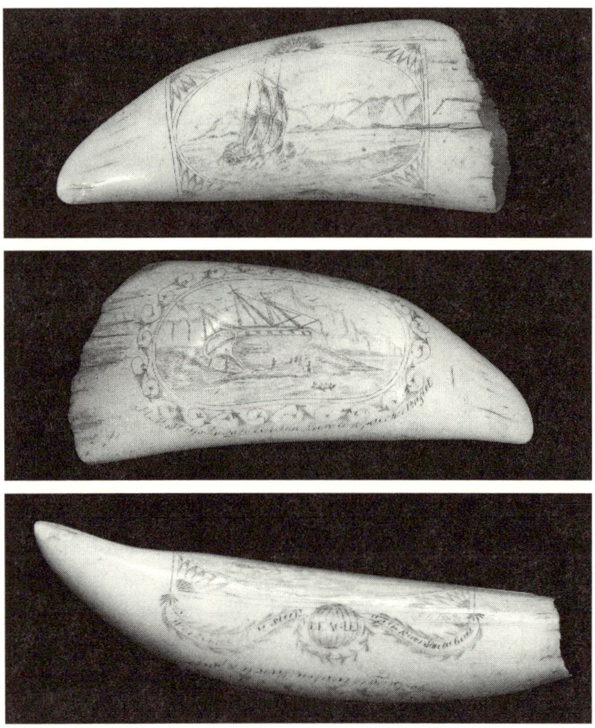

Fig. 6. **HMS *Beagle* Tooth by J.A. Bute.** There are several of these, signed by a Royal Navy sailor aboard the *Beagle* on the famous voyage commanded by Robert Fitzroy, with Charles Darwin aboard, in the 1830s. There were certainly adequate supplies of time and sperm whale teeth on the voyage, but Bute may have done some of the scrimshaw afterwards. Photo courtesy of Hyland Granby Antiques, Hyannisport, Massachusetts.

Braley, Jason L. (fl. circa 1840-64). New Bedford whaling master who in his journals (in KNB) mentions several times in passing, without providing any specifics, that during most of his career on shipboard he was occasionally engaged in making scrimshaw. The younger brother of whaling captain Samuel T. Braley (1817-1870), Jason was born in 1824 at Acushnet, Massachusetts, the son of Elisha and Delia (Sherman) Braley. The boys grew up on a family farm in Rochester, Massachusetts, where they moved when Jason was an infant. He shipped out at age 16 for the 100th lay as a green hand in the Rochester brig *Solon* (1840-41), seaman in the Mattapoisett bark *Willis* (1842-43), and boatsteerer for the 90th lay in the bark *Newton* (1843-46). This voyage is noted for the crew's "mutiny," refusing duty at Oahu; as a petty officer, Braley remained with the ship when, with consular sanction, the crew was discharged and another crew shipped. But the *Newton*'s woes did not end there. In December 1844 the captain fell ill and died at San Diego, and the voyage was disrupted until another commander could be installed. According to the *Plymouth County, Massachusetts Biographical Review* of 1897, Braley left the *Newton* in Hawaii at what must have been around this time, to become a boatsteerer in a vessel named *Crown Princessen* for about 20 months, which, if true, would have been a strange step; but no other information is provided. In any case, he was back in New Bedford in time to sign for the 60th lay as third mate in the ship *Stephania*, in which he was promoted to second mate during the voyage (1847-49). It was on this cruise that he began the journal in which his interest in scrimshaw is documented and in which he also transcribed a few songs and poems. He continued this journal as mate of the bark *Louisa* (1850-53), master of the *William Badger* (1853-57: his only complete voyage as captain), and as first mate and relief captain of the bark *Falcon* (1859-62). According to the *Biographical Review*, he was then first mate of the Edgartown ship *Vineyard* for about 18 months — which would have been during 1862-64 — until he was injured when a cask fell on him and he returned home for good. He had been living between voyages with his mother's kinfolk on the Martin Sherman family farm in Rochester when he married Hannah M. Hall in 1850, and while he was still whaling they lived on Mount Pleasant Street in New Bedford. But after Braley retired from seafaring he returned to farming in Rochester with his wife and four children. The farm they purchased in 1873 became especially noted locally for his strawberries. No specimens of his scrimshaw have yet come to light.

Braman, Lewis (fl. circa 1850-65). Elizabeth Stetson (q.v.) took an active role in the life of each of the ship's companies of which she was a part. The wife of Captain Charles Stetson (q.v.), she accompanied her husband on several whaling voyages; their son, Charles A. "Charlie" Stetson (q.v.), was actually born during one of them. Elizabeth performed such domestic chores as cooking, baking, sewing, and mending, not only for her own family, but for some of the men, too; she tutored Charlie year after year, and even did a bit of scrimshawing of her own. In her journal aboard the New Bedford ship *Erastus Corning* in 1864, she alludes to what appears to be scrimshaw done for her by one of the mates: "Mr. Braman marked 2 teeth for me." Or perhaps he literally *marked* the teeth for *her* to do the scrimshaw. The next day's entry includes the notation that she "helped Jose mend some pants for Mr. Braman." "Jose" was José Carascos, whom she describes as a "Spaniard" taken on board at Paita (Peru) as ship's boy; he was later promoted to steward. "Mr. Braman" was Lewis Braman, second mate. There was surely other scrimshaw going on aboard the *Corning*; in fact, Thomas Morrison (q.v.), who is reported to have done some scrimshaw on a later voyage, was a boatsteerer on the *Corning* at the time. But Braman's and her own family's scrimshaw pursuits are the only ones she mentions. Unfortunately, none of the actual pieces has ever surfaced.

Braman was born circa 1829, the eldest son of Norton and Phebe Braman, farmers in Ellington, Connecticut. He lived with his parents and was working as a machinist at East Windsor, Hartford County, until just before he shipped out in the bark *Mercator*, in July 1850, on the first of his five or six whaling voyages in New Bedford vessels. His whereabouts after returning with the *Mercator* in September 1852 are unknown until he embarked on his next voyage, as boatsteerer in the bark *Union* (1854-55). He made a second voyage in the *Union*, this time as second mate (1854-55), then in 1857 went as third mate in the ship *Hope* on what turned out to be a long and disastrous cruise. In October 1863, already a month more than an incredible six years out, the *Hope* was wrecked on what Captain Leonard S. Gifford's report in the *Whalemen's Shipping List* of March 8, 1864 names as Bampton Shoals, in latitude 19° 05' South and longitude 158° 30' East (this is in the Cook Islands, and is evidently neither the Brampton Shoals near Waitangi, New Zealand, nor Brampton Reef, off Queensland, Australia). The officers and crew, 29 in all, took to the whaleboats and landed at Brisbane, Queensland, whence they took a steamer to Sydney, N.S.W. Braman found his way to Tahiti, and there, on Christmas Day 1863, joined the *Erastus Corning* as a replacement second mate on a voyage already in progress. He was later amicably discharged at Tumbez (a recruiting port in Peru, on the border of Ecuador), where he joined the American merchantman *Porcia*, probably also as second mate. (The *Porcia* may have been a whaler at some point, but is not listed as such by Starbuck, or by *Whaling Masters* prior to 1869, when the vessel is credited to Chilmark, Martha's Vineyard.) Nothing is known of his later career, though he may have been the Lewis E, Braman, age 69, who with his wife Annie was running a boardinghouse in Hartford in 1900.

Britt, William W. (fl, circa 1836-38). On his only known voyage, sperm- and right-whaling in the Indian Ocean as a seaman in the ship *Martha* of Fairhaven, commanded by Daniel Borden, from September 1836 to April 1838, Britt engraved a splendid tooth, signed "W.W. Britt, Sculp" (private collection, reported by Peter Bump, a descendant). It has an original and fresh (that is, a completely non-derivative) sperm whaling scene, with a breeching whale prominently featured in the foreground, one whaleboat fast and approaching under paddles, another approaching under oars, and a third readying to strike; there is a ship with drooping sails in the background; and the scene is framed in a rectangle, brilliantly and expertly inscribed below: "SPERM WHALING SCENE OFF THE ISLE OF ST. PAULS. INDIAN OCEAN. / By the crew of the ship *Martha* of Fair Haven / Nov. 11th. 1837." The official logbook of the voyage (in NBWM) notes the ship's position the previous day as 34° 15' South, 83° 30' East, which is actually nearer to Amsterdam Island than St. Paul's; and it records the capture of the whale, presumably somewhat farther southwest, thus nearer to St. Paul's, but without supplying specific coordinates, on 15 November (thanks to the eccentricity of ship's time, where the new day often begins at noon rather than at midnight, this is the date *following* the date on the tooth); and it twice mentions the whale as producing 70 barrels of oil. A crew list transcribed into the journal in 1918 by the then-owner, New Bedford collector Andrew Snow, Jr., clearly lists "Wm. W. Britt" among the seamen; so too a reportedly contemporaneous crew list in NHA. What is particularly interesting about this fellow is that he appears to be the same William W. Britt who was working as a wood engraver active in New York City from 1844 to circa 1886 and who characteristically signed his engravings much as he signed the scrimshaw, "W.W. Britt, Sc."

This suggests that prior to going whaling he had likely undergone a formal apprenticeship (or a portion of a formal apprenticeship) as an engraver, which would account for the sophisticated composition and extremely refined technique of his scrimshaw, as well as his uncharacteristically formal signature; and that after the one voyage he returned to his original occupation in his home state. He was born in 1819 or 1820 in New York, and is listed in the 1850 U.S. Census as an engraver, residing in New York City, married to a woman named Mary, with an eight-year-old daughter named Adeline. After this the family temporarily disappears from view: neither Croce & Wallace (82) nor William Young (66) list William Britt as active after 1850. However, the 1860 New Jersey census has him living in Hudson City, in Hudson County. Indications are that he had been widowed some years before, and that, around 1860, he was married for the second time, to a New Jersey woman named Lucy, ten years his junior. After another unaccountable gap in the records, the 1880 U.S. Census lists William Britt, age 62, wood engraver still living Hudson County, but now in Jersey City (just across from Manhattan), with wife Lucy and two daughters, Ella, age 19, and Lily (Lillie), 15. This is a clear indication that such later wood engravings that are signed "W.W. Britt, Sc." — including illustrations in *Harper's New Monthly Magazine* for David Hunter Strother's "Personal recollections of the war. By a Virginian" (August 1867), Ernest Ingersoll's "La Villa Real de Santa Fe" (April 1880), Constance Fenimore Woolson's "At Mentone" (January 1884), and others — are by his hand. He died before 1889, by which time Lucy was working as a nurse (which may have been her original career) and living in Jersey City with her daughter Lucy, a music teacher. The reverse side of the tooth has the crudely engraved name "Richard Mae," who was probably a descendant but whose relationship to William Britt has not be ascertained.

Brookes, William Tolley (fl. circa 1810-42). A bone-and-ivory walking stick, a fid, and four teeth — one engraved, one relief-carved, and two undecorated — are "associated with William Tolley Brookes, commander of the London whaler *Active* in the late 1830's." According to his grandson, Major Cyril James Hastings Brook[e]s, late of the National Westminster Bank, London, who bequeathed the five pieces to NMM in 1978, Captain Brookes certainly owned them and may have done some of the scrimshaw himself. On the other hand, by the time he took over the *Active* Brookes was already a whaling master of long tenure in the London South Seas trade, perpetually in a position to be the recipient of such gifts from members of his crew and to commission such items as the walking stick by any ship's carpenter in his command. The engraved tooth has pictures on both sides, copied directly from popular illustrations — so faithfully that it is difficult to judge whether similar densely-engraved works in other collections are by the same hand. One side has a sailor climbing a ship's rigging beneath a stormy sky, cleverly framed by a ship's stern, complete with gallery and gunports overhead and keel below, with anchors at the top corners, inscribed below: "The Sailor Boy / Though the strained mast should quiver as a reed, / And the rent canvas fluttering strew the gale, / Still must I on … *Byron*," quoted from the Third Canto of Byron's *Childe Harold*. The other side has a portrait of a woman in a low-cut gown, with stipple-engraved red highlights on her lips and cheeks, labeled "MISS O'NEILL / IN THE CHARACTER OF BELVIDERA," representing stage actress Eliza O'Neill (1791-1872) in a revival of the nautical-theme play *Venice Preserved* by Thomas Otway (1682). The walking stick has a shaft of whale skeletal bone, a foreshaft and turk's-head (or monkey's fist) pommel of sperm whale ivory, and a brass ferrule. One of the other teeth has a classical figure carved in low relief; the other two teeth are polished but undecorated; the conventional panbone fid is perhaps less likely by the captain's own hand unless it were left over from a much earlier voyage, when as an apprentice or ordinary seaman he would have had daily use for such a tool.

Brookes's early whaling career remains a mystery and virtually nothing is known about him personally, but his record as a successful whaling master in an unbroken succession of London South Sea whalers is well documented. Before the *Active* he had the ship *Indispensable*, 351 tons, owned by Daniel Bennett (1821-24); ship *Recovery*, 420 tons, a converted former Royal Navy sloop-of-war, in which Brookes skippered two voyages for Bennett (1824-27 and 1828-31); ship *Matilda*, 483 tons, owned by Green & Co. (1832-36); and bark *Jane Eliza*, 419 tons, which was owned by Foster & Co. when she sailed in 1836 but was sold during the voyage to owners in Sydney, New South Wales, at which point Captain Brookes came home early by other means in 1837 or 1838. The *Active*, 494 tons, also owned by Green & Co., was Brookes's next and final command (1838-42).

Brooks, Timothy W. (fl. circa 1846-1850s). A whale ivory pickwick in NHS is attributed to Timothy Brooks. The overwhelming likelihood is that this was Timothy W. Brooks, born on Nantucket in 1831, the son of William Brooks, a cooper who himself almost certainly made at least one whaling voyage, and the former Emeline Wyer. The general expectation on Nantucket was that every young man would go whaling at least once, and, true to form, Timothy and at least two of his brothers — George, older by ten years, and William, ten years younger — made whaling their career for a while; so too their brother-in-law, Ferdinand Defriez. Even if the brothers did not serve formal youthful apprenticeships in their father's cooperage (which some may have done before going to sea), they certainly must have had some youthful tutoring, which accounts for where young Timothy would have acquired the requisite skills to produce the pickwick and probably other "built" scrimshaw. He made his maiden whaling voyage not in one of the vessels from his own Island, where the whale fishery was by this time in gradual decline, but as ship's boy in the New Bedford ship *China*, in which he embarked in 1846 at age 15 years and 3 months. Though the 1860 and 1880 U.S. Census continue to list his occupation as mariner and sailor (he is unaccountably absent from the 1870 census), his subsequent voyages have not been discovered. In 1880 he was living in Menlo Park, California, still working as a sailor and evidently still unmarried.

Brott, Lucien A. (fl. circa 1867-71). Ship's carpenter from upstate New York whose whaling journal mentions extracting sperm whale teeth and who probably did some scrimshaw, but by whom no specific works have as yet come to light. In December 1870, as carpenter in the *Young Phenix*, he records the capture of a bull sperm whale, and his entry for December 27th includes that he (individually or as part of the crew) "cleaned the teeth to-day." On January 1 they took two more sperm whales, one of which stove one of the whaleboat in its jaws, which evidently rattled the crew. The two whales yielded 150 barrels of sperm oil, and "we soon had the jaw on deck perfectly harmless. we then knocked off and shortened or rather took in sail and so ends my third new years day on board ship." What he did with his share of the teeth from the three whales — and all the other whales they took on that voyage — goes unmentioned. But as carpenter he was perfectly positioned to make something out of them, as whaleship carpenters customarily did.

Brott evidently only made the one whaling voyage. Born in Schuyler County, New York in

1847, he was the son of Aaron J. Brott, carpenter, and Caroline Brott. Soon after, the family moved to Dix, in Chemung County, then to Lodi, in Seneca County. He had one or two siblings and was evidently apprenticed to a carpenter, presumably his father. By 1870 his mother had died and his father was remarried — to Hannah Baker, a widow, who added her two young daughters to the brood. Lucien, who was still at sea at that time, is listed in the 1870 census as a "sailor and ship carpenter," age 23. In 1867, when he had signed articles as carpenter for what turned out to be a better-than-average voyage in the *Young Phenix,* he named Rochester, New York, as his residence; but after his return in 1871 he married an Irish immigrant named Jennie and settled in Ithaca, New York, where he worked as a carpenter. By 1900 they were living in Brooklyn, New York, where he worked as a machinist and had at least one daughter; and in 1910 he was retired and living with Jennie in Landis Township, Cumberland County, New Jersey.

* **Brown, George W.** (fl. 3rd-4th quarter of the 19th century). Based on two provenance documents that surfaced at auction from different sources 24 years apart, two very different works of scrimshaw are attributed to this man — or to two men of the same name — about whom nothing is known. The *Dictionary* reports "A wax-inlaid pictorial tooth inscribed with the name 'G.W. Brown' and incised with pictures of a man in sailor garb holding an American flag and a woman in exotic costume with a Chilean flag, bears the motto 'Acuerdate' (in effect, 'remember [me]') — seeming to signify an international romantic liaison between a Yankee mariner and a Latina lass; attributed from Bourne 14 March 1986 (#289)." More recently, a cane with a cylindrical wooden shaft and mushroom-shaped pommel of walrus ivory was consigned to auction, along with the holograph notation, "'Made by Grandfather Brown out of one of the timbers of the whaler *Rebecca Sims*' (Capt. George W. Brown)" (Eldred, 8-9-10 April 2010, #944). Unfortunately, the heirs and progeny of "Grandfather" Brown are not named, thus the weak provenance is tantalizingly inconclusive and the artist remains unidentified.

There were three American whaling captains named George Brown, with the middle initials B, E, and F respectively, but never one named George W. Brown. Unless either the provenance or the transcription gives the wrong initial, the scrimshaw-maker must have been a captain of something else — perhaps in the coastwise trade, or deepwater merchant voyages, or on ferryboats; or perhaps he was a harbor pilot (there was a pilot of this name in Rhode Island earlier in the century), any of which would have entitled him legitimately to be called Captain. He may or may not have gone whaling: the name is so common that there were George W. Browns from all over the country who served in whaling crews out of New Bedford and other ports — including an African-American sailor from Philadelphia who was cook in the bark *Elizabeth* of Freetown, Massachusetts, during 1844-45; a fellow from Providence who was a mariner in 1844 and a daguerreotype photographer in 1850; and a dozen others, from Hartford, Connecticut; Albany and Southampton, New York; Guilford, Maine; Little Compton and Newport, Rhode Island; and Nantucket, Falmouth, Gloucester, and Fairhaven, Massachusetts, all active during the 1840s-'60s — in addition to the two Boston shipwrights mentioned in the *Dictionary,* who may actually have been former whalemen in shore-side jobs. There were also a dozen or two George Browns who served on whaleships without any middle initial being recorded but any one of whom could conceivably be the George W. Brown who made the cane or engraved the tooth. None of them is known to have served aboard the *Rebecca Sims,* a merchant ship of 400 register tons, built at Philadelphia in 1807, converted for whaling in 1828, a veteran of eight whaling voyages out of New Bedford and Fairhaven. In the autumn of 1861 she became one of the "Stone Fleet": old, shopworn Yankee whaleships purchased by the U.S. Government to be sunk in the harbor of Charleston, South Carolina, as part of the Union effort to blockade Confederate shipping. Whatever "timber" Brown may have used for his cane must of course have been removed before the ship was filled with rocks and scuttled. How he obtained it and the whale ivory remains a mystery.

Brown, William R. [Browne] (fl. circa 1838-66). Though he was a whaling master for more than 28 years, there is no evidence that he ever practiced scrimshandering himself. However, in his manuscript memoirs (in KNB), in which he spells his surname *Browne* (as he also did in connection with his very last voyage), he did have one practical thing to say about teeth when cutting-in a sperm whale: "To obtain the valuable spermaceti, in the head of the sperm whale, the lower jaw is allowed to sink — unless we wish to save the teeth — for the sailors' carving, or to trade with the natives of some of the islands." His whaling career was long and distinguished. He was brother-in-law to two well known New London whaling captains, James B. Smith and John B. Rice, and he himself commanded ten whaling voyages to widely separated grounds: two in the ship *Hamilton* of Bridgeport, Connecticut, to the South Atlantic (1838-41), five in the ship *Peruvian* of New London to the Crozettes and Desolation Island in the Indian Ocean and to the Northwest Coast (1841-54), and one in the bark *Pioneer* to Desolation (1857-59). He then retired from whaling — temporarily as it turned out — and may have been captain or manager of the former Stonington whaler *Charles Phelps* from circa 1859 into the early Civil War years, during which the vessel was owned in New London and used as a government store ship. (The *Charles Phelps* was later owned in New Bedford, and with the name changed to *Progress* was exhibited at the Columbian Exhibition in 1893 in Chicago to typify the whaling industry of New England.) After the Civil War Brown came out of retirement briefly to skipper the New London whaling schooner *Forward* on a voyage to Hudson Bay, but the vessel was lost only two weeks out, all hands saved. As Bernard Colby points out, Captain Brown had his wife and two children with him on the *Peruvian*; and Nathaniel Taylor, in his firsthand account of a whaling voyage during 1851-53 in the New London ship *Julius Caesar*, remarks about encountering them upon his arrival at Desolation Island: "A spacious house is erected upon the *after* part of the deck" of the *Peruvian*, "and there, for aught I can see, Captain William R. Brown, his wife, Miss Mary with her piano, and Master Johnny with his playthings pass the time as pleasantly as if at home" (quoted by Colby, 17). In later life he was evidently on the lecture circuit for a while, talking about his whaling experiences and widespread travels. (Not to be confused with another, contemporaneous William R. Brown, born circa 1818 at Bridgehampton, New York, who was a steamboat pilot at Ledyard, Connecticut, on the Thames River adjacent to New London and Norwich.)

Bunker, Joseph F. (fl. circa 1828-71). African-American whaleman and former ship's carpenter from Nantucket who, as second mate in the ship *Gazelle* of New Bedford, is specifically mentioned as a participant in a joint scrimshaw project with the captain and first mate. Captain Daniel F. Worth (q.v.) had his wife on board, and on September 1, 1865, Frederick H. Lawrence, a green hand from Westport, Massachusetts, wrote in his journal: "A few remarks have been made about scrimshoning. For the last week the Capt[ain] and mate and second mate have been constantly employed in making something for his lordship and his lady ship and now they have got every thing about done for themselves." The mate was Thomas Foster (q.v.), and all three — Captain Worth, Foster, and Joseph Bunker — had been together on a previous voyage in the bark *San Francisco* when she was wrecked off Montauk Point, Long Island, in February 1862. They evidently formed a close-knit brotherhood on that trying occasion and made their next voyage together in the *Gazelle*, where they were now collaborating to produce some kind of scrimshaw for the captain and his wife — whom the diarist, barely 17, characterizes with a measure of sophomoric disdain (and with a pun that he may or may not have intended) as "his lordship and his lady ship." Unfortunately, we are never told what the three were making, and the diarist himself may not have known. However, as a trained carpenter and sometime ship's carpenter, Bunker must have played a large part in whatever it was. Nor could this have been the only time he turned his hand to scrimshaw, merely the only occasion for which we have direct evidence. He was born around 1811, may have trained as a carpenter in his youth, and must have made his early voyages from Nantucket, some of them as ship's carpenter. He was 44 when he sailed as boatsteerer and carpenter in the *San Francisco* under Captain Elisha Cudworth (1855-56). He sailed in her again under Captains Philip H. Omey and Edwin A. Perry (1857-59), and a third time in 1859, probably as third mate, under Captain Daniel Worth, on the voyage on which the *San Francisco* was lost in 1862. His voyage as second mate in the *Gazelle* (1862-66) may have been his last, or he may have gone with Captain Worth on *his* last voyage, as master of the brig *Para* of Salem, Massachusetts (1867-71). Unfortunately, nothing is known of Bunker's background, family life, or subsequent career.

Bunker, Obed R. (fl. circa 1830-63). Whaling master from one of Nantucket's great whaling families: in song and story, the Bunker name is virtually synonymous with the whaling trade. A baleen busk in KNB, incised with images of flowering plants, an urn, a hip-roof Federal house, and geometric motifs, is inscribed "Lydia Allen." This was a fairly common name in nineteenth-century New England, but remarkably, of the many Lydia Allens only one could have been the recipient of the scrimshaw busk, as she was of an appropriate age and was closely related to whalemen; and it is from this connection that the scrimshaw can be tentatively attributed. She was originally Lydia T. Morton, born on Nantucket in 1812, the daughter of Dr. Martin T. Morton (1783-1841) and the wife of Avery T. Allen, a merchant tailor of Nantucket, whom she married in 1836. When her younger sister Emily married whaling captain Obed R. Bunker in 1847, the couple moved in with Lydia and Avery Allen. It was probably around that time that Bunker (who was already a distinguished whaling master) made the busk for his sister-in-law, or perhaps had it made for her.

Obed R. Bunker was born on Nantucket in 1815, the son of Owen Bunker (1775 -1864) and the former Phebe Gardner (1780-1870). He appears to have been a kinsman of an earlier Captain Obed Bunker (1741-1812), who commanded Nantucket whaleships in the 1770s, and he was related to a host of other Bunker whalemen. In addition, his sister Mary (1801-1888) married Robert F. Fosdick, captain of three whaling voyages out of Fairhaven (1831-43); his sister Sarah (1812-1840) married William Henry Gardner, who became master of the ship *William Mitchell* (1839-43) and was away at sea when Sarah died; and his older brother, William P. Bunker (1809-1864), was relief captain on the 1844-48 voyage of the New Bedford ship *Mobile*. However, it was Obed himself who achieved the highest prestige among his siblings and in-laws, with command of three voyages in Nantucket ships: two in the *Constitution* (1842-47 and 1847-52) and one in the *Spartan* (1858-63).

* **Burdett, Thomas** (fl. circa 1833-62). Nantucket-born whaling master and merchant sea captain, by whose hand the *Dictionary* reports a sewing box and a swift, both dated 1851 and made while he was master of the New Bedford bark *Statira*. The box is said to be constructed of tamana wood from the Marquesas Islands, with a star motif on the top inlaid in dark wood and mother of pearl, and with whale ivory knobs on drawers that open to a compartment with whale ivory pegs to hold spools for thread. The swift is a tabletop type, made of whale skeletal bone and wood, with turned spools and gaskets, metal fastenings, a metal wing-nut on the clamp, and abalone shell and sealing wax inlay; the ribs are tied with pink silk ribbons that are evidently indigenous. The swift and the box were acquired by NBWM from the estate of Burdett's unmarried granddaughter, together with three other heirlooms: a miniature oil-on-bone portrait of Thomas Burdett as a young man, a photographic portrait of him taken in 1862, and a photograph of his father, Captain Barzillai Burdett. A private collector reports another, similar swift (but no box) by the same hand (not confirmed). Burdett was born on Nantucket in 1814, the son of Barzillai and Eunice [Robinson] Burdett. He went to sea in the New Bedford ship *Roscoe* (1833-36) and was first mate (1848-53) and captain (1853-57) of the *Statira* (Starbuck, 504, erroneously lists James Burdett as master of the *Statira* on that voyage), and captain of the Westport bark *Sea Queen* (1858-62). He married Caroline E. Prescott of Portland, Maine, in 1840, and later lived on Fourth Street in Boston, from which port he worked as a merchant captain in the 1860s and afterwards as a cooper. They had a daughter named Emma (born circa 1841) and a son named Charles (born 1849), who became a civil engineer and later a lawyer in Hartford, Connecticut. Thomas retired in the 1890s, when he and Caroline and a servant girl moved to Hartford, next door to their widowed son Charles and his two children, Ralph (born in 1879) and Emma (1884-1964). Charles died in a New York City hotel fire sometime between 1900 and 1903, after which Thomas and Caroline evidently moved back to New Bedford, where Thomas died in 1903. Their granddaughter Emma inherited the scrimshaw, which came to NBWM from her estate in 1964.

Burgess, Joseph Hathaway (fl. 1851). A native of Fairhaven, Massachusetts, he was briefly in the whale oil business in Rochester, New York, beginning in 1851, when he alluded to his familiarity with the scrimshaw and souvenir-collecting traditions of his whaleman father and whaling-port hometown (typescript in NBWM reported by Michael P. Dyer). Whether he actually did any scrimshawing himself is doubtful. He was born in 1828, the son of Paul Cooke Burgess, a mariner who died at sea three years later, in 1831, killed by whale. This is what may have dissuaded Joseph from ever making a whaling voyage himself; in any case, he never did. The 1850 U.S. Census lists him as an accountant, age 21, living in Fairhaven with his widowed mother, Ann Hathaway Burgess, 42, and widowed grandmother, Anna Hathaway, 81. Soon after, he married Eliza Caroline Kelso Platt of New York City; and in 1851, as a newlywed trying to establish himself as an oil merchant in Rochester, he wrote in a letter to his mother, "We are going to have a stall in the State Fair enclosure for the exhibition of our oils and we propose to put in a lot of teeth, shells, canes, clubs, &c &c &c &c to attract attention" — a use of whaling relics no doubt intended to set an appropriate mood, evocative of the whale fishery. Little is known of the specifics, but the venture in Rochester was evidently not the success he had hoped. They moved back to New Bedford not long after, where he fared better. By 1856 he was senior partner in Burgess & Smith, oil manufacturers, and by 1859 had become a soap manufacturer on his own, living with his wife, two children, and a maid. In 1880, at age 52, he was a widower, boarding solo in New Bedford and again listed as an accountant. He not only followed this profession as such, but was the proprietor of a small business school and teacher of bookkeeping. He later remarried and lived in New Bedford until 1907.

Busch, N. — see **Bush, Nicholson W.**

Bush, Nicholson W. (fl. circa 1841-50). A sperm whale tooth (in a private collection) pictorially engraved as a love token, utilizing pinprick-transfer images imported from published illustrations, is reportedly signed "N. Busch"; but as there are no whalemen on record utilizing this spelling of the surname, this almost certainly a variant or substitution or error for "Bush," indicating Nicholson W. Bush, the son of a New Bedford wool dealer and brother of a fellow-whaleman. Their parents were originally from Newport, Rhode Island, but Nicholson was born at New Bedford in 1823 and made three whaling voyages from that port, as a green hand for a 140th lay in the bark *Hope* of New Bedford (1841-42), as seaman for a 125th lay in the ship *Falcon* of New Bedford (1843-46), and as boatsteerer for an 85th lay in the ship *London Packet* of Fairhaven (1847-50). Between his second and third voyages he married Adaline Frazee of New York in 1847. On his third voyage his ship was formally condemned and taken out of service, likely stranding the crew in Sydney, New South Wales, leaving them to their own devices to find berths or passage home. (The *London Packet* must afterwards have been repaired, for it is reported to have been sold and put back into service as a whaler out of Sydney.) Nicholson Bush vanishes from view at this point, does not appear again in the New Bedford City Directories, and evidently did not make another whaling voyage (though his brother Thomas was a mate well into the 1850s): apparently, Nicholson left New Bedford and whaling to take up residence and another career elsewhere. He was evidently twice married. In 1853, when he was living somewhere in Rhode Island, his wife gave birth to a daughter named Gertrude. In 1870, at age 45, he was living at Portsmouth, Rhode Island, where he was employed at a local copper works, and was married to a woman named Mary, with whom he had a three-year-old son named Clarence.

* **Bute, James Adolphus** (fl. circa 1819-36). The *Dictionary* reported a tooth (in WAM) by J.A. Bute relating to the famous voyage in HMS *Beagle*, under Robert FitzRoy (1831-36), on which Charles Darwin developed the materials and theories that led to *The Origin of Species*. Bute was a Royal Marine on the *Beagle* at the time. Since publication of the *Dictionary* and *More Scrimshaw Artists*, four more such teeth from the *Beagle* voyage, signed by the same artist, have emerged. Two that have scenes of small craft and ship portraits (reported by Alan Granby) were exhibited in different years at the New York Winter Antiques Show. One of these ("Tracking the boats of HMS Beagle up the River Cruz, East Pategonia [sic]", mentioned by Fiona McWilliam, *Nation's Cities Weekly*, Jan. 1, 1999) was superficially deteriorated from losses of pigment and was expertly restored by conservator Jean D. Portell of Brooklyn, New York, utilizing pioneering new methods. She presented her findings at the annual Scrimshaw Collectors' Weekend (at KWM) in June 1999. The third (reported by William J. Boylhart in 2005) has on one side a colophon-style bust portrait of a Maori with weapons and rope motif, labeled below "New Zealand"; on the other side, a barren shorescape with a nearly naked standing human figure holding a spear and a bow, with a second figure paddling a kayak-like canoe in the water nearby, labeled below "Natives of Tierra del Fuego" and signed "J.A. Bute.";

and on the edge, a rose and thistle motif, inscribed in a riband below "BRITONS UNITED". The fourth, depicting the *Beagle* hove down and undergoing repairs, inscribed "H M Sloop Beagle laid on shore to repair her Forefoot," turned up at auction in England (Bonham's, 16 Sept. 2009). This brings the count to five, of which only two have been examined and vetted by SFL. Assuming that all five are authentic, Bute may have made multiples as mementos for shipmates and friends, not unlike the many Susan's Teeth of Frederick Myrick.

The *Beagle*'s surveys of Tierra del Fuego, Cape Horn, Diego Ramirez, and adjacent islands were the principal basis of an Admiralty chart of the region published in 1841. Little is known about James Adolphus Bute himself. He was likely of Scots ancestry, was born circa 1799, and joined the Royal Navy as a Marine private at age around 20. On a crew list of the *Beagle* in the journal of Syms Covington, Darwin's assistant (who was later postmaster of Pambula, N.S.W.), Bute is specifically listed as one of the Royal Marines. He evidently lived at Greenwich (London) and possibly at nearby Shoreditch, and died at Greenwich in 1859.

Caldwell, Sir James, Bart. (fl. 1731-84). Anglo-Irish aristocrat and political essayist. He is not known to have carved or engraved any scrimshaw himself, but in a book entitled *Debates Relative to the Affairs of Ireland, In the Years 1763 and 1764* (issued anonymously and privately printed at London in 1766), he wrote:

> *It is to be observed, that in the Sea off the Coast of Donegal, there are, besides the Whales, that yield only Bone and Blubber, the Finn-fish, the Porpoise, the Sun-fish, and the Sperma-ceti-Whale, besides Seals. The teeth of the Sperma-ceti-Whale, are shaped like a Cucumber, and are about 18 Inches long; they are as white as Ivory, take a fine polish, and make very beautiful and durable Handles for Knives and Forks.* (Citation provided by Michael P. Dyer.)

Like several other eighteenth-century commentators, Sir James seems to have confused sperm whale teeth and walrus tusks. Only exceptionally large sperm whale teeth ever exceed 9 inches (23 cm) in length; 11-inch (28 cm) specimens are extremely rare, and none has ever been found as long as 18 inches (46 cm); they are not really shaped very much like cucumbers in any case. Walrus tusks, on the other hand, while they may not precisely resemble cucumbers either, do commonly achieve and exceed 18 inches in length. Inaccurate though they be, Caldwell's remarks do reflect a rare eighteenth-century recognition of the qualities of beauty, utility, and durability of marine ivories that whalemen themselves would come to appreciate *en masse* two or three generations later. There are glorious Baroque examples of walrus ivory carved into handles for cutlery (in FSM); and there are even two sperm whale teeth scrimshawed by the great Edward Burdett that were converted into handles for carving sets (formerly in HMM, latterly in Rinaldi, now in a private collection in California).

Given his lofty station, it is unlikely that Sir James made such implements out of whale teeth himself: he was the sort of fellow who probably had people to do that for him. Sir James Caldwell, Bart. (circa 1720-1784), was the Fourth Baronet Caldwell of Castle Caldwell, in County Fermanagh, Ireland. Educated at Trinity College, Dublin, he served with distinction in the Austrian army — in recognition of which Empress Maria Theresa conferred upon him in 1749 the title of Count of Milan. Back in Ireland, he mostly managed his estates, pondered human nature, and wrote essays on economics and politics. These included his *Debates* (1766), which among other things was a groundbreaking endeavor to record for scrutiny and posterity the words spoken in Parliament, as well as *A proposal for employing cloathing, and furnishing with implements of husbandry, children, from the age of ten to sixteen; with a view to agriculture, the improvement of land, and gardening* (1770), *Essay on the character and conduct of His Excellency Lord Visc[ount] Townshend, lord lieutenant general, and general governor of Ireland, &c...* (1771), *Enquiry how far the restrictions laid upon the trade of Ireland* (1779), and a second edition of the *Debates* (1779) (www.irishartsreview.com; Library of Congress Online Catalogue). An amusing inscription on a whimsical stone monument at the family estate on Lough Erne (Ireland) reveals something of the baronet's character. This odd *memento mori* is shaped like a violin, whereof the text is self explanatory: "To the / memory / Of / Denis McCabe / Fiddler / who fell out of the / St Patrick Barge belonging / to / Sir James Caldwell Bart. / and Count of Milan, & / was drowned off this / Point August Ye 13 / 1770 / Beware ye fiddlers of the fiddlers fate, / Nor tempt the deep lest ye repent too late, / Ye ever have been deemed to water foes, / Then shun the lake till it with whiskey flows, / On firm land only exercise your skill, / There you may play, and drink your fill" (www.castlesbytheerne.co.uk).

Campbell, — (fl. 19th century). One of a pair of teeth monochrome engraved with naval engagements after Bowen's *Naval Monument* appears to be signed "Campbell" (reported by Gary Eckstine). The back of one is polished but undecorated, the other is very elaborately festooned with naval and patriotic paraphernalia, portrait miniatures, flags, horses, etc., and boldly inscribed with mottoes in fancy lettering (not legible in the photocopies submitted). Absent of any provenance the artist could not be identified by the signature alone; however, on stylistic grounds he certainly could not be the Naval Engagement Engraver and is very likely not the Naval Monument Engraver (qq.v.) but, rather, one of the many practitioners who based their pictures on the illustrations in Bowen, in this case a better-than-average draftsman with a flair for the ornate.

Cann, William (fl. circa the 1840s). Common seaman credited with a panbone busk, engraved by means of pinprick-transfer with simple, full-length, monochrome outlines of two standing women in gowns, which has on the back a crude, unfinished American shield and is inscribed "Cann," in the manner of a signature; in NBWM. In the absence of a provenance, the maker can only be provisionally identified through the process of elimination. Very few men of this surname served on American whaleships, and most of the ones in the NBFPL Whalemen's Index turn out actually to have been named Carr: Thomas D. Cann, the man listed as such as first mate of the Fairhaven bark *Bruce* (1848-51), was actually Thomas D. Carr, who was also second mate on the New Bedford barks *Milwood* (1842-44) and *Hope* (1845-47), and first mate on the *George Washington* (1851-52) and *Osceola 3d* (1852-54). Likewise, William S. Cann, named as a green hand in the ship *Henry Kneeland* of New Bedford (1854-57), was actually William S. Carr (he was indeed a green hand in the *Henry Kneeland*, but on an earlier voyage, 1845-48; it was actually Henry J. Carr who was the green hand in the *Henry Kneeland* on the later voyage). There was a career seaman actually named William Cann, born in 1831 in Sidney, Nova Scotia, who lived in Providence, Rhode Island, and Groton, Connecticut, married Mary A. Pendleton of Noank, Connecticut, at Mystic in 1855, and died at Sailors' Snug Harbor in 1906 — though whether it was Sailors' Snug Harbor in Boston or the one on Staten Island, New York, is not clear; and there is no record of him ever having gone whaling. Several men named Cann served as captains, officers, and seamen in merchant schooners and brigs out of Salem, Massachusetts, in the 1850s and '60s: John Cann of Newburyport, J.T. Cann of Weymouth, William Cann of Calais, Maine, and William M. Cann from Yarmouth, Nova Scotia; but there is no record of any of them in the whale fishery. Thus, by far the most likely candidate for maker of the scrimshaw is the William Cann who, at age 25, shipped as a seaman in the New Bedford whaleship *Barclay* (1840-43). Unfortunately, nothing else is known about him.

Carr Brothers (fl. circa 1820-50). The provenance of an important tooth that descended in the Carr family of Warren, Rhode Island, and is now in WHS (reported by Richard Donnelly) implies authorship within the family as it was donated by the youngest maiden sister, Mary Phillips Carr, at age 76 in 1891. However, any one of the five Carr brothers could theoretically have done the scrimshaw; or it could have been done by their brother-in-law, Mason Ingraham (q.v.), a career mariner; or by some other hand and merely been brought home as a souvenir or gift by any one of the sailors in the family. The tooth has complex cartographic and pictorial renderings of New York harbor from Sandy Hook to the Battery and Lower Manhattan, featuring Castle Garden, Governor's Island, and other fortifications, as well as a ship's route through The Narrows into the harbor. On the other side is an equally complex schematic representation of the "Roadstead at Gibraltar," with the British colonial establishment and the Rock clearly delineated. The lighthouses and waterborne traffic are reminiscent of the Pagoda Artisan (see the article on Silvanus Baker) and there is hardly any portion of the tooth that is not richly filled with images.

Of the six sons and five daughters born to Captain William Carr (1763-1845) and his second wife, Rebecca Phillips (circa 1774-1846), two were definitely sailors, the other four could have been, and at least five could theoretically have been scrimshaw artists; brother-in-law Ingraham makes six; but no whaling records for any of them are known. George Washington Carr (1808-1879) is a likely candidate because, according to the prestigious compendium *Representative Men of Rhode Island*, he was a career mariner in early life — the only one of the six Carr brothers anywhere so designated. He was also the one who became prominent in local affairs: a bank cashier for many years, a director of the Warren Manufacturing Company, and a town government official. The oldest brother, Nathan (1796-1850), died at sea — but whether as a passenger or member of the crew is not clear, and it is not known whether or not he was a sailor at any time. But that he "died at sea on a ship heading for New York" (Arthur A. Carr, *The Carr Book*, 1947) is suggestive in connection with the New York Harbor motifs on the tooth, as he may have been a regular on the North Atlantic route. Three of the brothers died young, two of them abroad: Henry Phillips Carr (1799-1816) at age 17 in St. Lucas, and Charles Carr (1813-1835) at 22 in Havana, but under what occupational circumstances is not known. Henry Phillips Carr II (1821-1863) died a soldier in the Union Army, in an action against Ft. Macon in Beaufort, North Carolina, but he had been a sailor in earlier years. As the unmarried kid sister (and sister-in-law), Mary Phillips Carr (1815-1893) would have been in a position to be the recipient of gifts as well as to be a residual heir of any of her brothers.

Carvalho, Celestino A. — see **de Carvalho, Celestino A.**

Caton, Manuel (fl. circa 1844-61). A knife-grip crimper with a two-piece whale ivory handle, three-tine fork, scroll saddle, and fluted whale ivory jagging wheel (in NBWM since 1916) has a notation in the provenance associating it with Manuel Caton, to whom it is accordingly attributed. Born circa 1829 on the island of Graciosa, in the Azores, he evidently joined his first whaleship, the *Albion* of Fairhaven, at St. Helena in May 1844, when the voyage itself was almost over and the vessel headed home. How he got to St. Helena at age 14 or 15 in the first place is not known for certain, though it may have been as a seaman or stowaway on a local packet, with the specific intention of securing a berth in a vessel bound for the Massachusetts whaling ports. The *Albion* had been out 21 months to the Indian Ocean and back. Jehaziel Jenney, who was making his first whaling voyage as captain, had been killed by a whale in March, and they called at St. Helena not only for routine provisioning but no doubt also to report the accident and take aboard a relief captain. Caton officially signed there as a green hand for the 195th lay, but he was aboard only five weeks before the *Albion* got back to Fairhaven in June 1844 and discharged the crew. It was not a good bargain in standpoint of pay, as they took no whales on the homeward passage: Caton must have gotten $\frac{1}{195}$th of nothing. But it was the kind of start that a young immigrant could use as the springboard for an entire career, which is exactly what he did. He immediately signed as a green hand again, this time on the bark *Elizabeth* of Mattapoisett (1844-46), commanded by Elisha Jenney, kinsman of the former captain of the *Albion* whom Caton had never actually known; and they sailed exactly 29 days after Caton first landed in Fairhaven. His next two voyages were as an ordinary seaman in the bark *Dumbarton* of Mattapoisett (1846-48), which was not a successful cruise, and the ship *Martha* of Fairhaven (1848-52), which was, modestly. During 1852-55 he was in either the bark *Mars* of New Bedford, or the bark *George and Mary* of Westport, or perhaps portions of voyages in both, it is not clear which. He then made his two final whaling voyages (but not necessarily his last as a deepwater mariner) as a boatsteerer in the New Bedford barks *Emily* (1855-57) and *Helen Snow* (1857-61). By this time he was married — to Mary E. Vescoucales, who was born in the Azores in 1831 and came to New Bedford in 1854 — and had become a naturalized U.S. citizen, as evidenced in his Seaman's Protection Paper (passport), issued in 1858. His descendants reside in New Bedford and Mattapoisett. (There was another mariner named Manuel Caton, born in the same place at the same time — at Graciosa, Azores, in 1829 — who married Clarissa Clark Munsey at Wiscasset, Maine, in 1854, and died in 1891, leaving descendants in Wiscasset and in New London, Connecticut.)

* **Ceres Artisans** (fl. circa late 1820s - 1840s). Thanks to painstaking analysis by Donald E. Ridley at KWM, KNB, and SFL, together with the collaboration of a small group of astute private collectors, also the faulty provenance of a busk that led to a preliminary attribution first published in *More Scrimshaw Artists,* and the recent emergence of a hitherto unknown Ceres A tooth that appears to be conclusive, the situation regarding the so-called Ceres Teeth has been further clarified, though by no means definitively solved. Affinities in layout, subject matter, and subsidiary features, with sumptuous interiors, proscenium arches, and rectangular ornamental borders, originally led scholars and collectors to group what turned out to be a large number of teeth (now numbering more than forty) as the work of a single, anonymous artist. In the absence of a known practitioner, the artist was nicknamed Ceres after the whaleship *Ceres* of Wilmington, Delaware, on which some of the iconography at least, if not the scrimshaw itself, was thought by Dr. Kenneth R. Martin of

KWM and Judge Paul E. Vardeman to have originated. Further comparisons, premised on the discovery of additional pieces in recent years, yielded the current consensus, which regards the best of the Ceres-type scrimshaw as the work of two different artists, distinguished as Ceres A and Ceres B. There are also pieces of slightly lower quality by the Ceres C Artisan, and other "Ceres-like pieces" by several lesser hands. Influence between and among A, B, and C is a possibility, between A and C a virtual certainty, but the extent, direction, circumstances, and significance of such hypothetical influence are thus far not entirely known.

All of the so-called Ceres scrimshaw is polished, engraved, and pigmented in the orthodox manner; none is inlaid or relief-carved, and there are no "built" components, add-ons, or moving parts. The Ceres A group — previously provisionally attributed to Shubael S. Spooner (q.v.) but now confidently attributed to William A. Gilpin (q.v.) — consists of 17 teeth, including two pairs; six of the singleton teeth are two-sided and 11 are one-sided, for a total of 23 "sides," in addition to a panbone busk that has several vignettes. All of the Ceres A pieces are pinprick-transfer work, engraved with a blade with undercuts visible in micro scale; several are polychrome or have polychrome highlights.

Pieces by the Ceres B Artisan — provisionally identified as William H. Meyers but possibly the work of John Cleland, Jr. (qq.v.) — are all incised with a point, rather than a blade, they have no undercuts, there is no evidence of pinprick transfer, and they are all pigmented in black monochrome. These number two busks and 17 teeth, including four pairs and two singletons that are two-sided, for a total of 21 "sides." Seven other pieces, of which three are engraved front and back (yielding a total of 10 "sides"), are similarly laid out and have superficially similar features, but are far inferior in concept and execution: in other respects, these vary considerably, and are grouped together as Ceres-like pieces (q.v.). The Ceres C pieces, numbering four teeth, are attributed to Edmund M. Chandler (q.v.).

All four of the attributed artists — John Cleland, Jr., who kept the journal in which the iconography originated; William H. Meyers, who probably did the actual drawings in Cleland's journal; William A. Gilpin, who was by far the best engraver of the four; and Edmund M. Chandler, about whom almost nothing is known — were shipmates on the 1834-37 voyage of the *Ceres* of Wilmington. Also, scrimshaw artist William Tallman (q.v.) was second mate on the voyage.

Ceres A Artisan — see Ceres Artisan, William A. Gilpin, and Shubael S. Spooner

Ceres B Artisan (fl. circa late 1820s - 1840s). Dr. Kenneth R. Martin and Judge Paul E. Vardeman have assembled substantial evidence that this artist, who originated the Free Trade and Sailors' Rights iconography and ship portraiture that characterizes the Ceres teeth, was William H. Meyers (q.v.) of Philadelphia, rather than shipmate John Cleland, Jr. (q.v.), of Wilmington, Delaware, in whose journal of the ship *Ceres* of Wilmington (1834-37) the originating watercolor sources appear. Known works currently attributed to this hand (catalogued and described by Donald E. Ridley at SFL) are 17 teeth and two busks, as enumerated above (see Ceres Artisans). They are all monochrome, cut with a point rather than a blade, with no evidence of pinprick transfer. Eight of the teeth are pairs: two pairs have the sailor-with-anchor on one tooth and woman-with-anchor on the other (in KNB; and BJ III:395); the third pair has a man in fancy garb on one tooth and a woman in a gown on the other (DAF); the fourth pair has a sailor on one tooth and a woman in a gown

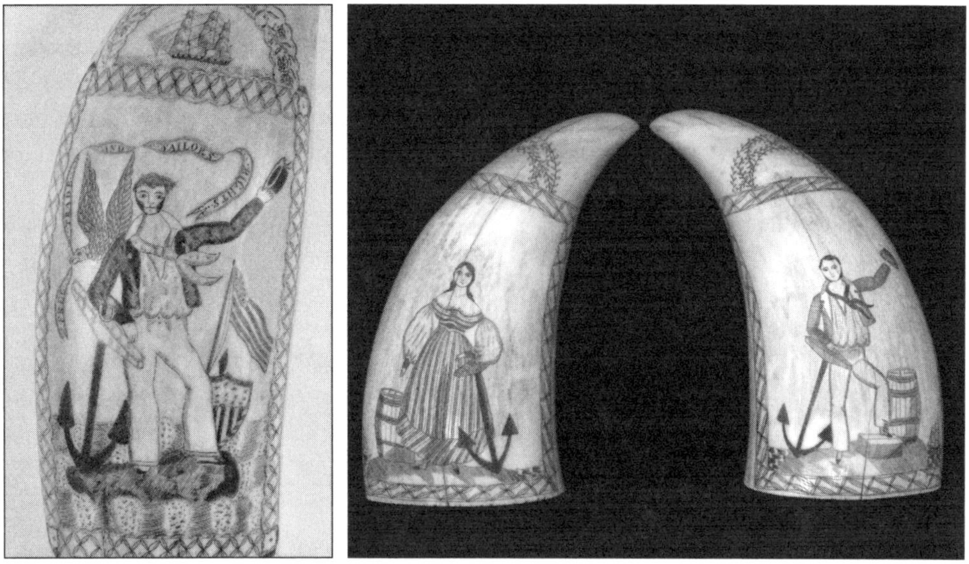

Fig. 7. "**Ceres Teeth**," comparing a sailor figure by the Ceres A Artisan, now known to be William A. Gilpin (left), and a pair of figures by the Ceres B Artisan, who was likely one of Gilpin's shipmates on the ship *Ceres* of Wilmington, Delaware, in the 1830s, but has not yet been identified. Courtesy of the Nantucket Historical Association; and the Kendall Collection, New Bedford Whaling Museum (photo by Richard Donnelly).

Fig. 8. **Two teeth by Manuel Enos.** The one on the left depicts a woman with a parrot, adapted from a fashion plate in the January 1860 issue of *Harper's New Monthly Magazine*. In the original the gown is monochrome and silky; in the whaleman's rendition the gown is brightly multicolored as though embroidered. The other tooth has an exotic image evocative of the Old Testament story of Rebecca at the Well, based upon "Arabia — the Arab Maid," after a painting by "Miss E. Carbeaux," engraved by Edward Finden for an edition of his *Tableaux of National Character, Beauty, and Costume* (London: T.G. March, 1843). It is also brightly colored, and inscribed on verso, "Jan. 25 / 1862 Off King Geo. Sound / Western Coast / of / **AUSTRALIA**." Kendall Collection, New Bedford Whaling Museum (photo by Richard Donnelly).

on the other (NBWM). Two Ceres B teeth are two-sided (private collections): a sailor and a ship portrait; and two Domestic Happiness couples with children, with a full-rigged warship (probably the USS *Pennsylvania*) on verso. The seven others are one-sided singletons. Three of these feature a sailor and a lady (Ashley, n.p.; Osona, Aug. 9, 2004, #70; Rinaldi, 1974, #8). Three have Domestic Happiness couples with varying numbers of children, with some of the men dressed as sailors (SIW; BJ IV:635; private collection); one of the charming features of these is a miniature sperm whaling scene hanging on the parlor wall. And one has a figure of Hope without an anchor (BJ I:339; Bourne Aug. 6, 1966, #157). The two panbone busks each have four vignettes, one with a full-rigged ship (NHA), the other with a ship and a brig (Osona, Aug. 8, 2004).

As noted, the identity of the Ceres B Artisan has not been definitively determined, but he was probably either William H. Meyers or John Cleland, Jr. Ceres A has been identified as William A. Gilpin (q.v.) and Ceres C as Edmund M. Chandler (q.v.), who were both shipmates of Meyers and Cleland on the 1834-37 voyage of the *Ceres*. The garments and décor represented on their scrimshaw are consistent with the early 1830s date and could not have been done earlier, and the scrimshaw bears resonant affinities with ink drawings in a shipboard journal of the voyage (in MMV) kept by Cleland, in which the watercolor and ink illustrations are attributed to Meyers. However, Ridley postulates that, as the attire and décor on the Ceres B pieces date from the late 1820s and early 1830s, Ceres B appears to be the earliest work by any Ceres Artisan and thus may be the source not only of motifs rendered by the other Ceres Artisans on scrimshaw (Gilpin and Chandler) but also some of the illustrations in the journal. The most notable of these is the Jack Tar / Free Trade and Sailors' Rights figure that is one of the principal identifying motifs on Ceres scrimshaw.

Ceres C Artisan — see Ceres Artisan and Edmund M. Chandler

Ceres-like Pieces (fl. circa the 1830s-'50s). This is a miscellaneous assortment of seven anonymous teeth that superficially resemble the Ceres A and Ceres B scrimshaw (see Ceres Artisans, above), but which are divergent in concept and execution. Whether any two are by the same hand has not been definitively ascertained. Only three, all one-sided, are in public-access collections: a soldier in a cocked hat (SPRI), a queen holding a Celtic harp (SPRI), and an inferior Domestic Happiness-like tooth, analogous to those attributed to William A. Gilpin (Ceres A), this one inscribed "HUMMINGBIRD" (KNB). Two others are known from auction records. One has the figure of a sailor with the inscription "FREE TRADE AND SAILOR'S RIGHTS" (Bourne, Aug. 5, 1981, #89; and July 31, 1989, #166) — a combination also found on several Ceres A pieces, but in this case the S is rendered backwards wherever it appears. The other is two-sided, with a figure of Hope-and-anchor on the front and a ship portrait on the back (Skinner, Nov. 6, 2005, #209). The two remaining teeth are two-sided: a Domestic Happiness type with a female fashion plate on the back; and a figure of Hope-with-anchor, surmounted by a Masonic symbol in a proscenium arch, with ship portrait on verso (private collections).

Chace, Charles W. (fl. circa 1847-67). Career whaleman from Westport, Massachusetts, who served as first mate of the *Charles W. Morgan*. He is credited with a dipper, made as a gift for his wife. The coconut shell bowl is elaborately relief-carved with two birds perched among leafy vines, two smaller birds on branches below, and inscribed in a riband "PRESENT TO RUTH M CHACE." It has an elongated heart-shaped mounting flange of whale ivory, with bands of wood and whale ivory on an octagonal foreshaft, a curved wooden handle of varying thicknesses with squared edges, and a plain whale ivory pommel with a wishbone-shaped pivoting whale ivory loop, to accommodate a lanyard or hook. It was donated to NBWM in 1976 by Mrs. Ruth C. Lang, a descendant, who also provided the provenance.

Charles William Chace was born in 1832, the son of Israel and Nancy Chace of Westport. His father was a carpenter in Westport and later a farmer in nearby Dartmouth, and Charles likely had some youthful training working wood; but he followed his elder brother Jonathan to sea and for the next twenty years or so made a career of whaling. Jonathan rose to command six whaling voyages in the 1870s and '80s. Charles never went so far, and the record of his voyages is only partially known: green hand, brig *Mattapoisett* of Westport (1847-48); boatsteerer, bark *Catherwood* of Westport (sailed 1853; lost on the Galapagos Islands, 1855); first mate, ship *Brewster* of Mattapoisett (1860-63); and first mate, ship *Charles W. Morgan* (1863-67), a voyage of which his journals are in MSM and NBFPL. After he left off whaling he was a farmer in Westport well into his seventies. He was thrice married and raised an entire new family each time. His first wife was Betsey; they were married when they were very young, he about 18 and she 16, and they had two children. They lived with Israel and Nancy Chace in Westport and Dartmouth, and it was not until his second marriage that Charles established a household of his own. The time and circumstances of Betsey's death are not known, nor is the date of his second marriage. This was to Ruth, the recipient of the scrimshaw, and it was probably around 1867. With Ruth he had two more children before she contracted consumption — sometime before 1880 — and she died not very long after. Around 1886 Charles was married for the third time, to Lusanna Wilcox, a widow 25 years his junior who already had a teenage daughter of her own; and with Lusanna he had two more sons and two more daughters. With regard to his honorific title "Captain" Chace in the provenance, local usage and local records in his hometown of Westport refer to him as such though he never commanded a whaling voyage. It may perhaps have been merely a courtesy because he held master's papers (though was never a captain in the whale fishery), or because he was master of some kind of vessel other than whaling. Another Charles W. Chase (not Chace) seems contemporaneously to have been a professional First Mate on whaling voyages in the 1850s-60s.

* **Champ, S.J.** (fl. circa 1836-39). Immigrant carpenter and ivory cutter in New York City whom the *Dictionary* was unable to identify satisfactorily but who is credited with two teeth. One is apparently Fraktur-influenced, described as "Polychrome tooth with a crudely rendered Pennsylvania Dutch female figure on one side and three vignettes (flower pot, woman with a bird, and two women) on the other side, inscribed 'S.J. Champ. N.Y.,' attributed in SSS" (illustrated in Hellman & Brouwer, 38); the other is "an unsigned tooth with a female portrait and praying figure, in a private collection." It should perhaps be added that, contrary to the description originally provided by SSS, the signature on the tooth from that collection is rendered in bold capitals, "S.J. CHAMP / N.Y."; that one of the vignettes on the back is patriotic in character, with the goddess-like figure of a Classical

nude, seated and draped, pouring refreshment into a goblet for an eagle (presumed to represent Columbia with her characteristic eagle accouterment), surmounted by an arch of stars; and that the other vignette is an enigmatic interior domestic scene of two women, one standing, the other seated and reading a book, labeled below, "ETERNITY." The two teeth are so orthodox in conception and execution that they could only have been produced by someone fully acquainted with the mainstream genre, almost certainly as a deepwater whaleman. However, no record of whaling voyages has been discovered.

Samuel John Champ was born in Staffordshire, England, sometime between 1806 and 1811. When he emigrated from Liverpool in the ship *Estelle* in 1836 he stated his age as 30 and his trade as laborer. He arrived in New York on 22 July 1836, and his whereabouts from that time until 1839 are not recorded. It is at that time that he may have gone whaling and made the scrimshaw. (If so, it was likely on an unidentified vessel out of Sag Harbor or Nantucket from which no crew list has come to light; there is no record of him in New Bedford or New London.) By 1839 Champ was in New York again, working as a carpenter and living on Spring Street; this was Ward 5 in Lower Manhattan, the heart of New York's notorious Sailortown district. Around that time he married a native New Yorker named Mary, fathered a daughter, and became a naturalized citizen (Superior Court of New York County, 13 Apr. 1840). In 1860 he was still living on Spring Street with his wife and a son named James, who at 16 was already working as a clerk; but Champ himself was employed as an ivory cutter, for which comparatively unusual trade one can only presume that whaling and shipboard scrimshandering had provided the rudiments. His neighbors on Spring Street at that time were Joseph Newman, age 37, an Irish immigrant identified as a manufacturer of whalebone (that is, baleen, undoubtedly for the city's thriving garment industry), and his American-born wife and family of five; however, unlike the Champs, the Newmans were evidently sufficiently prosperous to employ an Irish-born domestic servant.

Chandler, Edmund M. (fl. circa 1834-37). One of the four or more hitherto anonymous Ceres Artisans (q.v.) — so-called by reason of their association with the 1834-37 voyage of the ship *Ceres* of Wilmington, Delaware — his scrimshaw was previously designated Ceres C. Based on a signature on one of the four teeth by this hand, the artist is now confidently identified as Edmund M. Chandler, an Ordinary Seaman on that seminal voyage of the *Ceres*. He was thus a shipmate of seaman William A. Gilpin (q.v.), now identified as the Ceres A Artisan; John Cleland, Jr., in whose shipboard journal of the voyage various ink drawings appear that are remarkably analogous to the images on the Ceres scrimshaw — notably a Jack Tar figure bearing the mottoes "Free Trade and Sailors' Rights" and "Virtue, Liberty, and Independence"; and William H. Meyers, who likely did the actual journal illustrations and may have been the actual Ceres B Artisan (q.v.), whose work Donald E. Ridley convincingly maintains may have been the initial source and inspiration for the Jack Tar figure and other motifs, both in the journal and on scrimshaw by the Ceres Artisans (Ridley, Scrimshaw Collectors Weekend, NBWM, 17 May 2008). Additionally, "The Ceres C pieces number four teeth ... One of these pieces has a port- (or larboard-) quarter view of a ship bearing the name "CERES" on the stern" (Ridley, private communication, 11 Apr 2008). Chandler himself seems to have eluded the census-takers and genealogists, and the only known record of him is that his name appears on the crew list in John Cleland's journal: no further details have yet been discovered.

* **Chappell, William H.** (fl. circa 1838-56). He is described in the *Dictionary* as a ship's carpenter active at New Bedford and Newport, credited with a mahogany showcase trimmed with whale ivory, made on the Kamschatka grounds for Captain Ephraim Harding in the New Bedford ship *Saratoga* during 1852-56 (Bourne, Aug. 17-18, 1971, #450; acquired by NBWM in 1983). It is also noted that in his journal of that voyage (in NCP) he describes scrimshandering; and in his journal of the New Bedford bark *Wade* during 1840-44 (in KNB) he made what he calls a "List of the Principal Mechanical Work Expended By Myself On Board the Wade," which runs to eight pages in a tiny, beautiful hand, indicating that he also "made a portable writing desk, Length 1 ft 11 in., depth 8-½ in., width 10-¼ in.," as well as chopping knives, tools, and other items. It should be noted that though he was born in East Greenwich, Rhode Island (in 1819), and may have apprenticed at Newport (and certainly apprenticed somewhere as a carpenter or cooper), there is little evidence that he ever actually worked as a carpenter or cooper at Newport, especially after he married Esther B. Potter of Westport, Massachusetts, in 1844, and worked thereafter in New Bedford. Also, that in his *Wade* journal he mentions at one point that all hands were "working on the jawbone of a whale," presumably to prepare it for scrimshaw, and there, on several occasions, reports that he was "scrimshonting" himself, including that he "made two sweep brooms from whale bone [baleen]" and "turned and finished 26 clothes pins for the Mate from jaw bone." As noted in the *Dictionary*, Chappell was ship's carpenter in the *London Packet* (1838-40) and the *Wade* (1840-44). With regard to the *Saratoga*, the Whalemen's Index in NBFPL reports him as carpenter and shipkeeper for the 150th lay, rather too long for so experienced a man; accordingly, the official crew list for that voyage of the *Saratoga* (in NBFPL) names E.K. Childs as carpenter and shipkeeper for the 105th lay, while "Wm. H. Chappell" is listed as cooper and boatsteerer for the 45th lay, which certainly must be correct. Born at East Greenwich, Rhode Island, circa 1819, he likely apprenticed as a carpenter or cooper in his youth, went to sea at age 19, and made two whaling voyages. After he married he worked for a few years as a cooper in New Bedford until he went in the *Saratoga*. He later had a grocery store on Purchase Street in which he also advertised crockery, china, glassware, and fancy goods, and in which Arthur, one of his many children, clerked for him.

Chase, Josiah E. (fl. circa 1837-82). While at sea as captain of the New Bedford bark *Hunter* in 1870 he recorded in his journal that he was "scrimshonting" and "Empl[oyed] myself making Julia's swifts." Julia was his wife; it appears that there were at least two swifts (see the article on William Washburn, a captain who was also making two swifts simultaneously); and it is likely from the context as well as from the length of Captain Chase's distinguished career that this was not the only scrimshaw he produced during the course of it. By the time of the *Hunter* voyage he had been to sea for more than thirty years and had been married for fifteen, during which time, like most whaling masters, he had been away from his family far more than he had been home, and had had many causes and many occasions and a great deal of time to produce mementos for the loved ones left behind. In fact, he would take his wife and children with him to the Pacific on his next voyage, and his wife would keep a journal of her own; she would also bear him a daughter along the way. Unfortunately, Captain Chase provides no details about the swifts, and neither they nor any other product of his "scrimshonting" has turned up.

Josiah Elden Chase was born in 1819 at Limington, Maine, the son of farmers Josiah (1784-1851) and Deborah (1789-1838), whose maiden name was also Chase. His early voyages are not known, but he was whaling by 1837 at age 18. On his second or third voyage, in the ship *Adeline Gibbs* of Fairhaven (1841-45), he had already progressed to third mate, and his next voyage after that he was first mate of the New Bedford bark *Canton Packet* (1845-49), skipping a second mate's berth altogether. He then skippered a series of New Bedford vessels: the ship *Martha* (1850-53), bark *Elizabeth Swift* (two voyages, 1854-58 and 1859-1863), bark *Hunter* (1867-71), which he left before the voyage was completed, the ship *California* (1872-76), and finally the ship *James Arnold*, of which Chase was the replacement captain during 1878-82. At this point he retired from the sea and became a full-time farmer at Limington. In the meantime he had married Julia Ellen Brown (1832-1915) of Farmingdale, Maine. Their first child was a son named Stephen who lived only ten years, but they had four children who survived into adulthood, three daughters and a son. The chronology is interesting as it typifies the distended calendar of a professional whaleman's family life. Josiah and Julia were married in June 1854 when he was already a captain and had recently returned from a voyage. Son Stephen was born 14 months later, in August 1855, by which time Josiah was already at sea in the *Elizabeth Swift*. He returned in October 1858 when Stephen was already three years old. Daughter Florence Ada was accordingly born nine months later, in July 1859. But by this time Josiah was at sea again in the *Elizabeth Swift*. He arrived home in September 1863, and this time he stayed ashore for more than four years. Son Charles Nichols was born in June 1865, son Stephen died that August, and daughter Mary Emma was born in September 1867, shortly before Josiah sailed again, in the bark *Hunter* in December (it was in the *Hunter* that he mentions making the swifts). The family came along with him on his next voyage, in the *California*, and Julia, the youngest child, was born in February 1875, on remote Norfolk Island in the South Pacific. She was a year and one half old when they arrived back in New Bedford in August 1876. The family stayed home when Josiah was relief captain of the *James Arnold*, and he finally retired in 1882. He died in 1898 at East Limington, Maine.

Chase, R.D. (fl. circa the 1870s-1910s). A rolling pin (in KNB) with the barrel comprised of three different kinds of wood, with whale ivory ends and handles, has a provenance that claims it was "made by R.D. Chase," about whom no information has been found. There are records of only about 50 men in the entire United States who were surnamed Chase or Chace, had the initials R.D., and were born between 1820 and 1900, and there is no indication that any of them ever went whaling or was ever in a position to make or receive scrimshaw. Nor was there any female of that name (of only about fifteen in the whole country) who could reasonably have been the recipient of such a rolling pin. This being the case, it seems likely that the scrimshaw was made by someone else, most likely one of the several whalemen named Chase or Chace whose first initial was R and whose middle names and second initial is not known.

* **Childs, William** (fl. circa 1842-67). The maker of a large, original, polychrome engraved walrus tusk (in KNB), he was born circa 1824, probably at Maynard, Massachusetts, the son of mariner Thomas Childs of Falmouth and the former Mahitable Hatch. His earliest voyages are not identified, but he must have been at sea by around 1840 or 1842. His wife, whom he married in 1852, was Laura A. Hamblin (born circa 1834), from one of Falmouth's leading whaling dynasties, the daughter of whaling captain Thomas F. Hamblin. For the first several years of their marriage, while William was still at sea, the couple and their first two children lived with Laura's widowed mother and

younger brother Andrew (a carpenter) in the Waquoit community of Falmouth, and later had a place of their own in Waquoit, where they raised their four children. The woman and child on the scrimshaw, said to have been engraved when William was captain of the *Vigilant* during 1865-67 (the last of his seven voyages as captain), are taken to be portraits of his wife and one of their children. He may or may not be the same William Childs who later managed oyster beds in Waquoit and nearby Cotuit.

* **Christian, Stephen C.** (fl. circa 1820-51). His *Dictionary* article identifies him as a New Bedford whaling master credited with a whale ivory and bone swift (in KNB), inscribed "Abigail Christian," presumed to have been made on shipboard for his wife Abbie, née Abigail Hammond, whom he married at New Bedford in 1835. A second attribution has since come to light in a private collection: a tooth dated 1832, engraved with pictures and mottoes, which in standpoint of contents, iconography, and architecture (but not in engraving technique) resembles the Susan's Teeth done by Frederick Myrick (q.v.) during 1828-29. It has two portraits of the ship *Swift*, one on each side; one has boats lowered in pursuit and is inscribed in a riband, "Ship Swift taking two 80 bbls whales." Surmounting these is an American spread-eagle with shield, arrows, and olive branch, inscribed "E Pluribus Unum." One edge has a sailboat approaching a ship at sea from a headland with a lighthouse and a church. Beneath these, inscribed circumferentially around the tooth, is the famous motto "Death to the living / Long life to the killers / Success to sailors wives / And greecy [sic] luck to whalers," alongside a spouting sperm whale. On the opposite edge the tooth is signed and dated, "Engraved by Stephen C Christian off Cape Horn July 23rd 1832." The whys and wherefores of its resemblance to the Susan's Teeth have not been adequately explained. While the workmanship is decidedly by a different, lesser hand than Myrick's, the similarities are such that, were it authentic whalemen's work of circa 1832, direct influence or a common source would be a virtual certainty. But the quality and style of the engraving appear so out of phase with the era of its ostensible authorship that the majority of scrimshaw cognoscenti who have actually examined the piece are skeptical, suggesting that the resemblances to Myrick's work are the deliberate result of cynical fraud.[1]

Stephen Christian was born circa 1806, went to sea at age 14, and was thirty years in New Bedford ships: a maiden voyage in the *Traveler* (1820-21), then two voyages in the *Triton* (1821-25) followed by two or three others, specifics unknown (could one of them have been as a shipmate of Frederick Myrick in the *Susan*? Or on one of the other ships Myrick portrayed in scrimshaw?). Christian was a mate in the *Swift* during 1830-32, the voyage on which he presumably engraved the tooth; then first mate in the *Frances* (1832-35), and captain of two voyages in the *Frances* (1836-43) and one each in the *John and Edward* (1844-47) and the *Hope* (1847-51). He is said to have died in 1864. However, this may have been in confusion with his son, Stephen E. Christian, who was born circa 1844 and died in the Civil War: he is identified as a "student" on his Union Army enlistment papers of September 1862 and he served as a private in Company E of the 3rd Regiment of Massachusetts Infantry. In 1864, when he was a private in Company E of the 58th Massachusetts, his occupation is given as "photographer." He died that same year.

* **Clapham, G.** (fl. circa 1836-38). In *More Scrimshaw Artists* Clapham is characterized as an Australian whaling master based at Sydney, New South Wales, originally from Brigg in Lincolnshire

[1] Panel discussion at the 22nd annual Scrimshaw Weekend of the New Bedford Whaling Museum, May 14, 2011.

(England), commander of the brig *Tamar* of Sydney in the late 1830s, and later a resident of New Zealand. He is credited with a total of seven teeth: two in AMNZ depicting sailing vessels and signed "G. CLAPHAM," and at least five others, "whereabouts unknown" at the time. Now two of these "others" have come to light. According to Dr. Janet West, "The whaling journal of Captain W. B. Rhodes, barque *Australian* of Sydney, 1836-38" (Whitcombe & Toombs, Christchurch, 1954, 30, entry for 28 Nov. 1836) places Captain Clapham in the *Tamar* off Tonga in November 1836, when the *Tamar* and *Australian* "kept company for some time" and "Clapham gave Rhodes a number of articles to take back to Lincolnshire including 5 WHALES TEETH CARVED." One of these is now believed to be a tooth with "a very dark yellow patina," described as "depicting a woman (full faced) under a tree holding a basket of flowers"; the scene is "murky" but the face "very clear" and the picture is "squared off," typically of copywork from a magazine or book illustration, with floral motifs and leafy vines above and below; signed "G. Clapham Sc[ul]p[sit]" (private collection, reported by Frederick Mitchell). Another, also quite richly patinated, depicts the standing figure of a man in uniform and is signed in a tiny hand, "G. Clapham Scpt" (reported by Andrew Zarauskas). From a crude photograph of the former, the "murkiness" of the image appears to be the result of migration of the monochrome pigment through substrata of the ivory, a feature primarily associated with water- and alcohol-soluble colored inks only rarely encountered with black monochrome, which is usually oil-based lampblack and so not generally subject to substrata diffusion.

Clark, Benjamin Smith (fl. circa 1840-60). New Bedford whaling master who was almost certainly the actual maker of a hefty figurine of a pinto horse, full-round-carved out of a large sperm whale tooth with polychrome pigmented highlights. It was given to NBWM in 1933 by Miss Mary Thornton Pierce, who provided a flawed provenance that confuses the dates and reverses the maker's name. According to Miss Pierce the figurine was "made by Captain Clark Smith" and "given to Albert Pierce by [the] maker c[irca] 1864." First of all, however, Albert G. Pierce (1869-1948), the donor's father, was not yet born in 1864. Thus, either it was given to him at a later date; or, if the 1864 date be at least approximately correct, it might have been given to Albert's father, Andrew G. Pierce, who was the president of the Wamsutta Mills cotton textile works and a sometime mayor of New Bedford. In due course the figurine would thus have been given to or inherited by Albert G. Pierce himself or by his brother, Andrew G. Pierce, Jr., and then come from either of them to Albert's daughter Mary. Moreover, there never was a whaling captain named Clark Smith, no evidence has been found of a Clark Smith in the whale fishery in any capacity, nor of any Captain Clark Smith active circa 1864 in any other capacity, including in the Union Army and Navy. On the other hand, New Bedford whaling captain Benjamin Clark (1793-1881), who was originally from Bridgewater, Massachusetts, married Jane Ann Smith (1801-1872) of Edgartown; their children were Benjamin Smith Clark and Jane Ann Clark; and when the son also became a whaling master, to distinguish him from his whaling master father he was called Captain Smith Clark. The scrimshaw was almost certainly made by him — Smith Clark, not Clark Smith.

The father, Benjamin Clark, was master of two voyages in the ship *Abigail* and two in the bark *Clarice* during 1829-38; part of his compensation was ownership interests in the two vessels. The son, Benjamin Smith Clark, was born at Edgartown circa 1821 and first went whaling at age 15, as a green hand in the *Clarice* on his father's last voyage as captain (1836-38). In 1850, barely two weeks after he returned from a voyage as first mate of the ship *Coral* under Captain Gideon Allen

(1846-50) and a few months prior to sailing for the first time as a captain, Smith Clark married Elizabeth Blackmar of Rochester, Massachusetts, where the couple resided as long as he continued at sea, and where their son and three daughters were born. He was captain of the ship *Leonidas* (1850-54) and bark *Chili* (1856-60), in which, like his father, he also held modest ownership interests. When he left off whaling he took his family to live with his parents at North Bridgewater, Massachusetts, where he worked as a house painter. It is not known whether he had carved the horse figurine at sea years before and only now passed it along to the Pierces; or perhaps it was newly carved at around this time. After his mother died in 1872 Clark *fils* moved his father, wife, and children to Brockton, Massachusetts, where they took in boarders while he continued to work as a house painter. Captain Benjamin Clark died there in 1881, Captain Smith Clark in 1895.

* **Clark, George H.** (fl. circa 1839-62). As noted in the *Dictionary*, he was a New Bedford whaling master credited with an inlaid mantle decoration surmounted by a pair of teeth bearing the initials "A.F.C." and "G.H.C." respectively (Eldred 26-27 July 1989, #760). He commanded whaling voyages in the barks *Roscoe* (1839-42) and *Dragon* (1842-44), and ships *Sally Anne* (1844-47), *Henry Kneeland* (1848-51), and *Bartholomew Gosnold* (1858-62), and held shares in several whaling vessels. Sophia S. Spooner of New Bedford, whom he married in 1839, was his first wife and the mother of his two sons, both of whom became seamen. He was widowed in the 1850s and was remarried to a woman named Frances, who bore him two daughters, and after his retirement from whaling he was employed as a watchman in a New Bedford bank.

* **Clark, James M.** (fl. circa 1835-70). The *Dictionary* mentions a gavel in MSM, and a bone-and-whale-ivory swift inlaid with abalone and baleen, inscribed "R W Vose from Jas[s] Clark," in KNB, both of which are confidently attributed to this long-tenured whaling master from Mattapoisett (Rochester), Massachusetts. He was a whaleman for 35 years, 24 of them as the captain on seven whaling voyages, in addition to the Gold Rush voyage in the bark *Yeoman* of Plymouth (1849) mentioned in *More Scrimshaw Artists*. It is interesting here to note that the swift was not made for a wife or sweetheart or any of the other usual kinds of recipients, but for the wife of the man who was evidently Clark's pastor. "R.W. Vose" was Rachel Wild [Faxon] Vose, wife of the Rev. Henry Clay Vose, D.D., who was evidently a Universalist minister in Marion, Massachusetts, adjacent to Mattapoisett and Rochester, in the region of the South Coast known as Sippican. It is not known whether James and Maria Clark and their children were congregants in his church or simply personal friends of the Voses.

Reverend Vose was born in 1816 at Stoughton, Massachusetts, and in 1839 married Rachel Wild Faxon of Braintree, Massachusetts, who was two years younger. In the typical manner of clergymen, they moved from congregation to congregation, living successively at Taunton, Rochester, Watertown, and Clinton, until Vose was apparently settled in a Marion church sometime during 1853-55. There they stayed for the long term, at least into the 1880s. Of their children who survived into adulthood, Albert, born circa 1853, became a medical doctor, and Frederic, born 1855, a schoolteacher.

Records disagree whether James M. Clark was born at Groton, Connecticut, circa 1814, or somewhere in Massachusetts (probably at Mattapoisett) in 1819 or 1820; some of the confusion may be owing to his having falsified his age for his first seaman's passport: it was a fairly common ploy for too-young prospective green hands to add a few years and even to misrepresent their places of birthplace in order to qualify for a berth while escaping notice from the folks back at the actual birthplace. Or the confusion may be between Groton, Connecticut, and Groton, Massachusetts. In any case, the U.S. Census is consistent in assigning Clark to Massachusetts, circa 1819-20. This would have made him a few years younger than Henry and Rachel Vose. James Clark's wife, whom we know only as Maria P. Clark, was substantially younger, born in Massachusetts circa 1832.

Clark, Smith — see **Clark, Benjamin Smith**

Clayton, John H. (fl. circa 1839-42). He signed a tooth that has on one side a starboard bow-quarter portrait of a full brig or snow under plain sail, labeled below "W.W. [ ]" (illegible); and on the other side, under a spread eagle with the USA shield and crossed American flags, the inscription "John H. Clayton," presumed to be a maker's mark (reported by William E. Hughes). Unfortunately, migration of the black pigment in the substrata of the ivory has blurred the name of the vessel so that it cannot be definitively deciphered. Whatever the name, she was neither a whaler nor a warship, as there was no whaler that had a name compatible with the W.W. initials and there is no evidence of naval ornament or armament.

There are only two men named John Clayton on record in the whale fishery. The career of the first one, brief though it was (only one voyage), is consistent with the period and style of the scrimshaw; the other is not. The attributed maker was born circa 1817 in Charleston, South Carolina, and was thus one of comparatively few men from the Deep South ever to have gone whaling. However, in 1839, when at age 22 he signed articles for a voyage to the Indian Ocean whaling grounds in the bark *Palestine* of Salem, Massachusetts (1839-42), he stated his birthplace as Charleston but his residence as Salem. Both the captain and the first mate died on that voyage, but of John Clayton no further record and no other scrimshaw is known. (The other John Clayton, born circa 1834, had three Seaman's Passports issued to him in New Bedford between 1856 and 1860, all stating that he was from Troy, New York, though there appears to be no record of him there. Despite the three passports, only two whaling voyages are known, and those two overlap chronologically so that the same man could not have been present during all of both: in the barks *Ocean* of Sandwich [September 1859 - August 1861] and *George & Mary* of Westport [November 1860 - August 1863]. In standpoint of style and iconography, it is extremely unlikely that the scrimshaw would have been made as late as the 1850s or '60s, thus an attribution to John Clayton of Charleston and Salem is far the more likely.)

Cleland, John, Jr. (fl. circa 1834-37). Seaman aboard the whaleship *Ceres* of Wilmington, Delaware during 1834-37, in whose shipboard journal (in MMV) appear the Free Trade and Sailors' Rights and ship portrait illustrations upon which the so-called Ceres Teeth are based. These were originally thought to have been done by a single hand, dubbed the Ceres Artisan or Ceres Engraver. However, over the succeeding years four different hands were differentiated by Donald E. Ridley of SFL, who accordingly separated the teeth into four discreet groups, and the respective artists were designated Ceres A, B, C, and D (or "Ceres-like"). Based on the core iconography in Cleland's journal, the Ceres B Artisan was confidently identified as the originator or prime mover even though his name was not known. This may have been Cleland himself. However, according to a Euclidian reasoning process by Dr. Kenneth R. Martin (Executive Director of the KWM at the time) and Judge Paul E.

Vardeman in the late 1970s, it was shipmate William H. Meyers (q.v.) who illustrated the journal for Cleland and may have originated the Ceres scrimshaw — that is, if not Cleland, then perhaps Meyers was Ceres B. In either case, thanks to the sudden and unexpected appearance of a Ceres A tooth signed by William A. Gilpin (q.v.), Gilpin is now known to have been the Ceres A Artisan; and Ridley has attributed the Ceres C teeth to Edmund M. Chandler (q.v.). All four — Cleland, Meyers, Gilpin, and Chandler — were shipmates on the *Ceres*, from which fact the daisy-chain of evidence establishes some clarity in the attributions; and while the Ceres B Artisan has not been unequivocally identified — whether Meyers or Cleland — the evidence weighs more heavily on the side of Meyers. (The far less refined and more miscellaneous work relegated to Ceres D, and whether there was more than one hand involved in producing it, has not been established; and given the undistinguished quality of the work, it likely never will be unless some kind of rock-solid provenance should emerge.)

Of Cleland himself we know but little. He was born in 1816 in Christiana (not far from Newark), Delaware, the oldest son and second-born of the twelve children of John and Ellen Cleland, prosperous immigrant farmers from Ireland, both of whom outlived their son. John Junior made the one whaling voyage and died a few years later in 1842 at Wilmington.

Coakley, John T. (fl. 1887-1909). New Bedford whaleman and latter-day whaling master, originally from Boston, later a resident of Hyannis and New Bedford. His case is one in which, despite published claims to the contrary, family provenance indicates that he was *not* a scrimshaw artist. In the book *Thar She Blows!* (New York, 1951), author Chester Howland relates what purports to be a factual occurrence aboard the New Bedford bark *Canton* under Captain George L. Howland (q.v.) in 1889:

> *"We had been on a passage three days and were busying ourselves on deck and below," Mr. Coakley reports. "I was glad to get the chance to finish carving a sperm whale's tooth and the captain had been working for months on an Australian gumwood box."*

The narrative goes on to describe a series of events that have no bearing on scrimshaw, but these opening sentences suffice for the purposes here. First of all, the fellow referred to was not "Mr." Coakley: John Coakley was a sixteen-year-old green hand when the *Canton* sailed in June 1887, and in 1889 was only about 18. The captain would never have referred to him or any green hand or any common seaman as "Mr.": it would have been "John" or "Coakley" or perhaps "Young John," but not the "Mr." honorific, which was strictly reserved for officers and petty-officer idlers. Secondly, Coakley's grandson, Morgan Levine, reports that the bit about the sperm whale tooth is pure fiction, a literary device to impart color: "My grandfather didn't make scrimshaw, he wasn't interested in that sort of thing... The only thing he ever saved from a voyage was a sea elephant tooth" (private communication, April 2006). John T. Coakley was, however, a career whaleman in the declining years of the fishery. After his inaugural voyage in the *Canton* (1887-90) he rose steadily through the ranks in the *Canton* again (1891-93) and barks *Sunbeam* (1893-95 and 1895-97), and *Morning Star* (1898-99), from which, having sailed as second mate, he was honorably discharged to accept a berth as first mate of the schooner *Robert S. Graham* (1899-1901) under the near-legendary Captain Benjamin D. Cleveland (q.v. in the *Dictionary*). Some years afterwards Coakley was the captain of a two-month whaling voyage in the schooner *Margaret* of Norwich, Connecticut (June-August 1909); then, surprisingly, for the remainder of his career he was an optician in New Bedford.

* **Coan, Enard** (fl. circa 1834-49). A monochrome tooth dated July 4, 1841, in the John F. Kennedy Collection, has singular importance because of the presidential provenance. Contrary to Clare Barnes's misreading of the scrimshaw as a memento mori (Barnes 1964, 120), it is characterized in the *Dictionary* as "rather whimsical," with the remark that "Barnes's error likely arises from his mistaking the whalemen's typically ornate floral and geometric decorations for mortuary art." The artist's early voyages were unknown at that time, but it turns out (from crew registers kept by the New Bedford Port Society) that Enard Coan was on a Pacific Ocean sperm whaling voyage — almost certainly as second mate — in the New Bedford ship *George Howland*, commanded by Seth Weeks, from 24 April 1838 to 21 October 1841. This was surely the vessel on which he made the scrimshaw later owned by President Kennedy. Coan was born at Guilford, Connecticut, in 1812, was issued a seaman's passport (which must have been his second or third) at New Bedford in November 1834, married Caroline Smith at New Bedford in 1838, and following the *George Howland* voyage (with the *Whalemen's Shipping List* mistaking his name as Edward Coan) shipped out immediately afterwards, on November 9, 1841, as first mate of the New Bedford bark *Canton* (1841-45). He then made one voyage as captain of the New Bedford ship *Charles* (1845-49).

* **Coffin, George Cobb** (fl. circa 1835-51). The *Dictionary* mentions a panbone serving mallet inscribed "G.C. Coffin," attributed in NHA, noting that such an indispensable tool would have come in handy in Coffin's role as cooper aboard the whaleship *Barclay* of his native Nantucket (1847-51). Judith Lund's recent excavation of Fall River crew lists revealed that Coffin's maiden voyage at age 17 was in the ship *Gold Hunter* of Fall River, commanded by his father, Captain Jethro Coffin (1833-34), and that he followed it with a second voyage in the same vessel. Born on Nantucket in 1817, George was the son of Captain Coffin by his second wife, the former Mary Cobb. He married Selina J. Eldridge of Cape Cod in 1847 and continued working as a sailor well into the 1860s, at least some of the time reprising his earlier role as a ship's cooper. Meanwhile, when Captain Coffin retired from whaling he worked as a carman on Nantucket; and after he retired from that, he and George's mother moved in with George and his family, still on Nantucket. Afterwards, George moved his family to Providence, Rhode Island, where he and his son, J. Frank Coffin, were in business together as carpenters.

Coffin, J.M. (fl. 19th century). In the absence of any provenance it is not clear whether the inscription "J.M. Coffin" on a panbone busk refers to the maker or the recipient (Osona, 4 Aug. 2007, #324B, where the busk is listed in the addenda but not described). Even if the former, given the large number of Coffins who went whaling — not only from Nantucket, where the surname was particularly numerous, but from throughout New England and elsewhere — the inscription itself is clearly not sufficient to warrant an attribution. Most notably, James M. Coffin was master of the ship *Constitution* of Nantucket (1832-33) and bark *Alto* of Fairhaven (1840-43). Born on Nantucket in 1810, he was the son of Gardner Coffin and the former Mary Jackson Goodwin. He married Anna J. Swain in 1832, had two children by her, and after her death in 1839 married her distant kinswoman Emily Swain in 1842, left off whaling for farming by 1850, moved to Kankakee, Illinois, where he became a police judge and died there in 1880. (The John M. Coffin whom NBFPL lists as captain of the ship *Charles Drew* of New Bedford, 1846-49, appears actually to have been John *T.* Coffin, according to Lund and Sherman, the latter likely based on NCP.)

Coggeshall, George R. (fl. circa 1844-52). In his journal aboard the ship *Samuel Robertson* of Fairhaven during 1849-52, he mentions that in December 1850 he was "employed in fitting rigging and scrimshawning," and in December 1851 (with a change in the flexible spelling of the term) he was "employed in scrimshorning." In March 1851 he reports "the Captain making a pair of swifts and myself turning belaying pins." The captain was William Washburn (q.v.). Whether Coggeshall's own "scrimshorning" efforts ever amounted to anything more than such rudimentary carpentry as producing panbone belaying pins for the ship has not been ascertained, and no scrimshaw by his hand has emerged. However, though he sailed as an ordinary green hand in the New Bedford ship *Brighton* in 1844, on the ship *Friendship* of Fairhaven during 1846-49 he was ship's cooper, which in itself is testimony to his knowledge of wood and tools. So he certainly had the basic skills and just as certainly had the time; the only question is whether he also had the inclination. He was born at Tiverton, Rhode Island, in 1826, the son of Caleb and Emily Coggeshall, and was likely apprenticed to a cooper in his youth. After his three whaling voyages he lived in New Bedford, where he worked as a cooper and married a Rhode Island woman named Lydia Wales Gifford, eight years his junior, in 1853. Around 1861 they moved to a farm at Portsmouth, Rhode Island, where they raised a son and a daughter and had three hired hands. He died in 1890 at age 64.

Coggeshall, John E. (fl. circa 1812-34). New Bedford whaling master who, according to Philip Purrington (in "Bird's Eye View," NBWM Library), did some scrimshaw as first mate of the Dartmouth brig *By Chance* (1826-28). By extension he may reasonably be presumed to have continued the practice on subsequent voyages. Small wonder: his extremely fine ship portraiture — vessels sighted and ships spoken, drawn in miniature in his journal of the *By Chance* (in NBWM) — demonstrate the optimal scale, technical precision, and clarity of draftsmanship for pictorial scrimshaw; and as an engraver of pictures on whale ivory, he would have been among the earliest American practitioners. It is extremely unfortunate that none of his scrimshaw has yet come to light; but there are his magnificent ink-on-paper miniatures to testify to his outstanding proficiency as a ship-portraitist. A great deal is known of his seafaring career but little is known of his education, family life, and circumstances ashore. He was born circa 1799, probably in New Bedford, went to sea at age 13 in the brig *Sally* (1812-15), and made a career of whaling for the next 22 years. His early voyages were in the ship *Russell* (1818-20), brig *Dragon* (1820-21), ship *George and Susan* (1821-24), and ship *Ann Alexander* (1824-25), all of New Bedford. He was then first mate (1825-26) and captain (1826-28) of the brig *By Chance*. At this point, upon completion of his first voyage as captain in 1828, he married Sarah W. Allen — then, almost immediately, he went to sea again, as first mate of the Fairhaven ship *Albion* (2 voyages, 1828-29 and 1829-30), captain of a voyage in the bark *Amanda* of New Bedford (1830-31), and captain of three in the ship *Albion* of Fairhaven (1831-34).

Coit, George Martin (fl, circa 1835-57). What the auctioneer describes as an "Inlaid Mahogany Veneer Sailor-Made Trinket Box" is nicely inlaid with abalone and mother-of-pearl hearts, stars, tetraskele, and geometric shapes, and has a hinged lid inlaid with an oval plaque engraved with the name 'W.A. Coit'" (Skinner, Nov. 8, 2009, lot #264). The provenance consists of a typescript label on the bottom: "Waity A. Sanford born Feb. 3, 1821 of Royal and Mary A. Sanford of Warren [R.I.] married Aug. 15, 1842 George M. Coit 2nd"; thus, as the initials evidently refer to Waity A. *Coit,* the box must have been made either after they were married or in anticipation of the marriage, in any case in 1842 at the earliest. Authorship is only provisionally ascribed to the husband, and it should be noted that the workmanship closely resembles that of fellow Warren whaleman Spencer Pratt (q.v.). Coit was born in Newport, Rhode Island, in 1815, the son of David Ambrose Coit and the former Mary Williams. He was captain on two voyages in barks out of Warren: the *Smithfield* (1851-53), which he evidently left before completing the voyage, and the *William Henry* (1855-57).

Cole, Seth, Jr. (fl. 1848-53). He was an accomplished painter in Alton, Wayne County, New York, concerning whom Michael Dyer rightly points out that it would have been strange had a whaleman-artist of his ability and experience not tried his hand at scrimshaw on his one, career-shaping voyage. However, no scrimshaw by his hand has yet surfaced. He was born in 1829 in Great Valley, Cattaraugus County, New York, the youngest son of Seth and Lucretia Salisbury Cole. As a child moved with his family to the hamlet of Alton, which was his home for the rest of his life, and taught himself charcoal drawing: "by the age of seven was drawing exceptional sketches." At age 19 he shipped as a green hand in the New Bedford bark *Statira* (1848-53), and during more than four years at sea "sketched many scenes depicting events and highlights of his voyage." These shipboard works ostensibly include the oil painting "Whaling off the Islands of St. Antao and St. Vincent, Cape Verde" (NBWM), which is said to have been painted on sailcloth, using whale oil, lampblack, white lead paint, and other found materials — a more folksy genesis than may actually have been the case. For a common seaman to be painting in oils on shipboard was highly unusual in any case, but the artist's own annotation on the back is, "Drawn from nature on Jan 1st, 1849 by Seth Cole [foremast] hand on the whaling bark of New Bedford on the afternoon we took two small sperm whales Saint Anthony and Saint Vincent Cape Verdee." The career whaleman and scrimshaw artist Thomas Burdett (q.v.) was the *Statira*'s first mate at the time — another reason to surmise that Cole was introduced to scrimshaw and likely did some of his own. A couple of years after he returned he married Maria Elizabeth Shipman (1855), who bore him two children and died in 1869, then married Katherine Espenschied and fathered three more children. He continued to paint nautical scenes and landscapes, branched out into portraiture, "and made his living as an itinerant artist... He spoke several languages, his hobby was astronomy and he dabbled at inventing." He has been called "an artist of superior talent, a man of exalted intelligence, a poet of gifted thought and expression and the soul of honor." He died at home in 1903. (Additional source: Office of the County Historian, Wayne County, New York: www.co.wayne.ny.us/ Departments/ historian/ MFSethCole.htm.)

Coleman, Zenas M. (fl. circa 1830-70). One of the last of the great whaling masters of Nantucket, he may have scrimshawed his own shaving box or it may have been made for him (private collection; reported by Paul Madden). It is constructed of tropical primary and secondary woods, and has a top attached with handmade copper hinges and inlaid in whale ivory with the initials "ZMC" enclosed in a rectangular frame, with silhouette cut-outs of nautical symbols: two-draw telescope, speaking trumpet, anchor, and octant (quadrant), with whale ivory and wooden trim inlaid around the edges and on the sides. The interior has a mirror mounted in the lid and chambers for razors and shaving gear. Born on Nantucket in 1815, Zenas Morslander Coleman was the son of Robert Coleman and Deborah Morslander. He was raised on the Island and in Nantucket whaleships, in which he eventually commanded eight voyages: three in the *Atlantic* (1850-62), one in the *Rainbow* (1864), and four in the *Eunice Adams* (1865-70). He was married to a fellow-Islander named Phebe, raised a family on Nantucket, and died in 1878.

Collins, Hananiah W. (fl. circa 1855-60). He was a one-voyage whaleman, credited with a small whip, the handle carved in full round out of whale ivory in the form of a hand holding a ring; in NBWM, the gift of Miss Elsie Collins in 1958. The provenance indicates unequivocally that Elsie Collins was the daughter of the maker, Hananiah W. Collins, "brother of Parkman Lund"; however, little has been definitively ascertained about Hananiah's career after his one whaling voyage, or about Elsie Collins; and the enigmatic connection to Parkman Lund has not been established.

Hananiah W. Collins was born in 1838 at Dartmouth, Massachusetts, the son of Captain Edward Willson Collins and Esther D. Tinkham Collins. The Captain, born at Dartmouth, in 1809, followed his older brother Silas into the whale fishery, served two voyages in the New Bedford ship *Condor* (1832-34), married Esther D. Tinkham of Rochester, Massachusetts in 1834, and was master of whaling voyages in the ships *Phocion* of New Bedford (1839-40; Asa Gifford, q.v., was in the crew), *Stephania* of New Bedford (1841-44), and *Midas* of Fairhaven (1844-45); but he died at sea suddenly at age 35 aboard the *Midas* in 1845, bound for the Indian Ocean and Northwest Coast whaling grounds, when Hananiah was only about six years old. There was also a daughter named Sarah Jane — Hananiah's baby sister — who died in June that same year at age 3. At age 16, in November 1855, Hananiah embarked as a green hand for the 180th lay on what turned out to be an unusually long and not very successful whaling voyage of four years and about five months to the Indian Ocean in the New Bedford bark *Cherokee*, Captain Philander Smith (1855-60). Not much else is known about him. He lived in Acushnet, just north of New Bedford; he was associated in some way with Parkman Lund, another, somewhat older Acushnet resident; he was working as a clerk in New Bedford circa 1898-1900; he was married to Helen A. Collins and had at least two daughters: Mary, born circa 1876, who became a nurse; and Elsie, born circa 1883, who worked as a librarian at the New Bedford Free Public Library. Presumably, neither daughter ever married: the two women were living together in Acushnet in 1930, listed in the census under their maiden names, with Elsie, the younger one, named as head of household and Mary specifically designated as "sister." Elsie, who donated the scrimshaw in 1958, may or may not have been — probably was not — the same Elsie Collins who died at Lowell, Massachusetts, in March 1968. The Eugenia Collins who was a teacher at the Rogers School in Fairhaven in 1897 may or may not have been related.

Parkman M. Lund was a local fixture in Acushnet and New Bedford; he was mostly famous for being old. In fact, when he died at age 97 on September 4, 1926, that fact was printed right in the alphabetical listings in the New Bedford City Directory — a very unusual occurrence. But Parkman Lund had been listed in every volume since 1849. His older brother, Jonathan P. Lund, went into business as a tinplate manufacturer at "the Head of the River" in Acushnet Village by 1845. Parkman joined the firm as a tinplate worker around 1849, was promoted to clerk by 1856 (by which time Jonathan's sons, Jonathan Jr. and Edward were also employed there), and by 1865 the company was billed as Lund Brothers. They also owned a lot of shares in a lot of ships. By 1869 Jonathan Sr. was retired and both Edward and Jonathan Jr. had died; thus, Parkman became the sole proprietor, now identifying himself as a "stoves and tinware manufacturer." He seems to have retired soon afterwards, too — there are no business listings for him after 1870 — and moved to New Bedford, where for the next 56 years he lived with his son William, known as Willie. For a while in the late 1880s Willie was a student in Billerica, Massachusetts, but what he studied has not come to light, and for the duration he had no trade and no visible means of support other than living with dad. The Lunds Corner district of Acushnet got its name from their long-standing businesses there. Clearly, Hananiah Collins was not the actual brother of Parkman Lund; however — especially as the names of their wives are not known — perhaps they were brothers-in-law. Though how this relates to the scrimshaw, or why Elsie Collins felt compelled to mention Parkman Lund in the provenance, is anyone's guess.

Congdon, Joseph (fl. circa 1825-46). Nantucket whaling master credited with a watch hutch said to have been made aboard the ship *Alpha* of Nantucket in 1846 or 1848 (the date is probably in error in either case) and "descended through the family along with a simple whale ivory bodkin and tortoise shell flexible bracelet made for a slender female wrist" (reported by Charles Manghis, who restored the piece for a private owner). The hutch is a square of mahogany, pierced at the center with a round, framed aperture to accommodate a pocket watch with the face showing; the corners are ornamented with fluted overlays, fastened with copper tacks; and the whole is flanked by stout Ionian columns of whale ivory, surmounted by a peaked panel of tortoise shell trimmed at the junction with a strip of baleen and at the top with three turned whale ivory finials. The base is mahogany overlaid with a small diamond-shaped panel of whale ivory, fastened with copper tacks; and (Manghis adds) "laid in under the semi translucent tortoise is a printed image of a ship." Congdon is presumed also to have made both the bodkin and the bracelet. He is known to have commanded five whaling voyages, in the Nantucket ships *Alpha* (1838-41), *Pacific* (1832-34 and 1834-37), *James Loper* (1842-46), and *Alpha* again (1850-54). Biographical details are scarce, but some documents and journals from his voyages are in NHA and NBWM.

Cook, Henry (fl. circa 1835-67). Homeward bound in the bark *Napoleon* of New Bedford in August 1867, he wrote in his journal, "not much doing. Work about all done, some scrimschoning." It is not clear from the context whether he meant by "work" that the whaling was over and there was not much left to do as they headed for home; or simply that his own chores for the day were done and he was turning his hand to scrimshaw. In either case, no scrimshaw by Henry Cook has come to light, and almost the only things known about him for certain are connected with the *Napoleon* voyage. According to the NBPS crew list, he was from Tiverton, Rhode Island, born circa 1830, and was 34 at the time they sailed in 1864. He had probably made his maiden voyage in a Rhode Island ship in the 1840s, was probably boatsteerer in some combination of the ship *South America* of New Bedford (1851-55), ship *Richard Mitchell* of Edgartown (1856-57), or bark *Smyrna* of New Bedford (1853-57), and was probably in the *Isaac Howland* (1859-64) immediately prior to the *Napoleon* (1864-67), aboard which John S. Coquin and Warren Gifford (qq.v.) were his shipmates. Thereafter Cook disappears from view. (Not to be confused with Captain Henry Cook, who commanded at least six whaling voyages in Provincetown schooners during 1850-61.)

Cook, Isaac (fl. circa 1840-53). Whaleman from Tiverton, Rhode Island, credited with a baleen busk made for his wife and bearing her initials (in NBWM). It has four lobes at the top, a rounded bottom, and is incised on the front with geometrical, leafy vine, and heart motifs, also a hot-air balloon with two people in the gondola. The back has the initials "LC," presumed to refer to his wife Lydia, whom he married in 1846. (As her maiden name was also Cook, it is not known whether he made the busk for her in her capacity as wife or fiancée. The fanciful and slightly frivolous balloon vignette rather suggests the latter.) He was born in 1821 in Tiverton, Rhode Island, the son of Dr. Dennis Cook (1783-1841), physician, and the doctor's second wife, the former Mary Lake. (The first wife, who died in 1817, was also named Mary and her maiden name was evidently also Cook.) Isaac likely made a whaling voyage as a green hand in an unidentified vessel prior to the three successive voyages he is known to have made out of Westport, Massachusetts, as seaman (1841-42) and boatsteerer (1842-43) in the bark *D. Franklin*, and as boatsteerer in the brig *Catherwood* (1844-45). There was then a six-year hiatus during which he got married, set up as a farmer in Tiverton, fathered a daughter, and moved his family to Little Compton, Rhode Island. His last voyage was as second mate in the bark *Sea Flower* of New Bedford (1851-53), after which he was farming in Little Compton into the 1880s. The attribution of the busk is derived from a reconstructed provenance. It was an heirloom given or bequeathed to NBWM in 1967 by Bertrand L. Shurtleff (1897-1967) of Little Compton, a Brown University graduate who taught high school in East Providence and wrote animal stories for children. He evidently inherited the busk from his mother, Hattie Emma Cook Shurtleff (1859-1943); his father, Eugene Kossuth Shurtleff (1856-1942), originally from Wisconsin, was a house carpenter and farmer in Little Compton. The donor's grandmother — Hattie's mother — was Lydia née Cook, wife of the putative maker and the original recipient of the busk sometime before 1853.

Cooper, J. (fl. circa the 1860s). A tooth featuring a sketchily-engraved patriotic figure of Liberty, with a sailing ship in the background, surmounted by the broadside portrait of a *Monitor*-type ironclad warship (flattop with gun turret), is boldly signed in a fancy cursive hand, "J. Cooper" (in the Frankford, Pennsylvania, Historical Society; reported by Craig Bruns of Independence Seaport). Nothing specific has been discovered about the maker, who was undoubtedly one of the many young men named John, James, and Joseph Cooper from Frankford, in Philadelphia County, who served in the Union Army and Navy. The one who made the scrimshaw is presumed to have acquired that particular skill on at least one whaling voyage prior to or during the Civil War. Naval lore and iconography were popular among American mariners, including whalemen and former whalemen, whether or not they actually served in the Navy. Transcriptions of wartime songs and such ballads as "The *Monitor* and the *Merrimac,*" "The *Cumberland,*" and "The *Florida*'s Cruise" ("The *Florida*'s Crew") are occasionally found in whalemen's shipboard journals; naval subjects in whalemen's drawings and scrimshaw are fairly common; but a portrait of a *Monitor*-class ironclad on scrimshaw is very unusual and perhaps unique.

Cooper, Mercator (fl. circa 1818-55). Renowned Southampton, Long Island whaling master who is associated with important early American forays to Japan and Antarctica. The attribution of his double-cage, table-mount swift is based on a detailed provenance from the donor, Judge Mercator Cooper Kendrick, a direct descendant, according to whom the swift was made by Captain Cooper himself (NBWM accession file). It has a panbone shaft and ribs, a whale ivory clamp, whale ivory bushings and gaskets with multiple turnings, and a plain whale ivory finial, with the ribs tied with white yarn. He also made other scrimshaw. According to Judge Kendrick's daughter, Deborah Cooper Kendrick of Southampton (interviewed by Bill Bleyer in *Long Island Newsday* in 2002), most of the important mementos of Mercator Cooper's encounter in Japan went to NBWM, but "We still have some scrimshaw and the shell collection."

Captain Cooper is best remembered for having made the most extended and (from the Japanese point of view) certainly the most intrusive visit to Japan by any American-flag vessel prior to the opening of diplomatic and trade relations between Japan and the USA scarcely a decade later. Until the 1850s, when an American naval expedition under Matthew C. Perry coerced the Japanese into agreeing to establish trade with the West, the ruling Tokugawa Shogunate prohibited contacts with foreigners, including those whose motives may have been a magnanimous repatriation of castaways. Other British and American vessels had rescued shipwrecked Japanese fisherman and tried to bring them home to Japan, with mixed results, but despite the whalemen's perpetual curiosity about Japan itself, most of the rescuers were reluctant to try to land castaways in Japan as it meant going out of their way, losing time on the whaling grounds, and risking a confrontation with hostile local officials who were unequipped — and had no authority — to deal with foreigners and unwelcome returnees. For the castaways themselves, there was the fear of punishment for violating the embargo on consorting with foreigners, no matter how unwittingly. Putting such castaways ashore in Hawaii or some other Pacific landfall outside Japan was the usual solution. By the time Cooper landed his castaway fishermen in Japan in 1845, the castaway fisherman Manjiro (q.v.), known in modern-day Japan as "the man who discovered America," had already been rescued (in 1841) and brought back to Fairhaven, Massachusetts, by Captain William Whitfield in the whaler *John Howland* of New Bedford. Cooper's landfall, when he boldly sailed uninvited into a Japanese bay and tenaciously sought to set the refugees ashore, immediately became a local *cause celebre* that ultimately resulted in an amicable exchange. On consecutive days in March 1845, while whaling off the coast of Japan in the ship *Manhattan* of Sag Harbor, they took aboard the crews of two disabled coastal trading vessels, the *Koho-Maru* and *Senju-maru*. Cooper dispatched two of the castaways to report the rescue to Japanese authorities and forewarn them that the *Manhattan* would soon be bringing them back to Honshu. A spell of bad weather delayed them for a few days, but when he attempted a to land on April 16 the *Manhattan* was met by 170 armed Japanese boats, who towed the ship into the harbor of Tateyama at the mouth of Edo Bay (Tokyo Bay), then to Uraga, inside the bay, where they dropped anchor and continued to be surrounded by an armada of Japanese boats in full-dress decoration. As the calcified 17th-century edict that closed Japan to foreigners was still in effect, no one was permitted to land, not even the castaways, whose inadvertent association with the Americans technically made them outlaws no longer welcome in their homeland. However, on April 20, after much discussion, the authorities finally agreed to receive the castaways, and a legation of officials came aboard to escort them ashore. Gifts were exchanged, watercolors and scrolls commemorating the event were produced by Japanese chroniclers (several of these gifts, watercolors, and scrolls are still preserved in NBWM), and the *Manhattan* prepared to sail. When Captain Cooper asked what he should do with any Japanese castaways he might encounter in the future, the authorities instructed him, "Carry them to some Dutch port, but never return to Japan" (Frank & Sakurai, 2004: "Pacific Encounters: Yankee Whalers, Manjiro, and the Opening of Japan," exhibition text, NBWM). Perhaps the most remarkable object Cooper received in Japan — presumably from the local authorities at Uraga — is a large and sophisticated map of Japan by one Sekisui Nagakubo, which Judge Kendrick donated to NBWM along with the swift.

Mercator Cooper (1803-1872) was the second of five children and the eldest of three sons of Nathan and Olive (née Howell) Cooper. He has three claims to enduring fame: first, the rescue of the Japanese castaways in the *Manhattan* and the ensuing encounter at Tateyama and Uraga in 1845; second, that as captain of a whaling and sealing voyage in the Sag Harbor ship *Levant* a few years later he made the first-ever landfall on the Antarctic continent, at Victoria Land on January 26, 1853; and third, that one of his granddaughters, Clara Rowley Howell, married Robert Kendrick, a great-grandson of Captain John Kendrick (1781-1849), the first American ever to make a landfall in Japan: this was in the brig *Lady Washington* at Kushimoto, on Oshima Island in Wakayama Prefecture, for eleven days in April 1791. (Kendrick and the *Lady Washington* had previously been fur trading on the Northwest Coast in company with Captain Robert Gray [1755-1806] in the *Columbia Rediviva*, just after Gray's circumnavigation and just prior to his discovery of the mouth of the Columbia River in 1792. Like Mercator Cooper a generation later, as soon as Kendrick arrived in Japan he was invited to leave and never return.) Thus, Judge Mercator Cooper Kendrick, the donor of the swift made by his ancestor, was a descendant of both Mercator Cooper and Robert Kendrick, the two mariners responsible for the most significant American contacts with Japan prior to the 1850s, when a treaty between the USA and Japan established diplomatic and trade relations. In all, Mercator Cooper commanded nine whaling and sealing voyages in Sag Harbor ships: four in the *Phenix* (1832-38), two in the *American* (1840-43), and one each in the *Manhattan* (1843-46), *Franklin* (1847-50), and *Levant* (1851-55) — the latter voyage, his last, being the one on which they touched at Antarctica. He was twice married, first to Maria Jane Green (1806-1860), who bore him a son and a daughter, then to Sophia Jessup Foster (1813-1894), from which union there was no issue. After he retired from seafaring he lived on a farm in Southampton.

* **Coquin, John S., Jr.** (fl. circa 1864-79). The *Dictionary* cites the journals that this dedicated scrimshaw artist kept aboard the New Bedford barks *Napoleon* (1864-67) and *Globe* (1869-72), which "reveal many important details about scrimshaw practices on shipboard":

> *In one passage in the* ***Globe*** *journal quoted by Barbeau (5f) and excerpted by Gilkerson (frontis), Coquin indicates that he was "scrimshawing" off the Coast of Africa, making coconut dippers, jagging irons [?], jagging knives and jagging wheels, riding whips, rulers, canes, a violin bridge, skipjacks, and a bird cage. He also reports that "the capt[ain] made me three dippers" (see Alexander Augustus Tripp); and that Coquin "sold a cane [evidently of his own making] to the mate of an English brig" at St. Helena on 14 November 1871. In addition to the inventory of the varieties of scrimshaw, part of the significance of the journal is in its providing evidence of the exchange and sale of sailor-made scrimshaw objects among the mariners themselves.*

The *Napoleon* was Coquin's maiden voyage (1864-67), on which he embarked at age 16 and on which Henry Cook (q.v.) was one of his shipmates. Others of Coquin's journals (also in NBWM), kept aboard the barks *Globe* (1869-72), commanded by Alexander A. Tripp (q.v.), and *Merlin* (1872-76), commanded by Albert A. Thomas (q.v.), impart substance and additional specificity to his inventory of scrimshawing activities and products. He mentions "making cutters for scrimshawing" — that is, the actual tools to produce some of the other items he lists; that he "took my cocoanuts out of the hold" (he may be the only one ever to mention that he, at least, kept them there, presumably with permission to do so); and that he "cleaned the whale's teeth" and was "cleaning cocoa-nut shells" in preparation for scrimshaw. He frequently refers generically to "scrimshawing," and once to "picking oakum, & scrimshawing," but he is sometimes quite explicit: "making cocoanut dippers," "making dippers," "making dippers & jagging irons," "making picture frames," and — in a grand sweep in which he appears to be referring to an entire watch or even the entire crew of the *Globe* — "making picture frames, Jagging knives, & canes at sundown." Captain Tripp is described as having made a coconut-shell dipper and "three dolphins." He also reports of Albert Thomas, in addition to the dippers and cane already mentioned, "Capt[ain] makeing [sic] canes & riding whips" and "Captain making a bird-cage." Canes were common scrimshaw products, but whalemen's allusions to riding crops and birdcages (which he mentions more than once) are quite rare. Unfortunately, none of Coquin's scrimshaw has been identified since publication of the *Dictionary* and *More Scrimshaw Artists*. A native of Dartmouth or New Bedford born in 1848, his voyages were in the New Bedford barks *Napoleon* (1864-67), *Pacific* (1867-68; illustrated journal in KNB), *Globe* (1869-72 and 1872-76), *Merlin* (third mate, 1872-76), and *Europa* (second mate, 1876-79).

Corey [Cory], Andrew A. (fl. circa 1888-1920). Career schooner captain out of New Bedford. He is credited with two inlaid cribbage board boxes, one of which is signed with his surname spelled *Corey*, contrary to the way the name is spelled by most of the rest of the large *Cory* clan of Westport, Massachusetts, and contrary to the way his own name usually appears in the whaling records; on the other hand, the same box has a label on the bottom with the *Cory* spelling. One of the boxes is rectangular, in mahogany, with a sliding lid trimmed with darker wood corners and bands of bone, the top inlaid with domino-style rectangles pierced as a cribbage game board, and additionally inlaid with two whale ivory horseshoes and five whale ivory playing cards, four of which are facsimiles of the 5's of each card suit, with the king of clubs in the middle. This box has internal storage compartments for pegs (markers) and playing cards, and was given to NBWM by Captain Andrew A. Corey himself in 1936. The other (in KNB) was acquired from Mrs. Robert MacKenzie in 1972 as part of a large, unrelated lot, but is similar, is clearly by the same hand, and is inscribed on the top, in what appears to be a display signature, "Captain Corey / N[ew] B[edford]." It has sycamore sides, a white pine bottom, and is inlaid on the top and all four sides with whale ivory, baleen, and various woods in geometric patterns. Like the other box, the cribbage board here is a series of rectangular whale ivory inlays resembling dominoes; it also has four whale ivory pegs (game pieces; markers), and a paper sticker on the bottom, marked in holograph "A.A. CORY."

Captain Corey or Cory was born in Westport in 1861, the son of career mariner and sometime whaleman Joseph Corey (1831-1891) and the former Clarissa M. Royce (1833-). His older sister, Mary C. Corey (born circa 1860), became a schoolteacher. Andrew went to sea early and by 1888 owned a quarter interest in the schooner *Hastings*, which became his first command in either 1888 or 1890. He ran schooners out of New Bedford from then on — notably coastwise passages in the *Hastings* (1890-96) and both coastwise and international voyages in the *Frederick Roesser* (1902-08) and *Richard W. Clark* (1909-16). A major shareholder in all three of these vessels, he also acquired ownership shares in the schooners *Abel C. Buckley, Longfellow, Margarett, Edward R. Smith, Pedro Varela,* and *Valkyria* of New Bedford, *T. Towner* of New Bedford and Providence, Rhode Island, and *John G. Pettis* of Westport — shares held in partnership with some of the leading merchants of the region. Around 1887, at just about the time he graduated from mariner to sea captain and merchant entrepreneur, he married a woman named Susan (b. 1870), and they had one child, Robert Anthony Corey (b. 1888), who became a machinist and married a registered nurse. Andrew left off seafaring in 1916 but continued to manage his shares in comfortable retirement. He gave the cribbage board to NBWM in 1936 and died in 1938.

Cornell, Frederick P. (fl. circa 1835-60). Whaling master of Dartmouth, Massachusetts, and Warren, Rhode Island, credited with scrimshawing a hinged mahogany box (in NBWM). It has geometrical and architectonic devices inlaid in whale skeletal bone, tortoise shell, and wood, faux handles inlaid in whale ivory, a tortoise shell escutcheon, and the name "JANE CORNELL" rendered as pierced work with engraved leafy ornaments on bone, inlaid on the top and surmounted by a silhouette of a perched bird; likewise the pierced-work initials "F.P.C." (Frederick P. Cornell) inlaid on the front, forming the gate to a fence motif inlaid in wood and bone. The wooden interior is divided into four compartments, with the bottoms of each lined with black velvet, one with a hinged lid inlaid with wood and bone, engraved with the silhouettes of two birds and an urn, the other three with removable wooden lids. The subdivided central compartment contains a removable needle-case folder of tortoise shell and bone with handkerchief-like cloth inserts, embroidered with a leafy pattern encircling the initials "J.C."

Frederick Cornell was born circa 1819 at Dartmouth, Massachusetts. Though he obtained a Protection Paper in New Bedford at age 16 in 1835, his first two or three voyages (on which he rose from green hand to boatsteerer during 1835-40) have not been identified. His next three voyages were out of New Bedford, as fourth mate of the bark *Minerva* (1840-41), third mate of the bark *Canton* (1841-45), and second mate of the ship *George Washington* (1845-48). He was next probably first mate (1848-53) and then afterwards captain of the bark *Smithfield* of Warren (1853-55), then captain of the brig *Annawan* of Mattapoisett (1855-57) and bark *Charles and Edward* of Dartmouth (1858-60). In 1848 just after returning from his voyage as second mate, he married Sarah Jane Allen (born circa 1830) of Dartmouth, but was widowed in 1852, evidently without issue. He married again in 1853 or 1855, and it was this second wife, Jane Ray (born circa 1835), now Jane Cornell, whose name and initials appear on the box. She was the daughter of Diana and William Ray, the latter a native of Ireland, who were farmers in Warren. The couple settled on the Ray family farm, where their only son William was born circa 1856. In 1860 Captain Cornell retired from whaling and settled down to farming in Warren, where William, who became a painter, and later William's wife, Lavinia née Arnold, lived with Frederick and Jane for many years.

Corning, H. — see Cornings, H.

Cornings, H. (fl. circa 1850s). Scrimshaw artist specializing in naval subjects. His signature appears on a pair of teeth, one engraved with the scene of an abolitionist meeting, the other with War of 1812 naval engagements involving the frigates *Essex, Enterprise,* and *Boxer*; signed "H. Cornings, U.S."; in PEM (reported by Daniel R. Finamore). The USS *Essex*, rated 32 guns, Commodore William

Porter, harassed enemy shipping and especially the British whaling fleet in the South Atlantic and the South and Central Pacific during 1812-14. The USS *Enterprise*, 14 guns, Lieutenant William Burrows, defeated RMS *Boxer*, 14 guns, Samuel Blyth, on September 5, 1813. Nothing has been discovered about the artist, but the scrimshaw was certainly based on printed illustrations and rendered long after the actual events.

Cornings is a rare surname, almost nonexistent in nineteenth-century America, especially in New England. The surname Corning is not uncommon, but with the initial H it is also rare in the whale fishery. In the 1860s and '70s a Harvey H. Corning, born circa 1818, was a bookbinder in Poquonnock, Connecticut, a small community in the town of Groton, nestled among the whaling ports of New London, Mystic, and Stonington. At the same time there was also a Henry H. Corning, born circa 1830, who was a bookbinder in nearby Preston. As a skilled manual trade, bookbinding bespeaks a certain greater-than-average degree of manual dexterity compatible with the decorative arts, and thus with scrimshaw; while the proximity of three important whaling ports in that part of Connecticut attracted many young fellows to the whale fishery in ways analogous to the employment stream in any single-industry "company town," whether the industry be mining, manufacturing, logging, or tourism. If either of these Cornings was the artist in this case, he would not have been the only scrimshaw maker to become a bookbinder in later life. For example, Silas Davenport, Jr. (q.v. in the *Dictionary*) apprenticed as a shoemaker in his youth, made several whaling voyages on which he produced at least one splendid swift, served in the Union Army during the Civil War, and spent the remainder of his life as a bookbinder in Sharon, Massachusetts.

Corvello, Antonio C. [Corvelho; Corvelo; "Capitão Corvelho"] (1879-1920). American whaleman and whaling master originally from Fajãzinha, on the island of Flores in the Azores. Like many of the Azorean scrimshaw-makers of his era, his output consisted primarily of sets of checkers and dominoes carved and turned from whale ivory and bone. The justification for the claim that he was also "a highly experienced shipbuilder" is not clear, but he was reputedly "a skilled carpenter" and sculptor of whale teeth (Gomes Vieira 2003, 74). According to Gomes Vieira, at age 15 "Corvelho" shipped in the brig *Frances A. Barstow*, commanded by Azorean-born Captain Joseph T. Edwards (q.v.), who was also a native of Fajãzinha. This would have been the 1894-97 voyage, when the *Barstow* was sailing out of San Francisco; Antonio would certainly have joined her during an Azores landfall. His official date of entry into the USA was his arrival in the *Barstow* in 1897. He sailed with Edwards again on two voyages of the New Bedford bark *Greyhound* (1898-1902 and 1903-07), likely rising from boatsteerer to second mate, meantime becoming a naturalized U.S. citizen in 1905. He afterwards served as first mate of the New Bedford schooner *Pedro Varela* under Azorean-born Captain Henry Mandly, whom he relieved as captain on that voyage (1907-09) and succeeded as captain on the next (1910-12). He then had the *Greyhound* for three voyages (1913-19). He was married at Fajãzinha in 1915 or 1916 but did not bring his wife Maria and infant daughter back to Massachusetts until 1917. His many Azorean admirers customarily give his name as António C. Corvelho, in the orthodox Portuguese fashion, but the man himself did not. His American draft registry, processed at New Bedford in 1918, identifies him as Antonio Castano Corvello, his wife as Mary J. Corvello, his residence as New Bedford, his occupation as "Master Mariner – Goen [sic] Whaling," and his employer as John A. Cook (a former whaling captain and prominent managing agent based in Provincetown at the time). His signature there, as elsewhere, is *Antonio C. Corvello*. His name is also listed the same way, along with those of his wife "Mary G." and two-year-old daughter Floripas, on a passenger manifest of the S.S. *Cretic* on their passage from São Miguel, Azores, to Boston in June 1917. His citizenship is given there as U.S.A., his residence as Fajãzinha, and his occupation as farmer, a pursuit he seems to have followed in the Azores between whaling voyages. After 1918 the family resided in New Bedford. The U.S. Census for New Bedford, taken in January 1920, lists him as Antone Corvello, occupation "Captain – Whaler," married with the one daughter. He would live only a few more months. His premature death in September 1920 is said to have resulted from the great influenza epidemic of 1918-19.

Cory, Edward Gray (fl. circa 1830-54). New Bedford whaling master from Tiverton, Rhode Island. He may have made his scrimshaw letter seal or it may have been made for him: a lathe-turned, one-inch disc of sperm whale ivory nicely incised "E.G. CORY," surmounted by an anchor device, mounted on a simple four-inch wooden handle (in NBWM). The son of Andrew Cory and Jane Gray Seabury, he was born in Tiverton in 1816, is believed to have made at least some his early voyages in Rhode Island whalers, was master of three voyages in the New Bedford ships *Phocion* (1841-43), *Champion* (relief captain, 1844-47), and *South Carolina* (1848-51), and finished out his career as first mate under Captain Joshua Weeks, Jr., in the New Bedford ship *Europa* (1851-54). In December 1842, during his voyage in the *Phocion*, he was married in Australia to Mary Ann Banford, a native of Sheffield, England. She accompanied him home in the *Phocion* and over the next twelve years bore him two sons and four daughters. After his retirement they continued to live in Tiverton, where one of his sons was a fisherman and where the 1880 U.S. Census lists his occupation as "works in fish works" and that of his 32-year-old unmarried son as "Jack at all trades." Captain Cory died there in 1885.

Crapo, Reuben W. (fl. circa 1844-81). New Bedford whaling master. The testimony of his wife, Lucy Ann Hix Crapo, in a journal aboard the New Bedford bark *Louisa* during 1865-67 (in NBWM), indicates that the captain was quite a dedicated craftsman. (She refers to him as W and evidently called him by his middle name, William.) He was frequently engaged in carpentry and building projects of one kind or another on board: re-casing the mast and rudderhead with his own hands, building a scuttle, a dovecote (or pigeon house), an onion pen, a new cutting stage, and a bedstead and crib for a new baby, born at sea in 1867; he also mended stove boats, repaired jewelry, fixed the ship's clock, and performed other small miracles with which whaling masters did not usually occupy themselves. She also reports him having "caught a porpoise [and] saved the oil and the jaw," which may have been for some scrimshaw-like undertaking, and brought her the tooth of a shark struck by the crew. Meanwhile, Lucy was busy with handiwork of her own — mostly needlework, making a few dresses, a pincushion, a quilt, and clothing for the baby. Unfortunately, she mentions scrimshawing but is not specific about what the captain may have made. So far, none has been identified.

Reuben William Crapo was born in Dartmouth, Massachusetts, in 1829, the son of Reuben Crapo, a farmer, and the former Cynthia M. Devoll. His rise in the whaling trade was unusually rapid: green hand at age 15 in the bark *Theophilus Chase* of Westport (1844-45), shipkeeper in the New Bedford bark *Rhine* (1846-48), then third mate (1848-50) and first mate (1850-53) in the New Bedford bark *Cornelia*. At this point, in 1853, between voyages, he married Lucy Ann Hix (1833-1910), with whom he settled in Westport, then went as master of the *Cornelia* (1853-57) and the barks *Montgomery* (1858-62) and *Ospray* (1863-64). He brought his pregnant wife along with him on his next voyage, as captain of the bark *Louisa* (1865-68) — the voyage on which Lucy kept her journal; but this one was fraught with sadness. The couple had little luck with children. During the voyage, in November 1865, a son, Wilmer, was born at Fayal, in the Azores, but lived only a few days. A daughter, Louisa, was born at sea on the same voyage in April 1867, in latitude 6° 44' South and longitude 33° 14' West: she was named after the ship and survived the voyage but lived only until 1876. Meanwhile, a second daughter, Annie, was born back home in July 1869 but died the following year, when Reuben was at sea again as captain of the brig *Starlight* (1870-73). His daughter Louisa died while he was at sea on his next voyage in the *Ospray* (1874-76). Now childless, he commanded two more voyages, the barks *Linda Stevens* (1877-81) and *Gay Head 2d* (1881-82), then retired to Westport. He died in 1907.

Crosby, Shipley Wilson (fl. circa 1828-66). Whaling master from Martha's Vineyard to whom DCHS attributes a pair of tusks with portraits of Martha Washington and Mary Todd Lincoln. A crew list posted online by NBFPL lists him as captain of the New Bedford ship *Euphrates* in 1844; however, Starbuck lists no such voyage, and according to Lund, Crosby commanded four whaling voyages: in the *Euphrates* (1849-51) and the ships *Cornelius Howland* of New Bedford (1851-54) and the *Almira* (1855-58) and *Europa* (1862-66) of Edgartown. He was born on the Vineyard in 1822, was a lifelong resident of Edgartown, married Elizabeth G. "Lizzie" Coffin of Edgartown in 1849, and retired from whaling in 1866. He died in 1872; Lizzie died in Rhode Island at age 70 in 1895. There is an anonymous portrait of him in DCHS.

Crucifixion Artisan (fl. mid 19th century). Religious themes are comparatively scarce on whalemen's scrimshaw and most of the documented examples are by Azorean and Azorean-American Roman Catholic hands. However, three, possibly four examples (in private collections) have been reported of what appears to be the consistently pious work of a single hand, evidently not Portuguese, monochrome engraved on sperm whale teeth. The characteristic features are a very slender Christ in skimpy loincloth and disc-shaped halo, crucified on a very thick wooden cross, flanked above by anthropomorphic sun, moon, and star or stars, and alongside with two lit candles in candlesticks and two somewhat incongruous standing female figures in nineteenth-century gowns, one holding a book and both evidently engaged in oratory. These are flanked in turn by leafy trees, and in two cases surmounted by an architectural form and a basket of flowers. On verso in at least one and possibly two or more cases is a panoramic whaling scene, with three ships, three or more whaleboats, and a pod of sperm whales, with birds in flight in the distance. On the two examples examined photographically, the layout is suitably charming but the quality of the draftsmanship and engraving is only slightly better than average; and both are heavily patinated, with the jet-black pigment showing up sepia-toned through what appears to be an amber-gray surface translucence. (Reported from several sources, including reports and photographs by Bradford Bickley.

Curtis, C. (fl. circa 1912). He is credited with a five-inch (13 cm) tooth bearing a broadside view of a bark under sail, labeled on the bow "EVA" and festooned with nautical symbols — a crossed-anchors-and-heart device, telescope, compass rose, taffrail log, sextant, ship's wheel, etc. — all engraved in a broad, open, unshaded style and boldly inscribed "Capt. C. Curtis / 1912," with a shield device bearing the initials M.J.V. and F.H.C. (reported and attributed by Paul Madden). There is no record of a Captain C. Curtis in the whaling trade, there was no American whaling vessel named *Eva* — ship, bark or otherwise — nor any whaler of any nationality named *Eva* in that era; and no C. Curtis has been discovered in the whaling industry in any capacity more recently than a green hand of that name who completed a voyage on the *Bartholomew Gosnold* of New Bedford in 1870. From the inclusion of the title "Captain," the inscription seems more likely to refer to the intended recipient than to the artist, with M.J.V. or F.H.C. perhaps referring to the maker. A clue to his identity may be that a Captain C. Curtis was newly involved in logging in the Solomon Islands in 1927, under the auspices of an Australian firm based in Melbourne (Bennett 1996, 10).

Da Rosa, Clarence Moniz (1911-1966). Coastal whaleman and whaling-launch engineer at a shore-station on the island of Pico in the Azores. "According to his daughter, Professor Maria do Carmo Moniz da Rosa, among the works he made were chess, domino, and checker sets, liqueur services with six cups, a carafe and tray in jawbone, and permanent ink pens"; he also executed official commissions in ivory for the municipality and the Azores region. The son of Francisco Vieira da Rosa and Maria Moniz da Silva, he was employed at a naval dockyard in Lajes [Lages] do Pico and had only limited time for scrimshaw: "He only worked in the evenings, because he had properties to manage, and was the foremost mechanic in Lages do Pico, and like other craftsmen made nothing for his family" (Gomes Vieira, 2003, 99).

* **Daggett, Henry** (fl. circa 1828-52). Several additional swift attributions have recently been reported (by Charles Manghis, Sam and Rider McDowell, Dr. Rick Schafer, James Vaccarino, and Judge Paul Vardeman), amounting to a total of at least five — far more than were normally produced by a single hand or for a single family. Two outstanding masterpieces are the specimens owned by Paul DeCoste and Sam McDowell: the one in the McDowell Collection is not only magnificently executed but also has the initials of the maker's wife, and came its own wooden storage box nicely inlaid with whale ivory, accompanied by a panbone busk engraved with a spread eagle and floral arrangement, and inscribed "THO' LOST TO SIGHT[,] TO MEMORY DEAR" and with the wife's initials "M.A.D." — unique among Henry Daggett's known work.

The article on George A. Grant in *More Scrimshaw Artists* quotes a description of his making a scrimshaw birdcage, from which it is clear that birdcages can be so elaborate and complex that building even one was ordinarily a matter of months or even years. There is no equivalent narrative that chronicles the making of a swift on shipboard, but a swift is typically even more elaborate and complex than a birdcage, so that making a good one would require commensurately more time and, presumably, commensurately more skill. In light of all this, Daggett's output is remarkable, notwithstanding that he had a long career at sea and even if he was able to recruit some help in cutting, shaping, and polishing the myriad components that each swift requires. Some informants have speculated that Daggett's attributed output of five or more was so great that some of the swifts credited to him may not actually be by his hand. Closely observed, the moving, rotating, and expanding parts, the dozens of ribs and struts that consistently match and fit together precisely on each swift, and the innumerable joints that remain flexible and supple even after a century and a half, make him not only probably the most prolific of all scrimshaw swift-makers (even if not all the attributions are his), but also one of the most ingenious.

Henry Daggett was born at Fairhaven, Massachusetts, in 1811, the third surviving son of Captain William Daggett (1773-1858) and Jane Daggett of Tisbury, Martha's Vineyard. His two older brothers, William and Isaac, both became whaling masters, commanding ships from Edgartown and Fairhaven (Isaac had a particularly long and distinguished career). Henry went whaling in his youth, in the New Bedford ships *Lancaster* (1828-31) and *Nautilus* (1831-34). Between voyages, in 1834, he married Mary Ann Taber (1815-1886) (or Mary Ann Taber French: the records disagree about her surname), and Henry eventually followed in his brothers' wake as a whaling master: as first mate and relief captain of the bark *Elizabeth* of Mattapoisett (1844-46), first mate (1846-48) and relief captain (1848-50) of the ship *William Wirt* of Fairhaven, then finally as master of the bark *Malta* of Holmes' Hole, Martha's Vineyard (1850-52), Daggett's adoptive home town. But that voyage ruined him. He sent home 263 barrels of sperm oil from the *Malta*, but the ship returned "clean" — that is, with no oil at all on board — which ended Daggett's career as a whaling captain. He made one final voyage as first mate of the New Bedford bark *Elizabeth* (1852-54), then retired from the fishery. However, he did not retire from the sea, was still listed in the census records as a master mariner (presumably in the merchant service), and was evidently still working as a merchant captain in the 1870s. He died in 1873. His three sons, Henry (1843-1913), Josiah (1844-1909), and Abram (or Abraham; born 1847), and his son-in-law William M. Smith (born 1833), were all whalemen and career mariners.

Davoll, Edward S. (fl. circa 1841-62). New Bedford whaling master who commanded nine conventional voyages and played a small, perhaps inadvertent, but controversial role in the illicit Antebellum slave trade. It is not clear whether he was the maker or the recipient of a panbone busk polychrome engraved with hearts, trees, plants, a star, and geometric shapes, with a strand of laurel forming the border. The family provenance is documented in an accompanying notebook containing (in ink holograph) the names and the birth and marriage dates of members of the Brownell clan, inscribed (in pencil) "Captain Edward S. Davoll… born Sept. 21st 1822," with further particulars about his wife, Elizabeth Brownell Davoll, and daughter Carrie (reported by David R. Hillier).

Born in Dartmouth, Massachusetts, Davoll's first recorded whaling voyage was as ordinary seaman in the brig *Elizabeth* of Westport, Massachusetts (1841-42). After three more voyages, one in the brig *Leonidas* of Fall River (1842-43), one as boatsteerer in the New Bedford bark *Cornelia* (1843-46), and one presumably as first mate of that vessel (1846-48), he was appointed captain of the *Cornelia*, on which he was captain on two voyages (1848-50 and 1850-53). His next command was the ship *Iris* of New Bedford (sailed in 1854), which he lost in a shipwreck off Port Gregory on the Indian Ocean coast of Western Australia in June 1855. Then followed two voyages as master of the bark *R.L. Barstow* of Mattapoisett, Massachusetts (1856-58, 1859-61), the second of which produced a disappointing 297 barrels of sperm oil, scarcely 12 percent of a respectable catch. It was then that he became involved with the ship *Brutus* on a fake whaling voyage. The *Brutus* was actually a slaver.

> *To evade the authorities intent on putting a stop to the slave trade, there were only two strategies: speed, to outrun Navy patrols; or a disguise, to escape their notice. Whalers were typically*

> *ungainly and slow — not an optimal type of vessel to outrun a British gunboat or an American revenue cutter. On the other hand, in standpoint of their medium size and large cargo capacity, whalers were well suited to cramming dozens or hundreds of people belowdecks, under the same kinds of inhuman conditions for which the odious Triangle Trade "blackbirding" slavers were notorious.... One whaleship looks much like another, and there were so many of them on the high seas in the 1840s and '50s that masquerading as a whaler could be an effective disguise... Moreover, the on-deck tryworks (whale oil cookery) provided a convenient bonus for preparing the soup, rice, and gruel that were the staples of slave "cargoes."* (Stuart M. Frank, "False Whalers: Slavers and Fenian Patriots in Disguise," *Seaport*, 39:1, Winter/ Spring 2004, 18-23. See also Kevin S. Reilly, "Slavers in Disguise: American Whaling and the African Slave Trade, 1845-1862," *The American Neptune*, 53:3, Summer 1993, 177-189.)

There were only a handful of such renegade whaleships, several of them outfitted and managed by an arch criminal named Appleton Oaksmith. He recruited disgraced whaling captains as a cover for fitting-out his illegal voyages; one of them, William Jackson, who was already under suspicion by the authorities, signed articles as first mate of the *Brutus* — a former Rhode Island whaleship — which sailed from New Bedford in 1860 "under cover of [the] respected whaling master, Edward S. Davoll." But possibly according to the original plan, or possibly because Captain Davoll found out what the voyage was really headed to do, Davoll "left the ship in the Azores only a few weeks out," whereupon "Jackson assumed command and sailed for Africa."

> *.There he ran into trouble. The Brutus was boarded near the mouth of the Congo River by the USS Mohican, who suspected the Brutus of slaving. However, Jackson avoided seizure by claiming they were cruising the humpback grounds to train green hands. He managed to land about 700 slaves in Cuba in 1861. The nominal managing agent of the voyage, Pierre Pearce, faced criminal charges in New York and Massachusetts over the incident, but he went into hiding and was never prosecuted. Neither was Jackson, who probably made several more crossings in the Brutus before burning the ship in 1864.* (Frank, ibid.)

Davoll may not have been so fortunate and may have been the scapegoat. According to some authorities (as reported by David R. Hillier), Davoll "managed to get the ship out of New Bedford just ahead of Federal marshals" and was later "indicted for taking the *Brutus* to sea for the purpose of engaging in the slave trade, however before he could be brought to trial Davoll died of typhoid." But whatever his subsequent fate, Davoll made a final whaling voyage as captain of the New Bedford schooner *Palmyra* (1861-62). He then disappears from view.

An incidental sidelight is that among the relics of his career as a legitimate whaling master is his manuscript version of a kind of orientation speech outlining his shipboard rules and regulations aboard the *Cornelia*, presumably to be delivered to the crew at the commencement of the voyage. Some of the rules are quite harsh (see Appendix II), and one of them addresses scrimshaw directly: "No scrimshawing of any kind until I give orders to allow it." Many captains prohibited scrimshaw-making until late in the voyage. It is said that the custom on many vessels was that it could commence only after they had taken their first 1,000 barrels of oil; on some vessels it seems to have been reserved for the homeward passage only. Davoll must have allowed it eventually or engaged in it himself, as the busk that descended in his family is associated with the *Cornelia* and was presumably either a gift from someone in his crew or something made by his own hand.

Deblois, John Scott (fl. circa 1833-63). Whaling master from Newport, Rhode Island, who was captain of the New Bedford ship *Ann Alexander* when the vessel was stove and sunk by an angry sperm whale in August 1851. A variety of scrimshaw in NHS is attributed to his ownership without any claim that he made any of it himself (nor any evidence that he did not): as a captain he would have had many opportunities to acquire scrimshaw made by others as well as to make scrimshaw of his own. By far the most interesting of the NHS pieces is a plain tooth with a provenance claiming that it is from the whale that sank the *Ann Alexander*. In this instance, of course, it was the *whale* that dispatched the *ship*, and not the other way round; and the whale got away, presumably with all of its teeth intact. Meanwhile, the ship disappeared beneath the waves forever, the captain and crew escaped in the boats (they were later rescued by the whaler *Nantucket*), and there was nary a whale tooth trophy to be had. However, the Deblois provenance is vindicated by subsequent events. According to historian Leonard Bolles Ellis,

> *Five months later this pugnacious whale was taken by the Rebecca Sims, of New Bedford. Two of the Ann Alexander's harpoons were found in him, and his head had sustained serious injury, pieces of the ship's timbers being imbedded in it. Disease had robbed the whale of his propensity to resist attack… He yielded to his captors from seventy to eighty barrels of oil.* (*History of New Bedford*, 1892, 445)

So the tooth was likely recovered by the *Rebecca Sims* and could have been presented to Captain Deblois at some later time, in addition to which he could have done some of the other scrimshaw that came into NHS from his descendants and heirs.

The *Ann Alexander* was actually Deblois's first command, and her extraordinary fate does not seem to have hampered the captain's career. He was afterwards appointed to command three voyages in New Bedford barks — one in the *Vigilant* (1852-55) and two in the *Merlin* (1856-59 and 1860-63). He was born in Newport in 1816, the son of John Deblois (1790-1834) and the former Sarah Cookson Scott (1794-1835), and likely made his first few whaling voyages in Rhode Island vessels. He later served as third mate of the Fairhaven bark *Isabella* (1841-45) and first mate of the *Ann Alexander* (1845-49) before taking that vessel on the fateful voyage of 1850-51. Between voyages in 1845 he married Henrietta M. Tew (circa 1808/17-1883), romantically reputed to have been a distant relative of the famous Rhode Island pirate, Thomas Tew (fl. 1692-95). The couple were prosperous — they employed a series of domestic servants, one and two at a time — but evidently remained childless. (Some genealogical constructs erroneously claim them as the parents of John Edward Deblois, born in 1847, however he was actually a nephew, the son of John's younger brother, Edward Thatcher Deblois). Captain Deblois lived the remainder of his days in Newport and died there in 1885. The *Ann Alexander* incident is recounted in detail in C.C. Sawtell, *The Ship Ann Alexander of New Bedford, 1805-1851* (Mystic, 1962); there is mention of the event in the scholarly literature about *Moby Dick*, as news of the sinking arrived in New York very soon after publication of the novel and seemed to corroborate the plausibility of the *Pequod* ramming at just the time Melville's critics were expressing their doubts; and there is a long, humorous poem about the *Ann Alexander* in Daniel Ricketson's *History of New Bedford* (1858, 102ff), reprinted from 1851 issues of the *New Bedford Mercury* newspaper and London *Punch* magazine.

de Carvalho, Celestino Amorim ["Celestino Ernesto "] (1906-1995). Coastal whaleman on the island of Flores in the Azores, and sometime foreman of the Boqueirão whaling station there, who produced a large volume of traditional Azorean scrimshaw and other objects (reported by Gomes Vieira, 2003, 96). "His works in [whale] ivory consist mainly of turned pieces, such as liqueur sets with cups, photograph frames, jewelry boxes or document cases made in exotic wood with ivory, domino, checkers and dice sets, etc." Born in 1906 at Santa Cruz, Flores, he was the son of Ernesto Ribeiro de Carvalho, a woodcarver and engraver, and Maria Lopes de Carvalho. Celestino learned handcrafts from his father and became a noted jack-of-all-trades who "mastered all the techniques of the old arts and crafts, from goldsmith to caster to carpenter, from cabinet-maker to wood-carver... He worked as locksmith, blacksmith, and machine turner," carved altar pieces for two churches in Santa Cruz, and is reputed to have been the earliest engraver of sperm whale ivory on Flores (the tradition on the neighboring island of Pico being substantially older).

DeHart, Joseph [José Lobo] (fl. circa 1854-61). Azorean-born sometime whaleman credited with three pieces of scrimshaw (in NBWM) concerning which the family provenance and museum files are equivocal as to whether he was the maker or merely the collector during his whaling days: a finely engraved pair of sperm whale teeth, one with the standing figure of a military officer in uniform, with sword and two epaulets, the other with a mountain goat and kid standing on a rock on a pedestal (as though it were a sculpture); and a cane (walking stick) with a wooden shaft and a curved handle comprised of bands of whale ivory and baleen. The man known to the whale fishery as Joseph DeHart was originally named José Lobo, born in the Azores in the middle 1840s. The family provenance reports him as having joined the crew of a Yankee whaler as cabin boy at the tender age of nine, to have made three voyages in that capacity, and to have been adopted by or taken under the wing of Captain Abraham DeHart, going so far as to anglicize his given name and adopt his mentor's surname as his own. However, official records and crew lists do not entirely bear this out. Joseph's one documented voyage was as a seaman (cabin boy or green hand) for the 170th lay in the New Bedford ship *Roman 2d* during 1857-61. This could not have been a berth for a nine-year-old child and, in any case, must have been at least a second time out. Abraham DeHart was indeed the captain on that voyage, but it was his one and only voyage as captain — so "Captain" Abraham DeHart could not have adopted anyone as such on any previous voyage. If José /Joseph was on an earlier voyage as ship's boy, he may indeed have joined it in progress and thus not have had his name appear on the books; he could also have stowed away when a ship called at the Azores for water and provisions. But if he had shipped again — in any capacity, at any age — he would have had to sign articles and, as a matter of law, his name would be required to appear; and it almost certainly would be evident in the records somewhere. So if the boy did slip aboard a whaleship and was taken into Abraham DeHart's care — which is likely; after all, he did adopt the DeHart name — it must have been on the 1854-57 voyage of the *Roman*, on which DeHart was first mate. And, given this relationship, it makes perfect sense that the boy, now recast as Joseph DeHart, would have been taken along on Abraham's next voyage, his first as captain, also in the

Roman. So the probable scenario is that young José Lobo came aboard the *Roman* in the Azores during the 1854-57 voyage, when Abraham DeHart was first mate, was installed as cabin boy, made the voyage with the ship and returned with her to New Bedford, anglicized his given name to Joseph, adopted DeHart as his surname, and made a second voyage with Abraham when his mentor was promoted to captain. Captain DeHart, born circa 1822, a native of New Brunswick, New Jersey, was one of those comparatively rare out-of-state transplants who eventually rose to command a Yankee whaler. His relationship with Joseph was certainly that of patron, with Joseph a kind of apprentice; there was likely also a personal friendship of sorts; but it took on no official dimensions: Joseph was never formally adopted, did not live with the DeHart family, and was not a member of Captain DeHart's household ashore. When Captain DeHart left off whaling in 1861, it seems also to have spelled the end of the protege's whaling career. Joseph married Ann Crapo and raised a family in New Bedford. Meanwhile, Captain DeHart was still listed as a Master Mariner in the 1870s; but if he took up some other form of seafaring — say, as a captain of coastwise trading vessels, deepwater packets, or steamboats — there may be no way definitively to determine whether Joseph followed in his wake. As it stands, no such ongoing relationship is known. And later, after Captain DeHart had retired from the sea, residing in Dartmouth, making a living at farming and house painting, and raising a family — including a sailor son, Alexander — there is no trace of Joseph in the picture.

Delano, Seth (fl. 1833-45). On 28 June 1844, aboard the ship *Tuscaloosa* of New Bedford (1840-44), seaman George de Wolf wrote in his journal (in NBWM): "Mr. Delanoe [sic] made a turning lathe yesterday and has been turning cane heads all of today." This was the last stretch of the homeward passage of a successful voyage to the Pacific, and after four years of sperm whaling there was likely plenty of ivory and bone on board for scrimshaw. Delano was a fairly common name in the New England seafaring fraternity (President Franklin Delano Roosevelt was proud of his Delano whaling ancestors; and Captain Amasa Delano published his memoirs and was later caricatured by Herman Melville in *Benito Cereno*) and De Wolf does not provide this one's given name. But the fellow to whom De Wolf refers as "Mr." Delano must therefore have been one of the officers, and from this it becomes possible to identify the scrimshaw-maker with a fair degree of certainty.

No one named Delano appears on the outward-bound crew list (NBPS). Based on this and the fact that the lathe episode occurred less than a month before the *Tuscaloosa* landed at New Bedford, it is clear that Delano must have joined the ship at some port-of-call with the voyage already in progress. According to de Wolf's journal, the captain, Frederick C. Taber, was a classic bucko, much given to flogging and other, even crueler punishments. Not surprisingly, in such circumstances desertions of crew and turnover of officers in the outports tend to be more frequent than otherwise. Interpolating from the chronology of officers named Delano who were whaling contemporaneously from the New Bedford Port District, only Seth Delano of Fairhaven, Massachusetts, fits the criteria (and fits them very well). He would have been second mate or possibly a substitute first mate during the concluding few weeks or months of the *Tuscaloosa* voyage.

The only other viable candidate is Obed Delano, born in 1814 in Rochester, Massachusetts, one of the Sippican towns. Having already served as captain of the New Bedford ship *Mercator* (1840-43), he would certainly have been qualified and was theoretically also available to join the *Tuscaloosa* voyage-in-progress as first mate in 1843 or '44. However, he has no credentials as a carpenter or artisan, and, more significantly, is reported as having gone as first mate of the Wareham ship *George Washington* on 24 July 1844, only three days after the *Tuscaloosa* returned to New Bedford — an intolerably short layover for a married man with a large family. (He was later first mate of the ship *China* of New Bedford [1852-56], then captain of the brig *Hopeton* of Sippican [1857-59] and schooner *Cohannet* of Marion [1869-70]. He married Verona William Hedley in 1838 and was a life-long resident of Rochester and Marion — both in Sippican — where he was managing agent of the *Hopeton* and a Town Selectman in the 1860s. He died in 1889.)

There is no such chronological or occupational anomaly in the case of Seth Delano. He was born in Fairhaven circa 1817, was apparently trained as a carpenter, went as a green hand in the ship *Addison* of Fairhaven (1833-36), and was afterwards first mate of the bark *Mt. Wollaston* of that port (1844-45). However, his career between 1836 and 1844, incorporating the period of the *Tuscaloosa* voyage, is unknown. He wed Rhoda P. Davis sometime around 1840, and by 1850 was working as a shipwright and (later) ship carpenter in Fairhaven and Mattapoisett, where they raised a large family (their eldest son Seth, Jr., was also a ship carpenter and in later life a house carpenter). In the 1870s, Delano retired to farming in Fairhaven.

De la Rez, Joann (fl. circa 1806-16). French artisan and navy sailor of possible Spanish or Catalonian extraction, credited with a pierced-work ivory box, 8 x 6 ½ x 2 ½ inches (approximately 20 x 16 x 5 cm), made while he was a prisoner of war at the Norman Cross Depot in England circa 1806-16: "The carved hinged lid depict[s] a gentleman and woman hunting with hounds within a foliate border... with geometric designs on a foil background" (Henderson Collection; *Jack Tar*, 117; Northeast, 6 Aug. 2008, #845). According to the provenance, De la Rez was an ivory carver in the port of Dieppe, was impressed into Napoleon's navy, and was captured by the British in 1806. The box itself is not scrimshaw but there is reason to suppose that, as the artist was a sometime sailor working in a major seaport, and as walrus ivory and especially sperm whale ivory were coming into France increasingly since the 1790s, the artist may have utilized them in his regular trade as a worker in ivory both before and especially after the Napoleonic Wars.

de Mendonça, Manuel E. (fl. circa 1859-75). He was an Azorean-born cooper in New Bedford and sometime ship's cooper to whom several quite varied but fairly simple pieces of scrimshaw are attributed; these, along with his cooper's tools and so-called "sea chest" (which may actually have been a tool chest), and a ship model that he may have built himself, came to NBWM in 1958 from the estate of Clara Mendonca Black, a granddaughter. Consistently with his shipping papers, she reported his name as Manuel E. de Mendonca, but in the 1870 U.S. Census he is listed as Manuel Mendonca, age 35, cooper, with a wife named Amelia Servis, age 21, also born in the Azores, and three young children, named Willie, Mary, and Henry, all born in Massachusetts. From this it is clear that Manuel was born in the Azores circa 1835. He had certainly come to Massachusetts by sea, but it is not known from what island, or when, or by what means. His only recorded whaling voyage was as ship's cooper in the bark *Marion* of New Bedford (1859-63), and the inventory of artifacts is itself testimony to his vocational nautical interests and, in standpoint of the materials used and types of items produced, typifies mainstream whalemen's work. In all likelihood it was a whaleship that brought him to New Bedford in the first place, and certainly by the time he was ship's cooper in the *Marion* he had become acquainted with the orthodox forms of scrimshaw, which, with his skills as a cooper, would have been straightforward for him to produce. These are all carved and "built," without any engraved inscriptions or pictorial features: a plain panbone walking stick; an oval ditty box with wooden top and bottom, plain panbone sides and skirt, and scalloped tabs; a single-cage swift made of whale ivory and two types of wood, with a whale ivory cup finial and wooden base, the ribs tied with white yarn; and a stiletto knife with a contoured handle of whale panbone, a handmade double-edged steel blade that appears to have been adapted or reduced from some other weapon or tool, and an oblong scabbard (sheath) with beaded edges, constructed of two pieces of panbone and fastened with three rivets, two bands of twine wrappings, and a collar ferrule. He worked as a shoreside cooper in New Bedford in the 1860s and '70s, but his later life and subsequent activities have not come to light.

DeMontigny, Clarence W. (1885-1957). He was not a whaleman or a sailor, nor even the son or grandson of whalemen, but he lived in New Bedford in the final years of the whaling industry and was a devoted, self-taught painter and sketch artist specializing in whaling subjects and waterfront scenes. His watercolors and drawings are of variable quality, but surprisingly many of them are uniquely valuable for documenting the home front when the whaling industry was in precipitous decline, including such otherwise overlooked details as shoreside buildings, derelict hulks at the wharves, and the belowdecks and aftercabins of the last surviving wooden whaleships. One of his few known scrimshaw productions is a signed walrus tusk in NBWM engraved with a panoramic whaling scene that is among his best work. It has a ship underway, a vessel that seems to be missing its mizzen mast, and a bark, with two whaleboats attacking an crescent-shaped, upside-down sperm whale inspired by Benjamin Russell, and more whales in the offing. A hole drilled through the tip indicates that it was the product of barter with Eskimos.

Clarence Wilfred DeMontigny was born in 1885,[2] the son of Wilfred DeMontigny, a French-Canadian house painter in Fall River, who had immigrated with his parents as a child; and his wife Elizabeth, who was born in Massachusetts of Irish ancestry. Clarence married Anna Murphy and raised a family in New Bedford, where after working in a cotton mill as a youth and later in a local shoe factory, he was employed as a mechanic and "wood polisher" for the Pairpoint Manufacturing Co. until the mid 1920s, when his love of history and the arts led him to become an antiques dealer on Merrill's Wharf (now Homer's Wharf). He was later a "wood finisher in a New Bedford furniture store and exhibited his pictures at art fairs, notably at Newport, Rhode Island, in the 1950s. He is listed in Peter Hastings Falk, ed., *Who Was Who in American Art, 1564-1975.*

* **Dexter, Rodolphus W.** (fl. circa 1835-60) As a New Bedford whaling master he had a difficult and ultimately unsuccessful career. Born in 1816 at Tisbury, Martha's Vineyard, he was the son of Benjamin Dexter and Betsey Hillman (not, as the *Dictionary* implies, the son or namesake of a whaling master). He grew up on Martha's Vineyard, went whaling at age 15 in the New Bedford ship *Commodore Decatur* (1831-32), and in 1838 married Irena Clifford, with whom he had two children, a daughter born just before he went to sea as first mate in the ship *China* (1840-42), and a son born a few months after he was back at sea again as master of the *Chili* (1843-45). These two voyages were reasonably successful as commercial ventures and Captain Dexter certainly produced

[2] According to his World War I draft registration in 1917, DeMontigny was born in New Bedford on Nov. 20, 1886, but his World War II draft registration accurately lists his birth as Nov. 20, 1885, in Fall River.

his share of artwork along the way, in the form of watercolor ship-portraits in his journal (in KNB) and, evidently, scrimshaw, which he mentions in his journal but never describes. However, Dexter's whaling luck declined rapidly after this. He sailed as captain of the *Israel* in August 1846, but the vessel was wrecked eight months later in Table Bay, at the Cape of Good Hope; and though, according to Starbuck, the oil was saved, it cannot have been much after only a few months' whaling. His next voyage was even worse, in its way: no ship was lost, but even though he sent a meager 400 barrels of whale oil home ahead of the ship *Chili* (1848-53), he returned in April 1855 after 44 months at sea with no oil at all. Still, he was able to obtain another command, an Atlantic voyage in the 184-ton schooner *Alfred* — which was quite a step down from his previous two ships, of 357 and 291 tons respectively; and the voyage itself (1853-55) was pretty much a bust, returning only 86 barrels of sperm oil and 40 barrels of whale oil after 18 months at sea. It was to be was his last whaling cruise. It is his *Chili* journal, filled with references to "scrimshanging" and excellent vignette drawings of ships and barks, and in which he mentions that they had a lathe on board that could be used for scrimshaw as well as for ship's work, that mark Dexter's unfortunate career as memorable in the history of shipboard occupational arts. Had his whaling luck been better he might have produced more scrimshaw; as it stands, none of his scrimshaw work has come to light. Fortunately, he fared better as an officer in the Union Navy during the Civil War and in the merchant service afterwards, when he moved his family to Stockton, California. There, he continued to earn his livelihood as a mariner and lived together in one household with Irena, their son R.W. Dexter, Jr., who was also a sailor, their widowed daughter Abby Barclay, and her two children. (Stockton was also the postwar home of the New Hampshire-born whaleman-scrimshaw artist Charles H. Durgin, q.v. in *More Scrimshaw Artists.*)

Dias, Joseph, Jr. (fl. circa 1830-57). Whaling master from Martha's Vineyard who, as a young boatsteerer in 1844, remarked in his journal at one point, "nothing to do but make canes to support our dignity when we [get] home" (NBWM). Unfortunately, none of his scrimshaw has yet been identified.

Dias — also known as Joseph Dias III — was born at Tisbury, Martha's Vineyard, in 1822, the grandson of Joseph Dias, mariner, who had come to the Vineyard from the Azores around 1770 and served in the American Revolution; and the son of Sarah (née Manter) and Captain Joseph Dias, Sr., a mariner, harbor pilot, and veteran of the War of 1812. Young Joseph served his apprenticeship in the New Bedford ship *William Rotch* (1831-35) and probably a Vineyard whaler or two, was a boatsteerer in the Fairhaven ship *Clifford Wayne* (1841-45), the outing on which he mentions making scrimshaw, and after an intervening voyage on an unidentified ship, probably as second mate, he was first mate of the Vineyard ship *Ocmulgee* of Holmes' Hole (1847-50), then captain of the ships *Pocahontas* of Tisbury (1850-53) and *St. George* of New Bedford (1853-57). According to scientists at planktonforums.org, at the time of his *Pocahontas* voyage Dias was known as " the boy captain," on account of his comparative youth (however, he was 28 when the *Pocahontas* sailed, younger than average for a captain but surely not even close to a record). Off the coast of Argentina the ship was stove by an angry sperm whale: "he [the whale] hit the ship in [the] right [starboard] side, [the] whalers heard the sound of breaking wood and a huge hole appeared in the hull, nobody thought about [the] hunt anymore, only with big struggle could [the] captain get his ship to [the] nearest port." Dias may have been early to command but he was late to marry. It was not until 1864, two months short of his forty-second birthday, long after his retirement from whaling, that he wed Mary Norton Athearn (1839-1909), 17 years his junior. The couple lived in Tisbury, where they raised two sons and a daughter, employed two servants, and ran a grocery business. Meanwhile, he compiled the records of some 4,000 American whaling voyages covering the period from the late-eighteenth century to 1906 (Baker Library, Harvard Business School). Mary died in 1909 and Joseph died two years later, at Oak Bluffs in 1911. (Not to be confused with a later Joseph Dias of Mattapoisett, who served two voyages as second and first mate of the bark *Sun* in the 1840s.)

Dove Crimper Artist (fl. 19th Century). Anonymous whaleman-artist credited with at least three crimpers surmounted by one or two full-figure doves carved as silhouette outlines with relief-carved highlights. They are distinguished by the epithets "dove crimper" and "two doves crimper." In the first category is one (from the collection of Andrew Snow of New Bedford, Massachusetts, acquired by NBWM in 1919) with a lozenge-shaped handle comprised of a strip of mahogany sandwiched between two panbone cheeks, the ensemble fastened by a mortise and tenon joint and eight yellow-metal rivets to a whale ivory tailpiece; the tailpiece is tapered to a three-tine fork, and at the other end the shaft tapers to a saddle carved in the silhouette image of a dove, with monochrome engraved highlights and a yellow-metal axle forming the eyes. This saddle supports an elaborate openwork jagging wheel having a six-pointed Maltese cross hub and fluted rim. The two doves crimper is typified by a specimen (from the collection of Martha M. Hinsdale, acquired by NBWM in 1959) that has a massive handle and foreshaft of whale ivory that has ornamental carving, perfling, a geometric pattern incised along the edges, four metal rivets, and a baleen separator, terminating at one end in a whale ivory, a finial full-round-carved in the form of a fist holding a yellow-metal ring (useful for hanging), and at the other end in an architectonic pediment with red and green sealing wax highlights, surmounted by two back-to-back doves: these are relief-carved silhouettes, with engraved highlights and ten yellow-metal rivets: each of the doves is a saddle for a jagging wheel, with the birds' eyes formed by the two yellow-metal axles. One of these saddles houses a small wooden wheel with serrated rim, the other an elaborate openwork jagging wheel with a six-pointed Maltese cross hub and fluted rim. Another, quite similar, two-dove crimper was reported by the late Paul Madden (who interpreted the birds as eagles) and was illustrated in his online catalogue during 2004-05.

Drew, James (fl, circa 1810-20). Nantucket whaleman who made two or three voyages in the New Bedford brig *Ospray* and wound up as captain of one voyage in her (1818-20). Either he or, much more likely, his nephew John P. Drew (q.v.) may have been the maker of a polychrome tooth depicting a pastoral couple surmounted by a spread eagle and motto, and a sperm whaling scene in a brig, inscribed "J. Drew • Nantucket" (reported by John Rinaldi; Osona, Aug. 7, 2010, #180). James was born on Nantucket in 1791, the son of Gershom Drew (1750-1809) and his first wife, Mary Cobb (1754-circa 1791), who were married circa 1772, but he was raised by the second wife, Abigail Gardner (1754-1809), whom his father married in 1795. He may have made a youthful voyage in some Nantucket ship, as was the custom among young men weaned on the Island, but his only known voyages were in the *Ospray*, beginning in 1810. In 1811 he married Hannah Coffin, who bore him a daughter that died in early infancy; he was widowed soon after, and was remarried to Nancy Fosdick in 1820.

Drew, John P. (fl. circa 1820s). Nantucket whaleman, nephew of Captain James Drew (q.v.). By the process of elimination, he appears to be the likely artist of a monochrome tooth with polychrome highlights, engraved on one side with a sperm whaling scene that has a brig with two spouting whales, a stove boat, and cornucopia, surmounted by a proscenium arch device inscribed "J. Drew • Nantucket"; and on the other, a couple, the man in a brimmed hat, cutaway coat, knee breeches, and slippers, carrying a cane; and the woman in a feathered hat and gown; surmounted by a spread eagle inscribed "E PLURIBUS UNUM" (reported by John Rinaldi; also Osona, Aug. 7, 2010, #180). For the greater part of the nineteenth century there was essentially only one Drew family on Nantucket, and only four Drew men and no women who had the initial J. Captain Alexander Drew (1785-1872), who commanded two whaling voyages in the Nantucket ship *John Jay* during 1822-28, had two sons named James Bunker Drew, both of whom died in childhood: one born in 1819 who died in 1833, and a namesake born in 1834 who died in 1836. Alexander's younger brother was Captain James Drew (b: 1791), who made a Pacific Ocean whaling voyage as captain of the New Bedford brig *Ospray* (1818-20), but his whaling career was rather too early for him to have engraved such a tooth while he was still at sea. The only remaining candidate was the son of James and Alexander's older brother William: John P. Drew was whaling in the 1820s but his voyages have not been discovered. Born on Nantucket in 1802, he was the elder of the two sons of William Drew and Lucy Pinkham Coffin. He married Valina Dixon in 1824 and died young in 1830. (Valina subsequently married John's younger brother Alexander G. Drew, who left her widowed a second time in 1836). If John engraved the tooth, which of course would have to have been sometime before 1830, he may have intended the ship-portrait as his uncle James's former command, the New Bedford brig *Ospray*, on which there is reason to believe that young John made his maiden voyage; or it could be some other brig with which John was associated afterwards. It is in any case a rather early production of its type.

Duarte, Manuel (fl. circa 1888-1922). Retail merchant-entrepreneur at Monterey, California, who sold — and may have participated in making — souvenir items made from whale skeletal bone. He was the son and sometime partner of former California shore-station whaleman Rosario Duarte (q.v.), and assisted his father and eventually succeeded him in the grocery and general merchandise business in Monterey. They stocked various kinds of souvenirs made out of whale vertebrae from the Monterey Whaling Station, continuing to do so long after the station itself closed. These bone items were mostly covers for pocket-size souvenir booklets and photograph albums, with the paper pages sewn together with ribbons or twine. They were produced as a local cottage industry by Azorean Portuguese immigrant families, most of whom were involved at one time or another in the mostly-all-Azorean crews at the Monterey and Point Lobos whaling stations.

The Monterey station, established by Rhode Islander and former New Bedford and San Francisco whaling captain John P. Davenport in 1854, was the first shore-whaling operation in California. By the 1860s it had several 10-man, all-Azorean crews, each consisting of harpooners, oarsmen, flensers, processors, and cooks. Lookouts were posted on high ground; when whales were sighted — primarily gray whales — the lookouts signaled the crews, who launched six-man whaleboats, fastened onto the whales with harpoons — hand-wielded or fired from Greener gun-type bow-chasers, dispatched the whales with hand-wielded lances or bomb-lances fired from shoulder guns, flensed the carcasses on shore, and piled up the unwanted bones alongside while they retrieved the blubber and tried-out the oil. Oil was the objective; the tons of bones were mostly refuse. The station remained active until 1888, was intermittently revived during 1898-1910, and meanwhile spawned more than a dozen other mostly Azorean shore-whaling stations that dotted the California coast from Oregon to Mexico. The Point Lobos station, established in 1862 in nearby Carmel, was one of the offshoots, remaining productive until 1884. (It was briefly revived from 1898 to 1901 by an all-Japanese crew of professional abalone fishermen who later made a splendid success of abalone canning at Monterey.) But whether the stations were operating or not, nobody wanted most of the bones. Some were used as paving "stones" for sidewalks in various parts of Monterey (a few remain in place even today near the old whaling station), but they never had any real commercial value. The surplus was thus more than ample to provide the very modest quantities required for the small-scale production of souvenir booklets, and the makers must have continued to mine the piles of refuse bones even after active whaling had ceased. The most characteristic manifestation of the souvenir booklets was as an album of suction-mounted sea moss specimens from Monterey Bay and nearby Asilomar Beach, an item that seems to have increased in popularity with the rise of the Cannery Row seafood factories in the early twentieth century.

Manuel Duarte (1865-1949) was born at Monterey, assisted his father in the grocery business in his youth, and in partnership with one George Turner opened a grocery store of his own in nearby Pacific Grove in 1888, the same year the Monterey Whaling Station closed. Their merchandise included a wide range of non-comestible items, including dry goods and bait. Duarte also provided fishing guides and brokered other services for tourists. He married a daughter of German immigrants and eventually succeeded his father as proprietor of the original family store, established in 1865, which had become not only a grocery and souvenir shop but a ship chandlery, boat rental emporium, and local hangout. Known as M.R. Duarte's Marine Museum and Glass Bottom Boat Office, it was "part of almost a whole block of lots owned by the Duarte family." The 1900 U.S. Census lists Manuel as a "fish dealer," but the 1910 U.S. Census identifies him at age 42 as a "notions merchant" and his wife Annie, age 34 (she was actually 36 or 37), as "Saleslady Retail Notions." According to Manuel's obituary, written almost 40 years later, the store was quite a landmark. Calling the proprietor "one of Monterey's well known pioneers" (a characterization perhaps even more true of the paterfamilias, Rosario), it says of the Duarte store that it "served as an impromptu meeting place for fishermen as well as many city officials," and that Manuel himself was also "a collector of waterfront memorabilia which he kept, and sometimes sold, at his store. Each item was identified by a fabulous yarn, the telling of which invariably accompanied each sale, to the delight of the purchaser." (*Monterey Peninsula Herald,* Aug. 31, 1949)

Among the "retail notions" were the pocket-size whale vertebrae souvenir booklets, which the Duartes were evidently not the only merchants to offer for sale in Monterey, Cannery Row, or Pacific Grove. Examples in KNB include a booklet containing actual specimens of sea moss (seaweed), each one pressed onto a separate sheet of paper, with the cover stamped "Sea Moss Souvenir." Another is labeled in ink holograph "This is a specimen of whale bone from Monterey, the noted whaling station. The bones were used for side-walks over one hundred years." A third is a photo album dated January 1900, containing similar sea moss specimens and snapshots of tourist attractions in Monterey, Pacific Grove, and San Francisco, inscribed: "The cover of this book / is made of the vertebrae / of a whale." A double-wide variant in a private collection in nearby Carmel measures just under 5 x 6 inches (12.5 x 15 cm) closed and 5 x 12 inches (12.5 x 30 cm) open. Here the paper label is printed in a serifed typeface and pasted onto the inside back cover: "THIS IS A / SPECIMEN OF WHALEBONE / FROM MONTEREY THE NOTED WHALING STATION / The bones were used for side-walks over one hundred years. A few of the walks are still in use." It contains six specimens of seaweed and seven tipped-in photographs, including one of the local seacoast, four of local shore-whaling, and, anachronistically, two shipboard views of deepwater whaling that have nothing to do with the Monterey bay locale. However, two of the photos are of the Moss Landing Whaling Station a few miles north on Monterey Bay — which hunted whales with 90mm bow-chaser cannons fired from steam-powered vessels and only began operations in 1919, thus providing an earliest possible date for this particular specimen.

The 1920 U.S. Census lists Manuel Duarte as the proprietor of a ship chandlery — the same shop adapting to changing times. It operated under Duarte family auspices until 1922, when it was taken over by a Chinese merchant, who relocated it and specialized in dry goods. (Additional sources: Sources: Tim Thomas, Monterey Maritime Museum; City directories; Sanborn Map; Kent Seavey, "Report for the Cole House and Duarte Store Historic Preservation Program," 2003.)

Duarte, Rosario (fl. 1860s-c1915). He was a member of one of the original mostly-all-Azorean crews at the Monterey Whaling Station, established in 1854 — the first of more than a dozen shore-whaling stations operating on the California coast between 1854 and around 1910. He, "along with some innovative sport fishermen," is also said to have introduced salmon trolling to Monterey Bay in 1878. But Rosario Duarte is principally remembered as the founder and proprietor of a general store that was a popular local meeting place and a hangout for local whalers and fishermen. In the context of whale byproducts and scrimshaw, his principal interest is that the shop — at least by the time his son was running it — carried a line of souvenir booklets and albums with covers made out of whale vertebrae, the product of a local cottage industry (concerning which see the article on his son, Manuel Duarte). As a former whaleman and enterprising entrepreneur, it may have been Rosario himself who invented or inspired the use of the otherwise worthless whale bones for the making of souvenirs.

Another manifestation of whale bone carving that is a kind of local analogue of whalemen's scrimshaw and may have involved Rosario Duarte is the production of votive bonecarving ensembles depicting the Carmel mission church, formally known as San Carlos Borroméo del Rio de Carmelo (founded in 1771). According to Robert L. Santos in his history of California, among local whalers skeletal bone was used for votive purposes in a very practical context. He cites an M.A. thesis by Alvin Graves (Fresno State College, 1969) for the claim that the whale bones imbedded in Monterey sidewalks were placed there "as a religious offering for a whaler's survival"; and a Ph.D. thesis by Donald R. Taft (Columbia University, 1923) finds that Robert Louis Stevenson, who lived briefly on the Monterey Peninsula, "walked with Joaquin, a Portuguese whaler, to the local church [in Monterey], and the whaler said:

> *'Look at the whalebone pavement in front of the church, Señor Stevenson. The Star of Hope is there all in the bones of whales that Saint Anthony has sent us. Each time a whale is caught, Portuguese fishermen carry bones on their backs all the way from the beach and kneel before the church to set them into the pavement in honor of the Saint.'*

> *'I see,' Stevenson nodded and looked on the beauty at his feet. 'Perhaps a fisher for words can someday honor the Saint by telling all the world about the devotion of fisher folk who come to the Mission Church of Monterey to pray and pay tribute.'"* (repr., New York: Arno Press and *The New York Times*, 1969)

A more aesthetic but otherwise analogous expression of the whalers' piety are plaques cut and assembled from whale scapulae, vertebrae, and other bones, in a few cases with other "found" materials (notably, abalone inlay), forming three-dimensional, low-relief pictures and tableaus — mostly images of the mission church itself, but also landscapes, occasional human figures, and religious subjects. Some of these are sconces for candles, or have shelves mounted with oil lamps or candlesticks, and so on. Some of these were votive offerings to the San Carlos Borroméo Mission church and, presumably, also to other religious establishments; others were undoubtedly made as souvenirs for sale to tourists and pilgrims. Several still hang in the Mission, and three (one with a wooden backboard) are displayed in the Whalers' Shack museum at PLSR. The plaques were clearly made by several hands, but the authorship and donations appear to have been anonymous.

Duarte's advertisement in the Monterey *Argus* newspaper of December 15, 1883, sums up the scope of his business at that time:

> ROSARIO DUARTE, **Alvardo St. near Steamer Landing — Dealer in Fruits, Candies, Nuts, Pipes, Tobacco, Cigars Groceries and Provisions, Fishing Tackle and Fishermens Supplies.**

Rosario Duarte is frequently mentioned in connection with the Azorean-Portuguese community of Monterey, and as a whaler he was certainly a member of an Azorean crew; but his ancestry was certainly at least partly if not wholly Spanish. His father was born in Mexico, his mother in Spain, and he in Baja California circa 1827. He was living in Monterey by 1852 (as is duly recorded in the local census), and was married there in 1854. The bride, Maria Alta Gracia de la Torre (1834-1908) — known as Altagracia — was born at Monterey, a descendant of an old California Spanish family, the daughter of José Joaquin de la Torre and María de los Cota. The Monterey census of 1860 identifies Rosario as a hotel keeper; however, in the U.S. Census of 1870 and again in 1880 he is unaccountably listed as a laborer, which clearly he was not. He is reported to have started the general store in Monterey in 1865, but was evidently living for a while in Castroville — which today, much to the consternation of Italians everywhere, styles itself "The Artichoke Capital of the World" — a few miles north, near Moss Landing. A notice in the Castroville section of the *Argus* on October 2, 1869, reports, "Our old friend Rosario DUARTE has left us for Monterey, but shows his faith in Castroville and its future by preparing as he is doing, to erect several buildings on his lot situated between the Pioneer hotel and Mr. Joseph WATSON's Fruit Store." A later article in the same newspaper mentions the delivery of lumber for his building project. On the other hand, business was not necessarily always thriving, as Duarte's name appears on Monterey's Delinquent Tax List for 1878-79 in the amount of $4.58 — the same year Rosario is said to have been introducing salmon trolling to Monterey Bay. Manuel Duarte (q.v.), one of Rosario and Altagracia's many children, eventually took over running the family store.

Duquesnoy, François (fl. circa 1618-43). Baroque era sculptor born in Flanders (now Belgium) and working in Italy. Like his German contemporary, Leonhard Kern (q.v.), Duquesnoy was one of comparatively few academicians to sculpt in ivory; like Kern, he may have used walrus ivory as well as elephant ivory; however, also like Kern, most of his accessible works are in other media, and whatever works there may be in walrus ivory may not have been recognized as such. The son and pupil of a Flemish sculptor, Duquesnoy (1597-1643) received his early training in his father's studio at Brussels. In 1618, subsidized by Archduke Albert, he went to study in Rome and remained in Italy for most of the rest of his life. Unlike Kern, many of Duquesnoy's works were oversize sculptures for churches and public buildings. As a youth in Brussels he carved a statue of Justice for the chancellery and two angels for a Jesuit church. His mature works included statues for St. Peter's and Santa Maria di Loreto in Rome, a bishop's tomb for the cathedral in Ghent, and numerous other such commissions. He has been called "one of the most sought after sculptors of his day," and was accordingly bestowed with the moniker "Il Flamingo" ("The Fleming"); but he also did "small reliefs and statuettes in bronze, ivory, and wax" that "were often inspired by classical art" (*Columbia Enc.*). Unlike Kern, Duquesnoy's ivory carvings — whether rendered exclusively in elephant ivory or also in walrus — rather than primarily consisting of figurines, also took the more scrimshaw-like form of relief-carvings and friezes on drinking cups and goblets. In fact, among other things he was "famous for... his ivory carvings for drinking-cups" (*Catholic Enc.*). (For remarks about the likely presence of walrus ivory in this early Baroque genre that was contemporaneous with the first decades of Arctic right whaling, see the article on Leonhard Kern.) Duquesnoy died suddenly at Leghorn in 1643 while on his way to Paris, where he had been promised the patronage of the great and powerful Cardinal Richelieu. "It is reported that he was poisoned by his own brother, Jérôme [1612-1654], who was also a clever sculptor," and who, the following year, "was burned for unnatural crime, 24 Oct. 1654" (*Catholic Enc.*). (Sources: *Catholic Encyclopedia; Columbia Encyclopedia*, 6th Ed.; *Columbia Electronic Encyclopedia*, 2003.)

Eayrs, Joseph H. (fl. circa 1837-45). Whaleman from Boston who may or may not have practiced the scrimshaw arts, but whose journal as third mate in the New Bedford ship *Gratitude* (1841-45) sheds significant light on the reading habits of deepwater whalemen in the middle nineteenth century.

In attempting to characterize the female fashion-plate illustrations that whalemen seem often to have used as models for scrimshaw, Norman Flayderman remarks, "Such pictures were usually copied from *Godey's Lady's Book* or some other 'fashion magazine' of the time" (Flayderman, 187). It would seem so, as many of the whalemen's pictures greatly resemble the *Godey's* type. Published in Philadelphia by Louis A. Godey and edited by Sarah Josepha Hale, *Godey's* was an enormously popular national magazine at mid-century and certainly circulated in the whaling fleet, as Joseph Eayrs testifies in his journal (reported by Michael P. Dyer):

> *[We] have had some amusement this last week having got several Books (new to us) from the Ship Harrison, amongst which was The Phantom Ship and Frank Mildmay by Capt[ai]n Mar[r]yatt, The Outlaw, Museum of History and several numbers of the* Lady's Book*. The last is a fine work has three of the best Tales I have ever read. The May number for 1841 is excellent, the story of the False Teeth is OK! OK!*

The three novels — *The Phantom Ship* (1839) and *Frank Mildmay* (1833) by Captain Frederick Marryatt, and *The Outlaw* (1835) by Anna Maria Hall, were comparatively new at the time; and the May 1841 issue of *The Lady's Book* to which Eayrs refers was actually published a month *after* the *Gratitude* sailed (the *Harrison* sailed from New Bedford the following July).

Flayderman names only *Godey's* specifically, which inspired Dr. Jack H.T. Chang to compile a comprehensive inventory of virtually all of the *Godey's* plates and thousands of images of scrimshaw from institutional and private collections, proving three points: that *Godey's* accounts for only a minority of the fashion plates that served as models for whalemen's scrimshaw; that whalemen frequently edited and adapted the published prototypes to suit their own purposes and tastes; and that the majority of fashion-plate illustrations on scrimshaw must be based upon plates in the numerous "other" fashion magazines to which Flayderman alludes but does not name, most especially *Harper's New Monthly Magazine.*

Eayrs may have been a voracious and enthusiastic reader, but he is not known to have made any scrimshaw. Born circa 1814, his Seamen's Protection Paper, issued in June 1837, six days before he sailed in the ship *Mercury* of New Bedford (1837-40), indicates that he was from Boston, age 23 at the time, rather older than average for a first voyage. Then, in 1841, he signed articles as boatsteerer in the bark *Gratitude,* but he appears to have been promoted to third mate even before the voyage commenced, as he is listed as such both in the NBPS crew list and in the 1841 *New Bedford City Directory*. His brothers Augustus and Henry also made whaling voyages around the same time. The *Gratitude* voyage (1841-54) was evidently Joseph's last. Around 1855 he married a woman named Mary who was 19 years younger. At first they lived in her native New York State, where their first two daughters were born. Then, unaccountably for a Yankee family, during the Civil War and after, from 1861 to 1870, they were living in Confederate Texas, where they had three more daughters. They afterwards moved to Chicago, where Joseph worked as a cabinetmaker and where he died of Bright's disease in 1880 at age 66.

Eduardo — see **Edwards, Antone Thomas**

Edwards, Antone Thomas (fl. circa 1893-1923). New Bedford whaling master from the Azores credited with a variety of utilitarian and ornamental scrimshaw of unspecified types. He was born António Tomaz Eduardo in 1882 at Fajãzinha, Lajes [Lages] das Flores, the son of José Francisco Eduardo and Maria Tomazia Eduardo. He was the older brother of whaling captain Joseph F. Edwards (q.v. in the *Dictionary*) and the nephew of whaling captain Joseph T. Edwards (q.v.). At Flores "when he was very young," about eight years old, in fact, he shipped as cabin boy in the bark *President 2d,* commanded by his uncle J.T. Edwards (voyage of 1890-93), arriving in New Bedford in 1893. There he is said to have attended school (which must have been intermittently at best) and was whaling in the schooner *William A. Grozier* under John A. Dunham (1894) and brig *Frances A. Barstow* of San Francisco under J.T. Edwards again (1894-97). Rising steadily through the ranks, his first command was as relief captain of the New Bedford bark *Greyhound* (1903-07), in which he later made a voyage of his own (1909). He then had the schooner *Mystic* (1910-13), in which he held an ownership share, and six voyages of the bark *Wanderer* (1913-23), the last square-rigger to go whaling in American registry: he was captain, but was not yet on board, when the *Wanderer* was wrecked in a gale on Cuttyhunk Island, just outside New Bedford, outward-bound in August 1924 on what would have been his seventh voyage in her. Meanwhile, in 1910 he had married Estefânia Vasconcelos Rosa, from Provoação on the Azorean island of São Miguel. After the loss of the *Wanderer*, on account of Estefânia's poor health in combination with the end of Yankee whaling, they moved to Florida, but returned to New Bedford in 1931, where he served for a while as captain of the four-masted merchant schooner *Kirkland*. He died in 1936 in a traffic accident. (Partly reported by Gomes Vieira, 2003, 85).

* **Edwards, Joseph Thomas** (fl. circa 1874-1908). Whaling master of Azorean origin, the uncle of fellow New Bedford whaling captains Antone T. and Joseph F. Edwards (qq.v.). "On the Island of Flores there are known to be two walking sticks, in [whale] ivory, whale bone and exotic wood, a sewing box and some bodkins, which were made by this Captain. The walking sticks were given to two sailors from the barque [bark] *Greyhound* when they returned to Flores, João Rodrigues Henriques, the mate, and João Rodrigues Duarte, who served as boatsteerer" (Gomes Vieira, 2003, 159). Also, "In the house in Fajãzinha where he was born... there were some engraved whale teeth that he had bought for 25 escudos or so, for a museum in Flores... [He] took the teeth to California when he emigrated [to take command of a San Francisco-based whaler in 1894]. Some were sold, to return to the Pico Museum," but some of them disappeared (Ibid., 158f). J.T. Edwards was born José Tomaz Eduardo in 1857 at Fajãzinha, Lajes [Lages] das Flores, in the Azores, the son of Franciso Tomaz Eduardo and his wife Maria Izabel. In 1874, at age 16, he joined the crew of the bark *A.R. Tucker*, commanded by Amos C. Baker, Jr. (q.v.), returning with her to New Bedford in 1876. He was next on a merchant voyage to Venezuela in the schooner *Cohannet*, and in 1878 resumed whaling as second mate of the schooner *Mary Simmons* and bark *Peru*, then first mate of the schooner *E.B. Conwell* and bark *Tropic Bird*. He made six whaling voyages as captain, in the bark *President 2d* (two voyages, 1887-90 and 1890-93), the San Francisco brig *Frances A. Barstow* (1894-97), the New Bedford bark *Greyhound* (two voyages, 1898-1902 and 1903-07), and the Provincetown schooner *John R. Manta* (1907-08). He died in 1913. (Partly reported by Gomes Vieira, Op. cit., 158f.)

Eldridge [Eldredge], James T. [Jr.] (fl. circa 1838-65). One of three brothers from Nantucket who were captains of whaling voyages out of New Bedford and Fairhaven, he is credited with a wooden desk with whale ivory and mother-of-pearl trim, made aboard the bark *Congaree* in 1858, and possibly also a polychrome tooth engraved and inscribed on the same voyage in 1856. The narrow, lectern-shaped kneehole desk is of a type often erroneously known as a "captain's desk" (because it is only wide enough to accommodate the kneehole and resembles the desks sometimes built into ship's cabins), but in this instance is made in a graceful style usually intended for ladies, with mushroom-shaped knob drawer-pulls on the sides and delicate detailing (in NBWM, the gift of a direct descendant). The tooth is inscribed on one side, in a cursive hand "An 80 bbl Whale / that was taken / by the Congaree / of / N.B. / Lat[itude] 1. 41. N[orth] / Long[itude] 86. 27. / Aug. 7th 1856," enclosed in a leafy floral border, with a blank riband device below and surmounted by a cherub holding an unidentified object. On the back it has a woman, seated, with three girls arranging her hair with a garland of flowers.

James T. Eldridge, Jr., was born on Nantucket in 1821, the son of mariner James T. Eldridge (1798-1866) and the former Deborah Pinkham. He may have apprenticed as a carpenter in his youth: the desk itself is testimony to professional-quality woodworking skills, and following his retirement from whaling he earned his living in the carpentry trade. After a series of youthful whaling voyages on which he steadily rose through the ranks, and presumably upon his appointment to second mate in 1846, he married fellow-Nantucketer Mary H. Macy (1826-1901). He was afterwards second mate on an unidentified voyage (circa 1846-50), and first mate in the New Bedford ship *America 2d*, which sailed in September 1850 but was crushed in the ice in the Anadir Sea in 1851. By the time he returned home after the shipwreck his wife had given birth to a daughter, Lydia Macy Eldridge (1851-1916), who would eventually inherit the desk. Around this time James moved his family to Milford, Massachusetts, to live with Mary's relatives. This provided her a measure of security when her husband was at sea, and would provide him a livelihood after he retired from whaling. He was first mate of the New Bedford ship *Congaree* under Captain Martin Malloy (1851-54) and was made captain of the *Congaree* on her next voyage, on which he made the desk and may have scrimshawed the tooth, but which was otherwise unremarkable. His next time out, as captain of the Fairhaven ship *General Scott* (1860-65), he brought Mary and Lydia along — the kind of adventure that was uniquely available to the families of whaling masters. It was not a commercial success, returning only a total 145 barrels of sperm oil and 45 of whale oil after almost five years at sea. But it was a success of another sort, as the *General Scott* (unlike many Yankee whaleships in the Pacific at that time) evaded capture by the Confederate commerce raiders; and it must have been an uncommonly companionable cruise, as the ship "returned with all her original officers, an unusual circumstance" (Starbuck, 577). Captain Eldridge was afterwards a carpenter and roofer in Milford in partnership with his father-in-law, Frederick Macy. He died in 1896. Two of his brothers were also whaling masters: David P. Eldridge (b. 1816), ship *Midas* (1847-50) and bark *Winslow* (1852-55) of New Bedford; and William M. Eldridge (b. 1826), ship *Asia* of New Bedford (1864-65) and bark *Sea Fox* of Westport (1871-74). David eventually followed James to Milford with own wife and daughter, moved in next door, and joined the family firm of carpenters and roofers.

Ellison, George (fl. circa 1850-55). A tooth with the standing figure of a girl in a knee-length skirt and matching jacket, bloomers, and high button boots or gaiters, holding a brimmed hat with olive branch; framed by a garland of flowering vines; surmounting the inscription "BARBARA"; inscribed below in a riband, "GEORGE ELLISON" (reported by John Rinaldi). The only man of this name known to have been active in the whaling trade was born in England circa 1829 and stated his residence as Oswego, New York, in 1850, when he embarked on a Pacific Ocean whaling voyage in the New London ship *John and Elizabeth* (1850-55).

Emery, Alfred (fl. 1856-60). Sometime whaleman from Brooklyn, New York, reported by his descendants and heirs to have made a handle of sperm whale panbone for his sheath knife. The provenance and attribution are based on a typescript biographical sketch by his son, Harry Emery, written in 1954 (reported by Michael P. Dyer from Jane Mackay Johnson, Alfred Emery's great-granddaughter) — a naïve interpretation condensed from Emery's firsthand whaling journal. It provides only a few of the essential facts and no direct quotes. The knife handle may not be all of the scrimshaw Emery produced on his one and only whaling voyage but it does seem to be the only scrimshaw that the family knew about. (For example, Emery may also have made the sheath out of sperm whale pizzle, which the family would not have known about or been able to detect unless specifically told.)

Alfred Emery was born in 1836 "in the pine woods at Geneva, N.Y.," but was evidently raised by his English-born widowed mother, sister, and brother-in-law in Brooklyn. As the brother-in-law was a housepainter, Alfred was early exposed to the building trades. After a sickly youth, at age 20 he went in the New Bedford ship *Lagoda* on what turned out to be an undistinguished but financially successful whaling voyage (1856-60). After his return he was a sailor for a while longer, boarding in New Bedford and New York, shipping as a foremast hand on merchant voyages to Europe, and working between times at plastering, bricklaying, and stone masonry. He served a year in the Union Navy, notably on blockade patrol on the St. Johns River in Florida, and mustered out as a quartermaster in October 1863. He then moved back to New York, married Fanny E. Berrien in 1865, and lived in Yonkers, then Riverdale (now part of The Bronx), and Manhattan, making his living as a bricklayer and brick mason in partnership with Alex Forsyth until 1896, "when [according to Harry Emery] the partnership was dissolved in order for him to become [a] N.Y. Building Inspector." From 1902 until his death in 1907 he was the head of a night emergency gang in the Building Department. His wife Fanny died in 1910.

* **Enos, Manuel** (1826-1915). Azorean-born whaling master from Long Island, one of the greatest pictorial scrimshaw-makers of all time. His masterpieces are a pair of teeth polychrome engraved on the Australian coast as first mate of the New Bedford bark *Java* in 1862 (KNB) (they are illustrated together in color on the dust jacket of *More Scrimshaw Artists*). One, hitherto identified as a figure of Rebecca at the Well, an Old Testament matriarch in full flower of youth dressed in sumptuous Middle Eastern garb, is actually based on an engraving entitled "Arabia — The Arab Maid" in the 1843 edition of *Finden's Tableaux of National Character, Beauty, and Costume* by William and Edward Finden (2 vols., published in London, expanded from William Finden's edition of 1834) (reported by Dr. Jack H.T. Chang). The other is a patriotic image of Columbia, a classic nude majestically and demurely draped in an American flag. Enos is also credited with a brightly-colored standing female figure on a tooth in KNB; and four pieces in CSH: a pair of large walrus tusks stipple-engraved on the next voyage of the *Java*, and a pair of teeth beautifully engraved with full-length female portraits (illustrated in Malley 1993).

There were several mysteries about his biography and intermittent whaling career. There has never been any doubt that he was born in the Azores Islands, but according to Robert Farwell (1981, 108f) and hence my own *More Scrimshaw Artists*, it was on the island of Graciosa circa 1827. However, the 1860 U.S. Census for Huntington, Long Island, has him born on the island of Fayal circa 1826; and Donald Warrin turned up family sources indicating that he was actually born in Lajes, on the island of Pico, on 22 May 1826, one of eleven children of José Inácio Macedo and Maria Carmo. The latter is almost certainly accurate.[3]

Enos's early years are almost completely unknown, but some of the details can be partly reconstructed by working backwards from the few existing documents. He was third mate in the whaleship *Huntsville* of Cold Spring Harbor, L.I., during 1851-54, and he was also on the immediately previous voyage of the same vessel during 1849-51. That he was a mate on that second *Huntsville* voyage indicates that he must have been at least a boatsteerer on the previous voyage, which indicates that it could not have been his first: he must have made at least one prior voyage

[3] Warrin 2009 cites Rafael Enos Aguirre, "Orígenes e historia de la familia Enos," private document; Rafael Enos Aguirre to Donald Warrin, email, 18 Mar 2009.

as ordinary seaman or green hand, perhaps in the *Sheffield,* as Malley suggests. Also, that first *Huntsville* voyage does not account for how Enos came to America in the first place. He sailed in the *Huntsville* from Cold Spring Harbor on both occasions, so he must have been there already; thus, he must have been to sea at least once before, on the voyage that ultimately brought him to New York — probably, like so many of his fellow islanders, signing articles or stowing away on an American whaler calling at the Azores, perhaps the *Sheffield.* Having landed on Long Island, he settled in Cold Spring Harbor, part of the town of Huntington. Warrin's speculation is almost certainly correct that Enos likely met his future wife, Susan Brush, while he was ashore briefly between voyages in 1851, because he married her shortly after he returned in the *Huntsville* three years later. He arrived in April 1854, celebrated his 28th birthday in May, was naturalized a U.S. citizen in June, was married in July, and sailed again in September, this time as boatsteerer in the *Sheffield* (1854-59). This was an unusual reversion after having already made a voyage as third mate. On the *Sheffield,* "'Big Manuel' is said to have been a member of 'the heaviest whaleboat crew in the history of American whaling,' numbering, in addition to Enos, three Cold Spring Harbor men, a Hawaiian, and a Montauk Indian, who in the aggregate 'supposedly averaged 225 lbs. [93 kg], a keel snapping total of 1,350 pounds [558 kg] for the six men in the boat's crew!'"[4]

His next two voyages were the ones for which Enos is best remembered in history, literature, and the arts: first mate (1860-64), then captain (1864-69) of the New Bedford bark *Java.* A young sailor from Maine named Joshua Filleborne Beane, who was also on both voyages, later published an articulate narrative in which, in an excess of literary license, he conflated the two voyages into one, mixing up many of his shipmates' names, combining two or more into a single character, and leaving out others entirely (Beane 1905). Thus, while Beane's is one of the most literate, colorful, and informative of all American whaling chronicles, and provides an insightful assessment of Enos in action, as well as a likeness — a small ink drawing by the author himself — it is not strictly factual and perpetrates some misimpressions. One is that Enos was the captain on both voyages: Beane makes no mention of Edward B. Phinney, the real captain during 1860-64 — the voyage on which Enos was actually the first mate and did the scrimshaw of Columbia and Rebecca. Another is the speed and efficiency with which, under Enos's patronage, Beane rocketed from green hand to second mate in the space of a single voyage. That it actually happened over the course of two voyages is remarkable enough; it would have been an incredible achievement in only one. Meanwhile, it is clear that celestial navigation and logbook-keeping were not Captain Enos's strongest suits, and that Washington Fosdick (q.v. in the *Dictionary*), ship's steward, a fellow scrimshaw artist who was thirty years older than any other member of the crew, regularly assisted the captain with his calculations and taught the young, well educated Beane celestial navigation. But Fosdick was ailing (he died on the voyage at age 60 in 1869, and was buried in a shallow grave on the Okhotsk seacoast of Siberia). In the meantime, all along, Captain Enos had increasingly come to rely upon his young protégé, Joshua Beane, whom he elevated to second mate.

Beane speaks about scrimshaw in some detail (see the article on William Martin), as though just about everyone on board were doing it. Oddly, he never mentions Enos in this context. In fact, he refers specifically to only one of the crew in connection with scrimshaw, and never by name but only as "the carpenter" and as "Chips" (the sailors' universal nickname for ship's carpenters).

---

[4] Frank, Op. cit.; quoted from Farwell, Op. Cit., 108, who indicates that the yarn may be apocryphal.

From crew lists it is clear that the man was William Martin (q.v.) from upstate New York, age 29 at the beginning of the voyage — thus a good bit older than most of the men. Beane calls him "the best workman we had on board, and the most industrious," but also an example of a rare compulsion among some whalemen to rid themselves of the fruits of their labor as soon as they arrive on shore, regardless of the time and energy expended in producing them: "'Old Chips'... made it a rule to sell everything that he had manufactured during the season at the first port entered." Beane reflects in greater detail upon another, unnamed shipmate afflicted with the same syndrome:

> *I have known the labors of a six months' cruise to be disposed of for a few dollars or even shillings, and the proceeds spent in drink, in [fewer] hours than the months required to make the articles sacrificed. One case, I remember, where a very ingenious fellow worked all his spare time during a three years' voyage in making an ivory ship. The hull was ten inches [25 cm] long, modeled from a walrus tusk. The spars and sails were carved from whales' teeth. Every block and boom was in its proper place. Altogether it was a nearly perfect piece of workmanship. At the last port before sailing home his appetite for drink got the better of him and he sold this specimen of his handiwork for three pounds ($15.00) and before the day was gone had spent the last farthing.*

After the two *Java* voyages Enos retired from whaling — temporarily, as it turned out — and spent a few years ashore. Warrin catalogues his various business activities during 1859-77: storekeeper; master of the coastwise schooner *Flyaway*, and manager of a tannery and kid-leather factory. According to Farwell, Enos was also master of the merchant schooner *Francis Smith*. In all of these Enos was presumably the sole owner or principal shareholder. Accordingly, in light of Enos's chronic restlessness and evident unhappiness in these ventures, it is difficult not to agree with Farwell's compelling assessment, which is also quoted by Warrin: "Behind the façade of success... lay Captain Enos' permanent failure to cope with life ashore, and real inability to transfer his skills as a whaleman to the supervision of other businesses." Subsequent events suggest that this may have applied equally well to his marriage and home life.

The biggest mystery of his life — now ostensibly solved — concerns misimpressions likely created or encouraged by Enos himself about the endgame of his career and his disappearance. Dissatisfied ashore, he pulled up stakes and went to sea again in 1877 as first mate in the New Bedford bark *George and Susan* (1877-80). A family genealogy insists that he died at sea in 1878[5], which would have been on this voyage; but it is clear that he sailed again in 1880 as first mate in the New Bedford bark *John and Winthrop*, and that he resigned from that berth in 1882 at Talcahuano, Chile, to accept an appointment as captain of the former Dartmouth, Massachusetts bark *Matilda Sears*, now renamed and in Chilean ownership. The usual story is that in 1882 Enos sailed as captain of the *Matilda Sears*, now renamed *Machias Bramas*, and neither ship nor captain was ever heard from again. As Warrin puts it, "Even the most exacting historians of Cold Spring Harbor and its whaling industry have insisted that Enos... disappeared on the high seas with the vessel and crew." However, Warrin uncovered convincing evidence that the story is a complete fabrication. In actual fact, *Machias Bramas* was a garbled misnomer for *Mathieu y Brañas*, namesake of the firm of Chilean whaling agents who took over the *Matilda Sears*; and Warrin cites a Chilean source for the claim that the vessel "continued to

[5] Ancestry.com. awt.ancestry.com/cgi-bin/igm.cgi?op=GET&db=viccork&id=I6021

form part of the small Chilean whaling fleet operating out of Talcahuano until it was finally retired at the port of Paita, Peru, in 1905."[6] Meanwhile, Enos himself changed his name and was reborn into a new life. "Manuel Ignacio Enos de Macedo — as he became known in Talcahuano" — evidently continued whaling out of Talcahuano on vessels owned by Mathieu y Brañas "well into the next decade," and he "met and eventually married a young local woman, María Petronila Araneda, with whom he had six children and thus ended his days as the scion of a Chilean Enos family," though they did not actually marry until after Susan's death in 1904. He died in bed two months short of his 89th birthday in March 1915. Warrin also provides the coda: "Today there is a street in the town [Talcahuano] named in the honor of 'Capitán Enos'... Both the name of Manuel Enos and the seafaring tradition continued with Big Manuel's son, Manuel I. Enos Araneda and the latter's son, Manuel Enos Sosa, who, beginning in 1939, spent almost sixty years at sea, many of them as master of merchant vessels."[7]

Evans, E.T. (fl. circa 19th century). An eight-inch (20 cm) tooth engraved with Masonic symbols, an American eagle, and a fort, with red sealing wax highlights, is signed "E.T. Evans" (reported by Paul Madden). Nothing has been discovered about the artist. Of the many men named Evans on the New Bedford, New London, and Sag Harbor crew lists who had the first initial E, there is no reason to suppose that any had the middle initial T, and nothing to connect them (or any other known whaleman) with this tooth.

Fales, James A. (fl. circa 1847-54). Whaleman from Maine who was possibly the maker of a whale ivory crimper with the saddle carved in a roosting bird motif, a fluted whale ivory jagging wheel, and a wooden handle with non-ferrous studs set into one side forming the stippled inscription "DRACO," and on the other side forming the initials "J.A.F." (reported by Ronald Bourgeault, Northeast Auctions). The only man with the initials J.A.F. or J.F. who served on any of the twelve voyages of the bark *Draco* of Fairhaven and New Bedford (1839-80) was James A. Fales, born circa 1829, of Eastport, Maine. At age 18, in November 1847, Fales obtained a Seaman's Protection Paper in New Bedford, and sailed two days later as a green hand in the whaling bark *President* of Westport (1847-51). He may have made a second whaling voyage in an unidentified vessel (1851-54) prior to going as a seaman or boatsteerer in the *Draco* of New Bedford (1854-57), commanded by Charles Perry Worth (q.v. in the *Dictionary*). This is certainly the vessel and voyage to which the inscription on the scrimshaw refers. Fales may also have served part of a voyage as a boatsteerer in the New Bedford bark *Alice Frazier* (1855-59), where the name appears on the crew list as James Failey. No subsequent voyages have been discovered, nothing has been learned of his later whereabouts, and no kinship relation has been established with the James Fales who was a watch- and clock-maker and nautical instruments dealer at the corner of Elm and Water Streets in New Bedford (the son and namesake of a watchmaker and nautical instruments dealer in Newport, Rhode Island); or the James A. Fales who was born in 1845 at Rockland, Maine, and was married there in 1870.

Fenelon Engraver (fl. circa 1833-48). The name assigned to this hitherto anonymous whaleman-artist, maker of at least seven polychrome engraved works of scrimshaw, derives from a panbone

[6] Sandoval Hernández, "Talcahuano y los últimos balleneros" [Talcahuano and the Last Whalers], n.d.

[7] For these clarifications of Enos's latter-day circumstances, Warren cites: Rafael Enos Aguirre to Warrin, email, 29 Sept 2007 and 18 Mar 2009; Aguirre, "Orígenes e historia de la familia Enos" (private document); and "El Mar fue mi universidad," Manuel Enos Sosa, interview by Macarena Rojas Gómez, in the digital magazine *La Columna*, 19 Sept 2004.

busk (one of three in KNB) that has the name of the New Bedford whaleship *Fenelon* inscribed in a cursive hand. This appears in a riband above the central vignette, a starboard broadside view of a full-rigged ship under sail flying an American ensign at the taffrail, a swallowtail pennant from the foremast, a long pennant (homeward-bound pennant) at the main, and a rectangular flag at the mizzen. The flag is a red St. George's cross on a white field, with a rectangle in the canton that encloses a St. Andrew's cross formed by alternating blue and red triangles. The other vignettes are an angel-in-flight holding a scroll inscribed "Love"; the cursive inscription "When this you see / Remember me", with two arrows, in a scroll frame; a spread eagle with olive branches and arrows in its talons, surmounting a Celtic harp (Brian Boru harp) ornamented with a figurehead-like human-form pillar and leafy garlands (a deferential symbol of Ireland); and a basket of flowers on a table with tablecloth, two cut roses, and a knife. The whole is surmounted by a proscenium arch device enclosing an arrow.

There are six other pieces ascribed to the same hand (of which the identity of authorship was first suggested by Dr. Donald Boger and Rod Cardoza). A second panbone busk (also in KNB) has a similar ship portrait, tabletop flowers-in-a-basket vignette, and proscenium arch, but instead of the spread eagle it has a goose-like dove in flight with an olive branch. A third busk (private collection; illustrated in *The Whalers*, 129), appropriately dubbed the "Unity and Love Busk," recapitulates the distinctive features, notably the proscenium arch, ship portrait, table-with-flowers vignette, and goose-like dove-in-flight; it also has an eagle with Calliope and her lyre, an angel holding symbols of Unity and Love, and the cursive inscription in a scroll, "Remember me when far away." A fourth busk (in KNB) could be called the "Love & Unity" busk: it lacks the proscenium arch but has instead a bent shield with fouled anchor, surmounted by the word "Hope" and surmounting a pair of roses on leafy stems; it lacks the dove-in-flight but has an angel-in-flight holding a scroll inscribed "Love & Unity"; and in place of the other features it has an odd standing figure of Liberty with Liberty Pole, Liberty Cap (on the pole), cornucopia, and roses; and in place of the potted flowers, it has roses and rosebuds on a leafy branch. A fifth busk (illustrated in Ashley, n.p.) has the proscenium arch, ship portrait, spread eagle, Celtic harp, flowering plant, the cursive inscription "When this you see / Remember me" in a curly border, and a riband inscribed "Ship / Mary Ann." It also has a columnar monument on a pedestal with wreaths, surmounted by a patriotic ensemble of a star, shield, flags, and ribbons. Much the same column with pedestal and patriotic array also appears on a sixth panbone busk (Flayderman, 168), which is very similar. It has the same inscription in the same curly border, with the proscenium arch, ship portrait, and spread eagle; it also has an angel-in-flight holding a scroll inscribed "Love" in a cursive hand, and a riband with the name "A.V. Booth." "A.V. Booth" and "Mary Ann" also appear on a tooth by the same hand that incorporates several of the characteristic features and is polychrome engraved in the same style: on the obverse, the broadside portrait of a full-rigged ship under sail, surmounted by the inscription "SHIP / M. ANN" in a riband, a United States flag deployed as bunting with the same unidentified St. George's cross flag that appears on the *Fenelon* busk, and "A.V. Booth" in a riband, with a decorative olive-branch border at the top and a circumferential checkerboard band at the bottom. On the other side it has the goose-like dove-in-flight with olive branch, and the inscription "UNITY / LOVE" in ribands atop and below an angel-in-flight, all surmounting a flowering plant in a basket on a table with a tablecloth, with the borders continued from the other side.

Because the name A.V. Booth appears on one of the busks and on the tooth inscribed *Mary Ann*, those pieces were previously thought to be by an artist named A.V. Booth. However, there is no record of an A.V. Booth in the whale fishery from any port, nor any man by that name in the census records of New England in the middle nineteenth century. "A.V. Booth" was, in fact, Ariadne Victory Booth, born in 1818 at Middleborough, Massachusetts, the older sister of four, or possibly five whaling brothers, and presumably the intended recipient of some of the scrimshaw. The most likely maker of the scrimshaw was one of the Booth Brothers (q.v.), but it is not clear which. Francis M. Booth, the fourth brother, made two voyages in the ship *Fenelon* (1842-47); Amasa A. Booth, who was probably the fifth brother, was the only man named Booth ever to have served aboard the *Mary Ann* (1854-55); but based on the evidence at hand, the three older brothers cannot be ruled out, including Philander Gates Booth, who was the only career whaleman in the family.

The ship *Fenelon*, 328 tons, was built in 1828 at Kennebunk, Maine, entered the New Bedford fleet in 1833, and was condemned abroad in 1848. During that period she made eight whaling voyages under five different captains. Crew lists survive for several of these, yielding the names of more than 150 officers and crew (including Luther Southworth, q.v.); and four logbooks and journals are known. The name of the ship is from a place in France, Fénelon in Périgord, the site of a well known château and birthplace of the Roman Catholic cleric and theologian François de Salignac de la Mothe Fenelon (1651-1715). The ship *Mary Ann*, 335 tons, was built at Fairhaven in 1838 and made six successful whaling voyages from that port from 1838 to 1864, when the vessel was withdrawn from whaling and sold to Quebec.

Fernandes Silva, Ernesto ["Ernesto Flores"] (1906-1987). Coastal whaleman and whaling-launch mechanic at a shore-station on the island of Pico in the Azores (reported by Gomes Vieira, 2003, 105). His work in whale ivory and bone "included liqueur sets with carafes, ashtrays, pipes, cigarette holders, and chess, domino, and checker sets." The son of José Gonçalves da Silva, who was also an ivory carver, and Isabel Fernades Silva, Ernesto was born on Pico, and likely influenced the career of his younger brother, João Fernandes Leal ["João Flores"] (1919-1996), a vocational carver and engraver of whale ivory (reported by Gomes Vieira, 2003, 133).

Fidalgo Baptista, José Francisco ["Capitão Fidalgo"] (1841-1929). American merchant seaman and sometime whaleman originally from the island of Pico in the Azores. On the basis of family provenance, Gomes Vieira (2003, 152f) reports that "he worked a great deal of ivory, fashioning utilitarian items, such as doorknobs, furniture handles, napkin rings, clothes-pegs [clothespins], etc." The son of José Francisco Fidalgo and Felicidade de Coração de Jesus, he was born in 1841 at Silveira, on the Island of Pico, and at age 15 stowed away on an unidentified Yankee whaler (probably using an alias, now untraceable), attended school in New England, was awarded a diploma from the Boston Nautical School (now called the Massachusetts Maritime Academy) and served as a mate on a series of merchantmen. Gomes Vieira further reports that during the American Civil War Fidalgo "was the whaling captain they chose to escort the bark *F.B. Phillips*, much to the envy of most of the whaling captains of his time"; and that "he went on to command the *Valentine Rose*." However, there is no record that Fidalgo was ever a deepwater whaling captain, the *F.B. Phillips* and the *Valentine Rose* remain obscure, and the alleged Civil War incident is undocumented and unexplained. (It should also be mentioned that Valentine Rosa was the Azorean-born captain of the New Bedford barks *Canton 2d* and *Morning Star* during 1907-14.) Sometime after the Civil War Fidalgo married and retired to Horta, on Fayal, where he fathered five daughters and evidently continued scrimshaw-making.

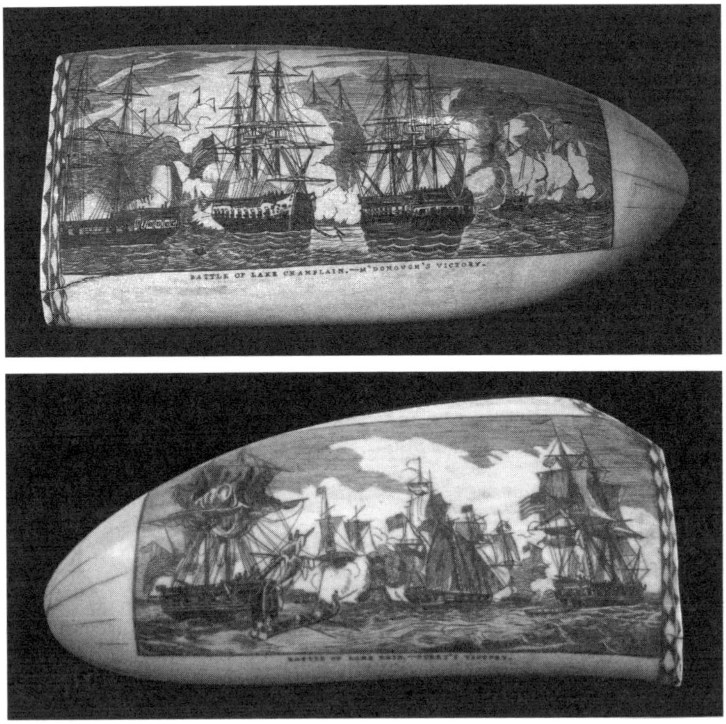

Fig. 9a. **N.S. Finney's War of 1812 naval engagements**, circa 1847-51: a pair of teeth with superb polychrome renditions, labeled "Battle of Lake Champlain — M'Donough's Victory"; and "Battle of Lake Erie — Perry's Victory." Judge Paul Vardeman discovered that both battle scenes were copied after wood engravings by William Croome in *The Book of the Navy* by John Frost (New York, 1843). The book was also the source for Finney's portraits of the commodores (see below) and for Nathaniel Currier's much larger "Battle of Lake Champlain" lithograph (New York, 1846). Harold H. Kynett Collection, Mystic Seaport; illustrated in Malley 1983, opposite page 81.

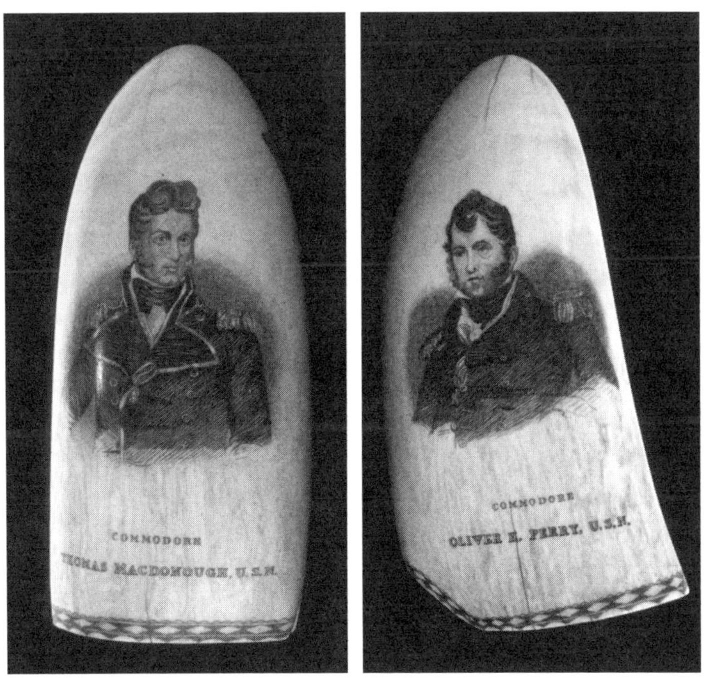

Fig. 9b. **Portraits of Commodores Thomas MacDonough and Oliver Hazard Perry**, the heroes of the battles of Lake Chaplain and Lake Erie, copied from contemporaneous sources, adorn the backs of Finney's War of 1812 teeth. These were produced at the tail end of Finney's whaling career, as second mate of the New Bedford bark *Bramin*, circa 1851, a few years before he started doing scrimshaw portraiture as a living. Harold H. Kynett Collection, Mystic Seaport.

* **Finney, N.S.** (fl. circa 1830-79). Though he is unquestionably one of the greatest scrimshaw artists of all time — some would say *the* greatest — Finney himself has been a perpetual enigma with many aspects of his life and career frustratingly elusive. His date of birth is differently reported in various official documents; he misrepresented his age when he signed articles to go whaling; his career is incompletely recorded in the whaling annals; the U.S. Census caught him only occasionally; there is almost no record of him at all during several years' residence in the Pacific; the San Francisco City Directories report his later whereabouts only intermittently and without adequate specificity; his name is as often misstated in period newspapers as not; and his unique career as a commercial scrimshaw artist has been ill documented at best. However, since the publication of *More Scrimshaw Artists* (1998), collector and scrimshaw historian Michael Gerstein has painstakingly unearthed a remarkable volume of hitherto unknown details that in the aggregate penetrate the mysteries of N.S. Finney to a greater degree than ever before. These have enabled a partial reconstruction of his career as whaleman and artist, resulting in a more complete picture of his activities and whereabouts than might hitherto have seemed possible.[8]

Finney's scrimshaw divides into two discreet periods. The first is his 27 years as an active whaleman, from 1830 to 1857, when he was making pictures on sperm whale teeth (no walrus tusks by his hand from this era have been discovered). The second is his two decades as a self-invented commercial scrimshaw artist in San Francisco, from 1858 to 1879, when he was executing commissions and working primarily but not exclusively in walrus ivory (a few sperm whale teeth and two 40-inch panbones are known). His scrimshaw comes in monochrome, polychrome, or monochrome with polychrome highlights, always meticulously engraved. Over time he increasingly used stippling to achieve subtle textures and shading. And while he was a superb copyist, as far as is known he was a copyist only: no original images of his have been identified. Apart from a few inscriptions — surprisingly few, in fact — all of his work consists of images recycled from illustrations in books, magazines, and documents, or faithfully copied from studio photographs.

Nathaniel Sylvester Finney was born in Plymouth, Massachusetts, on October 29, 1813, the son of Josiah Finney and Sally née Sylvester. He embarked on his maiden whaling voyage at age 16 in the ship *Hercules* of New Bedford, to the Brazil Banks (1830-31), then went to the Pacific in the whaleships *Charles Drew* of Fairhaven (1831-34) and *Lancaster* of New Bedford (1834-35). For reasons unspecified, he deserted the *Charles Drew* in Hawaii. (The captain on that voyage was fellow scrimshaw-maker Rodolphus Nye Swift, q.v. in the *Dictionary*; see also the article on R.G.N. Swift.) His activities over the next twelve years are not fully known. Whalemen "on the beach" in Hawaii in that era — including not only Americans, but also Australians, Germans, Englishmen, Scots, Polynesian Islanders not native to Hawaii, and, beginning in 1842, even a few Japanese — could earn a living by shipping for seasonal passages in American and Honolulu-registry whaleships. (Herman Melville, after deserting the *Acushnet* in the Marquesas in 1842, was a roving whaleman-and-farmhand-for-hire for a couple of years in the Pacific.) Finney may have been a whaleman-for-hire at this stage, which his later string of partial whaling cruises from Honolulu seems to bear out. Around this time he may also have tried his hand at art for pay, which was to become his trade in California a few years later. The records become clear again in 1847 when, back in New Bedford,

---

[8] Michael Gerstein's research is currently comprised of files, photocopies, field notes, charts, analytic diagrams, and correspondence, assembled over a period of years. Most recently he has been assisted by Dr. Jack H.T. Chang and a small, nationwide discussion group, in tracing Finney's pictorial sources in books and magazines. Some of the material has been presented at the annual Scrimshaw Weekends held at NBWM each May. Copies of the pictures and documents are housed in the Scrimshaw Forensics Laboratory® at the NBWM Research Library, and one hopes that sometime soon Mr. Gerstein will produce a biography and comprehensive catalogue raisonné of Finney's work.

Fig. 10. **N.S. Finney copied "The Sisters"** from the March 1843 issue of *Graham's Magazine*, where it was engraved by partners Thomas B. Welch and Adam B. Walter of Philadelphia as an illustration for a poem entitled "The Sisters" by Robert Morris, after a much older picture by the seventeenth-century Scottish painter John Michael Wright. The scrimshaw was a bequest of Nathan C. Hathaway in 1923 and the print was a gift of Dr. Jack H.T. Chang in 2010, collection of the New Bedford Whaling Museum (photos by Richard Donnelly).

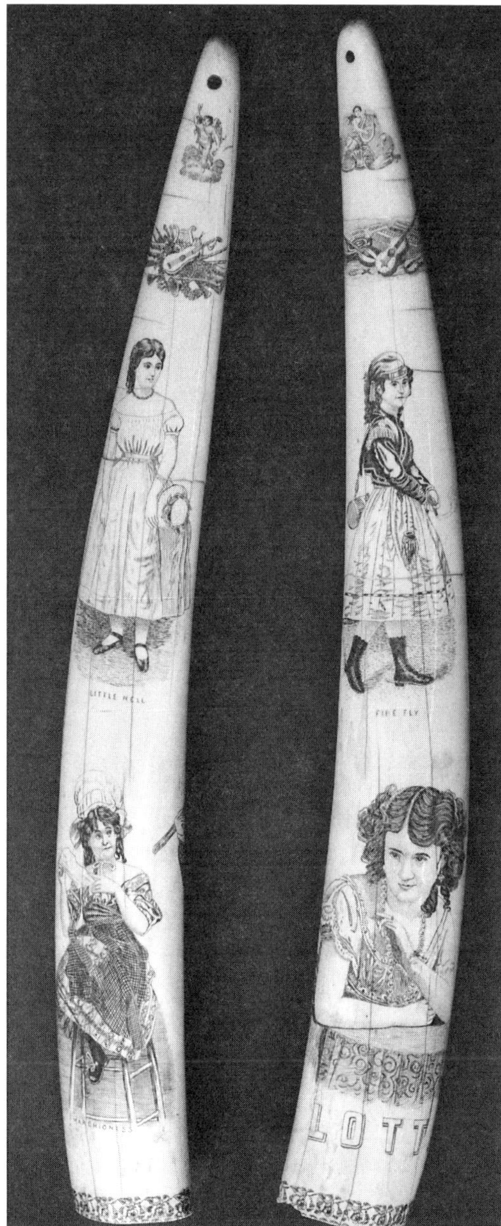

Fig. 11. **Walrus tusks by N.S. Finney** from his years as a commercial artist in San Francisco, when he was making a living doing scrimshaw on commission. This exemplary pair showcases Lotta Crabtree (1847-1924), a tumultuously popular stage performer closely identified with San Francisco, in a few of her characteristc costumes, faithfully copied from a poster compiled from illustrations in newspapers, magazines, and playbills, beautifully executed by Finney with near-photographic precision. Collection of Michael Gerstein.

he shipped as second mate of the bark *Bramin* (1847-51). It was on this voyage that he appears to have engraved his splendid pair of polychrome scenes of the War of 1812 Battle of Lake Erie, with portraits of Commodores Thomas McDonough and Oliver Hazard Perry on the backs, brought home by Captain Francis Butts of the *Bramin* (MSM; unattributed in Malley 1983, 74f and opp. 81). In fact, much of Finney's finest work on whale teeth must have been done around this time or shortly afterwards, in the 1840s and '50s: his "Sisters" tooth (NBWM) is based on a prototype published in *Graham's Magazine* in March 1843, and the model for his famous "Morn of Life" teeth (NBWM and private collections) was a steel engraving by Henry Cooke (1819-1890), after a painting by Sir William Charles Ross, R.A. (1795-1860), published in 1850. By this time Finney had developed the fancy urn-with-flowers motif that appears as a kind of trademark on the backs of some of his work. His next berth after the *Bramin* was second mate of the New Bedford ship *Rodman*, on which he sailed in October 1851, probably with the prior understanding that he was intending to work his passage back to Hawaii. Accordingly, he was discharged at Honolulu "at his own request." In November 1856 he signed articles to be first mate of the New Bedford ship *Bartholomew Gosnold*, which was then calling at Honolulu, again intending only a one-year circuit in the Pacific. He received a discharge from the *Gosnold* at Honolulu in December 1857, and that was the end of Finney's whaling career.

The following year a newspaper article in the San Francisco *Evening Bulletin* described a "curious caving on a whale's jawbone," to be raffled off for charity, "executed by Nathaniel T. [sic] Finney, mate of the whaling ship *Bartholmew Gosnold*," depicting "the civil heroes of the American Revolution," including George Washington, Thomas Jefferson, Gouverneur Morris, Richard Henry Lee, John Jay, Patrick Henry, John Adams, John Hancock, John Routledge, James Otis, Samuel Adams, and Benjamin Franklin (in MMV). By this time he had evidently settled in San Francisco. The 1860 U.S. Census lists Nathl. S. Finney, age as 47, sailor, living there with his older brother Josiah, a carpenter, Josiah's wife and two children, and a "master builder" named S.H. Bushee, age 31. A second panbone features a portrait of John C. Henan, "the Benicia Boy," the American bareknuckles champion in boxing stance, copied from the April 14, 1860 issue of *Frank Leslie's Illustrated Newspaper* (KNB). It must have been done shortly after the picture was published, while the biggest bout of the century was still headline news: Henan battled the English champion Thomas Sayers (1826-1865) to a hard-won draw on April 17, 1860, just outside London. The same panbone also has faithful, same-size copies of "The Constitution and the Guerriere," from Abel Bowen's *Naval Monument* (Boston, 1816), after a painting by Michele Felice Corné; a handsome American spread eagle; and a fashion plate of a woman and a running child, entitled "Promenade Costume & Boys Dress," from the June 1858 issue of *Harper's New Monthly Magazine*. The portraits of Union heroes — notably Abraham Lincoln, Ulysses S. Grant (both in uniform and in civilian attire), and William Tecumseh Sherman — for which Finney first became known, thanks primarily to three large tusks now in MSM that came from Abe Warner's Cobweb Palace saloon (described in detail in the *Dictionary* and in Malley 1983, 82f), are evidence that by the time of the Civil War Finney had already adopted his standard format of stacking portraits and patriotic vignettes vertically on walrus tusks and pairs of tusks. His style remained consistent throughout the remainder of his career even though his inventory of images varied: highly defined portraits copied from photographs, probably done on commission; pictures of show-business celebrities, usually in costume; mythological figures, genre subjects, and decorative patriotic and musical vignettes, all brilliant copy-work, mostly on walrus tusks but also a few on teeth. Whether such pictures were done on commission or on speculation is not known. While a few of them have found their way into KNB, MFA, and MSM, the majority are held in private collections. There are also two sperm whale teeth "blanks" in KNB: a matched pair, highly polished, signed on the backs, with one of Finney's characteristic circumferential borders along the bottoms, evidently prepared in advance, in anticipation of a commission he never got to before he died, which was on April 19, 1879.

Fish, John G. (fl. circa 1860s-70s). Merchant captain from Maine who, as master of the ship *Ada A. Frye* in 1869, engraved a tooth with an elaborate profusion of mathematical, architectural, and geometric symbols of Freemasonry, including stylized depictions of builders' tools — an example of scrimshaw made by a mariner working outside of the whale fishery and a prime specimen of Masonic iconography on scrimshaw (illustrated in Kevin D. Murphy, ed., *Folk Art in Maine*, 2008, 57). The scrimshaw came with two bonus dividends. The first is an ironclad provenance from Laura E. Fish, the Captain's granddaughter, who donated the tooth to the Farnsworth Art Museum in Rockland, Maine, in 1972, together with a painting of the *Ada A. Frye*. The second bonus is the scrimshaw-maker's journal of the *Ada A. Frye*, in which Captain Fish provides rare documentation of the time and means of its creation. Four months at sea, on a passage from Boston to San Francisco by way of the Straits of Magellan, in an entry dated April 19, 1869, he not only mentions working on the tooth, but specifies that it was "drawn in pencil and cut with a pen knife" (Farnsworth exhibition label, originally submitted by Thomas Conley). John G. Fish was born in Maine circa 1831, lived in South Hope, Knox County, worked both as sailor and mill hand, married a woman named Sarah around 1855, and had one son, Elwin (AKA Elwyn), born in 1861. He left off seafaring in the 1870s and moved his family to Boston, where he worked in the boat- and shipbuilding industry, in which Elwin was employed as a shop clerk. When the Captain retired he and Sarah moved back to South Hope, where they were still living in 1910. Elwin became an engineer and then a plant manager in the rubber industry, married a woman named Nellie, and lived in Bristol, Rhode Island, and Elkhart, Indiana. Their daughter, Laura, donor of the scrimshaw in 1972, was born in Boston in 1886 and died in Rockland, Maine, in 1974.

Fisher, — (fl. circa 1840s-50s). A typed label that was already pasted on the back of a mounted pair of polychrome engraved teeth when they were acquired by NBWM in 1919 erroneously makes the claim, "Scrimshaw by Capt Henry Fisher Ship Splendid." The scrimshaw did not come directly from a family legacy, but from the large private collection of Andrew Snow, assembled in the late nineteenth and early twentieth centuries and bequeathed to the museum. The ostensible provenance notwithstanding, there is no record of any Henry Fisher being the captain of any American whaling vessel. There were several whaling captains surnamed Fisher whose given names are not recorded, but none of these was ever captain of a whaler named *Splendid* (see Lund 2001, 123f). Two captains of whaleships named *Splendid* had the surname Fisher: John Potter Fisher (q.v.), who commanded the ship *Splendid* of Edgartown, Massachusetts, during 1851-54; and Thomas N. Fisher, who was replacement captain on that same vessel sometime during 1862-67. Henry B. *Fordham* commanded the ship *Splendid* of Cold Spring Harbor, New York, during 1848-51. Hence the scrimshaw could logically have been made by someone who meets any of three criteria. If the name Fisher in association with command of the *Splendid* be taken as the centrally significant criterion, then either John Potter Fisher or Thomas N. Fisher of the Edgartown *Splendid* could be the man. If it seems more likely that the name Captain Henry *Fisher* of the *Splendid* is a corruption of Captain

Henry *Fordham* of the *Splendid,* then Henry B. Fordham (q.v.) of Cold Spring Harbor would be the one. Or the scrimshaw could simply have been made by a sailor named Henry Fisher who was never a captain, who may or may not have served in a whaleship named *Splendid,* and who was inadvertently promoted to "Captain" Fisher in consequence of the usual kind of ancestor inflation that occurs when little-understood stories get passed down orally through several generations. To complicate matters still further, when one of the boatsteerers in the *Ospray* of New Bedford was Henry Fisher (1854-57), one of the other boatsteerers was named Charles Fisher, and the captain was Timothy Fisher. Without additional information there is simply no way definitively to determine who made scrimshaw, but the most likely candidates are John Potter Fisher and Henry Fordham (qq.v.).

* **Fisher, Henry** — see **Fisher, John Potter**; and **Fordham, Henry C.**

Fisher, John Potter (fl. circa 1830-58). Noted in the *Dictionary* article on Henry Fisher are a pair of teeth polychrome engraved with symbolic figures of Liberty and Justice, mounted on a wooden stand ornamented with a whale ivory fouled anchor; in NBWM. One tooth has a standing female figure of Liberty with staff, Liberty Cap, the obligatory American flag draped over her left shoulder, and an American shield at her right hand; the other has a seated female figure of Justice wearing a wreath, holding scales in her right hand and a sword in her left; mounted together on a chamfered wooden stand, ornamented with a fouled anchor carved out of whale ivory. A typescript label affixed to the back of the stand erroneously identifies the artist as Captain Henry Fisher aboard the whaleship *Splendid* of Edgartown, Massachusetts, thus dating the scrimshaw to circa 1851-54 — erroneously because nobody named Henry Fisher was ever captain of the *Splendid* or any other American whaling vessel; clearly, the provenance has the names confused. The actual captain of the *Splendid* on the 1851-54 voyage was not *Henry* Fisher, but *John Potter* Fisher; and he was not the only man named Fisher to command the *Splendid.* A man named *Thomas N.* Fisher was one of two relief captains on the *Splendid*'s 1862-67 voyage: the original captain, James B. Huxford, left the ship in mid-passage on account of illness; his replacement was Captain Cleveland, whose given name is not known and who died during the voyage. Thomas N. Fisher was Cleveland's replacement; and as it turned out, Thomas Fisher *also* died on the voyage and was replaced by yet *another* relief captain, Elial T. Fish. (To complicate matters still further, Elial belonged to the Fish family on Long Island that later changed its name to Fisher.) Subsequent research has shown that the figures of Liberty and Justice on the scrimshaw were copied directly from prototypes in *Gleason's Pictorial Drawing Room Companion,* which was founded in 1851 and became *Ballou's Pictorial* in 1854; or from the masthead of Gleason's Line-of-Battle Ship, where they were published together again in 1859. These Boston magazines and their New York counterparts, *Frank Leslie's Illustrated News* and *Harper's Weekly,* were widely circulated in the homeland seaports and throughout the Pacific; and it happens that the 1851-54 voyage of the *Splendid,* commanded by John Potter Fisher, coincided with *Gleason's* ascent to popularity. It is also generally the case that provenance, family tradition, collectors' lore, and amateur research are far more likely to result in confusion about a maker's given name than to mistake the name of a ship, especially a name so simple and memorable as *Splendid.* So, presuming that the basic elements of the provenance — Captain Fisher, *Splendid,* 1850s — were correct as received with the scrimshaw when it was bequeathed to NBWM in 1919, and in the absence of any indication otherwise, two factors combine to make it clear that John Potter Fisher is the only viable candidate among the three Fishers at issue here. Henry was never a captain and appears never to have been aboard the *Splendid*. Thomas was captain of the *Splendid* for only a very short time and died before the end of the voyage, thus making it unlikely that he would have had time to do any scrimshaw, and in any case his death preceded the customary homeward-bound scrimshaw-making activities. Even more to the point, John Potter Fisher was captain of the *Splendid* when *Gleason's Pictorial* was launched and when it soared to a popularity that persisted throughout the voyage and into the magazine's next incarnation as *Ballou's*, until it shut down in 1857.

To complicate matters further, however, there were two captains named John P. Fisher, each of whom was sometimes recorded simply as John Fisher, and a possibly third captain named John Fisher who had no distinguishing middle initial; and they all had overlapping whaling careers in the 1840s and '50s. John Potter Fisher, sometime master of the *Splendid*, had been skipper of two New Bedford ships, the *India* (1845-48) and *Abraham H. Howland* (1848-54), then commanded two from Edgartown: the *Splendid* (1851-54), on which he is credited with having made the scrimshaw; and the *Navigator* (1854-58). He may or may not have been the John P. Fisher who was relief captain of the *Bartholomew Gosnold* of New Bedford sometime during 1854-58: though he was presumably otherwise occupied (as captain of the *Navigator*), so was the *other* John P. Fisher, as first mate in the *Osceola 3d* (1854-56) and *General Pike* (1856-59). Presumably, the John P. Fisher late of the *Splendid* might have been available to take over the *Gosnold* briefly in 1858, and the other John P. Fisher between voyages briefly in 1856. On the other hand, the whole matter of the *Gosnold* is muddled, as some of the official records (such as the crew list in NBFPL) are also equivocal and list John Fisher not as relief captain but as the captain from the time of sailing. Unfortunately, while several logbooks and journals of various voyages of the *Gosnold* are extant, none is known to survive for this particular voyage. More is actually known about the early career of the younger John P. Fisher, the one who did not make the scrimshaw: green hand in the *Benjamin Tucker* (1846-49), boatsteerer in the *Triton* (1849-51), second mate in the *Citizen* (1851-54), first mate in the *Osceola 3d* (1854-56) and *General Pike* (1856-59), and finally master of the *General Pike* (1859-63) and *William Gifford* (1863-68).

Fisher, Thomas N. — see **Fisher, John Porter.**

Fleetwing Engraver (fl. circa 1877-81). His identity is not known, but according to a credible provenance he was originally an actual engraver by trade. Each one of two granddaughters of Adeline Heppingstone (q.v. in the *Dictionary*), wife of Captain John Heppingstone, inherited a pair of tusks, pertaining to which a handwritten provenance states: "These tusks were carved or scrimshawed aboard my grandfather[']s whaling bark *Fleetwing* by one of the sailors in the Ar[c]tic Ocean about 1878. He was a steel engraver who had to go [to] sea on account of liquor. This is as told to me by my mother who was on board the ship at the time." (The mother in question was John and Adeline Heppingstones' daughter, also named Adeline, born in 1868. She made at least three whaling voyages with her parents; in fact, her older brother John died aboard the bark *Julian* at age five in 1869.) On the voyage in question, the *Fleetwing* sailed from New Bedford in November 1877 and returned to San Francisco in October 1880. No logbook or journal is known to survive from the voyage, but from the catch statistics of Heppingstone's 1870 voyage in the *Julian* out of Honolulu (Hegarty, 1959, 50), and from daughter Adeline's journal of the 1880-81 voyage of the *Fleetwing* (NBWM) that Heppingstone customarily took many walrus as a matter of course, so too the several other whalers with whom he sailed in company; and that the oil and the ivory from the *Fleetwing* were sold on the San Francisco market (see Appendix VI).

Each pair of tusks is engraved on one side only with vignettes that appear to have been copied or traced from wood-engraved originals, probably from illustrations in magazines. One pair has a total of six female figures with polychrome highlights, three on each tusk: two bust portraits and four full-lengths, each of the latter wearing what appear to be theatrical or operatic costumes, each standing on a checkerboard floor or stage. The other pair has eight images, three on each tusk surmounting a much larger, dominant image at the base: two female bust portraits, three full-lengths of children at play (one with the standard rolling hoop), and one three-quarter-length figure in what may be a military uniform, surmounting (on one tusk) a charming pair of young boys in stereotypical sailor suits, standing in the masthead; and (on the other tusk) a young girl wearing a sailor suit, seated, holding a sailboat model. In standpoint of style and layout, if not workmanship, the four tusks are very much "in the manner of" the great master, N.S. Finney (q.v.), with the images stacked vertically and not connected, but here much less refined. In fact, rather than engravings on steel or copper, the execution much more closely resembles wood engraving, which could of course be a result of the medium, or wood engraving could have been the maker's actual original trade.

A list of the outward-bound crew survives in NBPS; however, a careful examination of what little background data is available about each did not turn up any evidence of a likely refugee from the engraver's trade. Most of the Americans were career mariners from southeastern Massachusetts and adjacent Rhode Island whose whereabouts at sea are accounted for from early youth, and most of the other Americans were too young to have been veterans of a previous career. The ten immigrants from the Azores, Cape Verde, and the West Indies may justifiably be eliminated as extremely unlikely former steel engravers. This leaves John F. Duryea, age 24, from Port Jefferson, Long Island; R.N. Kirk, 25, from St. Johnsbury, Vermont; John McGaul, 27, a Scots-born resident of Boston; and four European foreigners: Frank Luke, 23, from Bohemia; Frank Marth, 26, from Zurich, Switzerland; Vincent Miguey, 40, French; and Rudolph May, 50, originally from Prussia. Any of these could conceivably be the maker, who probably made only the one voyage. (However, none of their names appears in any of the basic compendia of painters, sculptors, and engravers published in English, French, German, or Dutch.) On the other hand, it seems possible, without seriously compromising the claim that the scrimshaw was done "about 1878," that the tusks were engraved on the next voyage of the *Fleetwing* (1880-81), of which John Heppingstone was also the captain and had his wife Adeline and daughter Adeline aboard. Unfortunately, no crew list of that voyage has yet surfaced for examination.

Flinn, Dana (allegedly active circa 1843-51). The name Captain Dana Flinn is connected with a series of scrimshaw fakes that were inadvertently published in the catalogue of a prominent and respectable auction house. As such, they warrant specific mention here as a caution, because — despite that as soon as the fakery was reported the auctioneer immediately withdrew the scrimshaw from the auction itself — the beautifully printed catalogue endures, threatening to hoodwink future historians and collectors.

Captain Dana Flinn was supposedly a New Bedford whaling master to whose hand several scrimshaw pieces are attributed in Skinner, 5 Nov. 2006. These include three polychrome engraved sperm whale teeth, "one depicting a three-masted whaling ship on the sea inscribed 'New Bedford' on a scroll at the bottom over the year '1843,' the reverse showing a blue and red flag over the inscription 'Ship ESSEX Sperm Whaling off the coast of New Holland' over the initials 'D.F.'; the second depicting a blue and red flag centered with a large 'D' over an American sailing vessel on a blue sea over the initials 'D.F.,' the reverse depicting several hoisted signal flags, the sides inscribed 'SHIP ESSEX 18/ NEW BEDFORD 43'; the third depicting a sailor and a harpoon flanking a large oval reserve surmounted with a bottle labeled 'GROG,' within the oval are the initials 'D.F.' over a three-masted sailing vessel, the reverse depicting a possible flaming torch, the tip engraved 'Sailor's Rights,' all three heightened with red and blue sealing wax, (age cracks)... " (lot #450). A fourth tooth is monochrome engraved with an unusual whaling scene, with a whaleboat going onto a monolithic breeching sperm whale, a whaleship in the immediate background, and the initials "D.F."; and a fifth tooth that has a broadside portrait of a full-rigged ship under partial sail, possibly by the same hand (lot #451). A small, oblong panbone panel "depicting a whaling scene with three sailing vessels flanking a whaleboat with figures poised to harpoon a sperm whale, above the inscription 'Capt. Dana Flinn N.B.,'" has polychrome highlights and the date 1851 (lot #453). There are also four logbook stamps carved out of whale ivory. One has the head of a sperm whale carved on each end, a three-masted schooner on the side, and the inscription "split case side," flanked by two five-pointed stars; another is a "carved sperm whale stamp with medial disk engraved 'ESSEX' over inscriptions 'DF' and 'SPERM'"; the third has "a carved sperm whale head on one end and a right whale figure on the other end, the handle inscribed 'F. FLINN,' and 'SPLIT'"; and the fourth has "a flag carved in relief on the bottom, the side with an engraved flag and the initials 'D.F.'" (lot #457).

There is no record of any whaling captain of any nationality named Dana Flinn, nor of any whaling captain with the surname Flinn (or Flynn), from New Bedford or any other port. It can be stated categorically that if there ever was a Dana Flinn on an American whaleship, he was not the captain. That no record has been found of anyone named Dana Flinn having served in the American whale fishery in any capacity from any port is not in itself damning or surprising, as crew lists for the outports are often absent or incomplete. However, there appears to be no census record, nor any other record, of anyone named Dana Flinn anywhere in the United States prior to circa 1880. Moreover, the only whaler *Essex* active in 1843 was a bark, not a ship; her registry port was Bristol, Rhode Island, not New Bedford; her 1842-43 voyage was commanded by Obadiah B. Davoll, not Dana Flinn; and it was a voyage to the Atlantic Ocean grounds that went nowhere near New Holland (the Indian Ocean coast of Western Australia). Added to which, the iconography of the pictorial pieces is suspiciously derivative, the inscriptions are trite and overdone, the calligraphy is forced, awkward, and unconvincing, the naval architecture equivocal and inexpert, the craqueleur (where it appears) is suspicious, and the whaling scene with the initials DF is certainly twentieth-century work. The whale stamps are even less compelling, not the least like any of the many authenticated specimens of sailor-made whale stamps. These shortfalls are not merely the results of bad draftsmanship or amateur craftsmanship, but, rather, they are serious errors of which no whaleman and no professional mariner, no matter how callow and unskilled, would be guilty. It appears that all of the pieces in all four lots are frauds: not antique, not whalemen's work, not sailors' work, and not what they superficially appear to be. The scrimshaw is of no aesthetic or historical consequence, and there is no evidence that Dana Flinn ever existed.

* **Folger, David** (fl. circa 1788-1805) — see **Folger, David [II]**

Folger, David [II] (fl. circa 1840s-80s). The *Dictionary* article on David Folger concerns a "Doll's bed of mahogany 'with scrimshaw finials,' said to have been made by Captain David Folger for his daughter (Flayderman, 236)." Based on Flayderman's declaration that the maker was a *captain* and the tacit implication that he was a *whaling* captain (of which there was only one eligible candidate of that name), the maker was erroneously identified as Captain David Folger of Nantucket, who was active circa 1788-1805, even though the type and style of the scrimshaw seemed out of phase with those dates. In fact, the piece is substantially later. It came into the NHA collection in 2003, when the maker was erroneously claimed to be a later Captain David Folger (1822-1897) and the recipient identified as his daughter Lydia. It is an outstanding example of scrimshaw doll furniture: a four-poster bed with plain whale ivory finials, a miniature crazy-quilt with a full set of linens, and a bisque doll, ostensibly original to the ensemble. However, there was no later Captain David Folger and the dates were incorrectly reported. The actual maker must have been the David Folger who was a cooper on Nantucket, where he was born on 3 September 1820, the son of William and Lucy Folger. He married Lydia Maria Wilber of Nantucket on 16 July 1844. Their daughter, also named Lydia Maria, was born circa 1847 (not in 1856, as is sometimes reported in the genealogical records). (According to the U.S. Census, she was three years old in 1850, but there her name and her mother's are both erroneously listed as Lydia Ann. She was correctly reported as Lydia M., age 13 in 1860 and age 23 in 1870.) David Folger the cooper may or may not be the David Folger of Nantucket who served as a Paymaster Steward in the Union Navy during the Civil War from August 1864 to June 1865. But, in any case, by 1870 he had become a farmer, still living on Nantucket with his wife and only child, Lydia, who was still unmarried and had become a teacher. Folger died not in 1897 (as originally reported by NHA) but in June 1908. In fact, in June 1900, at age 79, widowed and still living with his daughter, he was still working, now as an insurance agent. (The confusion in death dates may arise from the fact that his wife was born on 8 September 1821 and died on either 17 August 1896 or 20 May 1897.) Whether Folger was ever a ship's cooper on a whaling voyage is not known, but he appears never to have been a captain of anything. Given the family chronology and the year of the daughter's birth, the scrimshaw was almost certainly made in the early 1850s, probably on shore in Nantucket, using some of the Island's perpetually abundant inflow of whale ivory.

Fordham, Henry C. (fl. circa 1839-48). Whaling master of Sag Harbor and Cold Spring Harbor, Long Island, New York, who is one of two "most likely" makers of a mounted pair of polychrome engraved teeth (in NBWM since 1919), whereof an old typed label pasted on the back makes the claim, "Scrimshaw by Capt Henry Fisher Ship Splendid." There is no record of there ever being a Captain Henry Fisher on any American whaling vessel (see the article on — Fisher). John Potter Fisher was master of the ship *Splendid* of Edgartown, Massachusetts, during 1851-54, and Thomas N. Fisher was a relief captain on that same vessel sometime during 1862-67. However, Henry B. *Fordham* was captain of the ship *Splendid* of Cold Spring Harbor during 1848-51, and this may be the source of confusion leading to the erroneous attribution to Henry *Fisher* rather than to Henry *Fordham*. Captain Fordham was born circa 1807, lived at Southampton, L.I., with his wife Harriet and two children, and commanded whaling voyages in the ships *Romulus* (1839-40) and *Fanny* (1841-43) of Sag Harbor and *Splendid* of Cold Spring Harbor (1844-48). (His name is usually given in the whaling records as Henry *B.* Fordham, but it is clear from his journal of the *Fanny* in KNB, and from the U.S. Census records, that he was Henry *Charles* Fordham, son of Nathan and Mary Howell Fordham, born March 16, 1807, married to Harriet E. Cook in 1829.) In 1849 he joined the multitudes of Forty-Niners heading out to the California Gold Rush, and by 1850 was encamped with his late-teenage son Nathan among a bunch of other New England mariners at the Middle Fork of the American River in El Dorado, California. In fact, the 1850 U.S. Census lists Henry twice, once as a seaman still living on Long island, where Nathan's age is given as 15, and as a miner in California, where for some reason Nathan's stated age is 19. The records are unclear whether Henry died in 1853 or 1863, but he is absent from the U.S. Census of 1860.

Formiga—see **Garcia da Silva, Francisco**

Fortes, Jayme [Jaime; James] (fl. circa 1917). He was one of four brothers and their uncle who came to New Bedford in ones and twos from the island of São Nicolão (St. Nicholas) in the Cape Verdes, in the early twentieth century, and commemorated their 'Stateside reunion on a remarkable, oversize, stipple-engraved sperm whale tooth associated with his voyage in the whaling schooner *John R. Manta* of Provincetown, Massachusetts, in 1917. The front has a broadside portrait of a whaling schooner (similar to the *John R. Manta*) under full sail with a sunrise or sunset in the background, a handshake betokening friendship and camaraderie, framed by a proscenium arch and leafy floral devices, with the name and initials of the artist. On the back are inscribed the names of his three Fortes brothers and their uncle, Valentine Fermino. It was a gift to NBWM from the Dawn Blake Souza in honor of Evangeline Fermino Freeman Blake, daughter of Valentine Fermino. All five of the men were from São Nicolão, they were all career mariners and fishermen, and they all worked intermittently in New Bedford's cotton mills. A second, very similar tooth in an equivalent size, almost certainly from the same whale, descended in the family of Captain Henry Mandly, Jr. (reported by his son and heir, Captain Alvin Mandly). It is identically stipple engraved with the same schooner portrait, friendship handshake, and surrounding ensemble, and was certainly done by the same hand; but it is unsigned and has the stipple-engraved initials "J.L." above and "W.A.G." engraved in a medallion device below. Mandly family tradition attributed this one to John Lopes, one of Henry Mandly's sometime crew, but it is now clear that the the tooth was *from*, rather than *by* John Lopes; and that "W.A.G." refers to the New Bedford schooner *William A. Graber*, which Henry Mandly, Jr., commanded on three Atlantic whaling voyages during 1917-19 and on which John Lopes served in the crew.

Jayme or James Fortes was born in 1894, the son of Carlotta Fortes, whom the census lists as a widow by the time she came to America, and John Fortes, who evidently never emigrated. Jayme and his brother Henrique (Henry) followed their oldest brother Antonio to New Bedford. It is possible that Jayme was in the crew of the schooner *John R. Manta* out of Provincetown, Captain Manuel F. Santos, during April-August 1914, but he is not named on the crew list for this voyage or the *Manta's* next two voyages, from New Bedford, in 1915 or 1916. But Jayme did make at least one Atlantic sperm whaling voyage in the *Manta*, out of Provincetown under Captain Antone J. Mandly, during April-August 1917. In fact, his draft card, issued in June 1918, a year later than he was technically required to register, is explicitly annotated by the registrar, "On whaling voyage June 5, 1917 / Knew nothing about registering." Whether he left the whale fishery because he did not like it or because of a shortage of berths is not clear, but in 1918 he was an "operator" at the Quissett Mill 1918, and later — according to family lore — returned to seafaring for several voyages of the *John R. Manta* during her days in the merchant service as a Brava packet on the run between New Bedford and the Cape Verde Islands. He never married, and died at sea when the *Manta* was lost with all hands in 1934.

The uncle named on the scrimshaw was Valentine Fermino [Firmino], born at São Nicolão on St. Valentine's Day — hence his name — Feb. 14, 1882. He was the first to arrive in America — according to family tradition, at age 19 in the whaling schooner *Ellen A. Swift* of Provincetown in 1899. However, this is certainly a mis-recollection (the wrong date or the wrong vessel) in confusion with a full-scale sperm whaling voyage Fermino made in the *Ellen A. Swift* from April to August 1905. The *Swift* returned from an Atlantic voyage in September 1898 and did not go whaling again until June 1900, returning in July 1902. Fermino may have joined that voyage in progress — signing on when the schooner touched at the Cape Verdes — or could have arrived in a Brava packet, perhaps even the *Swift*, as a passenger or extra hand, around 1899 or shortly after. But by the time the *Swift* returned from her next whaling voyage in September 1904 Fermino was already working at the Quissett Mill, where he met fellow textile worker Domingas Fortes, whom he married at the Seamen's Bethel in 1904. He became a naturalized U.S. citizen, anglicized his surname to Freeman (thus sometimes appearing in the City Directory twice, both as Fermino and as Freeman), worked in the cotton mills, as a fisherman, and at miscellaneous jobs, and with Domingas raised ten children in New Bedford. He died in 1975 at age 93.

Valentine's sister-in-law, Carlotta Fortes, was the mother of the four Fortes brothers, three of whose names appear on the scrimshaw. That the tooth descended in the Fermino / Freeman family, rather than through the Fortes branch, suggests two circumstances: first, that this tooth, though engraved by Jayme Fortes, must have been presented to the uncle, Valentine Fermino; and second, that there may have been more such teeth, perhaps a whole set, one for each of the four men named.

Two of Jayme's three brothers — Valentine's nephews — are named on the tooth. Antone (1889-1979) was the oldest, a career whaleman while the fishery lasted, in the New Bedford schooners *Pedro Varela* (1910-12) and *A.E. Whyland* (1912-14), the barks *Bertha* (1916) and *Greyhound* (reported by the New Bedford Port Society; dates uncertain), and the schooner *John R. Manta* (1921), the last of her species, at this time almost at the end of her whaling career. Antone was a boatsteerer on the *Bertha* and third mate on the *Manta*, but despite his experience and steady rise the fishery was in precipitous decline and there were simply not enough jobs. So he was worked intermittently as a doorman, a driver, and — like his younger brothers — in the cotton mills and eventually in the sword fishing business. He was married to a West Indian woman named Ada de Grasse, who bore him six children. The second brother, Henrique (1892-1961), was also a career mariner who worked intermittently in the cotton mills, served in the U.S. Army during World War I, became captain of his own fishing boats, and raised a family in New Bedford. Jayme (1894-1934), the scrimshaw artist, was the third brother. The fourth brother, João Bautista (born circa 1898), called Bautista by his family but known in America as John, had not yet landed in America when the tooth was engraved. Once arrived he was a mariner, boatman, father of five, and sometime sword fisherman in association with his older brothers.

* **Fosdick, Washington** (fl. circa 1825-69). He had a long career — even longer than noted in the *Dictionary* — during which he made some mildly erotic scrimshaw. He was born in New York City, but his two passports (one issued to Washington Fosdick in 1839, the other bearing the name Washington Foster in 1844) differ with various ship's articles and other records regarding whether his birth was in 1808 or 1811. After many voyages, in the 1860s he served as steward on the New Bedford bark *Java 2d*. According to shipmate J.F. Beane, who chronicled the voyage perceptively in *From Forecastle to Cabin* (1887), Fosdick assisted the captain with his calculations and taught young Beane celestial navigation. Fosdick died at age 60 on the Okhotsk seacoast of Siberia in 1869:

> *The steward, who had been ailing since leaving the tropics, became suddenly very much worse and, although we ministered to his wants with rough, but kindly hands, the dissipations of years counted at last [he was nearly thirty years older than the next oldest member of the crew] and he shuffled off his mortal coil, uncounted miles from friends and home. We constructed a rough coffin and ... carried the remains on shore at Rocky Point and there deposited them in a shallow grave. A prayer was read, the grave was filled, and over it we piled a wall of stone to mark the place and protect it from being desecrated by wild animals that roam the beach in search of food.*

(Beane actually compressed two successive voyages of the *Java* into one, so that neither his own advancement from green hand to seaman, to boatsteerer, to second mate, nor perhaps Fosdick's decline, was quite as rapid as they may appear in the narrative.)

There were several scrimshaw artists aboard the *Java* at that time, notably Captain Manuel Enos (q.v. in *More Scrimshaw Artists*), who produced a string of masterpieces during his variable career; Fosdick, who may or may not still have been scrimshonting; Captain Timothy C. Spaulding (q.v.), under whom Fosdick served two voyages; Beane himself (q.v.); and the carpenter, William Martin (q.v.), whom Beane accounted "the best workman we had on board, and the most industrious."

Foster, Edward N. (fl. circa 1854-61). A watch stand in the form of a long-case clock, made of wood and presumed to be trimmed with whale ivory and bone, is known only from snapshots and latter-day diagrams of circa 1940 (reported by Richard Donnelly). According to a holograph provenance, it was "made at sea by Edward N. Foster, grandfather to Chas. H. Sullings." Foster was born in Monmouth, Maine, sometime during 1834-37. He was issued a Seaman's Protection Paper, presumed to be his first, in New Bedford in 1854, when he declared his age as 20; but there is no record of any voyage he may have made at that time. During 1859-61 he served as cook in the bark *R.L. Barstow* of Mattapoisett, his only documented whaling voyage. After he returned in 1861 he obtained a new Protection Paper, this time stating his age as 24; and, again, there is no record of any voyage thereafter, nor has any record of his subsequent activities been discovered. (Regarding the provenance, Charles H. Sullings was born in New Bedford circa 1857, the son of John W. Sullings, a partner in Sullings, Kingman & Co., hardware and cutlery merchants. He was at first a piano tuner in Boston and Providence, then a piano salesman in Providence, living there and briefly in Warren, Rhode Island. He married in 1888 but there seems to be no record of children.)

Foster, James (fl. circa 1785-90). The written provenance of a wooden chipwork trinket box with a finial turned from whale ivory, together with subsequent research by Karen Langberg of Skinner's, are the only information about this sometime whaleman from Rochester, Massachusetts He was born there in 1768, and at age around twenty produced a "round maple box wuth laped seams fastened with copper rivets, carved domed lid with b one [sic] finial, the cover with copper riveted date '1788' the sides of the box riveted with the name 'HULDY FOSTER' and two hearts, the cover and sides ornamented with geometric and compass chip-carved decoration, and an inlaid 'X,' a paper inside the box is inscribed: 'This box was made by James Foster for his sister Huldy during one of his sea voyages. He was born 7-25-1768. Drowned at sea 12-5-1790'" (Skinner's, Aug. 14-15, 2010, lot #840). The auction catalogue adds, "James and Huldah (Huldy) Foster were two of the eleven children of Deacon James and Mary (Lewis) Foster… Huldy was born August 23, 1766 and died February 15, 1867."

Foster, Jeremiah (fl. circa 1790-1822). A five+-inch (13+ cm) walrus ivory fid engraved "Jeremiah Foster's 1774" (reported by William J. Boylhart) is accordingly ascribed to Jeremiah Foster, Jr. (1774-1822), mariner of Beverly, Massachusetts, who was born in the year inscribed on the fid — though it could have been made by his father, Jeremiah Foster, Sr. (1750-1820), who was also a mariner from Beverly. The year 1774 is not known to have been particularly significant to Foster pers except for the birth of his namesake son, who was not his first, but rather the ninth of ten children and the third or fourth son. If the elder Jeremiah made the fid, that the year inscribed on it happens to be the year of his son's birth could be mere fortuitous coincidence. Nevertheless, the man born in 1774 is the more likely maker. Jeremiah Senior's father was Joseph Foster (1709-1755), who was twice married and died at sea; his uncle was evidently the Captain Jeremiah Foster who in the 1740s was commandant of the 6th Company of the 5th Massachusetts Regiment of North Shore militia (Hale's Regiment, mustering at Ipswich, Massachusetts). Jeremiah Senior (1750-1820) married Anna Lovett, who bore him at twelve children, of whom Jeremiah Junior (1774-1822) was the eldest surviving son. He married Lydia Standley and fathered nine children of his own, including a son named Jeremiah (1816-1885), who also had a son named Jeremiah (1839-1907). They were all life-long residents of Beverly, but apart from the one death at sea nothing specific has been discovered about their seafaring careers.

Foster, Thomas, Jr. (fl. circa 1850-79). What little is known about his scrimshandering is connected to his voyage as first mate in the New Bedford ship *Gazelle* during 1864-66. However, he was the son of a whaling captain and was to become a successful whaling master in his own right, with a career's worth of opportunities to create scrimshaw of his own. Aboard the *Gazelle* in September 1865, a green hand named Frederick H. Lawrence wrote in his journal, "A few remarks have been made about scrimshoning. For the last week the Capt and mate and second mate have been constantly employed in making something for his lordship and his lady ship and now they have got every thing about done for themselves." The captain was Daniel F. Worth (q.v.), the second mate was Joseph F. Bunker (q.v.), and Thomas Foster was the first mate. Unfortunately, neither the collaborative scrimshaw made on the *Gazelle* nor any other scrimshaw Foster may have made on his own has ever come to light.

Like Captain Daniel Worth, Thomas Foster was a native of Martha's Vineyard. He was born in 1834 at Holmes Hole in the town of Tisbury. His mother, Charlotte E. West (1817-1869), was a native Vineyarder; his father was whaling captain Thomas Worth, Sr. (1808-1858), a native of Farmington,

Maine, who commanded voyages in the New Bedford ships *Wilmington and Liverpool Packet* (1837-41) and *St. Peter* (1842-46). Thomas Junior went to sea at a very early age on a string of voyages in vessels whose names have been lost to memory. He was married in 1858 upon achieving the rank of second mate (few career whalemen ever married sooner, as earnings in the lower echelons were not generally considered adequate to support a wife and family). His bride was Virginia L. Manchester (1834-1897) of Tisbury, who bore him a daughter named Ella (born 1859) and three sons. Charles (1857-1922) worked on the family farm, but both Thomas (1863-1889) and Daniel (1867-1943) started out very young as whalemen and professional mariners. But before this family had materialized, Worth went as second mate in the bark *San Francisco* in 1859; and after that vessel was lost in 1862 he followed Captain Worth onto the *Gazelle* as first mate (1862-66) — the voyage on which he is reported as having collaborated in scrimshonting. He was then master of two voyages in the brig *Mercy Taylor* of Tisbury (1862-66 and 1867-68), and, continuing with what had developed into a specialty of whaling on the Atlantic and South Atlantic grounds, he next achieved the near apotheosis of being the master of New Bedford barks. He made two voyages in the *Sarah* (1871-73, 1873-75), one in the *Cicero* (1876-78), and a watershed voyage as captain of the brand-new *Alice Knowles* (1879-85), in which he brought his wife and his two sailor sons. Thomas, age 16, was signed as an ordinary seaman; and Daniel Worth Foster, 13 — named, of course, after the father's lifelong friend and boom companion, Daniel Worth — embarked as cabin boy. It was a hugely successful voyage that returned 2,370 barrels of sperm oil, 1,600 barrels of whale oil, and 7,145 pounds of bone. On the way home they called at St. Helena, where they visited the famous Napoleonic sites together: Longwood, Bonaparte's residence during his final exile; and the tomb where his remains were interred from 1821 to 1840. (These shrines on the remote South Atlantic island of St. Helena were, of course, very popular with homeward-bound whalers, who were among the few ever to have had any opportunity to visit them. Regardless of the whalemen's individual attitudes about Napoleon himself, which tended to be complex and often less than favorable, pilgrimages to Longwood and Napoleon's tomb were the frequent subjects of whalemen's journal entries and scrimshaw. Of the former, among the most articulate and most favorable are the St. Helena passages in J. Ross Browne's classic narrative, *Etchings of a Whaling Cruise*, published in 1846, which Foster and his family would likely have known) After the family cruise in the *Alice Knowles* Captain Foster retired to his Holmes Hole farm while his sons Thomas and Daniel continued their seafaring careers. Thomas made several voyages, had a narrow escape or two in the Arctic ice, worked his way up to third mate, and was well on the track to command when he died at sea en route to the Arctic in 1889. Back home, Captain Foster, retiree, was an active Freemason, and became a lodge brother of his former shipmate, fellow captain, and lifelong friend, Daniel Worth, when Worth returned to Martha's Vineyard following an absence of three decades. Foster was widowed in 1897 and lived alone thereafter for nine years. He died in 1906.

Foster, Washington — pseudonym of Washington Fosdick (q.v.)

Fraits, Emanuel A. (fl. circa 1830-45). Born on the island of Flores in the Azores, he was a career whaleman on Westport, Massachusetts vessels until his early thirties and is credited with a rosewood yardstick made circa 1844 (in NBWM). It has whale ivory tips and is inlaid on one side with a version of a bent-hearts-and-diamonds motif in whale skeletal bone. Abalone shell inlays mark the half and quarters of a yard, transverse bars of whale ivory mark the eighths, and dots formed by inlaid bone dowels mark the calibrations on the back.

Though the Portuguese surname is often spelled Frates (and is often Anglicized), and in any form Portuguese names are frequently misspelled, this fellow consistently listed himself as Emanuel A. Fraites. Born in 1813, he was the son of Antonio Alvares Freitas and Maria Josefa Azevedo, served as a boatsteerer in the brig *Mexico* (1841-42), and was second mate in the bark *Barclay* at the time he made the scrimshaw (1843-44), which was likely a gift for his fiancée, Massachusetts-born Henrietta A. Gidley, whom he married in 1845. Fraits evidently retired from seafaring at that time, and by 1850 was listed as a farmer in Dartmouth, Massachusetts, where he and Henrietta raised seven children and where he died in 1885. Their son Emanuel W. Fraits (born circa 1851) was also a whaleman who is listed in the crews of overlapping voyages, in the New Bedford barks *Arnolda* (1876-80) and *Frances A. Barstow* (1877-78). However, the family provenance is quite specific that the yardstick was made by Emanuel Fraits circa 1844, thus it is unlikely that they have the wrong ancestor in mind.

Frandson, Andrew (fl. circa 1898-1910). He is unequivocally associated with, and may himself have made all or portions of, a small walrus ivory cribbage board with a picture and inscription. The tusk has minor telltale staining, indicating fossilization from the tundra, and is monochrome engraved with a stylized totemic *wasco* figure of a sea creature, in imitation of the Tlingit (Northwest Coast Indian) manner, surmounted by the word "ALASKA" in a rudimentary riband; and is inscribed for presentation in a graver's fine cursive hand, "Triumph Lodge No. 32 / Presented by / Bro A Frandson / Skagway Alaska"; with two small gold nuggets embedded in the cribbage board (reported by a private collector, who traced the Frandsons to the 1910 Census for the City of Skagway). Frandson may have made the piece himself or had it commissioned; the fraternal order has not been identified (however, the name Triumph Lodge suggests the Freemasons or the Knights of Pythias). Andrew Frandson was born in Wisconsin in 1877 of Danish parents who emigrated there in 1870. (This particular family consistently spelled the name *Frandson*, rather than the *Frandsen* more commonly used by Danes of that name in Europe and America.) Andrew and his brother Frank, older by two years, appear to have come to the frontier town of Skagway in connection with the Klondike Gold Rush of 1898; the nuggets on the cribbage board may merely be intended as symbols of Skagway's Gold Rush heritage, or may betoken some specific event associated with the Gold Rush, of which Skagway was an epicenter, port of entry, and major depot. By 1910 Andrew was a partner with Prosper Ganty in the Ganty & Frandson Grocery, Frank was a boatbuilder, and they were living in Skagway with their widowed mother and two adult sisters, who had likely joined them only after things had quieted down from the Klondike aftermath. Living next door was an unemployed Irish immigrant sea captain; and, as the scrimshaw collector also reported, two doors down was Captain Peter Frandson, master mariner, age 42, a kinsman born in Denmark who emigrated in 1882 and by 1910 had a wife and two young daughters. It is not known when Andrew left Alaska, but he died at Highland, San

Bernardino County, California, in 1957. In his obituary his name appeared as Andrew Frandsen. (Sources: 1910 Census, Skagway, Alaska; Frandsen Genealogy, Rootsweb; Spude 1979.)

Freeman, Thomas (fl. circa 1830-80). A panbone seam rubber, six inches long, highly polished, with a contoured octagonal shaft, chamfered cube pommel, and a blade with contoured depressions for finger grips, is one of the most interesting pieces in NBWM, (where it was acquired in 1904) by reason of the very unusual monochrome inscriptions beautifully engraved on the shaft: "THOMAS FREEMAN / his Rubber," on one side, and on the other side "DROP IT YOU BUGGER." The craftsmanship and state of preservation are so perfect, and the inscription so ingratiatingly eccentric, that had it not come into NBWM in the very first year of the museum's existence — thereby establishing its rock-solid provenance when the American whaling industry was still a going, if faltering concern — it would certainly have come under suspicion as possibly a modern fake. On the contrary, while nothing much is known about the maker, the scrimshaw is entirely authentic. The biography of Thomas Freeman, to whom the seam rubber is attributed, is tenuous at best. In 1833, when he shipped as ordinary seaman in the Fairhaven ship *Albion* at age 21, he declared his residence as Fairhaven, a town for which the customary Vital Records have never been published; so his life and career are largely reconstructed from fragmentary records that may or may not all pertain to the same fellow. U.S. Census records indicate that he was born in Massachusetts circa 1811 — which would probably have been either Fairhaven or somewhere on Cape Cod — but crew lists in NBFPL indicates that he was from the island of Fayal, in the Azores, and there is no record of a Seaman's Passport (which was issued only to citizens, native-born and naturalized). He reportedly did not come home in the *Albion* from that voyage, but how he got back to New Bedford is not known. He is probably the same Thomas Freeman of Fayal who was in the crew of the whaleship *Condor* of New Bedford during 1834-35, but what he did and where he went for the next few years are not known. Years later he was shipkeeper in the bark *Janet* of Westport, Massachusetts (1848-51), and by that time was living in Wellfleet, on Cape Cod, with his wife, Hannah (whom he must have married around 1833), and three children. He continued working as a sailor for the next two decades and more, and they were still living in Wellfleet in 1880. (Not to be confused with other mariners who were active contemporaneously in New England: Thomas Freeman, born in 1806 at Eastham or Orleans on Cape Cod; and a Thomas A.J. Freeman, born that same year at Salem, Massachusetts, who was issued a Seamen's Passport at Salem in 1826. Neither of these is known to have gone whaling. Meanwhile, an English whaling captain named Thomas Freeman made a couple of South Sea whaling voyages in the 1830s and '40s for the Enderby Brothers firm of London whaling merchants, and during 1838-39 skippered the Enderby schooner *Sabrina* on an expedition into Antarctic waters south of New Zealand as sub-captain under John Balleny in the schooner *Eliza Scott*.)

Frizina, John (fl. circa 1830s). According to his journal as second mate in the whaleship *Golconda* of Bristol, Rhode Island (1835-38) (in NBWM), he made an ivory whistle and a "jagging knife" on the voyage. Not only has the scrimshaw not come to light, but no information whatever has been found about anyone of this name (or Frisina, Frizinha, Freizina, etc.) anywhere in America in the nineteenth century.

Gammons, Ephraim (fl. circa 1845-49). A New Bedford shipwright and ship carpenter, he was the son of a whaleman and may have gone whaling himself in his youth, but is in any case credited with a scrimshaw tooth featuring "portraits" of a type unspecified (reported by Michael Yates, a descendant, on the basis of a family provenance). He was not the only Ephraim Gammons in New Bedford or Fairhaven. According to the family provenance, he was Ephraim Thomas Gammons, born in Fairhaven in 1827, the son of Ebenezer Keen Gammons and the former Sarah Wetherell Taber. The father, Ebenezer, had made two whaling voyages, in the ships *George and Susan* (1819-20) and *Lorenzo* (1820-21), but no record of any voyage has been discovered for Ephraim. If he ever did go whaling, it must have been in the middle 1840s, for in 1849 he married Mary Sylvia Potter (1826-1907), known as Sylvia, the daughter of Pardon Potter 2d, a New Bedford ship carpenter, and his wife Hannah, with whom the newlyweds lived for the first few years of their marriage and in whose house the first of their several children was born. Ephraim later worked as a shipwright, ship carpenter, and house carpenter. According to a genealogy compiled by Winnifred Dassman, "The [Gammons] family moved to Abington [Massachusetts] for a time around 1857, but returned to Fairhaven and New Bedford, later moving on to Westport [Massachusetts]," where Ephraim was employed as a farm laborer and several of their older children, boys and girls, were working in cotton mills. In 1900 Ephraim and Sylvia were living in Dartmouth with an unmarried daughter, Ida; and after Ephraim was widowed in 1907, he and Ida lived together for a few years in New Bedford. He died in 1911.

Garcia da Silva, Francisco (fl. late 19th – early 20th centuries). He was "a well-known [whale] ivory craftsman" at Cabo Branco on the island of Pico, later at Horta on Fayal, and was known locally in the Azores as Formiga. According to João Gomes Vieira, it was "a time when almost all ivory was worked into utilitarian pieces: table games, tool handles, clothes pegs [clothespins], pipes and cigarette holders, etc." (Gomes Vieira, 2003, 171). Three of his sons by his wife Gerónima — Manuel (1913-1985), José (1916-2000), and Francisco (1922-1977) — were also Azorean carvers and engravers of whale ivory, all nicknamed Formiga.

Gardiner, Charles B. (fl. circa 1855-65). A glass-front display case intended for wall mounting contains, among 18 handmade objects of wood, whale ivory, bone, and metal: a miniature swift-in-a-bottle (a single-cage swift of wood, ivory, and bone, mounted on an ivory or bone barrel made up of individual staves, standing on a miniature four-legged table, in the manner of a ship-in-a-bottle); a 3-inch (7.5 cm) oval of sperm whale ivory, relief carved with a spread-eagle holding arrows in its talons, and flat and highly polished on the back (evidently intended for mounting as a finial ornament on a box or newel post); a napkin ring of marine mammal bone, oval in cross section, relief carved with two doves facing one another and suspending vertically between them three links of chain, with the relief-carved initials "MTG" framed in chain links; and two relief-carved bone finger-rings, one with the initials "TG," the other with three horizontal links of chain. It also contains a large folding knife with one wooden and one ivory cheek; and a variety of elaborate, superbly-made piercedwork wooden gewgaws. The ensemble came with an undated provenance, typewritten on the stationery of the Batavia Clamp Company of Batavia, New York (reported by Richard Donnelly):

> *The articles in this case were whittled [sic] by Chas. B. Gardiner, Grandfather of Dr. Chas. W. Gardiner. Note how the knife has worn from long use. The chain hanging from the circular frame*

> *was whittled inside the frame and then pulled out. Mr. Gardiner was a Cabinet Maker, whose tables were brought in to have casters put on, the ball on the bottom of the leg was sawn off so as to leave the table the normal height. He would pick up the ball and whittle a perfect ball inside leaving an outside basket. Note the original varnish remaining on the basket. One of the chains is a double chain, each link of one chain is inside the like [sic] of the other. All the contents of the bottle were put in through the neck of the bottle. The top of the table is all one piece. There are 14 staves in the barrel. The stopper is locked with a wooden key. / This work was done during the years from / 1855 to 1865.*

Charles B. Gardiner was indeed active as a cabinetmaker in Hamilton, New York, from 1850 to 1871, meanwhile also serving on the town's first Board of Education (elected in 1853). But whether he was ever a ship's carpenter or ever made a whaling voyage before 1850 is not known. According to James H. Smith in *The History of Chenango and Madison Counties*, New York (Syracuse, 1880), the first of Hamilton's several furniture factories was established by one James Higgins in 1810. Around 1825, Higgins sold out to his former apprentice, Erastus Wheeler; and in 1840 Wheeler took in Wilson Parker as a partner.

> *In 1850, Charles B. Gardiner bought Wheeler's interest and the business was continued by Parker & Gardiner till 1864, when Parker sold [out] to Madison Hall. In 1871, Gardiner sold his interest to Madison Leach, who in 1873, sold [out] to Archibald B. Campbell, who, in 1874, also purchased Madison Hall's interest.*

The grandson, Charles W. Gardiner, born in Ohio circa 1866, was a salesman and sometime superintendent of the Batavia Clamp Company — hence the stationery. He was evidently not a medical man, and the source of his title "Dr." Charles W. Gardiner has not been established.

Gardner, Abraham [Abram] (fl. circa 1810-43). New Bedford whaling master to whom two coconut shell dippers (in NBWM) are attributed. They are so much alike that they appear to be a pair, but almost certainly were not produced for the same recipient. Each has a large coconut-shell bowl with the outer surface relief-carved with a fluted pattern on the bottom, a band of cross-hatch cuts, and a name in raised serifed capitals, surmounted by a circumferential rope-and-tassel pattern. The name on one, which has a wooden handle carved in a spiral twist pattern, is, "ABRAM. GARDNER"; on the other, where the handle is absent, the name is "RHOBA HAFFARDS." Gardner was born in 1793 or 1794, went to sea by 1808 or 1809, was a boatsteerer in the Nantucket ship *Samuel* (1811-13), and, with his name listed variously as Abram and Abraham, command 13 voyages, mostly in New Bedford vessels: two in the brig *Cornelia* (1819-21), one in the ship *Camillus* (1821-22), two in the ship *Atlas* of Newport, Rhode Island (1823-25), three in the ship *Richmond* (1825-28), three in the ship *Canton* (1828-38), one as temporary replacement captain in the ship *George and Susan* (1838-39), and one in the ship *Zephyr* (1839-43). He married a woman named Rebecca in 1822 or 1823 and had several daughters, one of whom may have married into the Haffards (AKA Haffords) clan of New Bedford; and he died in 1869. Of the Haffardses, one named Jonathan served in the 2nd Regiment of Massachusetts Militia in the War of 1812; another Jonathan Haffards, evidently a son of the preceding, commanded a whaling voyage in the New Bedford ship *John Howland*

(1832-36). His kinsmen James and Stephen Haffards were whalemen, and Charles Haffards was a sailmaker. Rhoba Haffards, whose birthplace, birth date, and maiden name are unknown, married into the family and by the late 1830s is listed in the City Directory as a widow boarding at 96 Elm Street. She may have been the widow of Jonathan Haffards, Sr., and thus mother-in-law to one of Abraham Gardner's daughters. Meanwhile, James and Elizabeth Haffards had a daughter named Anna Rhoba Haffard, known as Rhoba or Roby, who married C.J. Page, Sr., and lived in Saline County, Missouri.

Gardner, George Washington (fl. circa 1790s-1828). Nantucket whaling master. A bodkin, turned from whale ivory, length 4-⅜ inches (111 mm), is attributed to G.W. Gardner as captain of the Nantucket ship *Globe* (reported by Charles Manghis). Gardner actually made three voyages in the *Globe* during a long and prosperous career as captain of a series of Nantucket whaleships: two voyages in the *Sukey* (1806-08 and 1809-11), one in the *William Penn* (1811-13), three in the *Globe* (1815-18, 1818-20, and 1820-22), and two in the *Maria* (1822-25 and 1825-28). It was not a pedestrian or eventless career. The two voyages in the *Sukey* were commercial successes: Starbuck records 1,000 barrels of sperm oil for the first one; for the second he records only that the ship returned "full" in 1811. The *William Penn* voyage turned out to be an ordeal. She was caught in the pincers of the Napoleonic Wars: she was captured at sea in December 1813 and was sent into Capetown as a British prize. Gardner's next voyage was in the brand-new *Globe,* in which he returned a record catch, the first ship ever to bring in more than 2,000 barrels (Starbuck, 217). Each of his next two voyages in the *Globe* also returned more than 2,000 barrels; and in 1822 he was given another brand-new ship, the *Maria,* in which he also returned excellent, 2,000-plus-barrel cargoes of sperm oil. In the meantime, he is credited with the discovery of a dozen or more hitherto uncharted islands and reefs encountered on his various whaling expeditions, about which he dutifully reported locations and sailing directions (the best known of these is Palmyra Island, in 5° 58' North and 162° 30' West, which became an important air base during World War II and remained a significant American weather station for a generation afterwards). Captain Gardner was born on Nantucket in 1778. He had two daughters and two sons by his first wife, Lydia Coffin (1779-1834), whom he married in 1801. Sometime after Lydia's death in 1834, he married Sarah [née Macy] Arthur Coffin (1788-1855), who had been widowed twice before. Both of George and Lydia's two sons, George Washington Gardner, Jr. (b. 1809), and William Henry Gardner (1812-1871), were whaling masters in Nantucket ships, George Junior as captain of the *Mariner* (1836-40), *Nantucket* (1841-45), and *Narragansett* (1855-60), and William as captain of one voyage in the *Richard Mitchell* (1839-43). Very oddly indeed, sometime after he returned from sea the younger brother, William, married their father's widow, Sarah (George Senior's second wife): it was his second marriage and her *fourth — to her step-son, 24 years her junior!*

Gardner, John (fl. circa 1832). He may or may not have made a walking stick in NBWM with his name on it. It has a wooden shaft, store-bought silver ferrule, and a turned whale ivory knob pommel with red and black sealing wax highlights, inset with an 1830 Liberty Head half-dime coin and engraved around the perimeter "JOHN GARDNER 1832." On the presumption that such a walking stick would more likely have belonged to a ship master than to a younger man or some lesser light, it is worth mentioning that there were three American whaling captains of that name, of whom only one was active as early as 1832: John J. Gardner of Nantucket, born in 1799 and married to Eliza Gardner, commanded seven voyages in Nantucket ships: the *Atlantic* (1825-28 and 1828-29), *Phoenix* (1829-31), *Orbit* (1832-36), *Baltic* (1839-43), and *Norman* (1848-49 and 1850-51). Of course while the 1830 coin is suggestive, its mere presence does not constitute absolute proof of anything beyond that it could not have been placed in the pommel anytime before 1830 (after all, it could be a random choice or a later addition or a later substitution). On the other hand, the 1832 date engraved on the ferrule can reasonably be taken to signify something specific, if not the date of presentation then perhaps the birth or wedding date of the owner or recipient, or the date of his first command. However, neither of the other two captains of that name was born as late as 1832, and none of the three was married that year. John Gardner II of Nantucket was master of the Nantucket ships *Harvest* (1840-44) and *Niphon* (1844-49), which latter he left before the voyage was completed; and John S. Gardner, who was born in Rhode Island circa 1820 and married Arabella W. Ellis at New Bedford in 1845, commanded three voyages in the Westport bark *Champion* (1847-48, 1849-53, and 1853-57), on the third of which he left before the voyage was completed. Surprisingly, apart from the three aforementioned captains (two of whom were not yet captains at the time), there were not many crew-men named John Gardner who were active in the Yankee whale fishery as early as the 1830s. One was from Warren, Rhode Island, born circa 1803, for whom the only known voyage was in the New Bedford ship *Russell* (1820-22). There were several John Gardners living on Nantucket, all mariners at one time or another. Two were African Americans, one born in New York circa 1808, the other from Providence, Rhode Island, born circa 1813; a white George Gardner was also born on Nantucket in 1813. Each of them was too young in 1832 for a walking stick of his own, but not too young to have made such a stick for a father, grandfather, or favorite uncle. And this walking stick probably was made in that way, perhaps by a sailor named Gardner for a relative named John. If it were made for a favored captain in 1832, it would have to have been John J. Gardner of Nantucket.

Gardner, Joseph (fl. circa 1815-36). A whaling master of Warren, Rhode Island, active during the apex of whaling from that port, he is provisionally credited (entirely on the basis of provenance) with four pieces now in WHS (reported by Richard Donnelly). The surest of the attributions is a panbone busk crudely engraved with geometric decorations, inscribed on verso (in ink holograph, in an early twentieth-century hand not the artist's), "Gift of Mrs. —— Gardiner [sic] / July 9, 1916 / probably originally of Capt. Joseph Gardiner"; and "From the Pearse House on [the] S.W. Cor[ner] of Broad & —— St. / Warren, R.I." There are also two well-proportioned, lathe-turned panbone fids, one small and one large; and a huskier-than-usual bone corn-husker with leather thumb-loop. These were donated in 1915 by "Miss Gardiner," one of the Captain's granddaughters. A fifth piece, which Gardner certainly owned but almost certainly did not engrave himself, was an earlier gift from another of the Captain's granddaughters, Lydia Maria Pearse, in 1891. It is a wide tooth featuring, on one side, an Old Testament scene of Adam, Eve, the Serpent, the Apple, and the Tree of Life, charmingly done in the manner of a sixteenth-century wood engraving. On the back is a highly ornamented ensemble of a recumbent lion (with an oddly human-like face) with a Maltese cross on its head, like a coronet, atop an urn-like device with floral decorations, surmounted by two serpents, ribbons, and two seraphim blowing trumpets (reminiscent of the trumpet-wielding angels on a Dutch tall clock). (The latter piece is apparently British and may be by the same hand as an anonymous, similarly decorated tooth in the Veldkamp Collection in the Netherlands.)

Joseph Gardner was born in Warren circa 1785 and commanded whaling voyages in the Warren ships *Rosalie* (1825-28), *Magnet* (1829-31), and *Luminary* (1832-36). There are also some references to the Warren ship *William* having been commanded by "Captain Gardner" in 1820, but this voyage is not confirmed by Starbuck or Lund. Gardner was married to a woman named Louica [Louiça], who bore him at least three children before he left her a widow in the 1840s. The eldest was Lydia (born circa 1812), who married a carpenter named Luther Pearse; and of the six Pearse children, the eldest was Lydia Maria Pearse (born circa 1837), donor of the Adam and Eve scrimshaw in 1891.

* **Gardner, William Bunker** (fl. circa 1835-56). The *Dictionary* reports that Captain Gardner "may have made the two pieces of scrimshaw furniture that he is known to have brought home as gifts for his wife — a small oak table with polychrome whale bone inlay, said to have been made on shipboard circa 1845-55; and a sewing stand with turned whale-ivory posts, supposed to have been made aboard the *Sarah Parker*." An exhibition label at NHA gives the year of Gardner's birth as 1813 (not 1811), and notes that the sewing stand (which NHA describes as a sewing box and spool holder) was made as a gift for his wife, Charlotte Coffin Gardner (1820-82), "who accompanied her husband and kept the ship's log during an 1852-55 voyage to California" in the *Sarah Parker*. It was given to NHA by Grace Brown Gardner, a descendant.

* **Gerrodette, Henry Vincent** (fl. circa 1847). Judge Paul Vardeman reports, "New information has surfaced" about Henry Vincent Gerrodette "which corrects my previous reference [hence the reference to him in *More Scrimshaw Artists*] to his service on the Wilkes Ex. Ex." — that is, on the Wilkes Exploring Expedition of the 1840s — an error that Vardeman attributes to "an erroneous label at the Smithsonian." Rather, it turns out that Gerrodette served in the Mexican War, a claim for which Vardeman cites a private communication from Paula Johnson of the SIW curatorial staff, to the effect that three pieces of scrimshaw associated with Henry Vincent Gerrodette are in the SIW collection: two teeth and a name stamp that is also fashioned from a sperm whale tooth. All three "are part of a donation made in 1956 by Miss Eleanor Gerrodette, of Washington, DC," who also donated at the same time knives, scabbards, and a pair of embroidered trousers that were worn by Gerrodette in the Mexican War, in which he served "with Commodore Robert Field Stockton on the old frigate *Congress*" in 1847. Gerrodette is presumed to have embroidered the trousers himself. About the scrimshaw Judge Vardeman remarks, "[Gerrodette's] work is unmistakable — bleeding heart enclosed by a wreath with flowers at the top" — features that are present on both of the teeth in SIW and on another in a private collection. The stylistic continuity between these and the name-stamp in SIW is also obvious. Of Henry Gerrodette little else is known. The only man of that name listed in the U.S. Census is a Henry *Gerrodett* of Brooklyn, New York, who was born in New York circa 1822. In 1870 he was working in a powder mill not far from the Brooklyn Navy Yard, married to a woman named Henrietta with a 16-year-old daughter; his 18-year-old son Isaac (or Isaiah) lived nearby and was apprenticed to a banknote printer. By 1880 Henry was retired, had evidently been widowed, and was living in Brooklyn with Isaac, who was now a married printer. No whaling voyages are known, nor anything regarding how he first came to make orthodox pictorial scrimshaw.

Gibbs, James (fl. circa the 1840s). Nantucket carpenter and sometime whaleman credited with a "carved bone and ivory swift in [its] original dovetailed West Indian mahogany box." The provenance and attribution arise from "Paper labels inside the lid [that] read: 'A swift/yarn winder complete with handmade case in mint condition. Made between 1840-1860 at sea by Uncle James Gibbs.' Signed by Wilma A. Tribau" (Northeast, 19-20 August 2006, #817). In fact, by 1850 James Gibbs, Jr., was evidently already finished with his youthful whaling adventures. He was born in 1823, the son of James Gibbs (1783-1842) and the former Martha Swift (1785-1841), made at least one whaling voyage in a Nantucket ship, married Charlotte M. Thompson (1824-1900) in 1844, and by 1850 was settled as a carpenter on Nantucket. He is listed as a Master Carpenter by 1860, and was accumulating quite significant holdings in real estate and other property. The couple had two sons. James W. (1852-1886), like his father, must have apprenticed as a carpenter in his youth, went whaling for a few years (in the bark *Herald* of New Bedford, 1869-72), and made carpentry his permanent career. The second son, Arthur C. (1858-1867), died in childhood.

Gibbs, John (fl. 19th century). A baleen busk (in NBWM) very crudely incised with images of a house with a chimney, a tree, a fouled anchor, and a series of geometric patterns rendered with a rough cross-hatch technique, is signed on verso "John Gibbs." There were several men of this name whaling out of New Bedford and New London in the nineteenth century, and no specific indication which of them might have made the busk: John Gibbs of Wareham, Massachusetts, born circa 1790, ordinary seaman at age 19 in the ship *Latona* (1809); John Gibbs of Somerset, Massachusetts, born circa 1797, obtained a Seaman's Passport at Newport, Rhode Island, in 1815; John Gibbs of Lubec, Maine, born circa 1819, sailed in 1838 on an unidentified vessel; John Gibbs of no known age or address, ordinary seaman in the ship *Callao* (1842-45) and boatsteerer in the bark *Mars* (1845-48); John Gibbs, mariner of New Bedford, who married Elizabeth Swift Spooner in 1842 but whose voyages are unknown; John Gibbs of Little Compton, Rhode Island, born circa 1822, passport issued at Fall River, Massachusetts, sailed July 1843 in the New Bedford ship *Lucas* which was lost on Madagascar in March 1845; John L. Gibbs, mariner of New Bedford, born circa 1827, son of Heamon and Martha Gibbs, married Sarah A. Shaw in 1847, voyages unknown; John J. Gibbs, born circa 1830, allegedly of Hartford, New York (though possibly Hartford somewhere else), green hand, ship *America* (1851-54); another John Gibbs of Wareham, born circa 1842, two voyages in the ship *Admiral Blake* (1860; 1860-62); and John Gibbs of New Bedford, born circa 1845, passport issued April 1862, voyages unknown.

Gifford, Albert A. (fl. circa 1842-57). Whaleman of Westport, Massachusetts, the son of a whaling captain, who brought home a variety of scrimshaw, at least some of which (and perhaps all of which) he is reputed to have made himself. The star piece is a small, double-cage, footed tabletop swift with handsomely carved whale ivory fixtures and beaded (purfled) slats, some of which (according to Richard Donnelly, who examined it) "were colored black with ink, paint or some blacking substance"; and, "Interestingly, the rounded ends of the black slats are natural white in color. This means that the ends were finished after the lengths of bone had been colored." There are three teeth, competently engraved but not so distinctively that the artist's individual style emerges as uniquely identifiable: one has a broadside portrait of a warship and a crucifix, one a ship portrait and spread-eagle, and the third, standing figures of a man and woman, an urn with flowers, and an eagle. Of four walking sticks, one has a spiral-carved panbone shaft and fluted mushroom pommel, the others have wooden shafts, brass ferrules, and whale ivory handles: one a plain transverse-curved grip; one a clenched right fist, dated 1856; and the third, a knob pommel with polychrome inlay. There are also: two whale ivory crimpers with fluted jagging wheels, one with a squared architectonic handle, the other surmounted by a full-round-carved turk's head (monkey's fist) knot; a curious folding toothpick of whale ivory in the form of a dancing Asian woman, and another with a polychrome anchor decoration; a hefty whale ivory bodkin; three brass letter seals with turned whale ivory shafts; three plain teeth, two polished and one raw; and miscellaneous scrimshaw tools. Additionally, two of Gifford's journals, of whaling voyages (in the *Mexico* (1844-45) and the *President* (1849-50), have whale stamps and watercolor recognition drawings of "the mountains and topography of the Azores." The journals, scrimshaw, and a daguerreotype portrait of the whaleman-artist came "directly from Gifford's ancestral home ... in Westport, Massachusetts" (Gould Auctions, 22 Sept. 2005, lots #102-117).

Albert Augustus Gifford (not Albert *Almy* Gifford, as reported by the auctioneer) was born at Westport in 1825, the son of Captain Anthony Almy Gifford, who was captain of three whaling voyages, in the ships *Constitution* of Newport (1833-36), *Hope* of New Bedford (1836-39), and *Benjamin Rush* of Warren (1841-45). The son's less distinguished whaling career was just beginning as his father's was ending. Albert may have gone as a cabin boy in the *Hope* under his father's command (1836-39), but his first fully documented voyages were in the Westport bark *Leader* (1840-41) at age 14, probably as a green hand, and as "oarsman" (Able Seaman) in the Westport brigs *Catherwood* (1842-43) and *Mexico* (1844-45). He was afterwards boatsteerer in the New Bedford ship *Metacom* (1845-48) and bark *President* (1849-50), and second mate in the ship *Herald* of New Bedford (1851-55) and bark *Mattapoisett* of Westport (1855-57). Meanwhile, his younger brother Samuel had also become a career whaleman with three voyages as a ship's cooper, afterwards climbing no higher than second mate. In 1848 Albert married Lucy Ann Sowle of Westport. Their children were Lafayette Leroy Gifford (b. 1849) and Alameda Jane Gifford (b. 1858). In an article entitled "The Galapagos Tortoises in their relation to the Whaling Industry: A Study of Old Logbooks," Charles Haskins Townsend reports,

> *Mr. Lafayette Gifford of Westport Point, Massachusetts, makes the statement that his father, who was a whaling captain, "visited the Galapagos in the 'fifties and saw there a renowned tortoise that was supposed to weigh over a thousand pounds. This tortoise had names carved all over its back. A British war ship finally took it away with the aid of tackles and a derrick. It was then but little longer than it was 150 years previously." Perhaps the original dimensions were carved on its back.*

Though Albert Gifford was never a whaling captain (neither was his brother Samuel), he evidently served on one or more voyages as a first mate, and the 1860 census lists him as "1st Mate Whaler." The circumstances of his later life are not clear. He was widowed sometime in the 1860s and by 1870 was remarried to a woman named Sarah, who was a few years older. He does not appear in the census after 1870 and likely died before 1880. In 1880 his son Lafayette, a fisherman, age 30, was living in Westport with his wife Ludevina and namesake daughter Lucy, but from the provenance it appears that Albert's scrimshaw and other whaling relics must have fallen out of the family at some point, to be discovered later in "Gifford's ancestral home ... in Westport."

Gifford, Asa Russell (fl. circa 1829-56). New Bedford whaling master credited with several pieces of scrimshaw donated to NBWM by his granddaughter in 1981: a tooth, polychrome engraved on one side with a broadside view of a full-rigged ship underway, on the other side with a monochrome pinprick-transfer picture of a trotting horse; a whale ivory letter seal bearing a ship under sail and five stars with the name of his father-in-law, James Harris Beetle (made circa 1849); a large bodkin lathe-turned from whale ivory; a whale ivory needle; and a tatting shuttle. These came to NBWM in 1980 together with an ambrotype photograph of Captain Gifford and a daguerreotype portrait of James Harris Beetle. Asa Russell Gifford was born circa 1812 at Dartmouth, Massachusetts, and made a career of whaling. His known voyages were all right whaling in New Bedford vessels: the ship *Pacific* (1829-32), on the Brazil Banks; bark *Pioneer* (1832-33) and ship *Hope* (1833-34 and 1834-36), in the South Atlantic; ship *Phocion* (1839-41), on which he was likely first mate under Captain Edward W. Collins (see Hananiah W. Collins), in the South Atlantic and Indian Ocean; and three voyages as captain, two in the ship *Mayflower*, the first in the Atlantic (1841-44) and the second to the Northwest Coast (1844-47); and, after a hiatus of several years, one in the bark *Roscoe 2d* (1853-56), also to the North Pacific. Still, on each of these voyages enough sperm whales were taken to provide the raw materials for scrimshaw made entirely out of sperm whale ivory. Between the *Mayflower* and the *Roscoe*, in 1849, he married Abby D. Beetle (born 1826) of Edgartown, Martha's Vineyard, daughter of James H. Beetle, Esq., and the former Betsy Worth; and he appears to have moved at that time to Edgartown, where their son James Beetle Gifford was born in 1853 and where Asa became a grocer after retiring from the sea three years later.

Gifford, Benjamin D. (fl. circa 1839-79). Whaling master who made a coconut shell dipper that has a twist-carved wooden shaft with a tip carved out of sperm whale ivory, and has metal overlay around the cup inscribed as pierced-work with the names of his father and mother, Captain Humphrey A. Gifford (1794-1868) and Phebe Davis Gifford (1799-1880). It was "made by Captain Benjamin Gifford of Westport on an unidentified whaling voyage as a young man" and was donated to NBWM by his nephew, W.L.R. Gifford of St. Louis, in 1941. Benjamin Davis Gifford (whose middle initial varies in the whaling records) was born at Westport, Massachusetts, in 1824. His father was a merchant sea captain, and Benjamin went to sea at age 15 as a green hand in the New Bedford bark *Hope* (1839-40), which he may have left early to transfer into his next ship, the *Florida* of New Bedford, in which he made two voyages (1840-41 and 1841-43). After one or two more voyages that have not been identified (1843-47), he was first mate in the Westport bark *Dr. Franklin* for the 25th lay (1847-49), then was her captain on two voyages (1849-51 and 1851-53). Neither of these was especially successful, particularly the second one. Thus, for his next voyage Gifford had to settle for a berth as a first mate in the New Bedford ship *Marion* (1855-59). But he was a captain again soon enough, on eight moderately profitable voyages in five barks, the *Mattapoisett* of Westport (1860-62), and the *President 2d* (3 voyages, 1862-67), *Glacier* (1868-70), *Spartan* (1872-73), and *Sunbeam* (1876-78) of New Bedford, capped by a partial voyage as relief captain of the *Laetitia* (1878-79). He married Hannah Rodman (born circa 1832) of Westport, and died in 1881. The couple were evidently childless, so it is no wonder that his scrimshaw passed to his younger brother, Humphrey Almy Gifford, Jr. (1828-1907), who like their father was a merchant sea captain. Humphrey and his wife, Alice Peckham Francis (1832-1903), were the parents of William Logan Rodman Gifford (b. 1862), the longtime head librarian of the St. Louis Mercantile Library and biographer of George

Gifford, Jr. It was he who donated his uncle's scrimshaw, as well as several pieces that had been owned by his maternal grandfather and others he had acquired from Henry C. Hathaway (q.v.).

Gifford, Warren (fl. circa 1859-77). Whaling master of New Bedford and Dartmouth, Massachusetts. Judging from his journals (in KNB) he was evidently an energetic scrimshonter, but only two actual specimens of his work have come to light. One (in NBWM) is a plain clothespin of whale skeletal bone (panbone) with diamond chamfering and triangular cuts at the top, said by the family to have been made by Warren Gifford while at sea and brought back to be used as a teething piece for a baby. The other (in KNB) is on a grander scale: a coconut shell dipper with the name and date "Ruth H. Slocum / 1871" carved in shallow relief, a heart-shaped mounting flange of sperm whale ivory, a tapered octagonal foreshaft with a baleen band, and a curved octagonal teak handle terminating in a full-round-carved turk's-head knot. Gifford mentions "scrimshonting" only in passing in his journal of three voyages during 1868-74, but is teasingly more specific in his earlier journal of the bark *Messenger* (1861-63), where in no fewer than twenty separate mentions of scrimshandering we find him "making schrimshon," "making canes," and reporting at one point that he "finished my schrimshoning, & stowed away my tools." One could wish that he had described the scrimshaw in detail, or that he might at least have inventoried the tools.

Warren Gifford was born circa 1838 at Dartmouth, Massachusetts, the son of farmers Allen and Deborah Gifford. If he made any whaling voyages prior to 1859 they are not recorded; but that year, at age 21, he got a seaman's passport in New Bedford and sailed in the bark *Pamelia* under Captain Henry W. Slocum, a kinsman of his future wife. The name Warren Gifford does not appear in the outward manifest of the voyage (NBPS), and the name William Gifford does — which must be an error, as Warren was certainly aboard; and when the *Pamelia* gammed the New Bedford bark *Messenger* in October 1861, he "made a deal" with Captain Jason W. Gifford (to whom Warren was evidently not closely related) to transfer to the *Messenger* as a boatsteerer for the 75th lay (1861-63). Captain Gifford later certified the transfer for the U.S. Consul at Port Louis, Mauritius (NBFPL microfilm reel #169). Warren Gifford's whereabouts during 1863-68 have not been established: no record of Civil War service has been located; he may or may not have been whaling the whole time, but his name does not appear in the surviving crew lists; and he may have spent some time in the merchant service. But he went whaling again a few years later, as a mate in the barks *Napoleon* (1868-72) and *Commodore Morris* (1873-74), and he left the *Commodore Morris* early, while the voyage was still in progress, to sail from New Bedford as captain of the bark *Janus 2d* (1875-77). In fact, his route home in 1874 to take up this new command surprisingly included a few weeks as captain of the brig *Oriana* of Shelburne, Nova Scotia, from Fayal to New Bedford with a cargo of oranges. The *Janus* voyage was a commercial success, but Warren went whaling no more. Not long after he returned in the *Janus* he married the substantially younger Lucy Jane Slocum (born 1852), who according to the U.S. Census was a tailoress, and set up housekeeping on a farm in Dartmouth with his wife and widowed mother-in-law. This was Ruth Howland (née Butts) Slocum, born circa 1825, the widow of Ephraim Gifford Slocum — the "Ruth H. Slocum" for whom he made the busk in 1871. There was no issue from the marriage, and the Captain was widowed himself a few years later. He then married a widow named Mary, whose daughter Maria became Warren's stepdaughter. They also had a daughter of their own, Lucy J. Gifford, born in 1884 and named after Warren's first wife. It was she who inherited the journal in which Warren mentions making scrimshaw. According to an inscription in the hand of William H. Tripp, who was curator of NBWM at the time, the journal was "left to" him by Lucy J. Gifford in 1938; and from him it went to KNB, whence it ultimately came to NBWM.

Gifford, William S. (fl. circa 1850-64). The *Dictionary* cites an anonymous logbook entry (quoted anonymously by Edouard Stackpole, 93; William Gilkerson, 12; and Norman Flayderman, 187) to the effect that both Captain Spooner Jenkins and his wife, Sarah Cornell Jenkins (qq.v. in the *Dictionary*), did some scrimshawing on the whaling voyage they made together in the bark *Benjamin Cummings* of Dartmouth, Massachusetts, during 1854-59. It turns out that the logbook entry is actually from the journal of third mate William Gifford (NBWM); and Philip Purrington's implication (in "Bird's-Eye View," NBWM) is that Gifford was also doing some scrimshaw of his own on the voyage; however, to date none of his scrimshaw has come to light. Gifford was born in 1831 in Westport, Massachusetts, the son of George A. Gifford, Jr., mariner, and the former Nancy Wilbur. William was the eldest of five brothers, all of whom went whaling at one time or another. (The others were Valentine, Charles, James, and Alexander. They also had two younger sisters and a much younger kid brother.) William's whaling career is not entirely known, owing to confusion with at least a dozen other men of that name in the New Bedford whale fishery. However, it is known that prior to his voyage as third mate in the *Benjamin Cummings* (1854-59) he had the twin responsibilities of boatsteerer and carpenter in the Dartmouth bark *Henry H. Crapo* (1852-54), and afterwards was third mate in the ship *Alfred Gibbs* of New Bedford (1854-58), and was one of the mates — probably second mate — in the ship *William Henry* of Fairhaven (1860-64). Meanwhile, he married a woman named Mary and moved to New Bedford. On his retirement from whaling he moved the family back to Dartmouth, where he worked as a ship carpenter and raised two daughters: Julia, who became a schoolteacher, and Susie, a stenographer.

Gilpin, William A. (fl. circa 1830s-'40s). Whaleman from a prominent Wilmington, Delaware family, a seaman aboard the ship *Ceres* of Wilmington during 1834-37, now confidently regarded as the master scrimshaw-maker hitherto known as the Ceres A Artisan. Several hands are known to have produced the so-called Ceres Teeth. The one who originated the genre, hitherto known as the Ceres B Artisan (q.v.), was probably either one of two of Gilpin's shipmates: John Cleland, Jr., who kept the journal in which the source illustrations appear, or William H. Meyers, who is believed to have produced the journal illustrations (qq.v.). The Ceres C Artisan has been identified as another shipmate, Edmund M. Chandler (q.v.). Until recently, based upon an unsubstantiated claim attaching to the oral provenance of an outstanding busk said to have been "made by Captain Spooner of Fairhaven," the Ceres A Artisan was thought to be Captain Shubael S. Spooner (q.v.) of New Bedford. However, in 2008 a classic Jack Tar "Free Trade and Sailors' Rights"-type Ceres A tooth emerged that has "W A GILPIN" inscribed in the border of the characteristic proscenium arch (reported by Robert Ballintine and Donald E. Ridley; Sotheby's New York, 26 Sept. 2008, #25). The attribution, coming after some 35 years of scholarly scrutiny, vindicates an hypothesis originally informally postulated in the 1970s by Dr. Kenneth R. Martin and Judge Paul E. Vardeman: that an ink drawing of the Jack Tar / Sailors' Rights figure in seaman John Cleland, Jr.'s journal of the ship *Ceres* of Wilmington on a whaling voyage of 1834-37 (in MMV) was the source of the defining image of the so-called Ceres Teeth (and is hence the source of the nickname by which the Ceres Teeth have ever been informally known to curators and collectors). Both Edmund M. Chandler and William Aratus Gilpin were in the crew on that voyage. The wrinkle here is that in the intervening years the various Ceres Artisans have been distinguished one from the other, and according to evidence convincingly presented by Donald E. Ridley, Ceres B (q.v.) may have been the original source of the motifs on the scrimshaw *and* in the journal. It is not known for certain who made the drawings in the journal — the best argument is Kenneth Martin's that it was William H. Meyers — but there can be little doubt that William A. Gilpin was the Ceres A Artisan, the most skillful of the four-plus hands that produced Ceres Teeth. (For inventories and comparisons of characteristics, see the articles on the Ceres Artisans and the individual artists; also Stuart M. Frank, "'Free Trade and Sailors' Rights': Americana Scrimshaw by William Gilpin," in *Important Americana* (New York: Sotheby's, 26 Sept. 2008, 39-41.)

Not a great deal is known about Gilpin himself. He was born in Wilmington in 1805, the fourth son and fifth of nine children of William Gilpin (1775-1843), farmer, and the former Ann Dunwoody (1777-1840). An older brother, Edward Woodward Gilpin (1803-76), would later serve as Attorney General (1840-50) and Chief Justice (1857-76) of Delaware. Appearances to the contrary and despite a Classical middle name from the annals of ancient Greece — Aratus of Soli (circa 315-240 BCE) was a poet whose most famous work is *Phaenomena* ("Appearances"); and Aratus of Sicyon (271-213 BCE) was a political figure famous for deposing the tyrant Nicocles in 251 — William Aratus Gilpin was actually named after two of his father's siblings who died in infancy in 1773, William and Aratus. Only two voyages are known for sure. The first of these, the seminal one in the *Ceres,* was undertaken in 1834, when William was already 29 years old, married, and an expectant father (he was by far the oldest of the four *Ceres* artists). It was almost certainly not his first voyage and possibly not his first whaling voyage. Then there is a three- or four-year gap in the record (1837-41), suggesting that Gilpin may have made another whaling voyage, as yet undiscovered. His last known voyage was in the whaleship *Jason* of New London (1841-42), for which, at the age of 36 (rather old for a whaleman), he was still rated as a lowly Ordinary Seaman, and was still living in Wilmington (misprinted in the NBFPL Index as "Arlington"). In the meantime, he had married Elizabeth Brown, on 8 May 1831 or 8 May 1834; and on one of the Ceres A teeth, featuring a full-length figure of Hope, the name "Elizabeth" is inscribed in the proscenium arch. The Gilpins's daughter, Anna Elizabeth, was born in 1834 or '35. She married Charles Elkitten Sparks in 1868, and it may be under that surname that some of his possessions and possibly some of his scrimshaw descended.

Of twenty known works attributed to William Gilpin — 19 teeth and one busk — 12 are engraved on one side only and six on both sides. There are only two pairs, but three or four individual teeth appear to be halves of pairs of which the other half is unknown. The sailor-with-anchor motif appears the most often (on seven teeth), the figure of Hope with an anchor appears on three teeth (but these may the missing halves of sailor-and-Hope pairs). Nearly identical "Domestic Happiness" scenes appear as fully-realized renditions on two teeth (in KNB and a private collection) and in an abbreviated form on a third (in the same private collection).

A tooth that once belonged to the late Captain Michael Rodgers (given to NBWM in his memory by his widow in 2003) typifies the flawless draftsmanship, distinctive layout, meticulous workmanship, and elaborate interiors of the "Domestic Happiness" teeth, but in an exotic mode. Internal evidence indicates that this one and two others like it were done shortly after 1837. On one side is "The Corsair's Farewell": a pirate and his lady-love in an embrace, standing in a sumptuously furnished room, framed by one of this artist's characteristic geometric borders. The image is based upon a print entitled "Conrad and Medora," depicting two principal characters in the tragic ballet "Le Corsaire," based upon Byron's poem "The Corsair" (1814), with music by the exiled French musician Nicholas Charles Bochsa (1789-1856) — he was official harpist to both Napoleon Bonaparte and King Louis XVIII — choreographed by François Albert (1787-1865), and first performed in 1837 at the King's Theatre, London. On the other side is a half-length female portrait (possibly the actress playing the role of Medora) in an ornate gown, flanked by luxuriant draperies and curtains, framed by a geometric border, and surmounted by one of the defining features of the Ceres artisans' work, a proscenium arch in which there is a larboard broadside portrait of a full-rigged ship under sail. On the foremast flies a flag inscribed "L", and on the mainmast another inscribed "NYE." The latter is a swallowtail burgee flown as the private signal ("house flag") of New Bedford whaling merchants T. & A.R. Nye and their successor, Thomas Nye; the L is the initial indicating the name of the ship. The Nyes managed only two vessels having the initial L, both of them ships. One was the *Louisiana*, whaling from 1850 until 1865, when she was lost in Kotzebue Sound; and because the other L vessel was already in service when the *Louisiana* was acquired, a mere L would not have done to distinguish one from the other; but *if* one and not the other, it would surely have been the one with seniority that kept the L as her name-flag — the earlier and more significant vessel, which was the *Lancaster*, acquired from merchant Jireh Perry in 1834. She made nine voyages under Nye auspices until she was condemned at St. Thomas in 1861. Thus, between 1834 and 1842, the era in which most of the Ceres scrimshaw was likely produced, the *Lancaster* was the Nyes' only vessel with the initial L, and she probably kept the L-initial flag right to the end, in 1861. What bearing this has on the life and career of William A. Gilpin is not known.

There are polychrome renditions of the same scene on two other teeth attributed to the same hand. One has an equestrian image of St. George and the Dragon on the other side (reported by John Rinaldi); the other has the Jack Tar with arms akimbo, eagle, and "Free Trade and Sailors Rights" motto that appears on other Ceres teeth (Skinner, Aug. 14, 2010, #930). The St. George motif also appears in a smaller size with other vignettes on a tooth that has the sailor-with-anchor figure on the other side (Phillips, 17 Jan. 2001, #115). Flowered vines decorate several of these teeth, while images of a Bethel ship and St. Paul's Cathedral, and the seminal busk (all KNB and NBWM) are, so far, unique.

In the absence of a clear provenance for any of the Ceres Teeth, a few mysteries remain. The names Elizabeth B. Ellis and J. Drew are associated with a Ceres-like tooth reported by John Rinaldi (Osona, Aug. 7, 2010, #180). Elizabeth B. Ellis (born circa 1818) became the wife of Elisha C. Leonard (1819-1894), whom she married at New Bedford in 1842. He was a native of New Bedford, the son of Nehemiah Leonard (1778-1869) and Hannah Tinkham Clark[e] (1792-1875), thus he was a kinsman of George and Henry Clark[e] on his mother's side. These were extended-family relations of Captain Shubael S. Spooner and could be clues to how Spooner may have come in to possession of the "Spooner" busk. Nehemiah Leonard became an oil dealer and moved with Elizabeth to Springfield, Massachusetts, where they lived with Frank B. Warner, head of the Chicopee Bank, in a boardinghouse presumably managed by Mr. Warner's wife Charlotte. (Fellow boarders were a lumber dealer from Maine with his wife and son, a grocer, someone styled as a "Market man," two Presbyterian clergymen, a day laborer, and four Irish immigrant women in their early twenties, three of whom were named Catherine.) Elizabeth B. Ellis Leonard died sometime after giving birth to their second son and fourth child in 1855, whence Elisha took the children back to New Bedford, moved in with his parents, and became the proprietor of a "carpet warehouse" downtown. Also living in the Leonard household at that time were his whaling captain brother-in-law, Alden G. Ellis with his wife and son: Alden had been master of three whaling voyages, in the New Bedford ships *Nautilus* (1838-42) and *William Thompson* (1842-46 and 1846-50). By 1856 Elisha Leonard was serving on the City Council, afterwards became a notary public and justice of the peace, and was Assistant U.S. Assessor and U.S. Assessor from the late 1860s until he retired around 1875, at which time his two adult daughters, an elderly aunt, and a domestic servant were running his household. He died in 1894.

"J. Drew" has not been definitively identified. The several men named James, John, Joseph, and Josiah Drew in the New Bedford and Nantucket whaling trade span the entire nineteenth century and then some, but none ever served in any of the vessels associated with William Gilpin, Edmund Chandler, Shubael Spooner, Alden Ellis, or the Clark[e]s, and none is known to have been associated with any of them in any other capacity. See articles on James Drew and John Drew.

Golden, Benjamin W. (fl. circa 1830-45). Towards the end of his whaling voyage in the ship *Sharon* of Fairhaven, in October 1839, he mentions in his journal that he was "employed in fitting rigging and turning bone fids." The latter is the original and most rudimentary form of scrimshaw: tools and fittings for use around the ship, in this case presumably made from sperm whale skeletal bone. Captain Albert Veldkamp of Vlissingen, the Netherlands, who was first mate on each of the two Dutch floating-factory whaleships named *Willem Barents*, from 1946 to 1961, reported of fids turned from sperm whale panbone (which were still very much in use on modern steamships in the twentieth century) that not only are they a great deal stronger and much less susceptible to chipping, splintering, or breakage than their wooden counterparts, but they are "self-lubricating": the indigenous natural oils increase their utility in reeving, splicing, and making grommets. And if such a fid "is broken or gets dried out, you simply throw it overboard and make another one easily," because "there is plenty of bone available" (private communication, West Terschelling, Netherlands, May 1996; and R/V *Professor Molchanov,* off Spitsbergen, June 2004).

Surprisingly little is known about Benjamin W. Golden. There is no Protection Paper (seaman's passport) on file in New Bedford, though he evidently made all of his whaling voyages from New Bedford and Fairhaven. According to his shipping records, he was born in Baltimore circa 1814, and went whaling at age 16 in the New Bedford ship *Hibernia* (1830-31), followed by the *Gratitude* of New Bedford (1831-35), an unidentified voyage (circa 1835-37), and the *Sharon* of Fairhaven (1837-40). In 1841 he went as second mate in the Fairhaven ship *Heroine*, but he evidently left that vessel somewhere along the way before the voyage was completed and returned to New Bedford. There, he married Julia A Tripp in April 1843, then sailed in June as second mate in the Fairhaven ship *Ansel Gibbs* (1843-45). So ends the record. (There is no reason to suppose any relationship between this man and the Benjamin Golden who was born in New York City circa 1834 and embarked on a whaling voyage in the bark *Dove* of New London in 1854.)

* **Grant, George A.** (fl. circa 1860s-80s). For another instance of an eccentric master craftsman who sold his scrimshaw — perhaps compulsively — see the article on William Martin.

Fig. 12. **Captain Joseph K. Green** made this small pan-bone-and-ivory swift with inlaid stand and matching sewing box circa the 1850s. The box has been in the New Bedford Whaling Museum since 1942, the gift of Mrs. Sara R. Greene. The swift descended in another branch of the family and was sold at auction for a record price (Northeast Auctions, Aug. 21, 2004, #849). Courtesy of the New Bedford Whaling Museum (photo by Richard Donnelly) and Ronald Bourgeault, Northeast Auctions, Portsmouth, New Hampshire.

Green, Joseph K. (fl. circa 1840-64). New Bedford whaling master renowned for his exquisite inlay in abalone and mother of pearl. (Green evidently spelled his surname without the terminal *e*, while at least some descendants adopted the spelling *Greene*. The name appears both ways in official whaling records and consular documents, but his signature is always *Green*.) An unusually ornate sewing box that has a hinged lid with the top, skirts, and sides inlaid in intricate floral and vine motifs with perching birds and numerous semicircles of shell, and has internal compartments with a plush pincushion and delicately carved-and-assembled pendant whale ivory handles on individual lids, was donated to NBWM by Mrs. Sara R. Greene in 1942. The recent attribution to Joseph K. Green is made on the basis of its descent in the Green[e] family, combined with the provenance of other objects from a parallel branch of Green descendants: a small whale ivory double swift mounted on a solid, stepped wooden base that is very clearly by the same hand as the sewing box, intricately inlaid with abalone and mother of pearl in an identical fashion, with floral and vine motifs, perching birds, semicircles of shell, etc. (The swift set a world record for auction prices realized for scrimshaw, at Northeast Auctions, Aug. 21-22, 2004, #849. In the same auction were an ambrotype portrait of Captain Green himself, a wood with wood-inlay knife box attributed to him, lot #851, and other associated items. He is also presumed to have owned a substantial pair of polychrome-engraved teeth depicting standing patriotic figures of Liberty and Justice, lot #850, which are not attributed to his own hand.)

Joseph K. Green was a career whaleman born at Dartmouth, Massachusetts, in 1822, the son of William T. Green, who was originally from Charlestown, Rhode Island, and his second wife, Dorcas Kendrick of Dartmouth. Joseph was first mate of the *Ann Alexander* under Captain John Scott Deblois when she sailed in 1850, and so was aboard when the vessel was stove and sunk by a whale in 1851 — a famous incident that, when reported in the immediate wake of the publication of *Moby Dick*, was taken to corroborate the plausibility of Melville's yarn. Green was now given command of the New Bedford bark *Susan* in which he skippered two voyages (1853-56 and 1865-57) on which his younger brother, William T. Green (born circa 1827), served as third mate and second mate, respectively. Joseph also brought along his wife Elizabeth and three-year-old daughter Mary on the second *Susan* voyage, and as it turned out, they were all shipwrecked together when the *Susan* was lost on the Esmeraldas coast of Ecuador in June 1857. This was plenty traumatic for Joseph, who after suffering the battering of the *Ann Alexander* now lost a command of his own; and for the owners (Starbuck points out that the *Susan* was "the sixth vessel lost by A.H. Howland in 8 years"); but it must have been especially traumatic for Elizabeth, now pregnant again and with a four-year-old in tow. Even so, the family, expanded by the addition of an infant son named Joseph, came along on the next voyage too, in the bark *Golconda*. This was an unlucky voyage in every respect, and proved to be their last. They sailed in October 1859, and Elizabeth gave birth to a son in Chile early along. But she and baby Levi died not long afterwards, though how long afterwards, and whether at sea or back in New Bedford, is not clear. In any case, Captain Green left the voyage and went home, presumably with the other two children in hand. He was relieved by Benjamin Winslow, and the *Golconda* continued whaling in the Pacific, only to have a disappointing catch of only 600 barrels of sperm oil, and to lose much of that when the *Golconda* was captured and burned by the Confederate commerce raider *Florida* in July 1864. This meant that they lost the 140 barrels of sperm oil that they still had aboard (fortunately, 460 barrels had already been sent home in advance) in addition to 1,100 barrels of sperm oil and 600 barrels of whale oil that they were carrying as freight; so that even though no lives were lost and all hands were put ashore safely, there would be little profit for anyone on this voyage, including Captain Green for his part in it. Meanwhile, another of Green's younger brothers, Abraham Francis Green (born circa 1831), was lost at sea in 1864. Joseph married again, to a woman named Mary (1835-1912) who was from Delaware or Pennsylvania (census records differ), and took up farming in his native South Dartmouth, where he fathered two more children. He died in 1888. On the *Ann Alexander* Captain John Deblois (q.v.) said of his first mate in December 1850, "Without doubt he was the smartest whaleman I ever saw"; and in 1851, "Mr. Greene is a first reat [rate] whaleman and a smart man and would like to have his way. I try hard to live in peace. I hav[e] to nip my tongue some times. He never has ben brought up to take good care of a ship" (quoted in Sawtell 1962, 66f).

Hart, Joshua. A crudely-rendered ship portrait on a rough and only semi-polished tooth (reportedly William J. Boylhart) is boldly but poorly inscribed, "TOSHUA HART" (sic), taken to signify *Joshua* Hart, about whose life and career nothing has been learned.

* **Haskins,** — attributed to "Haskins," mentioned in the *Dictionary*, has still not been identified. There are two theories about where to look. One is to concentrate on the several short-term seamen surnamed Haskins who served in whaleships of New London, which was heavily invested in Arctic whaling (thus occasioning a higher-than-otherwise incidence of opportunities to acquire walrus ivory) and which, if the MSM collection be a reliable barometer, seems to have produced an unusually high proportion of engraved walrus ivory (as distinct from engraved whale ivory), compared with, say, Nantucket or New Bedford. The other theory is to concentrate on the background, circumstances, skills, and longevity of whalemen surnamed Haskins, irrespective of home port, just so long as they were whaling in the Arctic for some part of their careers, and thus had sufficient opportunity to acquire walrus ivory. The idea here is that, statistically, a suitably skilled mariner in propitious circumstances would more likely be a scrimshaw-maker than a one-voyage neophyte, especially were he a career whaleman of long tenure (thus with many more opportunities to acquire the ivory and, presumably, more discretionary leisure for scrimshaw production). Neither theory is satisfactory, nor is either method guaranteed to produce the desired result, but in the absence of actual evidence a field of too many plausible candidates is perhaps better than no candidate at all.

In the first category — men who made a voyage or two in New London vessels — are: John A. Haskins, mariner, who lived in New London in the 1850s and likely made at least one whaling voyage around that time; Daniel Haskins of Rochester, Massachusetts, who embarked at age 18 in the ship *Dover* to the Pacific Ocean (1851-55); Erastus Haskins of Oswego, New York, age 19, who went in the bark *Laurens* to the Atlantic and Indian Ocean grounds (1857-58); and Leander Haskins, born in Dartmouth, Massachusetts and a resident of Charlestown, Massachusetts, who went in the brig *Isabella* to Hudson Bay at age 35 (1863-64). (As noted in the *Dictionary*, there were also two men named Haskins who served as boatsteerers on Western Arctic voyages out of San Francisco: Charles B. Haskins, bark *Abraham Barker* (1891-92), and another Daniel Haskins, bark *Hunter* (1893).

In the second category are two brothers, John C. and William H. Haskins, each a career whaleman for twenty years or more who served briefly as a captain. They were from Freetown, Massachusetts, born in 1827 and 1829, respectively. It appears that in his youth John served at least part of an apprenticeship as a cooper (William evidently did not), and certainly served as ship's cooper on at least one voyage, sperm- and right-whaling in the North Pacific aboard the New Bedford ship *Minerva 2nd* (1848-51) — signifying that he was a trained artisan more accustomed to handling edge tools than most sailors and statistically far more likely to have made scrimshaw than the average foremast hand. Moreover, for much of his working career he boarded with two accomplished whalemen-scrimshaw artists, Benjamin C. Blossom and John C. Reed (qq.v.) and their wives, who were John's sisters. His one voyage as a captain was in the New Bedford brig *Cossack* (1857-61) to the Pacific and Indian Ocean grounds, where he was unlikely to encounter much walrus ivory. However, all of his other known voyages were to the North Pacific, where they took bowhead whales aplenty and where a whaleman would typically have many opportunities to acquire walrus tusks by barter with the Natives. The younger brother, William Henry Haskins, has a less convincing claim. There is no evidence that he was ever a cooper or woodworker of any kind; he did not live with the two scrimshaw-artist brothers-in-law (in fact, he and his family lived on Martha's Vineyard); and his career as a whaling captain was something of a disappointment. His first command was the New Bedford ship *Louisiana*, which sailed in April 1864 but was wrecked fifteen months later in Kotzebue Sound, Alaska. They saved the oil, which they sent home by other means, but there was not yet much to save; and the wreck occurred too early in the voyage for there yet to have been much scrimshaw. Next, in June 1866, William sailed as captain of the Fairhaven brig *John Hathaway*, but the vessel was condemned soon after and the voyage was never completed — a sad, scrimshaw-less conclusion to William's unlucky career as captain. He was thus the less likely of the two brothers to have scrimshawed the Haskins tusk, though in theory either one of them *might* have done it, and either one or *both* of them could be among the myriad scrimshaw artists whose work has simply not surfaced or not been identified.

Hathaway, Henry C. (1842-1931). He became famous from having been third mate in the New Bedford bark *Gazelle* on one of the world's most famous whaling voyages, the 1866-70 expedition on which they rescued the Irish firebrand poet, political agitator, and journalist John Boyle O'Reilly (1844-1890) from penal servitude at Bunbury, Western Australia (1869). This led to Hathaway's befriending O'Reilly himself, with whom Hathaway shared a cabin during their time together homeward bound in the *Gazelle*; and to his activities seven years later as an integral collaborator in the even more notorious rescue of six other Irish Fenian political radicals from Fremantle, Western Australia, in the New Bedford whaler *Catalpa* (1876). Hathaway was not exactly a scrimshaw artist at any time, but he evidently did cut and polish at least one large pair of sperm whale teeth from the *Catalpa* voyage, and — along with a belaying pin from the *Catalpa* and a specimen of the 1876 lithograph of the *Catalpa* expedition by E.N. Russell — presented the teeth to his young collector-historian friend, W.L.R. Gifford.

William Logan Rodman Gifford, born in 1862, was a New Bedford native who had become head librarian of the St. Louis [Missouri] Mercantile Library. Being from New Bedford, he was himself the son, nephew, grandson, brother-in-law, and son-in-law of sea captains and whaling masters. Gifford's father-in-law was whaling captain John G. Dexter of Rochester, Massachusetts, under whom Henry Hathaway served as boatsteerer in the New Bedford bark *Hercules* during 1862-66, immediately prior to his Fenian adventure in the *Gazelle*. Gifford's paternal grandfather was merchant sea captain Humphrey A. Gifford of Westport; and his uncle, Captain Benjamin D. Gifford (q.v.) of Westport, was a whaling master and scrimshaw artist. W.L.R. Gifford himself collected whaling lore and whaling relics, he was the biographer of George Howland, Jr., in 1892, and became somewhat famous in his own right for having held his position longer than anyone else in the distinguished history of the Mercantile Library. He donated Henry Hathaway's *Catalpa* scrimshaw and other relics to NBWM in 1941. (David R. Gifford was captain of the *Gazelle* on two voyages on which Henry Hathaway served, including the famous O'Reilly rescue mission. He was born in 1826 at Savoy, in distant Berkshire County, Massachusetts, and if he was any kin to W.L.R. Gifford it could only have been a distant relation which the paucity of records render elusive.)

Ironically, Henry Clay Hathaway, the man who is best known for the spirited and patriotic but illegal *Gazelle* and *Catalpa* rescues, simultaneously became New Bedford's principal law enforcement officer. He was born in 1842, the son of a New Bedford blacksmith and edge-tool manufacturer, Braddock D. Hathaway (1806-1879), and the former Harriet Richmond (1805-1886). (B.D. Hathaway's famous overhead shop sign, shaped like a hatchet, is in NBWM and has been published many times.) Henry's two older brothers went into their father's blacksmithing firm; one fell at Gettysburg in 1863; but Henry went whaling. In August 1856, at the tender age of 14 he sailed as a green hand in the New Bedford ship *Lancer*, and only a short time later, on November 23, the captain, Aaron C. Cushman died. Owen Fisher stepped in as relief captain and the voyage continued, but Hathaway did not complete it. His name appears on the outward manifest, but his obituary reports that he spent only "about two years" in the *Lancer*; and as he is also listed in the crew list of a simultaneous voyage in the New Bedford bark *Callao* (1858-62), but is not listed on the outward manifest of that vessel, the likelihood is that he transferred from the *Lancer* to the *Callao* at some point when both voyages were in progress. By this time he was rated Ordinary Seaman. He was promoted to boatsteerer on his next voyage, the one in the bark *Hercules*, commanded by John G. Dexter (1862-66). Thus the stage was set for Hathaway to go as fourth mate for the 60th lay in the ship *Gazelle*, Captain David R. Gifford, on what Hathaway had no reason to expect would be anything but just another conventional whaling voyage. It was not. Under the guise of going whaling the *Gazelle* was actually in the control of a covert network of conspirators intending, through stealth or force, to liberate the Fenian patriot John Boyle O'Reilly. A member of the radical republican Fenian Brotherhood, in 1863 O'Reilly had

> *enlisted in the Tenth Hussars in Ireland for the purpose of spreading anti-British sentiments among the soldiers. He was sentenced to death on the charge of high treason in 1866. The sentence was commuted to 20 years' penal servitude, and he was sent out to the penal colony in Australia, where he arrived in 1868"* (*Century Cyclopedia of Names*, 1954, III:3033f)

Sentiment favorable to O'Reilly was especially prevalent in New England at this time, given the pro-Confederate sympathies of the British government during the recent Civil War — sympathies in which the general run of British citizenry did not share, by reason of their opposition to slavery, but which nevertheless raised the ire of many Americans. New Englanders tended to be anti-slavery and anti-royalist in any case. Accordingly — despite resistance to Irish immigration to America in many quarters — New Englanders tended to be pro-Irish and anti-British at this time on this issue. As many saw it, O'Reilly and his Fenians were fighting to liberate the downtrodden Irish people from 700 years of British imperial oppression; theirs was the cause of Freedom and Liberty, with O'Reilly their articulate spokesman. It is the resonance of this sentiment that imparts to Hathaway's otherwise innocuous pair of polished sperm whale teeth the status of a kind of sacred relic. So, too, the official logbook of the *Gazelle* voyage (in NBWM), in which passenger O'Reilly transcribed three long poems of his own composition in his own hand, signing and inscribing them to his crew of rescuers. That Hathaway was one of these and was soon the best known — especially after the death of Captain David R. Gifford in 1873 and the sensational *Catalpa* episode of 1876 – placed Hathaway among the titans.

Having returned to New Bedford in the *Gazelle* and with O'Reilly safely landed (he was hired to write for the *Boston Pilot* newspaper, and became editor-in-chief in 1874), Hathaway was ashore for six months between voyages in 1870, during which time he married Catherine Perry (1840-1922), then went to sea again as third mate of the *Gazelle* (1870-74). On this voyage Hathaway saw a captain die at sea for a second time, when David R. Gifford expired in mid passage in 1873. In most other respects it turned out to be just another conventional whaling voyage. Perhaps after the Fenian adventure such a commonplace cruise was simply too tame; in any case, it was Hathaway's last time whaling. Almost as soon as he came home he was appointed New Bedford City Marshal (1874-75), then captain of the night watch of the New Bedford Police (1875-76) — this at the same time that veteran escape-artist Hathaway was clandestinely plotting with John Boyle O'Reilly and John Devoy to organize another illegal mission to rescue more Fenian prisoners in Australia. The scheme was for Captain George S. Anthony to outfit a vessel and recruit a crew for a conventional whaling cruise to the Pacific, and only after the ship was already at sea would the ulterior purpose of the voyage be revealed to the officers and crew. This turned out to be the *Catalpa*. In 1876 — the very year the *Catalpa* brought six Fenians out of Fremantle, with guns ablazing and a Royal Navy patrol boat in hot pursuit — the Mayor of New Bedford, Alanson Borden, appointed Henry Hathaway the city's first Chief of Police (1876-78), its highest ranking law enforcement officer. In this newly-created berth Hathaway supervised two captains, two lieutenants, 26 officers on the regular force, and 83 Special Police.

In 1878 Police Chief Hathaway left the force to become Captain Hathaway, master of the brand-new merchant bark *Veronica*, 409 tons, built at Bath, Maine, in 1878. She was owned by some of New Bedford's leading merchants, and carried cargoes and passengers between New Bedford and the Portuguese islands — the Azores, Madeira, and Cape Verde — providing steerage accommodations for immigrants to America, return passage for whalemen from the islands who had become stranded in New England, and promoting the brisk exchange of the cultures and commodities of three continents. The celebrated New Bedford ship-portraitist Charles Sidney Raleigh painted the *Veronica* when she was new (in NBWM), and she naturally attracted the attention and admiration of the Azorean and Cape Verdean communities on both sides of the Atlantic, as she was by far the grandest vessel ever to have been in the Azores and Brava packet trade.

For Hathaway this lasted only about three years. In the next phase of his career he was involved in a wide range of business interests, as a sometime furniture dealer, real estate magnate, tobacco merchant, and auctioneer. In 1891 he acquired a carriage factory that was originally established by Forbes & Sears in New Bedford in 1862. Now, doing business under his own name, the Henry C. Hathaway carriage works had 15 employees and did fairly well for the few years remaining before the advent of the automobile. That same year, shortly after John Boyle O'Reilly's premature death in 1890, in recognition of his unique friendship with Hathaway, a consortium of prominent Boston merchants presented Hathaway with a commemorative bronze ship-portrait of the *Catalpa* in a fancy frame, on which a silver plaque is engraved with the inscription, "CAPT HENRY C. HATHAWAY / in grateful memory of / JOHN BOYLE O'REILLY / Whom he rescued twice from imprisonment and once from death. / Presented by a few friends in Boston, May 19, 1891" (in KNB). In addition, as the *New Bedford Standard* reported in his obituary on May 4, 1931, Hathaway was "Honored by Irish Societies in Many Cities," as he had become the principal living symbol of the Fenian rescues and American enthusiasm for O'Reilly's Irish republican spirit, which — oddly — seems to have been as popular in rarefied Boston Brahmin circles as it was among the Irish immigrant rabble. Meanwhile, he played a responsible role in civic affairs, serving as United States Shipping Commissioner until 1921, when the office was abolished; on the New Bedford Board of Aldermen; and as Chairman of the Committee of the City Council on Public Instruction, thus *ex officio* as a trustee of the New Bedford Free Public Library. This was the capacity in which he also had a professional relationship with librarian W.L.R. Gifford, who eventually donated Henry C. Hathaway's only known scrimshaw ten years after Hathaway's death in 1931 at age 89.

Hathaway, Nathan C. (1851-1923). There were many whalemen named Hathaway in a town brimming over with Hathaways, but this fellow was not one of them. He grew up in the late heyday of the whaling industry, in which he participated only indirectly, in a modest white-collar career in finance, as clerk, bookkeeper, and assistant cashier of the Mechanics' National Bank. He also served as treasurer of the New Bedford Port Society which operates the Seamen's Bethel and Mariners' Home, he was intimately familiar at first hand with the whaling industry in its declining years, and was active at the NBWM in its formative days, contributing substantially to building the museum's collection of scrimshaw, as reflected in the minutes of an early annual meeting:

> *Nathan C. Hathaway is constantly adding new treasures to his case of ivories, and it is safe to say that Mr. Hathaway's case, the case of jagging wheels and the case of miscellaneous articles made on shipboard form a collection of ivories which is most valuable and unique and one which it would be impossible to duplicate.* (*Proceedings*, Annual Meeting of the Old Dartmouth Historical Society, March 30, 1910)

What has not generally been known is that Hathaway also made at least one piece of scrimshaw of his own: a coconut shell bowl, with cutout lid, three legs turned from panbone, and a turned panbone mushroom-shaped knob threaded into a hole in the lid.

Born in New Bedford in 1851 — the year *Moby-Dick* was published — Nathan was the son of John A. Hathaway, the proprietor of a New Bedford livery stable, and the former Elizabeth A. Studley. He never married but traveled extensively abroad, in later life boarding with his brother Andrew and brother-in-law James H. Tallman, and retired circa 1918. Many additional pieces of scrimshaw came to NBWM from his estate in 1923.

Hazard, William (fl. circa the 1830s or '40s). Pair of small teeth, each circumferentially monochrome engraved with seaport views, looking seaward from the waterfront, with ships, boats, harbor activity, and staffing, each signed "W. HAZARD"; examined at the Newport [Rhode Island] Historical Society from a private collection in Newport. Of the many men surnamed Hazard involved in the whaling industries of Massachusetts and Rhode Island, one was William C. Hazard of Portsmouth, Rhode

Island, born circa 1813, who got his Seaman's Protection Paper at Newport in 1834. However, the most likely maker of the scrimshaw was William Rhodes Hazard, who gave his residence as Point Judith Rhode Island, when at age 19 he signed articles for a voyage in the whaleship *Meteor* of Mystic, Connecticut (1840-42). He was born in 1821, the son of Theresa née Clarke and Bowdoin Hazard, a merchant in South Kingstown who employed all four of William's younger siblings. He was afterwards a farmer in South Kingstown in association with his brother Edward, and he married Sarah H. Robinson in 1851. Contrary to a family genealogy posted on Ancestry.com, he was almost certainly not the Rhode Island native of this name who was living in St. Louis with his wife Rachel and working as a flour merchant in 1870; and he may or may not have been the Rhode Island native named William R. Hazard who died in Monmouth, New Jersey, in 1905.

Healy, George — see **George Heely**

Healy, Lyman (fl. circa 1831-45). Whaleman and ship's cooper. In his journal of the New Bedford ship *William Thompson* during 1835-38 (in KNB), Healy not only mentions "cleaning teeth" — that is, processing sperm whale teeth on deck, presumably in preparation for scrimshandering — but reports on one occasion, "cooper making whalebone broom"; on another, "cooper scrimshonting"; and even that the cooper made "a ship model for the captain." The captain was Hiram Weeks, and the outward-bound crew list for the *William Thompson* (in NBFPL) names Alexander McDonnell as cooper. McDonnell was certainly a ship's cooper is his subsequent career aboard the New Bedford ships *Honqua* (1846-49) and *Natchez* (1851-55). However, aboard the *William Thompson* in 1835 he deserted at Fayal within a couple of months of sailing, so early in the voyage that he could scarcely have had opportunity to do a lot of coopering, much less to indulge in scrimshaw. Neither the crew list nor Healy's journal provides any clue to the identity of the cooper after McDonnell's desertion, and McDonnell was the only man on board who is known ever to have worked as a cooper on any other occasion — except, ironically, Healy himself. This is one of several circumstances of this *William Thompson* voyage that are odd. First of all, of the twenty men named on the outward manifest when the ship sailed from New Bedford in June 1835, there are two whose ages are not recorded, but of the remaining eighteen, eight were older than 30, a remarkably high percentage; and eleven, a majority, were over the age of 25, which is more remarkable still. And of the original twenty, only seven — the captain, journal-keeper Healy, and five others — completed the voyage. All the rest, and also most of the ten or twelve replacement crewmen recruited along the way at Fayal, Pico, and elsewhere, deserted in various ports-of-call, from Fayal itself to Port Louis, Mauritius, in the Indian Ocean, and Bay of Islands, New Zealand, in the Pacific. In one instance several men lowered a whaleboat and slipped away all at once. What is most unusual about this is that such large numbers of desertions occurred in a crew comprised of comparatively mature men who were, for the most part, seasoned mariners who had been whaling before and can be presumed to have known what to expect. And it seems especially odd in that there is no other indication that Captain Weeks and his mates were anything but regular, garden variety ship's officers: no evidence of bucko punishments, worse-than-average provisions, or anything out of the ordinary for a blubber-hunter. Nevertheless, Alexander McDonnell, ship's cooper, age unspecified, was one of the first to run off, at Fayal in July or August 1835. So he never really made the voyage at all. He probably did make scrimshaw, as artisans on shipboard were wont to do, but not on this voyage. And as Healy was the only other man on board who is known ever to have worked as a cooper at any other time, it appears that he must have been the replacement cooper and, oddly, that it is to himself that he refers in the third person as the cooper who made the ship model and the scrimshaw.

As a sometime artisan himself Healy likely made scrimshaw on other occasions, even if not on this voyage. He was born at Tiverton, Rhode Island, circa 1808, and in his youth may have apprenticed as a cooper or caulker, the two trades he practiced later in life. His first known voyage was in the New Bedford ship *Ceres* (1831-33), in which he embarked at age 23. He was then in the New Bedford ship *Milwood* (1833-34); and by the time he returned in the *William Thompson* (1835-38) he was living in New Bedford. He may have made his next voyage (circa 1838-41) in a Rhode Island vessel, but in any case later went as cooper for the 44th lay in the New Bedford ship *Archer* (1841-45). This appears to have been his last voyage. The 1850 census lists him as Lyman *Haley*, age 42, born in Rhode Island, working at that time as a caulker in New Bedford, where he lived with his wife Sarah, a New Jersey native, age 38. In his later years, evidently widowed, he moved back to Tiverton, where he was a farmhand boarding at Josiah C. Durfee's farm.

* **Heely, George** (fl. circa 1853-56). As noted in the *Dictionary*, he was the maker of an important tooth that has on one side the stern-quarter portrait of an American warship under plain sail, copied from a cut on an official document, with the initials "W.J." (as if for presentation) overhead, framed in a wreath and surmounted by a spread-eagle; and, on the other side, an original standing figure of a woman in typical Peruvian ladies' attire, with shawl and mantilla, inscribed "Lima"; signed "George Heely" (KNB). He was born circa 1836 in New Boston, New York — though whether it was the New Boston in Cortland County or (more likely) the New Boston in Lewis County is not known for certain. He may have been the same George *Healy* who as a teenager in upstate New York, before he went whaling, worked as a wood sawyer, and he appears to have been a boatsteerer and ship's carpenter in the whaling bark *Sea Flower* of New Bedford during 1856-57, with his name erroneously transcribed in the ship's articles as George L. Heald. The boatsteerer's berth indicates that he had made at least one prior whaling voyage. In 1860 a George *Heely* was working as a mail carrier in Seneca, New York, but the maker of the scrimshaw appears to have been the George *Healy* who that year was working as a boatman on Lake Ontario, a career for which his deepwater whaling experience would have suited him nicely, and was boarding with the family of fellow-boatman Charles Coe in Volney, Oswego County.

* **Herendeen, Alonzo O.** (fl. circa 1847-89). New Bedford whaling master from Cape Cod. On the basis of one reliable provenance independently corroborated by another, he is known to have made two fine jewelry boxes, with a third confidently attributed. Each is a wooden oblong with hinged lid, contrasting wooden edges, and a leafy vine floral motif delicately inlaid on the top in whale ivory and mother-of-pearl. The insides of two are lined with velvet. According to the handwritten provenance on the bottom of a box in KNB, it was "Made from sandal wood from the Island of Juan Fernandez, South Pacific Ocean, by Captain Alonzo O. Herendeen, ship *James Arnold*, 1887." The provenance of a second box claims that it came from "Capt. Herendeen of ship *James Arnold* of New Bedford" (in DAF). A third specimen with a provenance from the Nye family on Cape Cod (reported by Paul Madden) claims no Herendeen connection but is attributed (by SFL) on the basis of shape, size, and style of the inlay. Additionally, a set of bone and ebonized wood dominoes in a

dovetailed wooden case with a sliding lid (Kranzler, Christie's-NY, 1 Nov. 1988, #423) is also attributed to Alonzo O. Herendeen despite that it is reportedly marked "Capt. A.W. [sic] Herendeen / Mar 2nd 1887": there was no Captain A.W. Herendeen, and as the box closely resembles three of Alonzo's known works, and as the date is perfectly consistent with the two of them, it is credible to assume that the provenance is mistaken with respect to the maker's middle initial.

Alonzo Herendeen was born in 1833 in Woods Hole in the town of Falmouth, Cape Cod, the second son (and the second of at least twelve children) of Sanford and Mary Herendeen. His father was a cooper, and both Alonzo and his brother Edward, two years older, apprenticed in the trade and worked at it into their late teens. Alonzo's earliest voyages have not been discovered, but he went to sea at age around 14, and as noted in the *Dictionary*:

> *... he was concurrently fourth mate, boatsteerer, and cooper in the ship* **Elliot C. Cowdin** *of Dartmouth (1855-60); then second mate and mate (1860-67) of the bark* **Mary and Susan** *of New Bedford. His first command was as relief master on that vessel (1866-67) after Captain Philip Howland died at sea, 11 Nov. 1866. Herendeen was given the* **Mary and Susan** *for two more voyages (1867-74), the second of which he interrupted (relieved by Captain Pliny B. Handy) in order to take the San Francisco brig* **Manila** *to the ground at Scammon's Lagoon, on Baja California: the only whaler to sail from California in 1871, the* **Manila** *was wrecked soon after. Rejoining the* **Mary and Susan**, *he returned with her to New Bedford in 1874, then took the bark* **Falcon** *(1875-79; relieved again by Pliny B. Handy and then James A. Crowell)...*

In 1886 he took command of the *James Arnold*, the vessel most closely associated with his scrimshaw. It was his last voyage. He died at sea on November 17, 1889, and was succeeded by Jesse T. Sherman. The scrimshaw box "Made from sandal wood from the Island of Juan Fernandez" in 1887 and any other pieces he may have had on board (that is, the ones that were not the products of previous voyages) would have been returned posthumously to his widow in Woods Hole, along with his other personal effects. Her name has not been discovered, nor whether they had children; and the initials "A.P.H." on one of the boxes have not been identified. In recent years several shameless and not very convincing scrimshaw fakes have been reported with the spurious signature "Alonzo O. Herendeen," mostly monochrome-engraved letter openers and other trivial implements made of generic mammalian bone that do not in the least resemble Captain Herendeen's actual work (debunked at SFL). One of these is crudely inscribed "Alonzo O'Herendeen, Bark Falcon, October 26 1875 – April 21, 1879. Pacific," proving that not all forgers are clever even if they have read a book.

* **Hersey, Joseph Bogart** (fl. circa 1843-51). Whaleman and whaling master on Atlantic voyages out of Provincetown, Cape Cod, Massachusetts. The *Dictionary* refers to two walking sticks attributed in KNB. Judging from the quality of the walking sticks and the drawings and vignettes in his journals, he was a talented amateur artist, but unfortunately no other product of his evidently large output of scrimshaw yardsticks, busks, and teeth has been identified. He was born in 1820 or 1821 in New York City, where he was likely apprenticed to a tailor. According to one of his later journals, his maiden voyage was in the schooner *Belle Isle*, which would have been circa 1841-42, and by 1843 he was a boatsteerer or third mate in the schooner *Esquimaux*. He was af-

terwards second mate of the brig *Phenix* (1845-46), first mate of the bark *Samuel and Thomas* (1846-48), and made three voyages as captain of the schooner *Shylock* (1849-51). His journals of all of his voyages except the first and last survive (in KNB), and his extensive and extremely articulate remarks about scrimshaw in the *Esquimaux* journal are anthologized here as Appendix III. In the 1850s he married Mary K. Dyer, lived at Provincetown and evidently also for a while at Sandwich, Massachusetts, owned a 1/16th interest in the schooner *Antarctic* and 1/8th of the *Shylock* and earned his living as a "trader" and later as a merchant tailor (from which arises the presumption that he must have had some training as a tailor in his youth). A daughter Naomi, born in 1857 died in 1862, and a son, Joseph O.B. Hersey, born at Sandwich in 1860, died in early 1861. A second son named Henry J. Hersey, born in 1863, was evidently the only child to survive Captain Hersey, who died in 1865 at age 44.

Hersey, William A. (fl. circa 1835-37). A medium-size sperm whale tooth (in KNB) is polished and boldly inscribed in a cursive ink holograph "Wm. A. Hersey" inside an irregular squiggly ink border, with no other adornments. It was evidently intended as a memento of a voyage and is attributed to a neophyte who, under the name Willie A. Hersey, kept a journal of a Pacific Ocean voyage in the whaleship *Endeavor* of New Bedford during 1835-37 (in NBWM). Edward W. Collins, father of Hananiah Collins (q.v.), was the first mate on that voyage and kept of a journal of his own that reveals nothing about "Willie." In fact, only two men named William Hersey have been encountered in the whaling records. The other was an African-American seaman from Lewistown, Pennsylvania, whose Protection Paper, issued at New Bedford in 1848, indicates that he was only 22 years old at that time, thus born circa 1826 and clearly too young to have been on the *Endeavor* in 1835. A large family of Herseys in Hingham, Scituate, Duxbury, and Plymouth, Massachusetts, is descended from a seventeenth-century English settler named William Hersey, hence William was a recurrent name in that Hersey family, but of the several Herseys from that clan who went whaling (mostly in the 1830s), no William is listed; nor is there a Protection Paper on file in New Bedford, nor any entry in the Port Society manifests. Much the same can be said of another clan of Herseys in New York State, from which scrimshaw artist Joseph Bogart Hersey (q.v.) emerged: they had plenty of men called William but no recorded whalemen of that name. Even Willie's journal fails to identify the keeper beyond giving his name and two "Mottos" [sic] with an enigmatic appendix: "1 Honesty is the best policy" and "2 Do to others as you would have others do to you / a new broom sweep / [signed] William A. Hersey."

Higgins, Samuel, Jr. (fl. circa 1831-34). A tooth offered at auction (Northeast, March 15, 2006) is reportedly inscribed "Samuel Higgins Junr. / Ship President / [Captain] Smith [or Swift] / Pacific Ocean, August 4, 1833. Latt. 4° 41' South / Long 115.58 West / Whale Made 80 bbls." The Nantucket ship *President* was indeed in the Pacific in 1833 during a whaling voyage of 1831-34. However, the captain on that voyage was Seth Cathcart, there is no record of any whaling vessel named *President* (of any rig or from any port) ever having been commanded by a captain named Smith or Swift, and no record has been located of any Samuel Higgins, Jr., in the whale fishery. However: see the article on Samuel *Huggins*, Jr.

Hogle, John T. (fl. circa 1840-44). His journal of the New Bedford bark *London Packet* (1840-44) implies that he was a participant in the scrimshawing activities on board, but none of his scrimshaw has yet come to light. On his Seaman's Passport, issued at New Bedford in November 1840 just prior to his embarking on the *London Packet,* he gave his age as 19 and his birthplace or residence as Cambridge, New York. However, the crew ledger at the Seamen's Bethel (NBPS) agrees as to age but gives his residence as North Adams, Massachusetts, c/o Vinal Hogle, who was probably his father. The *London Packet* was evidently his only whaling voyage, and the 1850 U.S. Census has him living in Canaan, New York, age 28, married to a woman named Laura and working as a mechanic. And that is all that is known about him.

* **Howard, H.** (fl. circa 1866). No new information has surfaced since the article on this man appeared in *More Scrimshaw Artists,* but evidently the analysis requires further clarification. The scrimshaw at issue is a tooth with a female three-quarter portrait on one side, and on the other side two winged cherubs embracing a flaming torch, with a signature reported as "H. Howord / New Bedford / 1866" (private collection). There being no record of anyone with this surname and initial ever having served in the New Bedford whaling industry, nor any listed in the City Directories at the time indicated, the presumption is that *Howord* must be an erroneous reading of the more common surname Howard. Given the surprising paucity of men with this surname and initial active in New Bedford or on New Bedford whaleships at any time consistent with the date 1866 appearing on the tooth (there were several men named Henry and Horace Howard in the 1830s and '40s who would have been too old to be the scrimshaw artist of 1866), by the process of elimination the scrimshaw is provisionally attributed to the only viable candidate: a Harry Howard, about whom nothing is known except that he served in the crews of four New Bedford whalers: ship *Contest* (1866-68), bark *John Carver* (1875-79), bark *Stamboul* (1881-82), and schooner *Abbie Bradford* (1882-83).

Howland, George L. (fl. circa 1870-93). New Bedford whaling master whom his son claims built at least one box on shipboard. In the book *Thar She Blows!* (1951), author Chester Howland relates what purports to be a factual occurrence aboard the New Bedford bark *Canton,* commanded by his father, George L. Howland, in 1889:

> *"We had been on a passage three days and were busying ourselves on deck and below," Mr. Coakley reports. "I was glad to get the chance to finish carving a sperm whale's tooth and the captain had been working for months on an Australian gumwood box."*

The statement about "Mr. Coakley" is a patent fabrication, excusable only by courtesy of poetic license. The man alluded to was the only Coakley on board, John T. Coakley (q.v.), who was later a whaling captain but at this time was a green hand, a kid on his first voyage — not yet "Mr." by any standard. In addition to which, Captain Coakley's grandson, Morgan Levine, born in New Bedford and a long-time resident of Nantucket, adamantly insists — based on firsthand testimony from Captain Coakley himself — that his grandfather never did any scrimshaw in his life. Thus, one is entitled to be skeptical about Chester Howland's implication in the same passage that his father was *also* a shipboard artisan, and that such a box of Australian gumwood (if George L. Howland ever made such a box) would typically have been ornamented with whale ivory or walrus ivory inlay, thus qualifying the box as scrimshaw and the maker as a scrimshaw artist. On the other hand, absent any material evidence or other testimony, for all we know Captain Howland could have been throughout his career a devoted and regular maker of inlaid boxes.

George Lyman Howland was born in New Bedford in 1853, the second of the two sons of George and Elizabeth Howland. His father was a house carpenter; his brother, Frederick A. Howland, four years older, preceded him into the whale fishery; but it was George who rose to first mate (1878-82) and then captain (1883-93) on four successive whaling voyages of the bark *Canton 2d* of New Bedford. Meanwhile, he was married and widowed with two sons; and after he retired from whaling he was a self-employed house painter in New Bedford, with his two sons working for him. There he remarried, fathered a second family, and eventually brought his new sons into the business. His sons by the first marriage were James Lyman Howland (1887-1964); and Chester Scott Howland (1891-1969), who married a woman named Dorothy, stated his occupation as Public Lecturer, and wrote the books *Thar She Blows! Thundering Adventures of Whaling and Mutiny* (1951) and *Whale Hunters aboard the "Grey Gold": A Tale of the Sea and of the Men Who Win Her Fortunes* (1957). (The brothers George L. Howland and Frederick A. Howland are not to be confused with George E. Howland and Captain Frederick S. Howland, who were whalemen in the previous generation and actually sailed together in the bark *Nye* of Dartmouth in the 1850s.)

Howland, William (fl. circa 1815-22). Whaling master who owned, and may have made with his own hands, a rather early swift and spool holder constructed of whale ivory, walrus ivory, and whale skeletal bone, inlaid with tortoise shell, and tied with red, white, and blue ribbons. It was likely made in the 1820s and was given to NBWM in 1945 by one of Captain Howland's granddaughters. Born in 1797 at South Dartmouth, Massachusetts, William was the son of Gilbert Howland of South Dartmouth and Sally Horton of Boston. He was a master mariner by the time he was in his early twenties, and later became a prominent merchant in New Bedford. He commanded three whaling voyages in the New Bedford schooner *Eliza Barker* during 1820-22, was captain of the brig *Sarah Herrick* for a while beginning in 1824, and the brig *Triton* for about two years during 1827-29, but evidently not on whaling voyages. However, reportedly after losing two fingers in a storm at sea, he retired from seafaring and went into the shipping business in New Bedford with his brother-in-law, Captain Cornelius Grinnell, with whom he dealt in a variety of provisions, stores, and cargoes, and participated in financing shipbuilding and whaling ventures. He was also master-of-record of several vessels in which he held ownership interests. As one of several men of his same name in New Bedford whaling circles, he is almost always referred to as Captain William Howland or William Howland II. He was twice married, both times to women named Abigail, both of whom were born in 1794 and thus were slightly older than he. Abigail A. Anthony (1794-1836), whom he married in 1820, was the mother of all of his children. After she died in 1836 he married Abigail W. Kirby (1794-1874) in 1838, and from this union there was no issue. Some Howland family genealogists, in addition to being hopelessly confused by the two Abigail wives (for the record, they were born on 14 Nov 1794 and 7 Sept. 1794, respectively), also erroneously claim that William died in 1840, when in fact he is clearly listed in the U.S. Census, New Bedford City Directories, and New Bedford Ship Registers up until his death on 28 February 1873, at age 76 years and 10 days. He had four children, and for a while in the 1850s and '60s the Howlands were also the guardians of yet another Abigail, Abigail C. Pope, who appears to have been the orphaned minor daughter of one of William's sometime business associates. One daughter, Jane (born circa 1831), remained unmarried, helped with the housework but had no particular occupation, lived with her parents throughout their lives, and afterwards went to live with her widowed aunt Anne B. Anthony and three adult Anthony cousins. But the scrimshaw — for which the provenance had to be reconstructed from fragments in the museum files — went to the younger daughter, Rebecca Wilbur Howland. She married Henry Martin Hayward, a saw manufacturer and ice dealer in Andover, Massachusetts; and the swift descended to their sixth child, the third of four daughters, Harriet Hayward (born circa 1869). She married Frank Anderson, a retail grocer in North Andover; and it was Mrs. Harriet H. Anderson who gave the swift to the museum in 1945.

* **Huggins, Samuel, Jr.** (fl. circa 1831-34). The *Dictionary* mentions "A tooth in MSM marked 'ship President 1833' ... presumed to refer to the Nantucket whaleship *President*, voyage of 1831-34," and notes that "Huggins was evidently not a native or resident of the Island." Another, quite handsome specimen of Huggins's work, made on the same voyage, has since emerged (reported by Ronald Bourgeault, Northeast Auctions): a tooth with a stern-quarter portrait of a full-rigged ship under plain sail, with three spritsail-rigged whaleboats lowered and in pursuit; and, on the other side, the bold, expertly rendered inscription in a graver's cursive hand, "Samuel. Huggins. Junr. / Ship. President. South / Pacific. Ocean. August. 4th / 1833. Latt[itude] 4,,41 S. Long[itude]. 115,,58 / Whale. Made. 80 Bbls." The ship portrait is presumed to be the *President* herself, but no further record of Huggins has been found. He must have been born between 1805 and 1815, but whether he was the Samuel Huggins born in Ireland around that time, or the one from eastern Pennsylvania, or upstate New York, or New Haven, Connecticut, or elsewhere, remains a mystery; and the *President* may have been his only whaling voyage. Even so, the name Samuel is particularly persistent in the Middletown, Connecticut, branch of the Huggins family, who were descendants of a Samuel Huggins born on Nantucket around the turn of the eighteenth century. There were other whalers in the clan, and the Middletown branch may well have maintained ties with their Nantucket kin, paving the way for a Middletown Huggins to go whaling on a Nantucket ship and become a scrimshaw-maker. (See also the article on Samuel Higgins, Jr.)

Hussey, Frederick W. (fl. circa 1820-40). Native Nantucketer, known to have been an inveterate maker of scrimshaw on a voyage as captain of the Newport, Rhode Island, whaleship *William Lee* (1836-40). Sereno Edwards Bishop (q.v.), age twelve, was a passenger on the homeward leg of that voyage, from Honolulu to Newport during 1839-40, and was impressed by the quantity and diversity of the scrimshaw on board. In his journal (in KNB) he writes that the captain " has shown us a number of articles made by himself and others out of whale teeth such as snuff boxes, bodkins, pie stamps [crimpers], needle cases, reels [sheave blocks], &c., all of which are done off very handsomely." One day in November 1839 Hussey "moulded [sic] a fife of lead and turned it; it did not make much noise however," so the next day "the captain made a wooden fife," but it was even more of a failure, as "it did not sound as well as the leaden one." In January 1840 Bishop reports that "Capt Hussey is making a bureau" and "has underway a swift and two work boxes"; and in February he was making a desk. Unfortunately, it is not known whether any of these objects survive; to date, none of them has been identified. Frederick William Hussey was born on Nantucket in

1806, the son of David Gorham Hussey (1783-1812) and Nancy [née Hussey] Hussey (1787-1867). He spent his youth on Nantucket ships, commanded only the one voyage, married Mary Joy Paddack (1810-79), and sometime around 1852 moved his family to a farm in Westfield, in Chautauqua County, New York, where he was widowed in 1879 and lived with one of his daughters until 1881.

Ingraham, Mason (fl. circa 1830s-60s). Sometime whaleman and master mariner from Warren, R.I., he was married to Rebecca Carr (1802-1882), thus was brother-in-law to the five Carr brothers and to Mary Phillips Carr (1815-1893), who donated an important tooth to WHS in 1891 (for full particulars, see the article on the Carr Brothers). While authorship of the scrimshaw more likely rests with one or another of the Carrs than with Ingraham (if only because the Carr brothers were actual blood relations of Mary Phillips Carr, and because Ingraham had a wife and children of his own while most of the Carr brothers did not, thus making Mary more likely their recipient and heir), it cannot be ruled out that Ingraham may have done the scrimshaw himself. He was born in Rhode Island circa 1801, probably in Warren or Bristol, married Rebecca Carr in 1833, and fathered her four children. The expanded family was evidently quite close, and several of the Carr siblings, including Mary Phillips Carr, lived with the Ingrahams at various times, in the same house or on adjacent properties.

Jeffers, William J. (fl. circa 1864). Deepwater sailor and sometime whaleman who made a walking stick (cane) that has a panbone shaft and a whale ivory pommel carved in full round in the form of a closed right fist. The provenance states that it was "made by the father-in-law of the donor, Mrs. Mary Jeffers, William Jeffers, while on a whaling voyage." William J. Jeffers, born at Dartmouth, Massachusetts, circa 1844, was the son and namesake of a teamer (teamster) born in County Somerset (England) and his Massachusetts-born wife Abby (Abigail). Nothing much is known about William's seafaring career other than that he was a professional mariner in early life. He likely made at several whaling voyages, but few specifics have been discovered. He obtained a Protection Paper (seaman's passport) at New Bedford on 29 Feb. 1864, stating his age as 20 and his residence as Dartmouth, and sailed in the New Bedford ship *Herald* on April 18; but the vessel returned on December 12 and there is no further record of Jeffers in the whale fishery until more than ten years later, when at age 30 he sailed in the New Bedford bark *Lancer* (1875-79). If he was whaling in the interim it must have been from some port outside the New Bedford Port District, on vessels of which the crew lists have not yet come to light. From purely circumstantial evidence (in census and genealogical records) it appears that Jeffers was married and widowed very young. So he and his son Orrin, who was born circa 1861 and was evidently left motherless not long afterwards, lived with William's parents in Dartmouth. Orrin had a brief whaling career — perhaps very brief. At age 17, on July 17, 1878 (when his father was still; at sea in the *Lancer*), Orrin sailed as a green hand in the New Bedford bark *Charles W. Morgan*. The Whalemen's Index in NBFPL specifies that he was "discharged at Faial" in the Azores, the *Morgan*'s first landfall, almost immediately after, on August 25; however, the comprehensive compendium of crew lists in John F. Leavitt's *The Charles W. Morgan* (1973) indicates that "Oren B. Jeffers" was among those who completed the voyage and returned with the *Morgan* on May 11, 1881. He later became a ship carpenter in Warren, Rhode Island; and his wife was the Mary Jeffers, born circa 1866, who gave the scrimshaw to NBWM in 1949.

Jenney, Andrew P. (fl. circa 1838-63). Fairhaven whaling master credited with three pieces of scrimshaw donated to NBWM by his daughter in 1942 and definitively attributed by his son the same year: a swift, evidently no longer extant, about which nothing specific is known; and a pair of polychrome engraved teeth. One of the teeth has images of a woman in a broad-brimmed hat with flowing ribbons, driving a horse cart, accompanied by two children; and a child in Highland tartan (kilt) with a horn, waving a tam o' shanter cap overhead and holding the leash of a very large recumbent dog, with a landscape background. On one side of the other tooth there is a woman in a low-cut gown with short sleeves, seven-layered hoop skirt, and bows with streamers on shoulder and waist, stepping on a remarkable geometrically patterned parquet or tiled floor, copied after an illustration in the October 1852 issue of *Harper's New Monthly Magazine*. On the other a young woman with long ringlets stands at an open balcony window, holding a sprig in one hand and reaching out with the other to a birdcage, all in sumptuous surroundings, with a concert harp visible in the background and fairly elaborate features of architecture, furnishings, and garden flora (a set of venetian blinds is distinctive): this is copied after a steel engraving entitled "Rosa's Canary" by W.H. Mote (fl. circa 1830-66) after a painting by Alfred Edward Chalon, R.A., (1780-1860), published in *The Gallery of Engravings* (3 vols., London, 1845-46); the image was later adapted as a lithograph entitled "The Canary Bird" by E.B. & E.C. Kellogg (Hartford, circa the 1850s). The daughter also donated a tub and a bucket made by her father, in connection with which her brother identified the scrimshaw as "more of Capt. Jenney's work." In addition, two interesting pieces donated by the daughter were collected by Captain Jenney during his seafaring days, but were almost certainly made by someone else. These are interesting because two ordinary scrimshaw objects of such different types were seldom produced as a matching pair: an oval ditty box with a wooden bottom and panbone top, sides, and skirt, polychrome engraved on the top with a coastal scene of a bark passing a high rocky promontory with a lighthouse at sunrise or sunset, encircled by acanthus leaf motifs, with the leafy motifs repeated around the entire circumference of the skirt, and with four oval polychrome vignettes of rocky coastal scenes the sides, each framed with acanthus and kelp leaf patterns; and a pie crimper with a double-fluted jagging wheel and beveled handle that has the same sort of polychrome engraved coastal vignettes with leafy trim: it was clearly made by the same hand, probably around the same time.

Andrew P. Jenney was born at Fairhaven in 1821, the eldest of five brothers, all of whom were sailors. Andrew made whaling voyages starting at age 17, as a green hand (1838-40), then seaman (1840-42) in the ship *South Boston* of Fairhaven. His kid brother John, age 16, was also a green hand on the first of these. Andrew was then five outings in New Bedford whaling vessels, where his progressive rises in pay on each successive voyage reflect his steady advances in rank: boatsteerer, 95th lay, ship *Copia* (1842-45); second mate, 53rd lay, bark *Frances* (1845-46), which burned at Mauritius in 1846; second mate, 47th lay, bark *Bartholomew Gosnold* (1847-48); and first mate, 20th lay, ship *Nautilus* (1851-52), a berth he left to become mate for an 18th lay in the *Copia* (1852-55). He was then master of two voyages in the Fairhaven bark *Joseph Maxwell* (1855-58 and 1859-63). David G. Mosher (q.v.) was his first mate on both voyages. During a layover ashore in 1858 he was married to a woman whose name has not survived in the official records, but who was almost certainly Sarah C. Akin of Fairhaven, born circa 1834 (she was kin to Captain Warren Aiken, q.v., through Akin and Ellis ancestors in Rochester and Fairhaven). A daughter named Emma came along soon after; but by 1860, when Jenney was at sea again in the *Joseph Maxwell*, he was a widower whose year-old child was living with Sarah's parents on the Henry Akin family farm. When Captain Jenney returned from this voyage it was for good. He settled on his own farm in Fairhaven, married Sarah's older sister Lucy (1830-1913), and fathered three more children. The youngest two of these, Bertha (born circa 1866) and Arthur (born circa 1868), were the ones who donated the scrimshaw and other Andrew Jenney whaling relics to NBWM. Captain Jenney died in 1895.

Jennings, Benjamin R. (fl. circa 1840-50). He was a cooper by trade and ship's cooper on two voyages — a shipboard artisan whose presumptive manual skills, training, and experience with tools betokens the ability and a likely inclination for scrimshaw. In this case, it is scrimshaw of a most complex, time-consuming, and labor-intensive type: a double swift with an elaborately inlaid box stand; donated to NBWM by a granddaughter of the maker. The swift itself, constructed of whale ivory, skeletal bone, and wood, has carved slats, abalone inlay, and sealing wax-filled turnings; the box is elaborately inlaid with abalone, mother of pearl, and tortoise shell in flowering vine and star patterns, has a drawer with whale ivory knob pulls, and stands on ball feet of whale ivory with wax-inlaid turnings, and is inlaid with a silver plaque inscribed "Susan W. Jennings." She was his wife, the former Susan W. Perry (born circa 1825) of Dighton, Massachusetts, who bore him three children. They were married circa 1847, at just around the time Jennings completed his last whaling voyage, so the name Susan W. *Jennings* could not have been relevant until that time; she would have been Susan W. *Perry* throughout his active whaling career. Which suggests that Jennings may have made the swift at sea on his 1844-47 voyage and put her name on it in anticipation of their nuptials; or made the swift at sea and put her name-plaque on it afterwards; or brought the materials home and made the swift ashore after the voyage.

He was born circa 1819, the son of Daniel and Elizabeth Jennings. He may have served as a cooper's apprentice in his youth, but in any case was ship's cooper for the 60th lay in the New Bedford whaleship *Hector* (1840-43) and for the 55th lay in the *Niger* (1844-47). Captain James Gray skippered both voyages, both were to the Pacific grounds, and both were quite successful — especially the first one, for managing agent Charles W. Morgan, which brought home 2,717 barrels of oil. The second voyage, for the partnership of Hathaway & Luce, in a brand new ship, returned a total of 1,545 barrels of sperm oil, 1,450 barrels of whale oil, and 5,000 pounds of bone carried and sent home. Jennings was already 21 when the *Hector* sailed, and the 60th lay is a rather large share for a maiden voyage; it therefore seems likely that he made at least one prior voyage as a green hand. (Unfortunately, crew lists for New Bedford voyages commencing in 1837 and especially 1838 are unaccountably scarce, so this hypothetical voyage has not been identified.) Apart from this, his two voyages as cooper appear to have been the sum total of Jennings's whaling career, and even at his still fairly junior level of compensation they may well have been sufficiently lucrative to set himself up as a cooper in New Bedford, which trade he followed from the time he came ashore at age 28 until he was past 70 (the City Directory still lists him as a cooper in 1892). He died in 1896.

Johnson, Charles H. (fl. circa the 1850s). A very odd 4-inch elephant seal tooth in NBWM has unusual top-to-bottom grooves and vertical rippling, with a large shattered section at the base; and it is hollow from base to tip inside. It is engraved on the convex curved side only, with a flowering plant, a cross-hatched band, and the bust profile of a gentleman, and is signed "Charles H. Johnson" vertically along one side. Among the many Charles Johnsons who went whaling out of New Bedford, there were two with the middle initial H, contemporaries, one black, one white, both from Plymouth County, Massachusetts. The one who almost certainly made the scrimshaw was Charles Holmes Johnson (1832-1910), who came from a large family in Wareham, the son of Benjamin Johnson, laborer, and Susannah née Haskins. The 1850 U.S. Census lists him as 16 [sic] years old and already a sailor: one older brother was a laborer and another was unemployed, but brothers Uriel, older, and William, younger, were sailors, too. Charles's early voyages are not known and were likely in the merchant or coastwise service. In 1851 he married Martha Chubbuck Bumpus (1832-1901), raised a family in Wareham, and in 1870 was still living there with his wife and four children, next door to the Bumpus clan, and was still listed as a sailor. In the meanwhile, he served as a green hand in the brig *March* of Mattapoisett (1853-54), steward in the New Bedford ship *Corinthian* (1854-58), and boatsteerer in the bark *Elizabeth* of Westport (1858-60). Less is known about the other Chares H. Johnson. Born circa 1833, he hailed from Rochester, Massachusetts, was African American (his Seaman's Passport, issued at New Bedford in October 1854, describes him as having a dark complexion, wooly hair, and dark eyes), and went as a green hand in the bark *Orozimbo* of New Bedford (1854-59). Any subsequent voyages these fellows may have made cannot be definitively identified from among the many voyages of other men named Charles Johnson.

Johnson, Henry (fl. circa 1820s-'30s). A small, rectangular plaque of whale skeletal bone, engraved with a technically proficient and highly detailed panoramic sperm whaling scene reminiscent of those by W.L. Roderick (q.v. in the *Dictionary*), in KNB, has a provenance from the Mylert Armstrong Collection, auctioned by Parke-Bernet at New York, Oct. 4-5, 1963, where the plaque is attributed "Made by Henry Johnson" (reported and submitted in photostat by John Rinaldi). The same auction catalogue also cites a "whalebone [sic] tip... engraved with trees and a Georgian house," implying an attribution to the same hand. On stylistic and iconographical grounds, the artist was almost certainly British, but nothing is known about him and the name is simply too common on both sides of the Atlantic to enable any reliable identification. At least one American whaleman named Henry Johnson — Henry M. Johnson — was something of an artist. He was born somewhere in Massachusetts circa 1824 and began his brief whaling career as a green hand in the brig *Lagrange* of Mattapoisett (1843-45). On his second and last whaling voyage, as a boatsteerer in the ship *Acushnet* of Fairhaven (1845-49), he kept an illustrated journal (in PEM) from which two watercolors of sperm whaling scenes are reproduced in Flayderman (1972, 25) and Creighton (1982, 23). John Rinaldi speculates that he may be the Henry Johnson who made the scrimshaw. However, the workmanship in the watercolors, while well above the usual standard of whalemen's amateurish drawings, is not nearly as highly refined and detailed as the scrimshaw, nor the draftsmanship so precise. The watercolors have a great deal more zip and vigor than the placid scene on the plaque; and the perspective, point of view, and scale are radically different, with the watercolors being close-up while the panbone is panoramic. In fact, the respective merits of the two are just about antithetical. The differences in media notwithstanding, it is doubtful that they could be by the same hand. On balance, the plaque is a typically British production while the action-packed watercolors are quintessentially American.

* **Johnson, Nicholas** (fl. circa 1880s-1900s). The *Dictionary* describes a "small tooth having a whaling scene with rising sun encircling the tip, below which is a decorated band and an anchor and line inscribed 'Wanderer,' taken to refer to the whaleship of that name," and "inscribed on reverse

'Ellen S. & Josephine S.'" It was given to PMS in 1925 with a provenance claiming it was "Engraved by Nicholas Johnson aboard [the] whale ship Josephine." No person of that name is recorded as ever having served in the *Wanderer* or the *Josephine* out of New Bedford. However, crew lists for the period 1882-1904, when the *Wanderer* and *Josephine* were based in San Francisco, are either not complete or not extant; and it is that era which is consistent with the stylistic character of the scrimshaw. So Nicholas Johnson could have been in the crew of one or both of those latter-day barks without his name necessarily being visible in the archives. Altogether, there were comparatively few Nicholas Johnsons in nineteenth- and early twentieth-century America, and none of them is known to have been a whaleman. That the scrimshaw was a gift to PEM in Salem, Massachusetts, suggests that the maker may have been a local man, which indicates the one North Shore fellow of that name, Nicholas Johnson, an immigrant fisherman living in nearby Gloucester, Massachusetts. He was born in Sweden circa 1848, but records differ as to whether his wife Anna was born in Nova Scotia or Sweden, and whether in 1849 or 1855. The 1920 U.S. Census gives 1879 as the year of their immigration and 1904 as the year of their naturalization as U.S. citizens, but they had a daughter Kate and son James born in Massachusetts between 1875 and 1878, so the parents must have been in Massachusetts before 1879. In 1880 they were residents of Gloucester, where Nicholas worked as a fisherman. As a second son, Charles, was born in Pennsylvania circa 1882, it is possible that the family was living there at that time; and as they are absent from the U.S. Census for Massachusetts in 1900 and 1910, it is presumed that they may have relocated to California at that time (as many whalemen did), but in that case their absence from the California census tallies remains unexplained. There does not appear to have been anyone in the immediate family named Ellen or Josephine. If the inscription "Josephine S." refers to the bark *Josephine*, the S remains a mystery; similarly, "Ellen S." could refer to a vessel, such as the Provincetown schooner *Ellen A. Swift*; but the two names more likely refer to people, as yet unidentified but possibly the intended recipient or recipients of the scrimshaw. As noted, the records are inconclusive whether and when Nicholas Johnson was whaling in the *Wanderer* or the *Josephine*, as the scrimshaw and provenance imply. Clearly, *someone* of this name likely made the scrimshaw and probably was whaling in one or both of those New Bedford barks. The Nicholas Johnson from Gloucester was not only a local man and a mariner, but became a bracelet maker in later life, in Attleboro, Massachusetts, in the outer periphery of the jewelry industry of Providence, Rhode Island. So he must have been an artisan of sorts all along, which adds weight to the tentative attribution of the scrimshaw.

Jones, Robert (fl. 1845-83). New Bedford whaling master from upstate New York to whom a scrimshaw crimper is attributed. It has a walrus ivory handle in the form of a hippocanthus — a mythical sea creature, with the head of a horse, two legs forward, and a curled fish tail aft, otherwise known as Neptune's Steed; it also has a two-tine fork and a double-fluted jagging wheel that has a piercedwork hub with six delicate spokes shaped like whaleboat oarlocks. The provenance (constituting the only substantive clue to its origin) declares that it was given to NBWM by "Mrs. A. Wilson Dods" in 1948. A. Wilson Dods, M.D., was a physician in Chautauqua, New York. He was born in Dumfries, Scotland, in 1854, retired from the practice of medicine by 1930, and died at the age of 91 in 1945. His first wife, whom he married in 1878, was Aura S. Porter (1857-1909), by whom he had three children. His second wife, the widow who donated the scrimshaw, was the former Helen T. Jones, daughter of Captain Robert Jones; hence the attribution. Helen was born in Hawaii in 1864 during a voyage commanded by her father in the New Bedford whaleship *George and Susan*, on which the captain had brought along his wife Caroline and two-year-old daughter Augusta. On the same voyage Caroline also gave birth to a third daughter, Bernice, born in Hawaii about two years after Helen.

Captain Jones had a long and distinguished whaling career, which he pursued while maintaining his permanent residence in Chautauqua County, first at Ellicott and later at Jamestown, New York. Born circa 1827, he first went to sea at age 18 as a green hand in the ship *Arab* of Fairhaven (1845-49). His remaining voyages were all in New Bedford vessels. He was a boatsteerer in the ship *Waverly* (1849-51), and did so well on his next voyage, as third mate in the ship *Scotland* (1851-54), that Captain George A. Smith took the unusual step of promoting him two ranks to first mate on the next voyage of the *Scotland* (1854-57). This set him up for a captaincy, which soon materialized in the ship *George and Susan* (1857-61). It was on the next voyage of this same vessel, prosecuted during the Civil War years (1862-66), that he brought along his wife and daughter and acquired two more daughters. He was afterwards captain of the bark *Concordia* (1867-71), and then he retired — but only temporarily, as it turned out. Ten years later, for reasons not explained, he went to sea as captain of the bark *Arnolda* (1881-82), then embarked a second time as captain of the same vessel in 1882 but died at sea before completing the voyage.

Joy, George F. (fl. circa 1815-45). Long-tenured Nantucket whaling master credited with a bone-and-ivory swift in a family legacy collection (reported by Tom Watlington). According to the provenance, in the form of a label written by descendant and heir John Williston Cook, the swift was made by Captain George Joy of Nantucket in 1850 [sic] and came down in the family through Mr. Cook to the current owner. Captain Joy was born on Nantucket in 1796, the son of William Joy and Jedida née Meader, and like so many of his fellow-islanders he was raised in the Nantucket whaling trade. At the height of his long career he commanded an unbroken series of six voyages in Nantucket ships: *Boston* (1822-25), *Golden Farmer* (1825-28), *Zenas Coffin* (1828-31), *Charles and Henry* (two voyages, 1832-36 and 1836-40), and *Columbus* (1841-45), after which he retired from whaling. He was intermittently thereafter a merchant sea captain and in that capacity made a Gold Rush voyage to San Francisco as master of the *Henry Astor* in 1849. In conformity with the custom on such voyages, the forty or so passengers and officers — all would-be prospectors in California —were "on shares," comprising a consortium of co-owners and unequal partners, of whom Captain Joy may have been one. He was also involved in the Nantucket Marine Camel Company, an outfit whose purpose was to use lift-barges called *camels* to float incoming and outgoing ships over Nantucket's famous sandbar, which threatened the livelihood of the island by impeding the larger-tonnage ships and barks that were now preferred for whaling and other oceangoing traffic. But he did not return to whaling. Thus, if he made the swift at sea (as almost all such scrimshaw productions were), it must either have been on the Gold Rush voyage circa 1849-50 (consistently with the date given in the family provenance), or was made at least a few years, perhaps many years earlier than the provenance indicates. In 1822, not long before embarking on his first voyage as captain, he married Anna Coggeshall of Nantucket, who was born in 1799 and bore him two sons, both named George, both of whom died young; and three daughters, only one of whom seems to have survived their parents. The oldest, Lydia (1823-1846), married Alexander M. Myrick by whom she had several children. Captain Joy was widowed at age around 60 and lived another twenty years with his unmarried daughter Mary. He died in 1876. Some of his papers are in NHA. Three journals of his voyages are in KNB, NHA, and NCP.

Kakarook, Guy (fl. circa 1894-1920). Inupiat (Inupiaq) Eskimo artist originally from the village of Atnuk, near Golovin, Alaska, who was active at St. Michael and is known for his ink and crayon drawings, pencil sketches, and watercolors (SIW, AMHA, SJM, etc.) as well as carved and engraved works on pieces of walrus ivory as well as on whole tusks (AMHA, ASM) depicting Native life and traditions, Alaska wildlife, and Arctic topography. The article in the *Dictionary* inadequately reflects his influence and importance as a slightly younger contemporary of Happy Jack (q.v.) in the first generation of Native Alaskan scrimshaw artists, and as one of the few early carvers who signed his work. In a review of an exhibition entitled "Eskimo Drawings" at AMHA in 2003, Julie Decker notes that "Inupiaq artist Guy Kakarook's drawings... on both ivory and paper, depict Native villages, fishing boats and indigenous animals," and she singles out as particularly noteworthy "a 1903 portrait of a Siberian couple rendered in ink and crayon and a drawing of an Inupiaq family standing before a fish rack" (*Anchorage Press*, Vol. 12, May 1-21, 2003). SIW has two volumes containing more than 30 sketches of life along the Yukon River and in the St. Michael area from circa 1894-1903, when Kakarook was working as a deckhand on a Yukon River steamboat. There are biographical sketches in the catalogue of the AMHA exhibition (Suzi Jones, ed., *Eskimo Drawings*, 2003) and in *Kakarook, Eskimo Artist* by Dorothy Jean Ray (1971). Guy Kakarook's sons Willie and Joe were also influential artists and scrimshonters.

Kamahiai, Joseph R. (fl. mid-19th century). Native Hawaiian mariner, one of the many Kanakas who signed on for seasonal rotation cruises on American and other whaleships from Honolulu and Lahaina to the South Pacific and Western Arctic grounds. He is the possible maker of a tooth that has a ship portrait on one side, the Hawaiian word *Moku* ("ship") on the other, and is prominently inscribed as a gift to William H. Hudson "from Joseph R. Kamahiai," reported by Susan A. Lebo in CCC. The tooth appears to be dated 1836 but the 3 is not clear and that year hardly seems possible, as 1836 is inordinately early for scrimshaw of this type and 1856 (for example) is a far more likely date in any case: William H. Hudson was a prominent U.S. Navy captain in the Pacific in the 1850s, cruising the coasts of California, Mexico, Panama, and the Hawaiian Islands. Around that same time (and no earlier), a Kanaka seaman named Kamahiai (no given name indicated) signed articles in Honolulu for seasonal passages in the New Bedford ships *William Badger*, Captain Jason L. Braley (q.v.) (1856); and *Magnolia*, Captain Leander Gershom Cox (1857). In 1870 a seaman named Kamahiai received a $40 advance when he signed for the 140th lay on an Arctic whaling cruise of the Honolulu bark *Paeia*, Captain Horace M. Newbury, but this Kamahiai may not have been the same fellow.

Keith, Charles Frederick (fl. circa 1850-80). The second of four whaling brothers, he was the most successful (the only one who became a whaling master) and, interpolating from the casual testimony in the journal of his younger brother, Marshall (q.v.), Charles may also have been a sometime scrimshaw-maker. He was born in Fairhaven, Massachusetts, one of several successive places of residence of his parents, Charles and Rachel W. (née Winslow) Keith. They were originally from Middleborough and later lived in Rochester and Mattapoisett. Charles may have made his maiden voyage in his early teens, for at age 17, he shipped as Ordinary Seaman in the Mattapoisett bark *Sarah* (1850-52), then made a second voyage in her as boatsteerer (1852-53). He was next second mate (1855-55) and first mate (1855-57) in the Mattapoisett brig *Annawan*, and at the very young age of 24 was appointed captain of that vessel, which he commanded on two voyages (1857-59 and 1859-62). By the time he returned, the Civil War had already broken out. Accordingly, in September 1862 he enlisted in the Union Navy as an Acting Ensign, was promoted to Full Acting Master in April 1864, and remained in the service until October 1865. He resumed his whaling career as captain of two voyages in the schooner *E.H. Hatfield* of Provincetown (1865-66 and 1867-68), then, after a hiatus of eight years in the merchant service, as captain of the New Bedford whaling barks *Triton* (1876-80) and *Charles W. Morgan* (1876-80). It was at sea aboard the *E.H. Hatfield* in August 1868 that he met up with his brother Marshall, who was first mate of the *Edith May* at the time, and promised to bring home a the crimper ("jagging knife") as a gift for his sister-in-law, Marshall's young bride. He is presumed to have made, or to have intended to make the crimper himself, but none of his actual scrimshaw has come to light. In 1859, between voyages, he had married Abby E. Bourne, the daughter of a house carpenter, and went to live with her parents in Mattapoisett. Twenty years later, after his voyage in the *Morgan*, he went into semi-retirement, living in Mattapoisett with Abby, their two sons, and his widowed mother-in-law. By 1900 he was widowed himself, still living in Mattapoisett, now with his widowed sister and her widowed daughter, and employed as a "caretaker of summer houses." He continued to live with the niece after her mother died, and by 1910 was joined by his youngest brother, William, now also retired. (William was the baby of the family and likely acquired some of his inculcation in sea ways from his three older brothers. A charming annotation in the journal of his first voyage reveals the small inventory of essentials he brought to sea with him in the 1860s: a "Pocket Clasp Bible"; a copy of "Worcester's Comprehensive Dictionery [sic]," evidently as yet unread; a copy of "Sargent's Fifth Reader," the most popular tutor of the day; a blank book "for songs," which turned out to be his combined journal and copybook; lead pencils, watercolor paints, and an ivory ruler.)

* **Keith, Marshall** (fl. circa 1853-70). Whaleman from Rochester, Massachusetts, whose journals mention his minor scrimshaw activities, though his older brother Charles (q.v.) appears to have been the more serious scrimshaw-maker. Marshall's is a sad story. He was the third of four whaling brothers. Their parents, Charles Keith and the former Rachel W. Winslow, lived successively in Middleborough, Fairhaven, Rochester, and Mattapoisett, Massachusetts, and had eight children, averaging two in each place. Albert, the oldest son, made several whaling voyages and rose to first mate. The youngest, William, made only one deepwater whaling voyage, then spent a few years on short Atlantic whaling cruises in schooners from Cape Cod and Boston, and in the merchant service. The second oldest, Charles Frederick Keith, had an eminent career, with six voyages as captain, including the barks *Triton* and *Charles W. Morgan*. Marshall, who became a kind of professional first mate, may well have been on his way to the quarterdeck too, when his life was cut short. He was a green hand in the Mattapoisett bark *Sun* (1853-55), boatsteerer in the New Bedford bark *Afton* (1856-58) on a voyage commanded by accomplished swift-maker James M. Clark (q.v. in the *Dictionary*), and rose steadily through the ranks in the Mattapoisett bark *Ocean Rover* (1859-62) and New Bedford barks *Smyrna* (1862-63) and *Brewster* (1863-65). In 1866 he married Sarah Pope Taber of Rochester, and on his next voyage, as first mate of the famous Dartmouth bark *Cape Horn*

Pigeon (1866-67), he kept a journal (in NBWM) addressed to "Dear Sarah." There, he mentions collecting a sperm whale tooth that he cleaned and polished, which he may have scrimshawed: "This fore-noon I was writing a letter to you and this afternoon I went on board the schooner Petrel and I got a very nice whales tooth which I shall bring home with me"; and, "This has been a nice pleasant day, Sarah. I have been to the mast-head six hours and the rest of the day I have been to work at various little jobs. Part of the day I have been cleaning that whales tooth." After he returned, presumably with the tooth in hand, and for the next couple of years — perhaps in order to be able to spend more time with his wife and infant daughter — he was shipmates with his brother William on shorter whaling cruises in the schooners *William Martin* of Boston and *Edith May* of Wellfleet (Cape Cod). On these, Marshall certainly made several whistles out of whale teeth, and his journals are again addressed to his wife Sarah. In March 1868 he writes, "The weather has been the same as yesterday thick and foggy. I have not been aloft. I have been making a little ivory whistle to pass the time off. I must close, so Good night Darling wife and Child." And a few weeks later, "This has been a pleasant day, Sarah, and I have been Aloft five hours. the rest of the day has been spent in idleness as you might say. I have coopered a barrel and made a Whistle. big business that. I must come to a close so kiss Susie for me and bid her good night Sweet Sarah Good night." The next day he reports, "I have been making a whistle for Susie," and the day after that, "another whistle." In August the *Edith May* encountered the *E.H. Hatfield* of Provincetown, of which his brother Charles was master: "Has been a pleasant day, Sarah, and what is more pleasanter to me, we have been gam[m]ing all day with Charlie. he told me he was going to make you a present of a Jag[g]ing Knife when he got home." Marshall himself got home not long after. Sadly, he died in 1870 at age 32; Sarah died two years later, at 30.

* **Kelley, William H.** (fl. circa 1863-91). Owing probably to its extremely high quality and specific inscription, both of which exceed the usual expectations for whalemen's scrimshaw, the authenticity of a unique whale ivory sculpture customarily attributed to Captain Kelley has occasionally been called into question: a hand, carved in high relief, grasping a sphere, with the face of the sphere handsomely engraved "Ship Gay Head of New Bedford Mass," signed in monogram "WHK," and mounted on a base of whale ivory decorated with Masonic symbols and inscribed "Abandoned at Point Belcher Sept 14 1871" (in NBWM). However, the authenticity and attribution are not only credible, but likely. Consistent with the outstanding character of the carving and the calligraphy in this instance is the fact that Kelley's credentials as an accomplished amateur artist are corroborated elsewhere: it was his original drawings that served as the basis for wood engravings in *Harper's Weekly* magazine illustrating *both* the 1871 *and* the 1876 Arctic whaling disasters, in both of which events Captain Kelley was a firsthand participant. Moreover, the character and quality of the *Gay Head* piece occasion the attribution of an earlier calligraphy-based tour-de-force (in KNB), made aboard the ship *Corinthian* of New Bedford in 1853, a voyage on which William Kelley served as blacksmith (1851-54): a walrus tusk lacking any picture, but engraved for presentation with an elaborately stipple-ornamented inscription: "THIS IS A WALRUS TUSK TAKEN / IN THE ARCTIC OCEAN. JUNE / TH[E] 24 - [18]53 BY A.N. STUART. MASTER / OF TH[E] SHIP CORINTHIAN. N.B. PRESEN / TED TO A.L. BASSETT[,] LEE. MASS. / LATT. 68 : 30 N. LONG. 170 - 30 W."

Various sources name Kelley as having been captain of the ship *Marengo* briefly in 1876: Starbuck (641) reports that the *Marengo* was "sold at San Francisco in 1874" and was "lost in the

Arctic 1876," but he does not give the date or name the captain. Could Kelley have lost two ships in the same year? In 1877 he sailed in the bark *Roman 2d* of New Bedford, but the vessel was wrecked at Magdalena, California, in 1878. So having lost three, or maybe even four ships in a row — the *Gay Head* in 1871, the *James Allen* in 1876, maybe the *Marengo* in 1876, and the *Roman* in 1878 — Kelley retired from whaling for a while. During his four-year hiatus he was occupied as skipper of the New Bedford towboat *Charlie*. In fact, the City Directory lists him as such from 1877 to 1882, when he moved to San Francisco and resumed whaling, making five consecutive voyages as captain of the bark *Coral* (1882-86) and four in the schooner *Jane Gray* (1889-91), of which the last voyage returned a disappointing catch and proved to be Kelley's final foray.

Kern, Leonhard (fl. circa 1613-62). German sculptor. He is best known for his small statuettes on religious and mythological subjects, and is distinguished for having worked extensively in ivory as well as boxwood and alabaster. In fact, as one of few academicians to have sculpted in that medium he is frequently described as a "well known ivory carver" ("den bekannten Elfenbeinschnitzer"), rather than as a sculptor, with more of a Renaissance than Baroque sensibility:

> *Leonhard Kern's shop in Schwäbisch Hall flourished, producing statuettes and small reliefs of high quality in boxwood, ivory, and alabaster. This output extended the precepts of Renaissance art well into the seventeenth century, thanks to Kern's memories of his study in Italy (1609–12) and his emulation of famous Italian masters....* (James David Draper, Metropolitan Museum of Art)

As such Kern was "an artist of European renown" ("einen Künstler von europäischem Rang"). Most of his sculptures that have been published accessibly are in other media than ivory, such as his boxwood figures of "Standing Woman" (18.6 cm, circa 1640; Cleveland Museum of Art) and "Diana" (23 cm, circa 1650; Victoria and Albert Museum, London), and an alabaster frieze entitled "The Deposition" (32.7 cm, circa 1640–50; Metropolitan Museum of Art, New York). His most famous ivory carving may be the figleaf-clad "Adam and Eve after their expulsion from Paradise," carved in full round from a single elephant tusk circa 1645-50 (Museum für Kunst und Gewerbe, Hamburg). However, it is not clear from the available documentation whether Kern worked exclusively in elephant ivory, or whether — as is more likely, given the comparatively small size of his sculptures and the general availability of walrus ivory from the Northern fisheries — he may have worked also in walrus ivory. Part of the unclarity may be owing to uncertainty among museum curators in former times about how to tell the difference — or that it might make a difference, at least from an historical if not an art-historical point of view. As Paul Davidson Phillips has remarked, "The techniques for carving walrus ivory were similar to those for elephant ivory but the former was apparently far more readily available" in the Middle Ages. It was imported to northern and central Europe from Scandinavia in increasing quantities from the ninth to the twelfth centuries, and even after the opening of trade with North Africa in the second half of the thirteenth century enabled Europeans to acquire elephant ivory more easily than before, walrus ivory remained a plentiful and less expensive alternative. This was perhaps especially the case after the regular seasonal Arctic whale fishery got underway around 1610-13, at first prosecuted by England and Holland but soon expanding to include Scotland, France, Spain, Germany, Denmark, and Sweden.

Thus, it remains possible, even likely, that such *Elfenbeinschnitzers* as Leonhard Kern and François Duquesnoy (q.v.) may have used walrus ivory at least some of the time.

Leonhard Kern (1588-1662), the son of a stonemason, was born at Forchtenberg, in Baden-Württemberg. He studied in Italy and traveled in North Africa and Slovenia during 1613-14, returned to Forchtenberg, where he married Amalia Zoellner, the daughter of a clerk, in 1614, and went to work in the shop of his older brother, Michael. He later worked in Heidelberg and Nuremberg, and finally established his own studio in the free imperial city of Schwäbisch Hall, in Baden-Württemberg. He died there in 1662, having fathered at least 17 children, few of whom survived their parents. (Sources: James David Draper, Metropolitan Museum of Art; Paul Davidson Phillips, "European Ivory Relief Carving"; R.H. Randall, *Masterpieces of Ivory from the Walters Art Gallery,* 1985.)

Kerns, J.A. (fl. circa 1871). Three sculptural miniature figurines of mythological subjects carved in full round out of walrus ivory are attributed, based on the signature on one piece; all three sold by Cowan at Sharonville, Ohio, Nov. 17-18, 2004, #245-247. A representation of Bellerophen riding the winged horse Pegasus is signed and dated on the base "J.A. Kerns 1871." A nude figure of "a mermaid with paired entwined tails" perched on a rock, holding a fluted scallop shell above her head, appears to be by the same hand and was acquired with the other. So too a semi-nude, crowned figure of a bearded Neptune, sans trident, standing astride a scallop shell, with the base engraved "Amie Ann P." The auctioneer speculates that the Neptune piece, at least, was "likely a whaler's gift to his sweetheart," but no record has been found of any whaleman of this name (nor any clues conrening the name of the whaleman, if he was not J.A. Kerns). Meanwile, "Amie Ann P." has not been identified and nothing is known about the artist.

King, Edward A. (fl. circa 1850-1905). A massive whale ivory crimper with pistol grip handle carved in the shape of a curled crescent, with a fluted whale ivory jagging wheel (in NBWM), "belonged to Capt. Edward King of the *Morning Star*"; and the provenance of a whale ivory napkin ring from the Batchelder Collection (in NBWM), "said to have belonged to Captain King of New Bedford," if it be correct, could only refer to that same man, Edward A. King. There were no fewer than fifteen American whaling masters named King between 1785 and 1905, of whom five commanded New Bedford vessels at one time or another; but of these, Edward A. King was the only one who lived in New Bedford, commanded the *Morning Star,* and was the captain of whaling voyages during the golden age of scrimshaw napkin rings, which was the late-nineteenth and early-twentieth centuries. There is no particular reason to believe that this or any other Captain King made his own napkin rings and crimpers, but there is also no particular reason to doubt it. If he were anything like his fellow latter-day whaling master, Ben Cleveland (q.v. in the *Dictionary* and in Appendix III of *More Scrimshaw Artists*), he may even have made napkin rings between voyages and borrowed a lathe to do so. On the other hand, the napkin ring in question matches a panbone jewelry box that traces to the brothers Edward and Luther Southworth (qq.v.), and was probably made by one or the other of them prior to 1851; and the box and napkin ring were acquired together from the same source by the eminent collector Charles F. Batchelder in 1937. The strong likelihood is that both the box and the napkin ring were made by the same hand, and that the hand was that of Edward or Luther Southworth, neither of whom is known to have had any social, professional, or kinship connection with any of the captains named King. If they had, the "Captain King of New Bedford" alluded to in the provenance would presumably have acquired the napkin ring from Edward or Luther (both of whom died before 1852), thus would almost certainly have been Godfrey King (q.v.), who was active as a master mariner from 1836 to 1864, having started out in Bristol, Rhode Island, but commanding New Bedford whaleships from 1839 on: he was the only "Captain King of New Bedford" who was contemporaneous with the careers of Edward and Luther Southworth. As for Captain Edward A. King, there is little doubt that the crimper was his, even if there be reasonable doubt that he made it himself. He was born in New Bedford circa 1844, the son of stonemason Simeon F. King and his wife Hannah. After the usual apprenticeship in the whale fishery and a reasonable rise through its ranks, Edward skippered nine consecutive New Bedford voyages almost without intermission: three in the bark *Stafford* (1873-83), followed by six in the bark *Morning Star* (1883-1905), in which he also held a $\frac{4}{32}$nds ownership interest from 1883 until 1912, when the vessel was sold to the Eastern Coal Co. to be used as a barge. By then he and his wife Lydia were retired and living on the income from his investments.

King, Godfrey. (fl. circa 1836-64). Whaling master of Bristol, Rhode Island, and New Bedford who may have made or owned a pierced-work whale ivory napkin ring in NBWM "said to have belonged to Captain King of New Bedford" (concerning which, see the article on Edward A. King). Surely, if there was one napkin ring there must have been others, perhaps a whole set of napkin rings and other tableware. He had a long but not very distinguished career as skipper of 11 whaling voyages. From Bristol he commanded the brigs *Governor Hopkins* (two voyages, 1836, 1837) and *Troy* (1838-39) and the ship *Leonidas* (1841-43); from New Bedford, he had the brig *Zoroaster* (1839-40), bark *Minerva* (1843-46), ship *Triton 2d* (1846-49), and barks *Osceola* (1851-53), *Malta* (1854-56), *Tropic Bird* (1857-59), and *Chili* (1861-64). Still, of the four candidates for maker of the scrimshaw — Edward Southworth, Luther Southworth, Captain Edward King, and Captain Godfrey King — Godfrey King seems the least likely.

L.

L. C. Richmond Engraver (L.C. Richmond Artist) — see **William Sizer**

Lacerda, João Soares (1887-1975). A man of many diverse talents, he was a whaling station manager, dentist, amateur photographer, and avocational scrimshaw-maker on the island of Pico, Azores (reported by Gomes Vieira, 2003, 138f). "At the lathe he executed chess and checker sets, fountain pens, pipes, and cigarette and cigar holders." He also made at least one walking stick with a whale tooth handle, and the Lajes do Pico municipal government commissioned him to produce part of the town's official gift for a presidential visit in 1941. His most distinctive work may be a beautiful folding lounge chair carved and assembled from sperm whale panbone (illustrated in Gomes Vieira, 139). A native of Pico, the son of João Soares Lacerda, Jr., and Josefa Carlota, he was a shareholder and manager of two Azorean whaling companies, the Nova Sociedad Lajense and the União Lajense Ltd. He married Maria Amélia Castro in 1912, fathered several children, moved his family to Terceira in 1947 to accommodate the secondary and university education of his children, and later retired to Pico. Manuel Rodrigues Quaresma (q.v.) was a contemporaneous whaling station manager at Lajes do Pico.

Lady Wellington Engravers (fl. circa 1833-37). Three teeth engraved by two different hands bear highly detailed portraits of the whaling brig *Lady Wellington*, aboard which it is presumed the artists served individually or together on at least one of her three short whaling cruises out of Sydney, New South Wales. One has a larboard broadside view of the brig under plain sail, framed by a plain oval line, inscribed below "L. WELLINGTON / 1834," with floral ornaments. On the back it has a coat-of-arms with viscount's coronet crest, flanked by the British lion and unicorn, with the motto "VIRTUS INCENDITVIRES" ["Virtue ignites strength"] in a riband below. On the top edge it has an oblong scene of four whaleboats being rowed, in various stages of pursuit, framed by a plain line. On the bottom edge is an elongated version of the coat-of-arms of the Order of the Garter, enclosing the motto "HONI SIT QUI MALY PENSE" ["Shame upon him who thinks evil of it"], flanked by the English lion and unicorn, with a Prince of Wales coronet crest, the motto "DIEU ET MON DROIT" ["God and My Right (Arm)"] in a riband below, and floral ornaments, in a plain oval frame (Bonhams, May 7, 2006, lot #1250). Another, clearly by the same hand, is laid out much the same way, with much the same ship-portrait but lacking the inscription. On the other side it has a full-blown rendition of the coat-of-arms of the Order of the Garter, enclosing the motto "HONI SOIT QUI MAL Y PENSE," surmounted with a knight's helmet coronet, with the motto "DIEU ET MON DROIT" in a riband below, and much the same oblong sperm whaling scene on the bottom edge, this time with a brig under sail in the offing (private collection). A third tooth, by a different hand, has a sperm whaling scene with two boats lowered in pursuit, inscribed "Lady Wellington Whaleing [sic]." On the back this one has a lateen-rigged, three-masted side-wheel steamer with a very tall funnel (smokestack), and with a lighthouse and headland in the background, inscribed "A View of the North Foreland from the North[war]d" (Sotheby's BJ:1 #485; Sotheby's, 22 May 2003, #755). From the naval architecture and the geographical reference, this odd steamer appears to be an English Channel ferry, thus connects the tooth with the *Lady Wellington*'s voyage to Australia, on which she embarked from London in 1832 and returned via Hobart (Tasmania) to Sydney in 1833; the scrimshaw may also been made on this passage or on the *Lady Wellington*'s first whaling voyage, which followed immediately after (1834-35).

The *Lady Wellington* was a brig of 142 tons, built in 1813 at Falmouth, Cornwall, and originally in the merchant service to Halifax, New York, and the West Indies (1813-31). (She was not the first such packet of this name; there was at least one other *Lady Wellington* on this same route in 1810 and 1811.) In 1831 she was registered at London and continued as a merchantman under Captains James Lockhart and Nathaniel H. Calker, carrying cargoes to and from Cornwall, Ireland, Canada, and the West Indies. In 1832 she sailed from London to Hobart, then to Sydney, and never returned to England. During 1833-37, still in London registry, she made three South Seas whaling voyages out of Sydney. The second and third of these (1834-36 and 1836-37), and perhaps also the first (1833-34), were under a Captain Cooper. When the brig returned to Sydney in August 1837 her whaling career ended. She was registered at Sydney in October of that year; and under captain and part-owner Arthur Devlin made several coastwise voyages from Sydney to Tasmania and South Australia, carrying passengers and cargoes. In August 1838 she was "wrecked at Port Adelaide [South Australia] when she was run in too close to shore to facilitate offloading; broke her back when stranded on the mud flat at low tide… ," then "was raised, condemned, and used as a store-ship, then as a lightship." (*Encyclopedia of Australian Shipwrecks*)

The motto *virtus incendit* vires belongs to the Anglo-Irish Smythe family, notably to Percy Clinton Sydney Smythe (1780-1855), 6th Viscount Strangford — which explains the distinctive coronet. His title in the Irish peerage was created for his ancestor in 1628. The 6th Viscount graduated Trinity College, Dublin, served as England's ambassador to Portugal, Sweden, Turkey, and Russia, and famously translated into English the lyrics of Portugal's greatest poet, Camoens. In the latter context he is mentioned in Herman Melville's *White-Jacket* (1849), the book that immediately preceded *Moby Dick*: A United States frigate calling at Rio de Janeiro receives on board, with suitable fanfare, a courtesy visit of Dom Pedro II the emperor or Brazil, and the narrator remarks,

> *A great pity it was, that in addition to all these honours, that admirer of Portuguese literature, Viscount Strangford, of Great Britain--who, I believe, once went out Ambassador Extraordinary to the Brazils [sic; he was the British ambassador to Portugal]—it was a pity that he was not present on this occasion, to yield his tribute of 'A Stanza to Braganza!' For our royal visitor was an undoubted Braganza, allied to nearly all the great families of Europe. His grandfather, John VI., had been King of Portugal; his own sister, Maria, was now its queen. He was, indeed, a distinguished young gentleman, entitled to high consideration, and that consideration was most cheerfully accorded him."* (*White-Jacket*, Chapter 56)

According to correspondence held by the National Library of Australia — notably a letter or letters of one James P. Webber of Patterson's River, New South Wales, in 1831 — Lord Strangford was somehow involved with the transportation of convicts for Australia's wool production. This may have been in connection with Strangford's diplomatic responsibilities; the *Lady Wellington*'s change of registry that same year, and her voyage to Tasmania and New South Wales the year following, may have had to do with conveying convicts or materials for the wool trade; but no direct connection has been discovered, and Viscount Strangford's connection to whaling and the *Lady Wellington*, and why he should be memorialized on whalemen's scrimshaw, remain unclear.

Lang, T.H. (fl. circa 1839). A superbly executed memorial tooth, monochrome engraved with an obelisk atop an architectonic pediment base, ornately inscribed in a graver's cursive hand, "In / Memory / of / Lithgow Townes / Who Died Sept. 20th 1839 / Aged 34 Years," signed below "T.H. LANG / ENGr[aver]. (Reported by Dr. Angelo DeFalco.) Nothing has been discovered about the artist or the deceased gentleman being memorialized, however it seems likely that the principals and the scrimshaw are English.

Larcom, Henry (fl. circa 1823-40). Mariner and sometime whaleman of Beverly, Massachusetts, who may have engraved a fine pair of polychrome teeth that descended in the Larcom family (held by descendants in Philadelphia, and shown on the PBS *Antiques Roadshow* in February 2007). Each tooth has two vignettes on recto (a whaling scene and birds) and a standing human figure on verso. One features a full-rigged ship under partial sail with a whaleboat lowered in pursuit, surmounted by a large red-winged blackbird in flight, and on the reverse side a man in a long coat, long trousers, waistcoat, and cravat, holding a top-hat and L-handle walking stick. The companion tooth shows a breeching sperm whale smashing a whaleboat, with the crew and gear flying through the air, and a second, fully-manned whaleboat approaching from behind, surmounted by two birds in flight. On the other side is a woman in an elaborate flowered hat and fancy gown. Some of the six pictures, especially the two vignettes of birds in flight, may have been based partly on printed prototypes, but the whaling scenes are authoritative and original, while the male and female figures, rather than being copies of generic magazine illustrations, were likely intended as actual portraits of a couple known to the artist.

A family provenance that traces through six generations identifies Captain Henry Larcom (1777-1862) of Beverly as the owner of the teeth, but it is uncertain how or when he acquired them and does not concern itself with who may have done the scrimshaw. Family tradition claims that he purchased them, but in the absence of actual evidence this is highly unlikely, as scrimshaw was rarely if ever bought and sold anytime during his lifetime. It is far more likely that he received them as a gift, but from whom? It was not uncommon for a whaling master to be presented with gifts from members of the crew, or even to commission an artisan aboard to produce scrimshaw or other objects for his own use. But Captain Larcom was not a whaling master, nor even a whaling merchant, thus would not likely have been in a position to receive a gift of scrimshaw as a normal matter of course. It is also unlikely that he made the scrimshaw himself, not only because there is no family recollection that he did, but, more to the point, because he was not a whaleman, and the authoritative whaling scenes on this pair are original and could hardly have been rendered by an amateur or neophyte. And even if Captain Larcom had made a youthful whaling voyage or two, engraved pictorial scrimshaw of this type did not appear on the scene until the late 1820s, and in this case the stylistic and iconographical evidence on the teeth indicates conclusively that the work could not have been done anytime before the 1830s — by which time Captain Larcom was in late middle age, a prosperous merchant long retired from actual seafaring. Meanwhile, none of his children or other descendants are known to have gone whaling or to have made any scrimshaw.

A far more likely candidate for maker of Captain Larcom's scrimshaw is a younger kinsman born in Salem circa 1803, identified in the 1840 U.S. Census as Henry Larcom 2d. A lifelong resident of Beverly, he was a career mariner who probably made at least one whaling voyage out of New Bedford (though only a few of his merchant voyages out of Salem are documented), and was of an appropriate age to have made or acquired scrimshaw of this type. He obtained a Seaman's Protection Paper in New Bedford at age 20 in 1823, and likely made a whaling voyage around that time; he may also have made others in the 1830s — if so, probably in vessels out of Salem. He married Nancy Allen at Beverly in 1826, and evidently died sometime between 1840 and 1850, leaving behind his wife and three children. His widow worked as a shoe binder, his eldest son and namesake was apprenticed to (and boarded with) a Beverly shoemaker, both sons eventually became fishermen, and one served in the Union Army and was afterwards a shoe manufacturer in Beverly, where he and his wife ran a boardinghouse.

By way of contrast, Captain Henry Larcom and his brood were at almost the other end of the social spectrum — which is worth mentioning if only to illustrate how far removed from the seafaring trades that prosperous family had become. Captain Larcom was the son of a mariner and Revolutionary War privateer who, according to his great-grandson and biographer, William Fitzhale Abbot, was captured by the British, confined "in the old Jersey Prison Ship," and later "died from the effects of a fever caught from a sick comrade, whom he had escorted to the latter's home in Marblehead upon their release." Captain Larcom himself was a successful sea captain and merchant who commanded and later owned a series of Beverly vessels engaged in the Mediterranean and coastwise trades. His account of a shipwreck and close escape was published as *Some particulars of the melancholy shipwreck of the Margaret, William Fairfield master, on her passage from Naples to Salem, having on board forty-six souls to which is added a short Occasional sermon and a hymn* ("Printed for the Author" in 1810). The story was summarized by Joseph Barlow Felt in the *Annals of Salem* in 1849, and was retold by Captain Larcom's daughter, Fanny Ellingwood Larcom [Mrs. Joseph Hale Abbot, 1807-1883], in the *Atlantic Monthly* issue of August 1871. She was the mother of Larcom's six eminent grandchildren. General Henry Larcom Abbot (1831-1927), a graduate of the U.S. Military Academy at West Point, was an Army engineer and Civil War veteran involved in scientific studies of the Mississippi River and railroads; his portrait miniature by Washington Blanchard is in the Metropolitan Museum of Art and his papers are at Harvard. Edwin Hale Abbot (1834-1927), a Boston lawyer and railroad executive, was a graduate of Harvard (B.A., 1855; A.M., 1858; LL.D., 1861), where his papers are housed. Francis Ellingwood Abbot (1836-1903) graduated Harvard (B.A., 1859; M.A., 1881) and the Meadville Theological Seminary (B.D., 1863) and became an influential Unitarian theologian. Emily Frances Abbot (1839-1899) married a grandson of Reverend Abiel Abbot and was known for charitable works. Edward Stanley Abbot (1841-1863) left Harvard in his sophomore year to attend the military academy at Norwich, Vermont, and as a first lieutenant in the Union infantry was mortally wounded at Gettysburg. William Fitzhale Abbot (1853-1922), another Harvard graduate (B.A., 1874), headed the Classics Department at Classical High School in Worcester, Massachusetts, for forty years, and authored the memoir of Captain Henry Larcom quoted above (MS in private family hands).

Latham, W. (fl. circa 1860). Canadian colonial mariner credited with two teeth similarly carved in shallow relief with British naval and patriotic symbols. One, in CMC, features an oval device incorporating the crosses of St. George and St. Andrew, but absent the cross of St. Patrick (as in the original British Union flag); this is flanked by two naval cannons, two stacks of cannonballs, and four British naval ensigns (a Union Jack in the canton and a St. George's cross quartering the fly), surmounted by a royal crown, and incorporating what CMC calls a "feather emblem" that "refers to the Prince of Wales, whose visit to British North America in 1860 created an outpouring of loyalty to Great Britain." The other tooth, in a private collection (reported by Anne B. Brengle), is much the same but the central device incorporates a full Union Jack set of crosses (St. George, St. Andrew, and St. Patrick): it is similarly framed by olive boughs, flanked by naval cannon, cannon shot, and the four British ensigns, and surmounted by the royal crown. This one has on the back the full-blown emblem of the Prince of Wales: a royal coronet enclosing three feathers, with the motto "ICH DIEN" ("I serve") in a riband below, and is signed and dated "W. LATHAM / Sculpt. 1860." The CMC acquired their tooth in Nova Scotia but were evidently unable to identify the artist. However, it appears that he was William J. Latham, born at Isaac's Harbour, Guysborough, Nova Scotia, the eldest son and second of six children of John Latham and the former Jane Davidson. His whaling career remains a mystery, but he was a fisherman by trade living at Seal Harbour, in Guysborough. He married Mary Jane Manthorne (1840-) circa 1858 and was the father of six sons and four daughters.

Lavare, William T. (fl. circa 1841-63). A provenance from one of his descendants that purports to document the source of two panbone busks by the Banknote Engraver is badly flawed in most of the details, conflates some of the circumstances of William's seafaring career with that of his father, and is ultimately unhelpful in identifying the artist. Dated 19 July 1973, it was written by Dorothy K. Swan in the form of a letter to William J. Boylhart, evidently based on information obtained from the owner-heir of the scrimshaw: "Re: Scrimshaw Stays [busks]. To answer your questions: 1. Source: China [sic]. 2. Her [the owner-heir's] great grandfather, William Tabor [sic] Levare [sic], was first mate sailing the Seven Seas. After he married her great grandmother, he brought home the stays from China [sic]. He came over here originally with Lafayette [sic] at the time of the Revolutionary War [sic]. He and his bride settled in her hometown of Little Compton [sic], Mass. [sic]. He was later lost at sea [sic]."

The Vital Records, Census, and whaling documents give the surname variously as Lavare, Levare, and Levere; but as *Lavare* appears in most of the official government documents, it would seem to be the preferred spelling. The ancestral middle name is Taber, not Tabor. Little Compton is in Rhode Island, not Massachusetts. The busks did not, and could not have come from China: they are orthodox panbone scrimshaw of a characteristically Anglo-American type, in this case unequivocally the work of the so-called Banknote Engraver. Some Lavare ancestor (perhaps William's grandfather) may have come to America with Lafayette at the time of the Revolutionary War, but the William T. Lavare who was first mate on a whaleship and brought home the scrimshaw was born in Westport, Massachusetts, on 31 May 1823, the son of Epaphroditus Lavare and the former Rhoda Manchester, who had been married at Westport in November 1816. (William's birth preceded by about a year Lafayette's famous American tour of 1824, when he was lionized nationwide and enthusiastically toasted as a national hero. The bust portrait of him rendered by the Banknote Engraver decades later on two or more sperm whale teeth, where the Marquis appears as a middle-aged, somewhat corpulent elder statesman with cropped hair, was copied from an illustration dating from the era of the 1824 tour.) Epaphroditus Lavare died in 1825, and in 1829 Rhoda was remarried, to James Clark of Little Compton, Rhode Island; so William and his brother Arnold Brightman Lavare, older by three years, may have been brought up there. (Rhoda was widowed again circa 1848, and in 1850 she was head of a household at Westport where her sons Arnold and William Lavare, and her three children by James Clark, were living.) According to the 1870, 1880, and 1900 U.S. Census, William's wife Sarah was born in Massachusetts, not Rhode Island; so whatever she may have regarded as her home town, she was not born in Little Compton. In fact, William and Sarah were living in North Dartmouth, Massachusetts, in 1870, and at Fairhaven, Massachusetts, in 1880; both of their children were born in Massachusetts (William, Jr., circa 1859 and and Anne circa 1876); and there is no evidence that the family ever lived in Rhode Island.

William was a whaleman, not a China trader. There is no evidence that he ever visited China, though he may have done so during one or more of the unexplained gaps between his whaling voyages. His brother Arnold preceded him into the whale fishery in 1839 at age 19 and made a couple of whaling voyages (including one in the Westport bark *President*, 1841-43). William obtained his first Protection Paper in New Bedford in 1841 at age 18, and made a career of whaling intermittently over the next 27 years. His first four voyages were in the barks *Champion* (1841-42), *Theophilus Chase* (1842-44, 1844-46), and *Janet* (1846-48), all of Westport. After what appears to have been a hiatus of two or three years, he went as third mate in the New Bedford ship *Henry Kneeland* (1851-54), commanded by his brother-in-law, William H. Vinal (1823-1869), who may have convinced Lavare to return to whaling. (Vinal was married to Lavare's only sister, Lavinia; in fact, at that time Lavinia and Vinal were living with Rhoda and the Lavare brothers in Westport, which was convenient and mutually supportive for the womenfolk while the men were away at sea). After another, longer hiatus William was first mate in the New Bedford bark *William Gifford* (1858-63) and schooner *D.N. Richards* (1867-68), then retired from the sea, this time for good. By 1870 he was working in what the Census calls a "car shop," and by 1880 he was a kiln operator and father of two. Meanwhile, he owned a ⅛th share in the Westport coastal schooner *Emma Clifton* (his brother and Captain Vinal also each owned a ⅛th share). He was not lost at sea; there is no record that William ever went to sea again after the *William Gifford*. He died in Fairhaven in January 1899 "of shock from injuries to his abdomen," and is buried at Riverside Cemetery in that town. But his *father*, Epaphroditus Lavare, *was* lost at sea, at age 36 in September 1825. Crew lists survive from the *William Gifford*, in which vessel the provenance implies that William brought home the scrimshaw; thus the Banknote Engraver could be among the 32 men named for the voyage specified. However, on stylistic and technical grounds the Banknote Engraver's scrimshaw appears to be much earlier than the 1850s-'60s era of the *William Gifford* voyage; and the provenance mentions only the two busks (what about the more than a dozen other teeth and several other busks?). The simple fact is that Lavare could have obtained the busks during his time in the *William Gifford*, or at some port of call along the way (in which case Bay of Islands or Honolulu would be the most likely), or from William Vinal, or from brother Arnold, or on any of his previous voyages.

Lawrence, John H. (fl. circa 1839-42). A so-called "whaling archive" featured on the PBS *Antiques Roadshow* television program, filmed in Los Angeles in August 2005 for broadcast in February 2006, contained three items of interest: an illustrated journal of the New Bedford ship *Phenix*, a portrait miniature purported to be of a John Lawrence, a panbone walking stick with an octagonal mushroom pommel of whale ivory, and a tooth engraved with a ship portrait, elaborately inscribed. The scrimshaw is quite good and the bound manuscript volume is clearly and prominently entitled in ink holograph, "Journal of A / Voyage Around the World, in / 1839, 1840, 1841, / Ship Phenix / By / John H. Lawrence" (the voyage commenced on April 4,1839 and actually returned on May 29, 1842). The implication of the provenance, as presented on TV by a descendant, is that Lawrence may have made the scrimshaw himself, ostensibly aboard the *Phenix* (not "Phoenix," as erroneously reported by PBS online). For some reason, despite that the years 1839, 1840, and 1841 are clearly stated on the title page and throughout the text of the journal, the descendant mistakenly described it as pertaining to a whaling voyage "from 1843 to 1847." However, as is often the case on the *Antiques Roadshow*, it was not the descendant/ owner but an ill-informed appraiser who irresponsibly made the wholly unwarranted assumption that John Lawrence was the captain on the voyage. Though Lawrence kept the journal and may have made the scrimshaw, he was not the captain on this or any other whaling voyage. Rather, he was a lowly green hand from New Rochelle, New York, born circa 1821 and aged 18 when the *Phenix* sailed. This was evidently his one and only whaling cruise, though he may have transferred to a Bremen whaleship for part of his time in the Pacific, circa 1842. The actual captain of the *Phenix* was a deepwater whaling veteran named Squire Sanford (brother of scrimshaw artist Ray Green Sanford, q.v.). Though a John *R.* Lawrence later commanded three voyages in New Bedford barks (two in the *Java*, 1852-60, and one in the *Draco*, 1862-65), there never was an American whaling master named John *H.* Lawrence. However, as the portrait and the journal descended in John *H.* Lawrence's family along with the scrimshaw, it may be presumed that the relevant connection here is John *H.* Lawrence (the young author of the journal who made only one voyage and was never a captain), rather than the real Captain John Lawrence (John *R.* Lawrence). Concerning the further adventures of John *H.* Lawrence, the historical record is silent.

LeBaron, Edmund (fl. circa 1850). In 1948 NBWM was given a heavy-gauge walking stick with a provenance from Church Holmes (born circa 1830) of Fairhaven, Massachusetts, and his daughter, Harriet E. "Hattie" Holmes (born circa 1857). The stick has a wooden shaft, of which the lower part is a tapered cylinder that modulates to an octagonal foreshaft inlaid with whale ivory teardrops and wooden triangles, and surmounted by a massive whale ivory mushroom-shaped knob pommel. As a night watchman who was later in the milk business and never made a whaling voyage, Mr. Holmes was in an unlikely position to have made a scrimshaw cane of his own, and (in conformity with family tradition) it is presumed that it was presented to him, perhaps by his brother-in-law, Edmund LeBaron. Remarkably for a clan living in New Bedford and Fairhaven, Edmund LeBaron appears to have been one of only two mariners in the family. The other was Edward LeBaron, who was a kinsman of some kind and made at least two whaling voyages in the 1850s.

Church Holmes, the owner of the walking stick, was born at Woodstock, Vermont, the sixth of eight children of Thomas and Patience [née Hammond] Holmes. The parents had moved to Vermont from Mattapoisett, Massachusetts, with their older children, and would move back to New Bedford with an enlarged family in the 1840s. By 1850 the two oldest children, Betsy and Thomas Jr., along with their spouses and Thomas's six-year-old son, were living with Thomas Sr. and Patience in New Bedford, while Church and his two younger siblings were boarding with James Moore, an English-born New Bedford ship-rigger who had married a Holmes relation. Betsy, the oldest sibling, born in 1817 at Mattapoisett, had married Edmund LeBaron, born in New Bedford in 1817. The 1850 U.S. Census lists him as a sailor living in New Bedford with Betsy, but with no mention of children. In the 1852 City Directory he is a boatbuilder, with Edward LeBaron, no occupation given and no relationship mentioned, boarding at the same address along with James S. LeBaron, who worked at Booth & Hathaway, a firm of lumber dealers, housewrights, and ship joiners. Edward was born in 1838 at Rochester, Massachusetts, the son of James and Sarah LeBaron; James A. LeBaron appears to have been his brother, and both of them appear to have been trained as carpenters. During 1856-59 Edward was a boatsteerer on the *Charles W. Morgan*, which means that he must previously have made at least one or two whaling voyages. These have not been identified, but the first was likely undertaken around 1852, at age about 14, when he was boarding with Edmund and Betsy in New Bedford. However, the nature and degree of Edmund and Edward's kinship has not been established (they may have been uncle and nephew), and nothing further is known of Edward. Edmund's career as a boatbuilder is also elusive. His run as an independent entrepreneur was evidently short lived, and while he may have been employed by others in the boatbuilder's trade in the 1850s and '60s, by 1869 he is listed as a moulding worker. Nevertheless, as one of only two sailors in the family, and also the only one for whom there is some modicum of evidence that he was handy with tools, he is the most likely maker of the walking stick. And if not he, it could have been Edward.

LeBaron, Edward (fl. circa 1852-59). He may have been, but probably was not the maker of an unusually large walking stick that belonged to Church Holmes of New Bedford, who was related by marriage to Edward's older kinsman, Edmund LeBaron (q.v.). His full name was Edward Sampson LeBaron, and he was born in 1838 at Rochester, Massachusetts, the son of James and Sarah [Atsatt] LeBaron. His voyage as boatsteerer for the 87th lay on the *Charles W. Morgan* during 1856-59 could not have been his first. However, though no prior voyage has been found, it (or *they*) must have been made during the period 1852-56, when Edward was boarding with Edmund in New Bedford. Unfortunately, the nature and degree kinship between the two LeBaron men has not been established, and nothing is known of Edward's life and career after the *Morgan* voyage.

Levare, William T. — see **William T. Lavare**

Lewis, Edward D. (fl. 1857-77). This distinguished captain of the New Bedford bark *Lagoda*, owned by Jonathan Bourne, Jr., is credited with three panbone canes and a coconut-shell dipper in NBWM, which also houses a half-size scale model of the *Lagoda*. The model was built in the newly-erected Bourne Building, named for Jonathan Bourne, Jr., in 1916. This was the same year that Pemberton H. Nye, ship chandler and descendant of sea captains, donated the first of the canes. It has a tapered shaft carved out of panbone with the lower portion smooth and the upper portion scored in a cross-hatch pattern, a foreshaft and handle comprised of alternating bands of whale ivory and baleen, and a whale ivory pommel, with the ensemble relief-carved and full-round-carved in the image of a snake (serpent): the eyes are inlaid in red sealing wax and the body twines around the foreshaft into a double coil at the top so that the two loops form a handle. The second cane was donated by E.H. Lewis, a descendant. in 1939. It has a panbone shaft, alternating bands of baleen and whale ivory, and a handle made up of nine pieces of whale ivory and baleen, cleverly full-round carved in the form of a woman's knee, calf, ankle, and bare left foot. The accompanying provenance declares, "Made by Capt. Lewis of the Lagoda," thus he likely made it sometime during 1873-86. The third cane came to the museum from Captain Lewis's nephew, Benjamin F. Lewis, through another kinswoman, Lillian Potter, in 1941 — the same source as the dipper, which has an ebony handle and whale ivory tip.

Edward Darwen Lewis was part of the first generation of a clan of Welsh immigrants who settled in Oriskany, New York. Born in Wales in 1839, he came to Oriskany with his parents at age 10. Three unusual things about him are that he was one of those rare fellows from the hinterlands who made a success of whaling and rose to command New Bedford ships; that he made the leap from green hand to captain in the space of only four voyages, spanning a period of 13 years; and that even at the height of his whaling career he continued to live in upstate New York, rather than follow the usual practice and relocate to New Bedford. Two things that were not so unusual are that he worked on Erie Canal boats in his youth, and he was recruited into the whale fishery by a *land-shark* — one of the often unscrupulous agents who collected bounties on each man he could coerce into signing articles for a whaling voyage. The agent "picked the boy up in New York and took him to New Bedford, Massachusetts, where he was put aboard a whaler" (obituary from 1927 reprinted in the *Utica Observer-Dispatch*, Apr. 12, 1947). At age 18 Lewis thus sailed as a green hand in the New Bedford bark *Peri* (1857-59), then made three voyages in the *Roscoe*, the first as a boatsteerer (1860-64) and the next as first mate (1865-70), both under Captain George H. Macomber, and he was barely 30 years old when he was given command. This third voyage in the *Roscoe* was a disappointing debut as captain. They sailed for the Pacific in November 1870 and managed to send home 470 barrels of sperm oil and 319 of elephant seal oil before the vessel was crushed in the Arctic ice in August 1872 with 800 barrels of sperm oil stowed. All hands were saved by a passing whaler but the oil appears to have been lost. Evidently, Captain Lewis was not blamed for the wreck: in the following year, not long after he returned from the Arctic disaster as a passenger, and not long after he married Mary A. Bennett in Utica, managing agent Jonathan Bourne, Jr., gave him command of the *Lagoda*. Lewis had her for three voyages (1873-86) on which his wife Mary accompanied him on the second and third (1877-86), and his memorable successes on all three voyages, and especially the third, were a large part of the reason why the *Lagoda* found such favor with her owners and why, out of all the ships in New Bedford, she was selected as the subject of the model in the Bourne Building. Captain Lewis, who in addition to his regular lay, also held a 1/16th ownership interest in the *Lagoda* as part of his compensation, thus profited from these voyages both as her captain and as a shareholder. He then retired from whaling in 1886 and was living in Utica, where he had purchased a grocery business, when in 1916 he and Mrs. Lewis were recruited by the designer of the *Lagoda* model to advise about details of the vessel. According to Zephanaiah Pease's landmark *History of New Bedford*, they "were able to supply … voluminous information as to the details of the bark's rig [and] the arrangement of her deck and cabin." Lewis was widowed shortly after, lived for a few years in a masonic home, and died in 1927. His obituary reported that he was "survived only by distant relatives," but among these were the two nephews and one niece who independently gave four pieces of his scrimshaw to the museum.

Lewis, Enos — see **Lewis, George**

Lewis, George (fl. circa 1838-53). A trove of polychrome pictorial scrimshaw, eight pieces in all (in KNB), was accumulated in six different transactions from a variety of sources over a period of several years, but on stylistic grounds they are attributed to the same hand. All of the intrinsic clues and extrinsic associations regarding their origin and provenance point to a maker with the surname Lewis; and while the identity of the artist has not been definitively ascertained, whaleman George Lewis of Walpole, Massachusetts, is the most likely candidate. Among the scrimshaw are three polychrome engraved panbone busks. One has a starboard broadside portrait of a full-rigged ship under full sail, flying an American flag at the taffrail and pennants aloft, with a potted flowering plant, interlocking hearts with leafy borders, and a palm tree. A second has a heart motif, a Norfolk pine, a diamond figure, seven flowers in a vase, with two of the flowers drooping, and a pentagram. Each of these is inscribed in pencil holograph on the back, "Lewis Family." The third busk has a heart and pinwheel motif, with baskets of drooping flowers and vines bracketing the name "MARY LEWIS," boldly inscribed; the letter A and the name "ANNIE" are also scratched onto the surface by a later hand. There are five polychrome engraved teeth, including two pairs. The single tooth has the starboard broadside view of a full-rigged ship under full sail, flying an American flag at the taffrail and long pennants from the main, with a tree and a bird on the back. One of the pairs is engraved on the obverse sides only with full-rigged ships under full sail, flying American flags at the taffrail and pennants from all three masts, with the names of the ships boldly inscribed below: a starboard broadside view is labeled "HECTOR" while the other is a larboard broadside view with the vessel identified as "CORAL." The second pair are ornamented on both sides with a starboard broadside views of full-rigged ships underway, each flying an American flag from the spanker and pennants aloft on all three masts; and on the other side of each, a flowerpot with seven red, heart-shaped flowers, of which two are drooping.

The keys to the attribution are the ship portraits on each piece, which have striking stylistic and iconographical affinities in macro and micro scale; and the potted plants with drooping flowers, which are distinctive. Side-by-side the ensemble forms a daisy-chain of features that are consistently reflected from one piece to the next. The key to the identity of the artist is nomenclature: the family name Lewis appearing both on the scrimshaw and in the provenance, combined with the ship names *Coral* and *Hector*, and the name Mary Lewis inscribed on the busk.

The *Hector*, 380 tons, was built at New York for the merchant service in 1818 and purchased and fitted for whaling at New Bedford in 1826. She completed ten whaling voyages (1826-60); on her eleventh was burned by the Confederate commerce raider *Shenandoah* at Ascension Island 1865. The *Coral*, 370 tons, was built at Newbury, Massachusetts, for the merchant service in 1819 and entered the whaling fleet in 1832. After eleven voyages from New Bedford (1832-75), in the course of which she was converted to a bark, the *Coral* was refurbished and refitted, thus enabled to make another eleven voyages out of San Francisco; she was finally withdrawn and sold in 1889. The careers of the two vessels thus overlapped for 33 years (1832-65), but as both are depicted on the scrimshaw as full-rigged ships the images must refer to the period before 1858, when the *Coral* was converted to a bark.

Though the records are not absolutely complete, evidently there was not even one officer or crewman named Lewis who served on both the *Coral* and *Hector*, and there was certainly no captain who commanded both ships; in fact, there were only three men surnamed Lewis who served on one ship or the other. Thomas Lewis and Enos M. Lewis were evidently unrelated but they were both aboard the *Coral* at the same time, on the voyage of 1850-54. Enos, a green hand for the 200th lay, was from the village of Easttown, in Chester County, Pennsylvania. His parents, Nathan and Hannah Goodwin Lewis, had buried a son named Enos who died in infancy in 1817, and in conformity with the tradition of giving a subsequent sibling the same name as that of a child who died young, Enos the whaleman was the namesake of his dead brother. His Seaman's Passport gives his name as Enos M. Lewis and his birthplace as Easttown, Pennsylvania, a clear indication that he was the second son named Enos in the Lewis family of Easttown. He also had an older sister named Mary (1815-1910). But this Mary Lewis was married and became Mrs. Randall Pratt in 1837, when Enos was only eight years old, long before he could have made a busk for her on a whaling voyage: if he ever did make such a busk it would have been inscribed "Mary Pratt." (Not to be confused with Enos M. Lewis of Philadelphia and the U.S. Navy, who was born circa 1834 and *may* have had a younger sister named Mary: she is identified in the 1870 census as Mary but in the 1880 census as Jennie, and her married name was Taylor. And not to be confused with Enoch Lewis, born circa 1826, an African-American mariner from East Walpole, Massachusetts, whose Seaman's Passport was issued at New Bedford in 1849, describing him as a mulatto, age 23, but whose voyages are not known. In any case, though he was from the same hometown, Enoch Lewis is not known to have been in the *Hector* or the *Coral* at any time.)

On the same voyage of the *Coral* that Enos Lewis was a green hand, Thomas Lewis was steward for the 120th lay. Aboard whaleships the steward was principally involved with food service and other comforts of the aftercabin; he ranked a notch or two higher than the cook and was slightly better paid than the cook and better paid than some of the foremast hands. However, in most whaleships the steward was not an idler; that is, he pulled an oar in the whaleboats and was called upon to work the anchor and sails when circumstances warranted. Thus, unlike many ship's cooks, the steward was often a capable seaman, and a steward's berth was often a steppingstone to higher rank and greater responsibility. For example, Thomas Albro (q.v.), steward on the ship *John Coggeshall* of Newport (1835-39), was not only a first-rate scrimshaw artist but also an accomplished seaman (his shipmates in the *Coggeshall* included his seaman-artist-brother Caleb Albro and Caleb's life-long friend J.N. Sherman, qq.v.). It is also worth noting that the Japanese castaway John Manjiro (q.v.) sailed as steward in the *Franklin* in 1846, but in testimony to his professional seamanship was afterwards elected boatsteerer by his shipmates. Apart from this, Thomas Lewis's voyage as steward in the *Coral* is the only thing known for sure about him. He may have been the same Thomas Lewis who served as cook for the 140th lay on an earlier voyage of the *General Pike* (1845-49); or the Thomas Lewis who joined the Fairhaven ship *London Packet* at Sydney, New South Wales, in 1846 for the 140th lay as an ordinary seaman; and he may or may not have had a wife, a sister, or a mother named Mary.

The case for George Lewis as maker of the scrimshaw is far the strongest of the three. First of all, with three deepwater voyages to his credit he was the whaleman of longest standing, thus the most accomplished professionally — which may mean only that he had more opportunities to make scrimshaw, but not necessarily the only ones or better ones. Secondly, he was married to a woman named Mary, which is particularly significant in the absence of any Marys associated with Enos and Thomas Lewis. Third, George is the only one of the three regarding whom there is some glimmer of known association with both ships, the *Coral* and the *Hector*. He was born circa 1817 at Walpole, Massachusetts (a stone's throw from the East Walpole birthplace of the black sailor Enoch Lewis). He obtained a Seaman's Protection Paper (passport) at age 21 in May 1838, but the ship in which he made his maiden voyage (1838-40) has not been discovered. He was an ordinary seaman in the *Hector* for a cruise of almost three years under Captain James Gray, from November 1840 to September 1843. (There was a George Lewis, age 22 but no residence indicated, who embarked in the *Stephania* in July 1839, which did not return until October 1841 — too late to have embarked in the *Hector* in November 1840 unless he left the *Stephania* early.) It is presumed that if George Lewis was indeed the artist, he must have made at least some of the scrimshaw at the time of the *Hector* voyage — but not necessarily the *Coral* and *Hector* pair, which may actually relate to a later phase of his career. After the *Hector*, he was an Ordinary Seaman for the 140th lay in the bark *Roscius*, (1843-46), which may have been his last whaling voyage (though not necessarily his last voyage at sea); or, more likely, he may be the same George Lewis who was a boatsteerer in the *Atkins Adams* (1846-50), and boatsteerer and shipkeeper in the *Jasper* (1850-53). Sometime while he was still active as a mariner, and in any case prior to 1850, he moved out to Fayette, Ohio, which was part of Gorham Township in Fulton County, where he lived on the farm of L.C. and Susan Rice and their toddler daughter. Susan Rice may have been George's younger sister. He married his Mary in the middle 1850s, turned his attention from seafaring to agriculture, and raised four daughters and a son on the Ohio farm. Nothing in his record has been discovered that would explain the significance of the *Coral* paired with the *Hector* on his scrimshaw, except possibly that Henry M. Rice, a kinsman of L.C. Rice, made a voyage as a green hand for the 200th lay in the *Coral* during 1854-58, which would have been just about the time George Lewis was living on L.C. Rice's farm and married the woman named Mary.

Lewis, James Russell (fl. circa 1855-57?). Credited with an engraved pictorial walrus tusk (reported by a descendant). Nothing is known of his life or career other than that he was a resident of Boston and probably went whaling. Of several men named James Lewis who served in the crews of American whaleships in the nineteenth century, one was a Boston resident born circa 1834 at Rehoboth, Massachusetts, who received his Protection Paper at Fall River in October 1855, sailed a few days later in the bark *Mattapoisett* of Westport, Massachusetts (1855-57), and made only the one voyage. But this may be James *M.* Lewis of Rehoboth, who later served three years as a private in the Union Army. The Boston City Directory lists only one James *R.* Lewis, a waiter in 1880. Other men named James Lewis (whose middle initials, if any, are regarded as unreliably transcribed in most cases) made the following voyages from New Bedford: seaman in the brig *Bramin* (1841-45) and bark *Newton* (1843-46); steward in the ship *Navy* (1843-45); green hand in the ships *Abigail* (1847-52) and *Henry Keeland* (1858-62). None are recorded from New London, Salem, or Nantucket, whereof the crew lists are incomplete.

Lewis, Thomas — see **Lewis, George**

Lincoln, James Lawrence (fl. circa 1838-62). New Bedford whaling master from Taunton, Massachusetts, who may or may not have been a scrimshaw maker. Sometime around 1853 he presented a scrimshaw walking stick (cane) to an older friend of the family, but the provenance is not specific about who actually made the stick. A captain can usually impose upon some skilled member of the crew to produce such an item on commission; but Lincoln was only a mate at the time, a berth in which it was more likely that he would have made the scrimshaw himself or bartered to get it — and, of course, any member of a ship's company might swap something to get such a walking stick from a shipmate. This one has a two-piece panbone shaft, the lower shaft plain with a wire ring at the bottom, the upper shaft and foreshaft, a baleen band separator, and an octagonal, tapered whale ivory knob pommel with scored ornaments. The provenance is inscribed by a later hand: "CARVED FROM A WHALE'S TUSK [sic] AND PRESENTED ABOUT 1853 BY CAPTAIN JAMES LINCOLN TO LEMUEL PERRY".

According to the Vital Records of Taunton, James Lawrence Lincoln was born there on June 11, 1820 (not Jan. 25, 1820, as has been reported on a family website), the eldest of the seven children of Benjamin Lincoln and Sophia Makepeace Lincoln. This is almost the only fact about him that appears in the records of his hometown, which is the seat of Bristol County, where New Bedford and a half-dozen other whaling ports are located. Though James Lincoln is, for reasons unexplained, entirely absent from the census records for New Bedford or Taunton, his whaling career is well documented throughout: maiden voyage in the bark *George and Martha* of New Bedfored at age 18 (1838-40); seaman (1840-41) and boatsteerer (1841) in the brig *LaGrange* of Mattapoisett; second mate in the brig *America* of Wareham for the 38th lay; then a voyage as third mate in the New Bedford ship *Enterprise* (1844-47) for the 60th lay. This latter voyage may appear to have been a step backward from his higher rank and larger share in the *America* of Wareham, but though this was a lower berth and a smaller lay, it was a much larger vessel with greater prospects for earnings and advancement. Sure enough, his next voyage (1847-49) was as first mate of the same vessel for the 27th lay under Captain Joseph C. Little (q.v.). He went one more voyage as a mate, in the Fairhaven ship *Ansel Gibbs* (1849-53), then had command of two modestly successful Indian Ocean voyages of the New Bedford bark *Elisha Dunbar* (1854-58 and 1858-62). It was at around the time he was serving as a mate in the *Ansel Gibbs* that Lincoln presented the walking stick to Lemuel Perry (b. 1787), a local dignitary in nearby Norton and friend of the family: he had served under James Lincoln's grandfather in the War of 1812, in a Norton unit that mustered at New Bedford, and he later held office as a Town Selectman and treasurer and trustee of Wheaton College.

Lindsey [Lindsay], Allen (fl. mid-19th century). A written provenance is almost the only surviving evidence of the putative maker of an oval panbone ditty box, four inches in diameter, reported from a private collection on Nantucket. The wooden top is inlaid with a five-pointed star of tortoise shell and trimmed with trunk tacks, the panbone skirt is engraved with hearts and geometric forms, and there is a later pencil holograph inscription inside: "Brought from the Arctic Ocean on a Whaling voyage by Allen Lindsay and given to his mother, who always said he made it. It is not known what year he brought it. He died 1863. Given to his daughter by an uncle 1910." Lindsay's whaling career has not been discovered, but he was almost certainly the man whom the U.S. Census records as Allen Lindsey, born circa 1818, a cooper in Bristol, R.I. He likely served as ship's cooper on at least one whaling voyage from that port. That he is listed as a passenger on an unidentified ship traveling from Matanzas, Cuba, to Providence in 1839, suggests that he may have been at sea up to that time and been returning from an abortive voyage; in any case, this is the only indication of approximately when he may have been at sea. His wife's name was Caroline; their eldest son and firstborn child came along circa 1845, suggesting that they were probably married around 1844; and in addition to two sons the couple had three daughters: Susan (born circa 1847), Serephine (circa 1852), and Hannah (circa 1855). The "uncle" may have been Captain Samuel M. Lindsey, who lived next door with his family.

Little, Charles (fl. circa 1830-52). New Bedford whaling master from Westport, Massachusetts, who, by virtue of a provenance that was transmitted orally through five generations of descent through the family, is associated with three pieces of nicely crafted scrimshaw; however, it is not clear whether he made them himself (which external circumstances suggest was likely the case) or simply brought them home from one of his voyages. These are: a pistol-grip crimper of sperm whale ivory, trimmed with baleen, the saddle terminating in a carved eagle head, on which the eyes are formed by the axle-hubs of the whale ivory jagging wheel; a rolling pin with handles turned from whale ivory and trimmed with sealing wax, the convex wooden barrel inlaid with diamond and lozenge patterns in whale ivory, wood, and mother of pearl; and a particularly fine and well-proportioned wooden cutlery box, inlaid with whale ivory diamonds and surmounted on the handle with a panbone plaque proficiently engraved "C. Little," undoubtedly a gift for his wife Cynthia.

Also known as Charles Little II and Charles Little, Jr., he was born in Westport in 1816, the son of Charles Little and Hannah née Chase of Dartmouth, Massachusetts (she was the widow of Richard Craw and already the mother of two). He went whaling at 16; and in 1840, at just about the time he was promoted to second mate, Charles married Cynthia M. Brownell (born 1821), who went along on at least one of his later voyages as captain. These were in the New Bedford ships *Congress* (1846-48), following a voyage on which he was first mate of the same vessel (1843-46); and *Emma C. Jones* (1849-53), brand new at the time. Meanwhile, Cynthia bore him a son named

George (born circa 1844), who also became a sailor, was later a house painter, and inherited the scrimshaw; a daughter also named Cynthia (born circa 1849), who married whaleman William B. Ellis, with whom she lived at first in the Little household (Ellis later commanded 17 whaling voyages out of New Bedford and San Francisco during 1872-1906); and a son Clarence (born circa 1854), who did not survive childhood. After the *Emma C. Jones* voyage Charles Little retired from whaling but he may have spent a few years as a merchant sea captain before leaving the sea altogether in the 1860s, when he turned to farming in Westport. He died before 1880.

Little, Joseph C. (fl. circa 1835-71). New Bedford whaling master credited with a variety of scrimshaw. Most distinctive is a disc-shaped butter mold of sperm whale ivory, carved in shallow relief with a floral pattern and his wife's name "ELIZA D. LITTLE" carved backwards, so as to print forwards when pressed on butter (in KNB). In addition, his daughter Elizabeth Howland donated an assortment of whaling relics to NBWM in 1961, including Captain Little's compass and charts, several Chinese lacquer boxes and tables, a *kiribatian* shark-tooth sword from Kiribati (the Kingsmill Group of the Gilbert Islands), a walrus tusk, a swordfish bill, 13 small sperm whale teeth, and four boxes of sea shells. These came to the Museum with her father's scrimshaw: a foot-long porpoise jaw dated 1861; a straight, turned wooden crimper with fluted whale ivory jagging wheel; a tiny "trick box" of whale ivory, with sliding top; a mixed-media sheave block; and two letter seals with raised letters, not unlike the butter mold — though how many of these he may have made himself, and which ones may have been presented to him by fellow master mariners or members of his crews, is not known.

A native of Dartmouth, Massachusetts, Joseph C. Little was born circa 1819 and went to sea in the middle 1830s. He embarked on his maiden voyage at age 16 in the ship *Maine* (1836-38), made another voyage in the *Maine* as a seaman or boatsteerer (1838-40), then was in the *Herald* of Fairhaven, probably as third mate (1840-42). He was next second mate of the same ship for a 38th lay (1842-44), first mate of the ship *Enterprise* of New Bedford for a 27th lay (1844-47), and was promoted to captain of the *Enterprise* on her next voyage. Between voyages, in June 1847, on the eve of his first outing as captain, he married Eliza D. Thomas, age 22, of New Bedford. They lived on a farm in Westport, where a hired hand evidently did most of the farming, Eliza tended to the household and the children, and Joseph spent the majority of his time at sea — but he did afford himself the luxury of a few longer-than-average breaks between voyages. After the *Enterprise* (1847-49), he was captain of the *Florida* (two voyages, 1851-53 and 1853-56), the *Hillman* (1857-61), and the *Marengo* (1866-71). When he retired from the sea he became a gentleman farmer in Westport, but he also held ownership shares in the *Marengo*, the New Bedford barks *Globe* and *Mabel*, and the Fairhaven schooner *Union*. Benjamin Blossom (q.v. in the *Dictionary*) kept a journal of a voyage as Captain Little's first mate in the *Hillman* (in KNB). Captain Little's daughter Elizabeth, known as Lizzie, who is credited with having donated the relics and most of the scrimshaw, was born in 1864, so if she really did make the gift herself in 1961 she would have been in the vicinity of 97 years old at the time. More likely the gift was made by some other relative in her name.

Locket Engraver (fl. circa the 1840s). Judge Paul Vardeman identified six monochrome engraved teeth in public and private collections that can be attributed to the same hand, and inspired the nickname for this otherwise anonymous artisan. An additional pair has since been identified by

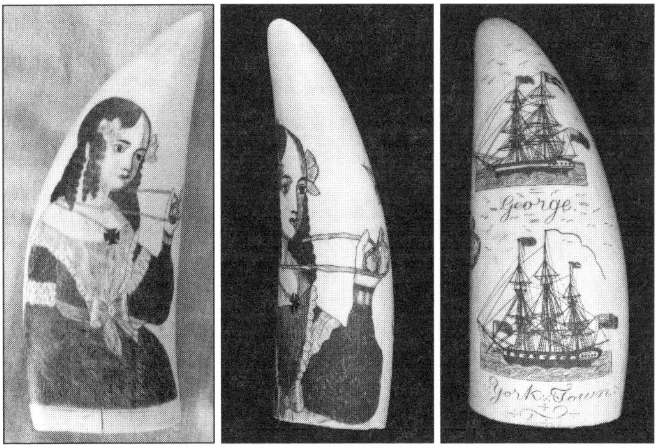

Fig. 13. **The anonymous Locket Artisan** was not the only scrimshaw artist to portray women wearing and holding lockets, but the characteristic features of his renditions are consistent: a dark-haired young woman looking at a locket (a Maltese cross or cameo brooch on a heavy cord) suspended from her neck and held outward in one hand, with one arm up and the other arm down; she has almond-shaped eyes with arched eyebrows, bowed lips, hair parted in the middle, long ringlets on both sides, bows at the temples, and a gown with puff sleeves, lacey ruffles low on the shoulders and sleeves, and a bow at the base of the bodice. One of the examples here (left) was provided by Judge Paul E. Vardeman, who was the first to identify this artist's hand. The other is from the Kendall Collection in the New Bedford Whaling Museum. The third photo shows the back of the Kendall specimen, an example of the Locket Artisan's finely engraved and carefully labeled ship portraits.

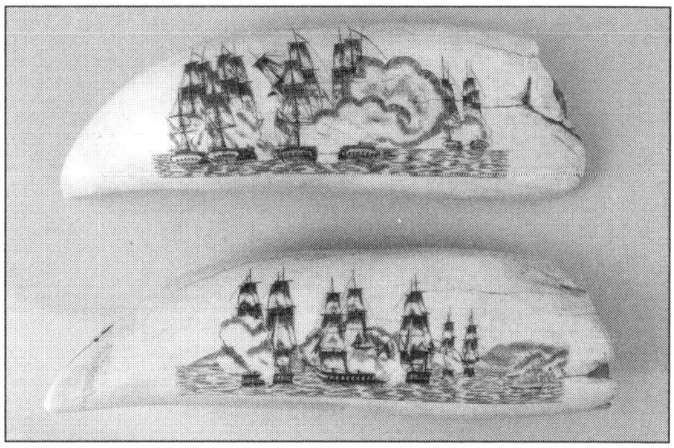

Fig. 14. **The anonymous Naval Engagement Engraver** specialized in War of 1812 naval battles, especially those involving entire squadrons (as here). His bold monochrome style with polychrome highlights is quite distinctive. The backs of some of his teeth have whaling scenes. Kendall Collection, New Bedford Whaling Museum (photos by Richard Donnelly).

Fig. 15. **The anonymous Naval Monument Engraver**'s approach to sea battles is more open and draftsman-like than the Naval Engagement Engraver's work. His teeth are characteristically based upon Abel Bowen's *Naval Monument* (Boston, 1816 and 1830) and rendered in color, with the forms outlined and with titles copied directly from Bowen. However, the scene on the top is labeled "ESCAPE OF THE CONSTITUTION FROM A BRITISH SQUADRON," which is how the scene is identified in Horace Kimball's *American Naval Battles* (Boston, 1831), but Kimball's scene is actually a copy of Bowen's "The *President* Engaging the *Endymion,* while pursued by the British Squadron." The other is "UNITED STATES SQUADRON UNDER COM. BAINBRIDGE returning triumphant from the Mediterranean in 1815." Collection of the New Bedford Whaling Museum, bequest of Martha Hinsdale from the collection of F. Gilbert Hinsdale, 1959.

SFL in the collection of the Norton [Massachusetts] Historical Society (based on photocopies submitted by Prof. Curtis Dahl). Though only some of the teeth (including one in SIW and one in NBWM) exhibit the lady-holding-a-locket feature that is the distinguishing feature of these teeth and gives rise to the name, other stylistic and iconographical affinities among the eight are also abundantly evident. "Five illustrate U.S. Navy warships active in the 1840s, often with another small vessel above. The reverse of two teeth has a young woman looking longingly at a locket," and another has the lady with the locket but no ship portrait. "The lady with the locket" is a young woman in ringlets who holds in one hand (sometimes the right, sometimes the left) a pendant oval miniature suspended from her necklace, thereby extending the loop of the necklace outward from her neck and upward to the level of her chin. She wears a Maltese cross brooch just below the neckline of her gown, and a large bow below the bodice; a male portrait is clearly visible on most occurrences of the locket. It is also notable that all of the named vessels served in the Pacific in the 1840s, and all were involved at one time or another in the Navy's efforts to suppress the slave trade on the Brazil, Cuba, and Africa stations. [1] The specimen in NBWM (acquired in 1923 from a private collector) has two ship-portraits on one side and the lady with the locket on the other. Significantly, the history of one of the named vessels indicates a fairly narrow time frame in the 1840s. The so-called sloop-of-war *Yorktown*, a full-rigged ship of 566 tons displacement, rated 16 guns, was launched at the Norfolk Navy Yard in 1839 and made three cruises. The first, under Cdr. John H. Aulick, was to the Pacific during 1840-43, when, according to the U.S. Naval Historical Society, she was "looking after the interests of the American whaling industry and of the nation's ocean commerce," and "called at the Marquesas, the Society Islands, New Zealand, and the Hawaiian Islands." These are mainstream Yankee whaling landfalls, and her record suggests the possible source of a whaleman's interest in the Navy. The *Yorktown*'s other cruises were from New York via Funchal and Porto Praya to join the American Africa Squadron in suppressing the slave trade during 1844-46, returning to Boston; and from Boston to Africa again from November 1848 to September 1850, when she struck an uncharted reef at Isle de Mayo in the Cape Verde Islands and was lost, with all hands saved. The other vessel on this tooth is a full brig labeled *George*, which has not been identified: the U.S. Navy lists no commissioned sailing vessel of that name at any time, nor were there any brigs named *George* in the whaling trade. [2] A tooth attributed to the same hand portrays the *John Adams* and an unidentified square-topsail schooner (brigantine) on one side, and an unidentified full-rigged ship on verso (Osona, 14 Aug. 1993, lot #86). This piece is technically and stylistically consistent with the other five, but adds little to revealing the chronology or identity of the artist, as two of the vessels are generic and unnamed, while the *John Adams*, according to Judge Vardeman, was a ship-rigged sloop-of-war launched in 1830 that was "referred to as 'the old frigate.'" [3] An example in a private collection shows the full-rigged ship *Boston* and a topsail schooner labeled *Swan* on one side, and the lady with the locket on the other. The sloop-of-war *Boston*, 18 guns, commissioned in 1826, was built at the Boston Navy Yard and served 20 years, on the Brazil Station (1826-29), in the Mediterranean (1830-32), the West Indies (1836-39), the East Indies (1841-43), and Brazil again (1843-46), until, en route to the Mexican War, she was lost in the Bahamas, with all hands saved, in 1846. The *Swan*, beautifully rendered on the scrimshaw, was evidently neither a commissioned U.S. Navy vessel nor an official hireling; nor was there a whaler of this name and rig at the time. [4] Another specimen (Bourne, 4 Aug. 1981, lot #139) has a portrait of the sloop-of-war *St. Louis* on one side and a figure of Alwilda the Female Pirate on the other.

The Alwilda picture corroborates the dating of the scrimshaw to the middle-to-late 1840s (for a brief discussion of the Alwilda and Fanny Campbell phenomena of the 1840s, see the article on William B. Sturtevant). The *St. Louis*, 20 guns, was built at the Washington Navy Yard in 1828, served all over the world, including in the Pacific and East Indies in the 1840s, served as a receiving ship after the Civil War, and was later renamed *Keystone State* for use as a training ship in Pennsylvania. She was finally scrapped in 1907. [5] A tooth of similar ilk portraying the USS *Independence* has an urn with flowers on the back and no lady with locket (McInnis, 1 Jan. 1993, lot #84; it was afterwards offered for sale by Samuel Herrup and illustrated in the *Maine Antique Digest*). The *Independence*, 90 guns, launched in 1814 at the Boston Navy Yard, was the first American ship-of-the-line and remained in service for 98 years, until 1912. [6] The tooth by this hand in SIW was "part of a large collection donated to the museum in 1935 by Frederic A. Delano." It has the lady with the locket on one side but the back is blank. The provenance is impressive but, given the pedigree of the donor and the large size of his collection, it reveals little or nothing about the authorship of the scrimshaw. Frederic Delano was the descendant of a prominent family of whalers and whaling merchants, among whom there would have been many opportunities to acquire scrimshaw of various kinds, and many potential sources: in addition to which, he was a collector who may have had some pieces that were connected in some way to his own family, certainly also acquired scrimshaw that had no such legacy. At the time Delano donated the scrimshaw to SIW, his nephew, Franklin Delano Roosevelt, was President of the United States. [7] Each of the pair in the Norton Historical Society has the lady-with-locket image engraved on one side — facing left on one tooth, facing right on the other. The back of one has a full-rigged ship under plain sail, labled *Eagle*, and an American warship flying pennants but no sails, labeled *Hornet*, the latter undoubtedly intended as the frigate of that name from the War of 1812. The other tooth has on the back a topsail schooner idenified as *John*, and a broadside portrait of the full-rigged ship *Boston*, so labeled. This second appearance of that vessel on scrimshaw by this hand suggests that the *Boston* may be the maker's own vessel; however, no corroborating evidence has been found. Likewise, while the Delano connection to FDR is interesting and suggestive, it does not really provide any substantive clues regarding the identity of the artist, nor to the genesis or significance of the lady-with-locket image itself. Judge Vardeman recalls seeing yet "another tooth with a Lady/ locket… but by a different hand," which suggests that it may have been generic, copied in both instances from an illustration in a magazine or newspaper, not yet identified.

Lovell, Austin (fl. circa 1835-90). Merchant sea captain from Barnstable and Osterville, on Cape Cod, who may have made a swift for his wife, of which only the whale ivory barrel clamp survives (in KNB). The clamp is engraved with the name of the intended recipient, "S.H. Lovell," which certainly refers to Sarah H. Lovell. But there were two women of this name at the time (and, remarkably, only two in New England who could have been the recipient of such a scrimshaw swift): one from Nantucket who was the widowed mother of mariner Edgar H. Lovell (q.v.), the other the wife of Austin Lovell. His real name was Robert Austin Lovell and he was born in 1818 to a distinguished family of Cape Cod mariners, the son of Ezekiel Lovell and Martha Cahoon; in fact, when his grandfather celebrated his eighty-first birthday, the event was considered worthy enough to be reported in the local newspaper: "Captain Austin Lovell of Osterville is celebrating today (in a quiet way) his 81st birthday" (*Barnstable Patriot*, Nov. 5, 1838). The younger man seems originally to have been known as Robert Lovell, but sometime in the 1850s he dropped the Robert and was known thereafter as Austin. No whaling voyages have been discovered under either name. After he left off seafaring in the 1870s he worked as a fisherman, and he was still listed in the U.S. Census as a "Retired Sea Captain" at age 82 in 1900. His wife, who would have been the recipient of the swift, was the former Sarah H. Wing, born in 1821, the daughter of Lot Wing and Clarissa Hallet. She became Sarah H. Lovell in 1842 and bore three children, but the descent and provenance of the swift — and the story of how only the clamp came to survive — have been irretrievably lost.

Lovell, Edgar H. (fl. circa 1840s). Nantucket mariner who may have made a swift for his mother, of which only the whale ivory barrel clamp survives (in KNB). The clamp is engraved with the name of the intended recipient, "S.H. Lovell," which certainly refers to Sarah H. Lovell. But there were two women of this name at the time (and, remarkably, only two in New England): one, born circa 1797, who was the widowed mother of Edgar H. Lovell, born circa 1822; the other the wife of Captain Austin Lovell (q.v.). Edgar was married to a woman named Phebe, they had a daughter named Ida May, and they lived on their native Nantucket; but nothing specific is known of his whaling career and he died comparatively young in the 1870s, after which Ida May went back to live with her mother.

Lovell, Henry S. – see **Sylvanus Henry Lovell**

Lovell, Sylvanus Henry (fl, circa 1846-50). An unusual, superbly crafted tooth, boldly incised in black and boldy highlighted in red (Northeast, 19-20 August, 2006, #1260), has a conventional provenance in the form of a handwritten letter. The scrimshaw features a port cityscape with a cluster of four- and five-story buildings and a large public building elevated behind, with the masts of a harbor crowded with ships, some flying American flags (the auctioneer claims that this is "Possibly New Bedford," but it is certainly not). On the back it has a military muster alongside "an American fort with cannon and soldiers, a lighthouse, and ships in a harbor." An accompanying letter signed "Aunt Hattie" implies an attribution to "Grandfather Lovell... born March 4th 1828," who made a four-year whaling voyage"; to which she adds, "On board the ship sailors did this work on whale's teeth. So it must have have been about the year 1846 or 1848."

The provenance leads accurately to the perpetrator. Sylvanus Henry Lovell was born in 1828 at Carver, in Plymouth County, Massachusetts, the son of Sylvanus Lovell and the former Joanna H Briggs. The family moved to Middleborough sometime before the son signed articles to sail as a green hand in the New Bedford ship *Congaree* (1846-50), using the name Henry S. Lovell (which he was to do for the rest of his life), evidently to distinguish himself from his father. (Incidentally, by way of corroboration: Henry, son of Sylvanus, was the only Lovell born on that date; and though he was not the only mariner named Lovell who had a close kinswoman named Hattie, he is the only Lovell known to have made a four-year whaling voyage in the 1840s.) Sylvanus Lovell (Sr.) became some kind of "trader" in New Bedford in the 1850s; meanwhile, "Henry" married Eliza Ann S. Dunham, who bore him two sons and three daughters. Hattie, born circa 1866, was the third child and eldest daughter (her married name and occupation, if any, have not been discovered). By 1870 the family was living in Jersey City, New Jersey, where Henry's occupation is not recorded, but they later returned to New Bedford — perhaps Henry inherited the family house from his widowed mother? In any case, he ran a restaurant on Achushnet Avenue in the 1880s and is said to have been on the Bristol County Grand Jury that indicted Lizzie Borden at Fall River in 1892.

Luce, Richard G. (fl. circa 1820-60). Whaling master from Tisbury, Martha's Vineyard, who may have made the inlaid wooden workbox in DCHS that he brought home for his daughter (reported by Brock Jobe). It has two drawers, turned whale ivory drawer pulls, and urn-shaped feet also turned from whale ivory and inset with sealing wax. The hinged lid and sides are inlaid and trimmed with abalone, mother-of-pearl, and tropical woods, including a delicate floral motif on the top, silhouette birds on the front, and silhouette horses on the sides (befitting a young girl); and a rectangular tortoise shell plaque set into the lid is inlaid in with the mother-of-pearl initials "ABL." The inside is divided into six compartments of unequal sizes, the central one surmounted by a large velvet pincushion and the others with lids of different tropical woods; and the inside of the lid is fitted with a mirror.

Luce was born in 1804, probably on Martha's Vineyard, and made whaling his career from an early age. He married Virginia Manchester of Tisbury in 1826, probably upon his promotion to second mate: the initials "ABL" refer to Abigail Bradford Luce, known as Abbie — born in 1828, the first of four children, the only daughter, and surely the recipient of the scrimshaw. Luce was given his first command in 1829 at the younger-than-usual age of 25, after which he made a succession of twelve whaling voyages in New Bedford vessels during a longer-than-usual stretch of 31 years as a captain (1829-60), with only a few interruptions: in the ships *Midas* (2 voyages, 1829-31), *Condor* (3 voyages, 1831-34), *Frances Henrietta* (1 voyage, 1833-35), and *Virginia* (3 voyages, 1838-43), and barks *Valparaiso* (1845-48), *Atlantic* (1851-54), and *Statira* (1857-60). He also had a long retirement on the Vineyard (he lived until 1885) but not an entirely happy one. According to memorial inscriptions in the Oak Grove Cemetery in Tisbury, all three of his sons became sailors — Richard G. Luce, Jr. (1831-1863), Charles W.M. Luce (1835-1868), and George B.M. Luce (1845-1868) — and, sadly, all three died at sea during their parents' lifetimes. Abigail's fate was brighter. She married steamboat captain Benjamin Coffin Cromwell in 1847, raised a large family of her own, and lived until 1904.

Ludlow, Elias (fl. circa 1800-05). The earliest known use of the word *scrimshaw* in any form is an entry of June 1805 in his shipboard journal, "All hands Scrim Shawnterin" (see Appendix I). The vessel is unidentified, though it may have been one of the Sag Harbor fleet; and whether Ludlow was including himself when he wrote "all hands" is unclear; so, too, what "all hands" may have been making. Not much is known about the man, either. He was born circa 1782, the second son of Anthony Ludlow (circa 1756-1809) and Elizabeth Ludlow (circa 1760-) of Bridgehamprion, L.I., New York, and as a young man earned at least part of his living from whaling.

Ludlow, Isaac (fl. circa 1837-54). Whaling master from Long Island, New York, credited with having produced scrimshaw aboard his last command, the bark *Monmouth* of Cold Spring Harbor; thus presumed also to have done scrimshandering at earlier stages of his career. He was born in 1807 at Bridgehampton, Long Island, the son and namesake of Isaac Ludlow, a local farmer. His early career is not definitively known, but he must have commenced whaling in the mid 1820s, as he embarked on the first of his six voyages as captain of Sag Harbor whalers at age 30, in the *Gem*

(1837-38). After another outing in the *Gem* (1838-39), he went two voyages in the *Hamilton* (1840-42 and 1842-44), then one each in the bark *Oscar* (1844-45) and ship *Arabella* (1847-49). His seventh and last command was the *Monmouth* (1851-54). With regard to scrimshaw the *Monmouth* voyage was perhaps Ludlow's most notable, but the name of that vessel is connected to the scrimshaw more than any other because Captain Ludlow is remembered primarily for his roles in two sensational events — one, lurid and contentious, aboard the *Oscar*, the other a noble act of heroism on the *Monmouth*. Each of them is commemorated in contemporaneous prints.

The *Oscar* incident was a notorious mutiny. In August 1845 the ship was at anchor in Ilha Grande, off Brazil, about seventy miles southwest of Rio de Janeiro, when a seaman by the name of Leonard Curtis threatened Captain Ludlow with an axe. The captain responded by shooting him dead with a rifle. When the *Oscar* returned to New York, Ludlow was indicted, tried, and acquitted of the charge of murder, amidst a tidal wave of publicity and controversy. An extremely rare contemporaneous lithograph, entitled "View of the Barque Oscar of Sag-Harbour, Capt. Isaac Ludlow. — Mutiny at Ilha Grande Aug. 18th. 1845. In which one of the crew Leonard A. Curtis was instantly shot," simultaneously shows the mutiny and its immediate aftermath (KNB; PEM; Brewington #4; Ingalls #259). The ship rests at anchor in a protected harbor, with sails furled and the Stars and Stripes fluttering from the spanker gaff; in a melee of officers and crew on deck, one man has an axe raised overhead while another man has a rifle aimed at him point blank. Meanwhile, in the water aft, above the marginal caption "Funeral of Leonard A. Curtis," a whaleboat bearing a coffin heads to shore with a crew of six; in the foreground (but not in perspective and much smaller than if they were drawn in correct proportion) are a church, a weeping willow tree (a habitual symbol of mourning), and a small cross that will mark the grave. The sympathies in the print are equivocal, but seem to lie more with Curtis than with the Captain.

According to historian James Truslow Adams, eight years after the *Oscar* mutiny Captain Ludlow "saved 105 lives from the British bark *Meridian*" (Adams 1918, 244). On August 25, 1853, the *Meridian*, crossing the Indian Ocean bound for Australia, veered off course and was wrecked hard aground on Amsterdam Island, one of the remotest landfalls anywhere in the world. The passengers and crew struggled through the powerful surf and onto the treacherous, rocky shore. A small, contemporaneous lithograph is entitled "The Wreck of the *Meridian* on the morning after the accident, showing how the passengers escaped and their encampment on the rocks"; it shows the castaways fetching water, retrieving provisions from the wreck, and erecting sailcloth shields against wind and weather, and a side panel shows "The passengers ascending the cliffs by ropes… ⅓ mile distant from the wreck" (Ingalls #260). As Elizabeth Ingalls explains,

> *Captain Ludlow, who was cruising for whales nearby on board the whaling bark* **Monmouth**, *spotted the shipwrecked passengers, and after some difficulty, effected their rescue on September 5. He then sacrificed the remainder of his whaling season to take the 105 passengers and crew safely to Mauritius, for which he and his crew were awarded medals.* (Ingalls 1987, 133)

A companion lithograph — the two were actually published at Port Louis, Mauritius, in 1853 — commemorates the rescue, with the caption "View of the N.E. portion of the Island of Amsterdam, with the place of embarkation and the last encamp[ment of the passengers, also the *Monmouth* standing off and on to receive them" (Ingalls #261).

Sometime around 1832 Ludlow married Phebe Pierson (1808-1894), with whom Isaac owned and operated a farm in Bridgehampton and fathered five daughters and one son, the youngest. Even while he was still an active whaling master in a community brimming over with mariners, farming was the occupation he declared for the census takers. His younger brother Jeremiah (1816-1895) was also a whaling master and had an even longer career, commanding six or seven voyages in Sag Harbor, Cold Spring Harbor, and New Bedford ships — and one Sag Harbor bark — beginning in 1841, when brother Isaac had already been a whaling captain on two voyages, until 1870, the year Isaac died.

Machado, Manuel (fl. mid-19th century). Azorean-born American whaleman whom a vague family provenance credits with a splendid oval panbone pierced-work sewing basket (in NBWM). The type is not uncommon, but attributed examples are extremely rare and this one is an unusually fine specimen. The shape and size (length about 8 ½ inches or 22 cm) are reminiscent of a seventeenth-century Dutch baleen *kapdoos* (oval or round hatbox), and the manner of construction is similar to the whalemen's oval baleen ditty-box. In this case, a strip of sperm whale panbone is pierced and carved to form open latticework; this is steam-bent around a wooden base, to which the bottom rim is nailed, with the ends overlapping and fastened with rivets on one side (in the manner of a Shaker wooden box). Unlike a *kaapdos*, baleen ditty-box, or Shaker box, however, the basket is open at the top and has a pivoting bail handle with matching latticework. This type of basket is a mainstream form extant in many manifestations, and here so well executed that it is difficult to believe that there were not others much like it by the same hand that have not been attributed. Unfortunately, the artist eludes identification and nothing more than his name is known. Two dozen men named Manuel Machado served on American whaleships from the 1850s through the '80s; all of them were from the Azores Islands (one of them by way of Brazil), few are known to have made more than a single voyage, and it is not clear which one may have been the maker of the basket. It was given to NBWM in 1986 by descendants — two maiden sisters, Mary and Cecilia Lewis — but the biography of their ancestor was as much a mystery to them as it remains for us today.

Only two men named Manuel Machado appear to have been more than one-voyage wonders. The one with the most highly developed professional whaling career was Manuel de Souza Machado, who made at least three voyages of which two are known, both in New Bedford barks, as an Ordinary Seaman in the *Robert Morrison* (1854-57) and fourth mate and boatsteerer in the *Mary and Susan* (1857-60). While he may be the most likely candidate for basket-maker, the namesake about whom the most is known was Manuel Silveira Machado, who with his twin brother Joseph Silveira Machado was born in 1833 on the island of St. George (São Jorge) in the Azores. He came to the USA in the 1850s, probably aboard a Yankee whaleship: the year of his arrival is uncertain, as the census page is illegible at that point, and his subsequent voyages are indistinguishable from those by other men of the same name. In 1870 he married Anna S. de Jesus Linias (1839-1915), a native of the island of Pico, in the Azores, and around 1879 they moved to Martha's Vineyard, where Manuel worked as a gardener, raised twin sons who became a carpenters, was naturalized as a U.S. citizen in 1894, lived with his son Joseph after being widowed in 1915, and died of arteriosclerosis in 1923.

Mackie, James (fl. circa the 1880s-'90s). He is not known to have been a scrimshaw artist and probably was not; but from listings in the New Bedford City Directory (citation provided by Michael P. Dyer), he is presumed to have been involved in retail sales of marine ivory, which suggests that even at this relatively early date there may have been commercial production of decorative or utilitarian objects of marine ivory. Mackie must have paid an extra fee to have his alphabetical listing appear in extra-large bold type, as it does in the 1889 edition at the top of page 287: "MACKIE JAMES, junk dealer, [business premises located at] 9 and 15 North Front, house 300 Acushnet ave. (see page 128)." The latter refers to his quarter-page display ad, which does not mention junk as such, but offers an astonishing variety of goods and services and is illustrated with a stock cut of a full-rigged ship under sail:

> JAMES MACKIE, / *Dealer in all kinds of* / PAPER STOCK, / Old iron, Brass, Copper, Lead, Pewter, / Whales' Teeth, Walrus Tusks, &c. / Old Ships bought and sold. Nos. 9 and 15 / No. Front St., New Bedford, / Orders solicited and satisfaction guaranteed.

This was precisely contemporaneous with the advent of picture frames and decorative objects made out of bone and ivory — including whale skeletal bone and marine ivory — by the likes of Charles Taber & Co. (q.v. in *More Scrimshaw Artists*). The Tabers were primarily stationers, framers, and sometime publishers, but early on became involved in selling of photographic materials and supplies, and in that very same year, 1889, were being called "the pioneer in the industry of art manufacturing in this country" (Pease & Hough, 1889). Other New Bedford merchants who perhaps had a somewhat lower profile may be presumed also to have been involved with the same kind of merchandise by that time or soon after.

According to the U.S. Census, Mackie was born in Ireland around 1830 (thus he is not the James Mackie who was born in New Bedford in 1825; nor the somewhat older James Mackie, AKA Magee, who commanded a five consecutive whaling voyages in the Fairhaven ship *Maine*, 1846-56), but it is not known when he immigrated, through what port of entry, or where he settled. His wife Adeline and step-daughter were both born in Massachusetts, but nothing much else is known about them, nor how or where the couple met or when they married. The early records of Mackie in New Bedford show him steadily employed in the city's extensive whale oil and spermaceti candle business: at the Marsh Candle Works in 1849, the C.H. Leonard Candle Works in 1856, and Fisher & Baker's oil and candle factory in 1859. By 1865 he had taken a job working for junk dealer William H. Cook, and circa 1869 he was made a partner in what was now reorganized as William H. Cook & Co., consisting of Cook and Mackie. James and Adeline were evidently separated at some point, as they had different addresses and separate listings in the City Directory in the 1890s. Even after Cook himself retired, Mackie continued until 1903 as proprietor of William H. Cook & Co.

Macomber, Stephen (fl. circa 1831-54). A baleen busk donated to NBWM by Lillian C. Andrew[s] in 1957, incised with serpentine leafy boughs and a starboard broadside view of a full-rigged ship under sail, bears the initials "R.A." and "S.M.," and the verse inscription "This is a present pretty girl for the[e] / Snatch'd from the bossom of the deep blue sea / And been fore many rugged [ ] afar / By thy true faithful friend a Tar." On the back it is clearly inscribed "Macomber" and lightly, almost illegibly inscribed "Rachel Macomber." The authorship has not hitherto been identified; in fact, the significance of the scratchings, and even the fact that the piece was inscribed at all, was lost to memory and evaded notice over the years; and it is remarkable how few parings of "S. Macomber" and "Rachel" there were in nineteenth-century New England — especially any connected to whaling; and especially when the intials "R.A." are factored in. Accordingly, the busk could only have been fashioned by whaleman Stephen Macomber ("S.M.") in the 1830s for his fiancee, Rachel Andrews ("R.A."), who was about the same age and whom he later married.

Stephen was born at Tiverton, Rhode Island, in 1816, the eldest of three children of Christopher and Eliphal Macomber. At age 15 he signed articles for his first whaling voyage, in the New Bedford ship *Gideon Howland* (1831-34), and after another voyage or two he became engaged to Rachel (1815-1872), the daughter of Stephen and Sarah Andrews of Dartmouth, Massachusetts. Stephen must have made the busk sometime during 1834-38, and the couple were married at Dartmouth on July 1, 1838. Meanwhile, Stephen's younger brother Job, born in 1818, had also become a whalemen, and the two served as mates simultaneously in different New Bedford ships during the 1840s and '50s. However, after a voyage as first mate in the *Frances Henrietta* under Captain Ephraim Poole, Jr. (1845-48), and another in the *Vernon* under Luther Little, Jr. (1851-54) — in fact, only a few months after returning from almost three years in the *Vernon*, and on the brink of possible elevation to command — Stephen died, on December 18, 1854, at age 38. Brother Job was already a captain and was at sea at the time as master of the *Montpelier* (1853-57). He was next given the *Majestic* in 1857, but, sadly, he also died young, at sea, aboard the *Majestic* at the age of about 40. After Stephen's death Rachel's widowed mother Sarah Andrews lived with her in Dartmouth; they were still living together in 1870, when Sarah was 81; Rachel died not long after, in 1872. Lillian Andrew[s], who eventually donated the scrimshaw, was evidently a collateral descendant in Rachel's family.

Macy, William H. (fl. circa the 1840s-'60s). A knife with a factory-made steel blade, wooden handle, whale ivory pommel and ferrule, and panbone sheath engraved "WILL MACY – HIS KNIFE" (reported by William J. Boylhart), is tentatively attributed to William H. Macy, who went whaling out of Nantucket in one or more unidentified vessels and was cooper in the ship *Albion* of Fairhaven (1854-57). A career mariner, he was born on Nantucket in 1826, the son of George Macy and Eunice Easton. In 1857, shortly after his voyage in the *Albion*, he married Phebe Ann Winslow, who was ten years younger and bore him seven children. By 1870 Macy became Register of Deeds for Nantucket, and after he was widowed in 1875 his maiden daughter Carrie took over as housekeeper for William and the six younger children. He died in Boston in 1891.

Macy, William J. (1827-1903). Whaling master from Nantucket, credited with a pair of sperm whale teeth polychrome engraved with images of a full-rigged ship under sail, a woman playing with a small child under a tree, a woman with broad-brimmed hat and fan standing beside a garden bench, and two young men carrying a young woman across a stream on a long tree branch; distinctively mounted together on an indigenous ebony platform, with vertical steel rods to support the teeth and six knob feet turned from whale ivory; in NBWM, donated by a great-grandson of the maker. William Jenkins Macy was born on Nantucket in 1827, the son of Charles Macy (1804-1887), a cooper, and Mary Jenkins. William was still living on Nantucket in 1850 and likely made his early whaling voyages from there, but in 1852 he married Ann Maria Mosher (1834-1862) and by 1860 had moved to New Bedford. Only the voyages late in his career are known. He was first mate (1855-59) and then captain (1859-64) of the *President*, a ship that was altered to a bark in 1859. He was widowed while he was at sea on this first voyage as a captain, leaving him with a son and a daughter. Thus, he was ashore for a few years, during which time he relocated and remarried, this time to Amanda Maria Peirce (born 1836), who bore him four more children, the first of whom came along in 1869 when Macy was again at sea as captain of the bark *Lancer* (1869-73). At this point he retired from whaling and by 1875 was running a variety store in New Bedford, selling "fancy goods," toys, and souvenirs for the next 20 years. Meanwhile, he was widowed again and married for a third time, to Delia [Cordelia] Luce Robbins, a widow who bore him a seventh child. He died in 1903.

Manchester, George L. (fl. circa 1842-59). Found pressed in the shipboard journal he kept as captain of the Westport, Massachusetts bark *George and Mary* during 1852-54, is a paper-cutout template for the handle of a pie crimper featuring pierced-work bent hearts and elongated crescents, with a pistol grip and a scroll end to accommodate the axle for a jagging wheel (KNB). The crimper was likely intended as a gift for Mary A. Palmer, to whom he was betrothed at the time and would marry not long after his return to Westport. It is presumed that Manchester made the template himself, but whether or not he ever made the crimper is not known; no exact match has yet been found. He was born in 1824 at Westport, the son of Hercules (1786-1873) and Abigail [née Tripp] Manchester (1788-1868), and the younger twin brother of James W. Manchester, who seems also to have made one or two whaling voyages in the 1840s (including as boatsteerer of the Westport bark *Harbinger*, 1842-44); but unlike George, James did not wind up making it his life's work. George was a career whaleman from the outset, and except for his maiden voyage, which must have occurred circa 1839-42, the record of his voyages, all in Westport vessels, appears to be complete. By the time he married Mary A. Palmer (born 1835) in 1854 or 1855 he had already been three or four voyages as captain. He was three voyages in the bark *Theophilus Chase*. The first was as ordinary seaman for the 105th lay (1842-44), the second was as boatsteerer for the 65th lay (1844-45), and on the third (1846-48) he shipped as third mate but early along was promoted to second mate for the 37th lay when the officers were reshuffled. He was then second mate in the brig *Thomas Winslow* (1848-49), first mate in the bark *Mattapoisett* (1849-50), then captain of the *Mattapoisett* (1850-51) at the comparatively young age of 26. After a second voyage in the *Mattapoisett* (1851) he commanded two in the bark *George and Mary* (1852-54 and 1854-55), one in the schooner *Kate Cory* (1856-57), and another in the *Mattapoisett* (1857-59). Both during his active career and after his retirement from whaling he held ownership interests in several Westport vessels, including two whalers he commanded (the *George and Mary* and *Kate Cory*) and three merchantmen he did not (bark *Janet*, sloop *Emma Clifton*, and schooner *Mary Chapin*). His brother James became a ship caulker and later a farmer, but George was listed in census records throughout his life as a Master Mariner.

Manchester, Isaac F. (fl. circa 1848-62). A panbone seam-rubber in NBWM is listed as having been donated in 1977 by Isaac F. Manchester, Jr., who attributed it to his namesake father; but the accession record may be flawed and the maker may actually have been the donor's namesake grandfather. In any case, it was Isaac F. Manchester, from Tiverton, Rhode Island, who likely made the seam-rubber on one of his three whaling voyages out of New Bedford, as a green hand in the ship *Archer* (1848-52), seaman in the bark *Statira* (1853-57), and boatsteerer in the ship *Fabius* (1857-62).

Manjiro [Nahahama Manjiro; John Mung; John Mungero] (fl. 1841-50). This Japanese castaway fisherman was in the crew on two Yankee whaling voyages, became an accomplished draftsman, and is well known in Japan as the first Japanese resident in the United States — "the Man who Discovered America." Especially in light of his skills as a carpenter, cooper, and naval architectural draftsman, there is no reason to doubt and every reason to expect that he would have attempted scrimshaw, along with everything else he tried on his two deepwater whaling voyages and his sojourns ashore as a Fairhaven schoolboy, cooper's apprentice, student of celestial navigation, California Gold Rush prospector, and deepwater mariner. Shipwrecked at age 14 in 1841 with four older fishermen companions with whom he was stranded for several weeks on a desolate, rocky island in the Pacific, they were rescued by the New Bedford whaleship *John Howland*, Captain William Whitfield of Fairhaven, Massachusetts,who took them aboard and landed them at Honolulu. On shipboard Manjiro was known as "John Mungero," which was shortened to John Mung. The other four elected to remain in the Hawaiian Islands, but Manjiro accepted Whitfield's invitation to remain aboard the *John Howland* and return with him to Fairhaven. There Whitfield and his wife virtually adopted the boy, enrolled him in school, brought him with them to the local Unitarian church, apprenticed him to a cooper, and provided the wherewithal for him to study celestial navigation. Manjiro later made a second whaling voyage, in the *Dr. Franklin* of New Bedford (1846-49), went gold prospecting in California — successfully, as it turned out — and, overcoming many obstacles, returned to Hawaii and then to Japan with two of his original fellow castaways, arriving about ten years after his inadvertent departure. Following twenty months of intensive interrogation by samurai officials in Okinawa and Japan, he was exonerated of espionage, was honored by being given the surname Nakahama, and being twice elevated to coveted samurai status. As the only man in Japan ever to have lived in the USA *as an American*, he is believed to have participated clandestinely, "behind the scenes," in treaty negotiations with Matthew C. Perry's American naval expedition in 1854, he was appointed a member of Japan's diplomatic missions to the USA in 1860 and 1870, and attempted — unsuccessfully, as it turned out — to introduce Yankee whaling methods in Japan, and with that intended purpose developed financial backing for, and personally commanded, two experimental offshore voyages from Japan in Western-style schooners. His influence upon the rapid modernization of Japan, leading up to and in the wake of the Meiji Revolution of 1868, is now widely considered to have been significant, with the result that Manjiro has been widely adopted in Japan as the personification of Japanese-American friendship.

No scrimshaw by his hand has come to light; but Manjiro the whaleman and cooper certainly possessed the requisite talents and interest to have experimented with the genre, and to have done so successfully on his two whaling voyages and several years ashore in Massachusetts, California, and Hawaii. However, his most important connection with scrimshaw is to have introduced it to Japan. He brought a few pieces home with him in 1850. Neither these nor the artists who produced them have ever been identified. The scrimshaw may have been confiscated during the long, arduous debriefing to which Manjiro and his two companions were subjected upon their return to Japan, but they are now lost, unknown even to Manjiro's reverent descendants. So too any scrimshaw Manjiro may have made himself that either remained with friends in Massachusetts or Hawaii, or accompanied him back to Japan. Nor has any scrimshaw been definitively connected with any of Manjiro's shipmates on either of his two whaling voyages, in the *John Howland* (1841-44) or the *Dr. Franklin* (1846-49). However, there are two pieces in NBWM, a panbone pierced-work jewelry chest and a panbone napkin ring echoing the same motif as the chest, that were made either by Luther Southworth (q.v.) of Dartmouth, Massachusetts, or, more likely, Luther's older brother, Edward Southworth (q.v.). Edward Southworth was second mate on the *John Howland* when that ship rescued Manjiro and his four castaway companions in 1841. There are several biographies of Manjiro in English: see especially his own autobiographical narrative "as told to Hyosun Kiryaku" in 1852, *Drifting Toward the Southeast: The Story of Five Japanese Castaways* (2003); also the biographies by Donald R. Bernard, *The Life and Times of Manjiro* (1992), Kaneko Hisakazu, *Manjiro: The Man Who Discovered America* (1956), and Emily V. Warriner, *Voyager to Destiny* (1956); and the expansive interpretive treatment by Christopher Benfey, *The Great Wave: Gilded Age Misfits, Japanese Eccentrics, and the Opening of Old Japan* (2003). The definitive and most detailed biography in Japanese is Tetsuo Kawasumi, *Nakahama Manjiro Shusei, Or The Manjiro Memorabilia* (2nd Ed., Tokyo, 1992).

Martin, William (fl. circa 1851-69). Ship's carpenter from upstate New York, whom J.F. Beane immortalizes in *From Forecastle to Cabin* (1887), a firsthand account of whaling in the New Bedford bark *Java* in the 1860s. First Beane characterizes the genre itself:

> *Another, and very interesting way of passing dull hours on board a whaler is "scrimshoning." This word, coined by the whaling fraternity for their private use, encompasses the making of everything from a plain ivory bodkin to the most elaborate inlay work imaginable. Boxes of fancy woods of different kinds inlaid with other woods, with pearl cut into diamonds, squares, crescents, and leaves, with silver, ivory, and bone, in designs simple or elaborate, as the taste of the maker might suggest.*

He then enumerates a few of the most familiar types of shipboard scrimshaw productions and the materials used for them:

> *Canes were made of ebony or other wood, of white bone from the jaw of the sperm whale, and of ivory from the teeth of the same animal... Swifts were manufactured of bone and ivory, riveted with silver wire, designed especially for a sweetheart or wife... Whales' teeth were ornamented with etchings and engravings in colors, many of them of more than ordinary merit.*

It is in this context that he remarks that "Old 'Chips'" — Martin was 29 at the outset of the voyage — "was the best workman we had on board, and the most industrious." Ship's carpenters on every kind of vessel were always called "Chips," and the *Java* was no exception. In this case "Chips" was William Martin; and if Beane saw any scrimshaw "of more than ordinary merit," with "some of the most elaborate inlay work imaginable," it must have been "the best workman ... on board" who produced the best of it. There were several other scrimshaw-makers on the *Java* at that time, including Beane himself (q.v.), about whose scrimshaw nothing is known. Washington Fosdick (q.v.), steward, the oldest man aboard, engraved a marginally prurient tooth on a previous voyage, and there is no reason to believe that he did not continue making scrimshaw throughout his career, including on the *Java*. And most notably, Captain Manuel Enos (q.v. in *More Scrimshaw Artists*), an immigrant from the Azores and a famous harpooneer, was one of the greatest scrimshaw artists of all time: his pictorial teeth are outstanding masterpieces of the genre.

Beane also discusses another eccentricity of Martin's: selling his scrimshaw at the first port-of-call. This is not only a rare instance of scrimshaw being exchanged for cash — it seldom was — but there is an underlying pathology in a whaleman's rush to rid himself of the fruits of his labor, regardless of the time and energy expended in producing them — scrimshaw "too often disposed of at the first port visited." The classic example is Nantucket whaleman George A. Grant, who spent three years at sea constructing a panbone birdcage as a gift for his ladyfriend, then impulsively sold it for $100 on the way home (see the article on Grant in *More Scrimshaw Artists*; and "The Last Harpooneer," a sketch by Austin Strong in *The Atlantic*, May 1942). Aboard the *Java* "'Old Chips'... made it a rule to sell everything that he had manufactured during the season at the first port entered." So, unfortunately, none of William Martin's scrimshaw has ever been identified as such: a whaleman who sold off all of his scrimshaw relegated his work to perpetual anonymity. Sometimes this was frivolous or impulsive, as it seems to have been in Grant's case; or perhaps Grant's story was entirely fictional, a self-deprecating yarn spun purely for the amusement of an audience. But sometimes there was a more self-destructive underlying cause, as in the analogous case of the Norwegian sailor character named Olsen in Eugene O'Neill's *Glencairn* plays (a part incongruously played by John Wayne in the 1940 film adaptation, *The Long Voyage Home*): Olsen saves his money for his whole life so he can return home and fulfill his dream, to buy a farm in Norway; but once on shore he fritters it all away on a binge and is forced to return to sea. Beane reflects:

> *I have known the labors of a six months' cruise to be disposed of for a few dollars or even shillings, and the proceeds spent in drink, in [fewer] hours than the months required to make the articles sacrificed. One case, I remember, where a very ingenious fellow worked all his spare time during a three years' voyage in making an ivory ship. The hull was ten inches [25 cm] long, modeled from a walrus tusk. The spars and sails were carved from whales' teeth. Every block and boom was in its proper place. Altogether it was a nearly perfect piece of workmanship. At the last port before sailing home his appetite for drink got the better of him and he sold this specimen of his handiwork for three pounds ($15.00) and before the day was gone had spent the last farthing.*

William Martin, from Lyons, New York, born circa 1834, was 20 years old when he was issued a Seamen's Protection Paper (passport) at New Bedford in November 1854, and sailed as boatsteerer in the ship *Corinthian* the next day. It could not have been his first voyage (green hands are not shipped as boatsteerers) and he may have left the *Corinthian* before the ship returned in 1858, as he is recorded as having gotten another passport at New Bedford in 1857 (but it may have been in 1858). He likely embarked on a third voyage at that time, probably as in the bark *Gratitude* (1858-62), on which the fourth mate and boatsteerer is identified as William R. Martin. He was 29 years old when he went as carpenter in the *Java* in 1864. Oddly, J.F. Beane (who for the purposes of his narrative compressed two successive voyages in the *Java* into one) never actually mentions Martin by name, but refers to him only as "Chips" and "the carpenter"; however, Beane does state explicitly that "Washington Fosdick, steward, claimed New York City as his home, and Otto Keller, the cabin-boy, was a Dutchman [i.e., German] from Elmira, New York State. The Carpenter, more familiarly known as 'Chips,' was also a New Yorker." It appears to have been his last voyage. Some inconclusive evidence implies that Martin had been trained as a cooper, and that he worked in a machine shop and lived in a sailor district of New York City in later life (he may have been living in New York City as early as 1857), but apart from that — which is largely speculative — nothing further is known about him, nor anything about his scrimshaw, which may never be identified. (Not to be confused with Captain William Martin, who commanded whaleships out of Warren, Rhode Island, in the 1850s; or with any of the many other contemporaneous William Martins in the crews of Yankee whaleships from various ports.)

Mason, C.D. (fl. mid-19th century). When retired sea captain Michael Rodgers died in 2002 he left an estate that included what has since become known as the "Sick of the Job" tooth: a sperm whale tooth (now in NBWM) that has, handsomely engraved on one side, a starboard broadside view of a full-rigged ship with sails askew, with another ship in the background off the larboard stern quarter, inscribed below with four lines of verse in a very small cursive hand.

> *O they who have felt it know how sweetly*
> *Some young women we sail to meet*
> *Sparkling on deck is no dry eye*
> *Ship a hoy   Ship a hoy our joyful cry*
> [signed:] C D Mason

On the other side is an elevated view of a countryside with houses, farmsteads, a mill building, church, river, roads, patchwork fields, and so on. Above, in a miniscule cursive hand, it says "sick of the job." The principal inscription is paraphrased from "The Meeting of Ships" by the Irish poet Thomas Moore (1779-1852), of which the full text of the original is:

> *When o'er the silent seas alone,*
> *For days and nights we've cheerless gone,*
> *Oh they who've felt it know how sweet,*
> *Some sunny morn a sail to meet.*
>
> *Sparkling at once is every eye,*
> *"Ship ahoy!" our joyful cry;*
> *While answering back the sounds we hear,*
> *"Ship ahoy!" what cheer? what… cheer?*
>
> *Then sails are backed, we nearer come,*
> *Kind words are said of friends and home;*
> *And soon, too soon, we part with pain,*
> *To sail o'er silent seas again.*

"C.D. Mason" may be the author of the parody and may also be the scrimshaw artist, but nothing whatever has been discovered about him or her in either context.

* **Mason, John B.** (fl. circa 1853-62). The *Dictionary* mentions him in connection with a walrus tusk monochrome engraved with an Old Testament Biblical scene of Rebecca at the Well on one side, and a recumbent dog on the other, inscribed "J. B. Mason Belleville N.J." (in KNB). No biographical details about the artist were discovered at that time. However, documents recently encountered now suggest a hypothetical reconstruction of at least part of his life and career. The key is his mother's birthplace: she was Catherine Macomb, born 1 Oct. 1805, in Belleville, Essex County, New Jersey, who married John Mason at Georgetown, D.C., on 5 April 1827. This is the only instance in which the place-name Belleville appears in the records in any relevant connection. John B. Mason, born circa 1839, was one of John and Catherine's nine children (he was probably the second son of that name, a namesake of an earlier son John who died in infancy). At age 20 J.B. was living on the Hoboken farm of Francis and Ann Dyer and their seven children, ages 12 to 28, including their son George, age 20. Hoboken is, of course, directly across the Hudson River from the great seaport of New York. It seems that J.B. was a friend or perhaps a relative of George Dyer, who was the same age and had been raised on the family farm; and that J.B. may have come to Hoboken so that he and George could ship out together as sailors (Edgar Alan Poe fictionalized an analogous situation in his *Narrative of Arthur Gordon Pym of Nantucket*); or, alternatively, that they had already met as shipmates and J.B. was now living with the Dyers as a mutual convenience. There is no evidence that the two ever actually shipped together; but if there was a whaling career it must have been around this time, in the latc 1850s and early 1860s. In fact, eight men named John Mason made whaling voyages from New Bedford around that time, but the lad born in 1839 was far too young to have been anyone but the John Mason who was a green hand for the 165th lay in the ship *James Andrews* (1853-57), which embarked when J.B. was 14 or 15 and returned when he was 18. This was his only attributed whaling voyage. And from here the story diverges. One version from the Mason family genealogy is that John Mason, the son of John and Catherine, married Anna J. Martin and fathered three daughters; no dates are ascribed to any of this. But according to another version of Mason family lore, J.B. married around 1862 and by 1870 was living at Sergeantsville, in Hunterdon County, New Jersey, with a wife and two sons, and was working as a clerk in a store. By 1880 he moved to Kansas City, Missouri, where he was proprietor of a "Tea & Coffee Store" with the older of his two sons, Henry, working there as a clerk. The odd thing here is that in the 1870 census the wife's name is given as Catherine and in 1880 it is Annie E.; but they are evidently the same woman (or twin sisters), born in New Jersey in 1836 and therefore three years older than J.B. And at this point the trail runs cold.

Matthews, Samuel (fl. circa 1860-64). A tatting shuttle, carved out of a single piece of whale skeletal bone, is engraved on one side with two pierced hearts pigmented in red and is inscribed "S. MATTHEWS." It came into the Charles F. Batchelder Collection from Osborn McArthur (one of Batchelder's regular sources), thence to NBWM in 1958. While "S. Matthews" could have been the name of the intended recipient, in this case it appears more in the nature of a signature. It is therefore provisionally attributed to one of the two New Bedford whalemen of this name, both of whom were named Samuel and both from Maine. The older one, from Sumner, Maine, was born circa

1820, went as a green hand in the Fairhaven bark *Benezet* in 1838, and deserted at Bay of Islands, New Zealand. He was evidently "on the beach" only a comparatively short time, as he was an ordinary seaman in the New Bedford bark *Marcella* not long after (1842-44). The other Samuel Matthews, from Eastport, Maine, was born in 1836 or 1837, the son and namesake of a sailor and (later) fisherman who was originally from Nova Scotia. His only known whaling voyage was as green hand in the New Bedford bark *Java 2d* (1860-64), commanded by T.C. Spaulding (q.v.). The surname on the tatting shuttle is clearly rendered as "Matthews," not "Mathews"; but in the whaling records and census reports the two spellings are used indiscriminately and interchangeably. However, the names also differ on their Seaman's Protection Papers, the official sailors' passports issued by the federal government that are thus presumed to be more reliable than the too-often casually rendered ship's articles and error-ridden census forms. The man from Sumner obtained his Protection Paper in 1838 with the surname spelled with only one T, while the younger man from Eastport got his in 1860 with the double-T spelling. This, and the fact that there is presumed to have been quite a bit of scrimshaw produced on the *Java 2d* on that particular voyage under Captain Spaulding (see also Manuel Enos and J.F. Beane), are the two bits of evidence that tend to tip the attribution in favor of the younger Samuel Matthews with two T's, from Eastport. It has also been suggested that a tatting shuttle of this type would likely have been more fashionable in the 1860s than in the 1840s, lending further weight to the Eastport man's claim. Unfortunately, there is no further information about either of them after their voyages.

* **Mattison, Malcolm G.** (fl. circa 1858-61) As time passes and additional research resources become available, the customary expectation is that revisiting a mystery may clarify it or perhaps even be lead to a solution (for example, see Donald Warrin's revelations in the article on Manuel Enos). However, the case of Malcolm Mattison is quite the opposite: new insights have exposed a mystery, or at least an historical anomaly, where none was known to exist before. And it all has to do with family history and family provenance.

Based on a solid family provenance, *More Scrimshaw Artists* credits Mattison with "Three teeth, beautifully engraved, featuring a portrait of a woman seated in a Victorian armchair, labeled 'Sallie'; American patriotic figures of Liberty (unfinished) and Justice; and a man's arm and hand placing a ring on a woman's finger, with the sleeve of her gown vaguely medieval in style, surrounded by floral ornaments and inscribed 'Per Contra, Que es lo.'" It is worth noting that, based upon the iconographical and stylistic characteristics of the three teeth, two lovely, goblet-like bud-vases in KNB, can be attributed to Mattison: two sperm whale teeth, inverted, hollowed out, mounted on turned whale ivory bases, and beautifully engraved with elaborately-costumed figures of children on one side and, on the back in each case, a man's left arm and hand placing a ring on a woman's left hand ring finger; framed by a delicate, heart-shaped garland of flowers and leaves; surmounted by a floral device (two erect flowers and four pendant Queen Anne's Lace-like flowers) embedded in a circumferential leafy vine. The attributions of the three teeth and two bud-vases remain intact and undisputed. The controversy is about the artist's biography.

More Scrimshaw Artists cites "an undated clipping from an unidentified upstate New York newspaper" to the effect that Malcolm and his younger brother, Lucius Van Schaick Mattison (1842-1910), "were raised on a 500-acre farm carved out of the forest near Scribia, New York; that the family 'lived in the blockhouse at Fort Oswego while their log house was being built'; and that Malcolm, who must have been born circa 1840, 'went to sea and died on a whaling expedition in the South Pacific before the Civil War.'" It is this latter claim that is the seed of the newfound mystery. As noted in *More Scrimshaw Artists*, "Mattison descendants report that Lucius Mattison's last will and testament, written in 1904 and probated in 1910, discloses that Malcolm was 'lost at sea from the ship *Louisianna* [sic] in 1861,'" which could only refer to the New Bedford ship *Louisiana* on a voyage of 1858-63. However, none of the official records list anyone named Mattison being on board when the *Louisiana* sailed; and of the three surviving journals of the voyage, none mentions Mattison's death, nor his being in the crew at any time. And if Malcolm died at sea (or anywhere else) in 1861 or thereabouts, it was evidently not reported to his father, who in September 1869 names Malcolm as a beneficiary of his last will and testament, with what appears to be a plea for a prodigal son to return home. After the usual introductory formalities and some initial bequests, he declares:

> *I give, devise and bequeath unto my beloved wife Amelia S. Mattison during her natural life all the rest and residue of my personal property of whatsoever name and nature and all my real estate whereof I may die seized or possessed and the use thereof during and for her natural life. And from and after her death I give, bequeath and devise the same to my son Lucas V. S. Mattison and to my son Malcolm G. Mattison, if the said Malcolm shall return to the said town of Scriba and report himself to my son Lucas V. S. Mattison within five years (5) after the death of my wife Amelia S. Mattison.*
>
> *And in case the said Malcolm G. Mattison shall not return to the town of Scriba and report himself to the said Lucas V. S. Mattison within five years after the death of my said wife then and in that case I give bequeath and devise unto my son Lucas V. S. Mattison, his heirs and assigns forever all the rest and residue of my personal property and real estate of which I shall die seized or possessed.*
>
> *Fourth — I appoint my wife Amelia S. Mattison Executrix of this my last will and testament hereby revoking all former wills made by me. In witness whereof, I have herunto subscribed my name this twenty-seventh day of September, one thousand eight hundred and sixty-nine.* [9]

Thus, the conclusion drawn in *More Scrimshaw Artists* holds even more forcefully today: "Unless Malcolm sailed under a pseudonym, his whaling voyage and death at sea must have taken place in some other vessel or at some other time; and so the true career of the scrimshaw artist remains a mystery." So, too, the significance of the remarks about the younger brother: "Lucius enlisted in the Union Army at age 17, rose rapidly through the ranks, won a field promotion for bravery, and as a lieutenant colonel led the 81st Infantry in an invasion of Richmond in April 1865 and participated the liberation of Libby Prison. His elaborate Civil War journal and memoirs (which were still held by the family in 1994) contain ink drawings and Latin inscriptions remarkably similar to the style of his late brother's scrimshaw engravings."

---

[9] Last Will and Testament of Truman G, Mattison (1812-1893), Town of Scriba, Oswego County, New York, Sept. 27, 1869; transcribed by Patty Groom, www.rootsweb.ancestry.com/~nyoswego/deeds/mattison.html. There is no record of a correction or codicil that might reveal further details.

Mayac, Charles ("Charley") (fl. circa 1919-70). An Inupiaq Eskimo hailing from King Island, Alaska, about 95 miles northwest of Nome, with Peter Mayac (q.v.) he was part of the first generation of a large clan of walrus ivory carvers specializing in local animals and, in particular, three-dimensional portrait miniatures of Arctic birds. He was born in 1905 and, as seems to have been the case throughout the four generations of his family since, started carving at a young age. He was of course strongly influenced by the so-called Nome School of Happy Jack and Billy Komoneseok (qq.v.). Charley Mayac was a close contemporary of fellow King Island carver Aloysius Pikonganna (q.v.), his "first wife's" name was Theresa, and his sons Andrew ("Andy") (1935-1983) and Earl were both carvers. Charley died at Nome in 1971. Earl became especially well known for his animal miniatures and sea birds in walrus ivory and fossilized ivory; also for walrus ivory jewelry, crochet hooks, and other small-scale items.

Mayac, Peter (fl. circa 1927-75). With Charles Mayac (q.v.), he was paterfamilias of a dynasty of Inupiaq Eskimo ivory carvers from King Island, Alaska, specializing in local animals and Arctic birds in particular. He was born in 1913 and, according to an Indian Shop run by the U.S. Department of the Interior, "learned to carve as a young man when he would go with other villagers to Nome. They would sit on the shore under their beached boats to sell their fish, and would pass the time carving ivory." He was of course influenced by older contemporaries, such as Charles Mayac and Aloysius Pikonganna (qq.v.), who were the second- and third-generation progeny of the so-called Nome School of Eskimo carvers — adherents of Happy Jack (q.v.), who died in 1918, and Billy Komoneseok (q.v.), who remained active into the 1940s. In turn, Peter trained or guided his sons in ivory carving. It also became the pursuit of his daughters, nieces, nephews, and grandchildren. Somewhere along the way he also built at least one full-size umiak (now preserved in BUW). He died in Anchorage in 1976. His sons Ted, Al, and George all became carvers — perhaps typified by the eldest, Ted, whom according to the USDI Indian Shop, was "carving ivory since childhood... has been fascinated by the beauty and the variety of bird life," and "began carving full time after he retired from the Alaska State Department of Transportation and Public Facilities in the fall of 1987." *His* son, Ted, Jr., known as Teddy, and the men and women whom Teddy describes as his "many many cousins and relatives who carve," all followed in the patriarch's footsteps — at King Island, and at Nome, Juneau, and Anchorage "after the state closed the school" on King Island; and several of the Mayacs have participated in academic meetings and consortia to help promote Native arts in Alaska. Much but not all of their work is signed. For the purposes of the often difficult task of distinguishing the work of one from another, some of the other names in the Mayac family are Agnes, Fred, Larry, Leona, and Rita.

Mayokok, Robert (1903-1983). Inupiat Eskimo artist from Wales, Alaska, who made his living producing pictorial souvenirs depicting scenes of Native whaling and hunting, Arctic animals, and typical genre subjects. These include engravings on fragments of walrus ivory as well as on whole tusks. Though he was a lifelong scrimshaw-maker, most of his prodigious artistic output was in the form of monochrome ink drawings on paper (as well as on velvet and on animal hide: rabbit, caribou, cowhide, and pig skin). These were not only marketed as such but also served as the basis for mechanically generated prints, ceramics (dishes, coffee mugs, teacups, saucers, teapots, ashtrays), and a variety of commercial products. Most of these, like most of his scrimshaw, he signed

"Mayokok." According to the California Academy of Sciences, "He had long been an ivory carver by trade, using walrus and fossil mammoth tusks," but only began doing artwork full time comparatively late in life. As a child he attended school through the sixth grade in Wales, likely received some instruction in drawing, and is reputed to have improved his English by studying Sears Roebuck catalogues. As a young man he was a traditional Native hunter and trapper, in which capacity he encountered Roald Amundsen in the Arctic pack ice, accompanied anthropologist Knud Rasmussen on an exploring expedition in the schooner *Teddy Bear*, served as interpreter for the Swedish Covenant Mission on Little Diomede Island, and traveled to Boston by rail with a herd of reindeer, which he trained for exhibition in Boston, touring Boston, New York, and Philadelphia on the way home. In 1939 Lomen & Co. (q.v. in *More Scrimshaw Artists*) sent him to the New York World's Fair with another herd of reindeer, with which Mayokok afterwards went on a national tour on which he lectured about Eskimo life. In middle age he was plagued by a recurrent tubercular condition for which he was confined in sanatoriums for months on end. This persisted throughout his life. In 1955, following a series of long hospitalizations, he moved to Anchorage and began painting and drawing as a livelihood. Again according to the California Academy of Sciences, he returned to the New York World's Fair of 1964-65 as an artist and interpreter of Eskimo culture, and beginning in 1970 he

> *included three small birds in all his drawings to symbolize the Holy Trinity, a testament to his Christian faith. In 1978, several of his drawings were selected for the public areas of the new Anchorage Sheraton Hotel. Italian sculptor, Neromi, enlarged Mayokok's drawings and interpreted them in the hotel's marble walls… Mayokok was extremely prolific during his lifetime. By his own estimates, he sold 2,000 to 3,000 drawings each year. When he had saved $500 from the sale of his artwork, he would buy a plane ticket and fly to different parts of Alaska to further promote himself.*

Both in and out of the sanatorium, Mayokok wrote children's stories of Eskimo life that were published in the 1950s and '60s. In Anchorage, during eighteen years as Resident Artist at the Alaska Treasure Shop, "he designed Christmas cards, stationery, wrapping paper, shopping bags, and record album covers… his sketches were commercially reproduced on pottery and chinaware … as well as on wooden napkin holders, wall plaques, and other items." His principal writings are: "Strong Current" (*The Alaska Sportsman*, Nov. 1949); "Seals" (*Ibid*, May 1950); "We Caught a Whale" (*Ibid*, July 1950); "My Life as an Eskimo" (*Ibid*, Aug. and Sept. 1955); and "A Marked Man: My Battle with Tuberculosis" (*The Alaska Journal*, 13:4, 1983). His artworks are in AMHA, the California Academy of Sciences, the Ketchikan Museum, the Kodiak Historical Society/ Baranov Museum, the Tongass Historical Museum, and UAM, and are widely held in private collections. See Susan W. Fair, "Robert Mayokok: Second-Generation Inupiaq Illustrator from Wales, Alaska," in Suzi Jones, ed., *Eskimo Drawings* (AMHA, 2003), 127-134.

* **McDonald, Orin L.** (fl. circa 1845-54). *More Scrimshaw Artists* cites a "Walrus tusk engraved with the figures of America, the goddess Diana, a fashionable lady, and other embellishments, inscribed on the back, 'Presented to… by O. McDonald 1854'; in Skinner, 15 June 1991, #53." This was undoubtedly Orin Levi McDonald, born circa 1826, from Norway, New York. He obtained a Sea-

man's Passport in July 1845 and sailed as a green hand in the bark *President* of New Bedford (1845-46), and was later in the ship *Henrico* on a Gold Rush voyage from Charleston, South Carolina, to San Francisco in 1849 (per Haskins, 297). He is also almost certainly the same man or a kinsman of the Orin L. McDonald who served in the Union Army as a private in the 7th Regiment, Illinois Infantry (National Park Service, *U.S. Civil War Soldiers*, 1861-1865, MS 539 roll 58).

McDonnell, Alexander — see **Healy, Lyman**

McCabe, Thomas (fl. 19th century?). Scottish seaman of unknown vintage, reported by Archibald A. Lawrie as possibly "a scrimshaw worker (bone carver) on whalers" who lived inland but "seems to have had his home or base in Edinburgh (Port of Leith)." Notwithstanding the speculation that McCabe may have "belonged to an earlier group of whale-fishers (at a guess, perhaps 1700?)," such an early date is highly unlikely. In the seventeenth, eighteenth and early nineteenth centuries Leith, the port of Edinburgh, was significantly involved in the Arctic whale hunt, which concentrated exclusively on right and bowhead whales, and thus did not normally acquire many sperm whale teeth; however, there may incidentally have been access to modest quantities of walrus ivory. But this was long before the advent of whalemen's scrimshaw and there is no evidence that carving or engraving bone or ivory (or even fashioning objects from baleen, as was sometimes the case among Dutch whalers after 1631) ever transpired on Scottish Arctic whaleships. In the twentieth century, Leith was the home port of the Christian Salvesen shipping empire, one of the largest players in the modern Anglo-Norwegian Antarctic whaling industry, in which there was a kind of revival of carving whale ivory and bone. But Leith (and Scotland in general) had no part in the nineteenth-century South Sea whaling trade, which was largely devoted to sperm and right whaling on the American model, was based in London, and produced scrimshaw on whale ivory, walrus ivory, baleen, and bone. (American-style sperm whaling was also prosecuted from a small handful of English outports but none in Scotland.) Such a shipboard artisan as McCabe, though his name is characteristically Scottish or Scots-Irish, and though he may have lived in Edinburgh or Leith, was far more likely the inmate of some nineteenth-century South Sea whaler out of London, or some deepwater sperm whaler from New England or Australia.

McIntire, John (fl. circa the third quarter of the 19th Century). The focal feature of a walrus tusk handsomely monochrome engraved on both sides with a ship portrait, leafy branches, anchor, and whaling implements, is the bold inscription in block letters that dominates one side: "by JOHN McINTIRE" and the diagonally-oriented coda, "A man / of / esteem" (Cowan, Nov. 12-13, 2003, #781). Both the iconography and manner are quintessentially American, and from all appearances the piece dates from the third quarter of the nineteenth century, thus is roughly contemporaneous and stylistically compatible with the work of N.S. Finney (though of lesser complexity and subtlety). The maker, presumed to be American, has not been identified. Little is known about the few men of this name in the whale fishery.

A man recorded in the crew lists as John McIntir [sic] was actually John McIntire of Lowell, Massachusetts, who was born there in 1829 or '30 and whom the U.S. Census lists as a machinist at Lowell in 1850; however, as he was only 20 years old at the time he was more likely a machinist's apprentice or machinist's assistant. Perhaps to escape his shore-bound trade he made two whaling voyages. The first was as a green hand for the 200th lay in the Fairhaven ship *Samuel Robertson* (1852-56), a long North Pacific voyage on which walrus ivory would likely have been readily available by barter from Native peoples (which was the way in which whalemen usually acquired it). His second cruise was evidently as third mate for the 50th lay in the New Bedford ship *Rapid* (1856-60) — remarkably, as this would have been an extraordinary advance in rank, and McIntire might justly regard himself as "a man of esteem" on that account. George F. Winslow (q.v.) was a boatsteerer on that voyage, which did not turn out well. It was a brand-new vessel, launched at Fairhaven in 1856, that embarked on a bowhead whaling voyage to the Northwest Coast under Captain David P. West on October 1 of that year. For the first 40 months or so it was a fairly commonplace cruise. However, as Starbuck explains, they "had a series of reverses in 1860" — at just about the time when they must have been preparing to head for home. For reasons unexplained, the ship "was fired by the crew" (which of course implies serious discontent), then "struck on a sunken rock, and run into the *Jeannette*" — three cataclysms that pretty well did it for the *Rapid*. Accordingly, after the ship had been burned, run aground, and collided, the voyage was abandoned and the vessel was condemned and sold. Nevertheless, it was not a total loss: most of the yield from more than three years of whaling was salvaged and sent home, a respectable catch of 1,512 barrels of whale oil and 15,660 pounds of bone. It was not only the end for the *Rapid* but seems to have concluded this John McIntire's whaling career too, and no further record of him has been discovered. In the meantime, a contemporaneous John McIntire from Boston was a green hand in the ship *Newark* of New Bedford (1855-59), but whether he was a man of esteem, or whether he made this or any other scrimshaw, is not known. He is far the less likely candidate, as this was his only whaling voyage and it was a sperm whaling voyage to the Pacific on which they evidently did not go to the Arctic, took no right whales or bowheads, and would have had little opportunity to acquire walrus ivory. Even less plausible is the candidacy of John McIntire of Onandagua, New York, who at age 23 in 1859 went as an Ordinary Seaman in the ship *Navy* of New Bedford (1859-63): this was also his only time whaling, an Indian Ocean voyage that ended abruptly when, as Starbuck reports, the vessel was "lost on Sandal Wood Island (Malay Archipelago) April 7, 1863." The crew had to take to the whaleboats for nine days and ten nights "with but little bread and water"; the net yield was a mere 76 barrels of sperm oil that they had previously sent home; and in the unlikely event that anyone had been able to get his hands on some walrus ivory on the Indian Ocean and do some scrimshawing while the ship was still seaworthy, it seems quite unlikely that he could have or would have smuggled it aboard the open boats in their desperate attempt to escape from shipwreck.

McKee, Raymond (1892-1984). He was a movie star in the days of the silent screen. With respect to scrimshaw he was mostly a collector, rather than an artist, and as a non-whaleman the scrimshaw he did produce was not really the McCoy. On the other hand, he was a kind of honorary whaleman. As the male lead in the first dramatic film about whaling, released at a time when even *Moby Dick* had not yet entirely emerged from its long obscurity and had not yet been filmed, McKee became an adoptive Native Son of New Bedford. *Down to the Sea In Ships* (1922) was set in New Bedford and filmed in New Bedford, using New Bedford vessels, New Bedford streetscapes, New Bedford waterfront locations, and New Bedford people as extras. McKee seems to have won the affection and admiration of all of the local denizens who were involved with the film in those last, declining days of whaling, including the veteran whalemen who served as technical advisers; and his experiences on location in New Bedford and the Caribbean implanted a lifelong passion. Unlike some film actors, who may play a role with synthetic enthusiasm and then step away when the cameras stop rolling, McKee's interest was genuine and infectious; and he did create some of his own original pieces of scrimshaw. It was partly this enthusiasm and the high regard in which McKee was held by the authentic whaling community in New Bedford that began his lifelong love affair with scrimshaw. Another reason was his love affair with costar Marguerite Courtot (1897-1986), whom he met in New Bedford during the filming. They were married in 1923 and stayed together for the rest of their lives.

He was born Eldon Raymond McKee at Lee, Iowa, in 1892, and was first featured in silent films in 1912 and 1913 under the name Roy McKee. Standard filmographies list him as appearing in no fewer than 148 films in a wide variety of roles between 1912 and 1932. Most were short and quick by modern standards, but by the time he was cast in *Down to the Sea In Ships* he had already done 85 or 86 of them and was well known. Marguerite Courtot was the female lead and love interest, a role the two played out in real life. The director, Elmer Clifton, was a sometime protégé of pioneer filmmaker D.W. Griffith: this was Clifton's finest hour and most enduring legacy. For Clara Bow, a future star who would be known as the "It" girl, this was a plum supporting part early in her career. The principal technical advisor, who also played the short-lived role of whaling captain, was George Fred Tilton of Martha's Vineyard, a former harpooner, sea captain, and celebrated local hero. (There is a bronze plaque to his honor at the New Bedford Seamen's Bethel, commemorating his trek across the Arctic ice to summon a rescue party for the whaling fleet that was frozen in and stranded in Alaska in 1893. Tilton's autobiography, *Cap'n George Fred Himself* was published in 1928.) Other notable stars of the silent screen in this film were two veteran whaling barks, the *Charles W. Morgan* (built 1841) and *Wanderer* (built 1878). This was the swan-song of the *Morgan*'s 83-voyage whaling career, which had ended in 1921. After providing a set for the wharfside and belowdecks scenes, she lay idle for three years until being acquired in 1925 for exhibition at the estate of Col. E.H.R. Green just outside New Bedford. (The last surviving Yankee whaleship, the *Morgan* has been preserved for posterity at MSM since 1941.) The *Wanderer*, still comparatively seaworthy at the time, was used for the scenes of the whaleship under sail, filmed in the Acushnet estuary and nearby coastal waters. Later, after an idle hiatus ashore, she was refitted for one final whaling voyage, which ended in shipwreck on Cuttyhunk Island on the very first day, outward-bound in August 1924. A third vessel, used for filming but not shown in the movie, was the generic gas schooner *Gaspé*, which was crudely fitted for whaling and brought the actors, film crew, technical advisers, and whalemen-extras to the Caribbean to shoot the whaling scenes.

The ambience of Old New Bedford, the romance of whaling, and the romance kindled by Miss Courtot while they were making the film, captured McKee's interest and imagination perhaps more than any other role he would ever play, and stayed with him throughout his life. Though he lived in Brentwood Heights, California, he was a paid-up member of the Whalemen's Club in New Bedford, which included on its roster many of the surviving former whaling captains, whaling merchants, and other local whaling notables, as well as such enthusiasts as William H. Tripp, future author and Curator of the New Bedford Whaling Museum, and Henry P. Kendall, future founder of the Kendall Whaling Museum (now KNB).

McKee's scrimshaw collection appears to have begun with a few pieces presented to him in New Bedford during the filming, which inspired him to continue collecting and to do some scrimshonting of his own. All of his known scrimshaw (reported by William N. Peterson and Rodi York), both the pieces that he did himself and the ones he collected, were acquired by MSM in 2001. His output comprises nine pictorial teeth, all signed with his name or initials or an anchor monogram device; and three carved pieces in skeletal bone, tentatively attributed. Of thc teeth, two commemorate the filming of *Down to the Sea in Ships*. One depicts a whaleboat, a New England house and church of circa 1850, a lighthouse, an anchor, a camera crew shooting film, and various actors in costume. These are actual identified portraits, including cameraman Alex Penrod, director Elmer Clifton with a megaphone, McKee himself, harpooning a whale, and others, all identified by name. Another, dated "5/13/22," has a portrait of the *Charles W. Morgan* and Caribbean Island scenes, inscribed "West Indies/ Apr. 7, '22" and a love note to Marguerite Courtot, "To/ Margot/ from Raymond/ McKee/ je t'aime." His other teeth are devoted to more generic types of nautical materials and whaling scenes: a schooner passing a lighthouse; a hut and palm tree bordered by starfish and jellyfish, inscribed "Vairai"; a starboard view of a whaleboat in pursuit, with harpooner at the ready; three dolphins; a sextant; a spread-eagle; and a British Union Jack flag device, dated "5/65." The attributed carvings out of bone are a spoon, a signet-type ring, and a miniature effigy of a sperm whale. From his personal collection came seven engraved teeth, most or all of which are latter-day, twentieth-century work, and some of which were evidently presented to McKee; and several pieces carved out of panbone. The latter are a necklace, described as possibly relating to "tramp art," circa 1921; an effigy of an axe; and a fid, a clothespin, a single sheave block, and a double sheave block. One of the teeth depicts a lighthouse, a banjo, and the schooner "GASPE ON THE ROCKS," presumed to have been made during the filming and probably presented to McKee. The others have a man on a rearing horse, labeled "EQUESTRIAN PORTRAIT OF THE EMPEROR OF RUSSIA"; a whaling bark, possibly intended as the *Wanderer* or *Charles W. Morgan*; a broadside view of a vessel under sail; a sailor holding a glass, standing near a cask inscribed "CHAS W/ MORGA... ", with palm trees and a building labeled "PIONEER INN BAR", set in Lahaina, Maui, Hawaii; a gaff-rigged schooner flying an American ensign, inscribed in a riband "ARIES" and dated 7/64; and a black sperm whale with zig-zag border, dated 9/64. Raymond McKee, who retired from films in 1932, not long after the advent of talkies, died in Los Angeles in 1984. Marguerite Courtot, who had been born in New Jersey in 1897 and made only two or three more films after her marriage to McKee, died at Long Beach, California, in 1986.

McKenzie, James H. (fl. circa 1846-71). New Bedford whaling master, the original owner and possible maker of an extraordinarily fine whale ivory crimper, full-round-carved in the form of a bare-breasted mermaid holding the jagging wheel, with the facial features, hair, and ichthyological portions stained in shades of brown (in KNB). The scrimshaw is in any case associated with McKenzie's voyage as captain of the New Bedford ship *Europa* (1871-76), aboard which it was reportedly made for the captain's wife, Susan A. McKenzie (1834-1927), to whom it surely belonged and from whom it descended. James was born in Scotland in 1828, emigrated to America as a child, resided in Dartmouth, Massachusetts, and spent his entire professional career in New Bedford vessels. He was evidently already a naturalized citizen when he obtained a Protection Paper (seaman's passport) at New Bedford and shipped as cabin boy and green hand in the ship *Brunswick* (1846-48).

He rose through the ranks in leaps and bounds, as boatsteerer (1848-51) and third mate (1851-55) on successive voyages of the ship *James Maury*, and first mate in the bark *Mars* (1856-60). He was then captain of the barks *Cherokee* (1860-64), *Eagle* (1865-69), which was lost on Sea Horse Island in the Sea of Ochotsk, and *Hercules* (1869-71), on which he came aboard about three years into the voyage as relief master for Isaac C. Howland; and finally the *Europa* (1871-76), which was registered in New Bedford but owned in Dartmouth — the vessel and voyage on which the crimper was made. While there is no clear record of children, the McKenzies appear to have had at least one daughter. In any case, after Captain McKenzie retired from whaling they took in a few nieces and nephews on their Dartmouth farmstead. (The 1880 U.S. Census also lists a James H. McKenzie, born in Scotland circa 1827, whose occupation at the time is given as miner; he was a head of household in a place called Oro, Butte County, California, where he had four boarders, from Wales, Cornwall, and Ireland, all miners, presumably prospecting for gold. This was probably not the same man.) Captain McKenzie died in 1898 and is buried in Dartmouth alongside his wife, who survived him 29 years.

* **Mechanic Artisan** — see **Pratt, Spencer**

Mendonça, Manuel E. — see **de Mendonça, Manuel**

* **Merphey, Thomas** (fl. circa 1835-62). A crudely engraved panbone busk with a five-pointed star, a six-pointed pinwheel device, and an unconventional and somewhat unclear arrangement of Christian symbols with cross, pentangle, and what appear to be Chi Rho initials (the Greek letters XP, a symbol of Christ), is dominated by the bold inscription "THOMAS MERPHEY" (reported by Paul Madden). There were several men named Thomas Murphy in the nineteenth-century whaling trade, but also several who evidently used this less conventional spelling of the surname. This may be the same man whose scrimshaw busk with emblematic decorations and engraved with the name "Thomas Merphey" is listed in the *Dictionary* (from Bourne, 7 Aug 1979, #40), and who may therefore be the same Thomas Murphy, born circa 1832 in New York State, who was a green hand in the New Bedford ship *Robert Edwards* (1849-51) and an Ordinary Seaman in the New Bedford schooner *Amelia* (1851-52). However, surviving crew lists are understandably equivocal about the spelling: all of the men whose name appears on their passports and in crew lists as Thomas Merphey also have their surnames recorded elsewhere as Murphy. Thomas Merphey of the Robert Edwards and *Amelia* was one of these. Another was born circa 1838 in Waterville, Maine, whose one voyage as a green hand in the ship *Empire* of New Bedford (1860-62) ended in shipwreck. But perhaps the most likely maker of the scrimshaw was career whaleman Thomas Merphey of Salem, Massachusetts, born circa 1812, whose early voyages are unknown, but who was later seaman, boatsteerer, and — significantly — carpenter in the New Bedford ships *Washington* (1840-45), *Charles Drew* (1842-44 and 1844-46), *Cortes* (1846-49), and *Midas* (1850-53), and was then probably third mate in the ship *Swift* (1853-56) and second mate in the bark *Dartmouth* (1858-62). Nothing has been discovered about his private life and personal affairs.

Méryon, Charles (fl. circa 1843-46). The Akaroa Museum in New Zealand has a tooth engraved with a view of Akaroa Harbour, "thought to be the work of Charles Meryon, a French artist who visited Akaroa on the French Naval corvette *Rhin* between 1843 and 1846." Given that Méryon was a mariner by trade, thus was theoretically familiar with whaling and scrimshaw — his visit to New Zealand was in his capacity as a lieutenant in the French Navy; and given that, when he later resigned his commission for a career in art, color blindness mandated that he work exclusively in monochrome, the scrimshaw attribution is plausible and attractive but purely speculative and circumstantial: there is little direct evidence. Méryon was born in Paris in 1821, the son of an English physician and a French dancer. His celebrated etchings include portraits, landscapes, and most notably a series of views of Paris. He has been called the greatest practitioner in 19th-century France. However, his health was not good and he died in a mental hospital in Paris in 1868.

Meyers, William H. (fl. circa 1834-48). Sometime whaleman from Philadelphia credited with ink and watercolor illustrations in the journal of John Cleland, Jr. (q.v.), aboard the whaler *Ceres* of Wilmington, Delaware during 1834-36, upon which the iconography of the so-called Ceres Teeth is based. He may himself be the Ceres B Artisan, originator of the Ceres-type scrimshaw, however the attribution is controversial. Aboard the *Ceres*, Meyers and Cleland were shipmates with William A. Gilpin and Edmund M. Chandler (qq.v.), each of whom produced teeth in conformity with the standard *Ceres* formula but with distinctive individual variations (see the articles on the Ceres Artisans and those individual artists). Meyers's illustrations from the whaling journal are reproduced in Kenneth R. Martin's *Delaware Goes Whaling, 1833-45* (1974); and it was Martin himself, in collaboration with Judge Paul E. Vardeman, whose Euclidian reasoning, based on Meyers's many nautical watercolors, attributed the journal illustrations and the Ceres B scrimshaw itself to Meyers, rather than Cleland, who kept the actual journal.

Meyers was born in Philadelphia in 1815. On his one and only whaling voyage he sailed from Wilmington in the *Ceres* in May 1834 but jumped ship in Honolulu in November 1836, then spent a couple of years in the merchant service, during which he was master of the brig *Lucy* in Caribbean waters. Kenneth Martin reports a journal at the New York Public Library "that covers the years 1838-39, immediately following the *Ceres* voyage, when Meyers was mostly aboard the merchant brig *Lucy*, apparently of Philadelphia" (private communication, 7 Nov. 2008), as described and excerpted in an article by Terry Walton entitled, "A Not-So-Ordinary Seaman: Intimate Pages from the Diary of William H. Meyers, on board and ashore" (1979) and as posted on the New York Public Library website. Meyers was next a civilian employee doing ordnance work at the Navy Yard in Washington, D.C., until he joined the Navy himself as a warrant officer in 1841. He was appointed gunner on the sloop-of-war *Cyane*, which was deployed with the Pacific fleet, participated in the capture of Monterey in 1842, and patrolled the West Coast and Hawaii. He was transferred to the sloop-of-war *Dale* in 1846, was in the *Cyane* again in 1847, saw action in the Mexican War, then resigned from the Navy in 1848 for reasons of poor health. He applied for reinstatement in 1849 but suffered a paralysis of his right side and a surgeon determined that he was unfit for duty (1850). The illustrations in his navy journals, published more than a century later in limited editions by the Grabhorn Press and the Book Club of California, in addition to informing the Martin-Vardeman attributions, trace his navy career: *Journal of a Cruise to California and the Sandwich Islands in the United States Sloop-of-War* Cyane*, 1841-1844 (1955); Sketches of California and Hawaii by William H. Meyers, Gunner, U.S.N., aboard the United States Sloop-of-War* Cyane *1842-1843 (1970); and Naval Sketches of the War in California, reproducing twenty-eight drawings made in 1846-47 by William H. Meyers, Gunner on the U.S.S. Sloop-of-War* Dale (with an introduction by Franklin Delano Roosevelt,

1939). Some of Meyers's pictures were also reproduced in an edition of a journal by one of his shipmates, *Philo White's Narrative of a Cruize* [sic] *in the Pacific to South America and California on the U.S. Sloop-of-War Dale 1841-1843*, edited by Charles L. Camp (1965).

* **Mickleburgh, Edward Robert** (1815-1890). He is primarily known as the maker of panbone plaques with beautifully detailed broadside portraits of Royal Navy warships at Portsmouth, each signed "E. Mickleburgh" notably "H.M.S. Victory 120 [guns] Entering the Sound," with coat of arms and other naval vessels, in KNB; and "A 74 [-gun naval warship] going into Portsmouth," with other vessels, among them an early paddle-wheel steamer, in TMH. However, since the publication of the *Dictionary* and *More Scrimshaw Artists*, an analogous plaque, centering on an analogous broadside portrait of a ship, labeled in a fine cursive hand, "Barque Terror Cruising / after Sperm Whales / Property of B. Boyd, Esq.," was acquired by ANMM, occasioning research by one of the curators that uncovered a few biographical details. Mickleburgh was born in 1814 at Margate, Kent (England), the son of the rector of a boy's school. He spent four years in the army, then went to sea, evidently in the merchant service, and by 1841 fetched up in Australia, where he married Mary Baker, also recently arrived from England. Whatever his career had been before, for several years thereafter he was the captain of merchant voyages out of Melbourne. The names on the scrimshaw indicate that he may somehow have been associated with Benjamin Boyd, a British expatriate merchant-entrepreneur who was trying to build a whaling empire on Twofold Bay, adjacent to Eden, New South Wales. It flourished for a time in the mid 1840s, especially for the years it was managed by Oswald Walter Brierly, a guest on a private yacht who landed in Australia in 1841. The *Terror* was evidently whaling out of Boyd Town during 1843-45, at the height of Boyd's short-lived success. But Boyd's widespread Australian land holdings and Boyd Town whaling station fell apart after Brierly went back to England in 1848 (where he became a distinguished marine painter, admired by Prince Albert and eventually knighted by Queen Victoria). In the meantime, Mickleburgh continued as a merchant sea captain, visited California during the Gold Rush, and eventually returned to England, where he was widowed, and in 1879 was admitted as a resident of Belvedere House, a seamen's retirement home in Surrey operated by the Royal Alfred Merchant Seaman's Institute. He died in 1890.

Mikhailov, Peter [Piotr] — pseudonym of Tsar Peter of Russia traveling semi-incognito as a commoner on his Great Embassy to Western Europe, 1697-98. See Peter the Great.

Mills, Charles (fl. circa 1853-57). One of few powder horns definitely associated with whaling is described in *Black Powder*, the journal of the Muzzle Loaders Association of Great Britain (Spring 2004, 35): 16 inches [40 cm] long, with German silver mounts, the body of the horn engraved with the image of "a harpoon over a decorated panel containing the inscription 'CHas MILLS HisHorn 1857,' which in turn is over an... albatross over a sperm whale. A foliate border then separates the next part of the design of the coastal map of New Bedford and a whaling ship with the compass bearings in and out of the port" (reported by Michael P. Scorey from a private collection in Great Britain; consigned to Bonham's, Knightsbridge, 25 July 2007). Charles Mills, born in Philadelphia circa 1832, was one of three men of that name who went whaling out of New Bedford in 1853 and 1854, and was possibly also one of the three or four men from Philadelphia named Charles Mills who served as privates in the Union Army during the Civil War. Whichever of those he may have been, there is little doubt that he is the Charles Mills of Philadelphia whose father was a barber and his older brother a house painter, and who worked as a painter himself both before and after he made his one and only whaling voyage, as a green hand in the bark *Franklin* of New Bedford (1853-57). He was married very young to Christiania Fowler (AKA Fuller), who was a year or two older than he. They lived with her parents for a while, and afterwards with her widowed mother. In the late 1860s their son George joined his father in the painters' trade. It is not known whether Charles ever produced any conventional scrimshaw.

Mills, W. S. (fl. circa 1843-49). The name appears on a pair of polychrome teeth donated to WHS by Mrs. James Mulcahy in 1891: the name may or may not refer to the maker, but in any case the teeth are associated with two voyages of the ship *South America* of Providence, Rhode Island, during 1843-49. One has a woman in a low-cut gown, seated, an urn, and a nest with two eagles; and a starboard broadside view of a ship flying a USA flag, with "South America" inscribed in a riband. The other also has a woman in a low-cut gown, seated, in this case with a harp on her lap, an urn with flowers and leafy vines; and a woman in a bonnet standing in front of a building with pillars. Nothing is known about the artist.

Milton, Anthony [Antone] (fl. circa 1840s-1900s). Azorean-American whaling master of New Bedford who transplanted to Oakland, California. A 24-inch [60 cm] walrus tusk with a "Scrimshaw image of Teddy Roosevelt with American flag [and] North woods animals" has the provenance "From Capt. Milton to his grandson R. Vincent Jeffreys of Oakland" (DeLuca, Feb. 19, 2005, #158). The only Captain Milton in the American whale fishery was Anthony Milton, who indeed lived out his golden years in Alameda County, California, in the vicinity of Oakland. And while Captain Milton may only have been the recipient, rather than its creator, the scrimshaw was done so long after his active career that it could not have been something given him by a crewman during a voyage (which was a common way for a captain to come into possession of scrimshaw that he did not make himself). At the time Milton retired from whaling, Theodore Roosevelt had not yet completed grammar school. TR was in the Whitehouse from 1901 to 1909, during which time Captain Milton passed his eightieth birthday. So the scrimshaw must have been made long after Milton's active whaling career. If the provenance be believed (and it seems tenuous), Milton must have commissioned it, purchased it, or made it himself in late retirement.

Milton is reported to have been "born in the Azores, Portugal, March 29, 1823" and to have settled in New Bedford at age 11. According to the U.S. Census of 1850 his birthplace was Rhode Island and he was living in New Bedford, an unmarried sailor, age about 28; however, in other census records concerning his son Joseph, Joseph's father is referred to as having been born in Portugal. Either way, Milton's parents were undoubtedly Azorean and he almost certainly arrived in New Bedford from Rhode Island around 1834. He made his first whaling voyages using the Portuguese form of his name, Antone, only later switching to the Anglicized Anthony. His was an odd career in two respects. First, he made six consecutive voyages, spanning almost 24 years, in the same vessel, the *Governor Troup* of New Bedford: it was not until he had already twice been a captain that he was assigned to any other ship. And on the way up he skipped ranks twice, an accelerated ascent to command. It may also be accounted as somewhat unusual for a New Bedford master mariner that all of his voyages were to the North Pacific and Northwest Coast for right and bowhead whales; so even though they took a few sperm whales on each of his voyages, walrus ivory (which was readily obtained by barter from Native peoples in Alaska and Siberia) would likely have been his regular medium for whatever scrimshaw he may have done at sea. If the Theodore Roosevelt tusk be any indication, and if Milton made it himself, it was certainly not his first and only piece: he may reasonably be presumed to have done some scrimshawing during his active career at sea; however, no such pieces have been identified. He was boatsteerer for the 100th lay on two successive voyages under Gilbert H. Jenney (1841-44; 1844-47). When Captain Jenney died at Honolulu on the second voyage in 1845 and was succeeded by first mate Francis J. Silvia (rather than by a newly appointed relief captain), a general reshuffling inevitably followed in which Milton would have been promoted to an unspecified junior mate's berth — probably fourth mate, possibly third mate. Then, without serving a single voyage as second mate, and probably not even serving anytime as third mate, he skipped to executive officer: the newly appointed captain for the *Governor Troup*'s next voyage, Frederick Coggeshall, assuming his first command, made Milton first mate. In that capacity Milton — now using the name Anthony, rather than Antone — served two voyages as mate under Coggeshall (1847-50 and 1850-53) before becoming captain of the *Governor Troup* on her next two voyages (1853-56 and 1856-59). Then, for the first time (or at least for the first time in more than 18 years of successive whaling voyages) he went in a vessel other than the *Governor Troup*: the *Europa* of New Bedford. They sailed in 1859, but Captain Milton did not complete the voyage. Sometime around 1864 he left the ship in the Pacific, probably at Honolulu or San Francisco (he was relieved by Severino D. Pierce), and settled in Alameda County near Oakland. A slightly flawed biographical sketch of him published in 1883 ruminates philosophically upon the ramifications of his upbringing and this change-of-life. His family came to New Bedford when Antone was 11 years of age, and

> *In that prosperous and busy seaport he grew up, with the ships of many nations around him, and following the example of hundreds of his fellow-townsmen, adopted a life on the ocean wave as a profession, and followed it in all parts of the world, until he found himself in California in the year 1865, when he purchased his present property in Alameda County, and took up his residence there. Here the worthy Captain has time to cogitate upon the mutability of things mundane, and have pass before him in vivid procession the personal recollections of stirring scenes full of adventure, and enjoy the fruits of a well-spent life. Married in September, 1867, Miss Alicia Healey, a native of Ireland, and has two children living, viz.: Manella [sic: Marietta], and Joseph P.* (*History of Alameda County, California*, Oakland: M.W. Wood Publ., 1883, 943; transcribed by Kathy Sedler)

Milton commanded at least one additional whaling voyage, out of Honolulu in the bark *Florence* of that port (1869-70) — a voyage not listed by Hegarty (1959) but known from Dr. Susan A. Lebo's research at the Bishop Museum in Honolulu. He lived for many years in the Oakland area. His son, Dr. Joseph P. Milton, was a physician in Oakland, and his unmarried daughter Marietta lived with her brother's family; but the ancestry of the putative grandson and donor of the scrimshaw, R. Vincent Jeffreys, has not been discovered.

Monteiro, — (fl. late-19th/early-20th century). A polished tooth bearing no picture but with the bold inscription, stipple-engraved in a cursive style, "Catharina / Monteiro Home / sweet Home" (reported by Adam Moniz; now in NBWM) was almost certainly produced as a memento for a loved one, leading to the reasonable but uncorroborated presumption that the maker was likely surnamed Monteiro. The name is Portuguese and stylistically the piece is consistent with the stipple-engraved scrimshaw in fashion among whalemen in general, and especially among Cape Verdean whalemen aboard Yankee whaleships in the last quarter of the nineteenth century and the first quarter of the twentieth (for two very different examples, see Jayme Fortes and Manuel J. Rogers). However, in this case neither the maker nor the intended recipient has been identified.

Moody, Daniel R. (fl. circa 1830s-'40s). "A Silk Reel [some kind of swift], carved out of whalebone, very neatly done" was submitted by D.R. Moody of Newburyport, Massachusetts, for exhibition in Boston in 1837, and is so described in the catalogue (*First Exhibition and Fair of the Massachusetts Charitable Mechanic Association at Faneuil and Quincy Halls, in the City of Boston* (1837, N° 1122, 79) (reported by Mark Foster). A variety of scrimshaw and scrimshaw-like articles are listed (see Appendix II), but without any claims about who actually made them; thus, in this instance there is no clear indication that Moody made the swift himself. However, in reference to a second submission, to a later manifestation of the same event, in 1844, the exhibitor's name is given as Daniel R. Moody of Boston — almost certainly the same man, only temporarily resident in Boston — and the clear implication is that he was the actual maker of "One Cotton Reel, or Swift, of Whalebone, made on board of a Whale Ship, on her passage home from the Sandwich Islands, with Tools made by himself. Shows much mechanical genius, and deserves encouragement" (Ibid., 1844 edition, N° 609, p. 120). However, while there were many mariners of that surname from the North Shore of Boston, no record has been found a Daniel or D.R. Moody whaling out of any port during that era. The Moodys were one of the Old Families of Newbury and Newburyport. Daniel R. Moody was born circa 1804, married Susan H. Webb in 1833, and, according to the U.S. Census, they were living in Newburyport in 1840 with three young children. He was likely the same Daniel Moody who is listed in the Newburyport City Directory (as late as 1858) as a ship carpenter — a clear indication that he would have had the training and presumably the skill to construct swifts out of whale skeletal bone, whether or not he actually made a whaling voyage himself.

* **More, A.P.** (fl. circa 1857-60?). The *Dictionary* attributes to him a work box (in KNB) comprised of pine secondary wood veneered with walnut, with 16 diamond-shaped inlays of walrus ivory and wood, surrounding a large diamond-shaped inlay ensemble in high relief; inside is a full-length till marked "A P. More [or A.R. More] / to Lilie HATHAWAY / Jun 14 1860 / BK TRITOn". A few suggestive facts about the recipient have come to light, but nothing has been discovered about the putative artist, and the meaning of the inscription has been only partly decoded. "Lilie Hathaway" refers to Lillian M. Hathaway, better known as Lillie, who was born at Wareham, Massachusetts, on June 14, 1860, the date inscribed on the box. "BK TRITOn" can only refer to the whaling bark *Triton*, which was launched as a ship and made 13 whaling voyages as such (1818-57), was converted to a bark in 1857, and under that rig made nine voyages out of New Bedford (1857-88) and five from San Francisco (1889-93). Thus, the box is presumed to have been made sometime during the *Triton*'s long career as a bark — possibly in 1860, the year Lillie was born. However, no A.P. [or A.R.] More [or Moore] has been found in Wareham or associated with the Hathaway family; and no one with that surname is recorded as having served in the crew of the bark *Triton* at any time. (All of the *Triton*'s regular crew lists survive, but they do not necessarily account for crewmen who signed on in some

outport while a voyage was already in progress. Even so, there is no indication of any sailor named More in the residual records of men recruited during voyages [in NBFPL]. As a point of interest, the crew lists further indicate that the only man from Wareham who ever served aboard her was a Barnabas E. Savory, age 19, during 1865-68.) It is significant that Lillie was the daughter of Charles H. Hathaway (q.v.), a professional sailor from Wareham who was a green hand in the whaling brig *Inga* of that port (1843-44). But he was never in the *Triton* and retired from the sea circa 1859, when he married a woman named Betsey and commenced earning his living as a peddler in Wareham. As a former whaleman, he was certainly in a position to make such a box himself; but the inscription clearly implies that the giver was A.P. More [or Moore]; no one of that name has been found anywhere in the whale fishery; and the significance of the bark *Triton* in the inscription remains unexplained. By 1870 Charles H. Hathaway was working on the railroad. Widowed circa 1872, he remarried shortly after (to a much younger woman named Mary), and by 1880, still living in Wareham, had become, according to the U.S. Census, a "small farmer" and the father of five.

Morgan, Richard H. (fl. 1848-52). In 1920 a cane made by Richard H. Morgan was given to NBWM by a namesake of the maker (probably his son). Two other canes in NBWM, acquired separately and much later, may be by the same hand. Distinguishing characteristics of the Morgan cane are a plain knob pommel turned from whale ivory, inlaid on the top with a disc of abalone; a tapered shaft consisting of a metal rod on which are "strung" twenty-five 1-¼-inch (3.2 cm) hollowed-out cylinders of whale ivory, interspersed with narrow baleen separators in the manner of a shark vertebrae cane; and a tip in the form of a tapered brass sleeve. The foreshaft of the Morgan cane is through-drilled to accommodate a wrist strap or lanyard, trimmed with disc-shaped abalone escutcheons. A second cane lacking any provenance is set up much the same way, but with only 13 ivory cylinders, without holes for a lanyard, and the disc inlay on the pommel is missing. A third cane is yet a third variation, again set up the same way, also lacking the hole for a lanyard and in this case with a shaft consisting of 15 cylinders with baleen separators; but of these the top half of the shaft is comprised of six wooden cylinders while the bottom half is made up of nine whale ivory cylinders; and the brass tip is smaller.

According to his Protection Paper (Seaman's Passport), issued at New Bedford in 1848, Richard H. Morgan was born circa 1825 and was from Tremont, Pennsylvania (he would thus have been about 95 years of age when the cane was donated, leading to the supposition that the donor was likely a namesake). He was a green hand in the ship *Abraham Barker* (1848-50) and an ordinary seaman in the ship *Florida* (1851-53), both of New Bedford. His captain aboard the *Florida* was Joseph C. Little (q.v.), and either he or his namesake also made a rigged ship model that the namesake donated to NBWM in 1917.

Morris, Frank C. (fl. circa 1876-1907). New Bedford captain of Azorean birth specializing in sperm whaling on the Atlantic grounds. William W. Manchester, second mate, homeward bound in the bark *Palmetto* of New Bedford (1880-83), wrote in his journal (in NBWM), "Nothing in sight and no sign of [there] ever being any spirm [sic] whales around here[.] the old man and the mate devote there [sic] time at Schrimshorning[;] that is all they think of." The "old man" was Captain Frederick P. Tripp (q.v.), the mate was Frank Morris, and unfortunately, none of their scrimshaw has come to light. Morris, born circa 1856, was a native of the Azores, though of which island is uncertain. His earliest recorded voyage was in the New Bedford bark *Arnolda* (1876-80), which he undertook at age 20. In any case, as his next voyage was the one in the *Palmetto* as first mate (1880-83), the *Arnolda* voyage could hardly have been his first; in fact, he was likely already serving as second mate in the *Arnolda*. After the *Palmetto* he may have made another, undocumented voyage (circa 1883-87) before serving two voyages as captain of the New Bedford schooner *Charles W. Morse* (1887-90 and 1891-95), one in the brig *Rosa Baker* of Boston (1895-99), and one each in the New Bedford schooners *Golden City* (1900-01) and *Eleanor B. Conwell* (1906-07). In 1900 he was living in New Bedford, married to a woman named Mary, but there is no record of children; and by 1910 he was evidently widowed and living in retirement at Fairhaven with a niece and grand-nephew who took in young children as welfare boarders. He was still with them in 1930 at age 77.

* **Morrison, Thomas** (fl. circa 1857-82). In his journal on two voyages of the bark *Avola* of New Bedford (in KNB), he wrote on Jan 21, 1873, "I am making a cane"; and three days later, "finished my cane today." He was slightly more expansive but no more specific on New Year's Day, 1876: "I wonder how the folks is at home this glorious New Year. I hope they are well and got a good dinner also enjoying themselves. We are trying to do so here by making rings and toothpicks, to kill time." No scrimshaw by his hand has been located, Morrison scarcely provides sufficient information ever to be able to identify any of it in the absence of a specific provenance, and nothing much is known about Morrison himself. His birthplace is not known, but he was an American citizen (unlike two other contemporaneous men named Thomas Morrison who were born in Ireland). From the time he was 15 his passports and shipping papers list his residence as New Bedford, which could as easily mean that he was a runaway as that he was an actual citizen of the whaling capital. No census records report him there. And despite that most or all of his voyages are known, his ranks and positions on the later voyages are not; neither is the year of his birth, as even his own shipping records differ about his age by a factor of six years, and no family data has come to light. What little is known is that he was born sometime around 1842, was living in New Bedford by the time he was 15 in 1857, and made the following voyages: as a green hand in the New Bedford ship *Thomas Nye* (sailed 1857), from which he came home early, in time to sail in the bark *Erastus Corning* (1860-66); the bark *Sea Queen* of Westport (1866-69), in which he was a boatsteerer; he was then a junior mate, specific berths unknown, in the New Bedford barks *Avola* (1870-74 and 1874-77), *Wanderer* (sailed 1878), and *Mermaid* (1880-82). (Not to be confused with a man of the same name who was born in Ireland in the 1790s and commanded whaling voyages out of New Bedford in the *Active*, *Daniel Wood*, and *Mary* in the 1850s and '60s.)

Mosher, David Green (fl. 1845-63). Career whaleman from Westport, Massachusetts, credited with at least three polychrome-engraved teeth distributed among Mosher descendants (one is now in NBWM). Each of the three known examples features standing figures of Bible-era Pharaohic Egyptian men holding weapons and battle standards (reported by Lorna Boulanger [Mrs. Donald Boulanger], a great-granddaughter). David G. Mosher was born at Westport in 1828 and made three Atlantic whaling voyages in the bark *Champion* — as Ordinary Seaman for the 115th lay (1845-46) and boatsteerer for the 65th lay (1847-48) while the vessel was owned and managed in Westport, and as second mate for the 35th lay (1849-53) after the *Champion* was transferred to New Bedford. On his next foray to the Atlantic grounds he was first mate of the Westport bark *Thomas*

Winslow (1853-55), after which, now having risen to a respectable station and evidently having accumulated sufficient income to wed, he married Lurana Esther Taber (1832-1900). He then made two Pacific Ocean voyages as first mate of the Fairhaven bark *Joseph Maxwell* (1855-58 and 1859-63), which were his last. The captain on both of these was Andrew P. Jenney (q.v.), and they were his last voyages, too. Mosher lived out the rest of his days as a farmer in Westport, fathering five children. He died there in 1899. A kinsman, Charles W. Mosher, kept journals of several of his own whaling voyages as ship's cooper and second mate, three of which survive (in NBWM), including one from the 1849-53 voyage of the *Champion* on which Charles was the cooper and David the second mate, in each case for the 35th lay. On the next voyage of the *Champion* (1853-55), with David serving as first mate, another kinsman, Sherman W. Mosher, was a green hand.

Mosher, Lester A. (fl. circa 1899-1922). He was a whaling master on five latter-day voyages out of New Bedford, but his greater fame accrues from a series of articles he wrote about whaling that were published in 1942. His interest in scrimshaw is known from a semi-fictionalized adaptation of the journal of his maiden whaling voyage in the New Bedford bark *Canton*, from May 1899 to September 1900. This flawed rendition was ghostwritten by Albert Hayward Young-O'Brien, using the pseudonym Brian O'Brien, with the somewhat misleading title *Scrimshaw and Sudden Death; A Salty Tale of Whales and Men*. It is sub-subtitled *Based on personal accounts and logbooks of Captain Lester A. Mosher*, and indeed it is loosely founded on Mosher's actual experiences. On page 162, the captain and officers are described as being engaged in making classic types of scrimshaw. Unfortunately, the ghostwriter camouflages the identities of the crew, as he does his own; and the names of the officers do not coincide with the actual crew list compiled by the New Bedford Port Society. Nevertheless, it is possible to identify at least some of the members of the ship's hierarchy whom Mosher caught red-handed making scrimshaw. William I. Shockley, the captain, is represented as working on a panbone swift. The mates are said to be making "bone canes worked to look like rope or bamboo, with handles of sperm teeth carved into sailor knots, swan necks, crowns, and bird's heads." In the book, Alex Nanton is implied to be the first mate and Herbert Reynolds is identified as the second mate, but both were actually boatsteerers on the real-life *Canton*. Nicholas R. Vieira was the real-life first mate (he was promoted to captain on the *Canton*'s next voyage), but he is not mentioned by name in the book. So the narrative implies that the first mate, Vieira, boatsteerers Reynolds and Nanton, and possibly others unnamed, were all making canes on the *Canton*. Meanwhile, a seaman pseudonymously called Nelson, who is not identifiable from the context, is supposed to have been making a panbone blackjack with a handle shaped like a fist: a very credible description of a standard whalemen's motif; and another unidentifiable crewman, pseudonymously called Owen, is crafting a classic panbone plaque, "a flat piece of bone on which he had made a drawing of the *Canton* with whales and boats all about her." This fellow is characterized as an alcoholic, desperate for drink and constantly running afoul of things on that account, "So it was good that he had the scrimshaw to work with; otherwise he would have been in trouble." Mosher himself, upon whose authentic journal O'Brien's story is based, has more pedestrian objectives: he is quoted as saying, "I as boatsteerer, made some chock pins of bone and polished them until they looked like ivory." Years later he donated a deformed sperm whale tooth specimen to NBWM, but none of his scrimshaw has come to light.

Lester Abiatha Mosher, a native of Dartmouth, Massachusetts, 20 years old at the time he went in the *Canton*, was born in 1879, the son of John F. and Adelaide F. Mosher. His father was Overseer of the Poor in Dartmouth; Lester was also a nephew of Captain William I. Shockley, who commanded the *Canton* on Lester's maiden voyage and likely acted in the capacity of mentor and overseer for the lad. Virtually all of Lester Mosher's seafaring career, spanning twenty years, was spent on sperm whaling voyages in Atlantic waters. In addition to the journal exploited as the basis for *Scrimshaw and Sudden Death*, he kept a journal of a second voyage under William I. Shockley in the famous New Bedford bark *Wanderer* during 1905-07 (in NBWM); and between whaling voyages — which were increasingly difficult to come by at the tail end of the fishery — he worked as a seaman in other trades. In 1911 Mosher was evidently given command of the bark *Wanderer*. (However, his part in the voyage is not recorded by Hegarty, who lists T.H. Jenkins as captain of a *Wanderer* voyage spanning 1910-12; but see Lund and *Whaling Masters*. The voyage returned an especially large and presumably profitable aggregate cargo of 3,150 barrels of sperm oil.) Mosher next served as replacement captain for Charles Brown in the *Valkyria*, a schooner owned and registered in New Bedford but on this occasion sailing from Portland, Maine (1912-14). Then, with the whale fishery already in precipitous decline, came another ruinous hiatus during World War I. Mosher's draft card, issued in 1917, gives his occupation as a "Master Mariner, John A. Cook Whaling Co.," but at the moment there were few whaling voyages to command and Mosher evidently spent most of the war years ashore. His swan song was during 1921-22, when he commanded three short voyages in the schooner *Athlete*, in which his father owned a 1/16th share. The first two of these were for managing agents Sylvia & Horvitz (Antone F. Sylvia and Samuel Horvitz) in 1921 and 1922, the third for James Avery in 1922. By then the curtain was about to fall for good, and Mosher had no further opportunities to skipper a blubber-hunter. Twenty years later — long before the advent of "Brian O'Brien" and his semi-fictionalized pastiche — Captain Mosher related his exploits and adventures under his own byline, in a series of articles published in 1942 in the *American Weekly*, entitled "'Thar She Blows!' Salty Tales of the Whalers in the Days When the Seas Were Free — and Romance, Peril and Fortune Beckoned the Deep Water Sailor From Arctic Ice and Tropic Island Paradise Alike." At some point along the way he married, probably around 1907; and in 1938 and 1940 he and his family donated to NBWM a deformed sperm whale tooth, a West Indian rubbing stone, and other souvenirs of his whaling days. (See also the articles about his shipmates Alexander Nanton, Herbert R. Reynolds, William I. Shockley, and Nicholas R. Vieira.)

Mung [Mungero], John — see **Manjiro, John**

Murphy, Thomas — see **Merphey, Thomas**

Murray, John (fl. circa 1856-70). Nantucket whaling master from Cape Verde. He is credited with a camphorwood document box that has a hinged top, with the top and sides inlaid with stars, diamonds, triangles, and circles in wood, whale ivory, and mother of pearl, and with an inlaid plaque inscribed "1856." The provenance states that it was "Made by Captain John Murray [and was] passed on to daughter Anna Murray from Orange Street, Nantucket" (William W. Coffin Collection, Osona, Aug. 8, 2004, #53). Born circa 1825, Murray evidently came to Nantucket as a young man, passed his whaling apprenticeship in Nantucket vessels, and served as a mate in the New

Bedford ship *Lapwing* (1860-63) before commanding two voyages in the Nantucket schooner *Abbie Bradford* (1867-68, 1869-70).

* **Myrick, Frederick** (fl. circa 1826-29). Thirty-six "Susan's Teeth" by his hand are now authenticated and reasonably well documented, bearing dates from 18 January 1828 to 4 September 1829. Of these, 31 bear portraits of the ship in which Myrick himself served, the *Susan* of Nantucket, while one has the *Barclay* of Nantucket, two the *Frances* of New Bedford, and two the *Ann of London*. One of the *Ann* teeth, one *Frances*, and 20 of the *Susan* are signed; both of the *Ann* teeth and 26 of the *Susan* are dated. (See Donald E. Ridley and Stuart M. Frank, *Frederick Myrick of Nantucket: Scrimshaw Catalogue Raisonné*; Donald E. Ridley, Janet West, Desmond T. Liddy, and Judith N. Lund, Frederick Myrick: *Physical Characteristics of the Scrimshaw*; Stuart M. Frank, "A Portrait of the Artist as a Young Man: Frederick Myrick (1808-1862)," and four other articles in a special issue of *The American Neptune* [Vol. 60, N° 4, Fall 2000], which anthologizes selections from the Proceedings of a Frederick Myrick symposium held at the annual Scrimshaw Collectors' Weekend at the KWM Sharon, Massachusetts, in June 1998.)

A brief article in an unidentified newspaper published in 1904 (NBW Scrapbook #2, 220), cited in the *Catalogue Raisonné*, describes one of the Susan's Teeth (Ridley #29-09-01) when it belonged to a William Crowley Russell of Hartford, Connecticut, and states erroneously: "This sailor [Myrick] was a consumptive and died and was buried at sea on this voyage" — i.e., the *Susan* voyage of 1826-29. The source of this false report is unknown. It is, of course, incontrovertibly established that Myrick lived for many years after his two whaling voyages — on Nantucket, in western New York, and possibly for a while in Michigan. Born 28 April 1805 on Nantucket, he was a green hand in the New Bedford ship *Columbus* (1825-26) and did his scrimshaw as a seaman in the *Susan* (1826-29). In 1833 he married Mary P. Folger, a descendant of one of the great Nantucketer families but a native of Sennett, New York, who was living on Nantucket at the time. He fathered three daughters and three sons, moved to Sennett sometime after 1847, may have lived for a while in Michigan, died in Sennett on 21 August 1862, and is buried there.

Perhaps the most interesting feature of the newspaper article is its account of how the owner obtained the scrimshaw in the first place: "It was given to him by his father, who received it from one of the owners of the bark [sic] Susan about 1835." This provides one of very few substantive clues about why Myrick may have engraved so many teeth with similar pictures and inscriptions, i.e., to distribute not only among shipmates (presumably) but also for presentation to at least one of the owners.

Naguruk (fl. circa mid-20th century). Dorothy Jean Ray lists this as one of the fictional signatures on commercially-produced, imitation Alaskan Eskimo scrimshaw. However, no such signature has been encountered on authentic or bogus scrimshaw: Ray's notion may have been based on false reports or in confusion with Nuguruk (q.v.).

Nakahama Manjiro: see **John Manjiro**

Nairne, Hugh (fl. circa 1847). On a whale ivory puzzle box in the form of a whaleship hull, on which the deck is a multi-part swiveling lid, polychrome engraved with the standing figure of a

Scottish warrior in tartan and full highland regalia. The internal layers are inscribed "Hugh Nairne / fecit / Newport, R.I. / 1847" and "Green Walden" (reported by Nina Hellman). Green Walden was master of the U.S. Revenue Cutter *Morris*, which was launched at Baltimore in April 1847 and sailed forthwith to Portland, Maine. Hugh Nairne is presumed to have been the artist and perhaps a member of the crew on this maiden voyage, for which no crew lists have been recovered; and Captain Walden was likely the intended recipient. However, the identity of Nairne himself has not been established. There were very few men of this name in 1847, most of them in Scotland, evidently none of them in Rhode Island or Maine, and only one immigrant on record, of whom there is no evidence that he ever was a sailor or was ever in Rhode Island; and what evidence does exist (including the variant spelling of the surname), suggests rather the contrary. This immigrant was Hugh Nairn, born in 1821 at Stewarton, Ayrshire, Scotland, the son of John Nairn, farmer, and Mary Ann née Parker. Hugh married Margaret Watt at Stewarton in June 1842 and they sailed to the USA immediately after, arriving at New York from Liverpool in August on the ship *Rosen*. They purchased farmland in Marissa, St. Clair County, Illinois, in 1843, where they had seven children, including a namesake son born around 1849. Margaret died in 1864, after which Hugh married Illinois native Je[a]nette McMillan, who bore him four more children. He served as an elder in the Presbyterian Church and died at Marissa in 1899. (His statistics are easily confused with a closely contemporaneous namesake from the same Ayrshire village, born in 1822 and died in 1894, having spent his entire life and career in Stewarton and not known ever to have left Scotland.) If that is all there is to it, how would either such fellow come to be making scrimshaw? and what might bring him to Newport? There was probably some other Scott named Hugh Nairne involved at some point in the Revenue Service and possibly the New England whale fishery whose record has been lost or has otherwise escaped detection.

Nanton, Alexander (fl. circa 1880s-1901). Career whaleman of West Indian birth and African ancestry. He is one of the officers described in the book *Scrimshaw and Sudden Death*, based on the journals of Lester A. Mosher (q.v.), as making scrimshaw aboard the bark *Canton* on a whaling voyage out of New Bedford during 1899-1900. Captain William I. Shockley was working on a panbone swift; Mosher himself, who was one of the boatsteerers, was making chock pins for his whaleboat; and the mates are said to be producing "bone canes worked to look like rope or bamboo, with handles of sperm teeth carved into sailor knots, swan necks, crowns, and bird's heads." Thanks to the ghostwriter's unaccountable effort to mask the identities of most of the officers and all of the crew, the names in the book are a jumble and most of the men are not identifiable. In the book, Alex Nanton is described as the first mate; however, Nicholas R. Vieira was the actual first mate at this time and was promoted to captain on the next voyage of the *Canton*; but Vieira is not mentioned in the book. On the 1899 voyage, Nanton was actually one of the boatsteerers and was promoted to third mate on the next voyage of the *Canton*, under Nicholas Vieira (1900-01). In any case, whatever the confusion of names and ranks in the book, and whether or not a boatsteerer can properly be described as an officer, Nanton was likely one of the men who were making canes.

Technically, boatsteerers are petty officers: they are always addressed as "Mister" like the officers, rather than by their first or last names like the crew; nor do they live in the forecastle with the common foremast hands; but they do not reside in the aftercabin with the mates, either;

rather, their place is in steerage, in the 'tweendecks just foreward of the cabin. Their station and their pay lies somewhere between officer and commoner. Nonetheless, as a boatsteerer himself and a proud professional whaleman, which that responsible station always implies, Lester Mosher seems to have classified boatsteerers more as officers than as crew. And for a colored man of African ancestry like Alexander Nanton, the meritocratic whale fishery was one of the few lines of work in the nineteenth century in which a black man could attain such a responsible station, out of respect to which all of the seamen, black, white, yellow, and brown, were required to address him unflinchingly as "Mister."

Alexander Nanton was born sometime around 1860 in the British West Indies. His voyages are not completely known, but he is recorded as having been three times in the *Canton*, the first probably as an able seaman under Captain Charles W. Fisher (1897-98), the second as a boatsteerer under Captain William I. Shockley — the voyage on which he is reported to have made scrimshaw (1899-1900) — and the third as third mate under Captain Nicholas Vieira (1901-02). Though the U.S. Census states Nanton's place of birth only as "British West Indies," and the shipping papers merely as "St. Vincent," it is likely that Nanton was actually from the island of Bequia, one of the Grenadines just south of St. Vincent that today is part of the independent nation of St. Vincent and the Grenadines. To the world at large the most famous thing about Bequia is probably the local whale fishery, which grew out of the island's involvement with Yankee whaling in the nineteenth century. Protracted contacts with visiting American whalers, and the recruiting of extra hands from among the local islanders that such contact seems inevitably to have generated (as it did also in the Azores, Madeira, the Cape Verdes, St. Helena, the Hawaiian Islands, and elsewhere), provided Bequia the wherewithal to develop its own home-grown, shore-based whale fishery. Bequian veterans of Yankee whaleships returned home and managed to adapt the technology to local conditions, using Yankee-type whaleboats and whalecraft to pursue humpbacks and pilot whales ("blackfish") in local waters, and flensing and processing them ashore. Lookouts were stationed on hilltops, rather than at mastheads; whaleboats were launched from beaches, rather than from shipboard; and whales were cut-in and tryed-out on little Petit Nevis Island nearby. This small-scale "subsistence" fishery became a mainstay of the Bequia economy, contributed to tourism, and persisted throughout the twentieth century and into the twenty-first. Whether Nanton himself ever participated in Bequia shore-whaling is not known; but it is not likely, as by 1920 he was gainfully employed as a lighthouse attendant in New Bedford, no doubt working for Charles A. Baker, the son of whaling captain, scrimshaw artist, and lighthouse keeper Amos C. Baker, Jr., and grandson of whaling captain, scrimshaw artist, and lighthouse keeper Amos C. Baker, Sr. (qq.v). In 1940 Nanton was still living at N° 6 Johnny Cake Hill in New Bedford. (See also: Lester A. Mosher, Herbert R. Reynolds, William I. Shockley, and Nicholas R. Vieira.)

Nanuk (fl. circa mid-20th century). Dorothy Jean Ray reports "Nanuk" as one of several fictional signatures on commercially-produced, imitation Alaskan Eskimo scrimshaw. However, this may be in confusion with "Nunuk." See the article on Nuguruk.

* **Naval Engagement Engraver** (fl. 19th century). In order to distinguish this first hand from various others who engraved sea battles on whale teeth — some of them equally skilled — and

especially to clarify the defining characteristics of scrimshaw by the newly identified Naval Monument Engraver (q.v.), it is worthwhile to recapitulate the article about the Naval Engagement Engraver in *More Scrimshaw Artists:*

> *Of the many whaleman-artists who scrimshawed scenes of naval battles… the anonymous Naval Engagement Engraver was one of the most prolific and consistent. As John Rinaldi was the first to point out, because the draftsmanship and style are straightforward and unornamented the hand tends to be readily recognizable; for the same reasons, his work is difficult to describe and often difficult to distinguish from the similar subject matter of other hands. His highly polished sperm-whale teeth sometimes have battle scenes on both sides, but more often there is a whaling scene on the back; in one instance, a broadside portrait of a sperm whale appears on the edge… His seas are engraved with confident, slightly curvilinear strokes tinted with a distinctive sea-green pigment (particularly visible under the microscope). Typically, a crudely-cut, strongly-colored red ensign with the Union Jack quartered flies at the taffrail of his victorious vessels (with no French, Dutch, or American flags so honored), which suggests that the artist [may have been] British.*

Four specimens are reported by KBP, one evidently depicting an action between British and Dutch warships (the latter may actually have been intended as French); others seem to portray British victories over American and French vessels.

> *The existence of a Naval Engagement Engraver is alluded to parenthetically in the* Dictionary *in the article on a British artist surnamed Foster (a whaleman later active in the fisheries at the North Sea port of Grimsby), to whom the Naval Engagement Engraver's hand is similar but who is not known to have specialized in naval battle scenes. Subsequent comparison reveals that there are at least two or three other artists with naval proclivities and superficially similar styles, whose separate identities could only be determined by an exhaustive forensic analysis of a majority of attributed pieces; and that at least one of these others* [the one whose hand most closely resembles Foster's, illustrated in *More Scrimshaw Artists*, 88; Flayderman, 71; Malley 1983, 73; and KBP] *is almost certainly American. It still remains to sort out and attribute the many naval engagement scenes in private and institutional collections in America and abroad…*

Though he remains anonymous, the Naval Monument Engraver is one of these artists whose scrimshaw now appears to have been "sorted out" as the work of a single hand.

Naval Monument Engraver (fl. mid-19th Century). Richard C. Malley, in his catalogue of the MSM collection, *Graven By the Fishermen Themselves*, 70-73, characterizes an entire species of scrimshaw that was copied after the widely circulated and immensely popular wood engravings in the two editions of compiler Abel Bowen's *The Naval Monument* (Boston, 1816 and 1837). Bowen's pictures, patriotic monuments to Yankee naval prowess in the War of 1812, were replicated on sperm whale teeth by various hands of varying skill at various times in the mid nineteenth century. The three examples in MSM illustrated by Malley, 72f, epitomize this diversity.

The third one is a representative work by the Naval Engagement Engraver (q.v.), one of the best and most prolific interpreters of the genre, notable for clarity and purity of line, sparing use of polychrome highlights, and, typically, the milky-white patina of the ivory. More recently, Judge Paul Vardeman has identified another able master of the Bowen genre: "six pieces by the same hand all copied from Bowen's *Naval Monument,"* faithful adaptations of Bowen's woodcuts on which the engraving technique is consistent, the sails appear sepia-colored, the scenes are labeled with comprehensive titles, with the labels distinctively stipple-engraved, often in red (private communication, 18 April 2005). In this engraver's work, the patina is subdued, rather than brilliant or milky, and the color of the ivory itself is characteristically (but not always) tawny, reminiscent of the color and grain of yellow pine. One of three examples in NBWM has on one side "UNITED STATES SQUADRON UNDER COM. BAINBRIDGE returning triumphant from the Mediterranean in 1815," and "HORNET BLOCKADING THE BONNE CITOYENNE in Bahia" on the other. A tooth in NCP pairs the same two scenes. There is also a third version of this pairing by the same hand (Sotheby's, 8 Dec. 1994, lot #190), regarding which the catalogue refers to "a similar scene" on a tooth in BJ:2 (Sotheby's, 24-25 Sept. 1982, lot #235); however, as Judge Vardeman observes, "that tooth is by a different hand. The Sotheby['s] tooth sold again at Bourgeault's [Northeast Auctions], Nov. 7 & 8, 1998, lot 892." A second specimen in NBWM has "ESCAPE OF THE CONSTITUTION FROM A BRITISH SQUADRON" on one side and a view of Venice on the back, a format — with one of Abel Bowen's naval battles on one side and a different kind of scene on verso — that the same artist also used on a tooth with *The President engaging the Endymion* on the front and a whaling scene on the back (Estate of Helen Palmer Lincoln, Wareham, Massachusetts, auctioned by Kenneth W. Van Blarcom, 22 Aug. 1993; and Osona, 13 Aug. 1994, lot #154). On another tooth by the same hand, *The Endymion and the President* appears on the front and the *Enterprise & Boxer* on the back (advertised by Charles L. Flint in the *Maine Antique Digest,* March 2005). Yet a third tooth by the Naval Monument Engraver in NBWM is stylistically identical but thematically and architecturally quite different. One side has a sperm whaling scene, with a full-rigged ship cutting-in and whaleboats lowered and in pursuit, boldly entitled below, " WHALERS DELIGHT," and inscribed above, "OUR LIVES YOU TAKE FOR LUCRE SAKE" (in effect, "you kill us [the whales] for money"). The other side has the same ship under plain sail passing a highland and lighthouse, boldly labeled below, "BUZZARDS BAY," and inscribed above, "HOME SWEET SWEET HOME," with an ornamental patriotic motif near the tip. Thus far, there are no reliable clues to the identity of the artist. A pair of teeth reportedly signed "Campbell" (q.v.) also has scenes from *The Naval Monument* has not been examined in this context, but they are almost certainly by a different hand.

* **Nelson, Horatio** (fl. circa 1836). The *Dictionary* makes note of a "Tooth engraved with a detailed map of Nantucket faithfully copied after the prototype in Obed Macy's *History of Nantucket* (1835), with derivative whaling scene on verso, signed (on the edge) 'H.E.C. Nelson, Steuben Co., N.Y.' (private collection)." Another tooth, signed "H.c.c. [or H.e.c.] Nelson" (private collection; reported by Ernest Helides) has a polychrome whaling scene circumferentially engraved in landscape format (that is, it is horizontally oriented on the surface and goes all the way around), set in the same geographical locale, and executed in the same manner, as W.L. Roderick's small masterpiece panbone panorama in MSM (illustrated on the cover of Richard Malley's *Graven By the Fishermen Themselves*).

There is no accounting for why or how the scene and the engraving technique, including treatment of the water and most details, are almost identical to the Roderick plaque, nor why the signatures differ on the two teeth signed by Horatio Nelson. Reservations have been expressed about the authenticity of the Roderick-like piece; however, based on his own close examination, Ernest Helides is convinced that the scrimshaw is genuine. Nothing further has been learned about the artist himself, who is still believed to be the Horatio Nelson (namesake of the British naval martyr) who obtained a Seamen's Passport at New Bedford at age 19 in 1836, indicating that he was born circa 1817 in Bridgeton, New Jersey, moved at some point to Steuben County, New York, and went whaling in an unidentified vessel in 1836.

Nickerson, Joshua (fl. circa 1840s-1880s?). Provincetown whaling master from Harwich, Massachusetts, on Cape Cod, and possible maker of two pieces of scrimshaw that descended in the family. While the provenance is clear, the heirs are uncertain whether the scrimshaw was made by or presented to Nickerson. One is a panbone busk with polychrome floral and patriotic vignettes and beaded edges; unfortunately, it is only shallowly engraved and has accordingly suffered significant fading and loss of pigment. The other is a light walking stick with a panbone shaft that has an octagonal foreshaft with fluted skirt, and a large, octagonal knob pommel of whale ivory.

The Provincetown whale fishery in the mid-nineteenth century consisted almost entirely of schooners making Atlantic Ocean voyages. The business both at sea and ashore was closely-held by a handful of interrelated families — a caste of owners, masters, and mates with few surnames and repetitive given names, such that individual records are difficult to sort out. There were at least a dozen Cape Cod mariners named Joshua Nickerson, of whom probably two were whaling masters. Their careers as captains spanned 33 years (1857-90); they were undoubtedly related but were not father and son. The scrimshaw maker — the one from Harwich — was the earlier of the two; the other, Captain Joshua S. Nickerson, from Provincetown, was the more likely master of the later voyages; but it is not certain which of the middle voyages were commanded by whom: the brig *Lewis Bruce* of Orleans (1857-58), and the Provincetown schooners *Union* (1863), *Alleghenia [Allegheny]* (1863), possibly the *Union* again (1866), *Arizona* (1872), *Gage H. Phillips* (three voyages, 1875-83), and *Angelia [Angelica] B. Nickerson* (two voyages, 1887-90). What is known about the scrimshaw maker is that he was born at Harwich in 1819, the son of Elkanah Nickerson, farmer, and the former Elizabeth Young; he married Mercy E. Small (1822-1915) in 1840; they had four sons and four daughters; and he died at Harwich in 1891.

* **Nickerson, T.** Contrary to indications in both the *Dictionary* and *More Scrimshaw Artists*, this name probably refers to the recipient, rather than the maker of a hinged wooden sewing box with a whale ivory plaque on the top engraved "T. Nickerson," profusely inlaid with stars, hearts, diamonds, and pinwheels of whale ivory, mother of pearl, and wood, and the inside fitted with thread spools so that the threads can pass through holes in the inlay on the front (Bourne, Aug. 1966, #405; Bourne, Aug. 1977, #521; J. Welles Henderson Collection; *Jack Tar*, 254; Northeast, 16 Aug. 2008, #859).

Nordenskiöld, Adolf Erik (fl. 1850s-80s). A geologist, mineralogist, naturalist, Arctic explorer, and world-class collector of maps and sea-charts, he is the most celebrated of the Nordenskiöld family of Swedish scientists. Surprisingly, perhaps, he made a walrus ivory paper knife, page turner, or mangle (in the Smålands Museum, Växjö, Sweden), described in Swedish as "A tribute from the High North to Christina Nilsson Rouzaud, in memory of the *Vega* voyage of Adolf Erik Nordenskiöld" (*"En tribut från den höga norden till Christina Nilsson Rouzaud. Minne af Vegafärden af Adolf Erik Nordenskiöld."*) It has the initials "CNR" expertly engraved in monogram, is prominently signed "A.E. Nordenskiöld," and was presented to the world-famous Swedish soprano Christina Nilsson (1843-1920) by Nordenskiöld himself following his polar expedition in the *Vega* (1878-80). Its very existence and superb quality suggest that he very likely produced — or oversaw the production of — other scrimshaw-like articles made out of walrus ivory, and possibly others made from fossilized mammoth ivory, which he mentions being plentiful in the New Siberian Islands:

> *"These islands are very remarkable from a scientific point of view, being very rich in the remains of the mammoth and other animals of the same period, which are found in greater abundance among them than on the tundra of the mainland. Some of the sand-banks on their shores are so full of the bones and tusks of the mammoth that the ivory collectors who for a series of years traveled every year from the mainland to the islands in dog-sledges, used to return in autumn when the sea was again covered with ice, with a rich harvest."* (Alexander Leslie, *The Arctic Voyages of Adolf Erik Nordenskiold*, London, 1879, 224)

When Nils Adolf Erik Nordenskiöld (1832-1901) was born to a Swedish-speaking family in Helsinki, Finland was still part of the Russian Empire. The son of Nils Gustav Nordenskiöld, a mineralogist and mining superintendent, Nordenskiöld *fils* was raised in the Finnish countryside, educated at a provincial school, and earned his bachelor's, master's, and doctoral degrees in the physical sciences at Helsinki's Imperial Alexander University (1849-57). However, his conspicuous and persistent advocacy of Finnish independence, in opposition to the prevailing Czarist Russian domination, resulted in his dismissal from a university teaching post and exile abroad. He fled to Stockholm, where he was appointed professor and curator of the mineralogical department of the Swedish Museum of Natural History. Over the next three decades he participated in, then led important expeditions to Spitsbergen (Svalbard) and the High Arctic, including two pioneering forays to Greenland, an unsuccessful but scientifically productive polar attempt, and the *Vega* voyage in search of a Northeast Passage across the Russian Arctic to China (1878-80). He published the scientific results of the *Vega* expedition in five volumes and a popular narrative in two. In recognition of his accomplishments, in 1880 he was created a baron and made a commander of the Order of the North Star, in 1893 he was elected to the prestigious Swedish Academy, the Nordenskiöld Crater on Mars was named for him, and he was elected to a two-year term in the Swedish parliament. He married Anna Maria Mannerheim in 1863 and produced four children, including the mineralogist Gustaf Nordenskiöld (1868-95). The A.E. Nordenskiöld Collection of 24,000 historical maps and cartographic items from the fifteenth through the nineteenth centuries is housed at the University of Helsinki.

Norton, Thomas Adams (fl. circa 1825-59). Whaling master from Martha's Vineyard to whom DCHS attributes a tooth featuring a townscape and a view of the State House in Boston that is associated it with his first voyage as a captain, in the ship *Hector* of New Bedford (1834-37). Born in Edgartown circa 1808, he served the usual apprenticeship and rose through the ranks on deepwater whaleships, married Lydia G. Kidder in 1837 shortly after the *Hector* voyage, and they raised a family in Edgartown as he went on to command a series of whaling voyages in New Bedford ships: *Alexander Barclay* (1837-39), *Hector* again (1838-40), and the maiden voyage of the *Charles W. Morgan* (1841-45) — his most famous exploit, because of the subsequent fame of the ship. He then retired from whaling — temporarily as it turned out. After ten years ashore he came out of retirement to skipper the first part of a voyage in the ship *Emerald* of Sag Harbor (1855-59) on which he was succeeded by relief captain Frederick M. Halleck. Following this, his retirement from whaling was permanent. The 1860 and 1870 U.S. Census state his occupation as Farmer, but in 1880 the listing reverted to the honorific Ship Captain. Fellow-Vineyarder and fellow-scrimshaw artist Willam Cottle (q.v. in the *Dictionary*) served under him in the *Hector* (1838-40). (Contrary to the report in *Foreign Ships in Micronesia,* it was Thomas Hawes Norton [q.v.], not Thomas Adams Norton, who was captain of the *South Seaman* of Fairhaven at Pohnpei in 1858. See: www.micsem.org/ pubs/ articles/ historical/ forships/ pohnpei. htm.)

Norton, Thomas Hawes (fl. circa 1830-64). Whaling master from Edgartown, Martha's Vineyard, who commanded five whaling voyages out of New Bedford and Fairhaven. The provenance of three busks, one made of skeletal bone and the other two of baleen, claims they "descended in the family of a Martha's Vineyard whaling captain" (Eldred, 8-10 April 2010, #1021 and #1022), but they were evidently engraved by three different hands. One of the baleen ones has images of a rose, a patriotic spread eagle, two female portraits, an exotic mask, and an inscription of six lines in a small, cursive hand, and is signed and dated "T.H. Norton / 1851." According to the 1850 U.S. Census Norton was born circa 1817 but other records indicate that he may have been as much as ten years older. After serving a voyage as mate of the ship *Callao* of New Bedford under kinsman James A. Norton, Thomas commanded two voyages in the ship *Menkar* of New Bedford (1845-48 and 1848-51). He was then captain of an ill-fated voyage in the ship *Citizen* of New Bedford (1851-53). Starbuck errs in naming the captain as Thomas A. Norton (the mistake is corrected in Lund) but accurately reports that the vessel was wrecked in the Arctic, 300 miles north of East Cape (Siberia) on October 14, 1853: six crewmen perished and a seventh died later. Meanwhile, the Fairhaven ship *Northern Light* sailed from New Bedford in 1851 on another ill-starred voyage. According to Starbuck, the "first mate, Mr. [William] Baker, and three men drowned in [the] Ochotsk Sea September, 1852"; one of the other mates, Isaac Briggs, whose name does not appear on the ship's outward manifest, died in August 1853; then, Lund reports, Captain William Stott left the ship, probably because of illness. So late in 1853 Norton was sent as replacement captain on the *Northern Light*. The sequel was a conventional conclusion of the voyage in April 1855. However, Norton's troubles were not over: his next outing would end in shipwreck for the second time. The ship *South Seaman* sailed from Fairhaven in August 1856 and had already sent home a more-than-respectable catch when the vessel was lost on French Frigate Shoal, almost 500 miles northwest of Honolulu, on March 13, 1859. Apparently undaunted, Captain Norton returned to New Bedford and was given command of yet another troubled vessel. The ship *Contest* had sailed under Captain Elijah B. Morgan the year before but returned to port because, as Starbuck relates, the captain "died suddenly of heart disease, March 4, 1861." So Norton was recruited to lead the *Contest*'s second attempt, which turned out to be a comparatively uneventful and moderately successful voyage (1861-64). It was also Norton's last. He was twice married, first to Jane Eliza Butler of Edgartown in 1837; then, in

1842, presumably after having been widowed, to Eliza W. Beetle, daughter of James H. and Betsey Beetle, with whom the couple lived in the 1840s and '50s.

Norton, William Henry (fl. 19th century). The orally-transmitted provenance of three objects in a family legacy collection claims that they were brought home to upstate New York from a voyage by "the only family member who ever went whaling": a generic, commercially-made set of bone-and-ebony dominoes in a cylindrical wooden box (the box is old but not indigenous), with the name "William H. Norton" in pencil holograph; a small, four-draw telescope with a leather sheath; and a medium-small tooth engraved with a circumferential sperm whaling scene, signed "William H. Norton"; the tooth has also been drilled in four places and two pendant brass rings were inserted, evidently for mounting (reported by Lawrence Tatro). Unfortunately, some later hand corrupted the whaleman's work by the addition of a badly drawn, inaccurate, amateur whaling scene that intersects with the competent original. Whether Norton made other scrimshaw that may have been given to shipmates or distributed to some other branch of the family is unknown. His whaling career is also unknown. Of several men named William Norton who went whaling from American ports in the middle 19th century, none of the records coincides precisely with the biographical details unearthed by this one's descendants. They have no record of the name of his ship or port, his family circumstances are only partially corroborated in the pubic records, and the census reports are inconclusive. He was born circa 1841 in Rochester, New York, the son of Horace Kent Norton, hostler, a native of Northampton, Massachusetts, who later lived in Westhampton. His mother was the former Margaret Polhamus, a woman said to be of Old Dutch ancestry whom Horace met in New York State. According to the family she was from Saugus, New York, but as Saugus is in Massachusetts and there is no Saugus in New York, her hometown may have been Saugerties, New York. The family identifies William's wife as Lavinia Pinch.

Nuguruk (fl. circa the second and third quarters of the 20th century). *Nuguruk,* which superficially resembles an authentic Eskimo name, is the most prevalent of several fictional "signatures" that appear on imitation Native Alaskan scrimshaw rendered on authentic ivory. Dorothy Jean Ray reports that scrimshaw resembling Eskimo work on which names like "Nunuk" and "Nuguruk" appear in the manner of a signature was actually "made in Seattle, usually mass-produced from a master copy by non-Eskimos in several manufacturing firms." There may have been some Native American artisans employed in this business, but many or most are said to have been immigrants from China and Japan. Such pieces customarily depict "typical northern subjects," such as Native villages, hunting and fishing scenes, local watercraft, and Arctic animals (polar bears, whales, seals, walruses, fish, and sled-dogs); they are evidently hand-engraved, pigmented in monochrome black, sometimes with red highlights, with the "signature" imperfectly incised in a cursive hand. In Ray's vast experience, these were "usually elephant ivory, with a tag 'genuine ivory,'" and were sold in Alaska, "where customers mistakenly thought they were buying Eskimo-made objects of walrus ivory" (*A Legacy of Arctic Art,* 1996, 148). However, it is now clear they were also marketed as such by retail souvenir shops in Seattle and elsewhere in the Pacific Northwest, and that several species of ivory were used (indiscriminately, it appears), including authentic walrus ivory. *Nuguruk* is the name on most of these pieces submitted for examination by the SFL between 1985 and 2007; *Nanuk* has been encountered on eBay and in flea markets; *Naguruk* and *Nanuk* have been mentioned but not seen. Of all such pieces submitted for examination by the SFL, the overwhelming majority — as well as virtually all of the ones encountered in antiques shops on both coasts over the years, and most of the ones listed on eBay whereof the material could be identified at all — were walrus ivory, a few were sperm whale ivory, and only very few of elephant or mammoth ivory were seen or reported. Ray's observation that "few Eskimos in the Nome vicinity signed their work, and if they did, they used a binomial" was certainly true of the first generation or two of Nome School artisans (such as Happy Jack or Billy Kamoneseok or Billy Billiken) but it was not necessarily the case with later practitioners — for example, Robert Mayokok of Wales, Alaska, a prolific mid-twentieth-century artisan who customarily signed his walrus ivory, ink drawings, and ceramics simply as "Mayokok." Objects bearing the Nuguruk "signature" seem to run the full gamut, across the entire range of typical, souvenir-grade Native Alaskan scrimshaw, including substantial, well made cutlery with fine blades of Swedish steel, but tending mostly to letter openers, paper knives, spreaders, napkin rings, salt shakers, ashtrays, and other smallish, somewhat utilitarian household articles. There is also Nuguruk "jewelry" (pendants, brooches, earrings, tie tacks, cufflinks, and such), and the same manufacturers may have produced billikens, totemic *tupilak* figures (which are actually more closely associated with Greenland and Canadian Inuit), game boards, shot flasks, and even Northwest Coast Indian totem poles, as imitative versions of each of these have been made of ivory by non-Natives in Seattle and points south. However, if these were made by the same commercial outfits that produced the Nuguruk or Nunuk lines, they were likely not signed as none bearing the Nuguruk or Nunuk signature has been reported.

Nunuk (fl. circa the second and third quarters of the 20th century). One of several faux Eskimo names that appear in the manner of holograph signatures on imitation Eskimo scrimshaw. See the article on Nuguruk.

* **Octuck [Octook], John** (fl. circa 1903-35). Native Alaskan artist, an early protégé of Happy Jack (q.v. here and in *More Scrimshaw Artists*), working in the hybridized Eskimo scrimshaw genre that combines traditional Yup'ik forms with figurative scrimshaw. In addition to the cribbage boards and other objects mentioned in *More Scrimshaw Artists*, a pair of figurines in KNB, carved out of marine mammal bone (species not identified) with monochrome black highlights, are faithful three-dimensional effigies of the two principal characters from the comic strip "Mutt and Jeff" created by Harry Conway "Bud" Fisher in 1907. Tall, lanky Mutt is depicted with his characteristic bushy moustache and sideburns, and wearing his customary top-hat. Short, stocky Jeff wears his signature homburg and is posed standing with hands in pockets and ankles crossed. Dorothy Jean Ray illustrates analogous examples in SIW attributed to John Octuck (*Eskimo Art*, 1977, #85), but is mistaken in her claim that they are a pair: in that instance the one she calls "Mutt" is indeed Mutt, but the one she identifies as "Jeff" is more like the dapper Monopoly board-game mascot figure with top-hat, beard, and handlebar mustache known as "Rich Uncle Pennybags," developed by Parker Brothers of Salem, Massachusetts, in the 1930s (note that the Monopoly character has both a beard and mustache only in some manifestations; in others he has a handlebar mustache but no beard). (See Evan Esar, *The Comic Encyclopedia*, 1978, 504; and Donald D. Markstein, "Rich Uncle Pennybags" and "Mutt and Jeff," Hasbro Games, 2003-04, www.toonopedia.com.) Ray's attribution of Mutt and Jeff figurines, which are carved from walrus ivory as well as skeletal bone, also extends to unnamed members of John Octuck's family. (Source: Henry Hornblower III.)

* **Pagoda Artisan.** The whaleman-artist hitherto known anonymously by this moniker and subsequently identified as S. Baker is now known to have been Silvanus Baker (q.v.) of Yarmouth, Maine. Furthermore, recent forensic examination and additional research have now differentiated this hand from that of the Albatross Artisan (q.v.), with which it was hitherto associated.

Palmer, H. (fl. circa 1831). A panbone busk beautifully engraved on one side with three ship portraits and a panoramic whaling scene, has on the other side the more crudely engraved inscriptions "JW," "DCB," "SHIP / Catherine / South Seas," "DB & HP," and "H. PALMER / OCTOBER 19th, 1831" (private collection; reported by Ronald Bourgeault and examined at SFL prior to consignment to Northeast Auctions, August 2007). Nothing much is known about it, and in the absence of a credible provenance the relevance of the following connection (with which all of the available evidence coincides) can only be surmised. In his *History of Essex County, Massachusetts* (1888), Duane Hamilton Hurd notes that "The ship 'Catherine' [of Salem, Massachusetts] Joseph Winn, Jr. [master], entered from Calcutta in October, 1831, consigned to Joseph Peabody." This was the homeward passage of a merchant vessel, concluding what may or may not justifiably be termed a "South Seas" voyage. The specific date in October on which the ship arrived at Salem is not recorded, but it could have been the 19th. The initials JW on the busk correspond to those of Captain Joseph Winn. Presuming that HP and H. Palmer refer to the same person, and that DB and DCB *may* refer to the same person, one theory is that H. Palmer was a member of the *Catherine*'s crew and maker of the busk, with DB / DCB the intended recipient — who in this context would most likely have been Palmer's fiancée.

On the other hand, there were two American whaleships named *Catherine*. The first was put into service in July 1831 and was whaling out of Nantucket until 1843, then out of New London until 1865, when she was captured and burned by the Confederate commerce raider *Shenandoah*. Given a sailing date in July 1831, October of that same year would have been far too early in the voyage for scrimshandering to have begun; in fact, it may even have been too early for there even to have been any new panbone aboard. But some other explanation could account for the October date, such as that a sailor named H. Palmer had panbone left over from a previous voyage; or, on some voyage at a later time inscribed the birth date of his lady-love, or the date that he and she became engaged. The other *Catherine* was a Salem ship known to have sailed on a Pacific Ocean whaling voyage in March 1832 but which may have been in service earlier (the records are cloudy and possibly incomplete). The salient clues being what they are, in the absence of a provenance ascription of authorship can only be educated guesswork.

Pardee, Warren W. (fl. circa 1846-48). A family provenance credits an H. or W. Pardee from Middletown, Connecticut, with two scrimshaw swift components, one unfinished, both said to have been made aboard the ship *William Tell* of Sag Harbor, Long Island, New York; in a private collection and until recently held by family descendants (reported by Charles A. Manghis). Each is lathe-turned from a single sperm-whale tooth in the form of a shaft 3 to 4 inches (7.5 to 10 cm) high; the turnings are inset with red sealing wax and surmounted by a shallow cup resembling the ones intended to hold balls of yarn on many scrimshaw swifts; the base in each instance is carved as a C-clamp with threaded whale-ivory turnbuckle (thumbscrew), evidently devised to fasten onto the edge of a table — all reminiscent of orthodox swift construction and ornamentation — with the rims of the cups drilled to accommodate tiny fastenings. They are accordingly thought to be intended as pincushions, of which the soft cushions themselves either were never added or do not survive; and perhaps to have been made to accompany a swift or swifts of similar design. It should not be surprising that the likely maker of these architectonic pieces turns out to have been a carpenter. As there were no other male Pardees with the initial H or W born or living in Middlesex County, Connecticut, anytime in the mid-nineteenth century, to whatever degree the family provenance may be relied upon the fellow in question could only have been Warren Washington Pardee, born in 1826. The whaleship *William Tell* made six voyages from Sag Harbor between 1843 and 1857, but Pardee's was likely the voyage of 1846-48, to the Pacific, as it was the only one that took an appreciable number of sperm whales, thus providing ivory for sailors' scrimshaw (the other five were all right whaling voyages to the North Pacific and Northwest Coast). This was Pardee's only known voyage. He may have been from Middletown originally, but by 1850 he was working as a carpenter and living with his two sisters at nearby Haddam. He was married later that same year to Sylvia A. Brainerd. Around that time he was operating a carding mill that stood on a stream in the Beaver Meadow section of Haddam, and "afterward made buttons there" (Richard M. Bayles, "Town of Haddam," in *The History of Middlesex County*, 1884).

Parker, George J. (fl. circa 1851-72). In his journal as captain of the New Bedford bark *Orray Taft*, wintering-over in Hudson Bay in February 1866, he mentions in his journal that he "Made an ivory whistle." Given his professional specialization in High Latitude North whaling, and that he was trapped in pack ice in the Canadian Arctic at the time, the whistle must have been carved out of walrus ivory (sperm whaling was not much of a factor in this branch of the fishery). Charles H. Durgin, in his contemporaneous journal of the *Monticello* of New London, provides comprehensive insights into the state of suspended animation in which the whaling fleet finds itself, banked in the snow all winter and almost completely idle while waiting for the spring thaw that will open navigable sea lanes into the whaling grounds; and the extraordinary significance of scrimshandering, musical performance, and amateur theatricals during those long, dark, icebound months. Happily, Durgin provides a gratifying multitude of details, including some account of the daily chores and extracurricular rehearsals that fill the time, and an inventory of his own scrimshaw as well as complete program bills of the various concerts and plays the Arctic thespians put on for the entire conclave of whalers on a regular basis. (Durgin's journal is printed in its entirety as an Appendix in *More Scrimshaw Artists*.) By contrast, Captain Parker was no common foremast hand like Durgin. In his role as captain he had charge of the voyage, and therefore of the welfare, safety, and productivity of his entire ship's company, as well as their livelihoods, the financial interests of the owners, and good relations around the fleet and with the Native people for as long as they remained icebound together. Accordingly, one could wish that he had seen fit to record on paper his thoughts about the advantages of bartering with the Natives for meat and ivory, the extent to which hunting and fishing locally could improve the shipboard diet as well as providing sport, and the importance of such diversions as music, theatre, and scrimshaw in maintaining morale during those long, idle months frozen-in at Cumberland Inlet. But, alas, like the stereotypical terse New Englander, all he imparts for posterity is "Made an ivory whistle," leaving us to draw our own conclusions.

George J. Parker, born in New Bedford in 1836, was the son of John J. Parker, who had a distinguished career (1822-44) as master of six whaling voyages out of New Bedford and two from Wilmington, Delaware. George embarked on his maiden voyage at age 15 in 1851, to the Pacific

Ocean in the Fairhaven ship *Zone*, which he evidently left early to transfer to a more lucrative and far more responsible berth as a boatsteerer on a North Pacific voyage in the New Bedford ship *Moctezuma* (1854-57). When, according to Starbuck, first mate Abraham Spooner was "taken out of his boat by a line," Parker may have been promoted again, probably to third mate. In any case, by 1861 he had earned an appointment as first mate on a Hudson Bay voyage in the bark *Antelope* (1861-63), after which he made three Hudson Bay voyages as captain of the *Orray Taft*. On the first two of these (1864-65 and 1866-67) he met with only modest success, and on the third he lost the vessel on Marble Island on September 14, 1872, barely two months out. Thus the curtain closed on his whaling career. He took up farming in Acushnet, Massachusetts, and was twice married, first to Elizabeth, who bore him nine children, then to Lillian, 33 years his junior, who bore him two more. At around 70 years old he moved with his second wife and youngest daughter to New Bedford, where he was still hiring out as a farm hand well into his seventies, and where, widowed for the second time, he boarded into his middle eighties.

* **Parmenter, John G.** (fl. circa 1866-67). The article entitled "J.G. Parmenter" in the *Dictionary* makes note of a tooth described as "depicting a Union soldier holding the flag, a topsail schooner, a ship and a whaler under sail; black with green water," with a label inside stating, "J.G. Parmenter whale's tooth Pacific, 1867" (Bourne, 29 Nov 1969, #50). This minimal information enabled only a provisional identification of the artist: "A John Parmenter of China, Maine, born circa 1845, received a Seaman's Protection Paper at New Bedford in 1866." Two more pieces have since surfaced from a direct descendant (reported by Henry Hornblower III; subsequently in Northeast Auctions, 19-20 August 2006, #1255), whereof the provenance corroborates both the attribution and the skeletal biographical data in the *Dictionary*, as well as providing clues to a few additional biographical details. One of these pieces is a tooth engraved with two standing figures; the other is a whale ivory crimper with fluted jagging wheel and a handle carved in the form of a lady's leg and foot with garter; it also has a polychrome engraved floral motif and the initials "JGP" (which may refer to the maker himself or to his wife Julia). The descendant also recalls seeing another tooth (possibly the one auctioned by Bourne in November 1969) in the family home during her childhood in Maine.

John Greenough Parmenter was born in 1844 at China, Maine, lived there and later at Vassalboro and Albion, Maine. During the Civil War he served three years and two months as a private in Company F, 7th Maine Regiment, Union Army (1861-63). Based upon the provenance and with a newly issued seaman's passport, he is presumed to have made a Pacific Ocean whaling voyage during 1866-70; but apart from having established that he did not sail from the New Bedford Port District, the voyage has not been identified, nor have many facts been discovered about his subsequent activities. (The suggestion that he may have made his whaling voyage aboard the ship *Mechanic* is clearly mistaken, as the only whaling vessel of that name was scuttled with the Stone Fleet of 1861.) By 1870 Parmenter was married to a woman named Julia and was living in Vassalboro, where he worked at a shovel handle shop. He died at Albion, Maine, in 1903.

* **Paul, Charles E.** (fl. circa 1878-84). The *Dictionary* refers to a writing-box (portable desk or lap secretary) in KNB, elaborately inlaid with wood and walrus ivory, which prominently features as the central ornament on the hinged lid the name "Regina" rendered in cursive script, boldly inlaid

in ivory and mother-of-pearl; and is identified "Made by Charles Paul New Bedford Mass." Constructed of wood, it is elaborately festooned with external and internal marquetry and inlay — geometrical designs, stars, fans, rope patterns, arrows, compass roses, fans, flowers, etc. — in a variety of woods, whale ivory, and mother-of-pearl, with a velvet writing surface and velvet tabs. Distinctive features are a series of cockleshells full-round-carved out of whale ivory and inlaid on the front face; and a bead pattern of discs of whale ivory alternating with convex discs of wood, with corners of whale ivory, framing the central vignette and inscription on the lid. Subsequent research corroborates the attribution to Charles E. Paul, born at New Bedford in 1862, who went to sea at age 16 and made three whaling voyages in New Bedford vessels, the schooner *Charles W. Morse* (1878-79) and the barks *Alice Knowles* (1879-83) and *Mars* (1883-84). "Regina" turns out to be Charles's older sister Regina Paul, born in 1857 or 1858; and it is not difficult to picture a young lad in his teens or early twenties spending long hours at sea crafting such a treasure as a gift for a favorite sister. Regina and Charles were the third and fifth of eight siblings; their father was Sylvester Paul, a New Bedford blacksmith who had immigrated from France; their mother, Esther W. Paul, was born in the State of Maine, where the parents lived at first and where their oldest son was born. The family records are sparse, but no evidence has been found that either Charles or Regina ever married, although, contrary to the usual pattern of Victorian spinsters, by her early twenties she was not living with her parents anymore. In the 1880s she had a job as a bookkeeper and a place of her own on Parker Street; by 1890 she was a teacher at the Acushnet Avenue School, a public school for the primary grades. In 1930, evidently long after brother Charles had departed the scene, Regina, at age 72, was still identified by her maiden name and was living in New Bedford with their younger brother John, an insurance agent ten years her junior.

Percival, Thomas (fl. circa 1835-62). Thomas Conley reports a coconut shell dipper with a baluster handle turned from two pieces of wood, a turned whale ivory finial, and a double-heart-shaped mounting flange cut out of sheet metal. The flange is continuous with two sheet-metal bands that are inset circumferentially around the bowl, the lower one of which flares out like a riband with the name "MARY PERCIVAL" in silhouette (private collection). Conley also attributes to the same hand a second dipper that has the motto "REMEMBER THE GIVER MAY 14, 1850" similarly cut out of sheet metal and inset circumferentially around the bowl (illustrated in Robert W.D. Ball, *Nautical Antiques*, 1997, 96); however, that one has a fist-and-loop finial, a spiral-cut, curved wooden handle, and the mounting flange is quite different. For a third example by another hand, see the article on Benjamin D. Gifford, who made a such a dipper with the cut-metal silhouette names of both of his parents inset circumferentially around the bowl.

The "Mary Percival" named on the scrimshaw was Mary née Chadwick, the wife of Captain Thomas Percival, a whaling master and one of several whalemen-scrimshaw artists from the lakeside hamlet of China, Maine. He was born circa 1819 in Vassalboro, Maine, and she in 1822, probably in nearby China. They were married in 1848 and lived on a farm in China, where their daughter Ella was born in 1849. They later moved to Augusta, Maine, birthplace of their son Frank in 1858. Percival's first youthful whaling voyage or two are not known. On a Seamen's Passport issued in 1841 at Salem, Massachusetts, in anticipation of his embarkation in the ship *Elizabeth* of that port (1841-44), his age is given as 22, his birthplace as Vassalboro, and his residence as Salem (which it probably was not). A second passport issued at Salem in 1844 prior to a second voyage in the same vessel, in which he was either a boatsteerer or third mate serving under Captain Worthin Hall (1844-48), gives Percival's age as 26, his birthplace as Vassalboro, and his residence as Edgartown, Martha's Vineyard (which it may or may not have been at that point). For his next voyage he followed Captain Hall to New Bedford to serve as first mate of the ship *Majestic* on a whaling voyage to the Northwest Coast (1848-51), after which Percival commanded the *Majestic* on two voyages to the North Pacific (1851-53 and 1853-57) and the Mattapoisett bark *Massasoit* on a voyage to the Atlantic whaling grounds (1858-62). He then retired from whaling. The 1860 U.S. Census identifies Percival as a soldier, for which no explanation has been discovered (he was on a whaling voyage at the time and could not have been in the Civil War military until 1862). The 1870 Census lists him as still a "ship master," but if he was active as such at that time it must have been in the merchant service. In either case, within the next few years he moved his family to Ulster County, in upstate New York, where he worked as a cabinetmaker and where son Frank was employed as a clerk.

Peter the Great (1672-1725), Tsar of Russia 1682-1725. Ivory carving was significant enough a pastime for European royalty in the eighteenth century that the *Encyclopædia Britannica* could report in passing, "Several German princes, as well as Peter the Great, carved and turned ivory in the lathe," resulting in "remarkable specimens of their work" (*Enc. Brit.*, 9th ed., 5:168). The difference between Peter and the others is that he was not only an authentic soldier, military field commander, and vice-admiral of the Russian Navy (which he created), but also an accomplished sailor, dedicated shipwright, and enthusiastic yachtsman in his own right; and unlike the other royal princes, he consistently and energetically practiced ivory carving throughout his adult life — every day, when he could; and his habitual medium was walrus ivory, obtained from Norway and the Russian White Sea coast. In fact, if his habitual behavior be any reliable indicator, he much preferred the mechanical crafts and sailoring to the conventional arts of governance and diplomacy, though of course he was the driving force, main focus, and autocratic arbiter of these in Russia. On his Great Embassy to Western Europe during 1697-98, he preferred to travel semi-incognito as Peter Mikhailov, shipwright and junior member of the legation, rather than suffer the irrelevancies and delays of pomp, circumstance, and ceremony that the visit of a crowned head would otherwise automatically have occasioned everywhere, and to indulge himself in the shipwright's and carver's trades. One nineteenth-century historian marveled at the dexterity of Peter the Polymath:

> *It is incomprehensible how this unwearied man could govern a great empire in all its details, establish manufacturers, build cities, dig canals, organize an army, a fleet, a host of public offices, found schools, academies, universities, theatres, and withal fine time to make these crosses, candelabras, and cups of ebony and ivory, and so to finish and polish every minute part, that any German guild would have pronounced it a masterpiece.* (Kohl, *Russia*, 76)

According to the Hermitage Museum in St. Petersburg, "Lathework was one of Peter's favorite pastimes, as it gave rein to his natural artistic bent and skill in scientific and technical invention"; and a biographer refers to Peter spending "several hours a day" turning wood and ivory, assisted by Andrei Konstantinovich Nartov (1693-1756) (Waliszewski, 199). During off-hours on a naval mission to Archangel in 1693, the Tsar "began turning the elaborate chandelier made of walrus tusks that now hangs in the Peter Gallery of the Hermitage" (Massie, 127). In his Summer Palace, built in 1710, "The most interesting room [of seven] on Peter's floor was the Turning Room, where the Tsar kept lathes to use in his spare time" (Ibid, 606); and on the way back to the Winter Palace from his marriage ceremony in February 1712, "Peter halted his sledge before he reached the front door so that he could go inside and hang over the dinner table his wedding gift to Catherine [née Martha Skavronskaya]. It was a six-branched candelabrum of ivory and ebony which he himself had made in two weeks of work" (Ibid, 570). In 1716, the Tsar commissioned Russian and Dutch translations of L'Abbe Charles Plumier's classic, *L'Art du Tourner* (Paris, 1706), identified by James Harris as "the first book dealing specifically with ornamental turning as well as 'plain' turning"; and in 1718 the Tsar sent Nartov to teach Russia's ally, King Frederick William I of Prussia, "the art of ornamental turnery." Sometime during 1717-21, "on the personal decree of Peter the Great," Nartov designed and built for the Tsar a complex contraption called a "medallic-guillocheur lathe" (Mokeeva, n.p.).[10] And in 1719, when Peter appointed a new envoy to Peking, he "sent with him as a present to the emperor four ivory telescopes which Peter had made himself" (Massie, 819).

The Tsar's stature as an ivory carver is no less impressive than his oversize physical stature. The Hermitage Museum regards him as a highly accomplished practitioner: "In the early 18th century, objects decorated with ivory became very popular in Russia. Turnery workshops were established at many European courts, where monarchs would pass their hours in simple pursuits, mastering various crafts. From the early 1720s Peter's 'Turnery Shop' was renowned as one of the best of the royal turneries." There are eleven lathes from Peter's workshops in the collection at the Hermitage, which also has "ivory objects made wholly or partly by Peter." An inventory of his lathe-turned productions, posted on the "Ornamental Turning" website, mentions goblets, candlesticks, measuring instruments, sundials, openwork pyramids with polygonal stars inside, scepters, columns, and engraved snuffboxes; and the compiler points out that Peter's successors to the throne, Catherine I (Peter's widow), Peter II, Anna I, and Elisabeth, also "turned at the lathe."

The materials included in the historians' unspecific term "ivory" are various. Walrus ivory was the most readily available and is the only type specifically mentioned by Peter's biographers or by the Hermitage. It had been imported into Muscovy from Norway since the Viking era, and in Peter's time was coming to Moscow and St. Petersburg from the Russian North and Siberia, where Semyon Dezhnyov, who died the year Peter was born, had developed Russia's territorial claims and exploited the region as a source of walrus ivory. Remarkably, there were sufficient quantities of it on hand in 1699 for Russia to include 400 lbs. of walrus ivory among bribes to Turkish officials (Bain, 523). Elephant ivory, more costly, could certainly be obtained from Russia's Venetian allies against Sweden, as well as from traders in the Middle East. Additionally, fossilized mammoth ivory was comparatively plentiful and, as Lister & Bahn point out, "The art of mammoth-ivory carving has a long tradition in Russia — both Peter the Great and Catherine the Great pursued it as a hobby" (Lister & Bahn, 138). It may also be significant that Tsar Peter had his own "collection of extracted teeth" (Hughes, 236). The species are not named, but the collection likely included sperm whale teeth from stranded carcasses in Holland and (given the vagaries of anatomical terminology and morphological specificity at the time) likely included narwhal tusks as well the teeth of terrestrial animals.

[10] According to Mokeeva, the lathe was destroyed by fire in 1747 and was reconstructed just after the Soviet era, in 1993, based upon Nartov's manuscript record of 1755.

The Hermitage has, in addition to the candelabrum (in Room 156), twelve tumblers from Peter's "Turnery Shop" and an ivory snuff-box with a written provenance indicating that it "was turned by Peter I himself and presented to Countess Chernyshova" circa 1712-20. There are also crosses: "The centre of one of these crosses is ornamented with a circular slide of ivory on which the crucifixion, with the mourning women below, are carved in bas-relief. A multitude of rays issue from this slide as from a sun, every ray is turned in ebony, in the ornamenting of which, with all manner of carving, an enormous degree of labour must have been expended" (Kohl, 76). The Brandenberg Museum in Copenhagen is also said to have several boxes and "a pair of compasses in an ivory box made by Peter," as well as boxes made by Kings Frederick III and Frederick IV of Prussia (Harris, Op. cit.).

* **Pettegrow, —.** The tooth mentioned in the *Dictionary* in connection with this name was neither on exhibition at the time of writing, nor had it been published, and it could not be examined at first hand: the description and attribution were based entirely upon rudimentary catalogue reports from PMM, to which the piece had been an anonymous gift years before. In the *Dictionary* it is described as: "tooth with red-orange stain at the root and bright orange at the tip, featuring a portrait of a bark labeled 'Emerald,' and with a metallic inset engraved 'Pettegrow, Rock Land, Maine." Its recent publication in *Folk Art of Maine* (Kevin D. Murphy, ed., 2008, 119) makes it clear that the *Dictionary* description is erroneous on crucial points: the vessel depicted is not a *bark*, but a full-rigged *ship* that may or may not resemble one or more of the several whaleships named *Emerald*. There is evidently no "metallic inset" integral to the scrimshaw itself, but the ivory is carefully inscribed in serifed capital letters in a riband, "PETTEGROW / ROCK / LAND / MAINE." More significantly, however, what has escaped PMM and the editors and compilers of *Folk Art of Maine* is that on stylistic and iconographical grounds, it is abundantly clear that the scrimshaw is a modern, twentieth-century production — what is euphemistically called "late work": not antique, certainly not whalemen's work, and not connected with any actual firsthand experience of the whale fishery. Based upon characteristics of the lettering in the inscription, the Pettegrow piece is almost certainly by the same twentieth-century hand as the phony pair of Ceres A Artisan teeth offered for private sale in 1993 that were debunked in June 2007 at the Scrimshaw Collectors' Weekend (NBWM). Not surprisingly, no whaleman named Pettegrow has been turned up in Rockland, Maine.

Phillip, Lewis (fl. circa 1850s-1870s). Likely maker of a rare work of scrimshaw from the Honolulu-based pelagic whale fishery: a monochrome tooth with a circumferential sperm whaling scene around the base, including a whaleboat with oars expertly tossed and a brig cutting-in to larboard, flying the flag of the Kingdom of Hawaii from the spanker gaff (a British Union Flag in the canton with horizontal stripes in the fly), and boldly inscribed above with a name that seems to indicate the maker, "LEWIS PHILLIP" (Osona, 4 August 2007, #285, where it is erroneously but understandably identified as "a British whaler cutting-in.") American whaleships almost universally cut-in on the starboard side (in the mid-nineteenth century, purpose-built Yankee whalers were constructed that way, with a gangway on the starboard side to accommodate a cutting stage). However, British, Australian, and Hawaiian vessels had no such standard and are known to have cut-in either to starboard or to larboard; and the brig rig was the one most commonly employed by Honolulu-based whalers. No record of Lewis Philip or Phillip has been discovered, but it appears that the scrimshaw was indigenous to the comparatively small Honolulu-based pelagic whaling fleet in the third quarter of the nineteenth century and that the maker was likely a member of one of the Honolulu-based crews. (Despite Susan A. Lebo's conscientious, quite valuable work unearthing and publishing the surviving crew lists of these voyages, many of the crew lists appear not to have survived.) The majority of crew on these vessels were Native Hawaiians but many of the vessels themselves and a significant portion of the masters, officers, and "mechanics" (ship's coopers, carpenters, and blacksmiths) were German, and an even larger plurality American; and many mariners of both nationalities became naturalized Hawaiian subjects. Thus, the vaguely German surname (Phillip or Philip, rather than Phillips) is further suggestive. There were in fact several immigrants named Lewis Philip or Phillip from Baden, Saxony, Hesse Cassel, and other parts of Germany working as blacksmiths, carpenters, and coopers in various parts of the USA in the mid-nineteenth century, there were certainly men of that name (or Phillips) who were of American birth, and there may have been others in the Hawaiian Islands, but none has been identified as a whaleman or a ship's cooper, carpenter, or blacksmith.

Phillips, Harvey R.C. (fl. circa 1840-85.) In his shipboard journal as mate of the *Minerva* during 1859-60 he provides testimony that entire ship's companies — officers and crew — were sometimes simultaneously engaged in scrimshandering. Homeward bound in January 1860 he observes at one point, "every body Scrimpshonting as the term goes… that is makeing Caines & Corset boasks & getting out whale boan hoops for presenting for their wives & sweet hearts." He adds about himself, "I have been polishing shells," but never specifies for what purpose. He appears to have been a thoroughgoing whaleman and quintessential vagabond, never long a resident in one place, evidently never married, occasionally an officer, and still sailing as an Able Seaman at age 63. Whether through absence of pride, lack of skill, or limited opportunities, he did not progress in the usual fashion through the shipboard hierarchy, ascending from one berth to the next in gradual steps, but rather, during a career spanning about 45 years, he alternated up and down, apparently serving in whatever capacity presented itself and moving from ship to ship rather more than was common. Then long past the age when most whalemen had retired to farming, shopkeeping, or one of the trades, Phillips embarked on a second whaling career.

Phillips, who gave his full name as Harvey R.C. Phillips, was born in 1818 or 1819 at Taunton, Massachusetts, the son of Richard C. Phillips (who died when Harvey was an infant) and Ruth Phillips. A career mariner, Harvey lived variously at Dartmouth, Westport, Taunton, Marion, and New Bedford. When he married Harriet B. Dean of Taunton in 1846, for some reason the bans were published in Providence, Rhode Island. He did not come from the Phillips family of New Bedford merchants who were managing agents of whaleships and owned (among many other things) about a half interest in the bark *San Francisco*, and he was not the same Harvey Phillips who commanded the *San Francisco* on her first whaling voyage (1852-54). Harvey R.C. Phillips was a sailor in the *Abraham H. Howland* and the *Gladiator* at that time, as his journals (in KNB) certify. His whaling career began with a long string of conventional voyages in New Bedford vessels. He may have made his maiden voyage in the bark *Amanda* (1830-31), embarking at age 12, other youthful voyages are unknown, and the following list of his known voyages in New Bedford vessels is undoubtedly incomplete: ships *Honqua* (1841-43), in which he was third mate; *Israel* (1846-47) and *Mercury* (1848-51), second mate; *Abraham H. Howland* (1851-52), third mate; *Gladiator* (1853-), first mate; *Eliza Adams* and *Morea*, short passages in 1858; *Minerva* (1859-60), first mate; and *Empire* (1860-62), which was wrecked on the Chatham Islands. Then, after a few years ashore, beginning at the age of around 50 he made a kind of second career in whaling schooners out of Marion: at least three voyages in the *Admiral Blake* (1868-75), two in the *William Wilson* (1876-79), and another in the *Admiral Blake* (1882).

Phinney, Edward B. (f. circa 1844-69). Whaling master and possible maker of a double-cage swift with a whale skeletal bone shaft and ribs, and a cup finial turned out of whale ivory, "supported on a square stepped base of ebony, ebony veneer with inlaid abalone floral and geometric segments, and panbone veneer, surrounded with a pierced panbone gallery, the ivory and panbone engraved with undulating vine and berry borders heightened with red and green sealing wax inlaid in the scribe lines (Skinner, Nov. 8. 2009, lot #237). The family provenance evidently associates the swift with Cape Cod (his birthplace and residence) and with his voyage as captain of the New Bedford bark *Java 2d* (1860-64). This was the voyage on which J.F. Beane (q.v.) embarked as a green hand and which, in his narrative, *From Forecastle to Cabin* (1905), he conflates with the subsequent voyage of the *Java* under Captain Manuel Enos (q.v.), never mentioning Phinney at all. Phinney had previously been a boatsteerer (1847-50) and second mate (1850-53) in the New Bedford ship *Iris*, first mate on the ship *Lapwing* (1853-56), and captain of the bark *Europa* (1856-60), and was afterwards captain of the bark *Desdemona* (1865-69).

He was born in 1826 in Falmouth, on Cape Cod, the son of Braddock Phinney and the former Mary "Polly" Bradford. He married Mariah H. Briggs of Dartmouth, Massachusetts, in February 1847, a few months before sailing in the *Iris*. There was evidently no issue from this marriage and Mariah appears to have died within a couple of years, almost certainly while Edward was still at sea, as the 1850 U.S. Census lists him as a master mariner residing in Falmouth but makes no mention of Mariah; instead, he is reported living with Harriet A. Smalley and two children, aged seven and five, with the same surname — evidently Harriet's son and daughter. An 1855 census of Barnstable County is insufficiently detailed to provide further clarification, and Phinney is absent from the 1860 U.S. Census. He must have married shortly after this, as the 1870 U.S. Census lists him as a master mariner, aged 42 (sic), residing in Waquoit (part of Falmouth) with his second wife, Ellen, 30, born in England, their five-year-old son William, and a Lavinia Phinney, 63, who must have been a female relative; no mention is made of Caroline, a daughter born in 1866 who may not have survived to 1870. Captain Phinney retired to Waquoit, where he died in 1899.

Phyfe, John (fl. circa the 1840s). His full-page advertisement in the *New York City Directory* for 1843-44 declares him a "dealer in ivory, and manufacturer of ivory goods" in his "manufactory" at the "Sign of the Golden Elephant," 10 Murray Street in lower Manhattan. In addition to the usual run of goods (billiard balls, dominoes, card boxes, tablets, piano keys, etc.), he offers "scrivella ivory," by which is meant *scrivello*, referring to small elephant tusks; "sea-horse and whale teeth," by which he means walrus tusks and sperm whale teeth; and various kinds of hardwoods. The census describes him as an "Ivory Turner" and "Manufacturer," indicating that he actually made some or all of the merchandise himself. What portion of his wares were whale or walrus ivory is not known.

John Phyfe, Jr., was born in New York in 1798, established his ivory-turning business on Murray Street around 1820, and was married in 1822 to Jane M'Niesh, born in Scotland in 1800, with whom he had several children. He was granted a patent in 1856, for "a new and useful Improvement in the Process of Bleaching Ivory," involving a table and reflector apparatus intended to capture and focus sunlight (U.S. Patent Nº 15,983, Oct. 28, 1856). His listing in the 1857 edition of *Trow's New York City Directory* indicates that he was retired by that time. After he was widowed in 1863 he lived with one of his daughters until his death in 1872.

Pierce, Eben (fl. circa 1839-65). Originally trained as a ship's carpenter, he became a successful whaling master and merchant sea captain who invented, and in 1865 patented the *darting gun*, a revolutionary whaling apparatus that combined the functions of a harpoon, a conventional hand-wielded lance, and a bomb-lance. A 15-inch (38 cm) scale model of a darting gun mechanism (in NBWM), carved and assembled out of three pieces of sperm whale panbone, is attributed to Pierce himself by virtue of his known competence as a woodcarver and a provenance from Frank E. Brown, Pierce's nephew, partner, and successor, leading to the supposition that the model is a patent model prototype of circa 1865. Of the many patents awarded in the nineteenth century for improvements to whaling harpoons and lances, the darting gun was one of very few invented by a seasoned whaling master based upon actual practical experience in the field. Perhaps for that reason it is one of the few "improvements" that was demonstrably effective and became popular with whalemen. Its use was nicely described by Arthur C. Watson in 1924:

> *The gun is darted in the same manner as the ordinary harpoon. As the dart enters the body of the whale, the long rod or primer brings up against the animal's skin. This pressure on the primer sets off the charge in the gun, and the bomb is shot into the whale. The gun is then hauled back into the boat, but the dart, to which the heavy whale-line is fastened, remains in the whale.* (*Old Dartmouth Historical Sketches,* Nº 23)

In partnerships with Selmar Eggers and Frank Brown, Pierce also developed, patented, and manufactured improved shoulder guns and bomb-lances that were widely used by New Bedford whalemen at the time and, remarkably, remain in use today by Alaska Eskimos hunting under so-called Subsistence Whaling Licenses from the International Whaling Commission. Accordingly, Pierce darting guns, shoulder guns, and bomb lances are still being produced in conformity with Pierce's original nineteenth-century patents (manufactured in Pennsylvania by the Naval Co., legitimate successors to Pierce and Brown).

The son of Eben [Ebenezer] and the former Charity Hines (or Hinds), Ebenezer, Jr., was born in Livermore, Maine, in 1817. At 14 he was apprenticed to ship's carpenters in a shipyard and at 21 he embarked on his first whaling voyage out of New Bedford, in the ship *America* (1838-40), after which his rise was meteoric. He was boatsteerer (1840-42) and second mate (1843-44) in the ship *Adeline,* first mate of the ship *General Pike* of New Bedford (1845-49) under his older brother, Captain Job Pierce (1810-1852), captain of the Fairhaven bark *Favorite* (1850-53), made a series of merchant voyages over the next twelve years, then returned to whaling as master of the New Bedford bark *James Allen* (1865-67). On the *James Allen* he field-tested his newly invented darting gun and afterwards went into the business of manufacturing darting guns and bomb lances in

New Bedford, with Selmer Eggers and nephew Frank E. Brown as partners in various aspects of production and sales. He died in 1903, by which time Frank Brown had taken over the business and his shop on Water Street in New Bedford had become a hangout for "the 'Spun Yarn Club,' a loose association of former whalemen, whaling masters, local tradesmen, and amateur whaling enthusiasts who, beginning in the 1890s, met [there] informally… to swap yarns and gossip about the old whaling days" (q.v. in *More Scrimshaw Artists*, Appendix III; and William H. Tripp, *There Goes Flukes*). Outside of whaling circles, especially in the yachting community, Pierce is best remembered for having given his derelict oyster sloop *Spray* to Joshua Slocum in 1892 for what became Slocum's single-handed tour de force, narrated in his *Sailing Alone Around the World* (1899). References: *Our County and its People: A descriptive and biographical history of Bristol County, Massachusetts* (1899).

Pikonganna, Aloysius [AKA Pikkunana] (fl. 1920s-80s). Inupiaq Eskimo elder from King Island, Alaska, well known locally as an ivory carver, storyteller, and traditional drummer. As a scrimshaw artist he may be described as a latter-day adherent of the Nome School of Happy Jack and Billy Komoneseok, producing cribbage boards (primarily) and other conventional walrus ivory carvings. His cribbage boards, each characteristically made from a whole tusk, typically feature engraved scenes of traditional Native hunting and fishing, surmounted by full-round-carved animal figures. Some have "fences" or "railings" of the type popularized by the early-twentieth century Nome School pioneers, and at least one has the standard map of the Alaska seacoast from Big Diomede to Unalakleet — including Nome and St. Michaels — in the manner of Billy Komoneseok. Another terminates at one end in a full-round-carved head of a polar bear, with bold red and black highlights, of the type frequently encountered as the ivory finial on an oosik, which is the kind of thing he may also have produced and which has elsewhere been adapted for salt shakers, letter openers, and other souvenir items. Pikonganna certainly produced walrus ivory letter openers himself, with animal carvings on the ends. Many of his works are signed; some are not. He was a traditional hunter, fisherman, and community leader, active in King Island cultural affairs. "In April 1976, KNOM [a Nome radio station] reported that King Island elder Aloysius Pikonganna, crabbing two miles from shore on the ocean ice, bagged 92 crabs in five hours," which was apparently a local record (KNOM online). According to reviewer Cortland Pell Auser, as one of four Native informant-spokespeople for the book *Ugiuvangmiut Quliapyuit. King Island Tales: Eskimo History and Legends from Bering Strait* (Laurence D. Kaplan, ed., 1988), Pikonganna "speaks of kayak hunting, warming houses with oil when no stoves were to be had, and trading skins and furs on the mainland." He was born in 1909 and died at Nome in 1986. His wife was Clothilde Pikonganna (1905-1983).

Pittman, Edward C. (fl. circa 1861-65). Whaleman of Cincinnati, Ohio. A baby rattle that was evidently originally accompanied by a lock of the infant recipient's hair is described as having a walrus ivory handle carved as a whistle and "decorated with pierced designs, incised lines and having a threaded cap with a ball finial." The provenance is based on "a handwritten note inside" asserting that the ensemble was a "Hair and rattle belonging to Marie Thompson Pittman Died 1865 — 6 months old." Sadly, little Marie did not live even long enough for her name to appear in any census; nor does it appear in the Pitman/Pittman family genealogies, and the provenance provides no specific clues as to which of the several whalemen named Pitman or Pittman who were active at that time may have made the scrimshaw. However, there was only one whaleman surnamed Pitman or Pittman known to have been active as such around that time; and as the scrimshaw surfaced in the unlikely venue of Cincinnati, where it was auctioned in 2005 (Cowan, Oct. 7-8, #777); and assuming that the provenance could be in error by a few months (e.g., that the baby could have been born in 1866), by far the most likely candidate is Edward C. Pittman (aka Pitman). He was born in Cincinnati circa 1840, his Protection Paper was issued at New Bedford in June 1862 listing Cincinnati as his residence, and his only known whaling voyage was as an ordinary seaman in the New Bedford ship *Janus* from July 1862 to October 1865. (Not to be confused with another Edward C. Pittman of Ohio, who had exactly the same name and was exactly the same age but was serving in the Union Army while the other Edward C. Pittman was at sea. At 21, in July 1861, Edward N° 2 enlisted as a private in Company H, 26th Ohio Infantry Regiment, and mustered out on 25 July 1864. While Edward C. Pittman the soldier was in the Union Army, Edward C. Pittman the sailor spent most of the Civil War years at sea on whaleships. Unfortunately, nothing further is known about either of the Edwards.)

Pope, Silas (fl. circa 1862-94). The provenance states that a rolling pin with a satinwood barrel and whale ivory handles, given to NBWM in 1935, was "Made at sea by Capt. Silas Pope." The donor was Mrs. John Ames Russell, née Maria Louisa Pope, Silas Pope's kid sister. She was five years younger than he, aged 83 in 1935. Her brother's only stint as commander of a whaleship was as a relief captain, succeeding Andrew R. Heyer on the 1886-90 voyage of the New Bedford bark *Palmetto*, but he was afterwards intermittently a captain-of-record in the merchant service and was first mate of the whaler *Platina* (where he was presumably poised to relieve Captain Thomas McKenzie) when he died at sea in 1894. He was born in 1847 at Dartmouth, Massachusetts, the son of Elihu Pope (1809-1895), blacksmith, and the former Rhoda Devol Taber (1819-1911). With one possible exception, his career was an unbroken sequence of New Bedford whaling ships and barks. His maiden voyage was in the *Three Brothers* (1865-69), followed by three consecutive voyages with Captain Gilbert B. Borden, as boatsteerer in the *Commodore Morris* (1870-73), third mate in the *Pacific* (1873-76), and second mate of the *Daniel Webster* (1879-80). He was next first mate of the *Bartholomew Gosnold* (1881-85), first mate and relief captain on the *Palmetto* (1886-90), and first mate of the *Mermaid* on a voyage on which they sailed from New Bedford but returned to San Francisco (1891-92), where the *Mermaid* was based from then on. But Pope himself returned to New Bedford.

Family and genealogical sources claim that Pope also sailed in the *Arctic* and the *Young Phenix*, but provide no further details. He is not named anywhere in the outward-bound crew lists of either vessel, which are complete during his lifetime. The only whaler named *Arctic* that was in service during Pope's lifetime was a ship of Fairhaven, built in 1850, wrecked and formally condemned in 1856, and withdrawn in 1861, when Pope was only about 14 years old and had not yet gone to sea. However, this same vessel later made eight short whaling forays from Honolulu during 1869-76, and if Pope sailed in her at all it would have been on one of these, squeezed in among his well documented string of deepwater voyages in New Bedford ships and barks. And given that unbroken sequence, he could not have made an entire voyage in the *Young Phenix*. If the family is right about this vessel he must have interrupted one of his other voyages as some kind of substitute and been aboard only temporarily.

Fig. 16. **Spencer Pratt** specialized in inlaid wooden boxes, each with distinctive inlay and probably a unique method by which the bottoms fit into a framework formed by the sides, but which are otherwise inadequately supported. At least four are known, one in the New Bedford Whaling Museum and three in private collections. Photo by Richard Donnelly, who first identified the artist.

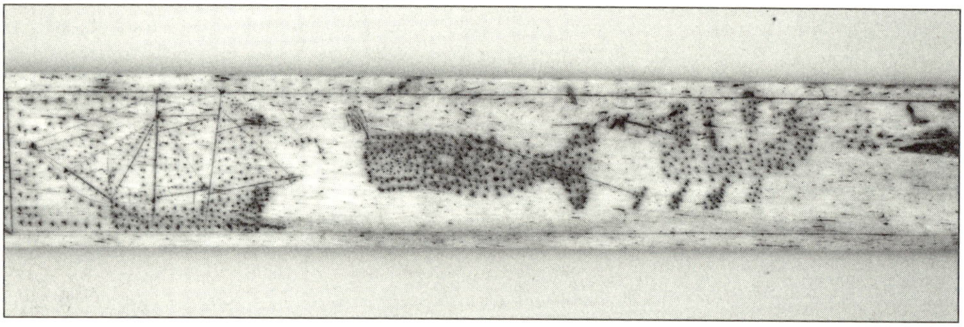

Fig. 17. **A landmark work in panbone by Alden Sears.** The earliest known pictorial scrimshaw on sperm whale byproducts is a busk or mangle by Alden Sears, produced in the late Colonial era. It has two stipple-engraved whaling vignettes and is boldly emblazoned with the name of the maker, who signed and dated it 1766. At that time sperm whale teeth were still regarded as a commodity and had not yet become available to the crew for their own pursuits, but skeletal bone was gradually being adopted as a favorite medium for whalemens' handiwork. Kendall Collection, New Bedford Whaling Museum.

Meanwhile, Pope lived with his parents in Acushnet until 1886 when, at age 39, he married Carrie D. Cushman. There is no record of children — hence, perhaps, the descent of the scrimshaw to the maker's sister (unless he made it for her in the first place). An unusually credible genealogical posting at Ancestry.com (which reads suspiciously like a newspaper obituary) claims that "Captain Pope was popular with his officers and men, a successful sperm whaleman and highly esteemed by all who knew him." According to the same source, "In the fall of 1893 he went to St. Helena where he joined the *Platina* as first mate. He became ill and died at sea on this voyage Feb. 8, 1894." After Carrie was widowed she worked a farm in Acushnet, where she had an elderly maiden aunt living with her.

Potter, Lemuel Milk (fl. 1846-63). New Bedford whaleman and whaling master from Dartmouth, Massachusetts, concerning whom a family history indicates that he was a scrimshaw-maker (reported by Tom Conley). He was born in Dartmouth in 1830, the son of Joshua Porter, farmer, and Deborah née White, served as a green hand in the ship *Benjamin Tucker* (1846-69), where his name was erroneously transcribed as Samuel M. Potter; boatsteerer in the same vessel on her next voyage (1849-51); third mate, ship *Alice Mandell* (1851-54); second mate, ship *Mary Ann* of Fairhaven (1854-58); and captain of one voyage in the *Mary Ann* (1858-63). He may have married around 1855 and been widowed shortly after, as Alden H. Potter, said to have been his son, was born circa 1856-57 but was living in Dartmouth with his Davis grandparents in the 1860s. Captain Potter registered for the draft in 1863 but evidently did not serve in the Civil War, and by 1868 he was married to the former Ann Maria Barker (1868-1955) of Dartmouth and had moved to Lafox, Illinois, where they raised a family. Meanwhile, Lemuel's younger brothers Alden Tillinghast Potter (b. 1832) and James Edwin Potter (b. 1837) were also whaling masters, Alden on three voyages (1862-75), James on two (1868-72). A family history associated with transcripts of Potter's journals of the *Alice Mandell* and *Mary Ann* (1851-58) declares that Potter "sang sailor songs with a twinkle in his eye" and "was interested in astronomy and worked at scrimshaw making swifts, rolling pins, cane heads, pie crust wheels, napkin holders and a fine wagon for [his son] Alden."

Pratt, Spencer (fl. circa 1825-55). Whaling master from Bristol, Rhode Island, credited with at least four inlaid wooden workboxes, dovetail-joined with hinged lids (attributed and reported by Richard Donnelly). One (in a private collection, with a provenance from Fall River, Massachusetts), size approximately 12 x 14 x 7 inches (30.5 x 35.6 x 18 cm), is inlaid on the top, front, and sides with mother-of-pearl and abalone stars, diamonds, circles, semicircles, bent hearts, teardrops, distinctive potted plants with flowering leafy branches, a double-heart-shaped escutcheon of mother-of-pearl, and straight borders of skeletal bone and wood (with distinctive T-shaped, rather than L-shaped corners); it has pendant ring handles of whale ivory; and centered on the top is a rectangular plaque of whale ivory, inlaid and framed with wood inlay, with a center rectangle of wood inlaid with the white metal initials "S.A.W.P." — the linchpin of the attribution, as these could only refer to Pratt's wife, Sarah Ann West Pratt. A box in KNB is confidently attributed on stylistic criteria premised on the preceding. It is slightly smaller in each dimension, has very similar motifs and borders inlaid in mother-of-pearl and wood, with the definitive potted plants (having slightly different rims on the pots), distinctive T-shaped corners, ring handles, a strikingly similar escutcheon, and a blank plaque inlaid on the top. An unusual feature of both boxes, thought to be characteristic, is that the bottoms were fastened with glue only — that is, without joinery, pegs, or other fasteners or supports. The first box has four ball feet; the other has had the bottom reinforced with wood strips to compensate the inadequate joinery — a later repair for which purpose the feet (if there were any to begin with) would have been removed. Two other boxes have also been located in private collections, including one that descended in the family of fellow Rhode Islander George M. Coit (q.v.) which has strikingly similar features and may have been made by Pratt rather than Coit.

Spencer Pratt was born in 1808 at Bristol, Rhode Island, the son of Stephen and Lavinia Pratt, and is presumed to have made his youthful voyages in Rhode Island vessels. In 1834, shortly after he completed a whaling voyage as second mate, he married Sarah Ann West, daughter of Jonathan and Sally H. West of Pawtucket, Rhode Island. A few weeks later he sailed as first mate of the ship *Mechanic* of Newport, Rhode Island (1834-38), the same Pacific Ocean voyage from which come the famous scrimshaw teeth by the so-called *Mechanic* Artisan (q.v. in the *Dictionary*), whose identity among the ship's company has not yet been discovered. It seems possible that the artist may have been Pratt himself, but the only evidence on either side of the issue is that Pratt made scrimshaw boxes — which is hardly sufficient proof.

A short-term member of the *Mechanic*'s company on this voyage was Paul Cuffe, Jr., son of whaleman, boatbuilder and merchant Paul Cuffe (1759-1817) of Westport, Massachusetts, who was in turn the son of a former slave who had purchased his own freedom, and a Native American mother. Thus, Paul Cuffe, Sr., became America's first African-American capitalist entrepreneur *and* America's first Native American capitalist entrepreneur. Paul, Jr. (born 1796), was at sea on whaling and merchant voyages from the age of ten, was captured and imprisoned by the British during the War of 1812, and shortly after whaling in the *Mechanic* wrote an autobiography that is now regarded as a classic (*Narrative of the life and adventures of Paul Cuffe, a Pequot Indian: during thirty years spent at sea, and in travelling in foreign lands,* 1839.) He joined the *Mechanic* voyage in progress at Paita, Peru, in 1836, stayed aboard a few months, and left the ship at the Society Islands.

While no comprehensive crew list of the *Mechanic* voyage is known to survive, the original captain, Henry Daggett, mentions "Mr. Pratt" and "Spencer Pratt" three times in his account book, in 1835 and 1837. Daggett later left the ship and was succeeded by a relief captain, Edward Harding; and Spencer Pratt was the captain on the *Mechanic*'s next two voyages, both to the Pacific (1838-42 and 1842-46). On the first of these, in 1841, the commander of the U.S. Frigate *Constitution* routinely boarded the ship at or near Talcahuano, Peru, and for reasons unknown identified the ship as being from Maine: "21 Feb 1841. Boarded US whaler *Mechanic* of Portland (Capt. Spencer Pratt), 30 months out with 1900 barrels of oil aboard" (USS *Constitution* Log, National Archives). Pratt seems to have retired temporarily after his second voyage in the *Mechanic,* but may have skippered the Nantucket schooner *Laura* on an Atlantic Ocean whaling voyage in 1848. He came out of retirement again a few years later to command the bark *D.M. Hall* of Fall River (sailed October 1853), and oversaw the sale of the vessel at Papeete, Tahiti, in 1855. At this point he appears to have retired permanently. His wife, Sarah, died in 1860 at age 47, with no issue from the marriage. after which Spencer lived or boarded with John, Mary, and Charles A. Coggeshall in Cranston, Rhode Island. Deteriorating mental health, diagnosed as "softening of the brain," resulted in his being declared *non compos mentis* in February 1868, whence he was placed in the care of his sister Betsey and her husband John N. Miller of Bristol, Rhode Island. He died soon after, in March 1868. According to his obituary in the *Bristol Phenix,* "He was a man of correct habits and a very enterprising and successful shipmaster" who left "no family and we believe no near relatives except one sister [Betsey]." Interestingly, when sister Betsey's estate was probated in 1880, the executor of her will was John S. Coggeshall, and among the items inventoried, but not further described, was "One Swift and Box" valued at $2.00.

Pugh, William (fl. circa 1865-70). An uncorroborated provenance, controversial in most of its details, credits a William Pugh with the scrimshaw ornaments on a factory-made viola. The top is inlaid with two ebony lozenges enclosing Masonic symbols, and the shoulders are overlaid with ebony, relief-carved in a leaf motif; the fingerboard (which the informant calls the "handle") is reportedly inlaid with abalone, whale ivory, and bone, and is engraved with an anchor device inscribed "Orion / 1865"; it has a unique, oversize nut of whale ivory engraved with the image of a full-rigged ship under plain sail, a bone tailpiece engraved with a roosting songbird, and a unique bridge consisting of a circular platform of whale ivory carved in the form of a belt and ornamented with two engraved silhouette profiles of whales; this platform rests on the top, encircling and supporting a bone bridge (privately held, sold on eBay, March 2007). A label inside the instrument indicates that it was manufactured by John G. Murdoch & Co. of London and Maidstone (England). The ebony overlay, ivory nut, and elaborate bridge platform are eccentric and give the appearance of dampening the sound quality. A typescript provenance declares: "Old viola made by William Pugh on board a ship about 1870 [sic]. Given to his son, Richard Pugh as a gift when he arrived at port after a year[']s absence. Given to me this day, Oct. 1, 1930 by Richard Pugh, my grandfather, at New Bedford./ Mrs. A.C. Hayes." There are also four additional documents that pertain to the family provenance: a small, handwritten booklet with various short essays, entitled "Men I Admire"; and three letters of recommendation for an Albert Hayes, all dated at Austin, Minnesota, on Oct. 14, 1899, including a handwritten one by an employee of the F.H. McCulloch Printing Co., and a typescript one from Rev. Edward F. Wheeler of the First Congregational Church.

In standpoint of methods and materials the piece would appear to be whalemen's scrimshaw, with respect to which the provenance is problematic in several particulars. First, the ship *Orion* in "the last third of the 19th century": The *Orion* of London, a Dutch-built prize of war taken in 1803, was whaling only until 1827, then disappears from view; the brig *Orion* of Rochester, Massachusetts, ended her career in 1840; the ship *Orion* of Nantes (France) was in service only until circa 1842; and the *Orion* of Nantucket was sold off to the merchant trades at San Francisco in 1850. The *Orion* of Hull, Yorkshire, went into service in 1850, but was whaling on the Greenland, Davis Strait, and Hudson Bay grounds, where scrimshaw was not much of a factor; no further record of her after 1850 has been discovered, and Hull continued whaling only until 1868. *Lloyd's Register* reports several vessels named *Orion* in 1865, none of them whalers (the *Orion* of Hull is not among them). If the scrimshaw is connected with a vessel named *Orion* in 1865, it must have been a merchantman, as yet unidentified. The instrument is British-made; however, there is no evidence addressing whether the putative scrimshaw-maker William Pugh was British or American (though his descendants clearly were living in America). There were two British whaling captains named Pugh. One was a D. Pugh, master of the *Nereiad* of London during 1826-27, for whom no subsequent voyage are recorded. The other, whose given name is not indicated in the records, commanded the brand-new ship *Foam* of London (303 tons, built at Newport in 1845) on a South Seas whaling voyage, departing London in June 1846, but with no further record. The surname Pugh does not appear in any other connection with the London whaling trade, including among the owners, masters, and harpooners. Men named Pugh in the American whale fishery were remarkably few. The only candidate from New London is a man named Henry whose surname *may* have been Pugh, age 30, born in one of the many places named Hanover (Massachusetts? Germany?), a resident of New London, served in the crew of the New London ship *General Scott* (1851-54). And only two ever sailed from the New Bedford Port District. One was a John Pugh of New York, who went in the New Bedford schooner *Petrel* (1867-68). The other was a Richard Pugh, who was a green hand for the 1/175th lay in the ship *Franklin* of New Bedford during 1853-57. Nothing further is known about this Richard Pugh, and while a search of crew lists and Protection Papers for ports other than New Bedford and New London has not been exhaustive, no trace of a William Pugh has been discovered on any American whaling vessel. (Just for good measure, regarding the names A.C. and Albert Hayes or Hayes, there was only one: Albert Hays from Springfield, Massachusetts, age 23, who was issued a Protection Paper at New Bedford in June 1851 but no voyages are recorded.)

Quaresma, Manuel Rodrigues, Jr. (1905-1982). Manager and associate director of the Estrela Lajense Whaling Company at Lajes do Pico, Azores, and "an expert in fine turning of whale ivory," including liqueur sets and pens with ivory nibs, both in vogue at the time (reported by Gomes Vieira, 2003, 177f). The son of Manuel Rodrigues Quaresma and Maria do Espírito Santo Quaresma, he was especially known for skillfully carved chess sets but also executed commissions to produce official gifts for visiting dignitaries, made at least one rosary with ivory beads, "a small model of a windmill complete with all the mechanism and cog-wheels, with sails in fine jawbone," and is credited with a sperm whale tooth carved in low relief in the form of an acanthus leaf. Gomes Vieira notes that Quaresma "was awarded a gold medal at an exhibition in Paris promoted by the Trade Council of Horta," but includes no specifics and reports nothing further about Quaresma's family circumstances. José Francisco Fidalgo Baptista (q.v.) was a fellow whaling-station manager at Lajes do Pico.

Reardon, H.S. (fl. circa the 1840s-'50s). A tooth engraved with a standing fashion-plate-like female figure on each side has the name "H.S. Reardon" beautifully engraved on one side (reported by Gordon Stanley from a commercial source which claimed it had come from an estate in Pennsylvania). Reardon's given name, age, residence, and voyages (if any) have not been discovered, and it is not known whether H.S. Reardon was the artist or the recipient of the scrimshaw. He was originally claimed to have been a sailor in the crew of the New Bedford bark *Marion* (1843-46), with his name listed in the ship's articles as H.S. Reardon and rated Ordinary Seaman for the 1/145th lay, indicating that it was probably not his first time in a whaling crew (that is, he had likely made at least one previous voyage, as a green hand). However, all of that appears to be erroneous. The only whaleship named *Marion* was not built until 1855 and commenced her first whaling voyage in that year. The vessel in question was actually the bark *Maria* of New Bedford, which was whaling in the Indian Ocean under Joshua Coffin during 1843-46. The only Reardon on board was *John* Reardon, Ordinary Seaman, for the 1/145th lay. This man's next voyage was in the ship *Leonidas* of Fairhaven under Captain John H. Tatch (1846-49). Perhaps John Reardon was the maker and H.S. Reardon the recipient. However, there were also five or six other men named Reardon or Riordon whaling out of New Bedford and New London in the 1850s and '60s, none of them with the initials H.S., none known to be from Pennsylvania, and none known to be connected with an H.S. Reardon. In any case, if H.S. Reardon was the intended recipient, chances are good that the maker had a different surname.

Reardon, John (fl. circa 1840-49). Possible engraver of a fashion-plate tooth bearing the name "H.S. Reardon" (q.v.). He was a seaman in the bark *Maria* of New Bedford (1843-46), the ship *Leonidas* of Fairhaven (1846-49), and probably at least one earlier whaling voyage, circa 1840.

Reed, John L. (fl. circa 1850-81). A career whaleman, professional first mate, and one of an extended clan of whalemen and scrimshaw artists comprised of four brothers and two brothers-in-law, he is credited with a variety of small but significant objects (chiefly sewing implements) made out of whale ivory, skeletal bone, and walrus ivory. In every instance, the provenance is impeccable. A whale ivory tatting shuttle by his hand was donated to NBWM in 1944 by John L. Reed's daughter, Mrs. Winnifred Reed Durfee, together with papers pertaining to Reed's stint as first mate of the bark *Eliza* of New Bedford during 1874-76 (the voyage on which she presumed Reed did the scrimshaw). It has faded polychrome engraving on both sides, depicting a thick branch with small leaves, and a single brass rivet intended to prevent the cheeks from rotating too freely. A handful of other objects arrived in 2008, the gift of Mrs. Durfee's daughter (John L. Reed's granddaughter), Mrs. Winifred Durfee Dimock (the two Winifreds spelled their names differently). These include handsomely crafted whale ivory and bone bodkins and tampers, and two walrus ivory tatting shuttles — one normal size, the other almost four times the average mass — both of them magnificently polychrome engraved with a vine-and-berry motif, and both bearing the fancily engraved initials "RCR."

John L. Reed was the youngest of four whaling brothers from Dartmouth, Massachusetts. The eldest, Wilson Reed (born circa 1826), was steward, then cook in the New Bedford bark *Bramin* (1844-45), followed by a voyage as seaman in the Fairhaven ship *Martha* (1845-48). Isaac M. Reed, two years younger, was cabin boy in the ship *Mercury* (1844-48) and seaman in the infamously badly constructed ship *Phocion* (1849-52). (This Isaac Reed is not to be confused with Isaac G. Reed of Westport, Massachusetts, who was a whaleship officer from the 1840s through the 1860s.) Israel Reed (born circa 1833) served as cabin boy in the ship *Minerva Smyth* (1848-52), seaman and boatsteerer in the ships *Triton* (1854-58) and *Black Eagle* (1862-63), then third mate and second mate on successive voyages of the bark *Morning Star* (1864-65 and 1866-67). John, born in 1836, was the only one of the brothers to rise as high as first mate. He was a green hand (1852-55) and boatsteerer (1855-59) in the bark *Isabella*, later (presumably after another couple of voyages) second mate in the bark *John Dawson* (1867-70) and first mate in the bark *Osceola* (sailed 1870). When that voyage ended in 1872 with the vessel being condemned at Mahe, Seychelles Islands, Reed was obliged to make a second voyage as mate — the one in the *Eliza* on which at least one of the tatting shuttles was ostensibly made (1874-76). That voyage was one of the longest on record: the *Eliza* sailed from New Bedford for the Pacific under Captain John M. Dimond in May of 1874 and did not return until November of 1882, fully *eight and one-half years later*. Perhaps needless to say, the officers and crew turned over several times in the meanwhile. Reed served as first mate on the outward passage and for about two years on the whaling grounds, then left the ship under honorable circumstances in 1876. At age 42 he shipped again in the New Bedford bark *Mars* (1878-81), and he may have been the same John Reed who made several voyages in the bark *Abraham Barker* out of San Francisco during 1881-88. In the meantime, Reed married Clarinda D. Blossom (born circa 1840), one of the two sisters of whaling captain Benjamin C. Blossom (q.v. in the *Dictionary*). The other, older sister, Alice Ann Blossom, was married to whaling captain John C. Haskins, master of the bark *Cossack* (1857-61) and relief captain of the ship *John Howland* (circa 1861-63). In the 1860s and '70s they all lived together — the bachelor captain Benjamin Blossom, John and Alice Haskins, and John and Clarinda Reed — on the Blossom family farm with their parents (and parents-in-law), Benjamin and Sarah Blossom. There was no issue from John and Clarinda Reed's union. By 1880 they were living in their own place in Dartmouth and had taken a boarder, a young teacher named Lizzie Ryder, who would have been good company for Clarinda if John was indeed whaling out in California. He was widowed a few years later, and in 1900, at age 64, he was living on his own, with one servant, on a farm in Dartmouth. But he was remarried soon after, to Hannah Macomber, a teenager 47 years his junior. She bore him three children, of whom the oldest, Winnifred, born in 1902, inherited the scrimshaw. In 1910 Reed was working as a gardener, and — together with his wife and children — Hannah's brother Arthur Macomber was living with them and working the farm. Reed died the following year.

Reynard, Owen (fl. circa 1826-48). New Bedford whaling master who certainly owned and used, and is credited with having made himself, a mahogany shaving box inlaid with wood and mother-of-pearl; in NBWM, donated by a descendant, Lucy Reynard Thornton, in 1951. The top and sides are inlaid with geometric and five-pointed star motifs in wood, skeletal bone, and mother-of-pearl; the drawer pulls and pendant loop handles are whale ivory; and the top is inset with a mother-of-pearl plaque engraved with the initials "OR." However, the most distinctive feature is an adjustable shaving mirror in a wooden frame set into the underside of the lid on brass hinges. When the hinged lid is open, the mirror swings down and rests on a wooden platform, which is covered with dark green velvet and mortised into grooves along the sides of the box: thus supported, the mirror can be angled to facilitate shaving. Whether or not Captain Reynard made it himself is not known for sure, but even if he did there are not likely other extant pieces by his hand. Though he rose rapidly through the ranks of the whale fishery and commanded three voyages, he died young. He was born in 1814 in New Bedford, the son of merchant sea captain John Reynard and his wife Mary, who were the parents of three whaling masters and the grandparents of a fourth. William Hathaway Reynard, their eldest, skippered three voyages during 1835-49; so too Owen, during 1838-48. The third son, Robert, was master of five voyages during 1842-59; and William's son, William Junior (q.v.), commanded a Westport schooner on one whaling voyage (1877-78). Owen went to sea at the uncommonly early age of 12 and made two successive voyages in the New Bedford ship *Young Phenix* (1826-29 and 1830-33). He made captain at the uncommonly early age of 24 and married Lydia (or Lucy) Hadley of Rochester, Massachusetts, the same year. Following his first command — the ship *Amethyst* of New Bedford (1838-40) — he was master of two voyages in the ship *Lalla Rookh* of New Bedford (1840-44 and 1844-48), but died soon after, in 1848.

Reynard, William Hathaway, Jr. (fl. circa 1860-78). In his journal as fourth mate in the bark *Pacific* of New Bedford in 1865, he described himself and other members of the ship's company engaged in preparations for making scrimshaw: On Friday, July 20th, "Broke out meat & Whales teet[h] and divided the teeth among all hands"; and on the next day, "myself & a few others were standing at the vice bench cleaning whale teeth" (reported by Sanford Moss). The journal also contains two sensational pencil drawings of human figures — one realistic, the other caricature-like — which not only demonstrate that the young man had some formal training, but also indicate that he was certainly capable of producing first-rate pictorial scrimshaw. Unfortunately, none of it has been identified.

Reynard was born into a prominent New Bedford whaling dynasty in 1844. His grandfather, John Reynard, born in England, was a merchant sea captain working out of New Bedford and a sometime POW in the War if 1812; his mother was the former Emily Howland Russell, descendant of several of New Bedford's founding families; his father, Captain William Hathaway Reynard (1808-1879), was master of three whaling voyages (1835-49), became a prominent ship owner and managing agent, was later the captain of merchant vessels, including the famous clipper ship *Flying Cloud*, and served as a New Bedford alderman and member of the Massachusetts state legislature; his uncle Owen (q.v.) was the captain of three whaling voyages (1838-48); his uncle Robert commanded five (1842-59). William Junior went to sea with his father "when a small boy," attended school at the Friends Academy in New Bedford, and at age 15 shipped before the mast in the whaleship *Scotland* of New Bedford (1860). Not all of his voyages are known, but he was a junior mate in the whaling bark *Orray Taft* of New Bedford (1869-72), first mate of the schooner *Thomas Hunt* on a sealing voyage out of Stonington, Connecticut, then master of the whaling schooner *Union* of Westport (1877-78), and was evidently a merchant sea captain for a few years (1878-85) before becoming a real estate agent in New Bedford. In 1886 he married Martha J. Robinson, a native of Cedar Rapids, Iowa. They moved to Padanaram in South Dartmouth in 1893, spending winters in Florida or California; and they had a son, who died in early childhood, and a daughter, concerning whom there is no report. (Partial source: W.W. Crapo, *Representative Men of Southeastern Massachusetts*, Chicago, 1912, 919f.)

Reynolds, Herbert R. (fl. circa 1876-1905). He was a career whaleman from Maine who lived at Brockton, Massachusetts, and punctuated his sea voyages with long intervals ashore, where he worked in a shoe factory. He is one of the men described in the book *Scrimshaw and Sudden Death* as making scrimshaw aboard the bark *Canton* on a whaling voyage out of New Bedford during 1899-1900. Captain William I. Shockley was working on a panbone swift; Lester A. Mosher, the boatsteerer on whose journal the published narrative is supposedly based, was producing chock pins for his whaleboat; and the mates are said to have been making "bone canes worked to look like rope or bamboo, with handles of sperm teeth carved into sailor knots, swan necks, crowns, and bird's heads." Thanks to the ghostwriter's unaccountable effort to mask the identities of most of the officers and all of the crew, the names in the book are a jumble and most of the men are not identifiable. Reynolds, named as the second mate in the book, was actually one of the boatsteerers; and whatever the confusion of names and ranks in the book, he may be presumed to have been one of the men making canes.

The details of his biography remain somewhat vague. He was born at Hartford, Maine, sometime between 1851 and 1855. His first known voyage was in the New Bedford bark *Cleone*, which sailed in 1876 and was lost in St. Lawrence Bay in the Western Arctic in 1879. The ship's articles list his birthplace as "Hartford" and his age as 25 in 1876. After the shipwreck, which may have discouraged him from making another whaling voyage right away, he moved in with his brother in Brockton, Massachusetts, and got a job as a shoe laster in one of that city's many leather-goods factories. He maintained his Brockton address even after he returned to whaling at age about 30, when he became a kind of perpetual boatsteerer on an uninterrupted series of voyages spanning the next ten years. He made one voyage out of New Bedford in the *Canton* (1883-86), then six in San Francisco barks: *Young Phenix* (1886), *Lucretia* (an auxiliary steam-bark; 1886-87), *Belvedere* (1887-88), *Lagoda*, on which he was fourth mate (1889-90), *William Baylies* (1892-1893), on which he was a boatsteerer again, and *California* (1893-1894). Then came an unexplained hiatus of about five years, after which he resumed whaling on two successive voyages in the *Canton* (1899-1900 and 1900-01), the first as boatsteerer and the second as third mate. His next berth was as boatsteerer in the bark *Kathleen* (1901-02), the fateful voyage on which the *Kathleen* was stove and sunk by a sperm whale (see the article on Joseph K. Green, who was first mate of the *Kathleen* on that voyage). There was another whaleman named Herbert Reynolds who was active at around this time who had been as a boatsteerer on the previous voyage of the *Kathleen*, and there has therefore been some confusion about which of the two was a boatsteerer on the *Kathleen*'s famous final voyage. However, the ship's articles of the previous voyage describe the other Herbert Reynolds as a "Mulatto," while the crew list for the 1901-02 voyage states quite explicitly that the boatsteerer on that occasion was Herbert Reynolds from Hartford, Maine, 47 years old, standing 5 feet 6 inches tall, with grey eyes, light hair, and a white complexion. This time, a horrendous shipwreck evidently did not discourage Reynolds from further whaling, as he shipped out again right away in the New Bedford schooner *Era* (1903-05), commanded by the celebrated Captain George Comer (q.v. in the *Dictionary*). This turned out to be Reynolds's last voyage. The 1910 U.S. Census has him single and living alone at age 59 in Hartford, Maine, evidently retired, with no occupation — after which he disappears from view.

Reynolds, Richard C. (fl. circa 1839-48). In his journal of the New Bedford ship *Janus* in the 1840s (in KNB) he confesses to "scrimshoning" without providing any specifics. But his journals are even more significant for the firsthand insight they provide into the whaling trade, and the warnings they offer to young would-be mariners. Born at Freetown, Massachusetts, in 1822, Reynolds embarked on his first whaling voyage at age 17 in the ship *Draper* of New Bedford (1839-42). It was on his second outing, as a boatsteerer in the *Janus* (1842-44), that he wrote four original ballads in his journal. Two of them narrate aspects of whaling voyages in a tone not altogether pessimistic. The other two, despite certain obvious literary and orthographic shortcomings, are notable for their cautionary advice about the pitfalls of whaling. Those two are presented here without changes to syntax or spelling, just the way the sailor wrote them:

Address to Young Sailors

1. *Come now brother sailors a warning take*
I would have you quit rambling and the seas forsake
If you donte you will be ondone
And curse the day you first began

2. *I have followed it for several years*
Its often filled my eyes with tears
I have often said when I returned again
That [I] would quite forsake the main

3. *But hear i am now caught again*
And for tow years or more i must remain
A catching whales it is my toil
For New Bedford onyrs [owners] to have the oil

4. *In doing this it is no fun*
For in a hundred barrels i have nary one
I do not think that this is right
For we must shurely work day and night

5. *To think of this it does me greive*
By cheating sailors they do live
They are not satisfied with their one
But take it all and leave me none

6. *The janus is the ship that I am now in*
As fine a little ship as dose on the ocean swim
Our mate will call jack crosstrese
He is always a yelling when it blows a heavy breese

7. *As I am now to end my yarn*
The weather grows cold insted of warm
I hope you will look before you leap
And see what dangers poor sailors escape

Another composition, untitled, could have been called "The Sailors' Advance," as it is a kind of Seaman's Complaint about the owners' method of advancing a sailor a portion of his pay before a voyage, to be paid back with interest as a deduction from the sailor's wages — or, in the whale fishery, as a deduction from his the *lay*, or fractional share in the proceeds of the voyage, which is customarily paid at the conclusion of the voyage.The deepwater sailors' characteristic attitude about this was that he would be working "for free" for the first three or four months of a voyage to pay off the debt, a debt that was often incurred to purchase an outfit for sea at usurious prices from the owners themselves, or merely to pay for board and lodging until sailing day. (The stereotypical owners' expectation, only sometimes justified, was that the advance would be squandered on liquor and loose women until it was all gone.) Then, during the voyage, fees for wharfage and pilotage as the ship traveled from port to port, and for gauging the cargo of oil and bone, were deducted from the profits of the voyage, thus detracting from the sailor's final cut. In the various songs and informal rituals staged on shipboard to commemorate the day when the debt was finally considered paid, the "dead horse" is a symbol of the debt. On some vessels an actual straw-stuffed canvas effigy was ceremoniously dunked, burned, or hanged from the yardarm, usually to the strains of a raucous song known as the "Dead Horse Chantey." Reynolds's little ballad endeavors to summarize the whole process:

1. *Come all my jolly Sailors wough [who] ever you be*
I will sing you a song uppon the high sea
On board of the janus wheare singing is free
The sailors are happy on land or at Sea

2. *All you that are to New Bedford a stranger*
Look out very sharp or you will fall into danger
Fine yarns they will tell and lead you astray
And then ship you of[f] your debts for to pay

3. *A small sum when you start you have to pay*
But a dead horse is a drug on the 200 hundredth lay
It will so encreace [increase] while you are gorn [gone]
When you return their will be ten to one

4. *Tis wharfage gauges pilotage and all*
And when you do settle things they will have it all
They will then say this is the first voyage
Go again my lad and keep up good courage

Reynolds did not take his own advice, at least not right away. Instead, he followed the owners' preference that he "Go again… and keep up good courage" on another voyage, this time as third mate the same ship (1845-48), probably also returning to scrimshaw; and when Captain Walter Taber was discharged sick at San Francisco in November 1846, Reynolds may have been promoted to second mate in the shake-up that inevitably ensued. When he returned from that voyage in 1848 he did take his own advice and gave up whaling, making merchant voyages instead into the mid 1850s. He married Susanna Gifford and was thereafter a farmer and stone mason in Little Compton, Rhode Island.

Rich, Lemuel F. (fl. circa 1840-50). Carpenter and ship's carpenter from Maine, credited with having engraved a tooth that has a dense, highly detailed circumferential scene and a circumferential diamond border at the base (Northeast, 19-20 August 2006, #905; reportedly also illustrated in Milton Simpson, *Folk Erotica*, Scranton, 1994, 36 and 25). One side shows an amorous couple in a landscape, surmounted by a wreath of roses framing the inscription "Love," and with "Love / 1850" inscribed below. The other side has a domed building with a standing female figure in the middle ground, inscribed below in a cursive hand, "Engraved by L.F. Rich."

Lemuel Franklin Rich — who, remarkably, appears to have been the only man in New England with that surname and those initials at the time — was born in Maine, probably in or near Bangor circa 1817 (the vital records and census reports disagree by plus or minus about five years). He was a carpenter by trade, may have had a junior partner named James Pennington, and was married, had a family, and was widowed in Bangor before he went to sea and moved to the Boston area. The crew list of his one recorded whaling voyage, undertaken at age 23 in the New Bedford ship *America* (1840-42), gives his residence at that time as Charlestown, Massachusetts. The rest of his whaling and seafaring career, if any, remains a mystery, but it may have been his first wife, Ruth, for whom the scrimshaw tooth was intended and some later voyage on which it was made. In any case, around 1855 Rich, presumably now a widower, married a woman named Margaret, who was born in Ireland and eventually bore him five children. He worked as a carpenter in Boston in the 1850s and '60s, then, by 1870, in the town of Franklin, in Norfolk County south of Boston, where two of his four daughters were employed in one of the several straw hat factories in Franklin and Foxborough while his three other children attended school. By 1880 they had moved back to Boston, where he appears in the City Directory as Lemuel F. Rich, occupation carpenter, but the U.S. Census reports him under his middle name as Franklin Rich. He maintained a carpentry shop through the 1880s while the two eldest daughters were working in a "bleachery" in Boston, and the third daughter had a job described as "working in a slipper factory." In the Boston City Directory for 1890, Margaret is listed as a widow.

Ricketson, Charles B. (fl. circa 1865-1930). Steamboat and steamship captain from Fall River, Massachusetts, and Providence, Rhode Island, tentatively credited with an oval panbone box, two oval baleen boxes, and an inlaid wooden box with hinged lid (in NBWM). The sides and skirt of the baleen boxes are elaborately incised with geometric shapes and floral motifs; one is inscribed "A.E. Ricketson" and is described in the provenance as a "needlepoint box" (not a common designation for such a scrimshaw object). It is presumed to have belonged to Abbie E. Ricketson (the only female A.E. Ricketson in New England who could plausibly have been the recipient), and to have been used by her for storing her needlepoint materials. It is accordingly attributed to her husband, Charles B. Ricketson, who is not known ever to have gone whaling, but who as a steamboat captain and sometime tugboat operator was closely associated with whaling people in southeastern New England. The other boxes, which are evidently by the same hand and were donated in the same lot at the same time (from the estate of Nathan C. Hathaway in 1923), are attributed on the basis of this explicit provenance. Charles B. Ricketson was born at Fall River in 1850 or 1851, the son of Sarah W. Ricketson and Master Mariner Charles L. Ricketson. There is no record of the father ever having gone whaling either, but the son was raised to be a mariner, went to sea in his teens, and worked in both sail and steam. In 1873 he married Abbie E. Dexter (born circa 1855, also known as Abby and Abigail), the daughter of a planer in a lumber mill at Bristol, Massachusetts. Captain Ricketson was based in Providence, where the couple raised three daughters, two of whom lived to maturity. He remained active even in semi-retirement at Rehoboth, Massachusetts, in his eighties.

Ricketson, John H. (fl. 1824-54). New Bedford whaleman and whaling master credited with a splendid commemorative tooth engraved while he was a boatsteerer aboard the ship *Timoleon* in 1835. The voyage itself was largely uneventful, beyond the usual hazards and occasional derring-do of sperm whaling in the Pacific; but it produced some remarkable scrimshaw. The classic Timoleon Tooth (in KNB) is signed by Josiah Sheffield, Jr. (q.v.) and beautifully inscribed, "June 1833 / Ship Timoleon / Joshua Bunker, Master, David B. Delano, Mate, Asa Hoxie 2d Mate, Ephm. Douglass 3d Mate" and "75 bbls. J. Sheffield Jr. Taken on West Coast Lat. 41. 30 N. Lon. 131.00 W"; three others by the same hand are known and several more are suspected. One of Sheffield's shipmates, boatsteerer John H. Ricketson, produced an analogous masterwork on the same voyage of the *Timoleon* (in NBWM). It has a starboard bow-quarter portrait of a full-rigged ship under sail on one side, and is inscribed on the other side with an abstract itinerary of the voyage: "SHIP-TIMOLEON / J. BUNKER MASTER SAILED FROM / NEW BEDFORD DEC. 25 1831"; below which, in tabular form, is inscribed (first column:) "PORTS / VISITED"; (second column:) "TIME OF / ANCHORING"; (third column:) "TIME OF / SAILING"; with the following tabular entries: [1] "PAYTA MAY 29 1832 JUNE 8" / [2] "JAMES ISL. JUNE 26 JUNE 30" / [3] "TUMBEZ OCT 23 NOV 4" / [4] "SANDWICH ISL MARCH 27 APRIL 16" / [5] "ST. BARBARA SEPT 19 SEPT 29" / [6] "TUMBEZ SANTOS OCT 3 OCT 9" / [7] "TURTLE BAY OCT 14 NOV 1" / [8] "SANDWICH ISL. APRIL 8 APRIL 24" / [9] "TODOS SANTOS OCT 5 1834 OCT 19" / [10] "TOMBEZ DEC 12 DEC 22" / [11] "HOOD ISL JAN 8 1835 JAN 14".

This was actually Ricketson's third or fourth consecutive voyage in the *Timoleon*. He was born at New Bedford circa 1807, the son of Charles Ricketson, merchant tailor, who took in John's older brother Henry as a partner in Charles Ricketson & Son. John likely apprenticed as a tailor for a while also, but at age 17, some years before he could have qualified as a full-fledged journeyman tailor, he went in the *Timoleon*, presumably rated green hand this first time out (1824-25). He likely made *Timoleon*'s next voyage (1826-28), when he would have been rated Ordinary Seaman, was definitely aboard on the voyage after that (1828-31), and was a boatsteerer on the 1831-35 voyage on which he and Sheffield did their scrimshaw. On Ricketson's first voyage Captain Charles Starbuck died at sea; on the third voyage the *Timoleon* was badly damaged in a storm while outward bound and had to return for repairs; and the fourth voyage was the first that was not primarily a right whaling voyage, but was exclusively devoted to sperm whaling. In other words, there was nothing remarkable about any of it, other than the scrimshaw, which is the outstanding feature of the *Timoleon*'s career. John Ricketson's career, on the other hand, appears to have been a bit bumpy. Only a short time after being a lowly boatsteerer in the *Timoleon* he was appointed captain of the New Bedford ship *Trident* (1838-42), and made a successful Pacific Ocean voyage for sperm whales; but then followed an unexplained hiatus of 20 months. He may have gotten married during this interval — his wife was Cynthia C. Ricketson — or suffered illness or family complications, but whatever the reason for his absence, he was not given another command right away, and when he returned to whaling it was on successive two voyages as first mate under Captain Elihu Russell in the barks *Emma* (1844-47) and *Peri* (1849-51), with an interval of 16 months between. He was then given another command of his own, the Westport bark *Janet* (1852-54), a moderately short voyage of 25 months of sperm whaling on the Atlantic that was only a modest success. With this he evidently retired and went into the grocery business in New Bedford, in which his wife Cynthia inevitably assisted. He appears also to have worked intermittently as a tailor in New Bedford, including a brief stint with Doane & Williams, merchant tailors, in the mid 1860s, and again in 1877. It is not entirely clear when he retired, for, grocer or no grocer, he continued to have himself listed in the City Directory as a master mariner until his death around 1885. (It is worth noting here that a much younger man named John H. Ricketson, born circa 1839, the son of farmers Benjamin and Lydia Ricketson, also went whaling for a while, was also a tailor in New Bedford, and also had a wife named Cynthia C. Ricketson. Of course, the *Timoleon* scrimshaw was produced before this John H. Rickson was born.)

Robinson, Fred W. (fl. circa 1876-88). A walking stick with a thick tapered redwood shaft, a large whale ivory knob pommel, and a disc separator that is possibly baleen (in NBWM), has a silver collar professionally engraved in a cursive hand, "Capt Warren Woods / Presented by / F. Robinson / Taken from the large Tree in California". The combination of a California association and the absence of other candidates strongly suggests that the maker was likely the only whaleman named F. Robinson known to have a connection with the Golden State: Fred W. Robinson, born in 1859 or 1860, probably at Chicago, was living in California and working as a whaleman from 1878 at least until 1888. The NBFPL index of whalemen indicates that he was in the crew of the bark *Charles W. Morgan* on the voyage of 1878-81, when the *Morgan* sailed from New Bedford and returned to San Francisco (which would remain her home port until 1906). However, Robinson's name is absent from the crew list for the 1878 voyage (Leavitt, 94f), which implies that he may have joined it at some port-of-call along the way, perhaps from the whaling brig *Heman Smith*, which sailed from Boston in May 1876 with an F. Robinson in the crew. This F. Robinson was 17 years old (thus was born circa 1859) and gave Cambridge, Massachusetts, as his residence at that time. Whatever his prior record, once Fred arrived in San Francisco he made several voyages under Captain George A. Smith in the bark *Abraham Barker* (1880-83) and probably two or three under Smith's relief captain and successor, John B. Tobey (1883-86). Robinson next followed Captain Smith onto the *Charles W. Morgan* when Smith took command (1886-87), at which time Fred's home town is listed as Chicago. He then rejoined Captain Tobey in the *Abraham Barker* (1887-88), after which he disappears from view. The only other candidates for attribution of the scrimshaw, far less likely, are a Francis Robinson who served as ship's boy in the New Bedford bark *Sea Breeze* and ship *William C. Nye* during the period 1853-57; and another Francis Robinson, born circa 1828 at Jaffrey, New Hampshire, who was cook in the barks *General Scott* of Fairhaven and *Marion* of New Bedford in the late 1850s. Warren Woods, named as the recipient of the stick, has not been identified. There was never a whaling captain of this name, and what he was captain of is not known. Sometime around the 1880s a Warren Woods who was born in California circa 1865 married Lily Pangburn (born 1865) of Suisun City, Solano County, not far from San Francisco, where Woods was a farmer and postmaster and where they were still living in 1930.

Robinson, J. (fl. circa 1845). Credited with a pair of teeth, each polychrome engraved on one side and mounted side-by-side on an indigenous wooden base relief-carved with leafy vines and stained black (reported by Sam McDowell). Featured on one is a starboard bow-quarter view of two full-rigged ships sailing in tandem, the foremost flying the British merchant red ensign. On the other is a larboard bow-quarter view of a bark sailing under plain sail, passing a headland that is almost certainly Mandly, on the north side of the entrance of the harbor of Sydney, New South Wales: this one also flies a merchant red ensign at the spanker as well as an illegible name pennant on the main, and is inscribed below, "WHALING BARGE LINDSEYS OF SYDNEY / LEAVING THE HEADS ON A CRUISE / 1845," and is signed "J. ROBINSON." The artist may reasonably be presumed to be Australian or Anglo-Australian but no actual information has come to light.

Robinson, Josiah, Jr. (fl. circa 1856-78). Whaleman and relief captain of Mattapoisett, Massachusetts, credited with an elaborately decorated rectangular wooden sewing box with hinged lid (in KNB). The top and sides are inlaid with whale ivory, abalone, and other woods in geometric patterns, vine motifs, flags, and a spread-eagle with a shield escutcheon; and with non-ferrous metal cutout letters forming the words "FRIENDSHIP'S OFFERING" and "OLIVIA", with floral and geometric trim. The inside lid has a 7 x 9-inch (18 x 23 cm) mirror, and a removable tray subdivided into seven compartments by wooden scroll work panels, one of which is a pincushion of calico and silk with a velvet button and lacy edging, and six of which have lids of multiple woods, abalone inlay, turned whale ivory button handles, and quarter-round banded moldings and supports of wood and sperm whale ivory. Found inside were a disc-shaped British paper of 36 pins, and a card with typescript provenance, "This box was made by Josiah Robinson when on a whaling voyage in ship [sic] Gen. Scott. 1860-1863." The *General Scott* was actually a bark of Fairhaven, commanded by James T. Eldridge (q.v.), a scrimshaw artist noted for an equally spectacular production. Josiah Robinson, Jr., of Rochester, Massachusetts, was third mate on the voyage (1860-65). "Olivia" was evidently the artist's older sister.

The NBPS crew list for the *General Scott* erroneously gives Robinson's age as 19, which would have made him something of a child prodigy as third mate. The age was probably copied directly from his Protection Paper issued at New Bedford in 1856, when he was in fact 19 and made his first voyage on an unknown vessel. He was born in 1837 at Rochester, the son and namesake of a miller who was originally from Harwich, Massachusetts. When he sailed in the *General Scott* he was actually about 23. He was afterwards mate on two voyages of the schooner *E.H. Hatfield* of Provincetown under Captain Charles F. Keith (1865-66 and 1867-68), then relieved captains Ichabod F. Hazard and Otis S. Snow as master of the bark *Cape Horn Pigeon* of Dartmouth (1872), and relieved captains Joseph D. Silva and Charles F. Keith as master of the New Bedford bark *Sarah* (1877-78). (His logbooks of the *Hatfield* and *Sarah* are in KNB.) He married Lucy J. Caswell, daughter of Elizabeth and Elbridge Caswell, a stonecutter in Mattapoisett, where they lived with Lucy's family for several years. His older brother Joseph, younger brother Benjamin, and brother-in-law George Caswell were also mariners. Joseph was later a boatbuilder in Mattapoisett, where brother-in-law Loring Caswell was a blacksmith. By 1880, after they had left off seafaring, Josiah and Benjamin were overseers and Lucy an Assistant Matron at the Massachusetts State Work House in Bridgewater. There is no record of children and no one named Olivia recorded in the family.

Rogers, Antone J. (fl. circa 1876-96). Cape Verdean career whaleman aboard New Bedford ships. From various whaling journals and such published narratives as Robert Cushman Murphy's *A Logbook for Grace*, it is clear that there were many whalemen from the Cape Verde Islands who were scrimshaw makers on American vessels — for example, João de Lomba (John Lomba), first mate on several voyages of the New Bedford brig *Daisy*, whom Murphy describes on the 1912-13 voyage as a "Homeric hero," and whose only known surviving scrimshaw is a stipple-engraved portrait on an elephant seal tooth in KNB. Antone J. Rogers is one of the few other men of Cape Verdean origin who are specifically named as having done some scrimshaw; however, no examples of his work have yet come to light. Equivocal records present various difficulties in trying to reconstruct his biography. He was one of several Portuguese-speaking whalemen and fishermen named Antone or Antonio Rogers living in New Bedford, Boston, and Gloucester: there was also an Azorean-born house carpenter named Antone J. Rogers who was approximately the same age and was active in New Bedford at exactly the same time. It is also clear that the U.S. Census records are not complete — less complete even than the New Bedford City Directories, which are nevertheless inconclusive. Concerning the whaleman Antone J. Rogers, all of his known voyages were from New Bedford, where the shipping records are specific about his birthplace, identity, and physical description, but are not consistent regarding his age. The various ship's articles are unanimous in describing him as 5 feet 6 inches tall, with a dark complexion, dark eyes, and dark hair. An annotation on the crew list for the bark *Stafford* in 1873 that his birthplace was "Buena Vista" is a common misnomer, deriving from a Spanish sensibility rather than a Portuguese; but it unequivocally denotes that Rogers was from the island of Bonavista in the Cape Verdes. (However, the crew list for the 1885 voyage of the *Greyhound* erroneously gives his birthplace as "Azores.") Inconsistencies in his stated age at the commencement of each of his five voyages provide no more specific an indication of his actual age than that he was born sometime between 1846 and 1853. The *Stafford* voyage (1873-76), commencing when he was ostensibly 22 years old, may have been his first; it is certainly the first known. This was followed by two voyages in the ship *Milton* (1876-80 and 1880-84) and one in the bark *Greyhound* (1885-87). He is likely also the man whose name is erroneously given as A.S. Rogers who served as first mate in the schooner *Eleanor B. Conwell* (1887-88); and he is surely the A.J. Rogers who, with his age recorded as 46, returned to whaling in an unknown capacity in the *Charles H. Hodgdon* (1894-96). Nothing has been discovered about his family life and later activities.

Rogers, George H. (fl. circa 1854-63). Avocational artist and scrimshaw artist in the Union Navy. A pair of porpoise jawbones engraved in polychrome on all four sides is inscribed "Lower jaw of porpoise — secured, polished and engraved by Geo H. Rogers in 1862 while in the Navy during the Civil War and while off the coast of Cuba cruising for blockade runners on board the U.S. Brig Bainbridge. / Ships of oak and hearts of steel / G.H.R."; and "G.H. Rogers native Newton Mass. / Enlisted in U.S. Navy Apr 1861 for term of three years as Apothecary" (Flayderman 1972, 8-9). After serving in the *Bainbridge* Rogers was a Pharmacist's Mate in the USS *Adela* on blockade service off the Florida coast during the winter of 1863. He produced sketches of both vessels (in USNH), on which the leftwards slant of the inscriptions, like those on his scrimshaw, exhibit strong holographic evidence that the artist was left handed. (He was not the same George H. Rogers who is listed in the 1865 New Bedford City Directory in Company E, 58th Massachusetts Volunteers,

Union Army: that man was a baker born circa 1844.) The navy pharamcist's mate who made pictures of the *Bainbridge* and *Adela* and inscribed the jawbones was born in 1838 and appears to have made at least one youthful whaling voyage out of New Bedford in the 1850s. This was possibly in the ship *John Wells* during 1854-57, or, more likely, in the bark *Morning Light* during 1856-59, but in either case it was as a green hand and was likely the occasion of his introduction to scrimshaw. He was probably a pharmacist's apprentice somewhere along the way, for not only was he a pharmacist's mate in the Union Navy, but after the war made his living as a druggist in Waltham, Massachusetts. He was twice married, in the 1860s to a woman named Grace, later to a woman named Ellen who accompanied him in retirement to California. He died at a very advanced age at San Diego in 1932.

Rogers, Jetur R. (fl. circa 1858-81). Long Island whaleman and master of one voyage, thus far credited with five scrimshaw items: an undistinguished panbone plaque; an unusual, possibly unique watch stand (watch hutch) of sperm whale ivory in the form of a miniature clock (with the name Jetur Rogers on verso); two pairs of bone knitting needles; and a classic oval panbone ditty box, nicely fastened (reported by Michael Gill and Nina Hellman). The hutch is especially intriguing, as it is carved out of a large tooth, and trimmed with ebony. Rogers was born in 1841 at Southampton, L.I., New York, the son of Albert Rogers and Cordelia née Halsey, the grandson of Herrick and Phebe Sayre Rogers, and Paul and Abigail Halsey, and evidently a nephew of Captain Jetur Rogers Rose of Southampton, who was captain of six whaling voyages from Sag Harbor and Nantucket (1850-71). After a generic rise through the ranks of the whale fishery, the younger namesake married Harriet E. Pierson in 1866, was captain of the bark *Stamboul* of New Bedford (1877-81), and afterwards lived on his brother-in-law's farm in Southampton with his wife and children. For 16 years (1899-1915) he was postmaster of the town and died sometime after 1915.

* **Rogers, Manuel J.** (fl. circa 1863-81). Whaleman of Cape Verdean birth or ancestry, who lived on Nantucket, sailed from New Bedford, and made a panbone ditty box and engraved a pair of teeth. The *Dictionary* mentions the ditty box, inscribed on the top in nail heads "*Manuel Rogers,*" in Sotheby's-NY 23 Jun 88, #115. At that time nothing was known about the artist. A pair of monochrome engraved teeth in KNB provide two additional clues from which the artist's identity becomes clear. One of the teeth has on one side a kind of whalemen's emblem: a whaleboat surmounted by a sheave block and an array of whalecraft (blubber hook, oars, harpoon, lance, and shoulder gun), with a larboard broadside view of a whaleship under sail, and the cursive inscription "Miss F. Rogers," surrounded by a leafy border. The other side is inscribed "Taken near / Juan Fernandez / Pacific Ocean 1881," with a compass rose and serpentine border. The second tooth, inside borders matching the first, has a whaleboat scene, poised to harpoon a whale, and is also inscribed "Miss F. Rogers"; the other side is inscribed "Bark / Mary & Susan / New Bedford." Incongruously, the whaleboat crew on the recto side is erroneously facing the bow — an error that one would not expect an experienced whaleman to make. However the scrimshaw is evidently genuine whalemen's work, and the probable attribution appears clear. Manuel F. Rogers was first mate of the bark *Mary and Susan* of New Bedford on a sperm-whaling voyage of 1877-81 commanded by Captain Edward E. Jennings. (Scrimshandering is typically a function of the latter part of a voyage, rather than the early part, for the obvious reason that, before scrimshaw-making can

commence, at least one whale has to be taken, to provide the raw materials; besides which, many captains discouraged the practice until some certain specified number of barrels of oil had been stowed or until the actual homeward passage. Thus, it is far more likely that any scrimshaw from the *Mary and Susan* that is dated 1881 was made on the voyage that *ended* in 1881, rather than the voyage that *began* in 1881. In this case it is a certainty. On the next voyage of the *Mary and Susan*, 1881-82, no one named Rogers was aboard, and it was purely an Arctic bowhead whaling cruise on which no sperm whales were taken; thus, the teeth and panbone for scrimshaw likely would not have been generated on the 1881-82 voyage.) The presumption is that Rogers made the box for himself on this or some other voyage, and engraved the teeth aboard the *Mary and Susan* for a sister or daughter. The problem is that the records of his life are so obscure that it is not known whether he had a sister or daughter with the initial *F.*

There were literally dozens of men named Manuel Rogers living and working in Massachusetts in the nineteenth century. Many were immigrants from the Azores; some were born in the U.S.A. of Azorean parents. One who served on the whaler *Sea Ranger* (1876-79) was born in Belgium circa 1840; another, who was approximately the same age and was living in New Bedford at around the same time, had been born in France. At least one was from Madeira, and a few were from the Cape Verde Islands, including a Manuel J. Rogers on Martha's Vineyard. However, for reasons likely having more to do with inefficiency and transience, rather than prejudice — that is, inefficiency of the recordkeeping process and transience of the seafaring populace — few of the men of Cape Verdean origin made it into the federal census. Thus, the Manuel J. Rogers who made the scrimshaw is elusive. Though he lived on Nantucket, all of his voyages were from New Bedford. If he was a U.S. citizen — born here or naturalized — he would have been required to carry a Seaman's Protection Paper (passport). If such a passport were issued at New Bedford, a record of it would likely have survived; but if he obtained his passport on Nantucket or elsewhere, the record may have been lost. So though the shipping papers imply that he was native born, no Protection or census listing has been found; thus, it is not certain whether he was or was not a citizen. Given that he served as first mate of the *Mary and Susan* in 1877, he is likely the same Manuel Rogers who had made previous voyages, as fourth mate of the *Brewster* (1863-65) and third mate of the *Abraham Barker* (1866-70); and that his stint in the *Rainbow* (1870-74) was as second mate. The articles for the *Rainbow* (1870-74) and *Mary and Susan* (1877-81) — but not those for the *A.R. Tucker* (1874-76), which is a voyage he also made — clearly gave Nantucket as his place of birth, but not necessarily his current residence. He was of Cape Verdean ancestry, if not Cape Verdean birth — one of the few Cape Verdean whalemen who are specifically credited by name with having made scrimshaw. And, in the final analysis, despite what little is known about his origins and his family, the Manuel J. Rogers who was first mate of the *Mary and Susan* is almost certainly the Manuel Rogers who made the box, though it is possible that the teeth were engraved by some *Mary and Susan* shipmate — perhaps a suitor of Manuel's as-yet-undiscovered sister or daughter.

Romanov, Piotr Alexeyevich – see **Peter the Great**

Rook, John (fl. circa 1825-75). Maine fisherman and former deepwater mariner, the recipient of an oversize powder horn inscribed (among other things) "JOHN ROOK HIS HORN" and dated 1836. The piece is attributed to Silvanus Baker (q.v.), a whaleman active in the 1830s who was later a merchant sea captain. It could conceivably have been engraved by Rook himself, but the cryptic inscription on it suggests that it was more likely a presentation to him, as it is hardly the sort of thing one would write to oneself: "YYURYYUBICURYYFORME" ("Too wise you are, too wise you be; I see you are too wise for me"). John Rook was born at Phippsburg, Maine, the second son and third child of three born to John Rook, Sr. (1780-1806), a sailor, and the former Frances Rogers (1781-1862). Sadly, the father never saw the child: John *fils* was born in November 1806, but by that time John *pere* was dead, lost at sea earlier that same year. Nothing is known of the son's early seafaring career, nor has anything been discovered about any youthful whaling voyages he may have made or any naval service he may have seen. By 1850 he was securely ensconced at Phippsburg as a fisherman with a wife named Jane (whose maiden name may have been Foster) and four children, of whom the oldest, James, would eventually follow his father's and grandfather's examples and become a sailor. In the first year of the Civil War, in December 1861, John lied and shaved ten years off his age — saying he was 45 when he had actually just passed his fifty-fifth birthday — in order to enlist as a lowly private in Company B, 15th Maine Infantry Regiment. His patriotism evidently exceeded his middle-aged endurance: scarcely six months later he received a disability discharge (5 July 1862) and returned home, where he lived into his seventies.

Rosa, Clarence Moniz da—see **da Rosa, Clarence Moniz**

Runels, George (fl. 1840-42). He was a one-time whaleman who became Mayor of Lowell, Massachusetts. The name appears as both Runels and Runnels, the latter mostly in the newspapers and census records (as it is the more common spelling); but in the official town records of Lowell and in the publications of the Lowell Historical Society it is consistently rendered Runels. A baleen panel or plaque in NBWM — a strip of baleen incised with vignettes of a full-rigged ship under sail, a farmstead scene with house, picket fence, orchard, barn, and paddock, a spread eagle with shield bearing the motto "E Pluribus Unum," a long foliate garland, and four bunches of flowers — has a solid family provenance to the effect that it was made aboard the ship [sic] *Benezet* of Fairhaven on her 1840 voyage by George Runels, the great-grandfather of the wife of the donor.

Runels (circa 1823-1911) was born in Warner, New Hampshire, in the southerly part of the state, "on what used to be spoken of, before the railroad was opened, as the old stage route from Boston to Windsor, Vermont" (Lowell Hist. Soc.). In his youth he must have been apprenticed to a stonecutter or stone mason, the trade he later followed with evident success. But at age 18 he escaped the Granite State and granite itself, and shipped on his one and only whaling voyage — which turned out to be more of an adventure than he had bargained for. The *Benezet* sailed from Fairhaven under Captain Charles A. Parker in December 1840 — 33 days before Herman Melville embarked in the *Acushnet* from the same port. They rounded Cape Horn for the Pacific and got in quite a bit of whaling during the next few months before disaster struck; which it did on August 9, 1842, when the *Benezet* was lost in the Fiji Islands with her entire cargo of 700 barrels of sperm oil. (From the fact that Runels had baleen for his scrimshaw, it seems that they must also have taken some right whales, but there is no mention of whale oil or bone in the records of the voyage.) Luckily, all hands were saved; but it meant no profits for the voyage, thus no pay for young George. Thus, Runel's whaling career was almost exactly coeval with that of Melville: their voyages not only began but ended mere days apart — Melville's own account of his desertion in the Marquesas,

Runel's because of shipwreck on the other side of Polynesia. Neither of them received any wages for their 20+ months at sea; and both of them wound up "on the beach" in the Pacific for far longer than either might have imagined. Runels, stranded ashore, penniless, 10,000 miles from New England, had to work his passage home — an odyssey of almost two years duration which finally repatriated him in a Salem brig. Notwithstanding that he later achieved recognition as a prominent local tradesman, and won election as mayor of a major manufacturing city, it is the shipwreck, already 69 years in the past, that was recounted in lieu of a normal obituary in a Boston newspaper in 1911:

WRECKED ON WHALING VOYAGE

Ex-Mayor Runnels of Lowell Dead at

Age of 88 Years.

> *George Runnels [sic], mayor of Lowell in 1882 [sic], who died in that city Monday, at the age of 88 years, sailed on a whaling voyage from Fairhaven to the South Pacific ocean. about a year and a half later, the bark was wrecked on the coast of the Fiji islands, and, after three days' exposure in open boats, the crew were picked up by a ship which left them in New Zealand. Mr. Runnels worked there for three months at pit sawing and wharf building — the first on the island — and shipped from there to the East Indies and the Fiji islands. He remained in this vessel a year, leaving for Manila and thence went to Canton, Singapore, and Calcutta, shipping from the latter place to Boston.* (Unidentified clipping in NBWM)

He must have had the scrimshaw with him the entire time.

Back in New England, he worked as a stonecutter in Lowell, where he married Mary A. Morrill, of Springfield, New Hampshire, in 1845. Their first two children were born in Lowell, but they were evidently living in Vermont for a while around 1850, where their third child was born. The family returned to Lowell by 1860, where George moved up from stonecutter to stone mason, where his son Charles followed his footsteps as a stonecutter, and where Runel generated sufficient public affection to be elected mayor for the 1883-84 term. He was apparently also something of a real estate entrepreneur, and built the Runels Building in 1892 at the corner of Merrimack and Bridge streets (unfortunately, this legacy was compromised when, a dozen years after his death, in the 1920s, it was renamed the Fairburn Building). He died in 1911, better remembered for his youthful voyage than for his many accomplishments as a Leading Citizen.

Russell, Abraham, 2d (fl. circa 1809-41). A large single-cage swift that has a shaft and ribs of skeletal bone, a finial, gaskets, tabletop clamp, and mushroom-shaped knob turnbuckle of whale ivory with sealing wax highlights, is inscribed on the clamp in stipple letters, "SUSAN P. RUSSELL," and is mounted on a later base with a brass plaque labeled, "MADE BY / CAPT. ABRAHAM RUSSELL / FOR HIS WIFE WHILE ABOARD THE SHIP / JOHN ADAMS / IN THE SOUTH ATLANTIC / 1835-1837"; private collection (reported by Donald and Mary Boger). There were two New Bedford whaling masters of this name (not three, as may be inferred from Lund; the other was Abraham B. Russell, captain of the bark *Bramin* during 1836-39 and ship *Bartholomew Gosnold*, 1839-43); neither of them has a wife named Susan. However, the provenance is clear that the maker of the swift was the Abraham Russell who was captain of the *John Adams* during 1835-37, a man generally known as Abraham Russell 2d to distinguish him from several others of that name. He was married only once, to a woman named Hannah. They did have a daughter named Susan (*Eliza Starbuck Barney Genealogy*, NHA); however, though the date of her birth is not recorded she was probably too young to have been given a swift in 1837; so the intended recipient remains in doubt.

Abraham Russell 2d, born in 1792 at Dartmouth, Massachusetts, was likely the son of Stephen Russell (not of Abraham Russell; nor of William and Hepzibeth Moiser Russell, as has sometimes been reported: coincidentally, William and Hepzibeth's son Abraham Russell was born in the same month of the same year, and died at age 52 only six months after Captain Russell's death at age 52). Russell spent his entire career in New Bedford vessels, the early portion of it evidently in the merchant service, notably in the ship *Ann Alexander* (from 1809). Thus he was already a seasoned mariner when he went whaling, first in the ship *Martha* (1818-19 and 1820-21), then as third mate of the ship *Milwood* (1821-22), the *Martha* again as second mate (1823-24), and the bark *Pacific* as first mate (1824-26). He was then captain of five successful whaling voyages: two to the Brazil Banks in the *Galatea* (1827-28 and 1828-29) and one each to the Pacific in the *Frances Henrietta* (1829-33), *John Adams* (1835-37), and *Falcon* (1838-40). In 1816, even before he ever went whaling, he married Hannah Smith (1792-1852), who bore him four children: Ruth Ann (born 1817), who later married Isaac Crapo; Stephen Giles (born 1826); and two more daughters, Hannah and Susan, whose birth dates and middle initials are not recorded. Susan may have been the recipient of the swift, for which there are only two other viable candidates. One is Abraham's mother, whose name is not known. The other is Susan Pollard Russell (born 1813), daughter of Roland Pollard of Nantucket, who married Edward G. Russell circa 1835-37, at just around the time Abraham Russell 2d was captain of the *John Adams* and made the "Susan P. Russell" swift. Susan Pollard Russell was the only surefire Susan P. Russell in New England at the time, and the swift would have made a glorious wedding gift, but no kinship between Edward and Abraham Russell has been established. In any case, Captain Russell died shortly after he retired from whaling, in September 1844; and the daughter named Susan died three months later.

Russell, Frederick T. (fl. circa 1865-81). Ellen Damon Russell Peters was the donor (to NBWM in 1966) of a panbone busk associated with and provisionally attributed to her father, Frederick T. Russell, whom she said "was a whaler during 1865-1881"; another panbone busk (acquired by NBWM in 1948 from an entirely different source) is by the same hand. The one directly from Russell's daughter is polychrome engraved with alternating floral and geometric motifs, a tree, two potted leafy vines, a checkerboard pattern, and an eight-pointed pinwheel in a circle. The other is also polychrome engraved: a planter and serpentine flowering vine, surmounted by a central checkerboard vignette strikingly similar to the one on the other busk, and three vignettes: a house with smoking chimney, a palm tree with hill and flowers, and flowers potted in a basket-like planter. The distinctive and distinguishing feature is the checkerboard motif, but other stylistic affinities between the two busks are unmistakable.

Frederick T. Russell, born circa 1847, was the youngest of four sons of New Bedford blacksmith Chauncey Russell and his wife Abigail. Frederick is known to have made whaling voyages out of

New Bedford in the 1860s and '70s, but the voyages themselves are elusive. A precise match with the dates 1865-81 specified in the provenance cannot be confirmed from the existing records, as there were several whalemen named Frederick Russell who were almost exactly the same age and were all active at the same time. The records themselves are internally inconsistent in standpoint of nomenclature and identifying features that might distinguish one Frederick from another; none of the crew lists, manifests, or other documents specifies the middle initial T., which would be a fairly reliable indicator; and where middle initials are given at all, they are clearly erroneous in some cases (as they are inconsistent and conflicting), but it is uncertain which are correct and which are incorrect. There was a Frederick Russell from Nantucket, another from Boston, and at least three, and probably four or more from New Bedford. Of the three principal candidates, both Frederick T. Russell and Frederick B. Russell were from New Bedford; Frederick H. Russell was from nearby Dartmouth. All three were born between 1846 and 1848 (a range that lies well within the margin or error for the approximations characteristic of census reports and shipping papers); all three embarked on their maiden whaling voyages in 1864; they each made several subsequent voyages, which overlapped one another's; and all three continued until around 1880 or 1881, then left the whale fishery. One of them was a boatsteerer on the 1866-67 voyage of the bark *President*, commanded by Benjamin Gifford (q.v.), but it is not known which; and this is the *only* voyage on which the berth or rank is specified. And it is unclear what any of them did after 1881.

Whatever may have been the specifics of Frederick T. Russell's voyages, it is certain that in midpassage of his whaling career, in 1875, he married Ellen A. Damon, daughter of Eunice [Adams] Damon and New Bedford ship joiner Doane W. Damon. For the first few years of their marriage the couple lived with Ellen's parents — at least until 1880 — which provided her the security of a family circle while her husband was at sea. And it is surely Frederick T. Russell and not any of the others who is connected to, and is the probable maker of the Ellen Damon Russell busk, for he was the one and only father of Ellen Damon Russell. She was born circa 1886 and married William J. Peters, a native of Michigan who was employed as a department store chauffer in New Bedford. She donated one of the busks to NBWM in 1966 and died in 1973.

Sanford, Abraham T. (fl. circa 1842-51). Whaleman, ship's cooper, and tight cooper in New Bedford, who as a skilled artisan may be presumed to have possessed the requisite skills, ample opportunity, and very likely the desire to produce more than only the one piece so far attributed to his hand. A rolling pin, with a barrel of dark mahogany and turned whale ivory handles inlaid with baleen dot patterns, has a written provenance: "Made by Abe Sandford [sic] and given to Louise Rogers Burlingame, with whom the sea captain [sic] boarded for a time" (in NBWM). Abraham T. Sanford was actually a seaman and ship's cooper in the 1840s-'50s but was never a captain; also, he is not known to have boarded anywhere outside his family except on shipboard and during a brief sojourn in California during the Gold Rush. He was born in 1819 at Dartmouth, Massachusetts, the son of Abraham Sanford and the former Hannah Briggs, and he must have been apprenticed to a cooper in his youth. A voyage he made in the whaleship *Science* of Portland, Maine (1839-41), was probably his first — a successful cruise from which, even as a lowly neophyte, he likely made some fairly good money. Still, it does not seem to have qualified him for a full-scale seaman's berth next time around, as his next voyage was as a green hand for a mere 185th lay in the New Bedford ship *Lancaster* (1842-45). His prospects were a great deal better when he shipped as cooper for the 43rd lay in the bark *Lebaron* in 1847; had the voyage been a success Sanford might have stuck with whaling. But it was not. They took few whales and the ship burned in 1851, stranding all hands — an ordeal that might have been enough to cure anyone of the urge to go whaling. However, by that time Sanford must already have left the *Lebaron*, as the U.S. Census reports him living at Middle Fork of the American River, in El Dorado County, California, in 1850, with no occupation listed — which means that he was prospecting for gold. He does not appear to have struck it rich. He was back from the Gold Rush by 1853, married Rebecca S. Monroe at New Bedford, and thereafter led a mostly landlubberly life as a family man and cooper in New Bedford — purveyor of tight barrels to the city's enormous whaling trade. But he did punctuate his career with one more whaling voyage, probably as cooper, in the New Bedford bark *Stella* (1860-62). This one turned out to be a modest success, with a total catch of 1,050 barrels of sperm oil gathered in only 26 months at sea, to be sold at wartime prices. He continued working at the cooper's trade into the 1890s, and died in 1895.

Louise Rogers Burlingame was evidently the same Louise Burlingame who was Mrs. Raymond C. Burlingame, wife of a New Bedford bridge manager in the 1920s and '30s. It is unlikely that she could have been Abe Sanford's landlord at any time: she would have been far too young, and as far as is known, unless there was some kind of domestic disturbance of which there is no surviving record, Sanford did not board anywhere away from his own home and hearth from the time he was married in 1853 to the time he died 42 years later. Moreover, Mrs. Burlingame's relation to donor Martha Rogers Alexander has not been established nor her identity discovered (they may have been sisters or aunt and niece). It is unlikely that the provenance is a fabrication, or that it was not Abraham Sanford who made the rolling pin. More likely, Louise Rogers Burlingame inherited it from someone who knew Sanford a generation or two before, possibly in some kind of landlord-tenant capacity.

* **Sanford, Peleg** (fl. circa 1828-50). New Bedford whaling master and older kinsman of Captain William P. Sanford (q.v.). A bone swift provisionally attributed to his hand (in PEM) is mentioned in the *Dictionary*. Additionally, the provenance of several pieces of scrimshaw of various types donated together to NBWM in 1971 declares that they came "from [the] donor's great uncles William and Peleg Sanford, whaling masters from South Dartmouth [Massachusetts] who in later years lived in the Pittsfield, Maine area." The donor, Sarah AKA "Sadie" McCrillis (1892-1981), was the wife of Lyle R. McCrillis (1892-1976), who owned a woolen mill in Pittsfield; however, the provenance is equivocal as to whether any of the pieces were actually made by Peleg or William Sanford, and if so, which ones by whom. Moreover, the relationship between the two has not been established beyond that they were not brothers but may have been cousins, or perhaps uncle and nephew; nor has Mrs. McCrillis's specific relationship to the two whaling masters been definitively ascertained. As captains, either would have been in a position to commission scrimshaw from among members of the crew, or to have received a piece or two here and there as gifts; and there are no stylistic or technical affinities to suggest that any two of the pieces were actually made by the same hand; however, there is nothing to suggest that they were not made by one or the other. The trove consists of an ornate table-mount swift of whale ivory and skeletal bone, the clamp in the shape of a fist inlaid with abalone, the turned spools with sealing wax highlights, the ribs tied with green and blue ribbons; a tooth, engraved on one side with a full-rigged ship under sail and (on the other

side) a whaling scene with a harpooned whale, a whaleboat poised for the strike, another stove by flukes with four men swatted into the air; three sperm whale teeth, one raw, one polished, and a polished pair; a blank for a panbone busk; a panbone fid, the upper half octagonal with a flat top; and a cane with a plain tapered panbone shaft and a small polished tooth set as a handle, with a wooden band separator. The blank for a panbone busk is a busk-size plank of whale skeletal bone that has been cut, planed, and polished, and is thus ready to engrave, and it would presumably be useless to anyone but a scrimshaw maker: it and the plain polished teeth are the best evidence that one or both of the Sanfords may have been interested in making scrimshaw themselves.

Peleg Sanford was born in 1810 at Westport, Massachusetts, the son of David Sanford and the former Eunice Simmons. He first went whaling in 1828 in the schooner *Regulator* of Westport, Massachusetts, married Sarah A. Sherman of Tiverton, Rhode Island, in 1831, made two or three voyages in the New Bedford ship *Herald* in the 1830s, and was given command of the *Herald* for a Pacific Ocean voyage (1840-44). His next voyage, to the Indian Ocean as captain of the *Mercator* of New Bedford (1845-50), was his last. In 1850 he retired to his farm in Westport, where he is listed in that year's census as a farmer (rather than as a master mariner) with a wife and five children. If the scrimshaw provenance be correct he later moved to the Pittsfield area in Somerset County, Maine; but no official record of him there has been located.

Sanford, Ray Green (fl. circa 1818-41). A shelf clock that was evidently originally built as a watch stand (watch hutch) circa the 1830s, housing a replacement mechanism of circa 1910, has a much faded and barely legible typescript label glued to the bottom, tentatively implying an attribution: "This Watch Stand was present / by [sic] Capt. Ray Green Sanford / about the year 1840. / He commanded these whaling vessels / on voyages from New Bedford, Mass. / Brig DELIGHT owned by Jona. Mosher / sailed Nov. 1, 1835 / Returned Aug. 30, 1836… etc.," the remainder largely illegible and overwritten in ink (however, the facts are recoverable from Lund and Starbuck). An ink holograph notation in a nineteenth-century-style cursive hand adds, "Capt. Sanford died in 1841 during this voyage." This is corroborated by Starbuck, who states merely, "Captain Sanford died November 1841"; and the logbook of the voyage (Kendall #323) is authoritative in noting that he suddenly contracted lockjaw from an injury to his finger on October 29, 1841, died the following day "without a struggle," and was buried at sea on October 31. The ornate case is wood, trimmed with red-and-black-pigmented engravings on whale ivory on the pediment, cartouche, skirt, edges, and sides, with a leafy vine motif, surmounted by a full-round carved and engraved spread-eagle and American shield; with side columns and claw feet derived from late neoclassical furniture styles. The tops of the whale ivory pediments on both sides are threaded to accommodate four finials (missing), with circular cutout "footprints" approximately 1 ¼ inches (3.2 cm) in diameter. The mechanism has a gothic face with chamfered glass; the works are a key-wound 8-day spring movement, in brass, with key on the back, manufactured by the Sessions Clock Co. (founded 1903) at Forestville, Connecticut, circa 1910. The piece may have originally have been made as a watch stand and later modified, with the aperture widened to accommodate a much larger clockworks; or it may have been built as a shelf clock and the original mechanism (if there was one) replaced in the twentieth century.

Ray Green Sanford was born in 1803 at Westport, Massachusetts, the youngest of the three sons of Philip Sanford (1743-1803), originally of Tiverton, Rhode Island, and the former Catherine

Tripp (born 1772) of East Greenwich. The father died a few months before Ray was born, and his mother was remarried, to Job Sowle (1757-1848) of Tiverton, when Ray was 15, which is about when he must have made his first whaling voyage. His brother Squire Sanford (1801-1870), older by two years, was also a captain of New Bedford whaleships, and was actually three years later than his kid brother in achieving his first command: he skippered two voyages in the *Phenix* (1835-42) and one in the *John* (1844-48) (John H. Lawrence, q.v., was in the crew on Squire Sanford's second *Phenix* voyage). Ray Sanford was captain on seven whaling voyages out of New Bedford, in the bark *Elizabeth* (1832-35), schooner *Delight* (1835-36), brig *Delight* (1836), brig *Sarah Louisa* (1836-37), brig *Delight* again (1837-38), and two more voyages in the *Sarah Louisa* (1838-41), on the second of which he died on board at age 38 (he was succeeded by Ebenezer Slocum, who had sailed as second mate in 1840; the brig returned in 1842). The rest of his biography is also rather sad. Nothing is known of his oldest brother, Philip (born 1799), who may have died in childhood; the three boys (or, by then, perhaps only two) were left fatherless as very young children, and as teenagers may have been *sent* to sea when their mother remarried in 1818. In 1831 Ray married Almira Jenny (born 1807) of New Bedford; they remained childless until June 1837, when Almira died four days after giving birth to a daughter, who was accordingly named Almira; but the infant died after only 15 weeks. In August 1840 Ray married his late wife's sister Elizabeth (born 1812), but seven weeks later, he sailed in the *Sarah Louisa* and never returned.

Sanford, William P. (fl. circa 1835-59). New Bedford whaling master, a younger kinsman of Captain Peleg Sanford, and possible maker of scrimshaw in a legacy collection in NBWM (q.v. in the article on Peleg Sanford). He was born at Dartmouth, Massachusetts, circa 1820, the son of Caleb and Content Sanford. He went to sea at age 15, married Mary H. Hervey [AKA Harvey] of Dartmouth ten years later, and, evidently throughout his active whaling career, lived with the Herveys in Dartmouth, where Mary would be secure in the family fold while William was at sea for three and four years at a time. His early voyages are not yet discovered, but just prior to his marriage he was second mate in the *Nimrod* of New Bedford (1842-45), and evidently conformed to the common practice in the whale fishery of waiting to marry until making the grade of second mate. Soon after getting married he went as first mate of the New Bedford ship *Hydaspe* (1845-48), from which, for reasons unknown, he was reportedly "discharged at Marques Island" seven months early — that is, seven months before the *Hydaspe* returned to New Bedford. If this enigmatic notation in the crew list actually means the Marquesas Islands, a common port-of-call for Yankee whalers in Polynesia, it would almost certainly have been for him to take a berth in another whaleship, which has not been identified. His activities during 1848-52 are not recorded: he may have made another voyage as mate or he may have been ashore; however, the 1850 census reports him still living with Mary on the Hervey farm in Dartmouth. In 1852 he went to sea again, as first mate on a North Pacific voyage in the New Bedford ship *Mt. Vernon* (1852-55). He was then given his first and only command, a North Pacific voyage in the ship *Draper* of New Bedford (1855-59). This was a much better-than-average catch and must have been a particularly lucrative venture, as the combined returns and cargoes sent home was 136 barrels of sperm oil, 2,734 barrels of whale oil, and 28,500 pounds of "whalebone" (baleen). At the average prices for oil and bone in 1859 this would have amounted to $74,196.92, of which Captain Sanford's share would likely have been enough to retire on. The provenance suggests that he eventually wound up in Somerset County, Maine, in the vicinity of Pittsfield, which is likely but unconfirmed.

Santos, John B. (fl. 1919). His only recorded whaling voyage was as steward on a successful Atlantic Ocean cruise in the schooner *Cameo* of New Bedford, skippered by Captain José M. Domingos, from February to September 1919. (William F. Joseph, q.v. in the *Dictionary*, who was later a renowned captain, was first mate on this voyage.) Along the way, Santos collected a porpoise jawbone and engraved it as a souvenir with the inscriptions "Lat[itude] 34° 47′ N[orth] Long[itude] 47° 47′ W[est]," "Sch[ooner] Cameo," and "1919," which accurately places the *Cameo* in the middle North Atlantic, a little more than halfway between North Carolina and the Azores. Santos was born in the Azores in the 1890s, married a fellow Azorean immigrant in New Bedford, and worked most of his career in the New Bedford cotton mills, where he may have been the same John B. Santos whom the 1930 Census identifies as a cotton mill foreman. Like many immigrants from the Azores and Cape Verde at that time, he may also have made one or more Atlantic whaling voyages from Provincetown.

Sawyer, Hugh N. (fl. circa 1833-50). A nicely crafted powder horn with ship portraits, signed and dated "H.N. Sawyer / May 8, 1838" (private collection; reported by Max Berry), is attributed to a fellow whose early whaling career is conjectural but, judging from the subject matter and technique of the engraving on the horn, probably learned scrimshawing on an unidentified Yankee whaling voyage in the 1830s. Little is known about him and no other work by his hand has been discovered. He was born in Maine circa 1814, either in Pownal, according to his U.S. Army enlistment record, or Portland, according to the later, less-reliable testimony of his brief whaling career. He gave his occupation as farmer when, at age 18, he enlisted in the Army at Ft. Preble in South Portland, Maine, on 4 September 1832 — suggesting that up until that time he was probably still living on the family farm in Cumberland County. He was assigned to the 3rd Artillery, Company F, under Captain (later Brevet Major) William L. McClintock. According to the official army record, Sawyer deserted twice, in March 1833 and March 1835. If there is any record of his having been apprehended after the first desertion it has eluded detection, but he was apprehended (again) in March 1838, slightly less than two months before the date on the powder horn. The circumstances and aftermath of his unspectacular army career are unknown. He may have gone to sea while he was AWOL, but he was issued a Seaman's Protection Paper (passport), which was likely not his first, at Providence, Rhode Island, in May 1840; and a couple of months later the U.S. Census listed him as a Mariner, age between 20 and 30 (he was actually 25 or 26), living alone as head of household (i.e., no wife or children are indicated) in New Bedford, Massachusetts, which strongly suggests an impending whaling voyage that has not been identified and which (given his highly developed scrimshaw technique in 1838) may not have been his first. He may or may not have been the H. Sawyer recorded as an ordinary seaman in the crew of the bark *Smyrna* of New Bedford during 1845-49. The only other snippet of data that has been unearthed about him comes from the U.S. Census of 1850, when Sawyer stated his age as 35 and his occupation as Mariner, was living in Durham, Cumberland County, Maine, with a wife named Mary J., age 33, and had no children (or no children yet). He then completely disappears from view.

Schwemer, Felix (fl. circa 1887). Whaleman of German origin. His name appears as a signature on a pair of five-inch [13 cm] teeth depicting nicely attired little girls, one sitting on a chair at a table, the other standing and holding a kitten, "each inscribed inside the rim 'Talcahuano / d[elineated] 18 April / 1887 / Felix Schwemer'" (Northeast Auctions, 20-21 August, 2005, #776). Schwemer was born in either 1868 or 1869 at Dresden, Germany, of parents from Mecklenburg and Hamburg. His early career is undocumented: he could have been recruited into the South Sea whale fishery on either side of the Atlantic. In April 1887, the date inscribed on the scrimshaw, he was evidently a whaleman ashore at Talcahuano, Chile — one of the blubber-hunters' favorite ports-of-call — but from what vessel is not known. He formally immigrated to the USA in 1889. In 1920, at age 52, he was president of a rubber manufacturing company in New York City, living at College Point in Queensborough with his Cuban-born wife Mercedes, who had immigrated in 1880. They were still living at College Point in 1930 (with their ages and years of immigration wrongly stated in the census), with Felix still at the same job and now joined by their adult daughter Anna.

* **Sears, Alden** (fl. circa 1760-92). Whaleman, whaling master, fisherman, schooner captain, and nautical jack-of-all-trades who made an extremely long and narrow panbone busk, monochrome engraved on both sides: on the obverse, a sperm-whaling scene with a two-masted schooner, a whaleboat under sail, and another in pursuit of a sperm whale, inscribed "A.S." and "1766"; and on the reverse, "ALDEN SEARS" (KNB). Captain Sears was born on Cape Cod in 1739, in a part of Harwich that is now West Brewster. He was the eldest son of Judah Sears (1699-1776) and Mary Paddock (1714-), and grandson of Captain Judah Paddock of Yarmouth. His parents moved to Rochester, Massachusetts, in 1769, but by that time Alden had forged a peripatetic career of his own. He married Hannah Bassett (1742-c1766) and, with his younger brother Nathan, moved to Nova Scotia where they were among the original proprietors of the Township of Liverpool circa 1761-64 and worked as schooner captains, whalers, fishermen, and traders. The busk, dated 1766, comes from this period and was presumably made for his wife Hannah. But she died soon after. Alden and Nathan returned to New England, where Alden lived for a while at Pawtucket and Providence, Rhode Island, working as a boatbuilder and distiller. In 1769 he was married again, to Phebe Walker (1748-1830), and moved to Dighton, Mass., where their seven children were born. At one time or another both brothers served in the Revolution, which of course meant forfeiture of their lands in Canada. Early on, Alden was still carrying cargoes at sea:

> *In returning from the West Indies with a cargo of molasses [he] was captured by the British, lost his vessel and cargo, and was held prisoner several years. An English officer, with whom he made friends, finally procured his release and supplied him with funds for his return. His wife is said to have had full faith during all the years of his absence that he would return, although others had given him up as dead. According to the superstitions of the times, there were many signs convincing her that he would return. One evening in her teacup, the peculiar position of the leaves was proof that he was then on his way home. She rose hastily, saying "Alden will be home to-night, and I must put the house in order, and dress and go to meet him." Upon opening the door, she really saw him in the distance approaching the house.*[11]

Meanwhile, brother Nathan is supposed to have been the captain of a company at the Battle of Bunker Hill; and at least for a while in 1780 Alden served in Captain Elijah Walker's Com-

[11] Samuel Pearce May, *The Descendants of Richard Sares (Sears) of Yarmouth, Massachusetts, 1638-1888* (Albany, New York, 1890), 120.

pany of Col. John Hathaway's Regiment of volunteers. After the war he seems to have resumed his nautical activities until 1792, when he and Phebe were part of a colony from the Dighton area who settled on farmlands in Ontario County, New York, where Alden is counted as one of the founding fathers of the town of Bristol. All seven of their children, ranging in age from 9 to 22 at the time, evidently went with them. Alden died there in 1803. All of the children lived to mature adulthood, and most spawned large families.[12]

Sewell, William (fl. circa 1842-45). A miniature jigsaw puzzle of whale skeletal bone (in KNB) is boldly inscribed "HUNTER N.B." and "WILLIAM SEWELL" — the former evidently in reference to the ship *Hunter* of New Bedford, the latter presumed to be the name of the maker, though possibly that of an intended recipient. However, the authenticity of the piece has been inconclusively questioned on both stylistic and historical grounds. Only one William Sewell is recorded as having been whaling in any vessel from the New Bedford Port District: he joined the Fairhaven ship *Eliza Adams* at Valparaiso as an Ordinary Seaman for the 165th lay in November 1842, and returned with the ship in December 1845. The *Hunter* was launched as a ship in 1851, entered the whaling fleet that year, was converted to a bark in 1867, and continued whaling until 1893, finishing out her career based in San Francisco; but there is no record of a William Sewell in her crew at any time; nor has any other trace of him in the whale fishery been found; nor is he identifiable from census and genealogical records. The scrimshaw itself is roughly rectangular, only about two inches (5 cm) long, irregular in depth, polychrome engraved with a sketchy though convincing whaling scene, and saw-cut into eleven interlocking pieces. The amateurishly ornate inscriptions and accuracy of the broadside ship portrait — which clearly shows the correct deployment of standing rigging, sails, reef points, and grommets, a square stern transom, davits with a whaleboat, and what appear to be bearers aft with at least one spare whaleboat — are the best evidence that the piece is authentic nineteenth-century whalemen's work. Moreover, the house flag flying from the mainmast is a fair approximation of the red-white-blue tricolor of Jonathan Bourne, Jr., managing agent of the *Hunter* throughout most of her career.

Shaw, Francis Marion (fl. 1844-48). Having made one whaling voyage in his youth, he later became a prominent industrialist in Brockton, Massachusetts, specializing in the machinery and apparatus for processing leather and manufacturing shoes. In his shipboard journal (in KNB), homeward bound in the New Bedford ship *William and Eliza* (1844-48), he wrote about "skrimshanding" — that on several occasions he was "markind [sic] whale's teeth" and "tinkering in bone and ivory," and that at one point he "was busy until 11 oclock marking a pair of teeth for a shipmate" (reported by Michael P. Dyer). In fact, Shaw was a devoted avocational artist and musician, his journal is profusely illustrated with drawings and watercolors, and he was an habitual maker of violins, which he played enthusiastically and, by all appearances, skillfully. His biography in *Representative Men and Old Families of Southeastern Massachusetts* (Vol. II, 668f) lauds him as

[12] In addition to the archives of the New England Historic Genealogical Society (Boston) and the Church of Jesus Christ of Latter-day Saints,.sources cited in various websites are: T.B. Smith, *Collection of Queens County Families*, Sears Family (MG 1, Vol 853), #S7, 8 Jun 1989 (Public Archives of Nova Scotia); L Ray Sears, III, *Descendants of Richard Sears*, Sears Family Association, 2002; Samuel Pearce May, *Descendants of Richard Sares (Sears) of Yarmouth, Massachusetts*, 1638-1888; Joel Albany, *Munsell's Sons*, 1890, 120;

> *for years a well-known businessman of Brockton, a gentleman of wide and varied experiences in life. He served his country in time of war in both the army and the navy; traveled far and journeyed in distant lands; and held numerous positions of trust and responsibility, serving the interests of important industrial enterprises, and lending a hand sagaciously to the conduct of public affairs.*

Francis Marion Shaw was born at Raynham, Massachusetts, in 1825, the second child and eldest son of Samuel Shaw, Jr. (1795-1881), a veteran of the War of 1812, and Rachel Barden Shaw (1791-1840). Francis was named for the celebrated Revolutionary War hero Francis Marion, and among his five brothers were other heroic namesakes whose military exploits must have appealed to the parents: William Wallace Shaw, Oliver Perry Shaw, and Andrew Jackson Shaw. Between the ages of 14 and 18 Francis worked in a local nail factory, then at the East Taunton Iron Works, in a factory near Philadelphia, and at the Duncannon Iron Works in Pennsylvania. (He was not the only whaleman-scrimshaw artist-engineer to have had his start in an iron foundry: see Robert W. Weir, Jr., in the *Dictionary*.) Shaw was 18 when he embarked on his one whaling voyage, to the Pacific Ocean in the *William and Eliza*. This eventful cruise was commanded by William H. Whitfield of Fairhaven, who is now famous for his previous voyage as captain of the *John Howland* (1839-43), with Edward Southworth (q.v.) in the crew, on which they rescued the Japanese castaway John Manjiro (q.v.) and his four Japanese companions, delivered four of them to Honolulu, and brought Manjiro home to Fairhaven. In the *William and Eliza* they sailed around Cape Horn,

> *stopping at Valparaiso and the Sandwich Islands [Hawaii], both on the outward trip and the return voyage, spending at one time six months in Honolulu. In 1846 they were taking in oil [off the coast of] Japan; while in the China sea they were in a typhoon, and had a narrow escape from destruction. At the Cannibal Islands [Fiji] they engaged in traffic with the natives, bartering beads for hogs; and young Shaw there sold the king's son one of the two violins that he had made himself, the other still [in 1912] being in possession of his son, Linus H. Shaw. Among other places that he visited were the Samoan Islands and New Zealand.* (Loc.cit.)

For five or six years following his return Shaw had various jobs in the shoe business, which was a mainstay in the economic life of Raynham and Brockton in those days; he then bought a farm in Raynham and built a small shoe factory on it. The factory burned down in 1860 and he moved to nearby Abingdon to start again, but soon afterwards he enlisted instead in the 9th Massachusetts Battery of the Union Army (1862). When that outfit was disbanded a short time later he went into the Union Navy. In his capacity as paymaster's steward in the USS *San Jacinto* — one of the navy's early screw warships, originally launched in 1850, now rebuilt and recommissioned — he participated in blockade patrols and abortive search-and-destroy assignments up and down the coast, from New Brunswick to Cuba and the Florida Keys. However, "On New Year's Day, 1865, the ship struck a reef near Great Abaco Island [in the Bahamas] and filled with water. Her guns, along with some equipment and provisions, were saved, but efforts to salvage the ship were unsuccessful" (*Dictionary of American Naval Fighting Ships*, VI:297). The castaway crew were stranded on Great Abaco for 18 days, subsisting by forage, until they were rescued by the USS *Tallapoosa* and taken to Boston. The Civil War ended that spring; Shaw was discharged in July and returned to Massachusetts to make his way in the shoe manufacturing industry, in which he rose to prominence. He was twice married: to Mary L. Eaton of Raynham, by whom he had six children and was then widowed; and to Harriet B. Bates of Abingdon, who bore him a son. Shaw's political and religious ideas were unusual: he was a member of the idiosyncratic Know Nothing Party in the 1850s but was later active in local and state political affairs as a "stanch [sic] Republican." An adherent of the millennialist Swedenborgian faith, he was also a lifelong member of the Grand Army of the Republic. He died at Brockton in 1900.

Shaw, John C. (fl. 1846-56). New Bedford whaleman, the probable maker of a panbone serving mallet, a wooden tabletop swift, and a wooden busk; he also collected a wooden war club from Tonga (Tongatabu), all of which descended in the family after Shaw's early death and were donated to NBWM by his grandson in 1917. Given that he made three full-scale whaling voyages during ten years at sea, it seems likely that Shaw would have produced other wooden objects and scrimshaw. He was born at Rochester (Marion), Massachusetts, in 1832, the son of Lewis Shaw, who was originally from Carver, Massachusetts, and the former Ruth Crandon of Dartmouth, Massachusetts. The Whalemen's Index (in NBFPL) reports him as having been on two successive Indian Ocean voyages of the New Bedford ship *St. Peter*, as seaman (1846-49) and boatsteerer (1849-52); however, his name does not appear on the New Bedford Port Society crew list for the latter voyage. This omission is almost certainly an error or oversight. The same list also omits the name of the captain, William H. Almy (q.v.), who may have signed articles after the original list was compiled. John C. Shaw, age 17, a resident of Marion, Massachusetts, was issued a new seaman's passport on October 4, 1849, and the *St. Peter* sailed on the 17th, almost certainly with both Captain Almy and boatsteerer Shaw aboard. His next voyage (1852-56) was also as a boatsteerer, either in the bark *United States* of Westport or the ship *Daniel Wood* of New Bedford. The two vessels sailed about five weeks apart in November and December 1852, both returned about five weeks apart in the spring of 1856, and there was a boatsteerer named John Shaw on each. The lay paid to the boatsteerer on the *Daniel Wood* was lower than what Shaw had received in the *St. Peter*, while the lay on the *United States* was higher — the statistical liklihood being that a professional boatsteerer would normally get a higher rate than on his previous voyage. However, the *United States* went to the Indian Ocean, while the *Daniel Wood* went to the Pacific; and if Shaw really did collect the Tongalese war club himself, as the family provenance implies, this would have been his only opportunity to do so, as it would have been his only voyage to the Pacific. In either case, this voyage appears to have been the end of Shaw's seafaring career. He did not go whaling again, perhaps for reasons of health: he died of consumption in Rochester at the age of 36 in 1868. His widow's name has not been discovered, but his son was John C. Shaw "Senior," a New Bedford physician. Dr. Shaw had two sons, whaleman John's grandsons: Thomas W., a New Bedford physician; and John C. Shaw "Junior," the source of the scrimshaw and other objects, a New Bedford bank agent and investment manager whose office was at 791 Purchase Street, in the old New Bedford 5¢ Savings Bank building that presently houses the NBWM Research Library, the Kendall Institute, and the Melville Society Archive. His wife, the former Clara Bourne — a daughter of the second-generation New Bedford auctioneer Standish Bourne — also donated objects to NBWM.

Sheffield, Charles G. (fl. circa 1831-57). A journal of the homeward passage of the ship *William Lee* to Newport, Rhode Island, from the Hawaiian Islands (1839-40) casually refers to "Mr.

Sheffield" as one of several scrimshaw-makers aboard. The journalist was Sereno Edwards Bishop (q.v.), the twelve-year-old son of Hawaiian missionaries, on his way to prep school, college, seminary, and a career in the clergy. On 24 Jan. 1840 he wrote, "A good many things are going on in the ship. Capt Hussey is making a bureau[,] Mr. V a work box, Mr Wyet a swift, [the] Steward a ship [model,] and Trip[p] an article. The captain has underway a swift and two work boxes[,] Mr Sheffield a box[,] and Mr V. another box." Mr Sheffield, one of the mates, was almost certainly Charles G. Sheffield of Newport, whom Bishop characterizes on another occasion (in a letter to his parents) as "religiously disposed." Unfortunately, Bishop provides no further description of the box. As for the maker, he was a career whaleman and sometime ship's cooper born in Newport circa 1810. Only some of his voyages are known, including one in the ship *John Adams* of New Bedford (1831-35) and two in the New Bedford ship *Hibernia*, as third mate and cooper (1849-53) under Captain Archelaus Baker (q.v.), and as third mate (1853-57). Nothing has been discovered about his life outside the whale fishery.

* **Sheffield, Josiah, Jr.** [Josiah C. Sheffield] (fl. circa 1828-35). The *Dictionary* describes the large so-called Timoleon Tooth, splendidly engraved with homeward-bound verse and the inscriptions "June 1833 / Ship Timoleon / Joshua Bunker, Master, David B. Delano, Mate, Asa Hoxie 2d Mate, Ephm. Douglass 3d Mate"; and (on the reverse side) "75 bbls. J. Sheffield Jr. Taken on West Coast Lat. 41. 30 N. Lon. 131.00 W," in KNB (illustrated in the *Dictionary*, opp. 119); and another tooth, unsigned, but confidently attributed to the same hand, which has a ship portrait inscribed "Ship Timoleon," names the mates, documents the whale, and is dated "July 3d 1833" (illustrated in Flayderman, 16, where it is erroneously credited to NBWM; it is actually in private hands; also in Bourne, 30 May 1990, #56). Another, extremely unusual pair, recently discovered in a private residence in "upper New York State on the shores of Lake Ontario," refers to the same vessel and voyage (in Julia, 26 Jan. 2006, #437). One is inscribed in a fine cursive hand, "No. 8 / N. West Coast / July 29 1833 / Lat. 37 10 N. / Lon. 125 00 W / Took 6 Whales," above a ship portrait labeled "Sept 20 1833 Anchored / in St Barbara / Sept 29 Sail'd for / Todos Santos Bay"; signed on the back, in an oval device, "JOSIAH SHEFIELD [sic] JR." The companion, from the same whale, is engraved "No. 9 / Oct. 3 1833 Anchor'd in / Todos Santos / Sail'd for / Turtle Bay / Nov 7 Off C. St. Lus. / Lat. 22.42 N. Lon 110.08 W. / Took 2 Whales 110 bbls.," with crossed American flags on arrow-tipped poles on a pedestal, inscribed below "Oct 14 Anchor'd in Turtle Bay. / & Cooper'd 1000 bbls. / 31 Sail'd for Cape St Lucas"; on the back in a vertical rectangular frame is a standing figure in long dress or gown, holding a small book or purse. This is a rare, perhaps unique instance in which a "journal" of a whaling voyage — that is, an itinerary of the voyage itself — is depicted on a series of scrimshaw teeth. That the teeth are numbered 8 and 9 indicates that there was originally a larger series chronicling the voyage, totaling an indeterminate number of teeth, of which only these two have as yet been discovered. The discrepancy between the two the names inscribed in fine, serifed capitals — "SHEFFIELD" on one and "SHEFIELD" on the other — is presumed to be a mere "typographical" error, as Sheffield is of course the normal spelling of the surname and the way it appears on Josiah's shipping papers and census records. In standpoint of stylistic and technical characteristics, the teeth and the signatures are by one and the same hand. Contrary to indications in the *Dictionary*, Flayderman is correct in suggesting that another, analogous Timoleon Tooth is by a different hand: in fact, this tooth, which endeavors to chronicle the same voyage and, remarkably, has

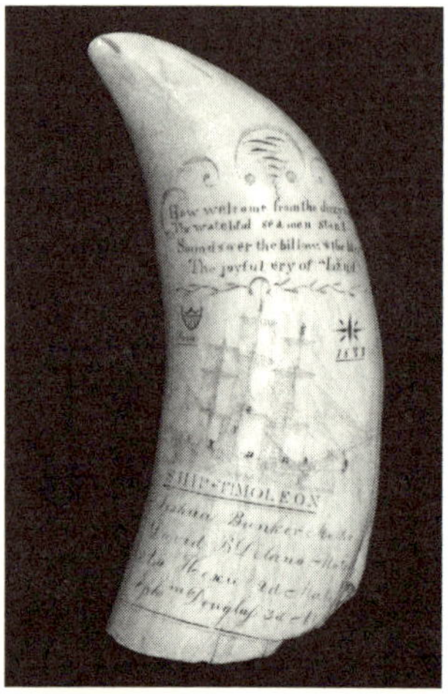

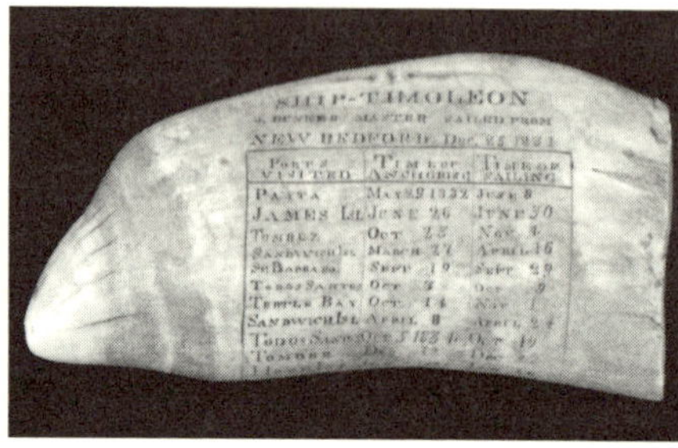

Fig. 18. **Josiah Sheffield, Jr., and John H. Ricketson**, shipmates aboard the whaler Timoleon in the 1830s, both produced beautifully engraved teeth documenting the voyage. Collection of the New Bedford Whaling Museum (photos by Richard Donnelly).

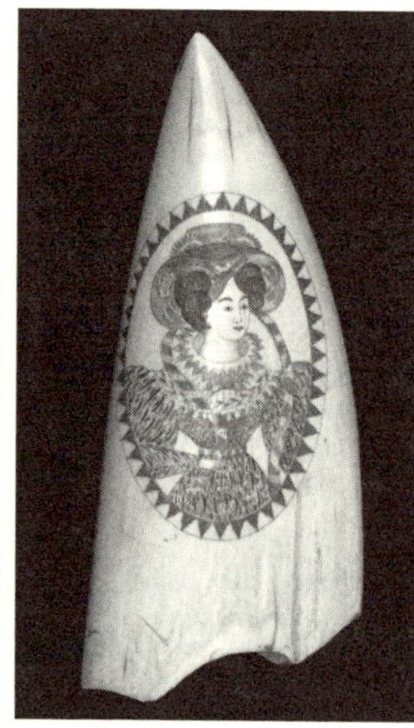

Fig. 19. ***L.C. Richmond*** **Tooth by William Sizer.** From the signature on one of his other teeth, Sizer has been identified as the scrimshaw-maker previously known only as the *L.C. Richmond* Artist. The two sides of a tooth in the Kendall Collection illustrate the principal identifying features of his pictures. Three teeth are known that have differing versions of a polychrome scene of the *L.C. Richmond* underway with whaleboats in pursuit. Two of these also have, either on the back or on a companion tooth, a half- or three-quarter-length portrait of a woman in a sumptuous, elaborately colored gown and fancy headgear, evocative of Renaissance costume. These similar but not identical images are the unifying feature enabling the attribution of several other teeth that have the female portrait only, with no signature or whaling scene. Kendall Collection, New Bedford Whaling Museum (photo by Richard Donnelly).

Fig. 20. **The anonymous Star Engraver**, first identified by Judge Paul Vardeman, is credited with five teeth, on which the characteristic stars are clearly visible. Courtesy of the Nantucket Historical Association.

engraving of equivalently high quality, is by Sheffield's shipmate, boatsteerer John H. Ricketson (q.v.) (illustrated in Flayderman, 17, where he erroneously omits that it is in NBWM, donated in 1971 by namesake descendant John H. Ricketson). The itinerary of the voyage indicates that the Ricketson Tooth could not have been done before 1835, suggesting that it may have been Josiah Sheffield's ambitious project (represented in teeth Nos. 8 and 9) that inspired Ricketson's more modest effort on what may have been his one and only scrimshaw tooth.

There are also clarifications to Josiah Sheffield's biography. Born on Nantucket in 1807 of Rhode Island parentage, he likely made his maiden voyage in an unidentified Nantucket whaleship. He was afterwards a seaman in the New Bedford ship *Averick* (1828-31), in connection with which he is erroneously listed in NBFPL as *Jonah* Sheffield Jr. of Nantucket (an error that evidently arose from a misreading of the handwritten documents; there are several such mistakes in the transcription of that particular crew list). The *Timoleon* voyage on which he made the scrimshaw was thus his third and last. The *Dictionary* is in error about his marriage to Judith C. Ray, who actually married Joseph C. Sheffield of Nantucket in 1839, and no corroboration has been encountered for a marriage to Hannah Castle. According to the 1830 U.S. Census, by that time Josiah was already living at Fabius, in Onondaga County, New York, where he eventually married a woman from Massachusetts named Mary and had two daughters, named Mary and Ellen, the latter of whom may have died in childhood. By 1870 Josiah and the two Marys were farming and taking in boarders in Maquoketa, Jackson County, Iowa, where Josiah died in 1880. How and why some of his scrimshaw may have remained in New York is unexplained.

Sherman, Albert C. (fl. circa 1865-99). Celebrated master of fifteen whaling voyages to the Central and Western Arctic from New Bedford and San Francisco, reputed maker of scrimshaw, and prodigious collector of Inuit artifacts from the Hudson Bay region and Eskimo artifacts from Alaska and Siberia. Most of his objects that are now in NBWM and KNB were acquired from or vetted by his three granddaughters, especially the late Hannah Sherman (afterwards Hannah Sherman Raffa). The largest and most complex piece of scrimshaw is a walking stick with a one-piece tapered panbone shaft, the lower part plain, the middle part and foreshaft relief-carved with octagonal bands flanking a cross-hatch diamond motif, culminating in a lyripipe motif surmounted by ten bands of whale ivory and wood in varying widths, inlaid with diamond shapes of whale ivory and tortoise shell. It came with a holograph note attached, stating merely, "Acquired from Capt. A. Sherman"; but Hannah Sherman claimed it was actually made by Captain Sherman himself. So, too, some or most of the minor pieces — such as napkin rings and bodkins — that were retained in the family for many years. From his voyages to Hudson Bay in the 1870s and early '80s he brought home Inuit-made garments of deer hide, elk hide, and fur, including jackets, trousers, moccasins, and hats, also a drawstring purse and several pouches made of elk hide, deerskin, cotton and wool cloth, velvet, felt, and silk, all hand-stitched in various combinations, some embroidered in the traditional Native manner, others elaborately decorated with glass trade beads in the style taught to the Native people by French missionaries in Quebec and the Labrador. On a later voyage to Alaska and Siberia he brought along his wife and young son, Albert Junior, universally known as "Bertie." They hunted bowhead whales among the ice floes, visited Siberian ports on the Sea of Okhotsk, and wintered-over with the whaling fleet at Herschel Island in the Beaufort Sea, beyond the farthest capes of Alaska. A daughter was born there — the first-ever in the Western Arctic whaling fleet.

The midwife was Sophie Porter, wife of Captain W.P.S. "Alphabetical" Porter; the daughter was named Helen Herschel Sherman, in honor of the place; and wintering-over was an altogether remarkable occasion, with baseball and soccer played on the ice, and with musical and theatrical soirees organized by the wives, with handwritten invitations and programs distributed around the fleet. From this voyage they brought home Eskimo-made fur coats, hats, skin mukluks, embroidered mittens, toys for Bertie carved out of walrus ivory (a manned kayak, a seal, and a tiny dogsled), and a smoking pipe fashioned of lead and wood by the Chukchi of Siberia, a region of the world seldom visited by any but the Yankee blubber-hunters of New Bedford and San Francisco.

It is worth mentioning here that in these final years of the nineteenth century the Western Arctic bowhead whale fishery (for oil and baleen) was in its heyday while the old New Bedford sperm whale fishery was in decline; and to take advantage of the proximity of California to Alaska, much of the fleet was transferred from New England to San Francisco. As John Bockstoce explains in *Whales, Ice, and Men,*

> *Some captains brought their families with them. They had to pay the owners $1000 for the privilege but it made their lives — and the lives of others at Pauline Cove [on Herschel Island] — far more pleasant. The winter of 1894-95 was the first with women and children in the fleet… The presence of women and children softened the hard edge of life that grows among men in isolation. At once the women began organizing parties, using every conceivable excuse for celebrations to leaven the gloom of winter.*

For this family the season was particularly memorable: "Certainly, one of the happiest events of those years took place on May 8, 1895, when Mrs. Albert Sherman gave birth to a 7 ½ pound girl, Helen Herschel."

Albert Case Sherman was born in 1849, the son of Peleg Sherman (1804-1862) and the former Hannah P. Case (1809-), farmers in South Westport, Massachusetts. A much older brother, Charles Frederick — to whom Albert was close throughout his life and with whom he and his family lived from time to time — was heir to the farm, and Albert went to sea. (In later life they later inherited and shared the famous old Ricketson House, built around 1680 in South Westport.) Sherman's first command was as relief captain for Holder C. Slocum on the New Bedford bark *Sarah B. Hale* (1877-80): the voyage was never completed and the vessel was condemned at St. Helena. Sherman was next given the bark *George and Mary* of New Bedford (1881-82) for a voyage to Hudson Bay, but all of his remaining voyages were to the North Pacific and Western Arctic, starting with the bark *Hunter* of San Francisco (1882-83), which, in addition to the conventional catch, returned 300 lbs. of walrus ivory; and the bark *John Carver* (1884-85), on which he was relieved by Horace B. Montross and which was his last voyage out of New Bedford. He now took rented lodgings in San Francisco, where he played out the remaining 15 years of his whaling career on seasonal forays to the Western Arctic grounds in a succession of newfangled auxiliary steam-barks. These were substantially larger than the wooden ships and barks that had hitherto typified the Yankee whaling trade: they had steel-reinforced hulls, better to withstand the chafing and pressure of the Arctic pack ice, and coal-fired steam engines, which theoretically made them more maneuverable and less vulnerable to being "nipped" in icy waters. Sherman made two voyages in the *Lucretia* (1885-86 and 1886-87), one in the *Belvedere* (1887-88), then three in the *William Lewis* (1888-91), on the first of which he joined the ship at Honolulu as relief captain for Cyrus Manter, and on the third of which the vessel was lost at Point Barrow in March 1891. He next had the *Beluga* (1892), the *Orca* (1893), and *Beluga* again (1894-96), including the famous wintering-over season of 1895-96 at Herschel Island; then *Orca* again (sailed 1897), a voyage that unfortunately ended in another shipwreck; and finally the *Thrasher* (1899), after which he retired from whaling and became proprietor of a livery stable in New Bedford. The wife who accompanied him to sea was the former Caroline L. Nye, popularly known as Carrie and the mother of his two children; but for some reason her name appears in the U.S. Census records as Ann C. Sherman, for which her daughter, Hannah Sherman, had no explanation. More puzzling is an unsubstantiated genealogy that claims that Caroline was actually his fourth wife — which Hannah Sherman was also unable to confirm; that he was married to a woman named Molly Ann on 5 August 1880, to Carrie L. Kirschbaum of Westport circa 1881, and to Hannah C. Brownell circa 1882 — the presumption being that each of the three ladies died before Sherman wed the next one. Some of all of these marriages may have been cited in confusion with other husbands named Albert Sherman. Whatever his prior circumstances, Albert married Carrie Nye around 1890. The scrimshaw and Arctic collections eventually passed to Bertie, a graduate of MIT in the class of 1913 and a professional musician; thence to his three daughters. Meanwhile, in 1930 Bertie donated to NBWM a modest but diverse inventory of the family's whaling souvenirs. Most were Native-made and a few had ethnographic significance: three Siberian baskets, a fishing hook, two stone sinkers, a spoon carved out of musk-ox bone, four fancy moccasins, 12 arrows for bird hunting, a fur parka, three odd gloves, two fur-tipped gloves, a walrus tusk cribbage board, and six fur rugs. There were also three pieces of scrimshaw that Captain Sherman may have made himself: two walrus ivory pointers and a very unusual crimper ("jagging wheel") made of musk-ox bone.

* **Sherman, J.N.** (fl. circa 1835-39). A one-voyage whaleman from the Massachusetts hinterlands who made an unusual walking stick aboard the whaleship *John Coggeshall* of Newport, Rhode Island, on a voyage celebrated for the illustrious scrimshaw of his shipmates, the brothers Caleb and Thomas Albro (qq.v. in the *Dictionary* and above). In fact, J.N. Sherman and Caleb Albro became lifelong friends on the voyage, and some 24 years after it ended their families were united in matrimony when Sherman's eldest son married Albro's eldest daughter.

The walking stick is beautifully made and has a charming provenance. It has a turned whale ivory knob pommel terminating in an octagonal base with an octagonal baleen separator band, a tapered panbone shaft with strips of baleen inset in a spiral pattern and geometric forms inlaid in abalone, mother-of-pearl, and baleen. It came to NBWM in 1976 from Everett B. Sherman in memory of his wife and son, Rachel M. Sherman and Richard E. Sherman, and was described at the time as having been made by his father's grandfather — "made by Waldo's grandfather, J.N. Sherman, when at sea" — that is, by Everett's great-grandfather. Everett was a great-grandson of both J.N. Sherman *and* Caleb Albro.

James Nelson Sherman was born at Bellingham, Massachusetts, in 1817, the son of Elisha Sherman (1780-1875) and Nancy Cooke (1790-), who were married in 1811. Elisha was a textile manufacturer in Bellingham and moved his family to the not-far-distant town of Foxborough to take advantage of an opportunity there. The Foxborough Cotton Manufacturing Company, for some reason nicknamed the Dighton Company, had been incorporated in 1814, but it "failed about 1820, and Elisha Sherman, Arnold & Ballou came from Billingham [sic] and run [sic] the factory for thread warp. Sherman soon bought out his partners, and for eight or ten years made cotton cloth and comforters" (*History and Directory of Foxboro*, Massachusetts, Needham, Massachusetts, 1890). James, the fourth of Elisha Sherman's eleven children, was thus raised in Foxborough and may have served an apprenticeship in textile manufacture. But rather than go into the mill for a living, at age 18 he obtained a Seaman's Protection Paper (passport) at Newport, Rhode Island, and sailed immediately as a green hand in *John Coggeshall* under Captain Seth W. Macy, 1835-39. Caleb J. Albro of Jamestown, Rhode Island, was an Ordinary Seaman on that voyage, his brother Thomas Albro was the steward, and, as noted in the *Dictionary*, "J.N. Sherman brought home an Albro tooth from the *John Coggeshall* in 1839" — a precious souvenir of the voyage and of their friendship, inscribed "Ship John Coggeshall Newport Sailed Oct 3 1835 Returned April 12 1839." It descended in the Sherman family along with J.N. Sherman's own inlaid walking stick.

For the balance of his career Sherman was a stone cutter and stone mason. He married twice, the first time in October 1839 — only seven months after returning in the *John Coggeshall* — to Catherine Drake of Newport. They lived in Foxborough until she died, probably in 1843. They had three children, the oldest of whom, James Stowell Sherman, was heir to the scrimshaw. J.N. Sherman's second marriage was in 1845 to Irene Bellows of Holliston, Massachusetts, where he moved his family, continued working as a stone cutter and stone mason, and fathered one or possibly two more children. Irene died in the 1890s, whence Sherman retired to East Providence, Rhode Island, where he spent his last years. He died in 1907 at age 90. The scrimshaw passed to his eldest son, James Stowell Sherman (1840-1908), who outlived J.N. by only a year. Born in Foxborough and raised there and in Holliston, in his late teens James went to live with and work for his father's old shipmate, Caleb Albro, who was now retired from whaling and a brief career as a merchant sea captain, and was farming in Portsmouth, Rhode Island. James served in Company F of the 29th Massachusetts Infantry in the Union Army, and in January 1863 married Albro's daughter, Mary Taylor Albro. Their eldest son — J.N.'s grandson — was Waldo Everett Sherman (born 1863), a locomotive engineer and later a machinist in a stove foundry at Milford, Massachusetts. He married Jennie Frances Linsey of Warren, Rhode Island. Their only son was Everett Bertram Sherman (1898-1976), who married Rachel Marble (1897-), worked as a machinist and automobile mechanic at Somerset, Massachusetts, and died in 1976. He bequeathed to NBWM the walking stick made by his great-grandfather, J.N. Sherman, and the tooth engraved by his other great-grandfather, Caleb Albro, who had been J.N. Sherman's shipmate on the *John Coggeshall* 140 years before.

* **Shiverick, Nathaniel** (fl. circa 1810-33). This "yeoman" maker of a straightedge of whale skeletal bone inscribed "N. Shiverick," "Nathl. Shiverick," and "N.S." (in KNB), was born at Falmouth, Massachusetts, in April 1783, the son of Samuel Shiverick (1755-1826) and Achsah Croel (1760-1821), and the grandson of Captain Samuel Shiverick (1716-1771). Nathaniel (q.v. in the *Dictionary*) built ships on Cape Cod, ran merchant schooners, married Olive Gifford in October 1812, and fathered three sons. One of his four brothers, Foster Shiverick, was a whaleman who died at sea in 1821 at age 30. (Not to be confused with Nathaniel Shiverick of Wareham, Massachusetts, a close contemporary who married Salome Fearing in 1811 and was the father of eight, including one called Nathaniel Jr.)

Shockley, William I. (fl. circa 1875-1907). He was one of New Bedford's better known latter-day whaling masters, whose involvement in scrimshaw is mentioned explicitly in the oddly contrived, semi-fictionalized book *Scrimshaw and Sudden Death*. The narrative is loosely based on the journals of Lester A. Mosher (q.v.) on the 1899-1900 voyage of the New Bedford bark *Canton*; Shockley was the captain on that voyage. On page 162 the captain, officers, and some of the men are described producing various classic types of scrimshaw. The mates (who in real life actually turn out to have been mostly the boatsteerers) were making canes with fancy handles, one of the men was engraving a panbone plaque with a whaling scene and portrait of the *Canton*, another was carving a panbone blackjack with a handle shaped like a fist, and Mosher himself, the boatsteerer on whose authentic journal the flawed narrative is based, was making panbone fittings for his whaleboat. Captain Shockley is said to have been working on a panbone swift, about which no further details are offered. Unfortunately, the swift itself has not come to light. Absent such firsthand testimony, one might have thought 1900 to be a bit late in the game for a swift, and the voyage itself too short to allow for its completion. Perhaps Mrs. Shockley was a bit old fashioned in her tastes, and perhaps the captain's work on it spanned more than a single voyage. (The others implicated in Mosher's accusation of scrimshaw are Lester A. Mosher himself, Alexander Nanton, Herbert R. Reynolds, and Nicholas R. Vieira, qq.v.)

There were two prominent Shockley families of New Bedford whaling masters, the Lakeville Shockleys and the Middleborough / Fall River Shockleys. The Lakeville Shockleys were two brothers who lived in that municipality a few miles north of New Bedford: Joseph Shockley, Jr., who commanded three voyages during 1837-41; and William Shockley, who had a much longer career as skipper of six voyages, from 1841 to 1860. William Irving Shockley, reputed maker of the swift, was from the other clan, consisting of father and son. The father was Captain Humphrey Alden Shockley (1815-1890), a contemporary of the Lakeville Shockley brothers and originally from Middleborough (his oil portrait by Joseph Whiting Stock is in NBWM). Ironically with respect to the present context, Humphrey's first command was the *Two Brothers* (1840-41). He was then captain of the *Lucas* (1842-43), two voyages in the *Roman* (1843-47), and two in the *William Hamilton* (1848-51). On his last voyage he left the ship before its completion and retired permanently with his wife, the former Hannah Gray Wilson, to a farm near Fall River. William I. Shockley was their son, the second of three sons and the sixth of eight children, born in 1858, a few years after Captain Humphrey Shockley had already retired from whaling. William's brother Hubert, older by about three years, joined their father on the family farm, but William was always a sailor, living at the farmstead between voyages. His career — the longest of any of the Shockleys — came along at a time when the market for sperm oil, spermaceti, and whale oil was in decline: New Bedford's traditional sperm whale fishery was no longer as profitable as it had been in his father's time, and in the 1870s and '80s much of the fleet and many of the resources were being moved to California to take advantage of its proximity to the North Pacific and Western Arctic grounds. This enabled shorter voyages to hunt bowhead whales for their baleen — so-called "whalebone" — for still-current uses in fashion and industry. So although William grew up in the New Bedford circuit and advanced extremely rapidly up the hierarchy — a voyage commencing at age 16 in the bark *Louisa* (1874-78), another, already promoted to third mate, in the *Charles W. Morgan* (1878-81), and another, possibly in the *Bounding Billow* of Edgartown (1881-82) — when he finally became a captain at the very young age of 25, he spent the entire first part of his career in San Francisco barks: one voyage in the

Fleetwing (1883-84), two whole voyages and two partial ones in the *Jacob A. Howland* (1885-88), one or two in the *Tamerlane* (1890 and 1890-91; see Hegarty 1959, 16, and Lund 2001, 287), and one in the *James Allen 2d* (1891-92). In 1887, when he was at Port Clarence, Alaska, in the *John Howland*, Captain Shockley posed for a group photo with nine other Arctic whaling masters (NBWM; illus. Bockstoce 1995, 225). But after he returned to San Francisco in the *James Allen* in 1892 he did not go whaling again for more than six years, hence was not present at the famous 1895-96 wintering-over of the Arctic fleet at Herschel Island. He returned to the fishery in November 1899, and on his last three voyages hunted sperm whales in Atlantic waters in three venerable New Bedford barks, among the last still extant: *Canton 2d* (1899-1900), *Sunbeam* (1901-02), and *Wanderer* (1905-07). With this, he left off whaling and took up dairy farming full time in Acushnet. In 1922 he and ten other renowned-and-retired whaling masters posed for a group photograph mounted to generate publicity for the silent feature film then being shot in New Bedford; the title of the photo is self-explanatory: "Famous New England Whaling Captains with John L.E. Pell, author of the epic screen feature, 'Down to the Sea in Ships,' Taken on the deck of the whaler *Charles W. Morgan*, August 1922." The male lead was Raymond McKee (q.v.), whom the film and the surrounding whaling milieux inspired to become a scrimshaw artist and scrimshaw collector; and of course Captain Shockley had been third mate on the *Morgan* more than 40 years before. Sometime in the 1920s William and Phebe Shockley left the farm in Acushnet and retired to Dartmouth.

Silva, J. (fl. 19th century). A bright polychrome tooth with a large five-pointed star, leafy floral ornaments, the broadside figure of a sperm whale, and two ship-portrait vignettes, is boldly signed "J. SILVA" (reported by Ryan M. Cooper). The name is Portuguese and the whaleman was undoubtedly of Azorean or Cape Verdean ancestry, but the name alone is far too common to provide the basis for any reliable attribution. On the other hand, Captain Joseph D. Silva (q.v.) is an Azorean of this name known to have made at least one piece of scrimshaw.

Silva, Joseph D. (fl. circa 1832-87). One of the earliest New Bedford whaling masters of Azorean birth, he is credited with an inlaid, hinged wooden box. The solid provenance from a descendant and heir describes it as inlaid with elephant ivory — an unusual and anachronistic medium for whalemen's scrimshaw (reported by Tim Sylvia, the species of ivory identified by Frederick Mitchell; now in a private collection). Silva was born on Fayal either in 1821 (according to the U.S. Census of 1900) or 1823 (according to Pat Amaral, *They Ploughed the Seas*, 1978, 120f). He was the son of Antone Francis and his wife, Louise Silva, who is said to have been a descendent of José Cardosa, sometime Governor General of the Azores. Joseph ran away to sea in 1832 as cabin boy in the whaleship *Brandt*. He landed at New Bedford and, like so many of his fellow-islanders, made a career of whaling, rising through the ranks eventually to become captain of eleven voyages: the New Bedford barks *Milwood* (1854-57), *George* (1857-61, 1862-64), *Edward Everett* (1867-69 and 1873-75), and *Sarah* (1876-78); the brigs *George J. Jones* of Fairhaven (1872-73) and *Varnum H. Hill* of New Bedford (three voyages, 1878-84); and the Edgartown schooner *Hattie E. Smith* (relief captain, 1885-87). According to Amaral, he may also have been captain of two outings in the whaling brig *Comet* of Honolulu (1870-71), on the second of which the *Comet* was lost with 32 other ships and barks in the Arctic disaster of 1871. Meanwhile, New Bedford artist Benjamin Russell produced a watercolor ship-portrait inscribed with the title, "Bark *Edward Everett*, Cap't Joseph D. Silva /

Bound in from Sea" (in NBWM). Joseph's younger brother, John D. Silva (1828-1893), who sailed with Joseph on at least one or two previous voyages, became captain of two New Bedford whaling voyages in his own right (1878-81). Joseph married Nancy Gould (1826-1895), a Bavarian immigrant. Their two daughters, Anna, born in 1855, and Caroline, probably born in 1868, both became music teachers. There is quite a lot of confusion about their later lives, affecting the provenance of the scrimshaw. Amaral claims that Caroline married Francis E. Stranburg, captain of four whaling voyages (1851-65). However, Amaral's dates are impossible (with the daughter born the same year as the mother) and the relationship remains unclear. Amaral claims that Stranburg was born in 1817 in Sweden; the U.S. Census has him born in Germany circa 1815 and living in Fairhaven in 1850 with a wife who was indeed named Caroline but is also reported as having been born in Germany, circa 1817. Joseph Silva was widowed in 1895 and is said to have lived thereafter with his daughter Caroline, surnamed Silva, who evidently remained unmarried. The 1900 Census, though it gives their surname as De Silva (an error obviously in confusion with Joseph *D.* Silva), specifies unequivocally that Joseph was born in Portugal in 1821 and Caroline in Massachusetts in 1868, that Joseph was married for 45 years, and that his father had been born in England and his mother in Portugal.

Simas, Manuel Francisco (fl. 1960s-2000s). Artist of Ponta Garça, Island of São Miguel, Azores (Portugal). João A. Gomes Vieira reports that scrimshaw formerly erroneously attributed to Maria do Espirito Santos Simas (Mrs. Manuel J. Madruga) of Lajes do Pico is actually the avocational work of Manuel F. Simas, a distant kinsman, who lived for many years in East Providence, Rhode Island, worked in a Massachusetts factory nearby, and later returned to the Islands. These include a sperm whale tooth relief-carved with the bust portrait of a traditional Azorean fisherman (from Bourne 1-2 Aug 1978, #568) and the full-round-carved effigy of an albatross head (Frank, "L'art du Scrimshaw," *Chasse-Marée*, N° 67, Sept. 1992, 61; and Frank, "The Art of Scrimshaw," *Maritime Life and Traditions*, N° 6, Feb. 2000, 57), both in KNB (illustrated together in *More Scrimshaw Artists*, 103). There are various other works in institutional collections at Lajes do Pico, Horta (Island of Fayal), and Santa Cruz (Flores), as well as private collections in the Azores, including engraved teeth in a distinctive monochrome stipple style, but most notably full-round-carved and relief-carved portraiture and religious figures in whale ivory and bone.

* **Simas, Maria do Espirito Santos** — see **Simas, Manuel Francisco**

Simmons, Manuel (fl, circa 1863-67). Possible maker of a tooth monochrome engraved with polychrome highlights: a circumferential sperm whaling scene of two whaleboats in pursuit, two floating carcasses marked with waifs, two whaleships in the background flying American flags at the main and house flags on the fore and mizzen, topped by "a swooping American eagle, grasping harpoons in its talons above the date July 10, 1864"; also inscribed "Ship Eliza / Adams," "Capt. J.W. Cornell," "off Coast Madagascar," and surmounted by the initials "M.S." (Sotheby's-NY, 26 Sept. 2008, #26). Among several mysteries concerning this tooth is the presence of the name of Captain John W. Cornell, who was captain of the *John Dawson* at the time (1862-64), the *Triton* next (1865-68), and not the *Eliza Adams* until 1876-78, which was the sixth and last of his whaling voyages as captain (1859-78). The actual captain of the *Eliza Adams* on the voyage of 1863-67 was Coddington P. Fish. The Sotheby's catalogue entry is followed by a series of narrative irrelevancies about John W. Cornell and the *Eliza Adams* that have nothing to do with the scrimshaw, which was almost certainly a product of the 1863 voyage. Also, it is not clear whether the initials refer to the maker of the scrimshaw or the intended recipient or someone else. The only man with the initials MS on either the 1863-67 or the 1876-78 voyage of the *Eliza Adams* was Manuel Simmons, a seaman on the earlier voyage about whom the crew list (NBPS) contains no further details. From the 1860 U.S. Census it is clear that he was born circa 1825 in Portugal (almost certainly in the Azores Islands), had a Portuguese-born wife named Mary, and had fellow-whaleman Manuel Thomas and Thomas's wife and two infant children living with them in New Bedford. There is evidently no further record.

* **Sizer, William** (fl. circa 1834-40). New England whaleman of Franco-Azorean descent who was almost certainly the artist hitherto known as the *L.C. Richmond* Engraver or *L.C. Richmond* Artist, one of the greatest scrimshaw picture-makers of all time. In the absence of a provenance and crew lists, an inscription on the scrimshaw itself is the only evidence that he was in the crew on the 1834-37 voyage of the whaleship *L.C. Richmond* (the vessel's only voyage out of Bristol, Rhode Island, before being sold to New Bedford owners). He produced brilliantly polychrome engraved teeth on this and possibly other voyages, several of which are provisionally identified. Inscriptions on two of the teeth specifically refer to the *L.C. Richmond* and three are clearly and explicitly signed. As noted in the *Dictionary*, one has images of Liberty and American patriotic devices, and is inscribed and signed "Wm. G. Pease, Eng[raved] by Wm. Sizer" (BJ:1, #441, from Bourne, Aug. 1966, #309). William J. Boylhart provided the description of another Sizer tooth: on one side, a monochrome hybridized standing female figures of Liberty, with Liberty Pole and Liberty Cap, and traces of polychrome highlights; and Hope, with fouled anchor; surmounted by a willow motif and the bold signature "ENG. / BY / W. SIZER." On the back (top to bottom) are: a leafy vine motif; a spread eagle with crossed flags, naval cannon, and USA shield, clutching in its beak a riband inscribed "EPLURIBUS / UNUM"; the starboard stern-quarter view of a 44-gun frigate flying the stars and stripes at the spanker, a commission pennant at the main, and a short pennant at the fore. And on the edges: a broadside portrait of a sperm whale and the inscription, "PACIFIC OCEAN / JULY.4.1834". The KNB specimen, which has exceptionally vivid color in sparkling, like-new condition, features a broadside view of the ship, whaleboats in the process of harpooning, birds in flight overhead, and an inscription below in bold, serifed capitals, "L.C. RICHMOND / CAPT. J[OSEPH] SHERMAN" (this was the voyage of 1834-37), and the characteristic female portrait in an oval frame on verso, but is not signed. A privately-held version that is virtually identical in size and is from the same whale shows the ship from the starboard stern quarter, with a breeching sperm whale "with chimney afire" (that is, spouting blood); there are no birds, the inscription reads "L.C. RICHMOND / W. SIZER Engr.," and the ship is, if anything, even more highly detailed and the engraving at least equally refined; however, the color is significantly faded with pigment losses; the reverse side is polished but undecorated (ex Niagara Falls Museum; ex Northeast Auctions, 2006). Two teeth recently discovered together in a private legacy collection are certainly by the same hand. One is a near twin of the obverse side of the well-known *L.C Richmond* tooth in KNB, a sperm whaling scene of a full-rigged ship with boats lowered in pursuit. The accompanying tooth is larger and the

back is polished and undecorated, but the front has a standing female figure in Renaissance-like garb that is unmistakably a mainstream variant of the several female portraits by this hand, including the one on the back of KNB tooth (reported by Kent Kopke). An analogous portrait by the same hand, this time in an oval frame, is partially illustrated in *The Craftsman in America* (National Geographic Society, 1975, 71). It is these strikingly similar, meticulously engraved female portraits in elaborate gowns reminiscent of the Renaissance — some in oval frames, some not — that connect the two *L.C. Richmond* teeth to the several teeth in private collections on which whaling scenes and ship portraits are absent, but which have analogous female portraits, enabling them all to be confidently attributed to the same hand, who is now known by the signatures to be William Sizer. One of these has the portrait in three-quarter length, as it appears on the KNB specimen (ex J. Welles Hemderson Collection, Northeast. Aug. 16, 2008, #672); another has the full-length version (reported by John Miklos).

Unfortunately, no complete crew list of the 1834-37 voyage of the *L.C. Richmond* is known to survive, and the name Sizer does not appear on a partial roster interpolated from a list of whales sighted on the voyage (in PEM, reported by Daniel R. Finamore). Thus, even Sizer's presence in the *L.C. Richmond* crew remains a matter of unconfirmed speculation, based on the evidence of the scrimshaw alone. Another complicating factor is that William G. Pease, to whom two of the Sizer teeth are inscribed, was afterwards captain of the New Bedford brig *Juno* (1839-40), of which there is also no complete crew list extant. This was Pease's only whaling voyage as a captain, his earlier career is not known (except that he may have been the William Pease from Chilmark, Martha's Vineyard, who was in the ship *Leonidas* of Fairhaven during 1820-23), and nobody named Pease appears on the partial *L.C. Richmond* crew list either. His name on Sizer's scrimshaw suggests that Pease may have been aboard the *L.C. Richmond* on the 1834-47 voyage, or Sizer may have done the scrimshaw while in the crew of the *Juno* on the later voyage under Captain William G. Pease. In any case, while much is known about his ancestry, the voyage in the *L.C. Richmond* and possibly the one in the *Juno* are the only two to which Sizer's name is in any way connected, and those circumstantial associations constitute almost everything that is known about his career.

Like virtually all Sizers in New England, William was a descendant of Anthony Sizer (1707-1753), who was originally Antonio DeSocieur or DeZocieur, a Frenchman born into a wealthy family on the Island of Terceira, in the Azores, in 1707. In 1726 Antonio shipped aboard an American vessel commanded by a Captain Henshaw and returned with the ship to Boston, anglicized his name, settled and married in Middletown, Connecticut, and worked as a sailor and later as a farmer. His namesake son, Anthony (1740-1764), was a career mariner, who on his third voyage "was drowned at sea by falling off the bowsprit of a sloop." Antonio's youngest son, William (1746-1826), was a sailor in the coastwise trade, a boatbuilder, a schoolteacher, and a captain in Colonel Jeduthon Baldwin's Regiment of Artificers in the Revolutionary War. His namesake son, William Sizer, Jr. (1770-1851) of Middletown, Connecticut, married Prudence Plum (1774-1814) in 1798 and moved to Chester, Massachusetts. It was their son, known as William III, born in Chester in 1801, who appears to have been the scrimshaw artist. A year after his mother's death in 1814 his father was remarried, to Charlotte Bassett (1790-1863). Not long afterwards, William III became a sailor and whaleman. Sadly, he "died at sea, April 16, 1840, and is buried in the Isle of Tahiti." According to Lillian Hubbard Holch, William left two sons, named John and Hiram, at least one of whom was born at Meadville, Pennsylvania, circa 1830; but she makes no mention of a wife or widow (Holch, Sizer Genealogy, 229).

Small, Leonard (fl. circa 1832-62). A whaling master of Cape Cod and Boston, he was the younger brother of Captain Nathan Small (q.v.): one or the other may have made a stipple engraved tooth with polychrome highlights that is attributed to "Captain Small of Provincetown"(private collection, reported by William J. Boylhart). One side has a sailor with short side-whiskers and beard, brimmed hat with ribbon, short jacket with brass buttons, white duck trousers, and patent leather slippers, standing on a balcony with a trellis railing and roses underfoot, dancing with a woman with her hair pulled back, wearing a low-cut, short-sleeve blouse with frilly edges and rose ornament, pendant earrings, a necklace of pearls or beads, a calf-length skirt with flowered border, and pump slippers. The other side has a rare cutting-in scene: three sailors standing on outboard platforms, flensing a blanket piece of blubber from a sperm whale, with three men wielding the upright pawls of a windlass forward. A garland of roses encircles the top of the tooth.

The brothers were born in Provincetown, the sons of Abraham Small and the former Mary Hopkins, and both brothers died on whaling voyages in their late forties. Nathan, the elder by four or five years, commanded a string of Provincetown brigs and schooners (circa 1840-60), some of which have not been identified (though his stints as captain on two voyages the brig *Phoenix* during 1845-47 are well documented). He died at sea in 1860. Leonard, born circa 1815, actually preceded his brother as master of the *Phoenix* on portions of four short voyages (1840-44), then commanded the brig *Gem* of Beverly, Massachusetts. (1849-50), followed by three or possibly four brief outings in the bark *Rothschild* of Boston (1850-52) and two longer cruises in the Provincetown schooner *Thriver* (1857-62). He lived in Boston and was married to a woman named Jane who bore him several children. They had a boarder from the Azores, a fish dealer born circa 1821, who must at one time have been in one of Captain Small's whaling crews and who Americanized his name by adopting Leonard's, calling himself Manuel Small. In January 1862, while captain of the *Thriver*, Leonard, the second mate, and two hands were killed by a whale.

It is not known which of the Small brothers may have made the scrimshaw. The association with Captain Small "of Provincetown" would seem to point to Nathan, who lived there, rather than Leonard, who was born there but lived in Boston. Both brothers commanded whaling voyages from Provincetown, but an implied association with the *Thriver* circa 1859-60 would seem to point to Leonard, who commanded several voyages of the *Thriver* during 1857-62. However, as some of Nathan's voyages are unknown, it is not certain whether he too might have commanded the *Thriver* at some point.

Small, Nathan (fl. circa 1828-60). Provincetown whaling master, brother of Leonard Small (q.v.), who may have made a stipple engraved tooth with polychrome highlights attributed to "Captain Small of Provincetown." Nathan was born at Provincetown in 1811, the son of Abraham Small and the former Mary Hopkins. Nothing is known of his early career and few details have emerged about the string of Provincetown whaling brigs and schooners he commanded (circa 1840-60), some of which have not been identified. However, his stints as captain on two voyages the brig *Phoenix* (1845-47) are well documented. He lived in Provincetown, married Jane Lancey in 1837, and died at sea in April 1860.

Smith, Charles F. (fl. circa 1855-61). He came from a family of whaling masters and farmers, made two whaling voyages in the 1850s, and produced a classic double-cage swift, given to NBWM by a granddaughter in 1986. It has an octagonal wooden cabinet base standing on four ball feet, containing four ebony-faced drawers with whale ivory knobs; an octagonal platform above the base is supported by eight turned whale ivory columns, and the tops of the base and the platform are inlaid with mahogany and ebony in the form of compass roses. The swift itself has a shaft turned from skeletal whale bone, surmounted by a whale ivory cup engraved with a serpentine leafy vine motif; skeletal whale bone slats (ribs), tied with twine; and a threaded brass fastener. As he was not married until several years after his whaling days, the supposition is that he may have made it for his mother.

George Smith, Jr. (1790-1870), and his wife, Sarah née Estes (1791-1867), were farmers in Dartmouth, Massachusetts, who married around 1815 and had a brood of children over a period spanning more than 20 years. Charles, born in 1837, was the youngest and had two much older brothers who were already veteran whalemen when Charles was still a schoolboy. In fact, Joseph E. Smith, born in 1817, became a captain when Charles was barely nine years old: he was master of one voyage in the Westport bark *United States* (1846-49) and five in the Westport brig *Solon* (1850-62). But when Charles was ready to try his own hand at whaling he went in his brother Leander's ship, the *Dr. Franklin* of Westport (1855-56), signing for the 135th lay as a green hand. This was actually the third command for Leander Smith (1825-1910), who had already skippered two voyages of the bark *Mattapoisett* of Westport (1853 and 1853-54) and would later serve as relief captain of the New Bedford ship *Benjamin Tucker* (1859-61). After the *Dr. Franklin* Charles went as boatsteerer for the 70th lay in the New Bedford bark *Cachalot*. They sailed in September 1857 as planned, but Captain William H. Perry left the ship on account of illness not long after and was relieved by Richard Wilson, during whose regime the *Cachalot* was sold abroad at Valparaiso in 1861, with no record of any oil returned to New Bedford. This cannot have been a profitable result for the crew, and it effectively ended Smith's whaling career. In fact, with the Civil War now brewing, his brothers Joseph and Leander would soon retire from whaling too. Around 1866 Charles married Ella C. Borden (1849-1912), daughter of mariner William Borden and his wife Hepsibeth. The couple lived for the next few years on the Borden farm in Dartmouth, where the first of their own children were born and which provided Ella and the family secure and familiar surroundings whenever Charles was at sea, in the same way the same farm had done for her own mother and sailor father. Charles and Ella's daughter Sarah, known as Sadie, came along in 1879, by which time they had a farm of their own and Charles had left off seafaring. By 1900 they had moved to New Bedford, where Ella managed a boardinghouse peopled by a diverse Americana menagerie, including Sadie, now 21 and soon to be married; a shop clerk, a bookkeeper, the superintendent of a local paper mill who had come to New Bedford from Ohio, a master mechanic from Rhode Island, an electrician, a machinist and his telephone-operator wife, and two young servants. Charles died in 1906 and Ella in 1912.

Smith, Clark — see **Clark, Benjamin Smith**

Smith, Washington (fl. 1821-25). A panbone busk polychrome engraved with floral and geometric motifs is inscribed on the back, "Made by Washington on Board a Whaling Ship During his Confinement for Talking Disrespectfully to his Captain. L.N.S." On the basis of the name and initials, the scrimshaw is provisionally attributed to Washington Smith, born circa 1802, a native of Taunton,

Massachusetts, and resident of Freetown, Massachusetts, who made four whaling voyages out of Fairhaven: two in the schooner *Telemachus* (1821-23) and two in the ship *Amazon* (1823-25). His brother Israel, a year younger, was a green hand in the *Amazon* on the latter voyage.

Soule, James M. (fl. circa 1839-68). Westport whaling master who either made or had made for him a wooden box that may only marginally be considered to be scrimshaw and has no other provenance (in NBWM). (Both Starbuck and Lund give the surname as Sowle, the U.S. Census gives it variously as Sowle and Soule, but in the whaling annals and genealogical records it is Soule.) The box has a geometric pattern inlaid on the hinged lid, and contains the label "CAPT. JAMES M. SOULE," along with dried flowers, artificial flowers made out of feathers, and carved-and-painted bone slats from a fancy Chinese fan — treasures of unknown origin and undocumented significance to the family. It is not insignificant that while he was at sea on a whaling voyage in 1852, his fiancée, Ruth Grinnell, in a letter describing events back home in Westport, asks him to "write when you are coming home" and "bring all the remarkable curiosities you can easily obtain, without much expense" (NBWM).

Soule was born in 1823, the youngest of the five sons and three daughters of Captain James H. Soule of Westport and the former Sophia Gray of Tiverton, Rhode Island. Three of the brothers and a brother-in-law became whaling captains: Gideon W. Soule (1804-1849), Edward Gray Soule (1809-1869), James, and Gideon Davis, Jr., who married their sister Abby in 1826. Their father is said to have committed suicide when James was only about five, and having lost their father early ages, Edward and James went to sea very young. Their maiden voyages are not known, but after at least one prior outing James was boatsteerer in the barks *Hope* of New Bedford (1841-42) and *Barclay* of Westport (1843-44), then second mate (1845-47) and first mate (1848-51) in the ship *Harbinger* of Westport, after which he was captain of the barks *Sacramento* (1852-54), *Mattapoisett* (1855-57), and *Greyhound* (1862-64) of Westport, and *Adeline* (1865-69) and *President 2d* of New Bedford (1867-68). He evidently did very well financially, for not only was he able to retire to farming in 1869, but he had a payroll that included an Azorean farmhand and several domestic servants to do the housekeeping. He was twice married, first to Ruth Grinnell, who bore him three children and died in the early 1860s, and afterwards to a woman named Phebe, who bore three or four more. The box is presumed to have been made for one or the other.

Southworth, Edward (fl. circa 1831-51). He was a career whaleman, a shipmate of the Japanese castaway Manjiro (q.v.), who was known as "John Mung" aboard the ship *John Howland*, and either Edward or his younger brother Luther Southworth (q.v.) made an exquisite panbone jewelry box and matching napkin ring that were donated to NBWM by their niece, Mary A. Southworth, in 1973. The sides of the oblong, hinged box are expertly planed and joined, with a pierced-work motif that is repeated on the napkin ring, and it is lined with pink satin that is visible through the piercings and thus highlights the design. If Edward made them aboard the *John Howland* they would have been among the hitherto unknown works of scrimshaw that Manjiro actually saw with his own eyes, and about which he reported enthusiastically when he returned to Japan in 1850. Southworth was born in 1815 at South Dartmouth, Massachusetts, the second son and the fourth of nine children of John Southworth (1784-1864) and the former Betsy Willis Harward or Haywood (1789-1860). Edward was the eldest child to survive past his teens, but both he and his younger brother

Luther Southworth (q.v.), a fellow whaleman, died young and unmarried, leaving no issue. In his short lifetime he made four voyages in New Bedford ships: a debut as a green hand in the *Robert Edwards* (1831-35); a voyage in an unidentified vessel, presumably as boatsteerer (circa 1835-39); the voyage in the *John Howland*, Captain William Whitfield, on which Manjiro and his castaway companions were rescued and on which Southworth was second mate (1839-43); and a final voyage as first mate under Captain David V. Coffin in the *Arnolda* (1844-48). He did not go whaling again after Luther's death in 1847, and he died himself in 1851.

Southworth, Jason (1848-52). A sometime whaleman credited with a tooth and a busk now in the hands of a descendant, who alleges that Southworth "carved" them aboard the whaleship "Charles Maxwell of New Bedford" — it was actually the *Joseph Maxwell* of Fairhaven — on a voyage of 1848-52 (reported on Public Television's *Antiques Roadshow* at St. Paul, Minnesota, in 2005). The tooth is engraved on one side with a woman and child in an elaborate leafy, floral border, surmounted by the inscription "BEAUTY AND INNOCENCE" in serifed uppercase letters; and on the other side with a crude but largely original scene of a whaleboat being crushed in the jaws of a sperm whale; there are two other boats approaching with lances poised at the ready, two other whales, one breeching and the other sounding, and a bark under sail in the background. The panbone busk is conventional, with star and heart motifs on one side, formed by a series of small dots (concerning which it cannot be determined from the visual and narrative information given whether the dots are inlaid or were engraved and pigmented).

The legacy horde includes photographs of the maker and his wife in later years, and letters from her son by a former marriage. The letters reportedly refer to what amounts to a family scandal, to the effect that Ann Jenison married a whaleman named Lorenzo Wood of Watertown, New York, and bore him a son and a daughter; she later became disillusioned and unhappy, ostensibly because of resentment over Lorenzo's long absences at sea. She established some kind of liaison with Jason Southworth (whether innocent or not was not specified on national television), and when Lorenzo was presumed lost at sea and Ann believed herself to have been widowed, she married Southworth. As the story goes, it later turned out that Lorenzo was not actually dead, but by the time he returned Ann and Jason had been married and (shortly after) moved to the Midwest. These factors, of course, are not accessible as such in the public records, and absent the letters themselves the story is impossible to verify. However, only two whaling voyages are recorded for Lorenzo W. Wood, both in New Bedford ships, as blacksmith in the *South Carolina* from June 1842 to April 1844, and boatsteerer in the *Hercules*, which he joined in progress at Mauritius in October 1846, returning to New Bedford in March 1847. How and when he got to the Indian Ocean between times, and on what ship, is not known. Perhaps he was a victim of shipwreck, though there were only two whaling vessels that sailed from the New Bedford Port District between April 1844 (when Lorenzo returned in the *South Carolina*) and October 1846 (when he joined the *Hercules* at Mauritius) that were subsequently lost. One was the ship *Averick*, which sailed in August 1844 (at just the right interval after the *South Carolina* voyage) and was wrecked in February 1845. The other was the bark *Frances*, which sailed in August 1845 (which would have been rather a long hiatus between voyages) and was burned by the crew at Mauritius in April 1846, which would have put Lorenzo in the right vicinity at almost the right time. But Lorenzo is nowhere listed as a member of either crew. In any case, he was home by March 1847, and Jason Southworth did not sail on his one and only whaling voyage until June 1848. If Ann Jenison Wood were really so despondent on account of Lorenzo's long absences (rather than because of something else), why would she marry another whaleman, who was also given to long voyages? And clearly, given the actual sequence of their voyages, there appears to be something amiss in the chronology of the situation, if not the rationale, as recounted by the informant. Whatever Ann's relationship may have been with Jason beforehand, he was away in the *Joseph Maxwell* during 1848-52, and they could not have been married before he returned in April 1852 — which was slightly more than *five years* after the conclusion of Lorenzo Wood's last known whaling voyage.

The few verifiable facts in the matter are that Lorenzo W. Wood was born at Lanesborough, Massachusetts, in 1809, worked as a blacksmith in Watertown, New York in the 1830s, in Durham, New York by 1840, on a whaling voyage or two at sea during 1842-44, and later again ashore. Ann Jenison was born in Vermont in 1811, married Lorenzo Wood at Watertown in 1830, and actually bore him two children Whether or not Lorenzo disappeared for a while and was presumed lost at sea, he disappears from the historical record around 1850.

Jason Southworth was also born in Vermont, at Rutland in 1815, which made him about four years younger than Ann Jenison. His early life is a mystery and he evidently made only the one whaling voyage, as cooper in the *Joseph Maxwell* at the comparatively advanced age of 31 (1848-52), after which he married the "widow" Wood and moved to Wisconsin, where they took up farming. Son Luther, age 19, evidently moved out there with them. The 1870 U.S. Census reports Jason — with his given name erroneously listed as Josiah — working as a "Jack of all trades" at West Salem, in La Crosse County. He died in Wisconsin, but there is no clear record of when or exactly where. Ann died there in 1881; and Luther, a farmer and hotel operator, in 1909.

Southworth, Luther (fl. circa 1840-47). He may have been the maker of the pierced-work panbone-and-satin jewelry chest and matching napkin ring (in NBWM) described in the article about his older brother, Edward Southworth (q.v.); and possibly a polychrome engraved panbone busk (in KNB). Luther was born in 1821, the fourth son and sixth of nine children of John Southworth (1784-1864) and the former Betsy Willis Harward or Haywood (1789-1860) of South Dartmouth, Massachusetts. He followed Edward into the whale fishery at age 17 in June 1838, when he received his Protection Paper at New Bedford; but in what ship he made his first voyage (1838-40) is not known. His next two ships were the *Fenelon* (1840-42) and *Tuscaloosa* (1842-44), the latter of which he evidently joined while the voyage was already in progress. He was next in the *Governor Troup* (1844-47), and when Captain Gilbert H. Jenney died at Oahu during the voyage Southworth may have been promoted from Ordinary Seaman to boatsteerer. An undated and unattributed panbone busk, festooned with polychrome engraved vignettes of an angel bearing a scroll inscribed "Love," a full-rigged ship under sail inscribed "Fenelon" in a riband above, a spread eagle with arrows and olive branches in its talons surmounting an Irish harp, a basket of flowers with tablecloth, two cut roses, and a knife, and the cursive motto "When this you see / Remember me" framed in scrollwork, may be by his hand. He died at South Dartmouth in 1847 soon after returning in the *Governor Troup*, unmarried and leaving no issue.

Sowle, James M. —see **James M. Soule**

Sowle, Nathaniel W. (fl. circa 1832-62). Rhode Island whaling master. On January 2, 1855, aboard the ship *Sea* of Warren, seaman John Jones wrote in the journal he kept in collaboration with first mate Clothier Pierce, "The Cooper & Capt[ain] Making Canes as usual." The cooper has not been definitively identified, but the captain was right-whaling specialist Nathaniel W. Sowle. He had previously been captain of two voyages in the Providence ship *South America*. The first of these (1843-46) produced what, according to Starbuck, was the "largest voyage on record up to date": a total of 270 barrels of sperm oil, 5,900 barrels of whale oil, and 58,000 pounds of bone, a portion of which was sent home ahead, a portion sold along the way, and the remainder carried home. The second voyage in the *South America* (1846-49) was also uncommonly lucrative, returning 200 barrels of sperm oil, 5,300 of whale oil, and 48,000 pounds of bone. His next voyage was the one in the *Sea* (1851-55), which at 807 register tons Starbuck calls "the largest whaler in service." This one also returned a larger-than-average cargo which could be characterized as mildly disappointing only by comparison with Sowle's previous triumphs in the *South America*: 54 barrels of sperm oil, 4,721 of whale oil, and 19,200 pounds of bone. His last whaling voyage was another impressive success, as master of the New Bedford ship *Montreal* (1857-62), returning a total of 83 barrels of sperm oil, 3,362 of whale oil, and 32,154 pounds of bone. The aggregate must have produced plenty for a comfortable retirement, but nothing is known of Captain Sowle's subsequent activities. He was born circa 1815, probably in Rhode Island, and died there in 1875 at age 60. From the record of his death it appears that he had a son named Henry and a daughter or daughter-in-law named Esther, but no details have emerged about his background, early voyages, or subsequent career, and none of his scrimshaw has been located. (Not to be confused with an earlier Captain Nathaniel W. Sowle, who was drowned at sea while fast to a whale on the third of his three voyages as captain of the ship *Bowditch* of Providence, 1839-44; or the later Captain Nathaniel P. Sowle, who commanded the New Bedford bark *Sea Fox*, 1887-89, and Provincetown schooner *Clara L. Sparks*, 1898.)

* **Spaulding, Timothy C.** (fl. circa 1844-72). In 1974 four of his great-grandsons — four brothers from California — donated to NBWM several objects collected, and some of the scrimshaw said to have been made, by Captain Timothy C. Spaulding of Fairhaven, Massachusetts. These included journals and disbursement accounts from all three of his voyages as a whaling captain; a pair of teeth monochrome engraved with the seals of the six New England states, provisionally attributed to Spaulding himself; another tooth engraved with dozens of miscellaneous faint images, unfinished, also attributed to Spaulding; a plain, polished sperm whale tooth; and a handle for a coconut shell dipper, with scroll ornament. The attributions are based on family lore and on the fact that one of the teeth is unfinished, hence would not have made a suitable gift, say, from a crewman to his captain.

Timothy Chase Spaulding was born at Thetford, Vermont, in 1826, the son of Vermont natives Timothy Spaulding and his second wife, Sylvia Cheney. That the father died at La Porte, Indiana, in 1838, when the future whaleman was only 12 years old and not yet gone to sea, suggests that the entire family may have moved out there for a time. Twelve would not have been inordinately young had Spaulding, like Melville, taken up a seafaring life in the wake of his father's death and his family's consequent financial reversals. As it happened, Spaulding did not. It was not until July 1844 that he obtained a Protection Paper at New Bedford, stating his birthplace as Thetford, Vermont, and his age as 19 (he was actually 18 years, 3 months, and 5 days old), and shipped for the

165th lay as a green hand in the bark *Martha 2d* of Fairhaven. He stuck with this vessel through four voyages, comprising his entire apprenticeship, 16 years in all, ascending by fits and starts to his first command at age about 30. His first three voyages were all sperm whaling ventures to the Indian Ocean under Captain Heman N. Stewart: as a green hand (1844-47); then bounding past Ordinary Seaman and Able Seaman to boatsteerer (1848-51); then, skipping a few ranks, second mate (1852-55); and remarkably, leaping over a first mate's berth to captain (1856-60). Ashore between voyages in 1855, while the *Martha* was refitting for sea, he married Rebecca Frances Stuart of Fairhaven, who bore him a son the following year, when Timothy was on the New Holland grounds of Australia. After the *Martha* Spaulding's sperm whaling expertise and Indian Ocean savvy continued to pay off on successful voyages as master of the barks *Java 2d* of New Bedford (1860-64) and *Elizabeth* of Westport (1867-70). The hiatus between these two voyages was undoubtedly occasioned by his wife's premature death, leaving Timothy a single father living far from his own kinfolk (who were still in Vermont and Indiana). But he was married again in 1865, to Fanny Laurinda Stowell, who bore him another son in 1866; and when Timothy got back to whaling in 1867, in the *Elizabeth,* he brought his 11-year-old son Charles Timothy along with him as cabin boy. It turned out to be quite a noteworthy cruise, for in addition to a respectable cargo of sperm and whale oils they "took 208 pounds of ambergris, worth $94 per pound" (Starbuck, 621). With this lucrative windfall crowning his career, he bowed out, retiring first to Fairhaven (where he had been living throughout his whaling career, but there is evidently no recoverable census record of him and his family in Massachusetts or Vermont during that period); then evidently to South Hadley, Massachusetts, where his third son was born; and finally to Chester, Vermont, where the fourth son was probably born and where Timothy died the following year, in 1879. His son Charles, the former cabin boy, continued in the whaling trade for a while. At age 18 he shipped as seaman on a Western Arctic voyage in the New Bedford bark *Josephine;* but when most of the fleet were crushed in the ice in 1876 and had to be abandoned — the *Josephine* among them — Charles escaped with his life but with little enough pay, and that was the end of whaling for him. He settled in San Francisco, married there the same year his father died, and — having inherited his father's whaling relics — it was his four grandsons who passed them along to the Museum 95 years later.

Spooner, Daniel Hicks (fl. circa 1830-45). A solid attribution of ownership and possible makership emanates from a provenance that at first appears wholly inadequate and inconclusive. Quoting directly, "A friend from Mattapoisett has [an inlaid scrimshaw] box which was passed down through his wife's family... This is all of the information they had: [Her] aunt's maiden name was Hazel Fraiser [sic]. Her mother's maiden name was Edith Spooner. They were from New Bedford. Hazel was born around 1900+. Not much to go on but it's all we have" (reported by Richard Donnelly). This account, minimal as it seems, clearly and unequivocally points to Daniel Hicks Spooner, career whaleman and master of two voyages in the New Bedford brig *Juno* (1842-43 and 1843-45). Not only was he the source of the scrimshaw in the family, but plausibly also the original maker. That he probably apprenticed as a carpenter in his youth, and certainly worked as a carpenter for at least forty years after he retired from whaling, suggests that he must have had the manual skills and likely also the creative inclinations to have produced scrimshaw earlier along.

He was born in 1814 at Dartmouth, Massachusetts, the seventh of eleven children and fourth of five sons of John Spooner and Catharine Gifford. In 1835, already well progressed in his whaling career (he was probably a second mate at the time), he married Rhumana Oman of Dartmouth, who was four years his senior and bore him seven children. After the *Juno* voyages he retired from whaling, lived at Acushnet, worked as a carpenter in the shipbuilding trade, and was later a house carpenter in New Bedford. His youngest son (of three), John Augustus Spooner (1854-c1948), was also a carpenter, and with his wife and children lived with his father after Captain Spooner was widowed in the 1870s. John was married twice, to Ruth A. Wright (1859-1883) and Susan T. Wright (1865-1915), and was the father of six. Captain Spooner's second daughter (of four), Lucy Ann Hicks Spooner (1845-1936), was also married twice: first, in 1866, to William Wilson Salisbury, who died later that same year; then, in 1868, to a distant relation, Charles Franklin Spooner (1830-1908), a local farmer who had made at least one whaling voyage, as a cabin boy in the New Bedford ship *Statira* (1843-45). (Technically, this marriage made her Lucy Ann Hicks Spooner Salisbury Spooner.) The couple had eight children. Their fourth child and eldest daughter was Edith Spooner (1877-1957), one of the two women mentioned in the provenance. She was a schoolteacher until 1898, when she married David Clow Fraser (1871-1946), a native of Nova Scotia. They lived at Lakeville, Freetown, and Mattapoisett, Massachusetts; and their eldest child, born in 1901 at Lakeville, was Hazel Spooner Fraser, the aunt named in the provenance, from whom the scrimshaw descended to the present generation.

* **Spooner, Shubael S.** (fl. 1832-59). He is the "Captain Spooner of Fairhaven [sic]" who was provisionally identified (in *More Scrimshaw Artists*) as the maker of the famous so-called Ceres A teeth and a similarly conceived, brilliantly executed busk upon which the Spooner attribution turns. This attribution was premised upon an unsubstantiated provenance that anecdotally ascribes the busk to "Captain Spooner of Fairhaven." However, new evidence has since emerged which tends convincingly to attribute the Ceres A scrimshaw to William A. Gilpin (q.v.).

On stylistic, iconographical, and technical grounds, the "Spooner" busk and the Ceres A teeth are demonstrably by the same hand. The case for Shubael S. Spooner is predicated on there being only one candidate for the identity of the "Captain Spooner of Fairhaven" mentioned in the provenance. Of several whaling captains named Spooner, none was from Fairhaven; however, Shubael S. Spooner, who lived in New Bedford, was master of the Fairhaven barks *Harvest* and *Favorite* in the 1850s. Evidently, no other whaling master named Spooner ever lived in Fairhaven or commanded a Fairhaven whaler. Part of the case against Spooner is that, while the garments, hair styles, interior decor, and other aspects of the Ceres A scrimshaw, including the busk, clearly date from the 1830s and thus overlap Spooner's youthful career, on stylistic grounds it all seems to belong to the previous generation (William Gilpin was fully ten years older). It is also a fairly reliable rule-of-thumb that such vernacular provenance associations as "made by Captain Spooner of Fairhaven" tend to be contemporaneous — that is, unless there is direct evidence otherwise, descendants tend to associate the artworks with the latter phases of the perpetrator's career, usually the last vessel under his command or the last vessel in which he served — which would place the busk in the 1850s, which it clearly is not.

The apparent fact that Shubael Spooner was not the author of the busk, and hence not of the Ceres A teeth, does not necessarily rule him out as a scrimshaw-maker. The provenance is vague and turns out to be in error regarding this particular busk, but is not necessarily false. It could simply have been made up by a devious purveyor, but it could also refer to some other piece and become attached to this busk in confusion with some other piece, the identity of which is now possibly lost forever. Indeed, given his own long career, and the extraordinary weight of topflight whaling experience in his immediate family (see below), it would seem remarkable if he did not make scrimshaw at one time or another. Whether he was any good at it remains to be seen.

Several features of Spooner's biography have been newly ascertained. Despite indications to the contrary in census records and shipping papers, Shubael S. Spooner was born at New Bedford in 1815 — September 28, 1815, to be precise — the son of Caleb Spooner (1782-1845) and the former Lydia Sherman (1781-1867), who married in 1805. Part of the confusion about his date of birth arises from the fact that he had five siblings — two brothers and three sisters — *all* of whom are listed in the *Vital Records of New Bedford* as having been born on the same day, September 11, 1817. The only reasonable explanation is that some or all of them were christened on that date. (Another sister, Avis, was born in April 1824.) It was a family full of whaling captains, including both of Shubael's brothers and his two brothers-in-law. The older brother, Gideon Spooner, commanded two voyages of the New Bedford ship *Iris* (1839-47), and the younger one, Caleb Spooner, Jr., was captain of the brig *Sea Fox* of Westport (1851-53), and the barks *George* of Newport, Rhode Island (1854-56), and *Cornelia* (1857-60) and *Joshua Bragdon* (1861-64) of New Bedford. Two of their four sisters were whaling masters' wives: in 1831 Charlotte married Henry B. Clark[e] of Somerset, Massachusetts, who was captain of the Somerset bark *Pilgrim* (1844-46); and in 1839 Sophia became Mrs. George H. Clark[e], who commanded five whaling voyages in New Bedford ships and barks (1839-62). As for Shubael, except for his two voyages as captain of Fairhaven barks, all of his whaling voyages were in New Bedford vessels: three in the ship *Hope*, as green hand (1832-33), ordinary seaman (1833-34), and boatsteerer (1834-36); third mate (probably) in the bark *Cornelia* (1837-38); second mate (it would appear) in an unidentified ship (1838-42); first mate in the ships *Charles Frederick* (1842-46) and *St. Peter* (1846-49); and captain of the barks *Harvest* (1850-53) and *Favorite* (1853-57) of Fairhaven. He had been living for a while in Newport when, in 1853, after his first voyage as a captain, he married Elizabeth P. Francis, daughter of Ezra Francis, a New Bedford mason, and the couple moved in with her parents, where brother Caleb Spooner (now also a whaling captain) and his wife and infant daughter joined them. After Shubael's second voyage as a captain he fathered a daughter of his own, Ella F. "Nellie" Spooner. But he knew her only briefly: she was born in March 1858 and he sailed away in October as captain of the New Bedford bark *Montezuma*, never to return. The 1860 U.S. Census records the Spooners and a few other miscellaneous family members living at the Francis homestead in New Bedford, but, ironically, by then Shubael, presumed to be at sea, was actually already deceased. The *Montezuma* went missing in a North Atlantic gale sometime in 1859, with no survivors.

Stanton, James E. (fl. circa 1837-83). Whaling master credited with a rolling pin that has a wooden barrel and flared bollard handles of whale ivory with sealing wax inlaid in the tips. It was donated to NBWM in 1935 by descendants who certified that it was "Made by Capt. James E. Stanton." The maker was the son of Captain Giles E. Stanton (1784-1854), a native of Newport, Rhode Island, who was evidently a master mariner, though not of whalers. (The source of the "captain" honorific is uncertain, but it is a title that is neither easily counterfeited nor casually regarded in such seafaring communities as were home to the Stantons: Newport, Nantucket, and New Bedford.) Having made a whaling voyage or two in his early days, in 1805 Giles married

Hannah Beebe (1786-1872), from one of the old Nantucket whaling families, and settled on the Island, working at the indispensable business of coopering. In the 1830s, when Nantucket's whale hunt was being eclipsed by New Bedford and its satellite ports, Stanton moved his family across the water and followed the cooperage trade on the mainland, moving occasionally from place to place. James Everett Stanton was born in Rochester, Massachusetts, in 1824; and in 1837, when at age 13 he got his first Protection Paper and embarked on his first voyage, they were living in Dartmouth, Massachusetts. Three of the five Stanton sons rose in the whale fishery, and all three became whaling captains (though one of them only briefly). William B. Stanton (1809-1877) was 14 years a whaling master, commanding three voyages in brigs out of Westport (1846-50) and three in New Bedford barks (1851-60). John B. Stanton (1816-1888) skippered only part of one voyage (during 1848-52). But the youngest, James (1824-1898), was awarded his first command at age 28 and strode the afterdeck for much of the next thirty years, as captain of the New Bedford barks *Pauline* (1853-57), *Ospray* (1857-62), and *George* (1864-65), then, after a hiatus of about seven years, the *Martha* (1872-74), *Cleone* (1876-77), *John Carver* (relief captain, 1877-79), and *Tropic Bird* (1881-83). Meanwhile, he accumulated ownership shares in most of these vessels as an integral part of his compensation, and also invested in shares of other whalers and merchantmen. He took his family to sea with him on some of his voyages; in fact, his second daughter, Henrietta, was born at Riyala, Peru, in 1859, during the *Ospray* voyage; and the first of his two sons, James, Jr., is said to have been born on a whaleship in 1863 — which would have been the *George*. The mother of his children (there were four in all) was the former Elizabeth W. Gifford of New Bedford; and after his whaling days Captain Stanton went into her family's business in New Bedford, the Gifford Brass Foundry, first as an engineer, later as an administrator, then as superintendent. What is not known is what they were all up to during the captain's seven-year sabbatical from whaling. Elizabeth died in 1892 and James in 1898, when the scrimshaw passed to James, Jr. (1863-1939), a cotton manufacturing executive at the Acushnet Mill and (later) the Bennett Spinning Company; he was afterwards an influential owner and managing agent of whaleships. His wife was the former Mary Thomas Cook (1863-1937), who donated the rolling pin to NBW in 1935.

Star Engraver (fl. circa mid-19th century). Five teeth in NHA, widely varying in size, but each quite white in color, oriented vertically, monochrome engraved on one side with polychrome highlights, and with a distinctive star device engraved on verso (reported by Tony Dumitru and Paul Vardeman). The star device is the distinctive identifying "signature" of this otherwise anonymous artist: an upright pentangle with the blades shaded, forming at the center a regular pentagon, within which is inscribed a small pentangle star also with the blades shaded, within which, in turn, is a regular pentagon with a bulls-eye dot centered. The Star Engraver epithet derives of course from this "signature." Two of these teeth have standing female figures of Liberty, with cap and pole, other American patriotic paraphernalia, and leafy motifs that appear in varying degrees on all five teeth. Two others have standing female figures, also with patriotic symbols and leafy forms. The fifth is an ensemble of human figures, decorative motifs, and leafy forms. Nothing is known of the artist or the provenance, but the iconography is mainstream Americana of the middle-nineteenth century, and the scrimshaw has appeared only in association with Nantucket.

* **Starbuck, Edward Cartwright** (fl. circa 1828-35). The *Dictionary* makes note of two teeth engraved by this prominent Nantucket whaleman: one has a whaling scene, twelve lines of verse, and is dedicated "Capt[ain] E. Smith / from his affectionate Nephew / E.C. Starbuck," in NBWM (Flayderman, 93 and 96); the other depicts a Seamen's Bethel and an elaborate sperm whaling scene, with a sailors' prayer for safe return home, inscribed, signed, and dated by E.C. Starbuck on the Nantucket ship *Mariner*, Captain Ebenezer Coleman, March 6, 1835, in NHA. The uncle was Captain Ezra Smith, Jr., who commanded five voyages in New Bedford and Fairhaven ships during 1826-44, and was at sea in the *Nye* at the time his nephew made the scrimshaw. Ryan M. Cooper reports a tooth by the same hand that is similar to the one described in the *Dictionary*, but unsigned: it has a Bethel on one side and a whaling scene on the other, with the Golden Rule inscribed underneath (private collection). There have also been further revelations about E.C. Starbuck's personality, character, and reputation. On a whaling voyage in the ship *Henry* of New Haven, Connecticut, during 1820-23, on which Starbuck was the mate, seaman George Attwater of New Haven kept a journal distinguished for, among other things, the earliest known description of whalemen's scrimshaw and one of the earliest known uses of the word. He consistently describes E.C. Starbuck and his fellow Nantucket whalemen with unrelenting disdain. In fact, "The character of Nantucketers as a self-appointed and self-important aristocracy of insufferable braggarts, is a point made so often by the long-suffering narrator that it becomes a recurring theme. This is compounded by Attwater's particular dislike of Nantucketer E.C. Starbuck (who later became a successful if unpopular whaling master) … " (S.M. Frank, "Introduction" to Attwater 2002, 15).

Starbuck, Reuben F. (fl. circa 1825-50). Nantucket whaling master credited with a carpenter's gauge (mortise gauge) that has a wooden head (fence), brass cheeks (sliders) on both sides, a brass turnbuckle, and a panbone stem (arm) calibrated in inches, halves, and quarter inches, bearing the engraved inscription "R.F. STARBUCK" and the date 1836 (private collection, reported by Sanford Moss). Starbuck was born on Nantucket in 1810, the second son (and the second child of four) of Thomas Starbuck (1784-1823) and Susannah Macy (1788-1824). His brother, Charles F. Starbuck, born in 1806, was also a career whaleman and made three voyages out of Newburyport, Massachusetts, as captain of the ships *Newburyport* (1834-37) and *Merrimack* (1837-39 and 1840-41). Reuben likewise went to sea in early youth and was given command at a younger-than-average age: at 25, in 1835, he married Mary Ann Swain (1816-1887) and later the same year embarked on the first of his four whaling voyages as the captain of Nantucket vessels: two in the ship *President* (1835 and 1838-42) and one each in the ship *Daniel Webster* (1843-47) and brig *Tyleston* (1849-50). No record of children has come to light, and while he evidently retired from whaling in 1850, family sources claim that he was lost at sea — which must have been in the early 1850s, as his widow married widower George Palmer sometime around 1854 or '55.

Stetson, Charles (fl. 1842-81). New Bedford whaling master from Kingston, Massachusetts. He was known in the whaling trade as Charles Stetson II because another man of that name was active as a whaling captain during 1831-42. His wife, Elizabeth E.H. Stetson (q.v.), and their son Charlie accompanied him on several deepwater whaling voyages, and Elizabeth reports in her journal of the New Bedford bark *Erastus Corning* during 1860-66 that all three of them, husband, wife, and son, were engaged in scrimshaw productions of one kind or another. She also mentions two teeth that were "marked" for her by "Mr. Braman" (Lewis Braman, q.v.), one of the mates. Her inventory of Captain Stetson's individual and collaborative output is almost certainly only partial — canes, cane shafts, cane handles, "whale bone needles," "tiny needles," and at least one tooth. On a few occasions she is fairly specific: "Charles pricked a tooth," "Charles made [a] head for [a] cane & bone needles," and "painted Charlie's tooth and varnished the figures." While her journals are the only explicit testimony to the captain's interest in scrimshaw, it may reasonably be assumed that he was likely a scrimshaw-maker for more than only that one voyage, perhaps for all or most of his more than thirty years at sea. Unfortunately, none of his scrimshaw has been identified.

Charles Stetson was born in 1825 in Kingston, near Plymouth, and went to sea at age 17, first as a green hand (1842-44), then as boatsteerer (1844-46) in the ship *Hibernia* of New Bedford, thereby skipping the ranks of ordinary seaman and able seaman. He next made two voyages under Captain Gorham B. Howes in the ship *Amethyst* of New Bedford, one as third mate (1846-50), the other as first mate (1850-54), thereby skipping the ranks of fourth and second mate. He certainly had Howes's good opinion of him to thank for his rapid promotion; and years later, aboard the *Erastus Corning*, Elizabeth reports that Charles was "making a cane for Uncle George & one for Capt. Howes," no doubt as a token of Stetson's enduring affection and respect. At age 29 Stetson was given his first command, the Fairhaven ship *Ansel Gibbs* (1854-59), followed by the *Erastus Corning* (AKA *E. Corning*, 1860-66), on which Elizabeth kept her journal; then the Boston brig *Rosa Baker* (1867-69), and the *Ansel Gibbs* again (1869-70). It was between voyages in 1850, as a newly appointed first mate, that he married Elizabeth. And not only did she accompany him on subsequent voyages, but their son Charles A. Stetson (q.v.) was born in Chile in 1855 during a landfall of the *Ansel Gibbs*. Aboard the *Corning* a few years later, "Charlie," as he was called, evidently joined his mother and father making some scrimshaw of his own. Captain Stetson's second voyage in the *Ansel Gibbs*, which ended in 1870, was to have been his last: the 1880 Census lists him as a "Master Mariner — Retired," living at Kingston with Elizabeth and a 15-year-old adopted daughter named Daisy Belle (Charlie was by then off somewhere on his own). However, Captain Stetson evidently came out of retirement in 1881 for an encore in the *Rosa Baker* again, which is the last that history knows of him. (Not to be confused with the earlier Captain Charles Stetson, mentioned above; or the Charles Stetson who was a contemporaneous New Bedford shipbuilder; or the contemporaneous New Bedford whaling master Charles F. Stetson.)

Stetson, Charles A. (fl. circa 1860-66). He is not known to have made a whaling voyage in any professional capacity, but he was the son of whaling a captain, Charles Stetson (q.v.), and was actually born on a whaling voyage. As a child aboard one of his father's ships, he appears to have made scrimshaw, some of it in collaboration with his mother, Elizabeth E.H. Stetson (q.v.). He was born in Chile in 1855 during a landfall of the Fairhaven ship *Ansel Gibbs* (1854-59), on which his father was captain and his mother a passenger; and between the ages of five and eleven he accompanied his parents to sea on the New Bedford ship *Erastus Corning* (1860-66). His mother's journal of that voyage implies that eight-year-old "Charlie," as he was called, made a tooth, which Elizabeth painted; he likely also made other scrimshander objects which his mother was either too busy or thought too trivial to mention. Between 1866 and the middle 1870s he attended school intermittently in his parents' home town of Kingston, Massachusetts, then moved to Brockton, Massachusetts, where he was a heel maker and later foreman of the so-called "heel room" of one of that city's many shoe factories. He married a dressmaker named Charlotte, and after being widowed (sometime after 1900) lodged in boardinghouse in Brockton and Plymouth, where he was still working in the shoemaking industry in the 1930s.

Stetson, Elizabeth E.H. (fl. circa 1854-70). Wife and shipboard companion of Captain Charles Stetson (q.v.), and keeper of an engaging shipboard journal aboard the *Erastus Corning* (1860-66) that alludes, all too briefly, to the scrimshandering activities of her husband, her son Charlie, Second Mate Lewis Braman (q.v.), and herself. Most of these few references to scrimshaw on what would turn out to be a voyage of five and one half years are crammed into the space of a few days in February 1863, and could not be exhaustive. But she was not feeling very well during those days and seems to have been more loquacious than usual regarding incidentals, commenting not only about scrimshaw but also about sewing, baking, cooking, ripping old, worn-out skirts and dresses into strips, presumably for later hooking or quilting, and other such domestic pursuits. Of scrimshaw, on the same day that she "sewed the bottom of [a] skirt" and "made button holes for Charlie's coat," she writes, "Charles [the captain, was] making canes" and "Painted Charlie's tooth and varnished the figure" — indicating that both her husband and their eight-year-old son were working simultaneously on scrimshaw projects of their own. The next day she writes, "painted 3 Pictures to day, 2 for Charlie and one in my Journal. Made 2 pans of buns... Charles making [a] cane for Uncle George & one for Capt. Howes." (The journal she refers to is her second journal of the same voyage, in MSM. "Capt. Howes" is Gorham B. Howes, who on two voyages in the New Bedford ship *Amethyst* a decade earlier had been Charles Stetson's captain and mentor.) Over the next few days, "Charles turned me 4 handles for swabs," presumably out of whale skeletal bone on a shipboard lathe; she herself "scraped a cane of spice wood, made a sheet, and picked a tooth," which may refer to *selecting* a tooth for some unspecified purpose, but more likely refers to *pin-pricking* scrimshaw on a tooth; and "Charles made a set of whale bone needles" and "a set of Tiny Needles." One can only wish that she had also accounted for the myriad other scrimshaw-making activities that must have occurred, among her family and other shipmates (such as Thomas Morrison, q.v.), as this and her other voyages progressed.

Her maiden name was also Stetson — Elizabeth E. Holmes Stetson, born in 1823 at Kingston, Massachusetts, the daughter of Wiswell Seabury Stetson, cordwainer, and the former Sally Adams Holmes. She married Charles Stetson, a distant relation two years her junior, in 1850, upon his promotion to first mate under Captain Howes; and beginning in 1854 she accompanied her captain-husband on several whaling voyages to the Pacific Ocean: the ship *Ansel Gibbs* of Fairhaven (1854-59), the bark *Erastus Corning* of New Bedford (1860-66), on which she kept two journals, and possibly also the Boston brig *Rosa Baker* (1867-69) and the *Ansel Gibbs* again (1869-70). She gave birth to her one and only son, Charles A. Stetson (q.v.), during a landfall in Chile on the first *Ansel Gibbs* voyage. After her husband retired from whaling in 1870, they adopted a daughter named Daisy Belle (born circa 1865) and lived in Kingston. It is unlikely that she accompanied Charles on his swan-song cruise in the *Rosa Baker* in 1881.

Stevens, G.W. (fl. circa 1852). Credited with a pair of teeth crudely but charmingly engraved: one with a navy tar wielding a cutlass on deck alongside a naval cannon, the other with a young girl holding flowers, one incised on verso, "G.W. Stevens / Pacific Ocean / 1852," the other "G.W.

Stevens / Pac. Oc. / 1852" (reported by Nina Hellman). There were not many men of this name in the whale fishery in 1852 but the attribution nevertheless remains elusive. An African-American seaman named George W. Stevens, born in New London, received his Protection Paper there age 38, in June 1834, but there is no record of voyages; and in 1852, at age about 56, he would likely have been too old to still be whaling. A George W. Stevens of Waterford, Maine, obtained his Protection at age 21 in New Bedford in May 1838, but there is no record of voyages and he may or may not still have been around in 1852. A George Stevens, age and residence unknown — possibly but not likely the same man — was an Ordinary Seaman on the New Bedford brig *America* (1843-44), joined the New Bedford brig *Juno* at Lahaina in April 1847 on a voyage already in progress (1845-48), then drops out of sight. There was a George Stevens, birth date, middle initial, and residence unknown, who was active at the right time, in the crew of the New London whaling brig *Topaz*, which sailed in June 1852 and was "Wrecked and condemned at Falkland Islands April, 1853" (Starbuck, 497); but this vessel never reached the Pacific. A man named George W. Stevens was a maker of coin silver implements and a sometime partner in the firm of Curtis & Stevens at Fall River, Massachusetts, in the 1820s-30s, but he had no namesake son who was a mariner. Another of that name, originally from New York, was a soap manufacturer on Nantucket in the 1860s, but no previous voyages are known. More likely than any of these is an as-yet-undiscovered G.W. Stevens who sailed out of Nantucket on a voyage for which the crew list has not yet been located.

Stewart, H.N. — see **H.N. Stuart**

* **Stivers, John O.** (fl. circa 1859-60). Master of a whaling voyage in the schooner *Tekoa* of Stonington, Connecticut (1859-60), to whom the *Dictionary* mentions "an architectural box elaborately inlaid with abalone, ivory, and baleen is attributed in MSM." It has since been learned that he was married to Helen B. Manchester in Rhode Island in 1881 but his actual residence has not been ascertained. (Not to be confused with Captain John R. Stivers, q.v.)

* **Stivers, John R.** (fl. circa 1860-80). The *Dictionary* notes that he was the master of several whaling voyages in New Bedford vessels, but provides no specific scrimshaw productions. MSM has since confirmed the attribution of a hinged wooden box inlaid with whale skeletal bone and mother of pearl, with an armature of whale skeletal bone, and a plaque on top engraved with the image of a child on a swing, said to have been made by Stivers on his voyage as captain of the *Cicero* in the 1860s (see *America and the Sea: Treasures from the Collections of Mystic Seaport*, 2005, 126). As previously noted in the *Dictionary*, he commanded whaling voyages in the ship *Cicero* (1860-65), bark *Henry Taber* (1868-71), ship *Eliza Adams* (1872-76), and ship *Milton* (1876-80). He was a resident of Mystic, Connecticut, where his widow Ellen was still living in 1912. (Not to be confused with Captain John O. Stivers [q.v.] or another John R. Stivers who was active in the New Bedford fishery around the same time [circa 1868-76; see Sherman #1517 and #2222].)

Stockbridge, Lebbeus, Jr. (fl. 1845-48). *More Scrimshaw Artists* reiterates in its entirety the provenance of an oval baleen box on an accompanying label: "Whalebone [sic] box. Made from the bone [sic] of a whale caught by the crew of the 'Bark [sic] Magnolia' which sailed from New Bedford in 1845. Fastened with pins made from ten cent pieces. Lebbeus Stockbridge, grandfather of Amy

Briggs, was one of the sailors" (reported by Michael Porlides). The article in *More Scrimshaw Artists* also states that Stockbridge was born in 1825 in Hanover, Massachusetts, served in the ship (not bark) *Magnolia* of New Bedford during 1845-48, married Mary T. Sylvester in 1849, and had a daughter, Ruthena (born 1854), who married a Charles Briggs and was the mother of the Amy Briggs mentioned in the provenance. For Starbuck the *Magnolia* voyage was a prime example of his claim that "instances are not wanting where whale men have undertaken yeomen's service for their country": Captains Bozer Simmons of the *Magnolia* and John S. Barker of the New Bedford ship *Edward*, "hearing that the garrison at San José, Lower California, was in imminent danger, landed their crews and marched to its relief" (113n). Starbuck places the incident in November 1846, but Bill Baccus, who has made a study of Captain Simmons and the *Magnolia*, reports that it was actually on 21 November 1847 (House Executive Document N° 1, 30th Congress, 2nd Session, 1112-15). In reference to the "several days in October 1846" mentioned in *More Scrimshaw Artists*, Baccus says, "The incidents of October 1846 are earlier, separate, and distinct from the Starbuck citation," and explains:

> *At that time the* **Magnolia** *was chartered by the US Military to move troops and volunteers from San Pedro to San Diego in defense of the town against the Mexican forces… On October 20, 1846 Stockbridge notes [in his journal], "The 'old man' made a purchase of some more land, bought an Island here in the harbour for $1,000." A deed supporting this sale from Pedro C. Carrillo to Capt. Bezer Simmons is recorded in the San Diego land records, October 20, 1846. The "Island" was, and remains today, Coronado Island and what is now the North Island Naval Station in San Diego Harbor. Pedro Carrillo was a supporter of the American conquest…* (private communication, 30 Dec. 2009)

Additional biographical details have surfaced since publication of *More Scrimshaw Artists*, including that Stockbridge's brief, unpremeditated stint in the Mexican War was not his only military experience. In 1849, newly married, he was farming in Hanover, and over the next five years actually had three children, of whom Ruthena was the youngest, suggesting the possibility of additional scrimshaw that may have descended through son Edwin or daughter Lucy. In May 1861 Stockbridge enlisted in Company K, 2nd Regiment Infantry, Massachusetts Volunteers, he was promoted to master sergeant in November 1862, and he mustered out in January 1864 (partly reported by Bill Baccus, from a history of the Hanover Academy, supplemented from *Massachusetts Soldiers, Sailors and Marines in the Civil War*). He then returned to his farm in Hanover. In 1874 he was admitted to the National Home for Disabled Volunteer Soldiers in Kennebec County, Maine (where the manager was General Benjamin Butler) and lived there and in at least one other disabled veteran facility until being discharged in 1882. He died in 1883.

Stocking, Dwight Clifford (fl. 1857-62). Neophyte sailor from Norwich, Connecticut, credited with a tooth that has a sedate polychrome portrait of a woman seated, wearing a gown with floral motifs, meticulously engraved using the pinprick-transfer method (in WHS, reported by Richard Donnelly). Young Dwight must have made it on his one and only whaling voyage, in the New Bedford bark *Camilla* (1857-62), where he is listed in the unusual berth of "ordinary boy" (higher in rank and pay than a cabin boy, about equivalent in rank and pay to a green hand). He was born circa 1841, the fourth of six children of Serenias Stocking, a manufacturer of some kind, and his wife Juliana. Just before or just after his whaling voyage, though both his parents were still alive, Dwight and two or three of his siblings went to live with James and Emily Bramby, who were likely relatives of their mother. Serenias and Juliana Stocking eventually retired to a farm in Canterbury, Connecticut, and were still living there in 1880, but nothing further is known about Dwight.

Stuart, H.N. (fl. circa 1820 – circa 1869). Fairhaven whaling master identified in various records as Heman N. Stuart and Herman N. Stewart. He is credited with a cane that has a globe pommel of whale ivory and an octagonal shaft descending to cylindrical, made up of alternating segments of skeletal bone, wood, and baleen. The provenance consists of a holograph tag: "Made by Capt. Stuart on board the bark Swallow in 1857" (Eldred, 8-9-10 April 2010, #956). H.N. Stewart was indeed captain of the *Swallow* in 1857 on what turned out to be his last complete whaling voyage. He was born circa 1804, probably in Sandwich, on Cape Cod, and lived there during his early career, later moving to nearby Falmouth (by 1832) and Fairhaven (in the 1840s?), where he married a woman named Rebecca and raised three children (as of 1850). His early career is only sketchily known: his first two or three voyages have not been identified. He served, probably as a boatsteerer and junior mate, in the New Bedford ships *Hydaspe* and *George and Martha* during 1827-30, but it is unclear which voyages and in what order. He was first mate in the New Bedford ship *William Rotch* (1830-31); then, over the next 30 years, he commanded nine whaling voyages: one in the bark *Bramin* of New Bedford (1832-34), two in the ship *Brunswick* of Providence (1834-36 and 1836-37), two in the ship *Leonidas* of Fairhaven (1837-39 and 1839-42), three in the ship *Martha 2nd* of Fairhaven (1844-47, 1848-51, and 1852-56), and one in the ship *Swallow* of New Bedford 1856-60, on which he reportedly made the cane. After the Civil War he came out of retirement at age about 62 to take command of the Fairhaven bark *Selah* (1866-69), but died sometime before completing the voyage.

Sturtevant, William B. (fl. 1854-77). The owner of a busk that features vignettes of an Alwilda- or Fanny Campbell-like female pirate holding a cutlass and characteristic skull-and-crossbones flag claims that it was made by a man named William Sturtevant, said to be buried in Milo, Maine (private collection; reported by Laura Pereira). The busk is boldly signed "William Sturtevant," who, while he may have been a kinsman of the Milo Sturtevants and could conceivably be buried in Milo, Maine, was definitely not one of the three generations of William Sturtevants who were *from* Milo, Maine. Two of the William Sturtevants from Milo were father and son, born circa 1787 and 1817, respectively. The father is not known to have gone whaling at all, and even if he had it would have been too early for him to have produced scrimshaw pictures of Alwilda or Fanny Campbell. Maturin Murray Ballou's fictional story of a female pirate from Lynn, Massachusetts, *Fanny Campbell, the Female Pirate Captain* — a yarn that was inspired by the newly popularized exploits of a legendary fifth-century Scandinavian pirate named Alwilda — was not published until 1845, ushering in a fashion for Female Pirate motifs on scrimshaw from the middle 1840s through the 1860s and '70s. The son, William H. Sturtevant, did go on a whaling voyage in the autumn of 1839: he was issued a passport (Seaman's Protection Paper) at New Bedford that October, listing his residence as Fayette, Maine, and his age as 22, and he made his one and only whaling voyage in the ship *Pacific 2d* of New Bedford during 1839-42 — still too early for Alwilda or Fanny Campbell scrimshaw. This chronology leaves only one possible candidate from Milo: William E. Sturtevant, son of Milo farmer Warren H. Sturtevant. This William was born circa 1847 but there is no evidence that he ever went whaling at all. No evidence could be found that he was ever issued a Seaman's Protection Paper, which was required of all American seamen on foreign voyages; in fact, there is no indication in the census records that he even survived childhood, and certainly none that he was ever a sailor. So all three of the William Sturtevants from Milo remain doubtful in connection with the busk. (It is also worth noting that though the tomb in Milo identifies the remains as those of a "Captain" William Stutevant, there was never an American whaling master of that name with that spelling at any time; that the William *Sturdevant* who skippered the New Bedford whaleship *Sophia* in 1831 is definitely not the man at issue here, was not from Maine, and is too early in any case; and that whatever this William Sturtevant of Milo, Maine was captain of, it was not a whaleship.)

On the other hand, a William B. Sturtevant of New Bedford, born there in 1840 or 1841, the son of carrriage painter Zachariah Sturtevant, was 29 years old in 1870 and boarding with his father in New Bedford, where the census indicates that the father had now become a grocer and specifically identifies the son as a sailor. In fact, William's record of voyages is almost completely known, and they occurred at just the time when Female Pirate motifs were fashionable. His first voyage was at the tender age of 13 as cabin boy in the New Bedford bark *Peri*, Captain Elihu Russell (1854-57). His next, sometime during 1857-60, has not been discovered, but the remainder of his whaling career, all in New Bedford vessels, is well documented. He was two voyages in the bark *Lagoda*, as a seaman (1860-64) and probably as a boatsteerer (1864-68): the crew list for the 1860 voyage lists him as from New Bedford, age 20, and the crew list for the 1864 voyage lists him as from New Bedford, age 24. He was next fourth mate in the bark *Adeline* (1869-74), and embarked on his final voyage at age 34 in the bark *George and Susan* (1874-77), likely as third mate. This professional deepwater whaleman was surely the author of the Female Pirate busk; in fact, he is the only plausible candidate.

Alwilda and Fanny Campbell may in any case be justly regarded as somewhat odd choices for the decorations on what amounts a ladies' intimate undergarment, a female accessory that was usually crafted as a tenderly-thought-of memento for one's wife, mother, sister, or fiancée. As far as is known, William Sturtevant had no fiance at the time he was whaling; but the coda of his story is unusual for a native-born Yankee whaleman. The Sturtevant genealogy is incorrect in claiming that he died at sea. Rather, after his final voyage he "swallowed the oar" about as completely as is possible to do in America. Sometime between 1877 and 1880, in his late thirties, he married a woman from Indiana named Annie, sixteen years his junior, took up farming in the district of Beaver City, Nebraska, hired a farmhand to help run the place, raised a family, and was retired there by 1910.

Summons, Ezra (fl. circa 1815-30). Career whaleman of color from Nantucket, credited with a panbone yard rule (originally 36 inches = 92 cm in length) calibrated in inches, halves, and quarters, made for his wife and inscribed "ALSA*SUMMONS," but broken off long ago at 29 inches (73 cm) (originally reported by Andrew Jacobson; now in NBWM). Such a yardstick, whether made of wood, panbone, or a combination of wood and bone, with or without engraving or ivory, bone, or mother-of-pearl inlay, is just the sort of thing a whaleman might typically make for a wife, mother, or sweetheart even before the advent of pictorial teeth and busks. In fact, yardsticks and straightedges are among the earliest American scrimshaw forms. The key to the identification and attribution here is the nomenclature. The surname *Summons* belonged principally to an African-American and Wampanoag family of native Nantucketers; and while the chroniclers, census-takers, and genealogists usually rendered it *Simmons* (or sometimes Simons), Ezra himself and most of his kinfolk persistently used the spelling *Summons*, which is probably also the way it was pronounced. In the eighteenth and nineteenth centuries *Alsa* was a not-uncommon diminutive for Alice (and for variants of Alice); and the only Alice (or Alicia, or Alissa, or Alison, etc.) with the surname Summons or Simmons or Simons (or anything like Summons) who had anything to do with the whale fishery, in any part of the country, was the former Alice Gutridge (AKA Alsa Goodrich), who became the wife of Ezra Summons in 1818. Thus, she was, uniquely, Alsa Summons. According to the *Vital Records of Nantcuket* and *Isabel Kaldenbach's Inventory of Black Nantucketers* (NHA), Ezra Summons was born on the Island circa 1796, the second child and eldest of four sons of Jeffrey Summons and the former Nancy Brock. Most of the young men born on Nantucket made at least one whaling voyage at one time or another, and Ezra was probably no exception, though no specific record has been found. Many made careers out of whaling; others eventually settled down to farming, shopkeeping, or one of the mechanical trades. It is not known what path Ezra chose, but he was probably still whaling when, at age about 22, he married Alice. He lived only until circa 1830, leaving behind his widow, his father, his father's second wife, named Martha, and a son named Jeremiah. (Alsa Summons of Nantucket was evidently the only woman of that name in America at the time, though there was an Alsa *Simmons* in Montgomery, Georgia, in 1840. Remarkably, apart from the Summons family of Nantucket, the only other men of that surname anywhere in the annals of American whaling prior to 1891 were Aaron Summons of New Bedford, who was in the ship *Parnasso* during 1825-26; and George Summons, Jr., born around 1820 in Philadelphia, the cook on three voyages, in the ship *South Boston* of Fairhaven [1845-48] and ships *Mercury* [1848-52] and *Gay Head* [1852-56] of New Bedford.)

Swan, Frank (fl. circa the 1840s). A swift previously attributed to Henry Daggett (q.v.), in a private collection, has a note bearing two anonymous holograph inscriptions and an accompanying storage box that together constitute a highly credible attribution and provenance indicating a different genesis. The first inscription is in pencil: "This Box contains an old fashioned article called a Swift made by my dear father on a sea voyage when he was a very young man Though in a terrible condition it is." The second, in ink in a different hand on the same slip of paper, identifies the author of the pencil inscription: "These words (with some more) were written in 1913 on the box holding a scrimshaw swift by Frances Swan Butterick who was born about 1860. So the swift was probably made 1850's" (reported by Dr. Rick Schafer). The two inscriptions establish the basis for a chain of evidence that leads back to a maker named Frank Swan. The woman named in the provenance, Frances Swan Butterick, was born in Massachusetts circa 1857. In 1910 she was a widow living in Bozeman, in Muscogee County, Georgia, with her 31-year-old daughter Anna, Anna's husband Harry R. Healey, a laboratory chemist, and their infant son Harry Junior. Frances had been shuttling back and forth seasonally between Massachusetts and Georgia around that time, and on Feb. 13, 1910 the Columbus, Georgia, society column in the *Atlanta Constitution* reported, "Mrs. Frances S. Butterick has returned from the east, and will be with Mr. and Mrs. Harry R. Healey for the remainder of the winter." The whole family moved to the Boston area two or three years after, and Frances continued to live with her daughter and son-in-law and evidently had some of her valuables shipped for her. The box in which the swift was stored in 1913, and in which it came to the collector some 90 years later, bears the printed paper label of the Jordan Marsh department store in Boston, clearly addressed in a contemporaneous ink holograph to Mrs. Harry Healey in Brookline, Massachusetts. By 1920 Anna Healey was also widowed and was boarding in Boston; and her mother, Frances Swan Butterick, whose father made the swift, had evidently departed the scene.

The maker, Frank Swan, was born circa 1824-25, but it is not known for certain whether in Massachusetts or Rhode Island. Unfortunately, nothing has yet been discovered about his whaling career, which must have been in the mid 1840s. By 1850 he was a butcher at Athol, Massachusetts, where his wife Mary gave birth to a son named William H. Swan. By 1870, still a butcher, he had been widowed and remarried, and was living in nearby Orange, Massachusetts, with his second wife, Julia C., son William, now 19, and daughters Ellen, 17, and Frances, 13.

Swift, R.G.N. (fl. circa 1866-70). As a seaman on two whaling voyages in the New Bedford ship *Contest* (1866-68 and 1868-70), he casually mentions "Scrimshoning all afternoon," as though only this longer, all-afternoon session, and not the activity itself, were sufficiently unusual to mention in his journal. Born at Fairhaven, Massachusetts, in 1845, Rupert G.N. Swift — who refers to himself in his journal as "Rupe" — was the son of whaling captain, scrimshaw-maker, and sometime live oak merchant Rodolphus Nye Swift (q.v. in the *Dictionary* and *More Scrimshaw Artists*), who made one of the finest of all scrimshaw birdcages (in KNB), probably for his wife Sylvia. Rupe's younger brother was marine artist and animal painter Clement Nye Swift (1846-1918), whose watercolors and drawings are held in several museum and private collections. The parents did well by their sons: both brothers were well educated and articulate, both were accomplished poets and humorists; so, too, presumably, a still younger third brother, Edward (born in 1855), who was a professional musician. The family sophistication is particularly evident in Rupe's eccentric and occasionally frantic shipboard journal. He was well read in Shakespeare, fairly knowledgeable about the Latin and Greek classics, and altogether as literary as his father was mechanical and his brother artistic. Many of his journal entries are verbal cartoons, there are two or three passages in schoolboy Latin and Greek, and a few are illustrated with zany caricatures. Clement was a skilled artist and gifted poet who was never a sailor and is not known to have done any scrimshaw. Rupe was as good or better as a poet but a far lesser artist: his shipboard poetic compositions are among the best ever written by a whaleman; still, his amateur sketches and caricatures are prominent features of his journal, and it is difficult to imagine that he could have made two whaling voyages without trying his hand at scrimshaw; or that, once having done so, he would be so embarrassed at their poor quality as to have thrown them overboard (he certainly had no such qualms regarding his zany scratchings illustrating the likes of the Bard of Avon and Hamlet's ghost, which are published in Kenneth Martin's *Whalemen's Paintings and Drawings*). Rupe made only the two whaling voyages, neither he nor Clement ever married, and they, along with their slightly younger sister Anna, continued to live with their parents in a house with servants on the Mattapoisett side of Acushnet, well into their parents' eighties. Clement earned a living as an artist, and Rupert as a coastwise merchant captain until he retired around 1870.

Tallman, Charles (fl. circa 1821-24). Born in 1802, he was the elder brother of Captains William Tallman, Jr., and Joseph Ricketson Tallman (qq.v.), but is only known to have made one whaling voyage himself, in the ship *Roscoe* of New Bedford, Captain Micajah Swain, sperm whaling in the Pacific during 1821-24. The three brothers were the sons of William Tallman (1761-1853) and Elizabeth Howland Tallman (1776-1818), and it is not known which of the three made which of the two panbone and whale ivory swifts and matching yarn-winder that descended in the Tallman family, each of which was engraved with the initials "DDT" (in NBWM). However, Charles is the most likely candidate for having made at least one of the swifts, and perhaps both. There were only two members of the Tallman family with the initial "D." Just before Charles left on his one whaling voyage, their widowed father remarried (in 1820), and thus Deborah Delano (born 1781) became their stepmother. At that time William was only 11 years old and Joseph only 9, both too young to have made such a gift at such a young age (though either one could well have made such a swift and yarn-winder later on). And almost as soon as Charles returned from whaling, he married Deborah D. Samson of New Bedford (in 1824), who became the second (and only other) D.D.T. in the family. Charles and this second wife Deborah may well have been affianced prior to his embarking, thus he may have made a second swift in anticipation of his nuptials — perhaps relishing the coincidence that his new stepmother and his intended bride would soon have the D.D.T. initials in common. Of course, it is possible that either of the other brothers could have made such swifts for their stepmother and sister-in-law at some later time, but not as likely. William followed the whaling trade for several years, and for Joseph it was an entire career. But Charles left it after his one brief foray and became a "trader" (so described in the City Directory) and later a bookkeeper in New Bedford.

Tallman, Joseph R. (fl. circa 1828-59). Captain William Tallman, Jr., mentioned in the *Dictionary* in connection with a whale ivory name stamp (in KNB), was the brother of Captain Joseph Ricketson Tallman and sometime whaleman Charles Tallman. Two panbone and whale ivory swifts and two yarn-winders matching one of the swifts, donated to NBWM (two acquired directly from the Tallman family, and a third attributed to the same hand) were almost certainly brought home by, and may have been made by one or another of the brothers, but it is not known which by which. All three pieces were engraved with the initials "DDT," indicating that they were made for one or both of the only two people in the Tallman family who had the initial D. Both of them were women who married into the family, and thereby acquired the initials D.D.T. The Tallman boys were all sons of William Tallman (1761-1853) and his first wife, Elizabeth Howland (born 1776). She died in childbirth in 1818, when Charles was 16, William Jr. 9, and Joseph 7. William Senior was remarried two years later (1820), to Deborah Delano (born 1781) of New Bedford; she thus became Deborah D. Tallman. Were there only one swift and only one D.D.T. in the family, this might explain things, as Charles (q.v.) embarked on his one-and-only whaling voyage the following year, and over the next three years at sea would likely have had ample opportunity to construct such a swift as a memento for his new stepmother. However, immediately after he returned he married Deborah D. Samson [Sampson], who became Deborah D. Tallman — a second D.D.T. Two swifts and a yarn-winder are a lot for one person to make in a lifetime, and are probably more than any one recipient would ever need; three such pieces by the same maker with the same initials is unprecedented. So it seems likely that there were at two makers and at two recipients, but which swift was made by whom and intended for whom is not part of the family lore.

Joseph Ricketson Tallman was born in 1811 at Dartmouth, Massachusetts. His older brothers preceded him to sea, Charles in 1821 at age 19, and William Junior the same year at the unusually early age of 12. Charles swallowed the oar after only one voyage, William rose through the ranks to become captain of a voyage in the New Bedford ship *Lewis* (1841-44), but Joseph rose higher than the others and commanded five full-scale deepwater whaling voyages of out New Bedford. At age 17 he went as a green hand in the *Cortes* (1828-30), then made an undocumented voyage, presumably as boatsteerer (1830-32), followed by the *India*, as one of the mates (1834-38), a berth as first mate in the *Nautilus* under Captain Alden G. Ellis (1838-42), and then a string of commands: the bark *Pioneer* (1842-44), ships *Lewis* (1844-48), *Hydaspe* (1848-52), and *Daniel Wood* (1852-56), and bark *Midas* (sailed 1857), which turned out to be his last. Meanwhile, he owned shares in all five of the vessels he skippered, some of which came to him as part of his compensation package and some of which were investments on his own hook. But his career ended sadly in the *Midas*. In January 1859 they were whaling in the vicinity of Micronesia, calling at the islands of Kosrae and Mokil for water and some friendly trade with the natives, and preparing to head north for the summer season of whaling in the Sea of Okhotsk. The journals of the voyage disclose no hint of what was to come, but on 15 August of the same year, at Ayan in Siberia, Captain Tallman, age about 48, died suddenly of an unknown ailment.

* **Tallman, William** (fl. circa 1821-44). Captain William Tallman, whom the *Dictionary* mentions in connection with a whale ivory stamp with his name on it (in KNB), was the older brother of Captain Joseph R. Tallman and the younger brother of Charles Tallman (qq.v.). One or more of the three surely brought home from their many voyages, and may have made with their own hands, two panbone and whale ivory swifts and a matching yarn-winder in NBWM, two of which came from the Tallman family in South Dartmouth, Massachusetts, the third of which is attributed to the same hand, and all three of which were engraved with the initials "DDT" in a manner certainly intended to personalize them for a specific recipient. The most likely candidate for maker of at least one of the swifts is Charles, who married Deborah D. Samson [Sampson] in 1824. But all three boys acquired a new stepmother in 1820, when their widowed father married Deborah Delano. Thus there were two Tallman women with the initials D.D.T. All three brothers went whaling, thus all three had the opportunity to acquire the materials and skills to make such swifts. The strongest argument for Charles as the maker of at least one or two of them is that he was actually married to one of the D.D.T. women. The strongest claim for William is that he was whaling from early childhood and is the attributed maker of the only other work of scrimshaw to have emerged from the Tallman clan, the aforementioned name stamp with his name on it. The strongest claim for Joseph is that he was the most successful whaleman of the three, made his entire career at it, and made more whaling voyages and was conceivably more thoroughly inculcated with whaling lore than his siblings. But none of these arguments is conclusive, none adequately explains there being two swifts (one with its matching yarn-winder), nor identifies for which of the Deborahs each swift was intended; so the mystery remains unsolved.

William, born in 1809, married Abby Kent of Bristol, Rhode Island, in 1833, just prior to sailing as second mate in the Ceres on the voyage of 1834-37 that produced the famous Ceres Teeth (see the articles on William H. Meyers, John Cleland, Jr., Willaim A. Gilpin, and Edmund M. Chandler). Eleven years later, after his voyage as captain of the *Lewis* (1841-44), Tallman retired from whaling, went into the hardware business in New Bedford, and was later the city assessor with an office in City Hall. He and Abby had seven children, none of their names beginning with D. One of his sons, William K. Tallman, operated a local livery stable; another, Edward G. Tallman, was one of New Bedford's pioneer generation of professional photographers.

Tasseok — see **Teseuke**

Taylor, Charles N. (fl. circa 1870s). Several auction lots were misleadingly described as "From the family of Captain Charlie Taylor of the whaling vessel *Rising Sun* of Provincetown, MA" (Eldred, July 29, 2005, #534-537 and #548). It was actually Charlie's father, Captain Thomas S. Taylor (q.v.), who was the celebrated Provincetown whaling master. Charlie probably went whaling in his youth, but Lund's uncertainty concerning the specious claim that he was briefly a whaling captain in his own right in 1878 is fully justified: he was likely aboard his father's vessel, the schooner *Rising Sun*, but he was a child of 12 at the time. Still, he could have been the original maker of some or all of the 14 pieces of minor scrimshaw described as having come from his family and the *Rising Sun*. See the articles on Thomas Smith Taylor and William Wilson.

Taylor, Thomas Smith (fl. 1853-97). Long-tenured whaling master of Provincetown, Massachusetts. Several auction lots were described as "From the family of Captain Charlie Taylor of the whaling vessel *Rising Sun* of Provincetown, MA" (Eldred, July 29, 2005, #534-537 and #548). These included two whistles carved out of sperm whale teeth, a damaged crimper handle, a pair of walrus ivory thread winders, two bone clothespins, a whale ivory ring, a small walrus ivory parasol handle in the form of a looped snake, a human hand carved out of bone, apparently made as a backscratcher, an ivory cane handle in the conventional form of a woman's leg and shoe, two bone bodkins, a whale ivory tamper with carved acanthus leaf ornaments (erroneously catalogued as a bodkin), and three raw sperm whale teeth. However, "Charlie" Taylor — that is, Charles N. Taylor (q.v.) — was never the captain of the *Rising Sun* or any other whaler. Rather, he was the twelve-year-old son of the captain in 1878. The actual captain, though not necessarily the more likely source of the scrimshaw, was Thomas Smith Taylor. Born at Yarmouth on Cape Cod in 1840, he was the son of mariner Charles Taylor and Hannah née Ellis. He went to sea at the age of about 13 in 1853 and had a long career of 44 years, including 32 as the captain of Provincetown whaling schooners: the *Mary E. Simmons* (1865-66), *Ellen Rizpah* (1866), *Quickstep* (1867), *Gage H. Phillips* (1867-68), *Sassacus* (1868-69), *Gage H. Phillips* again (1869-70), three successive voyages in the *Mary E. Simmons* (1870-73), and 16 as perpetual master of the *Rising Sun* (1873-97). He was also a ship owner who held shares in whalers and other vessels. He married Josephine E. West, who was born of American parents in Liverpool, Nova Scotia. They had four sons, all of whom seem to have gone whaling at one time or another, but none of whom made it his permanent profession: Charles R., Elisha Thomas, William W. (q.v.), and Hersey D. Thomas's brother-in-law, Newton P. West, born in Nova Scotia circa 1850 and thus six or seven years younger than his sister Josephine, lived with the Taylors for several years and also went whaling out of Provincetown. Beginning about 1898, after he had retired from whaling, Captain Taylor was an undertaker in Provincetown, where he died in 1919. (Sources: *Past Masters of King Hiram's Lodge*, Provincetown; Deyo, *History of Barnstable County*.)

Taylor, William Wilson (1874-1954). A sometime whaleman in his youth, the brother of Charles N. Taylor (q.v.), he may have made (but probably did not make) some of the family scrimshaw described in the article about his whaling captain father, Thomas Smith Taylor (q.v.) of Provincetown, Massachusetts. Despite that his local lodge of Freemasons credits him with being "a master mariner in his father's employ at the end of whaling in Provincetown" (*Past Masters of King Hiram's Lodge*), there is no record of him as a master mariner in the whaling trade. He likely made more than one whaling voyage on his father's schooners, perhaps in company with his brother Charles and uncle Newton West. In later years he may also have worked in his father's undertaker business, but by trade he was a fisherman. His father was the only whaling master in the nuclear family, and it was his brother Charles in whose line the family scrimshaw descended. (Not to be confused with the much earlier and evidently unrelated William W. Taylor who commanded five New Bedford whaling voyages during 1840-53, long before William Wilson Taylor was born.)

Teacup Swift Maker (fl. circa the 1820s). The nickname for this anonymous maker of double-cage swifts constructed of sperm whale ivory and skeletal bone derives from the elaborate and quite delicate engraved decorations on the cup (surmount), clamp, and other ivory components. These resemble the lightweight floral vine motifs on English bone china and porcelain tea services — hence the nickname for the anonymous artist — and (less so) their French, German, and Chinese export counterparts. Two such swifts in NBWM (one from KNB) are clearly by the same hand but were acquired years apart from entirely different sources. Nina Hellman sold at least two others in recent years (they are now presumably in private collections), and SFL has received unspecific reports of two or three others in museum and private collections. The unifying features are the materials (sperm whale ivory and bone), which are not in the least unusual; and the fine, teacup-like ornamentation, which is typically a floral or leaf-and-vine motif pigmented in one color only (they have been found in a pinkish red, green, and black) but sometimes also including black initials or highlights. (The one in KNB has the date 1822, which is probably the year the swift was constructed but could refer to the year of the recipient's birth, the year the couple was betrothed or married, etc.) The similarities are not in themselves sufficient to demonstrate definitively that the Teacup Swifts are all by the same hand, and as yet no systematic comparison has been undertaken to establish whether they also have other characteristics in common (such as architecture of the cage, design of the clamp, the relative size, type, structure, and mechanics of the sprockets, and the means of fastening the ribs to the sprockets). Several makers are known to have produced more than one swift, but it is not known why a single maker might have built so many, as swifts are among the most time consuming and labor intensive of all shipboard scrimshaw productions and were usually reserved as gifts for close family members.

* **Tennant, Moses A.** (probably fl. circa the 1820s-30s). The *Dictionary* mentions a "Sheraton table of cherry wood inlaid with whale ivory, baleen, and abalone, labeled 'This Table Was Made By / Moses Tennant / Great Grandfather of / John & Blake Tennant'" (Bourne, 10 Feb 1987, #72). Although Moses Tennant's voyages have not been discovered, genealogical records now make it possible to trace the scrimshaw back to its origins, and thus identify the maker. The two great-grandsons named in the provenance were John S. Tennant (born circa 1922) and Blake A. Tennant (1925-1992). They were from Newton, Massachusetts, the sons of Frederick A. Tennant (born circa 1871), a patent

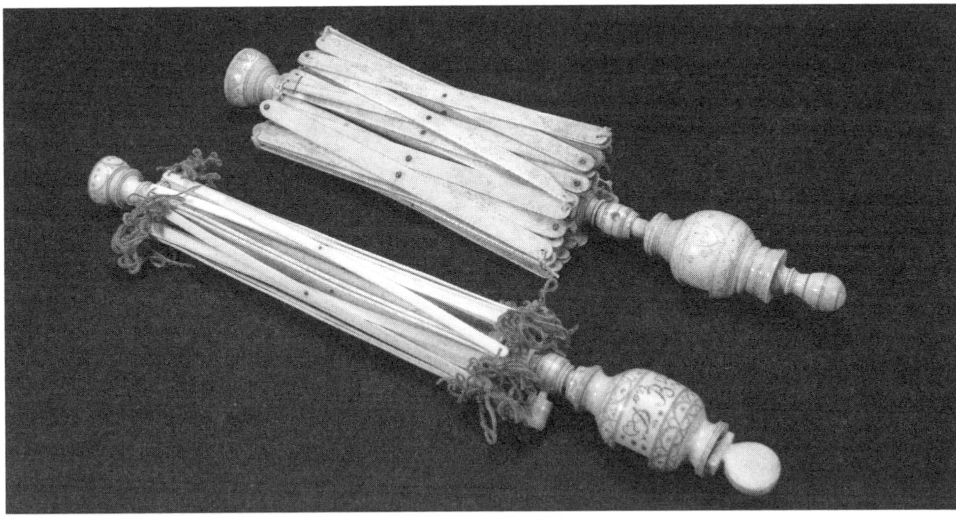

Fig. 21. **Swifts by the anonymous Teacup Swift Maker** are distinguished by delicate floral ornaments in magenta on the cup finial and table clamp. Kendall Collection, New Bedford Whaling Museum (photos by Richard Donnelly).

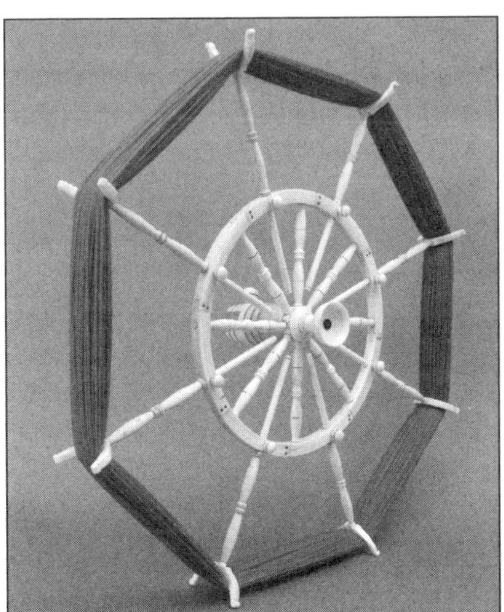

Fig. 22. **Seth Whelden, Jr.**, of South Dennis, on Cape Cod, is the attributed maker of this unique whale ivory and panbone *niddy-noddy*, which has his name and residence faintly written in pencil. The object is a yarn-winder in the form of ship's wheel, intended to perform much the same function as a conventional swift. Kendall Collection, New Bedford Whaling Museum (photo by Richard Donnelly).

attorney and former U.S. government assistant commissioner; and his second wife, Isabel B. Tennant (b. circa 1888). Frederick, in turn, was the son of John Tennant (b. 1839) and his wife Julia (b. circa 1838), who were farmers in Ripley, Chatauqua County, New York. John was the son of Moses A. Tennant (born circa 1802), who made the table. Moses married a distant relation with the same surname, Delinda Tennant, who was born the same year. Their son John, in whose line the scrimshaw descended, was the youngest of ten children. By 1860 — long after whatever voyages Moses may have made — he was farming and raising his family back in Chatauqua County. He died in 1876.

Teseuke [Tasseok; Tessioq], Ippaktuq – known as **Harry** (fl. circa 1895-1912). Inuit community leader, Chief of the Aivilingmiut in the vicinity of Cape Fullerton (Hudson Bay), Canada, and principal Inuit colleague and shipmate of George Comer (q.v. in the *Dictionary*). Widely known as "Harry," he was a prodigious carver and engraver of walrus ivory, primarily human and animal figures and at least one cribbage board. The provenance for these is partly documented in the Arctic diaries of Comer himself and in reports from the Canadian government's so-called *Neptune* Expedition to the Arctic in 1903-04. According to Maria von Finckenstein, two of the principals in that party, A.P. Low and surgeon L.E. Borden, collected ivory carvings now in CMC, and "one of the ivory bears in Borden's collection is signed 'Harry'" ("Harry Teseuke, Captain Comer's Mate"). His figures are rather less fluid than the more sophisticated animal forms of Happy Jack (q.v.), but are similarly deeply rooted in the indigenous traditions of Northern culture and have analogously been regarded as representing some of the best popular works by Inuit artisans. K. Ethel Borden calls him "an Eskimo genius" ("Northward 1903-04," *Canadian Geographic Journal*, 50:1 [Jan. 1961], 35). Comer, in a journal entry dated Jan. 20, 1904, reports, "My chief native Harry (Teseuke) has been making some ivory carvings for Commander Low, which he took over this evening" (Ross, *An Arctic Whaling Diary*, 90; see also A. P. Low, *The Cruise of the Neptune*). Harry appears often in Comer's many photographs, including scenes of working walrus ivory with a bow drill. His wife, known as "Patty," produced exquisite embroidery that Comer also collected for AMNH. Fred Calabretta included examples of Harry's and Patty's work his Comer exhibition at MSM in 2008, and there are representative pieces in several permanent collections, including AMNH. But the largest trove is CMC, which "bought a large collection of Comer's artifacts in 1913, including a group of animal ivories (fox, musk ox, narwhal, polar bear, wolf), most of which, if not all, were created by 'Harry' Ippaktuq Tasseok (or Teseuke), Chief of the Aivilingmiut…" (Von Finckenstein, 44). Many of these are posted on the CMC website www.civilization.ca.

Tessioq — see **Teseuke**

* **Thomas, Albert Alexander** (fl. circa 1853-76). New Bedford whaling master originally from Salem, New York. His known scrimshaw — which includes only those pieces attributed to him that descended in his family and were donated to NBWM by his grandchildren in 1979 — is prodigious in quantity and was produced to a high technical standard befitting the work of the trained artisan that he was in his youth. As might be expected from a professional carpenter, these works are primarily mechanical and architectural, rather than pictorial or purely decorative in character. Kitchen and food service implements include: two wooden rolling pins with whale ivory ends, one with whale ivory handles; a crimper (jagging wheel) with an open work handle of whale ivory, wood

inlay, three-tine fork (one tine broken off), fluted wheel, and whale ivory ring to accommodate a hook or lanyard; a small shovel-shaped whale ivory spoon; two coconut shell dippers, one with a wooden handle inlaid with diamond-shaped mother-of pearl, the other with a whale ivory shank, both with ornately carved whale ivory ends and ivory loops for hanging (one loop broken off); six stemware goblets of whale ivory, with slight variations in design and shape; three spreaders shaped like knives, with whale ivory blades and tortoise shell handles; and two lathe-turned whale ivory napkin rings. Domestic tools and sewing items include: a two-tine whale ivory pick or pickwick with a scalloped handle; three tatters, one of whale ivory, one of tortoise shell, and one of tortoise shell with an ivory spool; four lathe-turned bodkins varying in size and design; a two-section folding yardstick of teak with wood inlay, whale ivory ends, and a whale ivory hinge on a brass pivot, calibrated in inches on one side and fractions of a yard (for measuring yard-goods) on the other side; also several parts for a swift: a turned base of wood and whale ivory with three acorn-shaped brass legs, eight notched wooden ribs or struts, and six turned whale ivory posts. Purely decorative objects are two fists, full-round carved out of whale ivory, each with a shank that fits into a whale ivory base (one base present, the other absent); a whale ivory locket with mother-of-pearl cross; and a pin of tortoise shell and whale ivory. There is also a walrus ivory cribbage board inlaid with wood, ivory, and mother-of-pearl in a floral motif, whale ivory legs, six ivory pegs (markers); and there are three boxes: two puzzle boxes ("secret" boxes) of whale ivory with swiveling lids, one of tortoise shell overlaid with a whale ivory carving, the other ivory carved in the form flower with a brass center; and a round ditty box with panbone sides, and with a swiveling lid and stationary bottom that are laminated or veneered with tortoise shell.

Albert Alexander Thomas was born circa 1834 at Salem, New York, the son of a sometime cordwainer, Gold Rush prospector, and carpenter active at New Bedford circa 1841-52. By age 16 Albert was apprenticed to Joseph Walker, a carpenter at Taunton, Massachusetts, and as was common among apprentices since time immemorial, he lived in his master's home and became an adjunct member of the family. It appears that he may have run away to sea. In 1853, at age 19, almost certainly before completing his apprenticeship indenture, he obtained a Protection Paper (seaman's passport) at New Bedford, stating his residence as Salem, New York, and his age as 21 — perhaps to avoid detection for having run off before reaching legal age. On the other hand, the Protection was issued in his rightful name, and he evidently did not hide his carpentry skills, as he was signed for the 150th lay as ship's carpenter in the *Franklin* of New Bedford — a much better rate of pay than he could have gotten as a green hand or even as an ordinary seaman. He must have done well on the voyage (1853-57), as Captain Josiah Richmond hired him back for his next outing, this time for the 55th lay as a combination fourth mate and boatsteerer in the same ship (1857-59). Just before he sailed Albert got a new passport, still listing his home as Salem, New York, but this time giving his correct age. On this voyage the *Franklin* was wrecked on Pitt Island in the Chatham Islands (though Starbuck indicates that it was on Strong's Island — Kosrae — in Palau) in April 1859. This was often enough to inspire early retirement from whaling. But they had already sent home a quantity of oil and bone and managed to salvage some of the remaining cargo, which meant that it was not a total loss; and Albert stuck with it. When he sailed again in 1860 he obtained yet a third passport, which now stated his residence as New Bedford, symbolic of his faster-than-average rise and the decision he must have made around this time to remain in the whale fishery and make it his career. Captain Richmond remained his steadfast patron, and Albert made two more voyages under Richmond, both of them in the New Bedford ship *Daniel Wood*, as second mate (1860-64) and first mate (1865-67). His final two whaling voyages were as captain. On the first of these he sailed in the bark *Albion* of New Bedford on Christmas Day 1867, rounded Cape Horn to the Pacific, and took enough sperm whales to send home 287 barrels of oil (and possibly also to sell some in the Pacific); but at Auckland, New Zealand, the vessel was sold to become "the nucleus of a whaling company there" (Starbuck, 617), leaving the original inmates somewhat at odds. By what means Captain Thomas and his crew returned home is not recorded, but he was back in NB in time to be headed out to New Zealand again in July 1872 as captain of the bark *Merlin* on what turned out to be a fairly ordinary and reasonably successful four-year voyage (1872-76). By that time he had married Emma R. Wilcox and settled in New Bedford, where they raised their son Albert Ernest (born circa 1868), known as A.E., the father and namesake of the donors of the scrimshaw, Albert Ernest Thomas and Miss Sylvia E. Thomas.

Thomas, Calvin (1791-1864). Lot #307 in Osona, 2 Aug. 2008, is a sailor's canvas ditty bag containing a band saw, fid, and other implements made of skeletal bone, wood, and rope fancywork, dated circa 1850, alleged to have been the "Property of New Bedford whaling Captain Calvin Thomas of Freetown, Massachusetts (1792 [sic]-1864) and has descended in the Chase family." Whether or not Thomas is supposed to have made and used these items himself is not specified. But the provenance is fatally flawed and its claims thus cast in doubt. There never was a whaling captain named Calvin Thomas (or Thomas Calvin); in fact, there is no record of anyone of that name ever going whaling from New Bedford; and it is not clear which of the many Chase families is supposed to have owned the scrimshaw. The real Calvin Thomas of Freetown was actually born in Pembroke, Massachusetts, in 1791 (not 1792), the son of Nathaniel Thomas and the former Betty House. If Calvin was ever a master mariner it must have been in the merchant service or coastwise trade, but there is no visible record of that, either. And if he was a captain of something, it is not clear what (possibly the local militia). In 1822 he was married to Lois Maria Washburn, born at Middleborough, Massachusetts, in 1797, and they were farmers in Freetown all their adult lives. No record of any sea voyage has been discovered. The U.S. Census of 1850, the year in which the scrimshaw is claimed to have been owned by a whaling captain, lists Calvin as a farmer and his son, Calvin Junior, born in 1824, as a farm laborer at the same address. Junior later joined the Union Army and died in 1863. Clearly, the provenance is unreliable and, regardless of whether or not the individual pieces are authentic, the integrity of the ensemble is suspect.

* **Thomas, Thomas** (fl. circa 1865-67). The *Dictionary* reports that "The journal (in MSM) of Lucy Hix Crapo, wife of Captain Reuben W. Crapo (q.v.) of the whaling bark *Louisa* of New Bedford, 1865-67, indicates that during the voyage she 'Received a present of a pair of engraved whale's teeth from T. Thomas, the cook — his first attempt at such work.' From the original shipping paper [in KNB] this is known to be Thomas Thomas, born at Brooklyn, New York circa 1839." There is another holograph copy or version of Lucy Hix Crapo's journal in NBWM, entitled *Diary of Lucy Crapo*, which also mentions T. Thomas in the same context in the same words. Meanwhile, the teeth themselves have not surfaced. (Oddly, there was at least one other, earlier ship's cook with the same double name: Thomas Thomas of Campbell, Pennsylvania, African-American, born circa 1817, was cook in the New Bedford whaleships *Dartmouth*, 1841-44; *Bartholomew Gosnold*, 1844-

47; *Washington,* 1847-50; *Lagoda,* 1850-53; and *Logan,* sailed 1854, wrecked 1855. It is clear that the *Louisa*'s cook was Thomas Thomas of Brooklyn, New York, born in 1839, and was not the same man.)

* **Tinker, James Chapman** (fl. circa 1856-60s). An oval baleen box with spade-shaped rat-tail joints, the sides incised with a portrait of a bark under sail, a tree, and an obelisk monolith, in NBWM, bears the stipple-engraved initials "JCT." According to the family provenance it was made on the bark *John P. West* by James Chapman Tinker of Groton, Connecticut. The maker and vessel identified in the NBWM accession files, and hence repeated in the *Dictionary,* turn out to be questionable at best. There were at least two men of this name in the nineteenth-century New London whale fishery. One, born circa 1827, was evidenly born in New London, and his Protection Paper was issued there in 1857, when he was 30 years old. The other was born in Groton in 1839 or 1840, and was at sea when the 1860 U.S. Census was taken, hence he had no fixed address at that time and is accordingly listed instead — as James C. Tinker, age 20 — in a separate Seamen's Register of Groton sailors then at sea. However, there is no indication that either of them ever served aboard the *John P. West.* The name James Tinker (or James C. Tinker or James Chapman Tinker) does not appear on any of the crew lists for any of the eight voyages of the *John P. West* out of New Bedford (1858-88). Surviving crew lists for her four voyages out of San Francisco (1888-91) are not complete, but the name does not appear on any of those, either. The *John P. West* was built in 1857, and though she was registered in and sailed from New Bedford, her first two voyages (1858-63 and 1863-68) were commanded by Daniel G. Tinker, Jr., of New London, who may or may not have been a kinsman of one or the other James Chapman Tinker. The name of this captain may be the cause of the confusion, that is, the source of the notion among some Tinker descendants or museum curators that James Chapman Tinker was on one of these voyages of the *John P. West.* He was not; in fact, his name does not show up as ever having sailed in any vessel from the New Bedford Port District at any time. Whatever whaling voyages the scrimshaw-maker may have made were probably in vessels from ports in New London County, Connecticut: Mystic, Stonington, Norwich, or New London itself. Moreover, it is not clear whether it was the James Tinker of New London or the younger one from Groton who died in 1888, as reported in the accession files.

Tournaire, M. (fl. circa 1900). Like C.H. Wood (q.v. in the *Dictionary*) in an earlier generation, Tournaire was a graver of sea shells — which turns out to have been his second career. In his first career, in France, he was "a very talented forger of French bank notes," in consequence of which he "was exiled for life to a distant Pacific island [New Caledonia] where he carved shells with equally consummate skill": a specimen in PEM is a portrait of Queen Victoria, inscribed (in English) "Remember these presents that come from New Caledonia… ." (Reported by Daniel R. Finamore.)

Tripp, — (fl. circa 1836-40). A man identified only as "Mr. Tripp" was boatsteerer for Captain Frederick W. Hussey (q.v.) in the ship *William Lee* of Newport, Rhode Island (1836-40). Serrano Edwards Bishop (q.v.), a young passenger on the homeward passage of that voyage (1836-40), includes Tripp among the more active of several scrimshaw-makers aboard. While Bishop is none too specific about the "article" Tripp was working on, one important revelation is that he made his own lock mechanism for a box of his own construction. On 24 Jan. 1840 Bishop wrote, "A good many things are going on in the ship. Capt Hussey is making a bureau[,] Mr. V a work box, Mr Wyet a swift, [the] Steward a ship[model,] and Trip[p] an article. The captain has underway a swift and two work boxes[,] Mr Sheffield a box[,] and Mr V. another box." About a month later, on 22 Feb. 1840, he adds, "Trip[p] finished his box to which he made the lock and hinges[.] the lock is of copper and is done very neatly[,] the bolt and key are of brass[.]" Unfortunately, Bishop provides no first names or addresses, so this particular Mr. Tripp has not been singled out from the dozens of that surname, mostly from Westport and Dartmouth, Massachusetts, and adjacent parts of Rhode Island, who were serving in whaleships from Massachusetts and Rhode Island ports.

* **Tripp, Alexander Augustus** (fl. circa 1840-84). The *Dictionary* reports that as master of the bark *Globe* of New Bedford, 1869-72, Captain Alexander Tripp made coconut-shell dippers. The same original source, first mate John S. Coquin (q.v.), a prodigious scrimshaw-maker himself, indicates that the entire ship's company was scrimshawing on several occasions, and that in addition to the dippers, the Captain Tripp also made three dolphins. He probably scrimshawed other things as well that may have escaped Coquin's notice.

Tripp was born at Westport, Massachusetts, in February 1823 (as reported in the *Dictionary*, not 1828, as has sometimes been reported elsewhere), the son of Eliphalet Tripp and the former Phebe Petty. His father died at age 33 in September 1839, and to help support the family Alexander went to sea the following June, as cabin boy in the Westport brig *Elizabeth*. As a young sailor in the 1840s he resided with his widowed mother and younger brother, fellow-sailor John Henry Tripp, on the Westport farm of their older sister Emaline and her husband, Charles H. Hathaway. In 1854, at Jamestown, St. Helena — Napoleon's lonely isle of exile in the middle of the South Atlantic — on the last leg of his first voyage as a captain (of the ship *Dominga* of New Bedford, 1851-54), Tripp married Emma E. Kay (1838-1917), who had been born and raised there. They settled in Westport and raised seven children while Alexander continued his long and distinguished whaling career: five consecutive voyages in the bark *Globe* (1855-72), three in the bark *Pioneer* (1873-80), and two in the bark *President* (1881-84) of New Bedford. He died in 1889.

Tripp, Frederick F. (fl. circa 1859-88). New Bedford whaling master. Homeward bound in the New Bedford bark *Palmetto* in 1884, William W. Manchester, the second mate, wrote in his journal (in NBWM), "Nothing in sight and no sign of ever being any spirm [sic] whales around here[.] the old man and the mate devote there [sic] time at Schrimshorning[;] that is all they think of." The mate was Frank Morris (q.v.). The "old man," who was occupying himself with scrimshaw during the tedious lull between whales, was Captain Frederick F. Tripp. He was born in 1841, the son of William and Susan Tripp of Westport, Massachusetts, shipped out at age 17, and spent the major part of the next 30 years at sea, in the bark *Altamaha* of Sippican (1859-60), the New Bedford ship *Lancer* (1860-64) and bark *Mars* (1869-73) and at least one other (circa 1864-69), then was mate of the bark *Marcella* (1873-76). He was appointed captain of the *Marcella* in 1876, but the vessel was ultimately condemned at St. Helena. He next commanded the *Palmetto* (1880-84), the voyage on which he is reported scrimshawing (though he must surely have taken it up long before and merely escaped comment until now). His last outing was as first mate of the bark *James Allen* (1885-88) on a sperm whaling voyage that originated in New Bedford but returned to San Francisco, after which the *James Allen* was employed at bowhead whaling. The proximity of San Francisco to the

Western Arctic grounds, in waters off Alaska and Siberia, suited it well as a home port for the bowhead hunters, and as the value of "whalebone" (baleen) gradually outstripped the value of sperm and whale oil, the New Bedford fleet was transferring out there, one by one. But Frederick Tripp was a sperm whaler, and the bowhead fishery either did not appeal to him or he was not getting suitable offers, so he retired at this point. He had married Lydia M. Perry in 1876, lived in New Bedford and Acushnet, had three sons, and died in 1899.

Tripp, Frederick S. (fl. circa 1840-57). Whaleman tentatively credited with a large tooth that has a monochrome three-quarter-length portrait of a woman in a gown with low neckline and puff sleeves, sumounted by a riband meticulously inscribed in a cursive hand, "18 / Sarah. C. A. Tripp / 57"; with a garland of delicately curled leafy boughs as a circumferential border around the base (reported by Donald and Mary Boger). The attribution is based on the date inscribed on the scrimshaw (which distinguishes the maker from more than a dozen other men of the same name who went whaling out of New Bedford) and the identity of the recipient, who is probably also the subject of the portrait: Frederick Spooner Tripp married Sarah A. Cook (1827-1905) at Fall River, Massachusetts, in 1845. He was born in Westport, Massachusetts, in 1820, the second of two sons and the third of twelve children of Job Tripp and the former Mehitable Davis. He was one of two young men from Westport who had the same name, were the same age, and went whaling at the same time. Starting at age 20, he worked his way up to second mate on three successive voyages of the Fairhaven bark *Favorite* (1840-50), got married along the way and started a family of his own in Fall River, then served as first mate on the ship *Jireh Perry* of New Bedford (1852-56), after which he retired from whaling and spent the next 35 years as an upholsterer in Fall River, where he was still working in 1891. He died in 1893.

Trotter, Elias Willard (fl. 1845-47). He made one voyage to the Northwest Coast grounds in the ship *Illinois* of Sag Harbor, Long Island, Captain Daniel Jagger, during 1845-47, and on that basis produced a memoir of his whaling experiences (preserved as an edited but unpublished typescript in NBWM). In it he provides a rare and all-too-brief discourse on the use of sharkskin as sandpaper in scrimshandering, which also poignantly reveals the whalemen's prevailing attitudes about the shark itself:

> *I might mention that during the cutting-in of the whale & while the greedy shark hovered amid us in so great number[s], a shark of perhaps the largest size was struck & saved. Truly they are a disgusting & terrible animal & all of the inhabitants, myriads in number, that the deep ocean holds as its own, I know of none so loathed & feared as the shark. Willingly I aided in hauling him aboard, pierced as he was [with] 2 irons. He would measure 9 feet in length, had 2 rows of teeth & was in all respect[s] the terror I once dreamed of. The men soon stripped him of his skin & hung it up to dry. Since then it has thoroughly dried & they use it preparatory to polishing & marking their sperm whale teeth.*

While Trotter participates in the shark butchering, he gives no hint that he did any scrimshandering of his own; in fact, he distances himself from this as he does few other aspects of his whaling experience ("*The men*... stripped him of his skin & hung it up to dry... " and "*they* use it preparatory to polishing & marking *their* sperm whale teeth"). Elias Trotter, born in 1824, was originally from upstate New York in the vicinity of Albany, the son of Col. John Trotter and Sarah Ten Eyck Willard. His mother was born in Stillwater and his older brother belonged to the Dutch Reformed Church in Albany. In fact, that brother, John Henry Trotter (1813-1861), married Hester Elizabeth Van Vechten (1815-1891), who was descended from Gansevoorts and was thus a distant cousin of Herman Melville; they named a daughter born in 1839 Catherine Gansevoot Trotter. However, apart from the family context and one whaling voyage not much is known about Elias himself.

Trowbridge, A.B. (fl. circa 1840-45). A well executed tooth, with the broadside portrait of a whaleship on one side and a loving couple farewell scene on the other (not unlike the analogous vignettes severally employed on teeth and busks by the Banknote Engraver), is signed on the root end, "A.B. Trowbridge / At Sea 1840" (privately held; reported by Paul Oligschlaeger of Ivey Selkirk Auctioneers, St. Louis). Nothing has been discovered about Trowbridge except that he was a boatsteerer for a 1/85th lay in the New Bedford bark *Canton Packet* (1841-45). His rank indicates that the *Canton Packet* could not have been his first whaling voyage, and the date on the tooth indicates that it must have been done on the homeward passage of his previous voyage.

***Turner, Charles H.** (fl. circa 1858-86). New Bedford whaling master mentioned in the *Dictionary* as having made a sugar scoop and vase fashioned from coconut shells with whale ivory components, and a wooden workbox inlaid with whale ivory (Bourne 17-18 August 1971, #436, 465, and 464). A skeletal autobiography and two very different and rather unusual pieces of scrimshaw have since come to light: an ornate Victorian desk with a fold-out writing surface, profusely trimmed with whale skeletal bone, which descended in the family until 2009 with a written and orally transmitted provenance that attributes it to Captain Turner himself; and a tooth circumferentially relief-carved with American patriotic vignettes (private collection; reported by Louis Hammond). The desk is generally of the form and dimensions of a parlor organ or upright piano, with scroll-cut supports under the fold-out writing surface itself, two double-door cabinets above, six drawers below with pendant teardrop pulls, and escutcheons and ornamental trim of whale skeletal bone. According to Ron Clark, Turner's great-grandson, it "was built by ... Captain Charles Turner, the captain of the Bark Napoleon" and "is made of drift wood, the two doors that open in front have buttons from his wife's wedding dress inserted with small pieces of ivory [sic] and [mother of] pearl" (private communication to NBWM, Jan. 21, 2009). The work is supposed to have been completed aboard the *Napoleon* at St. Helena on the homeward passage; and as Turner was twice homeward bound as captain of the *Napoleon*, this could have been in 1878 or 1882. The notion of "drift wood" is certainly misleading, as the material is hardly the saltwater-logged, degraded stuff that washes up on ocean beaches. Rather, it appears to be some much higher category of lumber — perhaps foundling wood retrieved from the sea itself or from salvage or barter at sea or ashore. The joinery and ornamentation are more precise and far more elaborate than are ordinarily encountered on sailor-made furniture, and if any sea captain constructed it from scratch himself (rather than merely decorated or tinkered with it) he must have been a wonderfully proficient cabinetmaker with an unusually complete set of tools on board. In the absence of any direct evidence that Turner had apprenticed or otherwise received training as a carpenter or cabinetmaker prior to going to sea, the attribution remains speculative and opinion is divided about whether an amateur could have built the desk himself. Alternatively, he could have converted a commercially-manufactured piece into scrimshaw by adding the whale ivory ornaments himself, or commissioned the desk from one of his ship's carpenters or other underlings at sea, or perhaps he had nothing at all to do with its construction. The likelihood is that the captain purchased or commissioned the desk from someone else and added the scrimshaw features himself. In any case, it ranks among the largest pieces that in any way qualify as scrimshaw.

Charles Henry Turner was born in 1840 at Falmouth, Massachusetts, on Cape Cod, the son of farmers Japheth and Susan Turner. Both of his older brothers, Nathan and Samuel, were also mariners; all three went to sea at early ages. Charles made whaling his career, rose gradually through the ranks, and at the comparatively advanced age of 34, shortly after returning from his first voyage as second mate in 1874, he married Clementine F. Doty, a Falmouth dressmaker. Two of their several children were born in the course of voyages on which she accompanied him, in whole or in part. The Falmouth Historical Society holds a brief manuscript autobiography outlining his career:

> *Sailed my first voyage from N[ew] Bedford Sept 1st 1858 in B[ar]k Orray Taft, Capt M[icajah] C[hadwick] Fisher, absent 38 months. Got home soon after the civil war broke out, than went in Gover[n]ment transports untill the end of the war carrying forrage or cattle for the army & transporting troops untill the war was over. Was in the first sailing vessel that went in Charleston harbour after its surrender with a [contingent] of Negro troops. 1876 sailed my 2d voyage whaling as boatsteerer in Brig E[unice] H. Adams [of Nantucket], Capt. Coleman of Nantucket, arriving home Sep 27th 1878. My next voyage was in the B[ar]k Cornelia of N Bedford for the South Pacific Ocean, Capt. Edward P. Shiverick of Falmouth master. Sailed 1868 arrived 1871, went as 2d officer, took 2350 bbls of oil. My next voyage sailed in the same vessel as first officer under command of Capt. LaRoy S. Lewis Oct 10 1871 for the South Pacific. Condem[n]ed the ship at Paita Peru Feb 1874 & arrived home in April 1874 by steamer from Aspinwal. My next voyage sailed as first officer of Bk Napoleon, Capt. Jernegan of the Vineyard [Martha's Vineyard], July 13 1874 for the South Atlantic Indian & Pacific Oceans. Sept 1875 put into Honolulu to land Capt Jernegan sick. I was then placed in command & continued the voyage arriving home May 4th 1878 with 1750 sperm & 20 whale. My next voyage sailed as master of the same ship. Aug 1st 1878 took my wife with me for a cruise in the South Pacific. Arrived home July 28th 1882 with 1550 bls sperm 625 whale & 2300 lbs bone. One child born on this voyage. My next voyage sailed as master of Bk AR Tucker of N Bedford June 25 1883. My wife joined me at St. Helena when 15 months out. One child born on this voyage at St. Helena. Arrived home Aug 2d 1886 with 1450 sperm 280 whale & 1250 bls bone. I than retired from the sea after 28 years on the water. Anything more that you would like to know I shall be happy to tell you.* (Also posted on the Rootsweb and Ancestry.com websites)

On the *Napoleon*, Clementine (known as "Carrie") kept a journal of her own and gave birth to a child; and it was during the *A.R. Tucker* voyage that she came out to meet the ship and gave birth on St. Helena in July 1885. As captain of the *A.R. Tucker* Turner is credited with having taken the second largest sperm whale ever captured. Falmouth lore also claims that at some point he "chased a sea-serpent with a whale boat in the South Seas." The 1900 U.S. Census still lists him as a Master Mariner, but by that time he had actually retired and taken up farming and cranberry growing in Falmouth and possibly Sandwich. He is said to have died in 1909 but the 1910 census lists Charles and Clementine as still farming in Falmouth. (Not to be confused with whaleman Charles H. Turner, born circa 1839, the son of a Nantucket cooper.)

Tuthill, J.A. (fl. 19th century). A "Pair of Engraved Walrus Tusks, signed J.A. Tuthill, Cutchogue, Long Island, 19th century" (Skinner, 24 Oct. 1998; *Maine Antique Digest*, Nov. 1998, 5-I) are singularly interesting, as they feature not only three conventional ship portraits in a panoramic whaling scene, together with landscape, architectural, and equestrian vignettes, but also a railroad train comprised of a steam locomotive spewing smoke, a coal car, and three passenger coaches. It must have originated with one of the large Tuthill clan of farmers, tradesmen, and seamen who were widely distributed in the township of Southold, on the south shore of the North Fork of Eastern Long Island, New York, and notably in Cutchogue, a hamlet and postal district southwest of the main part of Southold. However, the identity of the maker has not been discovered. There were no whaling masters surnamed Tuthill, and no whaling records have been unearthed for any J.A. or J. Tuthill (however, see below). In the 1830 census a J.A. Tuthill, known only as such, appears as a resident of Southold (neighborhood unspecified), born sometime between 1800 and 1810, living at the time with a wife of about the same age, a boy of between 10 and 15 years of age (who may or may not have been his son; likely not), and (evidently) his adult sister and widowed mother. However, his occupation is not indicated (the census in those days did not report occupations) and the name does not appear as such again. The 1850 census (the first to designate occupations) lists a James Tuthill (no middle initial), born in 1803 or 1804. He is identified as a seaman living in East Marion, another hamlet in Southold, with a wife of about the same age and four children. Despite superficial similarities (however vague) in the vital statistics of J.A. and James Tuthill, neither is specifically identified with Cutchogue, while irreconcilable disparities in the numbers and ages of their children suggest that they are not likely the same man. But one or the other *could* be the James Tuthill who is known to have been involved in whaling at some indeterminate point. In reference to yet another hamlet of Southold, just southwest of Cutchogue, a local historian reports,

> *The name "Jamesport" has a vagrant history. James Tuthill first coined it about 1832 when he purchased Miamogue Point, laid out a street grid for an ambitious whaling port and named it "James' Port" after himself. After the railroad came through in 1844, the first post office was set up. Although it was located on the main road, it was called "Jamesport." The name replaced the hamlet's old names of "Old Aquebogue" or "Lower Aquebogue." Late in the century, when the inhabitants of the original Jamesport wanted their own post office, they had to settle for "South Jamesport."* ("The KeySpan Property," www.hallockville.com)

These remarks incidentally suggest a clue to the vintage and possible attribution of the tusks. Assuming that the local rail line may have inspired the railroad vignette on the scrimshaw (as it did James Fenimore Cooper's splendid introduction to *The Sea Lions*, his novel about Eastern Long Island's commercial seal hunt, published in 1849), the fact that the railroad did not "come through"

Southold until 1844 suggests a far later epoch than any whaling career that someone of J.A. or James Tuthill's age would have had. This is corroborated by the obviously later type of locomotive and coaches depicted. There were surprisingly few male Tuthills in Southold with the initials J.A., and even fewer plausible candidates. For example, Jacob A. Tuthill, born circa 1815 at Southold (postal district unspecified), and Julius A. Tuthill, born in Cutchogue circa 1849, were perhaps of compatible ages but there is no indication that either ever went whaling or was ever a sailor. And so on.

Vanderzee [Vandezee], — (fl. circa 1839-40). Whalers occasionally took on passengers as they crisscrossed the Pacific from one island to another, and even more often on the homeward passage. A man known only as "Mr. Vandezee (or Vanderzee)" is a rare instance of a whaleship passenger who took up scrimshaw — enthusiastically, it seems — during his brief time aboard. He was traveling with his wife from the Hawaiian Islands to Newport, Rhode Island, in the ship *William Lee,* commanded by Frederick W. Hussey (q.v.) during 1839-40. What little is known of him is told by a fellow passenger, Sereno Edwards Bishop (q.v.), the twelve-year-old son of Hawaiian missionaries on his way to prep school in upstate New York. Bishop's journal (in KNB) does not say exactly which Vanderzees these were (he provides neither Christian names nor addresses), but they were almost certainly members of the prominent Vanderzee clan in upstate New York, descendants of Dutch patroons living mostly in Coeymans and elsewhere in Albany County. On the *William Lee,* Mr. Vanderzee appears to be something of an amateur ornithologist, and collected bird carcasses from which taxidermic specimens were prepared for him on board. On several occasions Bishop describes him making and assembling a substantial stockpile of scrimshaw, the purpose of which, though nobody ever says so, must have been to serve as mementos and gifts for the folks back home. In January 1840 he was making a work box and "another box"; in February he "Bought of Anderson [one of the crew] a pair of whale's teeth[;] they are the largest that I ever saw," which he "is going to use his for a swift, which he is about to make. he is also at work on a small bureau which is to be made of bone"; and one day in March he traded with some of the crew, "getting the material for a swift," together with four teeth, a panbone cane, six or eight bone stays (i.e., staybusks), a shaft, a cup, and some kind of whirligig, "ready made" (see Appendix IV).

As Dr. Jack H.T. Chang has pointed out (private communication, March 2007), Bishop's description of scrimshaw activities aboard the *William Lee* unwittingly reveals a hitherto undocumented method of applying pigment. On some previous occasion the boy had swapped Vanderzee some paints and brushes. Now, in April, "Mr. V. took some of those Chinese paints... and ground them with oil and Sp[iri]ts [of] Turpentine, and painted the edges of the drawers to his bone bureau, they worked very well." However, because both the scrimshaw-maker (Vanderzee) and the informant (Bishop) were passengers and tyros, not regular members of the crew, it is uncertain whether this technique was ever used by actual sailors making mainstream scrimshaw on shipboard.

***Vieira, Nicholas R.** (fl. circa 1879-1911). Born on the island of Flores, in the Azores, Captain Vieira (1856-1913) was one of New Bedford's most distinguished latter-day whaling masters, and remains today very highly regarded on his native Flores as well as in New Bedford's Azorean community. A bilingual Portuguese-English biographical sketch by João A. Gomes Vieira (2003, 182f) refers to him by his original Portuguese name, Nicolau Rodrigues Vieira, and specifies, "Some engraved teeth and walking-sticks, attributed to him, were found in his family's house on the island of Flores." His work is represented in the Museu de Arte e Tradição Popular (Museum of Art and Popular Tradition) on Flores (this citation is misprinted in the *Dictionary*, appearing as MTA rather than MAT).

Though Vieira was first mate on the 1899-1900 voyage of the New Bedford bark *Canton*, he is not mentioned in Brian O'Brien's fictionalized account, *Scrimshaw and Sudden Death*, which is based on the journal of one of the boatsteerers, Lester A. Mosher (q.v.), and describes the captain and all of the officers as engaged in making scrimshaw (see also Alexander Nanton, Herbert R. Reynolds, and William I. Shockley). Gomes Vieira's account of Nicholas Vieira's whaling career is based on the *Dictionary* and Amaral 1978, hence imparts no additional insights and repeats Amaral's controversial assertion that the captain's son, Joseph [José António] Vieira (1891-1951), fourth mate, acted as relief captain of the *Bertha* in 1910. The standard story is that Captain Vieira became ill and was put ashore at Fayal, leaving Joseph in charge until a relief captain arrived. One version even claims that Captain Vieira specifically designated his son as relief captain. However, Lund (*Whaling Masters*, 2001, 407) does not indicate that Vieira left the ship early at all, and accordingly names no relief captain; and it appears that any departure of Nicholas Vieira, for illness or any other reason, may have been only temporary. In any case, the voyage ended in shipwreck on the homeward passage in 1911, fifteen months out, with the entire crew and even the vessel saved. Captain Vieira is said to have recovered from his illness, but he never returned to sea and died not long afterwards, in 1913. There are several images of him in NBWM, notably a large studio photograph by the Jordan Art Company of New Bedford (1894) and a scrimshaw portrait by an anonymous Azorean-American hand, rendered on a large sperm whale tooth.

Wade, John B. (fl. circa 1861-74). The implication of his journal of a whaling voyage in the ship *George and Susan* of New Bedford (1861-64) (in NBWM) is that he participated in scrimshawing activities on the homeward-bound passage; but none of his scrimshaw has yet surfaced. He was born in 1839 in Canton, Massachusetts, and at age 10 was apprenticed to a bootmaker, William S. Hall, with whom he lived in North Bridgewater, Massachusetts. He later worked for Joseph Harlow, a shoemaker in whose home in Halifax, Massachusetts, Wade was billeted until 1861, when at age 22 he obtained a Seamen's Passport and went to sea in the *George and Susan* — perhaps to escape the dreary confines of the mechanical trades, or perhaps to avoid military service in the Union Army. After the voyage — and at the end of the Civil War — he settled in Bridgewater, where he worked in a shoe factory. Then, oddly, after a hiatus of seven years ashore, already married to a woman twelve years his junior named Eliza, and now the father of a three-year-old son, Wade went to sea again on the same vessel for another whaling voyage of almost three years (1871-74). He was then a merchant seaman for a while, which is where the trail grows cold.

Waite, Crary B. (fl. circa 1835-64). New Bedford whaling master credited with a panbone cane that has a whale ivory handle full-round-carved in the traditional shape of a clenched right fist holding a bolt or wand, with a knot of baleen woven circumferentially around the foreshaft, and the maker's initials "C.B.W." inlaid in baleen dots around the cuff. The initials notwithstanding, the cane was reportedly given by Captain Waite to a friend of about the same age, Neverson Newton (1818-1890), a farmer in Somonauk, Illinois, and was recently found in storage at the Marie Louise Olmstead Museum in Somonauk (reported by trustee Bevin R. Wold).

Waite is briefly mentioned in the *Dictionary* as the unlikely maker of a tooth in TDM in England illustrating a sperm whale hunt, signed and dated "Waite 1833," but in this case the provenance makes an unequivocal attribution. Accompanying the cane was a photographic portrait of the maker and an obituary, published in an unidentified newspaper in 1892 and fraught with errors and misunderstandings. It has him born at Tiverton, Rhode Island, in 1818; he was actually born in adjacent Westport, Massachusetts, in 1819. The family moved to New Bedford a few years later, and there Clary's brother Benjamin eventually became a dry goods merchant and held ownership shares in whaleships and other vessels. Clary, however, made his career at sea, first as a green hand in the ship *Frances Henrietta* in April 1835. The obituary claims that the vessel was wrecked in the Falkland Islands, but Starbuck and Lund report her safely returned to New Bedford in June 1836 with a hefty cargo of oil. On his next outing Waite actually was shipwrecked in the bark *Elizabeth*, at Pico, in the Azores, in September 1836. He next went as boatsteerer in the ship *Virginia* of New Bedford (1838-40), then served time in what appears to have been the German ship *Augusta*, sailing out of Bremen on what may or not have been a whaling voyage or two (circa 1840-43). In fact, the New Bedford merchant John Avery Parker, whose son-in-law, Christian A. Heineken, was a merchant and sometime producer of harpoons in Bremen, was the managing agent of Waite's next voyage, in the New Bedford ship *Trident*, in which he likely went as third mate (1843-46). After that Waite was three voyages in the bark *Hope*, as second mate (1847-50), first mate (1850-53), and captain (1853-54). He married Emily Hill between voyages in 1853. He was ashore and away from whaling for a couple of years, then accepted command of the Mattapoisett whaleship *Brewster* (1857-60); and when he went next as captain of the *Robert Morrison* (1861-64) he took his family along, and on that voyage narrowly escaped being captured by the Confederate commerce-raider *Alabama*. Meanwhile, he held a 4/32nds owners' share in the *Brewster* on his own voyage and the voyage following. He retired from whaling in 1864 and purchased a grocery in New Bedford, he retired completely by 1870, and he died in 1892. His son, Charles H. Waite, became manager of the Norfolk [Virginia] National Bank.

Walsh, John (fl. circa 1850s). A tooth in a private collection, reported but not examined, is said to have a "waterfront scene of Boston [in] 1850" and, on the other side, "a large wright [sic] whale and other fish and animals, also the name John Walsh, Cove Head." The picture title is generic and, unfortunately, so is the place-name, with the result that the personal name is not sufficient to identify the artist, even in combination with these other features. There were seven or eight men named John Walsh [AKA Walch] in the crews of whaleships out of New Bedford, Fairhaven, Dartmouth, and New London in the 1850s — including one from New South Wales — and no additional clues by which to distinguish the scrimshaw artist from the others. The man that seems the most likely, because he had the best credentials both as a whaleman (he made at least three voyages) and as a mechanic and artisan (he was a cooper by trade), was from western New York State. He was born in Black Creek, Niagara County, probably around 1818 (the records differ widely), was a boatsteerer in the ship *Hesper* of Fairhaven (1848-53), which could not have been his first voyage, then ship's cooper and shipkeeper in the *Marcella* of New Bedford (1853-57). The only other John Walsh known to have made more than a single voyage was also from western New York. He was born around 1831 in Mentz, Cayuga County, and was in the crews of the New Bedford ships *Illinois* (1853-57) and *Abraham Barker* (1857-61). Around that same time there was also another John Walsh occupying the cooper's berth in a New Bedford whaler, but nothing else is known about him: he evidently made only the one voyage, and though his name appears on the NBPS crew list for the bark *Cavalier* (1855-58), uniquely in his case on that crew list, the usual data regarding his age, residence, and physical description are unaccountably missing.

Ward, William Denny (fl. circa 1846-59). He was a New Bedford native who at age 15 started out as a regular whaleman and later became a career ship's cooper, until tragedy overtook him. It is not surprising that a cooper might have a scrimshaw *bung starter* or *bungstart* — a simple mallet used to insert *bungs* (wooden plugs) in barrels, and to "start" a bung when removing it. The one credited to Ward has a crude head made of sperm whale panbone, and a flattened octagonal wooden handle. While the descendant who donated it (to NBWM in 1980) claimed only that it "once *belonged* to William Denny Ward," it is likely that the whaleman-cooper made it himself for his own practical use on shipboard. The donor, Fred C. Ward, also said that his ancestor "was lost at sea near Cape Horn from a whaling ship [on] December 18, 1859," which is highly credible if only for its specificity.

William Denny Ward was born circa 1831, the son of Jonathan R. Ward, a New Bedford baker, and Mary née Denny, a native of Nova Scotia. For William to have qualified as a ship's cooper in later life he may have served at least part of a formal apprenticeship in coopering prior to embarking on his first voyage, as a green hand in the New Bedford ship *Congaree* (1846-48). His next voyage was as an ordinary seaman in the ship *Ann Alexander* of New Bedford under Captain John Scott Deblois (q.v.), the famous voyage on which a sperm whale deliberately struck and sank the ship in the summer of 1851 — just in time for the news to reach New York and vindicate Melville's story for skeptical readers of the newly-published *Moby Dick*. Fellow scrimshaw artist Joseph Green (q.v.) was first mate on that fateful voyage. After the wreck Ward, like the rest of the ship's company, was forced to find other means home; and like only a few of the others, he soon went whaling again. But this time he stepped up to the higher pay, greater prestige, and far more comfortable circumstances of ship's cooper, first in the bark *Sacramento* of Westport (1852-54), then the ship *Pacific* of Fairhaven (1854-57), and finally the New Bedford bark *William Gifford*, which sailed in October 1858. He died at sea about fourteen months later.

Warren, Stephen H. (fl. circa 1882). A "scrimshaw box with various inlays" measuring is 9 x 4 x 6 inches (23 x 10 x 25.5 cm), offered for sale "with contents," was described somewhat opaquely by the auctioneer as having on the top inlay at the four corners and a name plaque inscribed "ELVIRA WARREN - LUDLOW," the front with three diamond inlays and five ivory inlays arranged to form four "negative circles" and an escutcheon, with "the same inlays" on the sides "spaced accordingly [to] form 4 element filfot in a negative manner on each side." The "contents" are a logbook of the bark *H.J. Libby* on a passage from Pananagua, Brazil, to Valpariso, Chile, in 1882, together with "typewritten documents relating to the purchase of 1150 bbls. of Sperm oil at 65¢ & 900 bbls. at 60¢, also a similar letter for purchase of more sperm oil, 2 canceled bank checks from [the] Mechanics National Bank [of] New Bedford, Mass." and "a large lot of ivory pieces and remnants" (DeLuca, Feb. 19, 2005, #228). H.J. Libby was Harrison Jewell Libby, a wholesale dry goods merchant from Limerick, Maine, who founded H.J. Libby & Co. in Portland in 1835. The firm reportedly "became very largely identified with the cotton and woolen manufacturers of Maine," and opened a branch in New York by 1862. The bark *H.J. Libby*, 621 tons, was built in 1873 by Hagen & Thurlow at Bath, Maine, and was in the Cape Horn trade to the Pacific, plying the routes between Samarang and Sydney in 1879, Brazil to Chile in 1882, and so on. Its relation to the namesake merchant and his dry goods firm is unclear. Stephen H. Warren, born in 1844 at Islesboro, Maine, was evidently the captain; Elvira née Tusler, born circa 1851 at Searsmont, Maine, was his wife and, as the inlay on the box indicates, the recipient of the scrimshaw. Stephen came from a whole clan of Warren mariners in Isleboro, the second son and namesake of a sailor and (later) fisherman whose brothers lived immediately nearby and were also mariners. Stephen served as a private in the 16th Maine Infantry in the Civil War but spent the rest of his adult career as a sailor. If he made any youthful whaling voyages they have not been identified. In the 1870s and 80s he, Elvira, and their son Eugene were living with her parents, Samuel and Lucy Fowles, along with some of her younger siblings, on a farm at Searsmont. They later had a homestead of their own nearby. By 1920 Stephen was widowed and retired, and he spent his last years as a resident of the National Soldiers' Home in Chelsea, Maine, where he died in 1931. It is not known for certain whether he actually made the inlaid box himself, but the presence of the "ivory pieces and remnants" indicates that he probably had them for making scrimshaw. The significance of "Ludlow" has not been discovered.

Washburn, William (fl. circa 1836-69). New Bedford whaling master. In a private journal aboard the Fairhaven ship *Samuel Robertson* in March 1851, the cooper, George R. Coggeshall (q.v.), wrote, "the Captain making a pair of swifts and myself turning belaying pins." The captain was William Washburn, who must have been a dedicated maker of scrimshaw: "a pair of swifts" is about as ambitious a scrimshaw project as could be undertaken. It is unfortunate that these swifts, if they survive, have not been identified. Washburn, born circa 1818 in Fairhaven, went to sea at age 17 in the brig *Ann Maria* of Fall River (1838-39), commanded by Angles Snell (q.v. in *More Scrimshaw Artists*). Washburn's other early voyages are not known but he had a distinguished career as a master mariner, specializing in bowhead whaling in the North Pacific and Western Arctic. He was first mate in the ship *Friendship* of Fairhaven (1846-49), then captain of two voyages in the Samuel Robertson (1849-52 and 1852-56) and one each in the *Arab* of Fairhaven (1858-60), *Ansel Gibbs* of New Bedford (1862-63, her first voyage after being transferred from Fairhaven), and *General Scott* of Fairhaven (1865-69). Like many whaling masters, as part of his compensation he customarily received an ownership interest (in his case usually a 1⁄16th share, expressed as 4⁄64ths) for some predesignated number of voyages of the vessels he commanded. All of these interests were held in partnership with Isaiah F. Terry of Fairhaven, who was managing agent of the vessels Washburn commanded, along with the usual consortium of other investors. Some captains were unable to obtain this potentially lucrative stakeholder benefit until they had proven themselves by commanding several voyages successfully. An unusual feature in Washburn's case was that he got the first of these ownership-based dividends, in the ship *Friendship*, when he was only a first mate. Another unusual feature is that they included a share in the schooner *Oxford*, which served as tender to the *Arab* (1858-60); another is that he did not hold onto such investments for very long: he seems not to have invested additional funds of his own, and his owner's shares had all expired by the time he retired from whaling in 1869. Meanwhile, he was twice married, first in 1846 to a woman named Elizabeth (probably Elizabeth Stoddard) for whom he likely made at least one of the *Samuel Robertson* swifts. He was widowed not long afterwards and evidently spent a lot more time ashore with his two daughters during 1856-58, when he hired Catherine Rose, a 25-year-old Azorean immigrant from Fayal, to help raise the children, and was captain of various merchant voyages (as in the bark *Antelope*, of which he was also part owner, in 1858). He remarried in 1857, and over the next few years his second wife, Sarah Terry, bore him a son and two more daughters, the youngest of whom, Helen (known as Nellie), remained unmarried and lived with her parents into their eighties. (The 1900 U.S. Census erroneously reports William as aged 82 and born in 1812, which are clearly mutually exclusive: the former is correct, the latter not.)

Wentworth, David P. (fl. circa 1850-60). A carpenter's scribe nicely crafted from sperm whale panbone and engraved with the initials "DPW" was found in Maine by Gordon Stanley. It has a written provenance claiming that it came out of "the Holbrook estate" in East Boothbay, Maine, and "most likely belonged to David P. Wentworth, a customer of the Holbrook Store and a neighbor in East Boothbay." Indeed, as Wentworth was a carpenter by trade, he probably made it himself. He was born in Maine in 1811 or 1812, married Abigail Decker in 1848, and is listed in the U.S. Census as a carpenter (in 1850) and joiner (in 1860) living in Boothbay with his wife and a step-daughter named Angela or Angelina Smith (there is no evidence that the union produced any natural issue). Several men surnamed Wentworth from Maine, New Hampshire, Massachusetts, and Connecticut went whaling out of New London, Salem, and New Bedford, but no record of a whaling voyage or of seafaring experience of any kind has been found for anyone named David Wentworth.

West, Bartholomew (fl. circa 1828-49). Career whaleman, master mariner, and possible maker of a tooth signed "B. West" picturing the harbor at Callao, which is the port of Lima, Peru (Rinaldi 2009, #194; reported by James Vaccarino); however, Benjamin West (q.v.) was the more likely maker. Bartholomew was born circa 1812, the son of William West of New Bedford, and during his short life listed his residence at different times as New Bedford and Fairhaven. He made three or four whaling voyages in his youth, all in New Bedford ships. The records of the first one or two are lost, but he went to the Pacific in the *William Hamilton*, probably as boatsteerer (1834-37), and the New Zealand grounds in the *Samuel Robertson*, possibly as third mate (1837-40). After he returned from the latter voyage in 1840 he married Freelove Peets, then sailed for a second time in the *William Hamilton*, probably as second mate (1841-44). A crew list in NBFPL lists him as captain of the ship *Moctezuma* on a voyage of 1844-47, but Starbuck, Lund, the NBPS ledger, and the NBFPL Index unequivocally name William E. Tower as captain on that voyage: West was actually first mate. He was next given command of the New Bedford bark *Emigrant*. She sailed on May 31 or June 1, 1848, but was lost with all hands under circumstances that remain a mystery. Starbuck's report is quoted almost verbatim from the NBPS ledger entry, that the *Emigrant* was "found in 1849 bottom up; crew never heard from."

West, Benjamin (fl. 1837-47). Merchant seaman, whaler, prospector, California pioneer, and saloonkeeper originally from Salem, Massachusetts, to whom a tooth is attributed that has a dandy panoramic view of the harbor of Callao (the port of Lima, Peru), a frequent port-of-call for American whaleships. The crenellated fortress dominating the roadstead and flying a Peruvian flag is prominently featured in the foreground, the city is delineated on the slopes behind, the harbor is punctuated with shipping, there are small, incidental vignettes on the back, and the tooth is signed "B.

West" (Rinaldi 2009, #194; examined and the locale identified and reported by James Vaccarino.) No other scrimshaw by this artist has yet come to light.

Of the several men named B. West known or suspected of having made at least one American whaling voyage in the 19th century, two emerge as the most likely candidates for attribution of the Callao-related scrimshaw; and of these, one is perhaps more likely than the other. Bartholomew West (q.v.), a career whaleman from New Bedford and Fairhaven, is the less likely because he died young, his voyages to the Pacific were early in his career and fewer, most of his whaling was in the Atlantic, and he is not known ever to have visited Callao; while Benjamin West not only visited the place on several occasions, but was actually ashore there for a while between voyages.

Of eight men named Benjamin West who are known or suspected of having been on American whaling voyages in the 19th century, only one is a viable candidate for the maker: the other seven can be eliminated on the basis of the incompatible circumstances of their lives and careers. A Benjamin West born in Salem, Massachusetts circa 1787, and a Benjamin West, Jr., born in nearby Gloucester a year or two later, were active before 1812, far too early to have made the scrimshaw. A Benjamin West born circa 1811 in the neighboring town of Beverly was a deepwater mariner but may or may not ever have gone whaling. Likewise the Benjamin West, Jr. (also known as Benjamin H. West), who was born in New Bedford in 1817 and was issued a Seaman's Passport there in 1838 but for whom no whaling voyages have been discovered. A Benjamin P. West born that same year in Tisbury, Martha's Vineyard, was the son of a deepwater mariner and was himself a career whaleman for more than twenty years in New Bedford vessels. At age 16 he went as a green hand in the ship *Java* (1833-34), later as boatsteerer in the ship *Moctezuma* (1841-44), first mate in the bark *Chase*, commanded by his cousin Abner West (1844-46), and third mate in the bark *Atlantic* (1851–54). In the meantime, another Benjamin West, age 19, from Somersworth, New Hampshire, served as a green hand in the ship *Almira* of Edgartown (1837-39), and a Benjamin West about whom nothing else is known was a green hand in the brig *Mattapoisett* of Westport (1847-48). However, none of the latter three is known ever to have made a Pacific Ocean voyage: their cumulative whaling exploits were limited to the Atlantic, so they would not have visited Callao on a whaleship.

This leaves only the Benjamin West who was born in Salem circa 1823 and evidently went to sea at an early age, possibly in the merchant brig *Eagle* in 1837, and certainly in the brig *Susan* in 1839 on a merchant voyage to the West Indies. After these he made two successive whaling voyages in the Salem bark *Henry*. West completed the first one (1841-45) and sailed again in 1845, but left the ship somewhere in the Pacific — probably at Callao — sometime before March 1846, when he joined the New Bedford bark *Dryade* in Callao. The *Dryade* landed him at Lahaina, on Maui, in August; and from there he went in the ship *Niger* on the homeward passage to New Bedford, where he arrived in January 1847. This concluded his whaling career, but not long afterwards he invested in one or possibly two Gold Rush voyages. Regarding the first of these his participation is uncertain. In June 1848 a Benjamin A. West of Salem — probably but not definitely the same man — is listed among the owners of the bark *Eliza* when she sailed for California under Captain A.S. Perkins. At 240 tons, she was built at Salem in 1823 and hers was "the second departure in 1848," a kind of historic voyage, as "It is said that the *Eliza* was the first vessel to reach San Francisco from Salem" (www.MaritimeHeritage.org). In the meantime, West was acquiring the former whaler *Ann Parry*, built in Salem in 1825, in which he would go to California himself on another historic voyage:

> *On August 10, 1848, the* **Ann Parry** *was auctioned off to Salem owners for $3,600, ending her long tenure as a whaler. The new owners, Benjamin West and John Hodges, departed Salem on June 21, 1849, for the Gold Rush in San Francisco. On December 29, 184 days later, she completed the trip around the horn. She was the last ship to arrive in San Francisco for the California Gold Rush.* (HistoryLink.org: The Free Online Encyclopedia of Washington State History.)

A.S. Perkins was captain on that voyage, and once they arrived West evidently went prospecting himself. According to a Crowley family genealogy (Ancestry.com), West married a Tolowa Indian in the Klamath region on the California-Oregon border: her name is not recorded, "reservation children" and a daughter named Emma (born 1865) are mentioned, but no further details are provided. However, West is recorded as having served on a jury in Crescent City, California, in 1854 (Anthony J. Bledsoe, *History of Del Norte County*, 1881; quoted in Edwin C. Bearss, *Redwood National Park*, 1969.) By 1860 he was working there as a boatman, and by 1870 as a saloonkeeper, having married a much younger woman named Mary and fathered a second family. He died in Crescent City in 1892.

West, Charles (fl. circa 1831-69). Whaling captain from Martha's Vineyard. During the first two years of a voyage as master of the New Bedford ship *Liverpool 2d* (1847-49) he kept a journal (in NCP), and pressed in its pages a ragged five-by-seven-inch (13 x 18 cm) fragment of lined paper, evidently torn out of some other ledger volume; and on it is a handmade pencil-sketch of an male equestrian figure in a cocked hat, labeled in a cursive hand, "General Taylor" and "The War Between the United States and Mexico" (reported by Judith N. Lund). The little portrait vignette, 2 ½ inches (64 mm) high, is a perfect size and shape for engraving on a sperm whale tooth. Significantly and perhaps uniquely among whaling relics, dots are clearly visible along some of the outlines, and some of the dots are punched through, as though with a needle — compelling evidence that the drawing was intended for, and was likely used for, scrimshaw. It is not known whether Captain West did the drawing himself or obtained it from one of the crew, nor whether he ever actually engraved the picture on a tooth; but it clearly does appear to have been used by someone, and strongly suggests that Captain West was interested in scrimshaw, whether or not he ever did any himself. If so, none has yet come to light.

Charles West was born in 1815 at Tisbury, Martha's Vineyard, a son of William West (1785-1854) and Mary Poole (1786-1855). His older brother William, Jr. (1812-1861), was a whaleman in his youth and later a merchant sea captain, but never a whaling master. Charles, a whaleman throughout his adult career, first embarked at age 16, made two early voyages in the New Bedford ship *General Pike* (1831-32 and 1832-34) and perhaps another unidentified voyage (1834-36) before going in the Fairhaven ship *Leonidas* (1836-37). Immediately upon returning in 1837 he married Betsey L. Dillingham (1815-1896) of Tisbury. Sometime during 1837-41 he must have made at least one voyage as a first mate (the vessel has not been identified), as he spent most of the next 28 years at sea as the master of eight whaling voyages, interrupted only by a wartime hiatus during the Civil War: three voyages in the ship *Delphos* of Holmes's Hole (Edgartown) (1841-46), the one in the *Liverpool* with which the scrimshaw is associated (1847-51), then one each in the bark *Helen Augusta* of Holmes's Hole (1852-54) and the ships *Ocmulgee* (1854-57) and *California* (1858-62) and bark

Marcella (1867-69) of New Bedford. In the 1870s West went into the retail grocery business with his wife, and died at Vineyard Haven in 1888. (Not to be confused with two other contemporaneous New Bedford whaling masters, Charles G. West and Charles B. West.)

Wetherell, Nathaniel (fl. circa 1771). A 36-inch panbone yardstick crudely incised with geometric ornaments is boldly inscribed on the two sides, "1771 NATANEL WETHEREL HIS RULE / SEPTEMBER / THE 13" (in WHS, reported by Richard Donnelly). This is one of the earliest known examples of mainstream American scrimshaw (see the article on Alden Sears) but the maker has not been definitively identified and nothing is known of his career. Most of the attributed legacy donations to WHS originated in Warren or Bristol, Rhode Island, and there were evidently mariners named Wetherell in Greenwich, Rhode Island, in the late Colonial era. However, indications are that this piece probably came from Norton or Taunton in Bristol County, Massachusetts (the same county in which the whaling ports of New Bedford, Fairhaven, Dartmouth, Westport, and Fall River are located, and adjacent to the Rhode Island whaling port of Little Compton, the seat of the whaling Richmond family). In Norton, a Nathaniel Wetherell (1717-48) married Dinah Lincoln (1722-50) around 1740 (he may have been the son, and was certainly a kinsman of Nathaniel Wetherel, 1696-1760, of Norton); a Nathaniel Wetherel married Hannah Richmond on 11 Aug. 1753; and a Nathaniel Wetherell married Mary May on 9 Oct. 1775. In nearby Taunton, a Nathaniel Wetherell married Hannah Stephens on 24 Mar. 1773; a Nathaniel Wetherell died on 12 May 1781; a Nathaniel Wetherel, Jr., married Lydia Dean on 7 Mar. 1812; and a Nathaniel Wetherel, Jr. — possibly the same one — married Deborah Smith on 13 Aug. 1814. Which of these may have gone whaling, and which may have been the scrimshaw maker, are unknown.

Wheeler, W. (fl. circa 1837). Irish or Anglo-Irish sailor in the Royal Navy credited with a name stamp intended as a kind of laundry marker, to identify a sailor's togs: a tooth with raised letters carved on the bottom forming the name "W. WHEELER," relief-carved on one side with crossed Union Jack ensigns surmounted by a royal crown, and a shield inscribed "H.M.S. / DUBLIN / 1837," surmounted by a stylized human face, with leafy and geometric border ornaments; on one edge, a British coat-of-arms and a bardic (Irish) harp; inscribed on the back, "Once the tooth of a Whale / That oft stood the Gale / In the wide Southern Ocean afar / Now would you suppose / I am used to mark clothes / That are stowed in the bag of a tar" (ex J. Welles Henderson Collection; *Jack Tar*, 106; Northeast, 16 Aug. 2008, #674). He may have been the same William Wheeler who was in the crew of HMS *Buffalo* from Spithead to South Australia in 1836 (Diane Cummings, *Bound for South Australia: Journey of the HMS Buffalo*, www.slsa.sa.gov.au) and/or the "W.T. Wheeler who was discharged from HMS *Sans Pariel* about the month of January 1855" (*Letter Book* of Admiral Sir Leopold George Heath, 1856).

Whelden, Seth (fl. circa 1834-45). Cape Cod whaleman credited with a yarn-winder or swift, of a type known as a *niddy-noddy*. It is constructed of panbone and whale ivory, carved, turned, and assembled in the unusual form of an exaggerated ship's wheel with eight spokes on a vertical axis, resulting in the wheel rotating in a horizontal plane (alternatively, the clamp could be fastened to support the apparatus so the wheel can turn in a vertical plane on a horizontal axis); with a turned whale ivory clamp, trimmed with red sealing wax (KNB). The attribution and provenance are reconstructed from a faint pencil holograph on the back, which has portions worn away and is thus only partially legible: "... Whelden... South Dennis Mass.... Care of K... ... aid". Even given this minimal data, the only possible maker was Seth Whelden, Jr., descended from a long line of Cape Cod Wheldens, of whom there seem to have been at least two or three Seths in each generation (e.g., see "Town of Dennis" in Deyo's *History of Barnstable County*, 507-577). The records do not agree about the year of this one's birth, but it must have been between 1813 and 1819, at either Yarmouth or South Dennis; and he was likely either the son and namesake of a sailor born at South Dennis in 1781, or of a farmer with the same name, born at South Dennis in 1787. Seth Junior went on at least two whaling voyages out of New Bedford: in the ship *Hercules 2d* (1834-36), at which time he gave his residence as Providence, Rhode Island; and bark *Smyrna* (1841-45), by which time he was living at Dartmouth, Massachusetts. Thus far, there is no further trace of him in the historical record, including that he likely made another whaling voyage or two during 1836-41 and some account of his subsequent activities.

Whittier, George (fl. 19th century). Credited with a carpenter's square and 13-inch (33 cm) folding ruler of whale skeletal bone, the ruler engraved on the back "George Whittier" (ex J. Welles Henderson Collection; *Jack Tar*, 119; Northeast, 16 Aug. 2008, #675).

Whelan, John "Rocky" (fl. circa 1840s-'50s). An Australian convict, "bushranger," and notorious outlaw in Tasmania, he was the possible maker of a club crudely carved out of sperm whale panbone — a material often encountered in Tasmania, where there was an active whaling trade out of Hobart and Launceston. The club is alleged to have been found in one of Whelan's hideouts and is now in QVM, which lists it among their scrimshaw and illustrates it handsomely on their website but does not specify the material, provenance, or circumstances of its discovery. The QVM "Scrimshaw Collection Guide" (by Kim Simpson, 2006) notes that

> *Whelan served part of his sentence at both Norfolk Island and at Port Arthur [Tasmania] penal settlements. He escaped from a labour gang in the 1840s, leading a life of robbery and violence. Whelan's most notorious hideout was on the slopes of Mount Wellington in Hobart; a cave on the mountain still known to this day as Rocky Whelan's Cave. This club was found in one of Whelan's hideouts.*

No record of any involvement by Whelan in the whaling industry has been discovered. Historian James Fenton calls him a "monster" and writes that Whelan "closed out his sanguinary career on the gallows" in June 1855, convicted of robbery and several murders. Whelan's confession is transcribed in Fenton's *History of Tasmania* (Launceston, 1884, 263f).

Whitecar, William B., Jr. (fl. circa 1855-59). In his firsthand narrative, *Four Years Aboard the Whaleship* (Philadelphia and London, 1860), Whitecar indicates that aboard the New Bedford bark *Pacific*, during tense hours of tempestuous weather on the homeward passage of from the Indian Ocean, New Holland, and New Zealand whaling grounds in 1859, he and the rest of the crew prepared souvenirs collected during the voyage and produced scrimshaw items intended as gifts for the folks at home:

All hands seemed suddenly transformed into a colony of curiosity-hunters. One would be seen with a box of shells, cleaning them; another with a Madagascar spear, polishing it, so as to be presentable; whilst others had articles of ivory, bone, and wood, and were busily employed in improving their appearance, so as to render them more creditable to the donor. Every man in the ship had more or less of this description of articles; the greater part of which had been constructed aboard from the jaws and teeth of the sperm whales. Our occupation with these things continued not only for hours, but for days, and in some instances whole weeks. (378)

Unfortunately, he does not specify which of his shipmates were especially avid makers, or name those whose scrimshaw work was particularly distinguished.

Whitecar was born in Philadelphia in 1833 or 1834, the son and namesake of a man the U.S. Census describes as a "conveyancer" and the former Rosanna Borden Smith. By age 17 the son was working as a druggist. He shipped to sea at age 22 and made only the one whaling voyage. As befit his original occupation, in the wartime Union Army he served as a hospital steward (in Company E, 81st Regiment of Pennsylvania Infantry). Oddly, his Civil War pension records indicate that he also used the alias William Benton at some point and also saw service in the Marine Corps, neither of which is further explained in the document. Meanwhile, in 1863 his father, William B. Whitecar, Sr., wrote a letter to President Lincoln urging him to protect the Pennsylvania coal fields from Confederate depredations.

Wilcox, Moses H. (fl. circa 1854-81). Intermittent whaleman and ship's cooper who, in his journal of the New Bedford bark *Osceola* (1870-72), mentions making scrimshaw of a type unspecified (reported by Philip Purrington in "Bird's Eye View," NBWM Library). He was born in 1836, the son of Seabury and Deborah B. Wilcox, farmers in Westport, Massachusetts, and may have apprenticed as a carpenter or cooper before going whaling at age 19. Like fellow scrimshaw artist and cooper A.B. Bean (q.v. in the *Dictionary*), Wilcox's career appears to have been a series of widely separated whaling voyages spread over a period of 25 years, punctuated by long stretches ashore. He was a green hand in the bark *Solon* of Westport (1854-56), cooper in the New Bedford bark *Kathleen* (1864-68), cooper and shipkeeper in the barks *Osceola* of New Bedford (1870-72), *Matilda Sears* of Dartmouth (1873-77), and *John Carver* of New Bedford (1880-81). His brother Thomas, younger by four years, was also a sometime whaleman. In their youth they appear to have taken turns, the one going to sea while the other remained at home to help on the family farm. Moses never married and in later life he lived with Thomas (who became a fisherman) and Thomas's wife and daughter.

Williams, Lewis W. (fl. circa 1854-83). He was the younger brother of Captain Thomas W. Williams (q.v.), made his maiden voyage in his brother's ship, *Florida 2d* (1854-58), and later became a whaling master in his own right. His niece, Mary Watkins Williams (Mrs. Edgar R. Lewis) — Thomas's only surviving daughter — donated to NBWM in 1935 a variety of whaling relics that had descended in the Williams family, but no scrimshaw. However, documents in a private collection allude to a cane or walking stick that was made by or belonged to a "Captain Williams" from this clan. It may have been made by Thomas, to whose whaling relics Mary was surely heir. But as Lewis had no children of his own, his only Williams niece may reasonably be presumed to have been his heir as well; thus, he must be included as a possible maker of the scrimshaw, which in any case is known only in the documents and has never been found.

Captain Lewis Watkins Williams (1838-1916) was born at Wethersfield, Connecticut, and unlike his brother Thomas, who was trained in the woolen mills and apprenticed to a blacksmith, Lewis was sent to Boston for a classical education, with the intention that he matriculate at college. But he went to sea instead and rose through the ranks to command a near-record 22 whaling voyages: one in the New Bedford bark *Fanny* (1869-71), one in the unusual capacity of relief captain on the Russian whaler *Tirgur* (1874), and twenty more conventional voyages out of San Francisco: one in the bark *Monticello* (1871), three in the bark *Florence* (1876-78), thirteen in the brig *Hidalgo* (1879-95). Then, well into his sixties and far past the usual age of retirement for whaling masters he went two voyages in the bark *Andrew Hicks* (1902-03) and one in the bark *California* (1906). Also unlike his whaling captain brother and whaling captain nephew, Lewis never settled in California permanently but went out to Oakland for only a couple of years in the late 1860s, then returned to Wethersfield. He finally retired at age about 68, and though he had married Hannah C. Woodhouse in 1866, he left no issue when he died in 1916.

Williams, Thomas W. (fl. circa 1851-79). A Welsh immigrant in Wethersfield, Connecticut, he was a whaling master whose brother and eldest son were also whaling captains, both of whom served their apprenticeships on vessels under Thomas Williams's command. In the aggregate the three captains skippered an astonishing total of 41 whaling voyages out of Fairhaven, New Bedford, New London, San Francisco, and Honolulu between 1851 and 1906. Their story is told in quite readable detail in a popular book by kinsman Howard Williams, *One Whaling Family* (Boston, 1964), which is largely based on journals of their voyages. A variety of objects donated to NBWM by a daughter of Thomas W. Williams in 1935 includes a specimen of whale skeletal bone but no scrimshaw, and there are no specifics about scrimshaw in *One Whaling Family*. And while letters in a private collection reportedly allude to a cane or walking stick made by a "Captain Williams" from this particular clan, there is no way to determine for certain which of the Williams whaling captains may have made it, if indeed any of them made it rather than have had it presented to him. Considering that the other whaling relics, including the bone specimen, descended through Mary Watkins Williams Lewis (Mrs. Edgar L. Lewis), the eldest daughter of Thomas W. Williams, he would seem to be the most likely original maker. On the other hand, his brother, Captain Lewis W. Thomas (q.v.), had no children of his own, so any scrimshaw in his possession, whether or not by his hand, may have found its way to his niece Mary.

There were two important figures in the American whale fishery named Thomas W. Williams, both from Connecticut. Thomas W. Williams of New London, who settled there in 1818, was one of that city's most prominent whaling merchants, both in his own right and as senior partner in the firm Williams & Haven. The other, Captain Thomas William Williams of Wethersfield, the hypothetical scrimshaw artist, was born at Hay-on-Wye, Brecken, Wales, in 1820, the eldest son and second child of William Williams (1794-1871) and Mary Watkins Williams (1797-1879). The family emigrated to America sometime between 1829 and 1834, but as with any family lore, there are inconsistencies in the collective memory. Harold Williams reports that the family "migrated to the United States in 1829 as steerage passengers in a sailing packet and, after spending a year or so on the eastern end of Long Island, they settled in Wethersfield, Connecticut" (Williams 1964, 385).

However, family sources also report that "On the trip from Wales, another passenger held her hands over Mary's ears so she would not hear the splash of the water as they buried her daughter, Catherine Ann at sea after she died of Scarlet fever" (Ancestry.com); but as Catherine Ann was born in February 1832, she could not have died on an Atlantic voyage in 1829. There were nine children in all, of whom the oldest and youngest sons became whaling masters — Thomas, born in Wales in 1820, and Lewis, born at Wethersfield in 1838. Howard Williams reports that in Connecticut "the family were employed in the local woolen mill as weavers" and that Thomas was apprenticed as a blacksmith and toolmaker but, with his mother's knowledge, "ran away from home to go to sea and shipped as a green hand on the whaleship *Albion*, Captain Austin Smith," of Fairhaven (not New Bedford), 1840-42. His next berths were as a boatsteerer and blacksmith in the *South Carolina* (1842-44) and second mate in the *Chili* (1845-48), both out of New Bedford; then second mate in the Fairhaven ship *South Boston* (1848-51) under Captain John M. Sowle, who promoted him to first mate during the voyage and whom he succeeded as captain on the next voyage (1851-54).

Williams had become a naturalized U.S. citizen in 1845, and his marriage to Eliza Azelia Griswold (1826-1885) of Wethersfield in April 1851 coincided with elevation to his first command. That year also marks the beginning of his career as a capitalist entrepreneur: from 1851 on he was also an ownership shareholder in each of the vessels he commanded; and it marks the beginning of his unbroken succession of voyages as captain, on most of which his wife and family accompanied him to sea — until two successive shipwrecks, in 1870 and 1871, dissuaded him from dragging his wife and children along on any more Arctic whaling expeditions. But while his seafaring was a family affair, three of his children were born on three separate voyages of the ship *Florida 2d*. And on Thomas's first outing in the *Florida* (1854-58) his younger brother Lewis, the future captain of a near-record 22 whaling voyages, made his maiden voyage as a green hand. This first *Florida* voyage also produced a son for Thomas and Eliza: Thomas Stancel Williams, called Stancel, whom Thomas would mentor and who would also become a whaling captain. The second *Florida* voyage (1858-61) produced a daughter, Mary, born in 1861, and ended on the eve of the Civil War with the ship being sold in San Francisco and the cargo sent home. Captain Williams was then given the *Jireh Swift* (1862-65), from which he sent home a respectable catch before the ship and additional cargo were captured and burned by the Confederate corsair *Shenandoah* in June 1865 — which was two months after the war had ended but before the news of Lee's surrender had reached the North Pacific. In accordance with the usual procedure, the *Jireh Swift*'s company were courteously put ashore. Williams was thus available for a stint as relief captain in the New London bark *Monticello* and to re-fit and provision his former command, the *Florida*, for Arctic whaling. The *Florida* voyage (1866-67) produced a successful catch and a second daughter born at sea. Williams then went on a several months' hiatus, during which he wrapped up his affairs back East and moved his family to Oakland, California. Thus, Williams was in the vanguard as the fishery increasingly focused its attention on Western Arctic waters off Alaska and Siberia, and, by reason of proximity, shifted its base of operations from New Bedford to San Francisco. He joined the *Hibernia 2d* at Honolulu as relief captain (1869-70), suffered shipwreck at Point Barrow, Alaska, in November 1870, and had his family with him again in the *Monticello*, now based in San Francisco, for a second Arctic disaster the very next year: the *Monticello* was one of 33 whaleships that got caught in an unexpectedly early onset of pack ice and were frozen in and wrecked on the Alaska coast in 1871.

(Howard Williams suggests that Stancel was probably the third or fourth mate on this voyage.) In all, Captain Williams commanded seven voyages in San Francisco barks: the ill-fated one in the *Monticello* (1870-71), four in the *Florence* (1872-75), one in the *Clara Bell* (1876), and a final voyage in the *Frances Palmer* (1879). On that voyage Stancel served as first mate, then succeeded his father on four voyages as captain (1880-83).

In the meantime, the senior Captain Williams had become a shareholder in whaling vessels deployed from Massachusetts, Connecticut, and California, including the *Jireh Swift, Florida*, and *South Boston*, as well as the barks *Peru* of New London and *Dawn* of San Francisco. He was also involved in real estate transactions on both coasts, and dabbled in toolmaking, wool manufacture, carriage making, and other speculations. His son attributes his premature death at age 60 to excesses suffered in experiments with "the first steamboat used in the Arctic for whaling":

> *On his last voyage, he took a small steam craft on the ship, a sort of tugboat, and used it to cruise in the ice fields looking for whales. He would be gone for days at a time and suffered hardships from exposure, poor food and water, which broke his health, and he died August 26, 1880 [in Oakland].* (Williams 1964, 383f)

His widow then returned to Wethersfield, where she died in 1885.

The sequel for their seaborne children was mixed. Thomas Stancel Williams (1852-1917) had a whaling career that was rocky at best. First of all, he "was struck in the leg by a bomb lance on one of his voyages and he had a wooden leg as a result"; secondly, except for the 1882 voyage the returns from his blubber-hunting did not cover the capital cost of outfitting, and the estate of Captain Thomas Williams, which had evidently been subsidizing Stancel's whaling ventures since the paterfamilias died in 1880, "could not afford to send him out in 1885." Consequently, the *Frances Palmer* "was sold in January 1886 after lying in Oakland Estuary since the fall of 1884" (Williams 1964, 394), ending Stancel's whaling days. Flora, the daughter born aboard the *Florida* in 1867, had not survived; she died of scarlet fever at Oakland in 1869. But the younger of the two surviving sons, William Fish Williams (1859-1929), had a distinguished career ashore. Born aboard the *Florida* in the Tasman Sea, he spent much of his childhood voyaging on his father's whaleships. "He was three years old before he went ashore to live during the Civil War… , sailed with the family on three voyages after the war, surviving two shipwrecks in the Arctic," and kept a journal on his last voyage, as a boatsteerer in the *Florence* (1873-74). But at age 15 he made a decision that was the opposite of that of his uncle Lewis, choosing college in preference to whaling. He graduated from Columbia University in New York in 1878 with a degree in mining engineering, took an additional degree in civil engineering in 1881, married Anna L. Connor of Marysville (not Oakland), California, in 1883, and settled in New Bedford, where he raised a family, worked as a civil engineer, and from 1894 to 1912 served as City Engineer. In the latter capacity he designed a bridge across the Acushnet River between New Bedford and Fairhaven, and afterwards, during two terms as Commissioner for the Massachusetts Department of Public Works (1922-28), supervised construction of the Cape Cod Canal. His sister, Thomas and Eliza's only surviving daughter, Mary Watkins Williams (1861-1938), had also been born on the *Florida* and made a series of voyages on her father's ships. She married Edgar R. Lewis, a native of Chilmark, Martha's Vineyard, who was a commission merchant in his father's firm, William Lewis & Son, managing agents for whaleships on both coasts, purveyors and distributors of whalebone (baleen), and diversified investors in shipping, manufacturing, and shoreside industries. Edgar lost a ship chandlery in the San Francisco earthquake and fire of 1906, and closed out his whaling interests by 1915. (Howard Williams claims that he did this in response to the Seaman's Act of 1909, which Edgar "thought would make the cost of whaling crews too expensive for whaling"; but it was even more a result of the collapse of the baleen market after 1904, when ladies' fashions changed, putting hoop skirts and corset stays out of style, thus suddenly eliminating the largest volume demand for whalebone.) Edgar and Mary lived for some years on an apple farm in Washington State, and when Mary was widowed in 1932 she returned to New Bedford, where she contributed the scrimshaw to the Museum in 1935 and died in 1938.

Wilson, Benjamin I. (fl. circa 1852-77). New Bedford whaleman who made a machete with handmade blade, whale ivory handle, and scabbard of wood and whale-hide. The handle is carved from a large sperm whale tooth, squared with chamfered edges; the scabbard (sheath) is carved out of two pieces of wood (two halves), joined together and covered with sperm whale *pizzle*, the only tanable hide that can be obtained from a whale; the blade was reportedly "ground out of Damascus steel by hand" by Captain Wilson himself; and the machete is supposed to have been used by him to quell a mutiny by his crew on his only whaling voyage as captain, on the New Bedford bark *Linda Stewart* (1875-77). It was given to NBWM in 1925 by Mrs. Caroline "Carrie" H. Wilson, the widow of Henry P. Wilson, an undertaker and presumed collateral descendant (the nature and degree of kinship is unclear).

According to his first Protection Paper, which he obtained at New Bedford in 1852, Wilson was born there circa 1838. A second passport, issued three years later, gives his residence as Dartmouth, Massachusetts. He went to sea at age 14 as a green hand in the New Bedford ship *Copia* (1852-55), was a boatsteerer in the bark *Rodman* (1855-59), then made a three or four unidentified voyages, presumably as a junior and then senior mate. He commanded only the one whaling voyage in the *Linda Stewart*; and while the crew's mutiny — a refusal of duty, with threats — may or may not have ended the captain's career, he died of typhoid fever at New Bedford shortly afterwards, in October 1879, at age 41. No record of a marriage or children has been found. (Not to be confused with Benjamin F. Wilson of New Bedford, a physician who was born at Dartmouth in the same year and was married to Lucy née Taber; nor with Captain Benjamin Rodman Carpenter Wilson, born circa 1805 South Kingstown, Rhode Island, who at a very young age commanded two voyages in the Fairhaven ship *Heroine* [1831-33] and died in 1869.)

Wilson, Richard C. (fl. circa 1850-68). It has not been ascertained whether Captain Wilson made the scrimshaw handle of his walking stick himself or had someone make it for him. It has a tapered knobby wooden shaft, the kind that shows (or is simulated to show) the knots from branches removed from the original bough; and a store-bought silver ferrule that is professionally engraved "R.C. Wilson," of a type that one would commission from a jeweler or stationer, a type that was common on both sailor-made and professionally-manufactured walking sticks in the nineteenth century. The scrimshaw part is an octagonal flared handle of whale ivory, terminating in an octagonal crown pommel, on the flat top of which a coin is inset, framed by a raised circle of the ivory. The coin is a now-rare 1855 "Type 2" gold "Indian head" U.S. dollar. (The Type 1 dollar coin, 13mm in diameter, was introduced in 1851 as a Gold Rush-era expedient, was found to be too small, and was supplanted in 1854 by the slightly larger Type 2, which has a diameter of 15mm.)

Wilson was born in New Bedford in 1834, grew up on a farm in Dartmouth, and embarked on his maiden whaling voyage at age 16 as a green hand for the 225th lay in the ship *William Hamilton* (1850-53). Remarkably, he had been only seven years at sea when, at age 23, he was made captain of the New Bedford bark *Endeavor* (1857-60), for which, in addition to a regular master's lay, he was to receive a 2/32 ownership share in the proceeds. This prodigious advance can only be explained by his having married the boss's daughter, Arzelia Ashley (born in 1837), daughter of Abraham Ashley, the New Bedford whaling merchant who was the managing agent and largest shareholder in the *Endeavor*. Yet despite that Wilson's voyage was a commercial success it turned out to be his one and only complete voyage as captain. He stayed ashore — living with Arzelia in her parents' substantial home in New Bedford, and probably working as a captain in the coastwise merchant trade — while Owen Fisher served as the *Endeavor*'s captain her next time out (1860-64). But the returns of that voyage were disappointing, so Ashley gave the vessel to Thomas Luce, who sailed in her in October 1864. But when Captain Luce became ill and left the ship, Ashley brought back his son-in-law as relief captain. Wilson produced another satisfactory catch of oil and bone and returned in the *Endeavor* in May 1868. Still, he did not go whaling again. He now became a farmer, and later a granite dealer, and then a building contractor, all in New Bedford, where they raised a family; and then, sometime around the mid 1880s, he and Arzelia moved out to Annawan, Illinois, where they ran a hotel. It is not known how the walking stick got into the scrimshaw collection of Andrew Snow, whence it came to NBWM in 1919; but it was likely purchased by Mr. Snow directly from the Wilsons at the time they were getting ready to move to Illinois.

Wing, Andrew J. (fl. circa 1837-60). New Bedford whaling master credited with two quite different scrimshaw productions, one an engraved tooth and the other a practical implement "built" out of bone. The tooth is a beautiful rendition of "A Family Party," an unattributed illustration of a young woman holding a young girl, a spaniel, and a cat, that appears in the August 1850 issue of *Godey's Lady's Book*, 50 (reported from a private collection by David Hislop, great-grandnephew of the artist's daughter; source identified by Laura Mathieu). Dr. Jack H.T. Chang observes that it is "a closer copy than any of the other scrimshaw versions of the same image, but by a different hand and the tooth from a different whale" than the anonymous version of the same image on a tooth in KNB. Captain Wing's other object is an inside measuring rod — a kind of oversize calipers device for taking the inside dimensions between outside perpendiculars — made of whale skeletal bone with walrus ivory trim and engraved numerals pigmented with lampblack, marked "Capt. Wing / Ship KUFF / May the 24th (?) 1856"; in KNB. Wing was captain of a North Pacific whaling voyage in the New Bedford bark *Kutusoff* during 1855-60 (his journal is also in KNB); the scrimshaw is tentatively attributed to his own hand aboard the *Kutusoff*, though it might have been made for him.

Andrew Johnson Wing, the son of Stephen Wing and Ruamy Gray Gifford, was born in 1820 — probably at Fairhaven, Massachusetts, but the records are inconclusive and the family seems to have moved around quite a bit from house to house and town to town. His first voyage or two may have been in the *George & Martha* around 1836-41, after which he was boatsteerer on three voyages the in Fairhaven ships *Heroine* (1841-43) and *Ansel Gibbs* (1843-45 and 1845-48), and was probably promoted to second mate on the third one. He was married at around this time, probably between voyages in 1848 (it seems that a second mate's pay and future prospects were considered by many to be suitable to taking on the support of a wife and family). The bride was Caroline Brown Ashley (born 1823) of Freetown, Massachusetts, and they lived in the part of Dartmouth that became Acushnet in 1860, by which time they already had five children; there were eventually seven, six of whom lived to maturity. Caroline's unmarried younger sister Betsy lived with them for years, presumably helping with the housekeeping and the brood, and keeping Caroline company for the long years that Andrew was at sea. A few weeks after the wedding, Andrew embarked on the first of two successive voyages as first mate for Captain James P. Allen, in the New Bedford ships *Condor* (1848-40) and *Canton* (1850-52). As was often the case with a qualified mate, Wing was promoted to captain of the same vessel on her next voyage, but the voyage did not end well. The *Canton* sailed in August 1852 and was whaling in the Pacific for more than a year when the objective of the voyage turned suddenly from profits to survival. In March 1854 the ship ran aground on a reef in the Kingsmill Group of the Gilbert Islands (Kiribati), forcing the captain, officers, and crew into open whaleboats for a life-threatening, 49-day passage to the safety of Guam. Captain Wing evidently was not blamed for the mishap, as he was given command of the *Kutusoff* not long after his return. This was the voyage associated with the measuring rod: it turned out to be a financial success and turned out to be Andrew Wing's last, as well as the last of the *Kutusoff* (1856-60). The ship was retired and sold, and Captain Wing retired to a farm in Acushnet, where his eldest son Charles helped with the farming while the younger one, James, went to sea. The third son, William, became a local teamster. Meanwhile, in 1872 Commander R. W. Meade in the USS *Narragansett* surveyed the island in the Kingsmills where Wing had gone aground, and named the place Canton Island in memory of the wreck. The *Canton* shipwreck was reported in the *Whaleman's Shipping List and Merchant's Transcript* of Nov. 7, 1854, appears in Alexander Starbuck's *History of the American Whale Fishery* (1876, 140 ff.), and is recounted dramatically in the *New Bedford Evening Standard* on March 22, 1914, where the headlines provide a cogent synopsis of the story:

> *VOYAGE OF SHIPWRECKED CREW OF BARK CANTON READS LIKE ROMANCE OF THE SEA. Thirty three Men Sailed for 45 Days in Open Boats Under a Hot Tropical Sun, Covering Distance of 3800 Miles — Attempted Assassination of Captain Wing of Acushnet Nipped in Bud When Mutineers Were Cowed with Knife — Party at Last Saved by Captain's Courage and Foresight.*

That account was based on the testimony of the captain's daughter, Mrs. Eugene White, and two men who had been green hands on the *Canton*, Thomas E. Braley and Alden H. Manter; and was retold by another former green hand on the voyage, later known as "Captain" Sylvanus S. Longley: "The Last Voyage and Wreck of the Whaleship 'Canton' of New Bedford" was published in three installments in a Kansas newspaper, and a version appeared in the *New England Quarterly* under the title "The Wreck of the Whaler Canton" (Vol. 13, 1940, 324-335). The list of re-tellings is extensive: an undated article by *New Bedford Standard Times* columnist Minna Littmann, "3800-Mile Voyage in Open Boats Saved Men of Canton After Wreck in the Pacific"; an article with no byline in the same paper, entitled "Canton Wreck Recalled Here by U.S. Action" (Apr. 3, 1938); and others by Chester S. Howland ("Capt. Wing's Nautical Feat," *Yankee Magazine*, March 1965, 57f), Herb Arral ("Acushnet man survived 49 days in an open boat," *Standard Times*, Apr. 18. 1972), Dr, George Woodbury,

"The Incredible Exploit of Captain Wing" (*Manchester Union Leader*, Sept. 9. 1971), and so on. The story was thus woven into the basic fabric of Yankee whaling lore, and mention of it appears often in the secondary literature.

Wing, Frederick A. (fl. circa 1830-56). Whaling master who may himself have made, or may have commissioned to be made, an inlaid mahogany sewing box bearing the initials "E.H.W." (reported by Richard Donnelly). The principal wood is mahogany, inlaid and trimmed with ebony and various secondary woods, with a small piece of mother-of-pearl inlaid on the lid; a well-constructed removable tray with compartments inside, under which are more compartments; and store-bought brass hinges and lock mechanism. An unusual feature is that the well-formed serifed initials are thickly inlaid in sealing wax and also framed with strips of sealing wax inlaid on the front panel. Another unusual feature is a two-inch (5 cm) whale ivory peg with dome finial and equatorial chamfered cube — function unknown — snugly mounted vertically in one of the drawer compartments. A minimal provenance insists that the box descended in the Wing family of Westport, Massachusetts, where Frederick A. Wing appears to be the only one of that town and surname whose vintage, career, and family circumstances fit the evidence here. The box was certainly intended for someone with the initials EHW, probably Captain Wing's wife, Eliza Hicks Wing, or (less likely) the younger of their two daughters, who was also named Eliza H. Wing and was born in 1847.

Frederick A. Wing was born at Westport in 1812, the son of Barnabas Wing (1788-1871) and Abigail Gifford (1792-1876), and the older brother of fellow whaling captain Perry G. Wing (1814-1888). Frederick obtained a Seaman's Protection Paper at New Bedford in November 1828, shortly after which he must have embarked on his first voyage or two (1828-32) — the details have not been discovered — followed by two short outings in the Westport brig *Mexico* (1832-33). He married Eliza Hicks in 1833, shipped as an officer in the ship *Cadmus* (1834-37), then seems to have gone on hiatus for a couple of years (1837-40). During 1840-43 he was first mate in the Westport bark *United States* under Captain William Hicks, who was evidently Wing's brother-in-law and was making his first voyage as captain. It may have been Hicks's influence that occasioned Wing's going to sea again. Hicks made only the one voyage as a captain, but Wing went on to make five, all in Westport vessels: two in the brig *Mexico* (1844-45, 1845-46), one in the bark *Mattapoisett* (1849-50), and two in the bark *Greyhound* (1851-53, 1854-56). The older of his two daughters was Julia, born circa 1834, with whom the Captain lived after he was widowed in the 1860s.

Wing, Noble P. (fl. circa 1825-49). Whaling master from Rochester, Massachusetts, to whom is attributed one of the finest of all scrimshaw yardsticks, made at sea for his wife while he was first mate of the New Bedford ship *Rebecca Sims* in 1848 (in NBWM). It is an ebony straightedge with whale ivory tips at each end. One side is conventionally calibrated in inches, halves, quarters, and eighths, but the other side has distinctive calibrations that elevate the piece to greatness: a series of whale ivory inlays in the form of right hands, each with different numbers of pointing fingers: one finger (the index finger) marks $\frac{1}{16}$th yard, two fingers indicates $\frac{2}{16}$ths or $\frac{1}{8}$th yard, three fingers is for $\frac{3}{16}$ths, and four fingers points to $\frac{4}{16}$ths or a quarter yard. There is also a paper label with the ink holograph "1848 Mrs. H. G. Wing," framed in whale skeletal bone and covered with a wafer-thin translucent plaque of tortoise shell, fastened with brass pins. "Mrs. H. G. Wing" was Hannah Gilbert Wing, née Leonard (1816-1879), whom Noble Wing married in 1839.

Noble Penn Wing was born in 1809 in Rochester, Massachusetts, the second son of Alden Wing, a sea captain, and the former Lucy Bates. He and two younger brothers were career whalemen. David Farnum Wing (born in 1813) died at sea in 1841 or '42 when he was still a junior officer. The youngest brother, George Washington Wing (1818-1885), had a long career and a comfortable retirement. He was first mate of the ship *Pantheon* of New Bedford when the vessel was burned by a mutinous crew at Nuku Hiva in the Marquesas Islands in March 1856, and was thus on hand and available — "on the beach" in the Pacific — when later that year he was recruited to be relief captain of the New Bedford bark *Byron*, succeeding William E. Tower, who had died at sea. David was the captain for the remainder of the voyage, the better part of four years, after which he retired. Noble's career was more extensive and eventually took an unusual turn. After rising through the ranks, he got his first command at age 28 on a short voyage of the brig *Orion* of Rochester (1837), then led three voyages of the brig *Solon*, sailing from the adjacent ports of Rochester (1839-40), Sippican (1840-41), and Mattapoisett (1841-42). The unusual turn was that he next went two voyages as first mate, in the New Bedford ships *Hope* (1843-45) and *Rebecca Sims* (1845-49), the voyage on which he evidently made the yardstick. Though this was his last whaling voyage, the census continued to list his occupation as "sailor" and "master mariner"; but if he made any subsequent voyages — perhaps in the coastwise or deepwater carrying trades — they have not been discovered. One version of the family genealogy claims that he died in 1891, however the 1870 U.S. Census lists Hannah as head of household without any trace of Noble, and it is likely that he died before then.

Winslow, George F. (fl. circa 1853-95). Whaling master out of New Bedford and San Francisco credited with three walking sticks made sometime during his 40-year whaling career; donated to NBWM by his widow in 1933. One is a cane with a tapered shaft of tropical wood and an L-shaped handle in the form of a bird's head with the beak slightly open, comprised of 12 pieces of whale ivory and baleen, with the pupils formed by a drilled-through non-ferrous metal rod. The other two are straight walking sticks, one with a turned wooden knob pommel with a bead at base, a tapered octagonal panbone shaft, with the foreshaft incised with herringbone and cross-hatch patterns, and a brass tip; the other with a turned whale ivory knob pommel with a long shank and raised bead at the base, tapered wooden shaft (with the stain oddly worn), recessed for a tip but since broken off and worn down, and a wide silver band ferule.

Captain Winslow was still paying homage to whale teeth and encouraging scrimshaw even after his retirement. Around 1906, at age about 70, he spoke about "the last of the Curios of my eventful career," which was the "Tooth of a sperm whale caught on the 'Commodore Morris' grounds, as may be recognized by its shape and size, peculiar to that boisterous, generally rugged, rough locality, say 750 to 780 miles [1225-1275 km] southwest of the coast of Ireland, 52° to 54° North, 23° to 25° West, as generally quoted, but my experience was not so far north for these big Whales, but 44° to 48° North, near enough the Steamers track that we saw smoke nearly every day, with several narrow escapes from being run down in thick weather... It came from a large young Bull Whale and was killed by me in a gale close under the stern of the bark 'Horatio' 349 tons, of New Bedford... " (Agard Papers, KNB).

This suggests four interesting things: In the first place, that this highly experienced and very successful whaling master — the veteran of 17 voyages, nine of them as captain, spanning 40 years of whaling — claimed he could recognize the habitat of a cachalot simply from the tooth being oversize and of a particular shape, even if he had not killed the whale himself; which is not a standard feature of the lore, does not take into account the sperm whale's wide-ranging, inter-oceanic migratory patterns, and remains uncorroborated. Secondly, he refers to the "Commodore Morris" whaling grounds, named, no doubt, for the New Bedford whaleship *Commodore Morris*, on which he himself made five voyages (1868-84) — as third mate, second mate, and three voyages as captain. "'Commodore Morris' whaling grounds" is also not part of the lore, and the fraternity of Yankee whaling masters did not customarily refer to those North Atlantic grounds by any such name. Third, Captain Winslow made those remarks to Charles Walter Agard (q.v. in the Appendix to the *Dictionary*), a New Bedford executive who conducted extensive oral history interviews with whaling captains as early as the 1880s — long before folklorists and anthropologists began taking to the field as part of their standard methodology. And fourth, and perhaps most significantly, Winslow evidently made his remarks in the act of presenting the tooth to Agard, in the dual contexts of it being a precious relic and potential scrimshaw, commenting, "… So you cut something on it that you care for, and not lose it, much less to give it away."

Winslow was a New Bedford native born in 1836, the son of Pardon Winslow, sailor, and the former Anna M. Gifford. The family lived with his maternal grandparents. his older brother Hallett Gifford Winslow was a career mariner, and, according to George's own account, he "worked in the plumbing business" in his youth and went to sea at age 16 as a green hand in the ship *Charles W. Morgan* (1853-56). He was a boatsteerer in the ship *Rapid* (1856-60) when, in the space of a single year, the ship was set on fire by the crew, struck a sunken rock underway, was run into by another ship (the *Jeannette*), and was condemned in a foreign port. (John McIntire, q.v., was third mate on that voyage.) Winslow returned to New Bedford as second mate on a merchantman loaded with an unglamorous cargo of guano, after which he was second mate on the ship *Kensington*'s Stone Fleet voyage to block Southern harbors. He joined the Union Navy on the rebound from a broken love affair, received training in the school ship *Ohio*, and served in the U.S. Ships *Marblehead, Mackinaw, Pontiac, Kansas,* and *Brooklyn*, not mustering out until 1868. He soon after married Fannie L. Willis, who bore him a daughter and a son. The rest of his sea time was in whalers: the five voyages in the *Commodore Morris* (1868-84), then five voyages out of San Francisco — as first mate of the steam-bark *Narwhal* (1884-86) and captain of the steam-bark *Balaena* (1887), bark *Wanderer* (1888), schooner *Norway* on a combined salmon-fishing cruise and scientific mission for the Smithsonian Institution (1890); two voyages as master of the New Bedford bark *Horatio* (1890-91), one as first mate of the San Francisco bark *Northern Light* (circa 1891-92), and, after a one-year hiatus ashore, a final voyage as captain of the New Bedford bark *Desdemona* (1894-95). He retired to a position as patrolman on the New Bedford Police force; enlisted in the navy again during the Spanish-American war and was commissioned a lieutenant in July 1898, serving as executive officer of the *Fish-Hawk*; then returned to the police force. He died sometime after 1910.

There were actually two prominent, roughly contemporaneous men of this name in New Bedford, and a third who was a mariner from Chilmark, Martha's Vineyard. The slightly younger one from New Bedford, George F. Winslow (1842-1928), was both a medical doctor and a rear-admiral in the U.S. Navy. A round ditty box, with wooden top and bottom and plain baleen sides, came with a handwritten card indicating that it was from "the collection of Dr. George F. Winslow," along with a ticket of admission to NBWM for Saturday, October 25, 1924. A handwritten notation on the back of the ticket states: "Whalebone diddy [sic] box / made by a sailor." Dr. Winslow had whaling ancestors, he was the son of a sea captain and the nephew of a whaling captain, and his older brother, Henry Alden Winslow (1835-1867), was a professional whaleman before he joined the Union Navy. Henry was later transport manager for a mining company in Montana, where he was killed in a conflict with the Sioux in 1867. However, there is no evidence that the scrimshaw originated with a Winslow family member rather than from some other source in New Bedford or from Dr. Winslow's distinguished service as a medical officer in the navy. He was born in North Dartmouth, Massachusetts, moved with his family to New Bedford in 1844, was educated at Friends Academy and Harvard College, received his M.D. at Harvard in 1863, and in the Civil War served as an Assistant Surgeon in the Union Navy, beginning in 1862. After the war he stayed on as a career medical officer, became Medical Director of the Navy in 1898, and retired in 1903 with flag rank. Meanwhile, in 1875 he married Virginia Shearman, who bore him four children. He visited NBWM in 1924 and may have donated the box to the museum himself before he died in 1928.

Wood, Frank (1851-1933). He was never a whaleman himself but was descended from whaling people (Captain Edward W. Howland, active in the 1830s, was his uncle), and though his father was a merchant who died when he was a child, Frank grew up in New Bedford surrounded by whalers and steeped in whaling lore. By trade he was a cotton broker in the vast textile manufacturing empire that gradually replaced whaling as New Bedford's largest industry and principal employer, but throughout his life he was a prodigious collector of whaling implements, relics, and curiosities, a sometime carver of whaling-related objects, and in retirement was curator of the NBWM for 18 years (1915-33). He is known to have made wooden half-hull models of various species of whales, mounted on wooden backboards. Full-round-carved models of whales are also attributed, and he may have done some paintings of whaling scenes. (Speaking about whaling pictures in a literary society paper entitled "Artists of This Vicinity," presented at the Roundabout Club in New Bedford in 1921 and the Colonial Club of Fairhaven in 1922, Mrs. Elwyn G. Campbell remarks, "Frank Wood, curator of Old Dartmouth Historical Society Museum, has painted some.") Whether or not he made any scrimshaw is not known for certain, least of all at which point in his career he may have done so, but if his wood-carving and scrimshaw collecting be any guide, it was likely contemporaneously with the whaling industry itself (he was no younger than many of the whalemen-artists scrimshawing on shipboard in the late-nineteenth and early-twentieth centuries). Michael P. Dyer (NBWM) interprets as a signature a name incised on the inside rim of an oval strip of panbone in a nearly illegible cursive hand, which he reads as "Frank Wood." Dyer theorizes that Wood may have enhanced at least one or two old pieces of utilitarian scrimshaw with sketchy miniature engravings of whaleboat scenes, including the panbone oval and a whale ivory seam rubber that has a similar picture, unsigned but possibly by the same hand (in PEM; McManus, 21). As curator of NBWM, Wood was assisted and ultimately succeeded by William H. Tripp (q.v. in the *Dictionary*). His best known publication may be the Introduction to George Francis Dow's *Whale Ships and Whaling* (1925). Just after Wood's death Robert Cushman Murphy (q.v. in the *Dictionary*), who was by then Curator of Oceanic Birds at the American Museum of Natural History in New York City, published his two-part article, "Floating Gold: The Romance of Ambergris, Dedicated to the Memory of Frank Wood, Curator of the Whaling Museum, New Bedford, Massachusetts" (*Natural History*, March-April and May-June 1933).

Wood, Lorenzo W. (fl. circa 1842-47). A tooth depicting an idealized mother and child, inscribed "Beauty and Innocence," was featured on the PBS-TV *Antiques Roadshow* in 2005, where the descendant-owners claimed that it had been made on a whaling voyage by an ancestor, Jason Southworth. However, in consideration of the kinds of confusion that frequently tend to corrupt oral history and family provenance — in this case perhaps occasioned by a scandal in the family — Lorenzo Wood may have an equal claim. The circumstances are explained in the article on Jason Southworth (q.v.). Lorenzo Wood made at least two whaling voyages, both out of New Bedford. He was born at Lanesborough, Massachusetts, in 1809, apprenticed as a blacksmith, and followed that trade at Watertown, New York, in the 1830s, at Durham, New York, by 1840, and as the ship's blacksmith in the whaleship *South Carolina* (1842-44). He was briefly a boatsteerer in the *Hercules*, which he joined in progress at Mauritius in October 1846 (probably as a means to get home from the Pacific), landing at New Bedford in March 1847. He then went back to Watertown and worked as a blacksmith again. He married Ann Jenison at Watertown in 1830, and she bore him two children: a son named Luther and a daughter named Harriet, who died in childhood. Whether and why Lorenzo disappeared for a while and was presumed lost at sea is not known for certain, and he disappears from the historical record around 1850.

Worth, Daniel F. (fl. circa 1840-71). New Bedford whaling master whose avid interest in scrimshaw while he was captain of the ship *Gazelle* in the 1860s is remarked by one of his crewmen and corroborated by the testimony of his own journal, which includes rare schematic plans of scrimshaw-to-come. One of the green hands, Frederick H. Lawrence of Westport, Massachusetts, age about 17, wrote in his journal on September 1, 1865, with more than a touch of disdain: "A few remarks have been made about scrimshoning. For the last week the Capt[ain] and mate and second mate have been constantly employed in making something for his lordship and his lady ship and now they have got every thing about done for themselves. Commence to growl about scrimshoning. Says its the only thing uppermost here. There was never anything said more true." On August 20 this same callow young fellow also wrote, with a measure of pride and self-satisfaction, "Most everybody is scrimshoning but me." The sophomoric diarist has only impatient and disparaging things to say about scrimshaw and never sees fit to reveal what the three officers were actually making (he may not have known). Meanwhile, there is insufficient evidence in Worth's own journal of a previous voyage (in NBWM), as third mate of the ship *Saratoga* (1849-52), to know whether his scrimshoning was habitual or if this was an unprecedented instance never to be repeated. But on the *Gazelle* the captain had his wife aboard and evidently recruited the two other men for whatever mysterious scrimshaw collaboration was afoot. Both of them, First Mate Thomas Foster (q.v.) and Second Mate Joseph F. Bunker (q.v.), had sailed with Captain Worth before. Bunker, a ship's carpenter by trade, must have been especially valuable to the project. The three, Worth, Foster, and Bunker, had been together when Worth was captain of the bark *San Francisco* and lost her on Montauk Point, Long Island, in February 1862. On that voyage and perhaps abetted by the shipwreck, they appear to have developed a special bond, about which the kid named Lawrence could hardly have known and which he could hardly have appreciated. In fact, fellow-Vineyarders Worth and Foster, both active Freemasons, were lodge brothers during the two long periods when both were living on the Island, and each named a son after the other. From the multi-faceted context of all of this, it seems likely that the three compatriots could well have been involved together in any number of projects, scrimshaw and otherwise.

However, it is clear from Worth's own journal of the *Gazelle* (Rinaldi 2004, #9; now in a private collection) that, whatever the collaboration may have been, he was also a devoted solo practitioner of painting, drawing, and scrimshaw. The journal contains fragments of several voyages, punctuated with watercolors, competent elevations of ships, barks, and brigs, including a fine vignette of the *Gazelle* herself cutting-in blubber; whale stamps, handwriting samples, and a handful of recognition drawings of islands and sea coasts. Only once, on January 25, 1865, does he actually mention what might be scrimshaw: "These 24 hours has been quite fine[,] a rain squall now & then[.] the land is in sight about 25 miles dist[ant]. Men have been employed in mending sails. I have been quite buisy [sic] this afternoon makeing [sic] a knife box." But scattered around elsewhere in the journal are a few pencil drawings of scrimshaw components — mostly what appear to be handles and shafts — and a fully developed, pistol-grip pie crimper with a fluted jagging wheel, a relief-carved animal head on the saddle, and a delicate leafy floral motif to be engraved on the handle.

Daniel F. Worth was born in 1829 at Tisbury, Martha's Vineyard, and lived a long and prosperous, though not entirely happy and trouble-free life. His father, Henry P. Worth, was the local U.S. Customs officer, and his brother, Henry F. Worth, older by 13 years, was the master of four deepwater whaling voyages out of Fairhaven and New Bedford (1848-70). Daniel followed Henry to sea in the early 1840s. His maiden voyage is not known, but he was a boatsteerer for the 80th lay in the ship *Heroine* (1845-49) (the official register lists this voyage as sailing from New Bedford, but Starbuck credits it to Fairhaven). He then joined the New Bedford ship *Saratoga* as third mate on a voyage already in progress commanded by Captain Ephraim Harding (1849-52). This was a tremendously successful venture, with a total of 209 barrels of sperm oil, 3,973 barrels of whale oil, and 80,400 pounds of bone (baleen) sent and carried home — a cargo that according to Starbuck sold for $124,000 (approximately five times the value of the ship itself). In 1852 Worth married Jane W. Harding (1835-1896) of Tisbury, who was known as Jennie. His journal entries are often interspersed with affectionate references to her, but their life together was colored by intermittent sadness. She bore him a daughter in 1853 and a son in 1859, each of whom lived only two years. While Jenny was pregnant with their ill-fated daughter, Daniel went as second mate for the 40th lay in the *Saratoga* on her next voyage (1852-56), which was again commanded by Ephraim Harding and was a better-than-average success. His little daughter was born while he was at sea and was dead by the time he returned home: it appears that he never laid eyes on her. With Harding's blessing and no doubt on the basis of Harding's strong recommendation, at this point Worth skipped over a first mate's berth entirely and was made captain of the bark *Helen Augusta* of his own home port of Holmes' Hole (1856-58), Martha's Vineyard. Having made a modest success of the *Helen Augusta* his first time out, he was given the New Bedford bark *San Francisco* for his next voyage, to the Atlantic grounds. It was disappointing on several counts. They sailed in May 1859 and managed to send home 2,000 pounds of bone, a mere fraction of their total catch, before the vessel, homeward bound, foundered off Montauk Point, Long Island, in February 1862. And sadly, the same thing befell him as it had on the previous voyage: his wife was with child on his departure, she gave birth while he was away, and the baby, a son, was already dead by the time he returned.

The *San Francisco* voyage, perhaps enhanced by the added incentive of a shipwreck that occurred so near its conclusion, evidently created a strong fraternal bond among the Captain Worth and his two officers, Thomas Foster and Joseph Bunker. This could only have been deepened by sympathy for the bereaved captain and his wife after their return. They all went together on their next voyage, with Worth as master of the ship *Gazelle* (1862-66), a sperm whaling expedition to the Indian Ocean with now childless Jennie as a passenger. According to the green hand's report, it was on this voyage that the three senior shipmates collaborated on scrimshaw; and it was the voyage on which Captain Worth reported working on a knife box and drew plans for a crimper, which he may also have made on the *Gazelle*.

His last whaling voyage was as master of the brig *Para* of Salem, Massachusetts, on a sperm whaling venture to the Indian Ocean (1867-71), but it is not known whether Foster or Bunker was with him on that occasion; Jennie evidently was not. Meantime, beginning in the early 1860s and through his first two decades-plus of retirement from whaling, for a total of thirty-something years, Daniel lived in Brockton, Massachusetts, where the 1880 census lists his occupation as "sea captain" and the 1900 census lists his occupation as "capitalist." Jenny died in the early 1890s, and a couple of years later Daniel married a woman from California named Nettie. Born circa 1876, she was only about 21 years old at the time, some 48 years younger than her husband. They remained together, from all appearances happily married, until he died at age 93, when she was 45. He brought his new wife home to Tisbury, where he was a Masonic lodge brother of Thomas Foster and where Nettie bore two sons: Thomas Worth (born 1898), who was of course named after his father's life-long friend Captain Thomas Foster, and Daniel F. Worth, Jr. (born 1899), whom Worth named after himself. Thomas became an electrical draftsman and Daniel an officer in the navy. Daniel Sr. and Nettie moved back to Brockton around 1906, not long after Thomas Foster died; then to Lynn, where Thomas and Daniel Jr. were still living with their parents in 1920, and where Captain Worth died in 1922.

Wyet [Wyatt], — (fl. circa 1839-40). Even as a passenger on the whaleship *William Lee*, "Mr. Wyet" was evidently swept up in the scrimshandering activities that occupied the captain, mates, boatsteerers, steward, and two other fellow-passengers as they traveled from the Hawaiian Islands to Newport, Rhode Island, during 1839-40. One of those passengers, twelve-year-old Sereno Edwards Bishop (q.v.), says of Wyet in a journal entry of 20 Jan. 1840 that he was making a swift, but gives no details: "A good many things are going on in the ship. Capt Hussey is making a bureau, Mr. V a work box, Mr Wyet a swift, [the] Steward a ship [model,] and Trip[p] an article. The captain has underway a swift and two work boxes[,] Mr Sheffield a box and Mr V. another box." Unfortunately, Mr. Wyet (or Wyatt or Wyer) has not been identified. See the article on Mr. Vanderzee.

Young, Horace (fl. circa 1832-56). An oval box made famous by repeated publication has a wooden bottom with panbone sides, lid, and skirts, with the overlap joints handsomely carved in shallow relief in the form of three hands, fastened with brass rivets; the top of the lid is trimmed with whale ivory dentil motifs and a tortoise-shell overlay, inlaid in the center of which is a scalloped rectangular whale ivory plaque, surrounded by four inlaid whale ivory stars; baleen inner rim; stained interior; in NBWM. The provenance is in the form of a holograph note enclosed, stating: "Horace Young ... made this ditty box on a voyage as a coffee box for his wife and it was always used as such and kept on 2nd shelf in kitchen closet until this year... . He was on a whale ship, one of Henry Coffin's ships one of which was the Katawba [sic]."

Horace Young was born circa 1815 in Kennebunk, Maine, the son of William and Nabby Young, and went whaling at age 17 in the New Bedford ship *Hope* (1832-33). His activities during 1833-44 are unknown but he must have made several whaling voyages, as he turned up as second mate of the ship *Mobile* during 1844-48, earning the 36th lay. On this voyage Captain Charles G. Smith left the ship four months out, probably because of illness, and the first mate, William P. Bunker, was promoted to captain; Horace Young, as second mate and thus next in line, was duly promoted to first mate, receiving the 26th lay for the duration of the voyage. Meanwhile, the ship *Catawba*, referred to in the provenance, was built at Mattapoisett in 1836 and made one whaling voyage for Nantucket merchant Charles G. Coffin (1836-39), then four for the partnership of Charles G. & Henry Coffin (1840-57). Taking into account the specific claims of the provenance, together with Horace Young's known record of service aboard New Bedford ships during 1832-33 and 1844-57, the 1840-43 voyage is the only one he could have made in the *Catawba*; and on that voyage he was almost certainly second mate. Young had settled on Nantucket, and upon that first promotion to second mate he married Caroline Riddell, age 19, in 1840. After the *Catawba* and *Mobile* voyages, he went as first mate again, this time for a 24th lay in the ship *Adeline Gibbs* of Fairhaven (1848-53). In 1853 he was at last appointed captain and given a 14th lay in the Westport bark *President* (1853-56), but he did not complete the voyage. Rather, reportedly "disillusioned with whaling," he left the ship in 1856, spent some time in Chile, returned to Nantucket for a while, and then in late 1858 or early 1859 he went back to Chile, where he sent for his family — his wife Caroline, their 14-year-old daughter Elizabeth (born 1845), and their infant daughter Ella (the future Mrs. Walter J. Spencer, born in 1858). Accordingly, the family — or at least Caroline and Ella; the family provenance makes no mention of Elizabeth (probably because she died without issue at a fairly young age, thus Horace Young's descendants are all descended from Ella and would not necessarily have any recollection of Elizabeth); so it was the wife and at least one of the daughters, probably both daughters, who set out in 1859 to join Horace in Chile. However, he perished at sea, evidently just before the family arrived or soon after: "After he arrived [in Chile] he and some companions built a boat and when they went out in it for the first time were caught in a typhoon, wrecked and all drowned.

His wife with baby had to find a way back to Nantucket and begin life over... " Elizabeth died unmarried and without issue in 1886, so the ditty box went to the second daughter, Ella. She eventually sold it to collectors Martha and F. Gilbert Hinsdale, who donated it to NBWM in 1959 — coincidentally exactly 100 years after the maker's death by drowning in Chile. It was exhibited in "The Flowering of American Folk Art, 1776-1876" at the Whitney Museum of American Art in New York in 1974, and is illustrated in McManus 1997, 111, where it is also featured on the dust jacket.

Young, Israel A. (fl. circa the mid 1840s). The family provenance for five pieces of scrimshaw sold at auction in three lots (Cowan, Nov. 12-13, 2003, #777, 779, and 780) attributes them to Israel Young, whaleman, of Killingly, Connecticut. However, he was not actually from Connecticut himself: his mother, probably his father, and certainly several ancestors on both sides were from Killingly; but while Israel may therefore have lived in Killingly at some time, and may have owned or inherited land there, he was born circa 1826 at Scituate, Massachusetts, married a Rhode Island woman in 1847, and raised a family of ten children, and earned his living as a farmer (1860 U.S. Census, Foster, Providence Co., Rhode Island; 1870 U.S. Census, Burrillville, Providence Co., Rhode Island). An Israel Young (c1786-1838) of Killingly served in Captain Sikes' Company of volunteers during the War of 1812 (Hale Collection: Headstones at the Mashentuck #1 Cemetery in Killingly); this was probably the whaleman-artist's grandfather. Another Israel Young, age and parentage not specified but likely the father of the scrimshaw artist, married a Killingly woman named Rachel on Aug. 14, 1825 (Barbour Collection, Vital Records of Windham County, 1; 108), and the Young family genealogy explicitly indicates that this branch of the family moved from Killingly to Scituate at some unspecified time. When whaleman-artist Israel A. Young of Scituate married Rebecca C. Hopkins (born circa 1828), of Foster, Rhode Island, on May 2, 1847, it was recorded in the Vital Records of Windham County, Connecticut, not because they lived there but because of the Young family's close connection to Killingly (Barbour Collection, 2; 41). But it was neither Scituate nor Killingly that gave rise to Israel's whaling career. The U.S. Census indicates that there was an Israel Young family living on Nantucket in 1840 who were not natives of the place, but no further specifics are given and they were gone by 1850. And there is no such Israel Young household listed for Killingly or Scituate in 1850. This would have been when Israel A. Young was about 16 years old, and would account for his having made a youthful whaling voyage in the early 1840s, as virtually every young man on Nantucket was expected to do — though on what ship or from what port he sailed is not known. Some Nantucket vessel is of course the most likely.

As for the scrimshaw, the five pieces are a substantial output for a rookie who is presumed to have made only the one voyage. The first in the catalogue, if not in the order of their production, is a tooth monochrome engraved with a buccaneer in a cocked hat and elaborately ornamented coat and trousers, holding a cutlass and pistol, standing on the deck of a ship, with a cannon and treasure chest alongside, framed with a geometric border labeled "KELLY." This is "Kelly the Pirate," the title and subject of a famous broadside sea ballad of the era, with the image faithfully copied from the frontispiece of the popular, pocket-size *Forget Me Not Songster*, which was published in various Boston, New York, and Philadelphia editions beginning around 1835. (For the ballad text and music, its history, and a facsimile of the prototype illustration, see S.M. Frank, *The Book of Pirate Songs*, 1998, #23, 61f. There is also another, anonymous scrimshaw rendition of the same Kelly the Pirate image on a tooth in a private collection illustrated in color on the dustjacket.) The second scrimshaw lot is a pair of teeth respectively engraved with monochrome bust portraits labeled "CALVIN" and "LUTHER," representing the Protestant Reformation theologians John Calvin (1509-1564) and Martin Luther (1483-1546), likewise copied from generic printed illustrations, both unsigned. The third lot consists of two unsigned busks, each dated 1843. One is polychrome panbone, with a heart motif framing an anchor and two flags, two mortuary monuments surmounted by obelisks, one with a weeping willow and the other framed by draperies, and a leafy tree. The other busk is baleen incised with a heart motif, three potted flowering plants, and a monument with obelisks and weeping willow. As the grandfather Israel Young died in 1838, it may be conjectured that his passing may have been the occasion for his son's family's move to Nantucket, and that at least one of the mortuary monuments on his grandson's scrimshaw may be for the sake of the grandfather's memory.

Zhuravlev, V. (fl. circa 1960-65). Among the very best work from the Soviet Antarctic whaling fleet is a four-piece ensemble consisting of a penguin figurine carved in full round out of whale ivory, mounted on a clear plastic platform stand, together with a sperm whale tooth engraved with a brightly-colored portrait of a factory-ship, signed "V. Zhuravlev" (in NBWM). The maker, one of few Soviet era whalemen-practitioners whose name is known, appears to have been the Ukranian artist Victor Zhuravlev (b. 1938), who evidently served in the crew on at least one Russian Antarctic whaling expedition in the early 1960s, a few years prior to his professional career as a portraitist and figure painter, primarily of women. Beginning in 1965 and continuing on after the fall of the USSR, his paintings have been exhibited at various galleries in Ukraine, notably in Kiev, also occasionally in Moscow, St. Petersburg, Oslo, and Cologne.

Zinke, Henri (fl. circa 1855-62). Ship's carpenter on two whaling voyages, in the New Bedford barks *Globe* (1855-58) and *Dominga* (1858-62), credited with a wooden box with hinged lid, inlaid top and sides with circles, stars, arrows, tetraskeles, sunbursts, and fan shapes of walrus ivory and whale skeletal bone, trimmed on the edges and sides with bone and ivory strips and sawtooth patterns, and inscribed in pencil on the bottom, "Bark Dominga 1862" (in KNB). Zinke was born in 1835 in France, where he may have apprenticed as a carpenter. He emigrated before 1855, when he went to sea in the *Globe*, commanded by fellow scrimshaw artist Alexander A. Tripp (q.v.), who may have inspired Zinke's own scrimshaw-making. George R. Abbott (q.v. here and in the *Dictionary*) was his shipmate in the *Dominga*. Zinke married a woman named Margaret, a New York native born circa 1841 of Canadian parents; the wedding likely took place between voyages in 1858. After his second voyage he worked as a piano-maker in New York City and fathered four sons, of whom the eldest, Henry, made a career in the U.S. Navy. Henri died sometime before 1900, at which time his widow was living in Manhattan with another son, Edward Ellsworth Zinke, a New York firefighter who was later an engineer in Schenectady, New York, and a machinist for the Federal Shipbuilding Corporation in Jersey City.

APPENDIX I

Earliest Appearance of the Word Scrimshaw

To date, the earliest known use of any form of the word *scrimshaw* is in an 1805 entry in Elias Ludlow's shipboard journal aboard an unidentified whaleship of Sag Harbor, Long Island: "All hands Scrim Shawnterin" (2 June 1805). There is no indication what the crew were actually doing, and whether it was assigned work for the ship (such as panbone belaying pins, thole pins, fids, tool handles, and sheave blocks) or recreational handcrafts for their own amusement and use.

The significance of this brief passage to scrimshaw history was initially recognized by Judith Navas Lund, from a self-published pamphlet by Rhys Richards, *Into the South Seas: The Southern Whale Fishery Comes of Age on the Brazil Branks, 1765-1812* (Paremata, N.Z., 1993). Owing to his refusal to adopt American spellings of American place-names, and his unfamiliarity with Long Island geography (despite that as a career diplomat he was posted in New York City for several years and was actually married there), in his attempt to identify the journal-keeper and the voyage Richards makes a minor error and some reasonable but not conclusive claims. First of all, he names the keeper as "Elias Ludlow of Bridgeport, Long Island," but of course Bridgeport is in Connecticut; there is no Bridgeport, New York. Bridgehampton is the township in Suffolk County, Long Island, in which Elias Ludlow and his parents and grandparents were born. Their English ancestors were Ludlums of Derbyshire who emigrated to New Jersey and New York in the seventeenth century. Elias was born there circa 1782, the second son among the ten children of Anthony and Elizabeth Ludlow. Sometime around 1803 he married a local woman named Sally Miller. The whaling port of Sag *Harbor* — not Sag *Harbour* — is actually a subdivision of Bridgehampton, and it was there that the Ludlow family lived from the eighteenth century at least until the end of the nineteenth.

That Bridgehampton and not Bridgeport was Ludlow's home town only serves to strengthen Richards's compelling contention that the unidentified vessel was likely a Sag Harbor whaler. However, Richards quotes the journal to the effect that they were outward bound in July 1804, were cruising the Brazil Banks from October 1804 to March 1805, and after a call at the Cape Verde Islands "this journal ends near home on 7 June 1805"; he then speculates that the vessel was likely the *Minerva* or the *Abigail* because Starbuck lists both of them as "returning home to Sag Harbour [sic] in 1804, but did not record [them] sailing again that year." His point is that, as "Starbuck had only a very sketchy knowledge of the whaleships from Sag Harbour [sic] frequenting the Brazil Banks and Patagonia at this time," he may have missed such a voyage of the *Minerva* or *Abigail* entirely. But if Starbuck is correct and there were no other 1804 voyages for the *Minerva* or the *Abigail*, it would demonstrate the opposite: if both ships returned home in 1804 and did not sail again that year, neither could have been the ship aboard which Ludlow was whaling on the Brazil Banks from October 1804 to March 1805. So *unless* Starbuck is mistaken it was probably not either the *Minerva* or the *Abigail*. In either case Ludlow's vessel remains unidentified.

APPENDIX II

Earliest Exhibition of Scrimshaw

The East India Marine Society of Salem, Massachusetts (which was founded in 1799 and evolved into PEM) acquired a scrimshaw sperm whale tooth by Edward Burdett and two "Susan's Teeth" by Frederick Myrick circa 1830 — the earliest known apperance of scrimshaw in any institutional collection. The three pieces are listed in the Society's 1831 catalogue and were presumably exhibited at around that time. Apart from these, the earliest public showing of scrimshaw of which any notice has yet been discovered was in 1837, as recorded in the remarkable catalogue of the *First Exhibition and Fair of the Massachusetts Charitable Mechanic Association at Faneuil and Quincy Halls, in the City of Boston* (Boston: Dutton & Wentworth, 1837) (reported by Mark Foster). The following items are specified:

In the section devoted to "SHELL, PEARL AND IVORY WORK, BRUSHES OF ALL KINDS, AND HAIR WORK," in addition to commercially-produced brushes and brooms with baleen bristles, there are "Whips, Canes, and Busks, of whalebone [i.e., baleen], curious specimens; and whale teeth," submitted by W. Adams, Jr., of Boston; and "A Walking Cane, manufactured from the bone of the whale, inlaid with shell; and whale's teeth and a bone, engraved in a superior manner," submitted by J.W. Osgood of Boston (N° s 33 and 384, 46). A section entitled "UMBRELLAS, CANES, AND FANCY TURNING" lists "Two Whalebone Canes, made on board a whale ship," from J. Dewing of Salem; and "One Silk-Winder. Made from the jaw-bone of a sperm whale on board a whaleship in the Pacific Ocean," submitted by A. Gifford of Boston, who further remarks, "This is worthy of notice as a specimen of work done under great disadvantage." D.R. Moody of Newburyport likewise commented on his submission of "A Silk Reel, carved out of whalebone," saying it was "very neatly done" (N° 1122, 79). One item in the fourth exhibition of the same organization (in 1844) is similarly phrased but a lot more specific, indicating that both it and the foregoing were specimens of one of the more familiar types of scrimshaw: in this instance the donor is listed as Daniel R. Moody of Boston (probably the same man), and the object is described as "One Cotton Reel, or Swift, of Whalebone, made on board of a Whale Ship, on her passage home from the Sandwich Islands, with Tools made by himself. Shows much mechanical genius, and deserves encouragement" (Ibid., 1844 edition, N° 609, 120).

APPENDIX III

Captain Davoll's Rules and Regulations

On his first voyage as a whaling captain, Edward S. Davoll wrote down an orientation speech outlining his rules and regulations governing shipboard behavior on the two voyages he commanded in the bark *Cornelia* of New Bedford (1848-50 and 1850-53). These rules extended even to scrimshaw and probably carried over to his remaining voyages, in the ship *Iris* of New Bedford (sailed in 1854, wrecked in June 1855), the bark *R.L. Barstow* of Mattapoisett , Massachusetts (1856-58 and 1859-61), and perhaps even the bark *Brutus* of New Bedford (1861), a false whaling voyage whereof Davoll was only aboard for the outward passage to the Azores. [1]

> *My men, you must be well aware that the object of this voyage is to get a cargo of oil. To do this, it becomes necessary that some system be established in order to effect our purpose, and it becomes my duty to lay it before you, which you will strictly observe and abide by through the voyage. Discipline is a thing that I must have on board at all times and in all places.*
>
> *Obey and respect each and every officer. Always give a respective answer to every call and order given, day or nights. Never fail to give an answer. Answer quick. Come quick. Go quick, and do as you are told and you'll find no trouble.*
>
> *I strictly forbid quarreling and fighting [and] sky-larking from daylight til dark. No books to be read at any time except Sundays. No scrimshawing of any kind until I give orders to allow it. No loud and noisy conversation allowed from sunrise to dark. No singing or whistling at any time through the day. No sneaking into the forecastle under pretense of getting something when it is your watch on deck, because I know all about those things. No sleeping in your watches on deck, day or night. I shall give you plenty [of] watch below expressly for sleep, so that in case you are caught sleeping in your watch on deck you may expect to be kept on deck in your watch below as a 'cure all.*
>
> *If any of you feel unable to stand your watch at any time, through sickness or inability, come at once and report yourself to me or whoever has charge of the deck, so that I may immediately know of it and give you relief. If you fail to do this and go off below without saying anything, you may rest assured that I do not believe you to be sick, and shall have you out of them tricks before you play them 'fine.'*
>
> *Don't let yourselves be heard to grumble in any way. I and the officers can do all that. Grumblers and growlers won't go unpunished. Your place when on deck is forward of the tryworks where you are to remain at all times unless you have orders to come aft. Remember what I have said to you from now to the end of the voyage. I now dismiss you. Go Forward.*

---

[1] About which, see Stuart M. Frank, "False Whalers: Slavers and Fenian Patriots in Disguise," in *Seaport* (quarterly journal of South Street Seaport Museum, New York), 39:1 (Winter/Spring 2004), 18-23; and Kevin S. Reilly, "Slavers in Disguise: American Whaling and the African Slave Trade, 1845-1862," *The American Neptune*, 53:3 (Salem, Massachusetts, Summer 1993), 177-189.

APPENDIX IV

The Analects of Joseph Bogart Hersey

Joseph Bogart Hersey (circa 1821-1865) was an uncommonly articulate journal-keeper and talented amateur whaleman-artist. Later in his career, the responsibilities of being captain seem to have afforded him less time for scrimshandering and less time to write about it in his journal. But the following passages are excerpted from the informative and nicely illustrated journal he kept as a young seaman, aged about 22, in 1843, aboard the schooner *Esquimaux* of Provincetown, Cape Cod, Massachusetts (in KNB). Here he had a lot to say about working sperm whale teeth and bone, as well as working wood. Interestingly, he specifically mentions *skrimshamping* only once as such, but refers to the art of scrimshaw engraving as *flowering*, and refers to both genres of sailor arts (that is, scrimshawing ivory and bone, and analogous woodworking activities) as *haberdashing* and *griddling*, words seldom if ever encountered in any such context elsewhere. The excerpts are here quotated directly from the writings of this rather well-educated young man, presented without alterations of spelling, punctuation, or syntax.

Lathe On Board

While going aloft this morning I was some what surprised at hearing a sound issue from the forecastle not unlike that occasioned by grinding coffee. I asked one of the crew what he was going to do with so much coffee, he replied "have it twice a day." When I came on deck, I went in the forecastle and there to my surprise saw a man turning a grind stone which had a belt around it that led to the wheel on the spindle of a ***wooden lathe*** *at which another of the crew was occupied in turning out a piece of ivory. Well might it be said that every generation grows wiser and wiser, for here we see the ingeniousness of two of these young fellows, who with the help of an auger, hatchet, and saw, have completed a lathe for turning, and got it in full opperation [sic].*

Making Articles Useful to the Fair Sex

"Go to the ant thou sluggard, consider her ways and be wise." A person who had an opportunity to observe the actions of the officers and crew of the Esquimaux at the present time might confidently assert that this proverb [accurately quoted from the Old Testament book of Proverbs, VI:6] was never intended for them. For they can be seen in the cabin, on deck, and in the forecastle studiously engaged in ***skrimshamping*** *or more properly speaking, manufacturing yard sticks, busks, knitting sheaths, &c. &c. for their old spoons, spudges, and crafts (I.E.) That is they are engaged in making articles useful to the fair sex, which they intend to present to their own especial favorites on their return. It is somewhat pleasing to see with what assiduous attention they bend their minds to the present employments in which they are now engaged, whereas but a few hours ago the courent [sic] of their intellectual faculties as rapidly flowed in the channel of Navigation and Mathematics. As for myself I have been swept in the courent by engraven [sic] a busk belonging to the cook.*

Remedy for Ennui

After breakfast in order to drive off the ennui occasioned by the inactive employment in which we are all engaged, I commenced working on a yard stick, which is the first **haberdashing** *in the wood line that I ever undertook to perform. On a voyage similar to this when you have been in pursuit [of whales] as long as we have without meeting with the object of your search, the mind becomes depressed, the spirits dejected, and a kind of a don't care feeling takes possession of the whole system. It may be said by some who are unacquainted with whaling that a close application of the mind to some useful study would be the best remedy for the desponding mind; that this would tend to alleviate the solicitous mind for a* **short time***. I will not attempt to deny, but as a perfect remidy [sic] nothing but a good [stock] of oil would prove subservient [sic].*

Mahogany Yardsticks

After breakfast all that could find tools went to work on the log of mahogany which we found on Saturday last. the yard sticks we sawed out with an edacity [audacity] well adapted to bring a smile upon the cheek of the lass who expects to be presented with one of these rods. So suitable to fill the place of a **three leg[ge]d stool***, or* **broom stick***.*

Preparing the Jawbones and Jaw Pans for Scrimshaw

At sun rise we commenced cutting in the remainder of our whale, and finished before breakfast, after which we sheared the jaws and dip[p]ed the case. The length of the jaw was eleven feet and contained forty two teeth. these we extracted with great dispatch and took particular care of, thinking how suitable the[y] would be for **haberdashing***. We also sawed off the pans and put them overboard to tow, in order to soak the blood out [of] them and whiten the bone; this circumstance gave rise to thoughts similar to those occasioned by the teeth.*

Immediately after breakfast we commenced washing out our boats the smoke had collected upon them in places where it would be difficult to distinguish the original color of the paint. they were also well besmeared with grease. After this job was accomplished and we had put our whaling implements in **apple pie order** *we then began to saw up and divide the the bone, scarcely any of which but what was held in such high estimation as the to prevent it from being wasted. The jaw and pans were dissected to such an advantage that nearly all had a piece which would answer to make a busk, or cane, and some were fortunate enough to get both.*

Show-and-Tell on a Gam

At 6 oclock p.m. our Captain in compliance with the rules of etiquette lowered his boat and returned the visit due to Capt. Smith [aboard the Belle Isle]. Not having left our vessel to go on board of another since our departure [from] home, and a good opportunity offering itself on the present occasion I seized upon it, and paid a visit to the ***old craft*** *in which I served my* ***apprenticeship****. While there the officers and crew showed us some boxes which they had manufactured in the cours[e] of their voyage. We returned home at ½ past nine oclock most pleased with our visit.*

Wasting Time

Today I disposed of my yard stick and resolved to devote more of my time to reading and study, and less to ***haberdashing****, knowing from experience the former to be much more beneficial.*

Haberdashing and Griddling

Several of our crew continue to ***haberdash****, or more properly speaking* ***griddling****.*

Once more our crew have taken to haberdashing or manufacturing busks. I employed a part of my leisure time in carving or flowering three.

Dividing Up the Teeth

In the morning we devided [sic] our share of the teeth from the last whale, some of our number were fortunate enough to get them which were nearly round; as for mine I did not consider it worth cleaning therefore threw it away. Our officers and crew appear to have received new animation of late, for they have once more bent their minds to ***haberdashing****. from this they were aroused by the sound of* ***breech oh****!! from the mast head.*

"Flowering" Busks

This afternoon we commenced sawing up the large whale's jaws that we captured in company with [schooner] Belle Isle on the 14th; the bone proved to be pretty good and yielded several canes, fids, and busks. I employed a part of my time in engrav[ing] or flowering two busks. Being slightly skilled in the art of flowering; that is drawing and painting upon bone; steam boats, flower pots, monuments, balloons, landscapes &c &c &c; I have many demands made upon my generosity, and I do not wish to slight any; I of course work for all.

APPENDIX V

Scrimshandering Activities, Scrimshaw Methods, and Collecting Specimens aboard the *William Lee*, 1839-40

As a passenger on the whaleship *William Lee*, traveling from Honolulu to Newport, Rhode Island, from October 29, 1839 to April 28, 1840, Sereno Edwards Bishop kept a journal (in KNB) in which, on several occasions, he comments briefly but importantly about scrimshaw-making (reported by Dr. Jack H.T. Chang). Bishop was the articulate, well educated, twelve-year-old son of missionaries in the Hawaiian Islands, on his way to school in upstate New York; he would afterwards graduate from college and seminary, marry, and return to Hawaii as a pastor, missionary, educator, and editor. Not only does his journal corroborate comprehensively the variety and proliferation of scrimshandering on board, but describes aspects that have ever been apparent but are nowhere else specified: that teeth, bone, and even finished scrimshaw were occasionally swapped and traded among the crew; that some whalemen customarily cut the bottoms off of teeth "so that they will stand up straight"; that teeth and bone were sometimes taken home to be scrimshawed ashore; that locks, hinges, and presumably other metal fittings were sometimes made by the whalemen themselves (though most are demonstrably store-bought); that "Chinese paints," store-bought watercolors, and turpentine were among the ingredients used for pigmentation; and that even cabin passengers were occasionally involved. In the present volume are brief biographical sketches of Bishop and each of the scrimshaw-making shipmates to whom he refers: Captain Frederick W. Hussey, the two mates, Charles G. Sheffield and a "Mr. Tripp," a foremast hand named Anderson, and two passengers, named Vanderzee and Wyet (qq.v.). However, as Bishop's remarks are significant for the light they throw upon the scrimshaw-making activities of a single voyage, they are anthologized here in the aggregate.

> *12 Oct. 1839: … [Captain Hussey] has shown us a number of articles made by himself and others out of whale teeth such as snuff boxes, bodkins, pie stamps [crimpers], needle cases, reels [sheave blocks], &c., all of which are done off very handsomely.*
>
> *3 Nov. 1839: I made me a small paper cutter of white whalebone[.] there is a considerable quantity on board but nearly all the teeth are worked up[.] the captain moulded a fife of lead and turned it; it did not make much noise however.*
>
> *4 Nov. 1839: the captain made a wooden fife today[.] it did not sound as well as the leaden one.*
>
> *24 Jan. 1840: A good many things are going on in the ship. Capt Hussey is making a bureau[,] Mr. V a work box, Mr Wyet a swift, Steward a ship[,] and Trip[p] an article. The captain has underway a swift and two work boxes[,] Mr Sheffield a box and Mr V. another box.*
>
> *22 Feb. 1840: Mr V. Bought of Anderson today a pair of whale's teeth they are the largest that I ever saw. Anderson has a number of them which he has scraped off clean and cut of[f] the bottoms so that they will stand up straight[.] he is going to carry them home to be carved. Mr. V. is going to use his for a swift, which he is about to make, he is also at work on a small bureau*

which is to be made of bone. Trip[p] finished his box to which he made the lock and hinges[.] the lock is of copper and is done very neatly[,] the bolt and key are of brass[.] Capt H[ussey] is to work on a concern which is principally a desk and I am making a small ship[.]

6 March 1840: Mr. V. has been trading today, getting the material for a swift; he got 4 teeth[,] a bone cane[,] 6 or 8 bone stays[,] a shaft, cup and whirls ready made. I had a bone cane given to me.

2 April 1840: Mr. V. took some of those Chinese paints (which I let him have sometime since, minus 4 brushes and a bowl[,] for a small box of water colors and $.50 to boot) and ground them with oil and Sp[iri]ts [of] Turpentine, and painted the edges of the drawers to his bone bureau, they worked very well.

* * *

Passenger Vanderzee, about whom nothing is known apart from Bishop's comments in his journal, appears to have been something of an amateur ornithologist. The journal presents some interesting sidelights on his shipboard collecting pursuits, in which the captain, officers, and crew were complicit. Surprisingly, at least one person on board (evidently not "Mr. V." himself) had the ability to prepare taxidermic specimens from the fresh carcasses he collected.

25 Nov. 1839: The booby that was caught last night was skinned and stuffed for Mr Vandazee. From the extremities of the wings it measured 4 ½ feet although it is not so large as a duck[.] we see great numbers of birds such as boobies, men of war, hawks, gannets, haglets, mother carey's chickens besides a kind of white bird[.] the captain tried a long time to shoot one of these but did not succeed.

8 Feb. 1840: A little bird was caught last night, which they prevented from flying into the fire, being attracted by the light[.] It was presented to Mr. V. it appears very much like a land bird, but has webbed feet; the bill is like a pigeon's.

10 Feb. 1840: They caught 3 albatrosses yesterday although it was Sunday[.] they cannot fly after they get on deck[.] it was ridiculous to see their attempts to walk[.] they would get up by the assistance of their wings and put one foot out; then as soon as they set the other out, over they would go. Mr. V. had one of them killed and skinned.

APPENDIX VI

Notes and Reflections on Marine Ivory and Baleen

Whalebone in Philadelphia, 1787

The following notice appeared in the 12 April 1787 issue of *The Pennsylvania Packet and Daily Advertiser*, published at Philadelphia by John Dunlap and David C. Claypoole, under a somewhat incongruous wood engraving of a bloated dolphin after a prototype by Pierre Belon published in Paris in 1553 (reported by Klaus Barthelmess). What the purveyor calls "whalebone" is, of course, commercial grade baleen, respecting which he claims the ability (unique in Philadelphia and perhaps unique in America) to provide the product fancy-cut in the British manner, along with an assortment of baleen, ivory, and horn implements:

Samuel Scotten,

WHALEBONE CUTTER,

At N° 383, Chesnut [sic] street, between Front and Second streets,

> *Has a good assortment of common cut whalebone; he also cuts and prepares whalebone in the English manner, equal to British to suit for bonnet, stay, umbrella and whip makers. He has also a good assortment of brushes, shaving boxes, black ball; ivory and horn combs, &c., which he will sell on reasonable terms. As no one here hath attempted manufacturing whalebone in the British manner, he apprehends few know the quality of such bone; but as there is little or no waste in it, he flatters himself the consumers will find it in their interest to encourage it, which will enable him to carry on the whalebone business in so extensive a manner, as to sell his dress'd bone at as low or lower price than common bone has sold for when the business was in one man's hand. A generous allowance to country shopkeepers and others, who buy to sell again. Orders from the country attended to with care and dispatch.*

Elephant and Walrus Ivory, 1794

A manuscript ledger entry of 1794, reported by Michael P. Dyer from the archive of New Bedford's founding firm of whaling merchants (in KNB), is entitled "Invoice of Oil & Bone Shipped by Wm Rotch Junr. on board Ship Barclay, David Swain, Master, for Home, consigned Homberg & Homberg freres for Sale." In addition to 50 casks of spermaceti oil, 138 casks of whale oil, 89 bundles of "Whale Bone" (baleen), it also lists cargoes of elephant tusks and walrus tusks: "Ivory. Ship'd same time 1 Cask Ivory Elephant & Sea Horse teeth 496 lbs left with Homberg & Homberg firm." Values are carefully tabulated for the whale products, but no values are given for the ivory.

Fossilized Ivory

Though it was not commonly used in scrimshaw, fossilized ivory was evidently known to many whalers who frequented and traded on the coasts of Alaska and Siberia. This included walrus tusks that had been frozen, stained dark, and structurally transformed in the tundra permafrost, as well as the huge fossilized tusks of the extinct mammoth. According to armchair historian Charles Walter Agard, quoting or paraphrasing an unspecified edition of *Chambers Encyclopedia* in 1906, "Mammoth ivory of commercial value is hunted for by ivory hunters in Siberia for Russian manufacture."

In 1905 or 1906, Agard interviewed Adeline Heppingstone, the wife of Captain John Heppingstone, herself a veteran of fourteen years on whaleships out of Honolulu and New Bedford with her husband during 1861-82. While she had no specific term for it, it is clear that it is fossilized ivory that, in a kind of diatribe about walruses, she describes as "the scraps, broken and worn off by surf, also old, old pitted, eaten, whole tusks in all stages of decay, of all colors, white, yellow, mottled, purple, even black found their way to trade centers, [notably] San Francisco" (Agard Papers, KNB; q,v, in *More Scrimshaw Artists*, Appendix III). In another context Agard adds, "Specimens [are] found in quagmires and quicksands of former days, as also in the ice — glacial ice and just [plain] Ice — also in various parts of the wide United States, as if mired in their day, mostly however in Alaskan and Siberian territory." He characterizes one particular specimen that was recovered by whalemen on the Arctic Ocean coast of Alaska: it was clearly much too large to be a walrus tusk, and was identified as prehistoric:

> *In August 1904, Mate Walter Ashley of New Bedford and of steam whaler 'Belvedere' [of San Francisco] went with his boat's crew to an abandoned Native village beyond Point Barrow [Alaska] which had been given up, its people going away probably [on] account [of] the ravages of measles or smallpox. In the usual Soldier of Sailor search for loot, souvenir[s,] or curios, an old piece of tusk was found stowed away overhead in a house that had nothing else to contribute.*
>
> *It was sent to the boat on the beach. The boatsteerer, a... man of intelligence, recognized the rarity of the subject, and naturally wanted a piece to work up into trinkets. It was very crooked or curved, its ends all gone, splintered, decomposed, disintegrating, shaling and cracked. The part measured seven feet — the balance was thrown away. This section was brought home as a relic of more ages B.C. than since...*

Agard, who was an inveterate collector of curios brought back from whaling voyages, also acquired a fossilized tooth gathered much nearer to home. James A. Barnes, a New Bedford attorney, wrote the following letter, dated 18 April 1894:

> *My dear Mr Agard*
>
> *I happened to come across this fossil tooth amongst my traps to day and the fact that I had promised the same to you some time since came to mind, therefore I at once enclose it to you fearing that I might be like some other promisers, but for whom you might now rival any Museum in the land — here's hoping you will.*
>
> *This particular tooth was found imbedded in the cliffs of Gay-head, Martha's Vineyard, by a former lighthouse keeper — I.N. Luce by name, whom I knew as a reliable man, perhaps an unusual qualification but a blessed one. The geology of the section you can study up, I dont care to give any pointers on that subject.*
>
> *He, the aforesaid Luce, stated that he had asked Prof. Aggasiz [Louis Agassiz, 1807-1873, of Harvard, America's most famous naturalist] and Prof. Shaler [Nathaniel Southgate Shaler, 1841-1906, dean of the Lawrence School of Science] of national renown, the probable age of*

this identical tooth and they agreed that it might be any where from ten to forty millions of years. [A]s such figures always take away my breath when I speak or think of them I will let you off right here.

Cordially yours,

Jas. A. Barnes

Ivoroid

Ivoroid is the brand name and adoptive trade name for a type of synthetic ivory made from cellulose (plant fibre), hence generically known as *celluloid*. Specifically, ivoroid is the form of celluloid that was intended to look and behave like ivory. It was used as a cheaper substitute for ivory (as well as for tortoise shell and bone) in a variety of decorative and practical applications.

In *An Introduction to Plastics* (2003), Greg Goebel describes the genesis of celluloid through something called *pyroxlin* [*pyroxylin*] a heat-moldable synthetic ivory "made from cellulose treated with nitric acid and a solvent," developed in England by one Alexander Parkes. He marketed it under the trade name Parkesine and won a bronze medal with it at the 1862 London World's Fair. However, it turned out to be susceptible to warping and cracking, and ultimately proved impractical. An American amateur inventor, John Wesley Hyatt, "took up where Parkes left off" and produced a more durable product that he called *celluloid*; but authorities disagree whether this was in 1863 or 1869. Goebel notes that among the early beneficiaries was dental prosthesis: "Sets of false teeth built around celluloid proved cheaper than existing rubber dentures. However, celluloid dentures tended to soften when hot, making tea drinking tricky, and the camphor taste proved to be hard to eliminate."

Celluloid was widely used in the manufacture of domestic articles from the 1870s to the 1920s, especially in ladies' dressing sets (typically consisting of a hairbrush, comb, hand-mirror, and dispensers for powder and facial tissues); handles for straight-razors, shaving brushes, carving knives, and fish-service sets; for the "white" keys on cheaper pianos and organs; and as a substitute for ivory inlay and trim on furniture, household implements, picture frames, and musical instruments. When used for trim, such as patterned inlay on furniture, or purfling on guitars, it can be pure white or "ivory" in color and without discernible grain. Likewise in its many applications to the kinds of things in which there was no need to make the material *look* like ivory, such as shirt collars, cuffs, corsets, etc., where the desirable virtues were that it be waterproof and stain resistant. However, in its commonest manifestations, where celluloid or ivoroid was intended as a substitute for ivory (piano keys, organ keys, dressing sets, shaving gear, and handles for cutlery), it often has artificially-induced amber–, tawney–, or honey-colored graining, and even faux Schrager lines (the honeycomb-pattern grain distinctive to elephant and other pachyderm ivory). It does not lend itself well to carving or engraving, tends to be more susceptible than natural ivory to heat, scuffing, and abrasion, perhaps less so to cracking and breakage. According to anthropologists at the University of Utah, "Celluloid is distinguished from ivory by a carbolic or menthol odor produced by heating or rubbing the surface of the [object]"; and it has been used for veneering, such as a two-piece button made after 1900, "by placing a thin piece of celluloid over another type of material."

Relative Value of Walrus Ivory as Cargo

The final financial tally for a voyage of the bark *Elizabeth Swift* of New Bedford in 1868 (reported by Michael P. Dyer) lists among the "Cargo brot [sic] home": "343 lbs Walrus Teeth [walrus tusks]. / Sold at S[an] F[rancisco] / @ 40¢ ," amounting to $137.20. This was, of course, in addition to the more mainstream cargoes and revenues: 6,615 gallons of "Humpback oil and Dark wh[ale] oil @ 65¢ " ($4,299.75), "20,681 gallons of whale oil @ 70¢ " ($14,476.70), and freight charges for oil carried home from the whaling bark *Eugenia* ($3,259.30); plus the much larger proceeds from oil and bone shipped home by other means ($129,268.81). This total, less customs charges ($8.17), pilotage ($49.50), wharfage ($26.01), incidental coopering ($25.69), oil gauging ($14.34), and commissions ($221.72), amounts to a very handsome net total of $151,093.32 ("Statement of Bark *Elizabeth* Swift's 3rd whaling voyage, Reuben Portius master, Sailed Novbr 12th 1863, arrived April 13th 1868. voyage 52 months & 1 day or 1611 days"; NBWM). The value of walrus ivory returned ($137) against the total value of the voyage ($151,093) is an extreme case — it was an uncommonly long and lucrative voyage — but is probably a fair indication of the comparatively trivial value of walrus ivory on such a voyage. There is no mention of whale ivory as a commodity.

Returns of Walrus Ivory

Returns of walrus ivory for the commercial market are scarce and incomplete, however Reginald B. Hegarty (1959) does present a few representative statistics from whaling expeditions originating in Honolulu. These were generally seasonal rotations: bowhead whaling in Arctic waters off Alaska and Siberia in the northern summer, alternating with whaling and trading in the Central and South Pacific during the off season. Thus, in addition to conventional cargoes of sperm oil, whale oil, and baleen ("bone"), the schooner *Liholiho,* Captain Halsey, in 1855, and brig *Hero,* Myer, in 1861, are credited with unspecified quantities of walrus ivory; and the brig *Victoria,* Captain Milton Fish, which brought in 500 barrels of whale oil, 14,000 pounds of bone, and 3000 pounds of walrus ivory in 1859, is the first of seventeen Hawaii-based whaling voyages for which quantities (but not values) of walrus oil, ivory, skins, and furs are specified:

Year	Vessel	Rig	Tons	Master	Sperm	Whale	Bone	Walrus ivory and miscellaneous
1859	Victoria	brig	200	Milton Fish	---	500	14,000	3,000 lbs ivory
1870	Count Bismarck	bark	453	Eduard Dallman	---	1200	16 000	2000 lbs ivory
1870	Comet	brig	255	C.H. Warren	---	---	---	Walrus oil + 600 lbs ivory
1870	Eagle	bark	382	H.S. Comstock	---	1000	10 000	100 lbs ivory
1870	Onward	brig	180	T.H. Norton	140	500	9 000	800 lbs ivory
1872	Arctic	bark	431	A. N. Tripp	140	660	12 000	394 bbls walrus oil
1872	R. W. Wood	bark	287	Whitney	---	550	12 000	2000 lbs ivory
1873	R. W. Wood	bark	287	Whitney	50	600	10 000	2400 lbs ivory
1874	Victoria	brig	200	Tripp	---	100	5000	3500 lbs ivory
1875	Desmond	bark	301	Smith	---	550	9 000	5000 lbs ivory, 600 bbls walrus
1875	Onward	brig	180	Gilley	---	1000	7 000	300 lbs ivory
1875	Giovanni Apiani	schr	86	G.F. Dority	---	130	5 500	13,300 lbs ivory + 364 furs
1876	Giovanni Apiani	schr	86	Fuller	---	---	14 477	8652 lbs ivory
1877	Giovanni Apiani	schr	86	Whitney	---	---	7 000	4000 lbs ivory
1878	Giovanni Apiani	schr	86	Weeks	---	---	750	220 lbs ivory + trade
1878	Onward	brig	180	Smithers	---	225	3 000	1500 lbs ivory
1879	General Harney	schr	86	Tripp	---	---	1 100	3500 lbs ivory + 400 skins

Commercial Value of Walrus Ivory

"[In 1904,] Mate Walter Ashley of New Bedford and of steam whaler 'Belvedere'... fancied $15.00 as a small value for a pair of large walrus tusks, cleaned and polished, weighing say 8 pounds, and say 29 inches long, on oft quoted $1.00 to $1.20 per pound for good ivory in San Francisco. Local ship owners quote 60 cents on Hudson Bay ivory, commercial, peradventure settlement rate with crew. So after weary waiting of weeks on display in a store window, [Ashley] was glad to get ten dollars Christmas money for his family." (Papers of Charles W. Agard, KNB)

Sperm Whale Teeth and Skeletal Bone as Commodities

The latter-day commercial value of walrus ivory notwithstanding, sperm whale teeth were seldom regarded as a marketable commodity after circa 1816, when China traders were no longer seeking them for barter in the South Pacific (see Stuart M. Frank, "The Origins of Engraved Pictorial Scrimshaw," in *The Magazine Antiques*, 142:4, Oct. 1992). Accordingly, records that specify any kind of commercial transaction involving sperm whale ivory (especially prior to the 1870s) are rare. A significant instance is a whaling merchant's ledger entry of May 30, 1864, under the heading "Account Sales Sperm Oil Stored from Ship Alfred Gibbs [of New Bedford] / 3rd Voyage on Acct. Capt. Edwd. Nichols & the Owners" (NBWM; reported by Suzanne Finney), which shows prices calculated per the individual tooth: "Sales to William O. Brownell / 220 Whales Teeth @ 25¢/ $55.00." This contrasts with the next entry, immediately following, dated Feb. 15, 1865, showing that the ivory amounted to a miniscule percentage of the total value of the cargo: "Sales to Charles H. Leonard / 5,938 ½ Gallons Sperm Oil @ $2.40 / 4 months with interest / $14,252.40." Thus, the value of the teeth comes to approximately 0.004% of the total value, which tiny fraction turns out to be a fairly consistent proportion in extant records for the next forty years. William O. Brownell (circa 1818-1880) was a ship chandler and, according to the New Bedford City Directory, a dealer in "old junk." To what use he may have put the sperm whale teeth is not recorded.

A few years later prices for whale ivory on the New Bedford market were calculated differently. At sea during a voyage of 1866-71 the ship *Ohio* sold 40 lbs. of whale teeth at 40¢/lb., for a total of $12.00; and 1178 lbs. of walrus ivory for $245.54, which is just under 20¢/lb. The "Cargo brot [sic] home" in the bark *Canton* in 1875 included "187 lbs Whl Teeth" at 40¢/lb. (total $74.80). In 1890 the *Canton*'s tally was "45 ½ lbs Whales teeth" at 40¢/lb., a total of $18.20; and (in a separate entry), sold "5 lbs Whales teeth" for $1.00, or about 20¢/lb. (NBWM; reported by Suzanne Finney). These totals, of course, were a mere pittance compared with the value of the oil and "whalebone" (baleen).

New Bedford merchants J. & W.R. Wing's financial accounts for the bark *Sunbeam* span several years, with the sale of sperm whale teeth noted with variable specificity (reported by Suzanne Finney):

Date	Item	Amount	Price
11 Nov. 1896	Sale whales teeth (quantity not specified)	6.35	—
17 Sept. 1897	198 lb whales teeth Not Paid	118.80	60¢/lb
17 Sept. 1897	3 lb whales teeth	2.25	75¢/lb
13 Aug. 1898	2 whales teeth	1.50	75¢/each
15 Nov. 1898	6 lb whales teeth	3.00	50¢/lb
20 Dec. 1899	240 lb whales teeth	121.80	50¢+/lb
15 Dec. 1900	whales teeth (quantity not specified)	13.00	—
15 Dec. 1900	125 lb Jaw bone	6.13	<5¢/lb
3 May 1902	Sale whale teeth (quantity not specified)	139.95	—
26 Sept. 1902	Sale Jaw bone (weight not specified)	74.86	—
10 Nov. 1902	Sale small whales teeth (quantity not specified)	4.80	—

The total balance for the period February 1894 to May 1897 was $20,806.70, of which a mere $6.35 — a truly microscopic fraction — came from the sale of teeth. The heftier balance for the slightly overlapping period January 1896 to January 1901 was $58,984.00, of which only $251.98 — about 0.004%, the same percentage as in 1864 — was realized from the combined sales of teeth and skeletal bone. Financially speaking, this was an inconsequential pittance. Almost exactly the same percentage is reflected in the tally for the final period covered by these *Sunbeam* records, July 1901 to May 1903: $219.61 for teeth and skeletal bone, against a total $45,283.33.

Slight differences are evident in the method of calculating the value of teeth brought back from two successive whaling voyages of the New Bedford brig *Leonora* in 1902 and 1906. The first of these was to Desolation Island in High South Latitude (1901-02) under veteran captain Benjamin D. Cleveland (q.v. in the *Dictionary*), who was also part owner of the vessel. The second, commanded by another shareholder, William B. Ellis, was an overlong Atlantic Ocean voyage from December 1902 to June 1906, on which "seven of the crew died of beri-beri and ten others [were] landed at St. Helena to be placed in hospital" (Hegarty 1959, 36). In managing agent Timothy C. Allen's financial ledgers (in NBWM, reported by Michael P. Dyer) , one tally specifies that of 300 teeth returned (the approximate yield from eight whales), 45 were "held back" (that is, not sold, for reasons unexplained), leaving 255 teeth valued at the following rates: 216 large teeth at $0.60/each = $129.60; and 39 small teeth at $0.30/each = $11.70; for a total of $141.30. In addition, there are two formal receipts signed and dated June 22, 1906, which specify eight "Whale Jaws" (presumably the same lower mandibles from which the 300 teeth had been extracted). As typeset headings on the printed receipts proclaim, these were all "WEIGHED ON FAIRBANKS SCALES" belonging to James T. Kiernan, a local tack maker, harness maker and saddler, preparatory to their sale by Captain Allen to New Bedford commission merchant William H. Bartlett, the son and successor of Ivory H. Bartlett. (Allen and Bartlett likely had the jawbones brought to Kiernan for weighing because he was one of a few local merchants who had scales capacious enough to take the load. And the loads must have been large. The tare itself — the "deduction from the gross weight of the contents made in allowance for the weight of the container" — weighed the better part of a ton.) The bone tally from the two *Leonora* receipts is:

1st receipt:	3,775 lbs. gross, less 1,610 lbs. tare = 2,165 lbs. net
2nd receipt:	2,895 lbs. gross, less 1,610 lbs. tare = 1,285 lbs. net
Total:	6,670 lbs. gross, less 3,220 lbs. tare = 3,450 lbs. net

The 3,450 pounds of bone was valued at $0.08 per pound, for a total of $276.00. Thus, the grand total for the jawbones ($276.00) and teeth ($141.30) was $417.30 — again, only a miniscule portion of the total value of the cargo. The buyer, William H. Bartlett (1830-1912), is known from local accounts and a newspaper obituary to have been a dealer in ivory and bone, but for what ultimate purpose he bought these teeth and bones remains unexplained.

Sperm Whale Teeth and Scrimshaw as an Attraction

Joseph Hathaway Burgess, a native of Fairhaven, Massachusetts (across the Acushnet River from New Bedford), was an oil merchant in Rochester, New York. In a letter to his mother in 1851 he explained, "We are going to have a stall in the State Fair enclosure for the exhibition of our oils and we propose to put a lot of teeth, shells, canes, clubs, &&&& to attract attention" (NBWM MSS94/5G3/Ser. A/4).

Sperm Whale Teeth as a Prize

An unidentified retired whaleman, interviewed around 1905 by Charles Walter Agard (q.v., *More Scrimshaw Artists*, Appendix III), relates how he had won a prize of cash and whale teeth aboard the bark *Sarah* in the 1850s:

> *After recruiting [taking on water and provisions] at St. Helena, we cruised around the Island. The Capt[ain] had offered $10.00 and the largest pair of teeth as a bonus to whoever raised a Whale. All hands strained their eyes all day. I had just come on deck and thought I saw something in the sun glare, and sure enough it was a spout. "Blows, oh, ohs" it was, haul aback the main yard, and get into your boats. Oh, it was dead easy, and by the next Friday evening we had his 100 barrels stowed down and the Ship cleaned. Next day was Saturday and I made my premium in the morning on a 90 barrel sperm whale. Oh, I was playing in great luck.* (Agard Papers, KNB)

Softening Ivory

Mackenzie's Five Thousand Receipts In All the Useful and Domestic Arts... by an American Physician (Philadelphia, 1853) is one of dozens of nineteenth-century American do-it-yourself guides to home remedies and domestic alchemy. Many of the recipes would now be considered toxic, carcinogenic, or unsuitably caustic for household use. Others remain effective for the purposes stated, whether or not they have been superseded and made obsolete by more recent concoctions. The perpetrator, Dr. Colin MacKenzie, also provides formulas for softening, polishing, gilding, and silvering ivory, which typify the home-remedy genre and likely apply just as well to whale and walrus ivories as they do to the elephant ivory for which they were originally intended. (MacKenzie also has a long section on painting ivory, including cleaning, preparing, and polishing the surface such that the pigment will adhere. This would have been fairly useful at the time, as the centuries-old method of painting watercolor portrait miniatures on wafer-thin slices of elephant ivory mounted on card stock, though well past its heyday and soon to be eclipsed by the newfangled phenomenon of daguerreotype photography, was still being practiced in the 1850s.) Some of the instructions for polishing and softening ivory are none too specific, and some may be hazardous to the ivory if not to the practitioner; in any case, they are probably no longer the most practical means to achieve the desired result.

To polish and soften ivory.

This article is polished with putty and water, by means of a rubber, made of hat, which in a short time, produces a fine gloss. ... [T]o soften ivory: Let it stand in a warm place 48 hours, and you will be able to bend the ivory in any form. (30)

To soften ivory.

Slice half a pound of mandrake, and out it into a quart of the best vinegar, into which put the ivory; let it stand in a warm place for 48 hours, and the ivory may be bent in any direction. (60)

To gild silk, satin, ivory, &c. by hydrogen gas.

Immerse a piece of white satin, silk, or ivory in a solution of nitro-muriate of gold, in the proportion of one part of the nitro-muriate to three of distilled water. Whilst the substance to be gilded is still wet, immerse it in a jar of hydrogen gas; it will soon be covered by a complete coat of gold. (15)

Curious mode of silvering ivory.

Immerse a small slip of ivory in a weak solution of nitrate of silver, and let it remain till the solution has given it a deep yellow colour; then take it out and immerse it in a tumbler of clear water, and expose it in the water to the rays of the sun. In about three hours the ivory acquires a black colour; but the black surface on being rubbed, soon becomes changed to a brilliant silver. (393)

MacKenzie also provides a surprising remedial use for unwanted scrimshaw:

Jelly from the raspings of ivory.

The raspings of ivory impart to boiling water a very pleasant jelly, which has been found more easy of digestion, and more nutritious than that of the hartshorn shavings, or isinglass. Mixed with the jelly of the arrow-root, in the proportion of one part to seven, it is much recommended for weakly and ricketty [sic] children, and consumptive or emaciated invalids.

The standard method of softening ivory for commercial use in the nineteenth century is probably the one described briefly in a loose-footed, anonymous ink holograph in the Papers of Charles Walter Agard (in KNB). A second holograph in the Agard Papers, written in the same hand, has the mysterious heading "Frankie Bubbles" but otherwise repeats the same material verbatim — a formula that remains unascribed and untested:

> *Ivory. In small pieces laid in strong Phosphoric Acid till transparent, rinsed in water, dried in pure linen, when dry is translucent & hard. Softens as often as desired in warm water or milk.*
>
> *Time of immersion depends on size. Varnish what is not to be acted upon.*
>
> *To harden Ivory boil for some time in solution of Gelatin.*

An anonymous filler article in the March 1890 issue of the periodical *Manufacturer and Builder* (Vol. 22, N° 3, New York: Western & Co., 51) offers a somewhat different version of the same recipe, attributed to the eminent British zoölogist Sir E[dwin] Ray Lankester (1847-1929), FRS, which appears to corroborate Agard's suggested method:

> TO SOFTEN IVORY. — *Dr. Lankester recommends phosphoric acid, of the usual specific gravity, which renders ivory soft and nearly plastic. When washed with water, pressed, and dried the ivory regains its former consistency, and even its microscopic structure is not affected by the process.*

Cursory experiments conducted at the Scrimshaw Forensics Laboratory® at NBWM in July and August 2007 included immersion of one-inch (2.5 cm) salami-slice discs of whale ivory in whole milk for several days, which was proven a remarkably effective means to soften the ivory temporarily, while simultaneously creating a detestable stench that makes the process hardly worth pursuing. Discs of 8 and 10 grams were weighed and measured, immersed for seven days, then removed and the surface wiped dry, then weighed and measured again immediately, showing a net gain of 1 gram of weight attributable to moisture; they were then allowed to dry out for two weeks, then were weighed and measured again. Moisture retention was virtually nil at the end of the two weeks: the discs had been reduced to their original weight (at a scale tolerance of 1 gram, no measurable difference could be detected), while the ivory surface appears to have re-hardened on its own within the same span of time.

Milkshaw

The following notice, concerning the manufacture of faux ivory from ordinary milk, is quoted directly in its entirety from the *St. Helena Guardian* newspaper of March 2, 1893, n.p. (NBWM, Folder 1, Folio Shelf 95; reported by Michael P. Dyer):

> MILK IVORY.— *The latest American industry is the manufacture of ivory from milk by the process of coagulation, as in making cheese. The solid portion is mixed with borax, and the mass subjected to high pressure. The resulting product, upon which the curious name of Lactitis has been bestowed, is said to be hard, durable, and well suited for the manufacture of combs, billiard-balls, penholders, pipe mouthpieces, and so forth.*

APPENDIX VII

Sample Sales of Walrus Ivory from the Western Arctic Whale Fishery on the San Francisco Market, 1873-1882

Based on research by Dr. Susan A. Lebo in Honolulu, submitted March 2005.
Source: New Bedford Whaling Museum, Mss 5, S-g3, Series B, S-s1, Box 11, Vol. 4.

Year	Vessel	Item @ Price per Pound and (Remarks)	Total	Page
1873	*Cleone* and *Helen Mar*; etc.	940 lbs walrus ivory sold at San Francisco @ 35¢	$329.00	162
1874	*Camilla*	2125 lbs walrus ivory sold at San Francisco @ 45¢ (Settlement with Captain Palmer)	$956.25	133
1874	*Mt. Wollaston*	253 lbs walrus ivory sold at San Francisco @ 55¢	$139.15	129
1877	*Mt. Wollaston*	716 lbs walrus ivory sold at San Francisco @ 32 ½¢ (Whalebone shipped home via Central Railroad)	$232.70	n/a
1880	*Helen Mar*	2126 lbs walrus ivory sold at San Francisco @ 40¢	$850.40	170
1881	*Helen Mar*	Whale teeth $9.30; walrus ivory $57.60	$66.90	174
1882	*Abbie Bradford*	Skins, walrus ivory &c $434.00; storage bone $2.00; amount paid natives for bone $213.50; amount paid natives for ivory, furs, &c. $108.50 (Settlement of Captain William H. Murphy's voyage*)	$110.00	—
1882	*Helen Mar*	Trade bone $30; walrus ivory sold by Wright & Bowne at San Francisco; 1055 lbs [walrus] ivory sold @ 90¢ (Statement for Helen Mar, Dec. 13, 1882)	$949.50	182
1882	*Helen Mar*	Walrus ivory sold at San Francisco 1000 lbs ivory less 10 lbs trade ivory; thus 990 lbs sold @ $1.10 (Statement for Helen Mar, Dec, 27, 1882)	$1,089.00	183

* Source: Mss 18, Series B, S-s1, Folder 3

APPENDIX VIII

Sperm Whale Teeth in the Fiji Islands

To the Fijians in the eighteenth and nineteenth centuries, the single most valuable and most highly prized possession was the *tabua* (pronounced *TOM-bwa*), a whole, polished sperm whale tooth, drilled at each end to accommodate a braided necklace of sinnet fibre, to be worn as a pendant at tribal council meetings and other ceremonial occasions. *Tabua* were often cryptically incised on one side with seemingly random and ill-formed Latin letters, of which the meaning and significance in this context are unclear even to the Fiji Museum at Suva. Typically, they could become quite beautifully patinated in rich amber hues, resulting from the aromatic smoke of countless council fires. *Tabua* functioned as symbols of social status, wealth, and rank, were used as dowries, as collateral for loans, to secure mortgages and seal other major transactions, as payment for significant debts, as restitution for social transgressions and major crimes, and as ceremonial gifts of the highest order. Accordingly, though whale teeth had little or no value as ivory in Europe or America, up until the end of the Napoleonic era they were a trade commodity in the South Sea whale fishery. Many Yankee whalers hoarded the teeth and returned them as cargoes to New England, where they were sold to China traders, who, in turn, could use them for barter in the South Pacific to obtain such trade commodities as sandalwood and *beche-de-mer* (edible sea slugs) for the Canton market. However, in Commodore David Porter's memoirs, published in 1816 and reissued in 1822, he divulged not only the high value placed on whale teeth by South Sea islanders, but also suggested where and how they could be obtained easily; thus (even though they were not as easily obtained as Porter indicated), a surplus soon developed and the market for teeth declined. (One result was that sperm whale teeth now became widely available to the whalemen themselves, for the first time, for their own handiwork: this was the true genesis of whalemen's scrimshaw. See Stuart M. Frank, "The Origins of Engraved Pictorial Scrimshaw," *The Magazine Antiques*, 142:4 [Oct. 1992], 510-521.)

The Fijians also had two other quite common types of sperm whale tooth necklace. The *wasekaseka* is made from one large tooth, "julienne cut," as it were, lengthwise, into long, narrow, wedge-shaped spikes. These are drilled through at the wider (root) end of each and strung on a cord of sinnet fiber, so that the pointy ends flare out like great claws, arranged with the longest in the middle and the sizes tapering down on each side — fierce- and ferocious-looking, not unlike the (smaller) bear's tooth necklaces of some Plains Indian tribes. The Fijian *wase gale*, on the other hand, is a necklace comprised of several whole teeth of the cow sperm whale, which are substantially smaller than the bull whale teeth used for tabua and wasekaseka: usually between five and eleven of these smaller teeth are drilled at the root end and strung on sinnet fiber, also arranged in order of size, with the longest in the middle and tapering down on each side.

The Fijians were not themselves whale hunters, and prior to the arrival of foreign whalers must have obtained the teeth primarily from stranded carcasses and drift whales. Their appetite for sperm whale teeth for all of these purposes remained strong, and the Fiji Islanders could be depended upon as a market for whale teeth throughout the nineteenth century, even after the China trade market for teeth declined.

Oeno of Nantucket, 1825-28

The Nantucket ship *Oeno*, Captain Samuel Riddell, fitted out for whaling at Edgartown, Martha's Vineyard, and sailed in November 1824. They rounded the Cape of Good Hope in December, intending to cross the Indian Ocean and arrive at the Bay of Islands, New Zealand, the following spring.

> *That was the last heard of her for nearly six years, and it was thought she was lost at sea with all on board. In 1830, however, the owner at Nantucket received a letter from William S. Cary, one of the crew, bringing the startling information that the ship had been lost on Turtle Island and that all of the crew had been massacred by the natives with the exception of himself, and that he was living among the islanders.*

"Turtle Island" is Vatoa, in the Fijis, where the wreck occurred on 5 April 1825 and the massacre a few days later. Cary kept a journal of the voyage which became a detailed diary of his experiences ashore afterwards, "a most graphic description of life among the Feejee Islanders." This became the basis of a serialized narrative published in the *Nantucket Journal* in 1887, which was reissued as *Wrecked in the Feejees: Experience of a Nantucket Man, a Century Ago, Who Was Sole Survivor of Whaleship "Oeno" and Lived for Nine Years Among Cannibals of South Sea Islands* (*Nantucket Inquirer* and *Mirror Press*, 1922; reprinted with an introduction by Harry B. Turner, 1928). This, in turn, appeared as an undated modern edition published by Ye Galleon Press of Fairfield, Washington, described as "One of the true tales left to posterity by the hardy men of Nantucket who went to the far corners of the earth in search of whales."

Among the instances the castaway mentions in which sperm whale teeth figure into what Cary calls "Customs of the Islanders," is that "Sometimes for very great crimes, in addition to [ritual penance] they are required to make liberal presents of whale's teeth. This is in cases of murder or for enticing away another man's wife, which is always visited with the heaviest punishment." (47) On several occasions during his captivity he was recruited to participate in tribal warfare, and in two instances the native use of whale teeth figures importantly. The first was in the heat of battle, where the teeth were part of an attempted peace offering, which failed when the bribe was refused:

> *Our army was composed of about 4,000 warriors, of whom about 100 had muskets... As soon as we drew near enough the enemy attacked us with arrows and showers of stones. We then opened fire with the muskets, which frightened them so that they made offers of peace, offering all their whales' teeth and the chief's daughter, but their offers were declined, and when they found we were going to storm the town they fled to the woods.*

The second was in 1828, when with fellow Nantucketer David Whippey and a few other American and Fijian sailor-castaways Cary was involved in a skirmish for which whale teeth were given in partial payment for their mercenary services:

We soon arrived near the enemy's village... and attacked them with arrows. They returned the attack with interest, adding to their arrows showers of stones which seemed mostly to be directed at me. On account of my having clothes on, they they apparently selected me for a mark.

I had several hairbreadth escapes from their missiles, but fortunately they were escapes. Eight or ten of us who had muskets marched up, dodging behind trees and stumps until within easy musket shot. David, dressed like a native, led our party. He got shelter behind a stump, singles out one of their chief warriors, fired and shot him through the head. As soon as their chief fell the enemy fled for the woods and mountains. Then we rushed forward, broke down their bamboo fence and entered the village. We killed all who had not made their escape, plundered the town and set it on fire, then marched back to Navarto, singing songs of victory. Here we were paid for our services with hogs, turtle, fishing nets and whales' teeth. (68f)

Dan Elias (PEM), who provided the original citation (private communication, 27 Dec. 2006), concludes convincingly that this transaction is at least one clear manifestation of a rare circumstance in which a *tabua* could have been acquired legitimately by a visiting whaleman *from* a Fijian, rather than the other way round (a raw tooth or scrimshawed tooth being traded *to* a Fijian). Thus it helps explain how a precious *tabua* could later become whalemen's scrimshaw — as must have been the otherwise inexplicable case of a Susan's Tooth that was first a *tabua*, was later scrimshawed by Frederick Myrick, and descended in the family of Captain William Swain.

Miverva of Sydney, 1829

The whaleship *Minerva* of Sydney, New South Wales, sailed in August 1829 and was wrecked in the Fiji Islands the next month, some 250 miles southwest of Tonga on what had hitherto been officially known as Nicholson's Shoals and Nicholson's Reef but henceforth came to be known to mariners as Minerva Reef. The castaways took to the boats and eventually fetched up on Turtle Island — Vatoa — the same island where the *Oeno* crew had been marooned and massacred four and a half years earlier. Two of the *Minerva* men produced narratives of the shipwreck and their several months' sojourn ashore in its aftermath. Both accounts — *A Narrative of the Wreck of the Minerva*, by Peter Pays, Sailing Master (Cambridge, England, 1831); and *Shipwreck and Adventures of John P. Twyning [Boatsteerer] among the South Sea Islanders* (London, 1849) — shed light on Fijian and Tongalese attitudes, customs, and practices. Twyning's narrative is especially informative regarding sperm whale teeth in Fijian culture (quoted here from a modern combined edition of the two narratives, entitled *Wreck of the Minerva*, introduced by Kieth Huntress and published in 1996 by Ye Galleon Press at Fairfield, Washington):

We often received presents of turtle shell, sennett [plant fibre], and other articles from the natives, in return for various things we did for them, and these we again exchanged for whale's teeth, which are important articles among the natives of the Feegee Islands, who not only used them as money, but pay them a kind of religious homage. After I had been sometime in the island, I obtained the possession of a very large tooth. Tooinehow [High Chief or "king" of the Lau Group] wished to have it and offered me a large pig for it. But the next day, when I took the tooth to him, I found that the pig he promised me had been killed. He then offered me an-

other, but a much smaller one. I refused to take it, and kept the tooth. This was bad policy in me, so it so vexed the king that he turned from me muttering something I did not understand; but a native soon took the opportunity of informing me that that the king was so highly incensed at my refusing to give him the tooth, that he had given orders to a Friendly Islander [Fijian] in his service to waylay me and take my life, when out among the Islands. In this emergency I applied to a Tongatabu chief named Maula Newballave ... much esteemed by Tooinehow, and one in whom he placed great confidence... I was therefore fortunate in being able to induce this important person to become my mediator. After hearing my case, he asked me for the tooth, and having given it to him, he told me to follow him to the king. Having arrived at the king's house, we were immediately admitted into his presence, when Maula Newballave presented the tooth to him, and asked him if that was the cause of his order to kill the king of Tonga's relation, he called me thus to indicate that that monarch had embraced Christianity, and that as I was a Christian, he called me his relation. Tooinehow hung his head in being thus spoken to, and replied, that he had been angry with the white man, but it had subsided now, and he was willing to forgive him. I excused myself, by relating our European mode of making bargains, and told him I should be happy to make him a present of the tooth. Maula Newballave immediately tabooed me, that is, adopted me as his son, and gave me the name Maula-tare, i.e., the White Captain. This was to me a great protection, for none after this could offer me any injury without incurring the enmity, and rendering himself liable to the revenge of so influential a chief. The king immediately pardoned my offense, and our reconciliation was cemented by drinking kava together. (46f)

We went to the king and presented him with a musket and a whale's tooth, [and] asked his permission to build a Schooner. He gave his consent freely, and promised to provide us with provisions during its construction. (52)

Tarnore, the king of Anbow ["a small rocky island"] arrived at Lakembo [in the Lau group] with a fleet of twenty one war canoes, manned with his warriors. ["They styled themselves warriors, but they were in reality a band of robbers subsisting on the plunder which they obtained from other chiefs, exacting it under the pretext of affording them protection against the attacks of other, less powerful chiefs than himself."] The bustle and excitement consequent on his arrival presented a very handsome and imposing spectacle… An assembly of the chiefs was convened, and preparations were made to solemnize [Tarnore's] coronation with as much pomp as possible. A large piece of tapper [tapa] cloth was manufactured for the occasion. It was almost twenty yards long and three yards wide. This was spread on the ground on an immense plain… Tarnore was placed in the center of this large carpet, and was attended by two priests who were to conduct the ceremony. Baskets were placed near him, filled with rolls of tapper cloth, sennett balls, and whale's teeth, which were to be presented to him. The whale's teeth were by the priests hung on all parts of his body; on his neck and arms, and in such profusion that he staggered under the weight of them. This loading him with riches was the sign of his being acknowledged the head of all chiefs… He soon freed himself from the burden, and let the teeth fall from his arms into the baskets, and at the end of the ceremony, he distributed these riches among his chiefs and warriors." (54f)

USS *Tuscarora*, 1867

The Friend was a weekly newspaper intended primarily for sailors, published by the Oahu Bethel Church at Honolulu beginning in the late 1830s, with the support of the American Seamen's Friend Society in New York. It had a very wide circulation among whalemen in the Pacific and among English-speaking mariners generally around the world. An anonymous article in an April 1868 issue reveals the extraordinarily high official esteem in which whale teeth were held in Fiji (submitted by Michael P. Dyer):

> *FAMOUS WHALE'S TOOTH FROM THE FIJI ISLANDS. — When the United States steamship Tuscarora, Capt. Stanley, visited Honolulu a few months since, he exhibited this famous tooth. We have no doubt, in the estimation of King Thakombau, that tooth is of equal importance to the 'great seal' of other nations. We copy the following from a late American paper* [1867]:
>
> *"The treaty with the Fiji Islands has reached the Department of State. It is a whale's tooth, richly variegated in color, with strongly twisted grass at the end. By it the King mortgages his islands to the United States for three years as security for payment of the remaining installments of indemnity on account of his subjects having eaten some American sailors many years ago. The President is to prevent the rival King from bringing war against the legitimate sovereign of the Fijis. The King's instructions are that if the President accepts the tooth, the treaty is to be considered established, otherwise it's to be returned."* (*The Friend*, New Series Vol. 18 [Old Series Vol. 15], No. 4, 1, Honolulu, April 1868)

APPENDIX IX

Bartering Sperm Whale Teeth in Polynesia

In his journal of a whaling voyage in the ship *George Home* of London under Captain Thomas James, the ship's steward, Edward Harris, relates two instances of bartering sperm whale teeth. On 9 November 1833, just off Hurd Island (in the Kingsmill Group of the Gilbert and Ellis Islands; now in Kiribati), they had an all-afternoon-and-evening gam with the American whaleship William Penn of Falmouth — actually their fourth in three weeks. This time, Captain Swain and a boat crew from the William Penn went aboard the George Home, while the chief mate of the George Home and his boat crew went on the William Penn. They "stopped until late when each returned to their Respective Ships," after which "Canoes came off [the island] and brought Mats, Cocoa Nuts &c which we purchased for Iron Hoop, Whale Teeth &c."[2]

A few months later, on 17 April 1834, at Agrihan Island in the Marianas (Ladrones), Captain James and the second mate "went on Shore to try to get some fresh Provisions." They returned two hours later "with some Pigs and 4 of the Natives." These were not natives of this particular island, but were among the 21 castaways living on Agrihan — twelve men and nine women — who a few years previous had been blown off course and set adrift at sea. They were rescued on May 1831 by the whaleship *Rambler* of Nantucket, Captain William Worth II, who found them in very poor condition. Later, presumably after they were somewhat restored to health, the *Rambler* put them ashore on Agrihan with "a few articles that he thought would be useful to them" — and this evidently enabled them to set up a livelihood bartering with visiting mariners:

> *... with the help of a Dog they have they catch Wild Pigs & Pen them up and sell them to any Ships for Cutting Articles such as Axes, Knives, Whales teeth, Fish Hooks, Chisels, Iron Hoops &c. They gave us 5 Pigs for a Axe and one for a Whales tooth etc. We got off this Day 28 Pigs and all for about the Work of £7 in England.*

[2] Journal in the collection of the Littlehampton Museum, West Sussex, Kent, United Kingdom, transcribed by Mrs. Christobel Smith, and stored in the archive of Canterbury Cathedral; courtesy of Anne Savours Shirley.

APPENDIX X

Nineteenth-Century Ivory Dealers

Nineteenth-century wholesale and retail dealers in ivory, and in goods made of ivory, tended to trade not only in elephant ivory but also in marine ivories. The species is not always clear on their lists of wares, and the designation "ivory" cannot be presumed always to signify "elephant ivory unless otherwise indicated." One prominent New York ivory merchant placed the following full-page advertisement in the 1843-44 *City Directory*, illustrated with a broadside woodcut vignette of an Indian elephant with uncommonly large tusks, standing on a riverbank jungle foliage and palm trees:

MANUFACTORY
OF
IVORY BILLIARD BALLS, TEN PIN BALLS AND PINS, &C.
(Sign of the Golden Elephant.)
J O H N   P H Y F E,
DEALER IN
IVORY, AND MANUFACTURER OF IVORY GOODS,
No. 19 Murray Street

The many items offered for sale specifically include: ivory billiard, pool, bagatelle, and roulette balls; "ivory checks [checkers game pieces] in great variey, of new and fancy patterns"; ivory dominoes in rosewood and mahogany cases; ivory backgammon men and dice boxes, both "richly carved and plain"; fancy wooden card boxes, both "highly ornamented and plain"; ivory martingale rings and miniature sheets; ivory writing tablets; ivory paper folders and page markers; ivory teething rings and whistles; piano ivory, "well dried and put up in sets of different qualities; "ebony sharps" (that is, wooden "black" piano keys, to go with the ivory white keys); ivory ten-pin balls, "a new and splendid article"; lignum vitae ten-pin balls; hardwood ten pins; also, notably: "SCRIVELLA IVORY, SEA-HORSE and WHALE TEETH, BOXWOOD, EBONY, COCOA, SATIN, and other Hard Woods." *Scrivello* ivory is elephant ivory; *sea-horse* teeth are walrus tusks; and *whale teeth* are sperm whale teeth.

John Phyfe (circa 1797-1872), a New York native of Scottish ancestry, was one of six brothers, some of whom were from time to time associated with him in business. The U.S. Census lists his occupation as "Ivory Turner" (1850) and "Manufacturer" (1860). He married Jane McNeish, born in Scotland, the daughter of John and Janet (Drisdale) McNeish; and by 1870 he was a widower, retired and living on a farm at Westfield, on Staten Island, with one of his daughters doing the housekeeping.

Phyfe was neither the first nor the only ivory dealer to stock a line of goods that included marine ivory. Those whose names have survived most visibly were the ones who were (among other things) toy- and game-makers — such as colonial merchant-artisan Charles Shipman of New York City, active in the 1760s as a dealer in ivory and wooden billiard balls, cups, balls, drumsticks, alphabet cubes, chessmen, backgammon pieces, and game markers; J. Ruthven, another

Scot in New York City, a metal, wood, and ivory turner, who produced billiard balls, bagatelle balls and cups, teething rings, whistles, and drumsticks, circa 1820; the James H. Hawes Manufacturing Company, makers of ivory and wooden toys in both Towanda, Pennsylvania and New York City in the 1840s, Newark, New Jersey in the 1850s, and Pennsylvania again from the 1860s on; S.M. Comstock & Co., active as "ivory fabricators" in Centerbrook, Connecticut, in the 1850s, who appear to have specialized in brushes and combs for dolls; and Edward Kelsey, who produced dominoes, ivory novelties, doll accessories, and toys in the 1860s, also in Centerbrook, Connecticut (www.toyhistory.com/thelist.html).

In New Bedford in the 1870s and '80s, William H. Cook and James Mackie were partners in Wm. H. Cook & Co. Cook, an Englishman born circa 1819, was married to a woman named Lydia from New Hampshire. Mackie was born in Ireland circa 1830; his wife Adeline was a Massachusetts native. The U.S. Census lists them as "junk dealers," but the partners were more explicit, referring to themselves as "Dealers in all kinds of Paper Stock, Old Iron, Brass, Copper, Lead & Pewter." Their printed sales receipts also took pains to advertise, in fancy typefaces enclosed in an ornately engraved frame of ribbands and leafy floral motifs, "Whale's Teeth, Walrus Tusks, &c." as well as "Old Ships Bought & Sold."

The presumption is that if these dealers had even a small market for whale teeth and walrus tusks, there must have been standard uses to which these materials were put, perhaps in preference to other types of ivory, perhaps as substitutes for elephant ivory (which was presumably costlier), perhaps by professional artisans and cottage-industry practitioners, irrespective of any maritime connections the makers may have had.

Ivory makers of various kinds are named in the directories of cities and towns all across nineteenth-century America. Likewise in England and Scotland, perhaps most notably in London, Birmingham, Glasgow, and Edinburgh, where compilations from the 1830s onward have surprisingly numerous listings for such narrowly defined trades as "ivory box and caddee [sic] maker," "ivory turner," "bone and ivory turner," "bone and ivory toy and fancy brush maker," "pocket ruler manufacturer," "box and ivory rule maker," and so on. The occupations specified for defendants and victims in the Proceedings of the Old Bailey, London's famous law court, include ivory brushmaker, ivory spoon-maker, ivory turner, ivory-turning and hardwood-turning, and whalebone merchant — along with the (non-specific) designations "box-maker," "brush-maker," "brush turner," "rule-maker," etc. The degree to which whale ivory, walrus ivory, or marine mammal skeletal bone may have been used in any of these manifestations is nowhere disclosed in the product descriptions, but whale ivory, walrus ivory, and marine mammal bone are sometimes unmistakably evident in the surviving products themselves, such as cane handles and pommels, billiard balls, tool handles, umbrella handles, brushes, candle snuffers, and ornaments for furniture.

APPENDIX XI

A Nineteenth-Century Baleen Dealer

James A. Sevey of Boston was a prominent dealer in baleen ("whalebone") and a maker of finished baleen products. He also held at least one patent on planing tools used in his esoteric trade. To the right is his 1878 wholesale price list for unfinished, cut-and-polished strips of baleen — raw materials offered in quantity in a wide range of sizes, from which to manufacture a variety of finished goods. On the back (next page) is a list of his own line of whalebone products, which both in number and in diversity exemplify the multiple applications of baleen at the height of American whaling in the Western Arctic. Sevey was born in Maine between 1809 and 1820, and married twice: to Mary Woodruff, who bore him seven children, all born in Washington County, Maine; then to Fannie Ford (1834-1901), whom he wed in Boston in 1861. In 1880 the Seveys were living in Boston with one daughter and Fannie's younger brother, a railway station agent.

LIST PRICES
H
DRESS WHALEBONE.
JULY 1, 1878.
J. A. SEVEY,
No. 40 Essex Street - - - - - - - - - Boston.
FOR SIZES 1 to 10, AS FOLLOWS:

	SIZE 1.	SIZE 2.	SIZE 3.	SIZE 4.	SIZE 5.	SIZE 6.	SIZE 7.	SIZE 8.	SIZE 9.	SIZE 10.
Inch.	Narrow, Ex. Finish.	1-4 in. wide, Ex. Finish.	5-16 in. wide, Ex. Finish.	3-8 in. wide, Ex. Finish.	5-16 in. wide, Finished.	5-16 in. wide, Ex. Finish.	5-16 in. wide, Heavy.	5-16 in. wide, Ex. Heavy.	3-8 in. wide, Heavy.	3-8 in. wide, Ex. Finish.
8	1.10	1.35	1.65	2.00	1.80	2.00	1.90	2.20	1.90	2.55
9	1.20	1.55	1.85	2.20	2.00	2.20	2.25	2.60	2.25	2.80
10	1.35	1.75	2.05	2.55	2.30	2.55	2.65	3.00	2.65	3.20
11	1.55	1.90	2.25	2.90	2.65	2.90	3.05	3.50	3.10	3.50
12	1.75	2.15	2.45	3.30	3.00	3.30	3.45	3.95	3.50	3.85
13	1.90	2.25	2.65	3.55	3.15	3.55	3.80	4.30	3.80	4.25
14	2.05	2.45	2.80	3.85	3.50	3.85	4.10	4.60	4.10	4.60
15	2.20	2.65	3.00	4.10	3.75	4.10	4.40	4.95	4.40	4.90
16	2.40	2.85	3.30	4.35	4.00	4.35	4.65	5.35	4.65	5.20
17	2.65	3.00	3.50	4.65	4.25	4.65	5.00	5.60	4.95	5.55
18	2.75	3.25	3.80	4.90	4.45	4.90	5.20	6.00	5.35	5.85
19	2.90	3.40	3.95	5.20	4.75	5.20	5.55	6.30	5.60	6.15
20	3.10	3.65	4.10	5.45	4.90	5.45	5.90	6.65	5.95	6.55
21	3.25	3.80	4.35	5.70	5.15	5.70	6.10	6.95	6.15	6.80
22	3.45	4.00	4.55	6.00	5.45	6.00	6.45	7.30	6.55	7.15
23	3.55	4.20	4.80	6.20	5.70	6.20	6.70	7.65	6.75	7.40
24	3.75	4.40	5.00	6.55	6.00	6.55	6.95	7.95	7.05	7.75
36		7.20	8.35	10.85	8.95	10.85			12.30	

Per inch. Per inch.
Gross 1-4 in. wide, 21 quality, .12 1-4 in. wide, 18 gauge. .23
" 1-4 " No. 1, 21 gauge, .11 5-16 " 18 " .24
" 1-4 " " 1, 19 " .15½ 3-8 " 18 " .29
10 to 14 " 5-16 " Stay Bone, 16 " .27½ 3-8 " S'y Bone, 16 " .34

24 Gross 1-4 in. wide, 19 gauge, 5.40, 5-16 in. wide, 18 gauge, 8.30, 3-8 in. wide, 17 gauge, 10.70
30 " 1-4 " 19 " 6.70, 5-16 " 18 " 10.10, 3-8 " 17 " 13.45
31 " 1-4 " 19 " 7.40, 5-16 " 18 " 11.10, 3-8 " 17 " 14.75
36 " 1-4 " 19 " 8.30, 5-16 " 18 " 12.75, 3-8 " 17 " 17.00
42 " 1-4 " 19 " 9.45, 5-16 " 18 " 14.00, 3-8 " 17 " 18.70
48 " 1-4 " 19 " 10.85, 5-16 " 18 " 16.25, 3-8 " 17 " 20.50

Per inch. Per inch.
12 to 36 Gross Round Dress, light, .38, Bdls. 1-8 to 3-16 in. wide, White Dress Bone, .21
" " " medium, .48, " 1-4 " " " " .37
" " " heavy, .58, " 5-16 " " " " .42

Copyright, by J. A. Sevey.

ARTICLES MADE OF WHALEBONE
BY
J. A. SEVEY,
40 Essex Street - - - - Boston.

No.
1. Whip Makers' Bone.
2. Whip Makers' Bone (Patent).
3. Parasol Makers' Bone.
4. Umbrella Makers' Bone.
5. Gross Dress Bone.
6. Samples to sell by.
7. Dress Bone in Boxes.
8. Round Dress Bone.
9. White Dress Bone.
10. Corset Makers' Bone.
11. Corset, showing Place of Bone.
12. Corset Clasps.
13. Hip Busk Bone.
14. Cap Makers' Bone.
15. Hat Makers' Bone.
16. Whalebone Hats.
17. Ribbon Weavers' Bone.
18. Suspender Makers' Bone.
19. Neck Stock Makers' Bone.
20. Bonnet Makers' Shurs.
21. Whalebone Canes.
22. Whalebone Riding Whips.
23. Whalebone Rosettes.
24. Ribbon Bone.
25. Billiard Cushion Springs.
26. Fishing Rod (New Style).
27. Fishing Rod Tips.
28. Landing Rods for Nets.
29. Divining Rods.
30. Drill Bows.
31. Ferules.
32. Busks.
33. Back Supporters.
34. Fore Arm Bones.
35. Probangs.
36. Tongue Scrapers.
37. Pen Holders.
38. Plait Raisers.
39. Paper Folder and Cutters.
40. Painters' Graining Combs.
41. Boot Shanks.
42. Shoe Horns.
43. Bone Fibre Shoe Brushes.
44. Fibre of Whalebone.
45. Fibre Curled for Beds.
46. Brush Makers' Bone.
47. Flue Brushes.
48. Caterpillar Brushes.
49. Whalebone Shavings for Beds.
50. Policeman's Clubs.
51. All Bone Whips.
52. Twisted Whip Handles.

53. Rio Corset Bone, all lengths and sizes.

Copyright, by J. A. Sevey.

APPENDIX XII

Twentieth-Century Scrimshaw Artisans of the Azores Islands and Madeira

Unlike the American and British whale fisheries, where occupational practitioners of scrimshaw were characteristically far away at sea on three- and four-year voyages, in the Azores the lines were not so finely drawn between those who went whaling and those who stayed home. With the exception of a handful of deepwater voyages from Horta, on Fayal, Azorean whaling was a shore fishery prosecuted in elongated Yankee-type whaleboats within sight of the home islands. It was a part-time, supplementary, seasonal pursuit of men whose principal livelihoods mostly lay elsewhere. They were farmers, fishers, artisans, boatbuilders, and shopkeepers who slept at home every night in their own beds. Not only was Azorean scrimshandering practiced ashore, but the wider community was more centrally involved, several skillful practitioners in recent generations have been able to make an actual living at it, some of them were casually or formally apprenticed as artisans under the supervision of more experienced carvers and engravers, a few even received formal training from credentialed art teachers on the Portuguese mainland, and in the late twentieth century the roster increasingly included women. American occupational scrimshaw came to an end with the demise of the Yankee whaling industry in 1927, but whaling continued in the Azores into the 1980s, and occupationally-rooted scrimshaw along with it. Traditions and conventions were handed down the generations in an unbroken continuum and have continued into the twenty-first century.

João António Gomes Vieira, an Azorean sailor, artist, historian, and collector, has endeavored to document the community of scrimshaw-makers in the Portuguese islands, both in the Azores and Madeira. While only those who were principally and vocationally engaged in whaling are given articles in this volume, it is appropriate here to mention those twentieth-century practitioners in the Azores and a few from Madeira who were legitimate, occupationally-rooted practitioners, whether or not they were direct participants in the whale fishery itself.

The best known and among the most accomplished are the late Frank Barcelos, whose engraved teeth span a wide spectrum of subjects and styles and are celebrated on his native Terceira, throughout the Islands, and in New Bedford and Fall River, where he worked for many years (his scrimshaw is widely represented in institutional and private collections in the USA, the Azores, and Europe); Fatima Madruga, noted for her magnificently engraved portraiture and fine Azorean genre scenes (and whose work is absent from private and institutional collections in North America and Australia only because of international prohibitions on the importation of modern ivory); and Juvenal Castro, an art teacher still (in 2008) very active on his native Terceira, whose engraved whaling scenes and ship portraits are among the Islands' most original and dramatic (and who has likewise suffered from lack of wider exposure because of legal restrictions on ivory).

The following list (which excludes living artists) is based on Gomes Vieira's *Man and the Sea: Portuguese Scrimshaw Artists in Whale Tooth Ivory and Bone / The Azores and Madeira — Their Lives and Works* (Lisbon, 2003). The artists are listed alphabetically by patronymic surname, followed by given name, matrilineal surname (where relevant), occupation (where known), island of origin, other relevant places of residence, and page references in Gomes Vieira's book [in brackets]. Where no occupation is specified the artist may be presumed to have made a living (or attempted to do so) by his or her art. A select few, by reason of their direct vocational involvement in the whale fishery itself, are represented by articles in this volume. An asterisk (*) indicates that there is a biographical sketch in the *Dictionary of Scrimshaw Artists;* a dagger (†) signifies a biographical sketch in the present volume.

Alberto, Adalberto Carlos (1938-1992). Island of Pico; eventually emigrated to California. [65]

Alves Soares, João (1919-1964). Whaler, fisherman, and telegraph engineer on Pico. [125]

André, Gregório Luís (1932-1990). Soldier, coast guardman, and artisan on Corvo, later working at Taunton, Massachusetts [119]

Ávila, Manuel Gualberto (1933-2000). Cattle breeder and maker of dental prosthetics on Pico. [173]

Barcelos, Francisco José Borges [Frank Barcelos] (1926-1993). Renowned scrimshaw artist from Terceira, later active at New Bedford and Fall River, Massachusetts. Some of his rare early work on whale ivory is highly symbolic, executed in vivid polychrome with engraved surfaces pigmented with bright primary colors, including heraldic, commemorative, and souvenir pieces. His mature work tends more towards representational whaling scenes and genre subjects, and in his later years he produced quite a lot of jewelry and pictorial works on a miniature scale. [111]

Belo, Roberto Bettencourt de (1956-2000). Terceira. [189]

† **Corvelo**, António C. (1879-1920). New Bedford whaling captain from Flores. [74]

Costa, António (1897-1985). Cabinetmaker on Fayal; later emigrated to Richmond, California (Richmond is where the last American whaling station was operating until 1972). [75]

Costa, António, Jr. (1929-1998). Electrician/mechanic on Fayal; later emigrated to San Pablo, California. [77]

Cunha, Manuel de Paiva e (1910-1987). Scrimshaw artist and forger on Madeira. Despite their clandestine origin, his engraved teeth are much sought after and highly collectible. (See Joshua Basseches, *Scrimshaw of Manuel Cunha,* 1988.) [165]

† **da Rosa**, Clarence Moniz (1911-1966). Launch engineer at a shore-whaling station on Pico. [99]

da Silva Geraldes, Jordão José (1926-1992). Fayal. [141]

† **de Carvalho**, Celestino Amorim [Celestino Ernesto] (1906-1995). Foreman of a whaling station on Flores; emigrated to New Bedford in the 1920s. [96]

de Freitas Henriques, Ângelo (1914-1991). Jeweler and watchmaker on Flores. [72]

† **Edwards**, Antonio T. [António Tomaz Eduardo] (1882-1936). New Bedford whaling master from Fajazinha, on Flores. [85]

† **Edwards**, Joseph T. [José Tomaz Eduardo] (1857-1913). New Bedford whaling master from Fajazinha, on Flores. [158]

Fagundes, Manuel Daniel (1949-2000). Pico. [168]

Fernandes Leal, João [João Flores] (1919-1996). Pico. [133]

† **Fernandes Silva**, Ernesto [Ernesto Flores] (1906-1987). Whaling-launch engineer on Pico. [105]

† **Fidalgo Baptista**, José Francisco (1841-1929). New Bedford whaling master from Pico. [152]

Garcia da Rosa, João Ladislau (1903-1982). Mechanic on Fayal, later at Oporto on the Portuguese mainland. [135]

Garcia da Silva, Francisco [Francisco Formiga] (1922-1977). Pico. [109]

Garcia da Silva, José [José Formiga] (1916-2000). Pico. [155]

Garcia da Silva, Manuel [Manuel Formiga] (1913-1985). Pico; Fayal. [171]

Gomes Francisco, José Augusto (1931-2003). Artisan and shopkeeper on São Miguel, originally from Cova da Piedade on the mainland. [144]

† **Lacerda**, João Soares (1887-1975). Whaling station manager and dentist on Pico. [138]

Loureiro, António Teles de Lima de Silveira (1927-1999). Civil servant, São Jorge. [79]

Machado Alves, Albino (1914-1990). Whaler, Pico. [69]

Moniz Barreto, Gualter (1936-1990). Artisan, Pico. [120]

Pereira, José Dias [José Boquilha] (1902-1982). Soldier and artisan, Graciosa. [148]

Pereira Goulart, António [António Cebola] (1876-1964). Carpenter and sailor living successively on Pico and at Horta, on Fayal. [84]

Pereira Goulart, António [António Sabão] (1916-1972). Cabinetmaker, Pico. [85]

Pimentel, Constantino (1923-). Blacksmith, Flores. [100]

Pimentel, Francisco José (III) [Francisco Capitão Novo] (1915-1988). Carpenter, blacksmith, and boatbuilder on Flores. [116]

Pimentel, Francisco José, Jr. [Francisco Capitão] (1882-1957). Evidently an unusually versatile artisan in his time, he was known as the "Man of Seven Crafts." Flores. [118]

Pimentel, José Francisco (1920-). Lighthouse keeper, Flores. [153]

† **Quaresma**, Manuel Rodrigues, Jr. (1905-1982). Whaling station manager on Pico. [177]

Raposo dos Santos, Aníbal (1922-2001). Policeman, São Miguel. [73]

Ribeiro de Carvalho, Ernesto (1869-1937). Civil servant, cabinetmaker on Flores. [106]

Rodrigues Vieira, Manuel (1925-1994). Sailor and local whaleman, Flores. [179]

Silveira, Orthon Rosa de (1940-1987). Fayal; later living at New Bedford and Fall River. [185]

Silveira da Rosa Bettencourt, Patrício (1934-1997). "Road-mender," São Jorge. [188]

Simas, Manuel Francisco (fl. 1960s-). Ponta Garça, São Miguel. Lived for many years in East Providence, Rhode Island, worked in a Massachusetts factory nearby, later returned to the Islands.

Soares, Dimas José Alves (1929-1996). Stonemason and sculptor, Pico. [103]

Soares, João Baptista Alves [João da Armanda] (1928-2002). Cabinetmaker and musician on Pico, later emigrated to Canada. [128]

* **Vieira**, Nicolau Rodrigues (1856-1913). New Bedford whaling master from Flores. [183]

Vieira Soares, Manuel, Jr. (1916-1972). Whaler and artisan, Pico. [181]

CUMULATIVE LIST OF BIOGRAPHICAL SKETCHES

References are to the three volumes: (i) *Dictionary of Scrimshaw Artists*, (ii) *More Scrimshaw Artists*, and (iii) *Scrimshaw and Provenance*

T

V

W

Y

Z

BIBLIOGRAPHY

Adams, James Truslow. *History of the Town of Southampton.* Bridgehampton, New York: Hampton Press, 1918.

Afonso, João. "Marfinos do mar: Enquanto a Baleia não surgia—a pequena arte dos baleeiros." *Panorama: Revista de Arte e Turismo,* 22:4 (June 1967), 65-68.

Agard, Charles Walter. MS papers in KNB and NBWM, including interviews with veteran whaling masters and whaling wives, and essays on various historical topics, 1883-1913.

Amaral, Pat. *They Ploughed the Seas: Profiles of Azorean Master Mariners.* St. Petersburg, Florida: Valkyrie Press, 1978.

The American Neptune. Special Issue on the Frederick Myrick Symposium (1998), 60:4 (Fall 2000), passim.

[Anonymous.] "Canton Wreck Recalled Here by U.S. Action." *New Bedford Standard Times,* Apr. 3, 1938.

[Anonymous.] "Prominent Russians: Semyon Dezhnyov, 1605-1672." russiapedia.rt.com/ prominent-russians/exploring-russia/ semyon-dezhnyov/

[Anonymous.] "'Scrimshaw': Hvalfangernes hvaltannarbeider /Scrimshaw: Whaling Men's Work in Whale Teeth.'" *Norsk Hvalfangst Tidende,* 45:2 (Feb. 1956), 61-65.

Arral, Herb. "Acushnet man survived 49 days in an open boat." *New Bedford Standard Times,* Apr. 18. 1972.

Ash, Christopher. *Whaler's Eye.* New York: Macmillan, 1962.

Ashley, Clifford W. *The Yankee Whaler.* Garden City, New York: Halcyon House. [1926] 1942.

Atlanta Constitution. Columbus, Georgia, society column, Feb. 13, 1910.

Attwater, George. *The Journal of George Attwater before the mast on the whaleship Henry of New Haven, 1820-23.* Kevin S. Reilly, ed. New Haven: New Haven Colony Historical Society, 2002.

Bain, R. Nisbet. "Peter the Great and His Pupils," *Cambridge Modern History,* 1903, Ch. 17.

Ball, Robert W.D. *Nautical Antiques.* Atglen, Pennsylvania: Schiffer, 1994.

[Ballou, Maturin Murray.] *Fanny Campbell, The Female Pirate, by Lieutenant Murray.* Boston: F. Gleason, 1845.

Banks, Charles Edward. *The History of Martha's Vineyard, Duke's County, Massachusetts.* 3 vols. Boston: George H. Dean, 1911.

Barbeau, Marius. "All Hands Aboard Scimshawing." *The American Neptune,* 12:2 (April 1952); repr. Salem, Massachusetts: Peabody Museum, 1966.

Barnes, Clare, Jr. *John F. Kennedy, Scrimshaw Collector.* Boston and Toronto: Little, Brown, 1964.

Bartley, Theodore D. *Life on a Canal Boat: The Journals of Theodore D. Bartley, 1861-1889.* Russell P. Bellico, ed. Fleischmanns, New York: Purple Mountain Press and the Lake Champlain Maritime Museum, 2004.

Basseches, Joshua. 1988. *Scrimshaw of Manuel Cunha: Late Work from Madeira Revealed* (Kendall Whaling Museum Monograph N° 2, Sharon, Massachusetts).

____________.; and Stuart M. Frank. *Edward Burdett, 1805-1833: America's First Master Scrimshaw Artist.* Kendall Whaling Museum Monograph Series N° 5, 1991.

Bayles, Richard M. "Town of Haddam," in *The History of Middlesex County* (q.v.), 368-417.

Beane, Joshia Fillebrown. *From Forecastle to Cabin: The Story of a cruise in many seas, taken from a journal kept each day, wherein was recorded the happenings of a voyage around the world in pursuit of whales.* New York: Editor Pubishing Co, 1905.

Benfey, Christopher. *The Great Wave: Gilded Age Misfits, Japanese Eccentrics, and the Opening of Old Japan.* New York: Random House, 2003.

Bennett, Judith A. "Logging Labor on Vanikoro, Solomon Islands: The Achievements of 'The Most Feeble In The Commercial World,' 1923-1964," *Pacific Studies,* 19:2 (June 1996).

Bernard, Donald R. *The Life and Times of Manjiro.* New York: McGraw-Hill, 1992.

Bertão, David E. *The Portuguese Shore Whalers of California, 1854-1904.* San Jose, California: Portuguese Heritage Publications, 2006.

Berton, Pierre. *The Arctic Grail.* New York: Viking, 1988.

Biographical Cyclopedia of Representative Men of Rhode Island, L.E. Rogers, ed. New York: National Biographical Publishing Co., 1881.

Biographical Review, Containing Life Sketches of Leading Citizens of Plymouth County, Massachusetts. Boston: Biographical Review Publishing Co., 1897.

Blasdale, Mary Jean. *Artists of New Bedford: A Biographical Dictionary.* New Bedford: Old Dartmouth Historical Society, 1990.

Bockstoce, John R. *Furs and Frontiers in the Far North: The Contest among Native and Foreign Nations for the Bering Strait Fur Trade.* New Haven: Yale University Press, 2009.

____________. *Steam Whaling in the Western Arctic.* With contributions by William A. Baker and Charles F. Batchelder. New Bedford: Old Dartmouth Historical Society, 1977.

____________. *Whales, Ice, and Men: The History of Whaling in the Western Arctic.* Seattle and London: University of Washington Press, 1986.

Bodfish, Hartson H. *Chasing the Bowhead.* "As told to" Joseph C. Allen. Cambridge: Harvard University Press, 1936.

Borden, K. Ethel. "Northward 1903-04." *Canadian Geographic Journal,* 50:1 (Jan. 1961), 35.

Bowen, Abel. *The Naval Monument.* Boston, 1816 and 1831.

Brewington, Dorothy E.R. *Dictionary of Marine Artists.* Salem, Massachusetts: Peabody Museum, 1982.

Brower, Charles D. *Fifty Years Below Zero: A Lifetime of Adventure in the Far North.* In collaboration with Philip J. Farrelly and Kyman Anson. New York: Dodd, Mead, 1942.

Browne, J. Ross. *Etchings of a Whaling Cruise.* New York, 1846. (Repr. ed. by John Seelye, Cambridge: The Belknap Press of Harvard University Press, 1968.)

Burns, Rosemary H. "Popponesset by the Sea," undated, in *Mashpee Commons Courier,* 2004.

Butsch, Richard. *The Making of American Audiences.* Cambridge University Press, 2000.

Calabretta, Fred. "Captain George Comer and the Arctic." *The Log of Mystic Seaport,* 35:4 (Winter 1984), 118-31.

Caldwell, Sir James. Bart. *Debates Relative to the Affairs of Ireland, In the Years 1763 and 1764.* London: privately printed, 1766.

California Academy of Sciences. [Robert Mayokok, Eskimo artist] http://research.calacademy.org/research/anthropology/eskimo/mayokok.htm

Carpenter, Charles H., Jr.; and Mary Grace Carpenter. *The Decorative Arts and Crafts of Nantucket.* New York: Dodd Mead, 1987.

Carr, Arthur A. *The Carr Book.* New York: Toconderoga, 1947.

Cheever, Rev. Henry T. *The Whale and His Captors; or The Whaleman's Adventures, and the Whale's Biography.* New York: Harper, 1850; and London: Thos. Nelson & Sons, 1851.

Chang, Jack H.T. xxx

Cliff, Nigel. *The Shakespeare Riots: Revenge, Drama, and Death in Nineteenth-Century America.* New York: Random House, 2007.

Colby, Barnard. *Oil and Buggy Whips: Whaling Captains of New London.* Mystic, Connecticut: Mystic Seaport, 1990.

Crapo, W.W. *Representative Men of Southeastern Massachusetts.* Chicago: J.H. Beers & Co., 1912

Crawford, Mary Carline. *The Romance of the American Theatre.* New York: Halcyon, 1940.

Creighton, Margaret. *Dogwatch and Liberty Days: Seafaring Life in the Nineteenth Century.* Salem, Massachusetts: Peabody Museum, 1982.

Croce, George C.; and David H. Wallace. *The New York Historical Society's Dictionary of Artists in America, 1564 1860.* New Haven: Yale University Press, 1957.

Cutler, Carl C. *Greyhounds of the Sea: The Story of the American Clipper Ship.* [New York, 1930.] Annapolis: U.S. Naval Institute. 1967.

____________. *Queens of the Western Ocean: The Story of America's Mail and Passenger Sailing Lines.* Annapolis: U.S. Naval Institute, 1961.

Cyr, Paul A., compiler. *The 1860 Census of Acushnet, Massachusetts.* Acushnet Historical Socoety, 1985.

Debates Relative to the Affairs of Ireland, In the Years 1763 and 1764. Issued anonymously and privately printed, London, 1766.

Decker, Robert Owen. Whaling Industry of New London. York, Pennsylvania: Liberty Cap, 1973.

Deyo, Simeon L., ed.. *History of Barnstable County, Massachusetts.* New York: H. W. Blake & Co., 1890

Dodge, Ernest S. *Northwest By Sea.* New York: Oxford University Press, 1961.

Dow, George Francis. *Whale Ships and Whaling: A Pictorial History of Whaling During Three Centuries.* Salem, Massachusetts: Marine Research Society, 1925.

Draper, James David. Metropolitan Museum of Art Collections Database, www.metmuseum.org/ works_of_art/collection_database/european_sculpture_and_decorative_arts/the_deposition_leonhard_kern/objectview.aspx?collID=12&OID=120027084.

Ellis, Leonard Bolles. *History of New Bedford and Its Vicinity, 1602-1862.* Syracuse, New York: D. Mason & Co., 1892.

Ely, Ben Ezra Stiles. *There She Blows: Narrative of a whaling voyage in the Indian and South Atlantic Oceans.* Philadelphia, 1849. (Repr. ed. by Curtis Dahl, Middletown: Wesleyan University Press, 1971.)

Encyclopædia Britannica, 9th ed., Vol. 5, New York, 1833.

Esar, Evan. *The Comic Encyclopedia.* New York: Doubleday, 1978.

Exhibition and Fair of the Massachusetts Charitable Mechanic Association at Faneuil and Quincy Halls, in the City of Boston. Boston: Dutton & Wentworth, 1844.

Fair, Susan W. "Robert Mayokok: Second-Generation Inupiaq Illustrator from Wales, Alaska," in Suzi Jones, ed., *Eskimo Drawings* (AMHA, 2003), 127-134.

Fairburn, William Armstrong. *Merchant Sail.* 6 vols. Central Lovell, Maine: Fairburn Marine Educational Foundation, Inc., 1945-55.

Falk, Peter Hastings, ed. *Who Was Who in American Art, 1564-1975.* Madison, Connecticut: SoundView, 1985.

Farwell, Robert D. "Manuel Enos: Cold Spring Whaleman," *Long Island Forum* (June 1981), 108f.

Felt, Joseph Barlow. *Annals of Salem,* Vol. 2. Salem and Boston, 1849.

Fenton, James. *History of Tasmania.* Hobart (or Launceston?): J. Walch & Sons, 1884.

First Exhibition and Fair of the Massachusetts Charitable Mechanic Association at Faneuil and Quincy Halls, in the City of Boston. Boston: Dutton & Wentworth, 1837.

Flayderman, E. Norman. *Scrimshaw and Scrimshanders, Whales and Whalemen.* New Milford, Connecticut: N. Flayderman & Co., 1971.

Forget Me Not Songster (The); Containing A Choice Collection of Old Ballad Songs, as sung by our Grandmothers. . . . Boston: G.W. Cottrell, n.d. [circa 1835].

Forget Me Not Songster (The); Containing A Choice Collection of Old Ballad Songs, as sung by our Grandmothers. . . . New York: Richard Marsh, n.d. [circa 1835].

Forster, Honore. *The South Sea Whaler: An Annotated Bibliography of published historical, literary and art material relating to whaling in the Pacific Ocean in the nineteenth century.* Sharon, Massachusetts: Kendall Whaling Museum; Fairhaven, Massachusetts: Edward. J. Lefkowicz, 1985.

____________. *More South Sea Whaling: A Supplement to The South Sea Whaler.* Canberra: Australian National University, 1991.

Frank, Stuart M. *Ballads and Songs of the Whale Hunters 1825-1895, from Manuscripts in the Kendall Whaling Museum.* 2 vols. Ph.D. Thesis, Brown University, 1985.

____________. *The Book of Pirate Songs.* Sharon, Massachusetts: Kendall Whaling Museum, 1998.

____________. "Captain George Comer's Scrimshaw." *The KWM Newsletter,* 8:2 (Summer 1990, 6-9)

____________. *Dictionary of Scrimshaw Artists.* Mystic Seaport, 1991.

____________. *Fakeshaw: A Checklist of Plastic "Scrimshaw."* Kendall Monograph N°1, [1988] 1993, with 1996 Supplement, Sharon, Massachusetts: The Kendall Whaling Museum.

____________. "False Whalers: Slavers and Fenian Patriots in Disguise." *Seaport,* 39:1 (Winter/ Spring 2004), 18-23.

____________. "'I'm One of the B'hoys': A Song about New York Firefighters in the Age of Sail." *Seaport,* 37:2-3 (South Street Seaport Museum, Spring/Summer 2002), 34-41.

____________. *Ingenious Contrivances: Scrimshaw in the New Bedford Whaling Museum.* Boston: David R. Godine, 2013.

____________. *Jolly Sailors Bold: Ballads and Songs of the American Sailor.* East Windsor, New Jersey: Camsco Music, 2010.

____________. *More Scrimshaw Artists.* Mystic Seaport Museum, 1998.

____________. *"Musick on the Brain": Frederick Howland Smith's Shipboard Tunes, 1854-1869* (Kendall Monograph N° 12), Sharon, Massachusetts: Kendall Whaling Museum, 2000.

____________. *Oooh, You New York Girls! The Urban Pastorale in Ballads and Songs about Sailors Ashore in the Big City* (Kendall Monograph N° 9), Perth, W.A.: Australian Society for Maritime History; and Sharon, Massachusetts: Kendall Whaling Museum, 1996.

____________. "The Origins of Engraved Pictorial Scrimshaw." *The Magazine Antiques,* 142:4 (New York, October 1992), 510-521.

____________. "Scrimshaw." *Encyclopedia of Marine Mammals,* William E. Perrin, Brend Würsig, and J.G.M. Thewissen, eds. (San Diego: Academic Press/Harcourt, Inc.), 2002, 1060-1066.

____________. "Scrimshaw: An Introduction and Overview, A.D. 800-1960." *Whaling & History: Perspectives on the Evolution of the Industry,* edited by Bjørn L. Basberg, Jan Erik Wexelsen, Sandefjord (Norway): Kdr. Chr. Christensens Hvalfangst-museet, 1993.

____________. "Scrimshaw: 'Ingenious contrivances… in the hours of ocean leisure,'" in *New England Antiques Journal,* XX:8 (Ware, Massachusetts, Feb. 2002), 68f.

____________. "Scrimshaw Like a Phoenix: A Love Story." *KWM Newsletter,* 8:2 (Summer 1990), 3, 11.

____________. "Les scrimshaws: Tradition artisanale des chasseurs de baleines." *Le Chasse-Marée,* 67 (Douarnenez, France, 1992), 46-61.

____________. "Scrimshaw: Occupational Art of the Whale-Hunters." *Maritime Life and Traditions,* #7 (London, March 2000), 42-57.

____________. "Scrimshaw: The Whalemen's Art." *Early American Life,* 37:3 (June 2006), 8-19.

Freeman, Frederick. *The History of Cape Cod: The Annals of Barnstable County and of Its Several Towns...* 2 vols. [Boston, 1858.] Yarmouth Port, Massachusetts: Parnassus. 1965.

Freud, Sigmund. *Civilization and Its Discontents.* (Repr., New York: W.W. Norton, 1962.)

Gilkerson, William. *The Scrimshander: The Nautical Ivory Worker and His Art of Scrimshaw, Historical and Contemporary.* San Francisco: Troubadour, 1975.

__________; and John R. Bockstoce. *American Whalers in the Western Arctic.* Fairhaven, Mass.: Edward J. Lefkowicz, Inc., 1982.

Gomes Vieira, João Antonio. *O Homem e o Mar: Artistas Portugueses do Marfim e do Osso dos Cetaceos... [Man and the Sea: Portuguese Scrimshaw Artists...].* Lisbon, 2003.

Goode, George Brown, ed. *Fisheries and Fishery Industries of the United States.* 5 vols. Washington, D.C.: GPO, 1887.

Guthman, William. *Drums A-Beating, Trumpets Sounding: Artistically Carved Powder Horns in the Provincial Manner, 1746 1781.* Hartford: Connecticut Historical Society, 1993.

Haring, Jacquelin Kolle; Gayl Michael; and Amy Rokicki. *Guide to the Manuscript Collections of the Nantucket Historical Association.* 2nd Ed. Nantucket, Massachusetts: Nantucket Historical Association, [1986] 1992.

Harris, James. *A Brief History of Ornamental Turning.* www.ornamentalturner.com/history.

Hartwig, G. *The Polar and Tropical Worlds.* Springfield: A.C. Nichols, 1875.

Haskins, Charles Warren, *The Argonauts of California.* New York: Fords, Howard & Hulbert, 1890.

[__________, compiler.] *Libera Martina Spinazze's Index to "The Argonauts of California."* New Orleans: Polyanthos, 1975.

Hegarty, Reginald B. *Returns of Whaling Vessels Sailing from American Ports: A Continuation of Alexander Starbuck's "History of the American Whale Fishery" 1876-1928.* New Bedford: Old Dartmouth Historical Society, 1959.

__________. *Addendum to "Starbuck" and "Whaling Masters." New Bedford Customs District.* New Bedford: New Bedford Free Public Library, 1964.

Hellman, Nina; and Norman Brouwer. *A Mariners; Fancy: The Whalemen's Art of Scrimshaw.* New York: South Street Seaport and Balsam Press; Seattle: University of Washington Press, 1992.

Henderson, J. Welles; and Rodney P. Carlisle. *Jack Tar: a Sailor's Life 1750-1910: Marine Art and Antiques.* Antique Collector's Club, 1999.

Hermitage (State Hermitage Museum, St. Petersburg). www.hermitage museum.org and hermitage.informbureau.com/ russian_culture_1700.

Hezel, Francis X., S.J. *Foreign Ships in Micronesia.* http://www.micsem.org/pubs/articles/historical/forships/index.htm

History and Directory of Foxboro, Mass., for 1890. Needham, Massachusetts, 1890 (repr. Foxborough Historical Society).

The History of Middlesex County, Connecticut, 1635-1885. Chicago: J.H. Beers & Co., 1884.

Hohman, Elmo P. *The American Whaleman.* New York: Longmans, Green, 1928. (Repr., Clifton: Augustus M. Kelley, 1972.)

Holch, Lillian Josephine Hubbard. *Sizer Genealogy: A History of Antonio De Zocieur, Who Changed His Name to Anthony Sizer, and Abel Sizer, Daniel Sizer, Lemuel Sizer, Sara Sizer Bill.* New York: n/p, 1941.

Howe, Octavius T., M.D.; and Frederick C. Matthews. *American Clipper Ships 1833-1858.* 2 vols. [New York, 1926.] New York: Argosy. 1967.

Howland, Chester S. "Capt. Wing's Nautical Feat." *Yankee Magazine,* March 1965, 57f.

Hughes, Lindsey. *Peter the Great: A Biography.* New Haven: Yale University Press, 2002.

Hurd, Duane Hamilton. *History of Essex County, Massachusetts.* Philadelphia: J. W. Lewis & Co., 1888

Hussey & Robinson. *Catalogue of Nantucket Whalers: Voyages from 1815 to 1870.* Nantucket, 1876.

Index of Seamen's Protection Papers, Special Collections, New Bedford Free Public Library.

Index of Whalemen and Seamen, Special Collections, New Bedford Free Public Library.

Ingalls, Elizabeth. *Whaling Prints in the Francis B. Lothrop Collection.* Salem, Massachusetts: Peabody Museum, 1987.

Irish Arts Review. www.irishartsreview.com

"Johnny the Painter." *The Bulletin from Johnny Cake Hil,* (New Bedford, Spring 1974), 14-16.

Jones, A.G.E., et al. *Ships Employed in the South Seas Trade.* 2 vols. Canberra: Roebuck Society, 1986 and 1992.

Journal of the House of Representatives of the Commonwealth of Massachusetts. Boston, 1886.

Kaldenbach, Isabel. *Inventory of Black Nantucketers.* Nantucket Historical Association archive. http://www.nha.org/library/NantucketBlacksdatabase2.htm

Kaneko, Hisakazu. *Manjiro: The Man Who Discovered America.* Boston: Houghton Mifflin, 1956.

Kaplan, Laurence D., ed.*Ugiuvangmiut Quliapyuit. King Island Tales: Eskimo History and Legends from Bering Strait.* Fairbanks: Alaska Native Language Center and University of Alaska Press, 1988.

Kawasumi Tetsuo. *Nakahama Manjiro Shusei, Or The Manjiro Memorabilia.* 2nd ed., Tokyo, 1992).

Kimball, Horace. *American Naval Battles.* Boston, 1837.

Kohl, Johann Georg. *Russia: St. Petersburg, Moscow, Kharkoff, Riga, Odessa, the German Provinces.* London: Chapman & Hall, 1842.

KWM Newsletter, the journal of the Kendall Whaling Museum, edited in succession by Robert L. Webb, David Cruthers, and Beth Macgregor, executive editor Stuart M. Frank, published quarterly, 1982-2001; archived at MSM, NBWM, NHS, NMM, PEM, and elsewhere.

Larcom, Henry. *Some particulars of the melancholy shipwreck of the Margaret, William Fairfield master, on her passage from Naples to Salem...* Salem, Massachusetts: for the Author, 1810.

Leslie, Alexander. *The Arctic Voyages of Adolf Erik Nordenskiold.* London: R. Clay, Sons and Taylor, 1879.

List of Officers Composing [the] Whaling Fleet [of] San Francisco, Cal. San Francisco: James Laflin. Annual volumes 1887-1908.

Lister, Adrian; and Paul G. Bahn. *Mammoths: Giants of the Ice Age,* London: Francis Lincoln Ltd., 1994.

Littmann, Minna. "3800-Mile Voyage in Open Boats Saved Men of Canton After Wreck in the Pacific" *New Bedford Standard Times,* n/d (scrapbook in NBWM).

Lomen, Carl J. *Fifty Years in Alaska.* New York: David McKay Co., 1954.

Longley, Sylvanus S. "The Wreck of the Whaler Canton" New England Quarterly, 13:2 (June 1940), 324-335.

Loomis, Chauncey C. *Weird and Tragic Shores: The Story of Charles Francis Hall, Explorer.* New York: Alfred A. Knopf, 1971.

Low, A.P. *The Cruise of the Neptune: Report on the Dominion Government Expedition to Hudson Bay and the Arctic Islands 1903-1904.* Ottawa, 1906.

Lund, Judith Navas. *Whaling Masters.* Gloucester, Massachusetts: Ten Pound Island Books; New Bedford: New Bedford Whaling Museum; Sharon: The Kendall Whaling Museum, 2000.

____________ et al. *American Offshore Whaling Voyages 1667-1927.* 2 vols. New Bedford: Old Dartmouth Historical Society / New Bedford Whaling Museum. 2010.

Lyon, David. *The Sailing Navy List: All the Ships of the Royal Navy, Built, Purchased and Captured, 1688-1860.* London: Conway Maritime Press, 1993.

Mackrell, Alice. Art and Fashion. London: B.T. Batsford, 2005.

Macy, Obed. *The History of Nantucket.* Boston: Hilliard, Gray, and Co., 1835.

Malley, Richard C. *Graven by the Fishermen Themselves: Scrimshaw in Mystic Seaport Museum.* Mystic Seaport, 1983.

____________. *In Their Hours of Ocean Leisure: Scrimshaw in the Cold Spring Harbor Whaling Museum.* Cold Spring Harbor, New York: Whaling Museum Society, 1993

Malloy, Mary. *"Boston Men" on the Northwest Coast: The American Fur Trade, 1788-1844.* Fairbanks: Limestone / University of Alaska Press, 1998.

Manjiro, John. *Drifting Toward the Southeast: The Story of Five Japanese Castaways.* Junya Nakaguni and Junji Kitadai, transl. and eds. [Edo, 1852] New Bedford: Spinner, 2003.

Markstein, Donald D. [Hasbro Games, 2003-04:] www.toonopedia.com

Martin, Kenneth R. *Delaware Goes Whaling, 1833-45.* Greenville, De.: Hagley Museum, 1974.

____________. *"Some Very Handsome Work': Scrimshaw at the Cape Cod National Seashore.* Eastham, Massachusetts: Eastham National Park and Monument Association, 1991.

____________. *Whalemen and Whaleships of Maine.* Brunswick, Maine: Harpswell, 1975.

____________. *Whalemen's Paintings and Drawings: Selections from the Kendall Whaling Museum Collection.* Sharon, Massachusetts: The Kendall Whaling Museum; Newark, Delaware: University of Delaware Press, 1983.

Massie, Robert K. *Peter the Great: His Life and World.* New York: Ballantine, 1980.

Mathieu, Laura. *2006. Fashion Depicted on Scrimshaw in New England Collections: 1825-1890.* Unpublished master's thesis, University of Rhode Island, 2006.

Mattapoisett and Rochester, Massachusetts: Being a History of These Towns and also in Part of Marion and a Portion of Wareham. New York: Grafton Press, 1907.

McCauley, Edward Yorke. *A Manual for the Use of Students in Egyptology,* 1883 (repr. Princeton University Press, 1942).

McLaughlin, W.R.D. *Call to the South: The Story of British Whaling in Antarctica.* London: George C. Harrap & Co., 1962.

McManus, Michael. *A Treasury of American Scrimshaw: A Collection of the Useful and Decorative.* New York: Penguin Books, 1997.

Melville, Herman. *Moby-Dick; or, The Whale.* New York: Harper, 1851.

____________. *Omoo: A Narrative of Adventures in the South Seas.* New York, 1847.

____________. *Redburn, His First Voyage.* New York, 1849.

____________. *Typee; or a Narrative of a Four Months' Residence Among the Natives of a Valley of the Marquesas Islands; or a Peep at Polynesian Life.* New York, 1846.

____________. *White-Jacket; or, The World in a Man-of-War.* New York, 1850.

Meyer, George H., ed. *Folk Artists Biographical Index.* 1st Ed. Detroit: Gale Research, 1987.

Meyers, William H. *Journal of a Cruise to California and the Sandwich Islands in the United States Sloop-of-War Cyane, 1841-1844.* San Francisco: Book Club of California, 1955.

____________. *Naval Sketches of the War in California.* Dudley Wright Knox, ed.; intro. by Franklin Delano Roosevelt. Grabhorn Press. New York: Random House, 1939.

____________. *Sketches of California and Hawaii… 1842-1843.* San Francisco: Book Club of California, 1970.

Mitchell, F. "Cape Cod." *Century Magazine,* 26:5 (Sept. 1883), 643-658.

Mokeeva, Valeria. Catalogue of the exhibition "Rose and Cross." Moscow: Kremlin, 1996-97.

Monterey Argus, December 15, 1883

Monterey Peninsula Herald, August 31, 1949.

Moore, Thomas. Poems

Murphy, Kevin D., ed. *Folk Art of Maine.* Camden, Maine: Down East Books, 2008.

Murphy, Robert Cushman. *A Dead Whale or a Stove Boat: Cruise of Daisy in the Atlantic Ocean, June 1912 - May 1913.* Boston: Houghton, Mifflin, 1967.

____________. "Floating Gold: The Romance of Ambergris." *Natural History,* (March-April and May-June 1933).

____________. *Logbook for Grace: Whaling Brig* Daisy, *1912-1913.* New York: Macmillan, 1947.

New Bedford Standard-Times, "South Coast Today" columns and obituaries (as noted in the text).

O'Brien, Brian. *Scrimshaw and Sudden Death; A Salty Tale of Whales and Men, based on personal accounts and logbooks of Captain Lester A. Mosher.* New York: Dutton, 1959.

O'Neill, Eugene. "Glencairn Plays" Five Plays of the sea

O'Neill, Eugene. "Ile." Five Plays of the sea

Olmsted, Francis Allyn. *Incidents of a Whaling Voyage.* New York, 1841. (Repr., New York: Bell, 1969.)

Ornamental Turning. www.ornamentalturning.net/history.

Our County and its People: A descriptive and biographical history of Bristol County, Massachusetts. Published by the *Fall River News,* the *Taunton Gazette,* and the Boston History Co., 1899.

Past Masters of King Hiram's Lodge, 1796-1930 (in Provincetown, Massachusetts; chartered by Paul Revere, Grand Master, in 1795). http://freepages.genealogy.rootsweb.ancestry.com/~mjhiggins/mass.htm

Pease, Zephaniah W.; and George A. Hough. *New Bedford, Massachusetts: Its History, Industries, Institutions, and Attractions.* William L. Sayer, ed. New Bedford: Mercury Publishing Co. for the Board of Trade, 1889.

Penniman, T.K. *Pictures of Ivory and other Animal Teeth, Bone and Antler; With a brief commentary on their use in identification.* University of Oxford: Pitt Rivers Museum, Occasional Paper on Technology N° 5, [1952] 1984.

Phillips, Paul Davidson. *European Ivory Relief Carving,* n.d. http://www.alsnetbiz.com/acc/articles.html

Poe, Edgar Alan. *The Narrative of Arthur Gordon Pym of Nantucket.*

Proceedings, Annual Meeting of the Old Dartmouth Historical Society, Annie Seabury Wood, ed., March 30, 1910.

Putnam, George Granville. *Salem Vessels and Their Voyages.* 4 vols., repr. from Essex Institute Historical Collections. Salem, Massachusetts: Essex Institute, 1924- .

Randall, Richard H., Jr. *Masterpieces of Ivory from the Walters Art Gallery.* New York: Hudson Hills Press, 1985.

Ray, Dorothy Jean. *Aleut and Eskimo Art: Tradition and Innovation in South Alaska.* Seattle: University of Washington Press, 1981.

____________. *Artists of the Tundra and the Sea.* Seattle: University of Washington Press, 1961.

____________. *Eskimo Art: Tradition and Innovation in North Alaska.* Seattle: University of Washington Press, 1977.

____________. "Happy Jack and His Artistry." *American Indian Art,* 15:1 (Winter 1989), 40-53.

____________. "Happy Jack: King of the Eskimo Ivory Carvers." *American Indian Art,* 10:1 (Winter 1984).

____________. *A Legacy of Arctic Art,* Seattle: University of Washington Press, 1996.

Reilly, Kevin S. "Slavers in Disguise: American Whaling and the African Slave Trade, 1845-1862." *The American Neptune,* 53:3 (Summer 1993), 177-189.

Representative Men and Old Families of Southeastern Massachusetts, Vol. II. Chicago: J.H. Beers & Co., 1912.

Ricketson, Daniel. *The History of New Bedford, Bristol County, Massachusetts: Including a History of the Old Township of Dartmouth and the Present Townships of Westport, Dartmouth, and Fairhaven.* New Bedford: Published by the Author, 1858

Ridley, Donald E.; and Stuart M. Frank. *Frederick Myrick of Nantucket: Scrimshaw Catalogue Raisonné* (Kendall Monograph N° 13), Sharon, Massachusetts: Kendall Whaling Museum, 2000.

____________ et al., *Frederick Myrick: Physical Characteristics of the Scrimshaw* (Kendall Monograph N° 14), Sharon, Massachusetts: Kendall Whaling Museum, 2000.

Robbins, Charles H. 1899. *The Gam: Being a Group of Whaling Stories.* Salem, Massachusetts: Newton & Gauss, 1913.

Ross, W. Gillies. 1984. *An Arctic Whaling Diary: The Journal of Captain George Comer in Hudson Bay, 1903-05.* Toronto: University of Toronto Press, 1984.

Santos, Robert L. *Azoreans to California: A History of Migration and Settlement.* Denair, California: Alley-Cass Publications. 1995.

Sawtell, Clement Cleveland. *The Ship Ann Alexander of New Bedford, 1805-1851.* Mystic, Connecticut: Marine Historical Association, Monograph N° 40, 1962.

Sayle, C.F. 1985. "Gamming," *KWM Newsletter,* 3:1 (Spring 1985), p. 3.

Scammon, Charles M. *The Marine Mammals of the North-western Coast of North America, Described and Illustrated: Together with an account of the American Whale Fishery.* San Francisco: John H. Carmany & Co.; New York: G.P. Putnam's Sons, 1874 (repr., New York: Dover, 1968.)

Sears, Robert. *The Historical and Scientific American Miscellany: A Book of Universal Knowledge.* 2 vols. Columbus, Ohio, 1865.

Sherman, John H. *Sherman Directory.* 4 vols. Baltimore, 1991.

Sherman, Stuart C., et al. *Whaling Logbooks and Journals 1613-1928: An Inventory of Manuscript Records in Public Collections.* (Garland Reference Library of the Humanities, Vol. 682.) New York and London: Garland Publ., 1986.

Sherman, Thomas Townsend. *Sherman Genealogy.* New York,. 1920.

Smith, James H. *The History of Chenango and Madison Counties, New York.* Syracuse, 1880.

Spude, Robert L., "Management Decisions at Klondike Gold Rush National Historical Park," *Cultural Resources Management Bulletin,* U.S. National Park Service Technical Bulletin, 2;3, (September 1979), 1-2.

Starbuck, Alexander. 1878. *History of the American Whale Fishery, from Its Earliest Inception to the Year 1876.* Report of the U.S. Commission on Fish and Fisheries, Part IV, Washington, D.C.: GPO, 1878. (Repr. 2 vols., preface by Stuart C. Sherman, New York: Argosy, 1964. Repr. 1 vol., Secaucus, New Jersey: Crown, 1989).

Strong, Austin. "The Last Harpooneer." *Atlantic Monthly,* 169:5 (May 1942).

Taylor, Nathaniel W. *Life on a Whaler: Narrative of a Whaling Voyage from New London, Connecticut, August 18, 1851, to June 4, 1854.* Howard Palmer, ed. New London: The New London County Historical Society, 1929.

Townsend, Charles Haskins. "The Galapagos Tortoises in their relation to the Whaling Industry: A Study of Old Logbooks." *Zoologica,* 4:3, 1925.

Tripp. William Henry. *There Goes Flukes: The Story of New Bedford's Last Whaler....* New Bedford: Reynolds Printing, 1925.

Trumbull, Henry. 1819. *History of the Indian Wars: to which is prefixed a short account of the discovery of America by Columbus, and of the landing of our forefathers at Plymouth, with their most remarkable engagements with the Indians in New England, from their first landing in 1620, until the death of King Philip, in 1679... To which is now added, a historical account of the sufferings of the inhabitants of the frontier settlements by the savages, during the French and revolutionary wars; and also the particulars of every important engagement with the Indians, in the southern and western states and territories, to the present time* (Boston, [1812] 1819, 1828, 1832, etc.).

Updike, Richard W. 1970. "The Walrus and the Commodore — A Puzzle in Scrimshaw," *The Magazine Antiques,* 98 (August 1970), 263f.

Van Horn, Walter.

von Finckenstein, Maria. "Harry Teseuke, Captain Comer's Mate: Historic Ivories at the Canadian Museum of Civilization (II)." *Inuit Art Quarterly,* 17[4], 2002, 43f.

Vital Records of various Massachusetts towns and cities, circa 1900-1925.

Waliszewski, Kazimierz. *Peter the Great.* New York: D. Appleton & Co., 1897.

Walton, Terry. "A Not-So-Ordinary Seaman: Intimate Pages from the Diary of William H. Meyers, on board and ashore." *Seaport* (Summer 1979), 22-27.

Warrin, Donald. 2009. *So Ends This Day: Portuguese in American Whaling, 1765-1927.* Dartmouth, Massachusetts: University of Massachusetts Dartmouth, 2000.

Warriner, Emily V. *Voyager to Destiny.* Indianapolis: Bobbs-Merrill, 1956.

Watson, Arthur C. [Eben Pierce.] *Old Dartmouth Historical Sketches,* N° 23. New Bedford.

Webb, Robert Lloyd. *On the Northwest: Commercial Whaling in the Pacific Northwest 1790-1967.* Vancouver, B.C.: University of British Columbia Press, 1988.

West, Janet; and Arthur G. Credland. *Scrimshaw: The Art of the Whalers.* Hull City Museums & Art Galleries / Hutton Press, 1995.

White, Philo. *Philo White's Narrative of a Cruize [sic] in the Pacific to South America and California on the U.S. Sloop-of War Dale 1841-1843.* Charles L. Camp, ed. Denver: Old West Publishing Company, 1965.

Whitecar, William B., Jr. *Four Years Aboard the Whaleship. Cruises in the Pacific, Atlantic, Indian, and Antarctic Oceans, in the Years 1855, '6, '7, '8, '9.* Philadelphia: J.B. Lippincott & Co.; London: Trübner & Co., 1860.

Who's Who in New England. Chicago: A.N. Marquis & Co., 1908.

Williams, Howard. *One Whaling Family.* Boston: Houghton Mifflin, 1964.

Winslow, Helen L. *The Folk Art of the American Whaleman.* Nantucket Historical Association Bulletin 1:3, 1955; repr. from *Historic Nantucket,* July 1954.

Wise, Terence. *To Catch a Whale.* London: Geoffrey Bles, Ltd., 1970.

Woodbury, Dr, George. "The Incredible Exploit of Captain Wing." *Manchester Union Leader,* Sept. 9. 1971.

Work Projects Administration. *Ship Registers* of various American ports.

Young, William, ed. *A Dictionary of American Artists, Sculptors, and Engravers; From the beginnings through the turn of the Twentieth Century.* Cambridge, Massachusetts: William Young & Co., 1968.

GEOGRAPHICAL INDEX

TAXONOMIC INDEX

INDEX OF VESSELS

References are to the articles and not necessarily to the specific individuals named

Whaling Vessels

Other Vessels

Yes Jesus

365 Days of Loving and Serving

BroadStreet Publishing

BroadStreet Publishing Group, LLC.
Savage, Minnesota, USA
Broadstreetpublishing.com

YES JESUS

9781424569229
9781424569236 eBook

Devotional entries composed by Sara Perry.

Typesetting and design by Garborg Design Works | garborgdesign.com

Editorial services by Michelle Winger | literallyprecise.com

Printed in China.

25 26 27 28 29 30 31 7 6 5 4 3 2 1

Love each other with genuine affection, and take delight in honoring each other.

ROMANS 12:10 NLT

INTRODUCTION

It isn't always easy to say yes. But when Jesus is your leader, your helper, and your friend, you can walk in obedience every day. He is good! You can trust him with the details of your life; he knows you intimately, and he always has your best in mind.

Spending time with God allows you to give generously to others out of the overflow of his heart for you. Rely on him to be your source as you are inspired to spread compassion, generosity, and hope through your service. As you read these devotions, Scriptures, and prayers, make it your intention to engage in acts of love. When you reflect God's character to a world that often seems harsh, you bring encouragement to people who may otherwise feel forgotten or hopeless.

Say yes to Jesus each day and watch as the world around you is drawn into his love!

JANUARY

"If you love me,
keep my commands."

John 14:15 NIV

HE IS SPEAKING

Then I heard the Lord asking,
"Whom should I send as a messenger to this people?
Who will go for us?"
I said, "Here I am. Send me."

ISAIAH 6:8 NLT

When Isaiah overheard the Lord asking who he should send as a messenger, it is likely that he was filled with both reverence and interest. God was the one who qualified Isaiah. He was looking for someone willing; he didn't need a list of credentials. The fact that Isaiah heard the Lord in the first place was significant. He heard and answered.

God is still speaking today. He is still asking who will go. If you hear him and feel compelled to answer, that is your permission. *Here I am. Send me.* This was not a flippant agreement Isaiah made. It was full-hearted and committed. When your heart jumps at the invitation of the Lord, don't hesitate to offer yourself to him. He will guide you and equip you; all you need to do is follow him.

Father, open the ears of my heart that I may hear you when you speak. I want to honor you with my whole life. I love you, Lord!

THE WAY

Jesus answered, "I am the way and the truth and the life. No one comes to the Father except through me."

JOHN 14:6 NIV

If we want to know the Father in spirit and in truth, there is one sure way to do it: Follow Jesus. He is the way. He is the truth. He is the life. There isn't another door we have to find. He isn't hiding in the compounds of the rich and famous. He is close to the brokenhearted and the vulnerable. God is accessible here and now through Christ. You don't have to earn a thing or prove yourself.

Come to Jesus. That's all you need to do. With an open heart and a receptive mind, take him up on his invitation. You will find more riches in relationship with him than you will in quick fix programs. He longs to lead you into the powerful peace of his presence.

Jesus Christ, I believe that you are the way, the truth, and the life. You are the representation of the Father, and I yield my life to your leadership and your love.

CALLED AND EQUIPPED

We know that for those who love God all things work together for good, for those who are called according to his purpose.

ROMANS 8:28 ESV

Whatever God has called you to, he offers the help and guidance you need. You can't avoid the unexpected challenges of life, but you can be sure that the one who called you will work all things together for good. Have you ever gone through a particularly hard time, and through the lens of hindsight saw how God brought beauty from the ashes of your pain and struggle? It may be hard to see in the moment, but God is working in the details.

If you feel ill equipped for what God is leading you into, you are in good company. He loves to guide his people as they pair their faith and trust with his wisdom and steadfast love. He will never leave you. He gives solutions for problems, clarity for confusion, and strength for weakness.

God, I can't do this on my own, and I'm so thankful that I don't have to. Lead me and work even the most painful parts of my story together with your wonderful mercy.

STRENGTHENED TO SERVE

"Fear not, for I am with you;
Be not dismayed, for I am your God.
I will strengthen you,
Yes, I will help you,
I will uphold you with My righteous right hand."

ISAIAH 41:10 NKJV

God does not expect you to have every step figured out. He created you, and he knows the limits of your humanity. Instead of expecting yourself to be strong all the time, remember what his Word says. He will uphold you with his righteousness. You don't have to do any of it on your own.

Does that take the pressure off a bit? It should! Everything that God asks of you, he provides the strength, fortitude, grace, and wisdom to do it. He holds on to you through thick and thin. You can lay down the pressure to perform, and instead rest in his confident help. He's got you with his gracious grip, and he will strengthen you with his own Spirit.

God, thank you for the power of your provision. As I hold on to your Word, you uphold me with your righteous right hand. Strengthen me today in your presence.

CONTINUE TO SURRENDER

Continue to walk surrendered to the extravagant love of Christ, for he surrendered his life as a sacrifice for us. His great love for us was pleasing to God, like an aroma of adoration—a sweet healing fragrance.

EPHESIANS 5:2 TPT

When we give our lives to Christ, we follow in his loving lead. He offered himself as a sacrifice, laying down his very life so that we could see, experience, and know just how extravagant his love is. It's not always easy to choose to walk in love, but it is always, always worth it.

When you go about your day, don't forget to stay yielded to the leadership of the Lord. When you are tempted to bite back at someone, remember what Jesus would have done. When you want to avoid a hard but necessary conversation, take heart that God is with you in it and that clarity is kind. You can be loving and tell the truth. The loving choice can, and often does, require discomfort. Stay open before the Lord, letting the extravagant mercy of his love guide you.

Loving Lord, teach me to walk in the kindness of your love and to extend grace to others.

IN ALL WAYS

Trust in the LORD with all your heart
And do not lean on your own understanding.
In all your ways acknowledge Him,
And He will make your paths straight.

PROVERBS 3:5-6 NASB

God is full of infinite wisdom. There isn't a problem he can't solve or a challenge he can't help you overcome. He holds the keys to every locked door and the answer to every lingering question. You can trust him fully, for not only is he perfect in wisdom, power, and strength, but also in love.

Humble yourself before the Lord today and remember that he sees the details you miss. Say yes to his ways and trust him to lead you in his goodness. He will not fail you. Psalm 37:4 serves as a reminder that even when the righteous stumble, they will not fall. So go ahead and make God the leader of all your ways.

Good Shepherd, I humble myself before you today. Lead me in your love and show me the next steps to take. I trust you!

HUMBLE GENEROSITY

"When you give to the poor, don't be like the hypocrites. They blow trumpets in the synagogues and on the streets so that people will see them and honor them."

MATTHEW 6:2 NCV

Generosity is a kingdom value. It is reflective of what the Lord's mercy looks like in our lives. When we choose to give to the poor, we should not do it to be noticed or honored by the people who see what we do. With humble hearts, we can serve and honor others in generosity, not needing anyone to validate it. God sees. He knows, and he honors those who live out his love.

What motivates you to act generously? God gives generously to us out of an overflowing heart of love. He doesn't give in order to receive anything in return. Oh, that we would be more like him, practicing open-hearted generosity. Let's keep our giving quiet but our hearts loud with love.

Generous Father, I want to be more like you in giving. Help me to open my heart and my resources, letting your love pave the way for sharing all that you have so freely offered me.

EXPRESSIONS OF LOVE

With all humility and gentleness, with patience, bearing with one another in love, making every effort to keep the unity of the Spirit through the bond of peace.

EPHESIANS 4:2-3 CSB

Saying yes to Jesus and his ways means walking on the path of his love. It means choosing to remain humble before God and others. It requires gentleness, laying aside the need to be harsh in our estimation of things. Patience is paramount, as it creates space for others.

When we bear with one another in love, it does not mean that we always feel happy. Our patience will be tried, our humility will be tested, and our gentleness will run out. Does this mean we should stop trying to live in unity with others? By no means! We are many parts of the same body, and we might not always work seamlessly together, but we can certainly try. There is room for repair, rebuilding, and respect. What marvelous expressions of love!

Savior, I don't want to be so caught up in my own idea of what is important that I lose sight of love's many expressions. Help me to live humbly, gently, and with patience.

EMBODIED GRACE

The Word became human and made his home among us.
He was full of unfailing love and faithfulness.
And we have seen his glory,
the glory of the Father's one and only Son.

JOHN 1:14 NLT

Jesus Christ is the living expression of the Father. There is no better reflection of God in humanity than his very own Son. Let's be sure that we measure everything we do in his name against his character. He is the ultimate example we follow; there is none better, truer, or more loving than Christ.

Jesus did not come to this world to condemn it but to save it. Who, then, are we to take on judgment instead of love? It is not our place to condemn others. Jesus reveals the grace of God, and we are all in desperate need of it.

Gracious Jesus, help me to remain gracious and loving toward others today. When I jump to judgment, remind me that your love is better.

SHINING DEEDS

"In the same way, let your light shine before others, that they may see your good deeds and glorify your Father in heaven."

MATTHEW 5:16 NIV

Jesus said that our lives light up the world. Let's not hide the love that has transformed our own lives. God's extravagant mercy lights up our lives with grace, hope, peace, and joy. Let's live unashamed of the power of this love and let our own deeds reflect the power of God's transformative kindness as we move in kind to those around us.

Perhaps you can reach out to someone in need of encouragement. Maybe it's leaving room in your schedule to listen to those who need an ear. Choose compassion and patience rather than biting back at someone today. Let love lead the way and you will find ways to do good to others.

Glorious God, I want to reflect the life-changing love that you so generously show me each and every day. Open my eyes to see opportunities where I can do good to others, reflecting your kindness, generosity, and grace.

RUNNING OVER

"Give, and it will be given to you.
Good measure, pressed down, shaken together,
running over, will be put into your lap.
For with the measure you use
it will be measured back to you."

LUKE 6:38 ESV

When we give out of generosity, we open ourselves to receive in the same measure. We shouldn't hold tightly to what we have, hoarding it for ourselves. We become bogged down by our own control when we do, missing out on what is available because we haven't made room.

When we are in desperate need, surely we feel the acute relief of receiving provision. They work together: we are never only on one end of the spectrum. There will be times when we are able to give more than others, and there will be times we are more reliant on the help of others. Let's allow both to be true, and let's practice opening our hearts and eyes to see ways that we can give to others.

Lord, thank you for stretching my compassion and generosity through giving to others. I trust you with the rest.

BEAUTY OF BELONGING

"Blessed are the poor in spirit,
For theirs is the kingdom of heaven."

MATTHEW 5:3 NKJV

We all long to know that we belong. We long to be understood and valued. Though the world has certain criteria that it deems attractive and worthy of attention, the kingdom of God does not put the same requirements on our belonging.

You don't have to be in a certain class in society or have it all together—you don't have to have anything together—in order to know what it is to be welcomed into the kingdom of heaven. You have only to put your trust in your Savior and follow the lead of his love through your life. You belong to Christ, and he will never cast you away because you don't meet the criteria others say you should. Follow his lead and welcome others in compassion.

Compassionate Christ, thank you for how you answer everyone who calls on you, and you won't stop. Thank you for the belonging I have found in you. Help me to be a safe place for others today.

KEEP LOOKING

Seek the LORD and His strength;
Seek His face continually.

1 CHRONICLES 16:11 NASB

As we follow the Lord through the ups and downs of this life, there is one important thing that we keep doing: seek his face continually. We were created for close relationship not for distant aspiration. Christ has brought us into fellowship with the King of kings. We need never be alone in this life. We have access to God the Father, Son, and Holy Spirit.

When you are weak, you can find your strength in God. Continually search for the Lord. As you do, you will find that he is closer than you knew. His presence is near, and his help is already on the way. Press in to the presence of your Maker, for he loves you, and he is all that you're looking for. There isn't a need he won't fill.

Holy Spirit, I want to know the power of your presence in my life. As I look for you, open my heart to see where you are already at work.

BREAKTHROUGH IS COMING

Let the sunrise of your love end our dark night.
Break through our clouded dawn again!
Only you can satisfy our hearts,
filling us with songs of joy to the end of our days.

Psalm 89:14 TPT

When the dark nights drag on longer than we expect, let's not give up hope. The one who shines forever bright is still as strong, vibrant, and present as he ever has been. Just as surely as the dawn comes each morning, so will the light of his love shine on us once more. We can be sure of it!

If your yes to Jesus today is simply to trust that he will break through your clouded dawn, that is a beautiful thing! Partner your faith to his faithfulness, refusing to believe that he has abandoned you in your time of need. He always comes through. He will satisfy your heart once more, and you will sing songs of joy again.

Shining One, you are the hope of my heart, even as I long for the refreshing pools of your presence to wash over me again. Break through, Lord, and I will dance for joy as your light meets my gaze.

TRANSPARENCY

If we confess our sins, he will forgive our sins,
because we can trust God to do what is right.
He will cleanse us from all the wrongs we have done.

1 JOHN 1:9 NCV

We cannot hide a thing from God. He knows our imperfections better than even we do. When we see the error of our ways, it is always good to confess them to the Lord. He is not surprised or disappointed, though others may be. He loves us thoroughly, and he will not stop just because we mess up.

If instead of denying our shortcomings we confess them, there is no shadow of shame to hide in. There is freedom in his forgiveness, and there is powerful restoration in taking responsibility for our part. God will always do what is right. It is in our best interest to be honest with ourselves, others, and God, and to walk in the freedom of his redemption and love.

Lord, you already know the reality of my shortcomings and faults. I don't want to let pride or perfection keep me from the freedom of walking in the light of your love.

FOLLOW HIS EXAMPLE

"Even the Son of Man did not come to be served, but to serve, and to give his life as a ransom for many."

MARK 10:45 CSB

Serving others is not an option in the kingdom of Christ. It is the very example of Jesus, and if we want to follow in his footsteps, we will not miss both the opportunity and the privilege of looking for practical ways to serve others.

Jesus rejected the notion that leadership needed to equate to power and wealth. When he walked this earth, his ministry had many followers. He did not promise them riches. He didn't promise them success. What he did promise was peace with God, the powerful ministry of the Spirit, and fulfilled hope in him. Let's be sure that we don't miss out on what matters most: living a life of love shown through acts of service that reveal the kindness of God.

Lord, I don't want your love to be something I talk about only but something that is seen and experienced through how I live and interact with others. Be glorified as I serve you.

VARIETY OF GIFTS

God has given each of you a gift from his great variety of spiritual gifts. Use them well to serve one another.

1 PETER 4:10 NLT

Every one of us has unique talents and gifts. We need each other to thrive in community. No person is the fullness of God's reflection. We get a much fuller perspective of who God is through the diverse representation of personalities, gifts, and talents.

Don't dismiss the power of your offering because you are busy comparing yourself to others. If you need a reminder of what it is you have to offer, ask the Lord to highlight the things that come easy to you. You can also ask your close friends what they see as your strengths. Armed with the knowledge of your gifts, look for ways to walk in them and serve others.

Father, thank you that I am a unique reflection of your image. Help me to value the gifts of others with honor and not discount my own. I choose to serve you and others with my talents.

FREE IN LOVE

You, my brothers and sisters, were called to be free. But do not use your freedom to indulge the flesh; rather, serve one another humbly in love.

GALATIANS 5:13 NIV

There is so much freedom in the love of Christ. When God removes our guilt, he puts it away from us. Let's refrain from taking on the shame of our past, for God has forgotten it. Instead, we can move in the liberation of his love.

What wonderful freedom! Let's use our freedom to do what Christ has called us to: serve one another humbly in love. This is the way of Christ: we show the powerfully extravagant mercy of God to others because we have experienced it ourselves.

Redeemer, thank you for the power of your liberating love in my life. Help me to walk utterly free today with no shadows of shame or guilt.

A SHIFT IN PERSPECTIVE

Work with enthusiasm, as though you were working for the Lord rather than for people.

EPHESIANS 6:7 NLT

Some days it is harder to serve the people around us than others. In these times, a shift in perspective can help tremendously. Instead of grumbling about the dirty dishes that have to be cleaned again, can you do it for the Lord?

God is abundant in patience and so very tender with us. If we remember that it is for him we do even the most menial tasks, perhaps the annoyance can be tempered with gratitude. When it is hard to serve those who are ungrateful, let's remember that God sees every act and every movement of kindness. He does not overlook our sacrifices, even the ones that look ordinary or expected. He is close, he is attentive, and he is worthy of our offerings.

Present One, thank you for the power of your presence that never gives up on me. In light of your love, help me to remember to continue to serve others.

YOUR CHOICE

As for me and my house,
we will serve the LORD.

JOSHUA 24:15 NKJV

Everyone is serving something: whether a goal, someone else's approval, or a certain set of values. Who and what do you serve? Look at the values that guide your decisions. What do they say about what you believe and hope for? If you find a discrepancy between the life you actually want to live and the values you are upholding in practice, you can reevaluate and adjust those today.

Every day you are presented with choices in how you treat others, how you use your time, and what you are building toward. If you find that power and prestige have become more important than love and justice, perhaps it's time to reassess. When you serve the Lord, you choose to partner with his kingdom purposes.

Lord, your ways are better than the ways of this world. Help me to choose your purposes, ways, and loving lead every single day.

HE SEES

God, the Faithful One, is not unfair. How can he forget the beautiful work you have done for him? He remembers the love you demonstrate.

HEBREWS 6:10 TPT

God is not unfair. He is full of truth, wisdom, and justice. He does not act the way feeble humans do. He doesn't grow impatient with us, as much as we feel as though he might. He is long-lasting in love; he will never run out of mercy.

Do you question how impactful your service to the Lord is? When you choose love, you choose his ways. He sees every movement of kindness, every sacrifice and surrender, every single act of service to others. Even when others overlook your efforts, he does not. You can trust the Lord's leadership in your life. Even if you don't understand the trajectory, if you are yielded to the Lord and his love, you can trust that he will bring you into his goodness.

Lord, you are the God who sees. You see every detail that others miss. I trust you more than anyone else, for you are faithful and true.

CLARITY OF PURPOSE

"No one can serve two masters; for either he will hate the one and love the other, or he will be devoted to one and despise the other. You cannot serve God and wealth."

MATTHEW 6:24 NASB

There is nothing wrong with making a living. That is not what this verse addresses. If the main motivator in our lives, however, is to increase our wealth by any means, we cannot claim to love God more than we love money. Money is a powerful tool, and it is necessary to get by in this life. But if we choose to pursue money over the well-being of both ourselves and others, then our priorities are not based in the kingdom of Christ.

The Lord is not impressed by our bank accounts. He was not bought by prestige and power back when he walked this earth, and he still isn't. His love is free to all, and we reflect his mercy when we prioritize his love over our own personal gain. Economies will fail, but the love of God never will!

Great God, I say yes to your purposes over my own comfort. Your love is better than life.

REMEMBER

You must honor the LORD and truly serve him with all your heart. Remember the wonderful things he did for you!

1 SAMUEL 12:24 NCV

A beautiful way to practice gratitude in your walk with the Lord is to remember the wonderful things he has done for you. Look back over your history with God, as long or as short as it may be, and ask the Spirit to highlight the power of his presence in your life. As he brings things to mind, write them down or simply thank him. Let it serve as a well of thanksgiving for when you need a boost of hope.

It is easier to say yes to the Lord when we know his nature. He is good, he is faithful, and he is ever so kind. How have we known this goodness, this faithfulness, and this kindness? When we actively remember, we fuel our hearts with renewed hope and faith to keep going. Peace settles over our hearts as we dwell in his presence. Let's not rush past the remembering today.

Good Father, open my eyes to see how you have faithfully met me in miraculous provision and mercy throughout my life.

WHAT AN HONOR

"The greatest among you will be your servant."

MATTHEW 23:11 CSB

It is no small thing to choose to humbly serve others. In fact, it is the most honorable thing to do. We all know the servants among us: those who work behind the scenes, not for accolades or attention, but for the love of what they do. They look to add value to others, not to make themselves look better.

On the other hand, we also know the types of leaders who do the opposite. Instead of leading by example or helping others, they make demands they would never act on themselves. Servant leadership puts the focus on others first. Let's follow the Lord, who is the ultimate servant leader, and look for ways to serve others in love today.

Jesus, I want to follow your example of humble leadership. Help me to make a difference by the way I serve others.

GLORIFY GOD

Do you have the gift of speaking? Then speak as though God himself were speaking through you. Do you have the gift of helping others? Do it with all the strength and energy that God supplies. Then everything you do will bring glory to God through Jesus Christ.

1 Peter 4:11 NLT

It is possible to glorify God through what you do no matter what it is that you do. In your workplace, you can use your gifts, talents, and skills with integrity to reflect the likeness of your heavenly Father. What do your actions at work say about what and who you value?

We can get caught up in the false idea that the only type of service that directly honors the Lord is ministry. That's simply not true. How we do anything is important. The way we live, treat others, and what we value is important no matter where we are or what we are doing. Let's be sure to deepen our fellowship with the Lord and to look to honor him in every facet of our lives.

Lord God, help me to be full of integrity, walking in the light of your truth, mercy, and justice no matter where I am or what I am doing.

LIVING SACRIFICE

Offer your bodies as a living sacrifice,
holy and pleasing to God—
this is your true and proper worship.

ROMANS 12:1 NIV

Worship is not about what we say, but about what we do. Anyone can say one thing and then turn around and do the opposite. Words only matter when they are backed up with action. This is where faith is shown—not only in what we say we believe, but in how we live it out.

God has called us to be living sacrifices, offering our bodies and souls to his leadership. When we follow the example of Jesus, our choices become aligned with his love. The purposes of Christ's kingdom become more important to us than our own comfort. Let your worship be on display through your surrendered life!

Lord Jesus, you are worthy of my trust and my affection. Teach me to walk in humility and integrity, following your Spirit every step of the way.

FULLY EQUIPPED

All Scripture is breathed out by God and profitable for teaching, for reproof, for correction, and for training in righteousness, that the man of God may be complete, equipped for every good work.

2 TIMOTHY 3:16-17 ESV

There is a wealth of wisdom in the Word of God. Hebrews 4:12 says, "The word of God is living and active, sharper than any two-edged sword… discerning the thoughts and intentions of the heart." The living Word of God is accessible through his Spirit, for God makes the simple truths of his kingdom come alive through revelations that only he can give.

Have you ever experienced a light bulb moment? This is what the powerful wisdom of God is like at work within your heart and mind. All that was fuzzy now becomes unquestionably clear. Whatever you need today—whether it's direction, hope, solutions to a problem, or an understanding ear—you will find it in the fellowship of God.

Holy Spirit, as I read Scripture, speak to my heart and bring clarity to my mind. I want to take the next right step today. Thank you for your leadership.

FAITHFUL STEWARDSHIP

"His lord said to him, 'Well done, good and faithful servant; you were faithful over a few things, I will make you ruler over many things. Enter into the joy of your lord.'"

MATTHEW 25:21 NKJV

As humans, we often don't perceive ourselves truthfully. We either overestimate or underestimate ourselves. Some of us may struggle to see any weakness at all. Others of us may not be able to confidently walk in our strengths. No matter what it is we have or don't have, we all have something to steward. Instead of planning for what we will do someday, let's use what we have wisely, faithfully watching over it.

Jesus illustrated many of God's values and truths through storytelling. Today's verse illustrates the importance of faithfulness even in the little things of life, and how that sets us on a trajectory of increased trust and partnership with the Lord.

Lord, I don't want to get so caught up in what-ifs that I miss out on what I already have. Help me to focus on what is mine to steward here and now and to faithfully follow through.

Treasure of Giving

"I've left you an example of how you should serve and take care of those who are weak. For we must always cherish the words of our Lord Jesus, who taught, 'Giving brings a far greater blessing than receiving.'"

Acts 20:35 TPT

When you hear the phrase, "it is better to give than to receive," what is your initial reaction? Perhaps you had a loved one tell you this in response to wanting something as a young child. Maybe it is an overused saying that doesn't mean much of anything to you anymore. Perhaps it rings true in your experience.

Whatever your reaction to this expression, the power of it is not in hearing it but in actually experiencing it. Whether or not you have put it into practice recently, take the opportunity that today offers. Look for a practical way to serve and take care of those who are weak. Be creative and specific. There are opportunities waiting for you to experience the power of generosity and compassion in action.

Lord, I don't want to get stuck in consumption. Open my eyes for creative and practical ways to serve others in love today.

Whose You Are

"Truly, truly I say to you, a slave is not greater than his master, nor is one who is sent greater than the one who sent him."

John 13:16 NASB

Jesus did not come to be served, catered to, or to judge others. He came to serve others and give his life as a ransom: to set the captive free, and to show us what the love of the Father truly looks like. When we see Jesus for the beauty of his love, as well as the power of his self-sacrifice, choosing to live to serve our own interests over the well-being of others just doesn't line up.

Jesus has given us the greatest example of God's love. No worker is greater, or more important, than his. We cannot evaluate our success or our priorities based on society. If we want to follow Christ, we have to uphold his kingdom values over the values of this world. When we need a reminder of why, all we have to do is look to Christ. He is our reason.

Lord, thank you for the power of your love that liberates me from shame, sin, and fear. You are my hope, and I choose to follow you.

WORKING TOGETHER

We are God's workers, working together;
you are like God's farm, God's house.

1 CORINTHIANS 3:9 NCV

Work is more efficiently done when we work together in harmony. We may have different roles to play, but our purpose remains the same. Do you know your part in the purposes of God's kingdom? You don't have to complicate the issue. Look for ways to show his nature in the life you already have, and watch how he transforms your heart, mind, and life with his mercy.

Instead of going it alone today, look for ways to partner with others. We are so often independently focused, but there is so much beauty, power, and solidarity in community action. If you don't have something specific you are working toward, keep your eye out for those already in the trenches and partner with them. Take a step of faith and put it into action.

Lord, thank you for the part I get to play in your kingdom. Show me where I can partner with others to further your purposes.

FEBRUARY

This is love for God:
to keep his commands. And his
commands are not burdensome.

1 John 5:3 NIV

SURE PROMISES

Every one of God's promises is "Yes" in him. Therefore, through him we also say "Amen" to the glory of God.

2 CORINTHIANS 1:20 CSB

You can count on God's promises because they are backed up by his faithful character. He never errs or backs out. He doesn't overlook a vow or forget a single thing he has said. Even if you don't remember what God said, he does. He holds himself accountable to his Word.

God's faithfulness is his signature, and it is our confidence. If we don't have to worry about whether God will follow through, we can move that energy to our own partnership with him. There will be times where we simply must wait on him to show up. Even in this, we can tend to the more mundane areas of our lives with attention, presence, and love. Let's not overlook the power of simply showing up as we wait in faith for God to bring breakthrough.

Faithful One, there is no one like you. You keep all your promises, and I don't have to worry about them. Give me peace and clarity to tend to what I can.

TAKE INTEREST

Don't look out only for your own interests,
but take an interest in others, too.

PHILIPPIANS 2:4 NLT

Directly before today's verse, Paul admonishes the Philippians to not be selfish. He encourages them to not even try to impress others. Instead of being overly focused on what people think of us, love turns the tables to consider what makes them tick.

Today's verse doesn't say don't look out for your own interests at all. It is human nature to look out for ourselves. Most of us don't have to put extra work into that category, but taking an interest in others requires effort. When we seek to know someone, we let our curiosity and compassion lead the way, and this is just what Jesus does with us. Follow his lead and take an interest in those around you today.

Jesus, help me to not be consumed with my own interests, opinions, and desires. I want to reach outside of myself and know others.

STAND STRONG

Stand firm. Let nothing move you.
Always give yourselves fully to the work of the Lord,
because you know that your labor in the Lord is not in vain.

1 CORINTHIANS 15:58 NIV

There are many forces at work in this world that fight for our attention. We have endless information available to us, quite literally at the touch of our fingers, twenty-four hours a day. It's too much for all of us, no matter how efficient we think we are. If we want to live with focus, intention, and peace, we have to manage our attention.

One way to do this is by being clear about what is important to us. What are our values? These are the things we should order our lives around. If making sure our families know that they are loved and cared for is important, we have to create space for quality time together. If we want to make a difference in our communities, we must make time to actively be a part of them. Let's be sure that our intentions are not just wishes and put limits on frivolous things that add little value to our lives.

Lord, thank you for the reminder that standing firm in you requires effort. Help me focus today.

WALK IN GOODNESS

We are his workmanship,
created in Christ Jesus for good works,
which God prepared beforehand,
that we should walk in them.

EPHESIANS 2:10 ESV

Our lives are not a mystery to God and neither are our hearts. He knows us best, and he has so much goodness in store if we will follow his loving lead. What's even more powerful than this is to know God's redemption in our lives. It doesn't matter what we have or haven't done in the past. There isn't anything that God can't turn around in his mercy and bring new life out of.

You are God's workmanship—yes you! What God has made, he knows exactly what to do with. He has good works already prepared for you to walk in. If you need leadership, look to your Father! He will guide you every step as you lean on his presence.

Father, thank you for the power of your love in my life. Where I see weakness, you see opportunities for redemptive growth. I look to you today for strength, peace, and wisdom.

SHARE IT

Do not forget to do good and to share,
for with such sacrifices God is well pleased.

HEBREWS 13:16 NKJV

God delights in our praises. He loves our expressions of gratitude. They mean something to him. But our praise cannot be only found in what we express through words. We must also do good. One way to do good is to share with others. Simply put, look for ways to share with those who are in need. Everyone benefits from this.

God sees and honors your sacrifices of praise as you offer tangible kindness and compassion to those around you. Let go of excuses that do nothing but pad your comfort and reach out to share what you have with others today. God is well pleased when you do!

God, open my eyes to see the opportunities around me to share what I have with others. I say yes to you by giving of myself today.

EMPOWERED TO HELP

Love empowers us to fulfill the law of the Anointed One as we carry each other's troubles.

GALATIANS 6:2 TPT

All of us experience moments in life that are seemingly unbearable. Whether it's due to the loss of a loved one, a prolonged illness, or the loss of a job or property, we can be sure that troubles will come our way. It is in these very times that the support of others matters most. A shared burden is a lighter load.

We are empowered by the love of God to help carry the heaviness of others. None of us was meant or made to do it alone. Let's be sure to reach out for help when we need it, and let's also be ready to help carry the troubles of others when we see the opportunity. This is the power and beauty of the family of God: no one has to suffer alone!

Father, thank you for the power of community and support I find in you and your kingdom.

LOVING ACTION

Little children, let's not love with word or with tongue, but in deed and truth.

1 JOHN 3:18 NASB

Much can be said of the power of God's love in our lives. When we talk about what love means to us, how it transforms, soothes, and moves us, it is often not in the space of ideas. It is in the muscle and the matter—the ways it is shown and experienced.

Love is incredibly practical. It is in the caring hug of a loved one, in someone offering to cook when we are too tired, in the "I'm sorry" or "I'll do better next time," in following through on what we say we'll do, in listening when we'd rather give advice. It is in all these things and so much more. Look for ways to take loving action today. There is power in your lived-out love.

Lord Jesus, when I start to feel as though love is a whim and a wish rather than care and kindness, remind me that I get to choose to love in action.

NO ONE BENEATH YOU

"Then the King will answer, 'I tell you the truth, anything you did for even the least of my people here, you also did for me.'"

MATTHEW 25:40 NCV

The least of these. What comes to mind when you read this phrase? Sit with it for a moment and let your mind wander a little. Whether it's children in war-torn lands or the panhandler on the street, there is no one more or less worthy of love than we are.

Let's not neglect our compassionate responsibility toward those the world dismisses. We cannot have the same cold attitude of overlooking their humanity simply because they are different, have less access to resources, or have no one to help them. It is important that we keep our hearts humble and look with eyes of love at those around us. Then we can more readily help those who need it.

Jesus Christ, your standard is the one that truly matters. Transform my heart so powerfully in your love that I look at others and see reflections of you.

OVERFLOWING

May the God of hope fill you with all joy and peace as you believe so that you may overflow with hope by the power of the Holy Spirit.

ROMANS 15:13 CSB

We are filled to be poured out. Not so we will be empty, but so we will actually live out of the overflow: the abundance of God's love, his presence that is full of joy, peace, and hope, as it spills out to others.

If you are empty today, there is hope for you. The God of all hope fills you with the power of his Holy Spirit, offering you the lavish kindness of his presence. He fills you with joy and peace as you pair your faith with his faithfulness. Don't worry if you have little to offer. God never runs out or runs dry of the empowering grace you need. Go to him and be filled.

Holy Spirit, fill me up with your love, the grace I need to walk in courage, and the empowering hope of your comfort and nearness.

RENEWED

Those who trust in the LORD will find new strength.
They will soar high on wings like eagles.
They will run and not grow weary.
They will walk and not faint.

ISAIAH 40:31 NLT

Some days we are overflowing, while others leave us depleted. On the hard days when nothing seems to be going right, let's remember that nothing lasts forever. Though grief remains for a night, the dawn of a new day is coming. When we are limited in strength, the rest of God becomes our place of refreshing.

God's grace gives us the strength we need to face what is necessary. We can certainly do our best to plan our schedule in a way that honors our limits, but there are certain things we cannot move to another day. It is in these moments when we need the new strength that today's verse speaks of. Instead of giving up, let's call on the Lord. He will renew our strength.

Lord, when I am depleted, I don't want to give up. Help me to rely on you for the strength I cannot conjure up.

SAFE PLACE

You are my refuge and my shield;
I have put my hope in your word.

PSALM 119:114 NIV

When you need the shelter of God's presence, it is always available. There are some storms that come in quick without warning. Others we see a mile off. No matter the state of your troubles today, God is nearer than you know.

God will never ask us to depart from the ways of his nature. If, in our fear, we feel the pull to judge others, ridicule them, or push them down in order to protect ourselves, we can be sure that it is not the presence of God at work in our hearts. It is the pull of fear. Love expands and makes things clearer. Fear muddies them and makes us feel rushed. Let's find our refuge in the presence of God, where love and peace reside.

Father, I know that you are unchanging. Your mercy is forever, and your kindness cannot be quenched. You are my safe place.

PREPARED

In your hearts honor Christ the Lord as holy, always being prepared to make a defense to anyone who asks you for a reason for the hope that is in you; yet do it with gentleness and respect.

1 PETER 3:15 ESV

When we honor the Lord as holy, we take his Word seriously. The hope of Christ is not a theory; it is alive and well within us. This is revealed through how we live: how we treat others, how we do our business, and what we prioritize.

When we consider the ways of God, the patience, tenderness, and grace of his love, we become more acquainted with the fingerprints of his mercy in this world. May we be arbiters of his goodness and loving representations of his truth. Always with gentleness and respect, let's be prepared to share the powerful hope we have, for it is life-changing and true.

Lord Jesus, continue to transform me by the power of your mercy in my life. Help me to be gentle and respectful as I share the incredible hope I have in you.

HOPE OF THE OVERLOOKED

The needy shall not always be forgotten;
The expectation of the poor shall not perish forever.

PSALM 9:18 NKJV

What is your attitude toward the poor? Jesus was a friend of known sinners, and he spent time with the lowest of society—those others overlooked. This included the destitute. He could have spent the bulk of his time with kings and in the places of highest honor, but this is not what he did.

If you find yourself in the halls of the powerful, don't run away. But do you also interact with those who have nothing to offer you? Let love be your guide in all things. Don't surround yourself with powerful people so you become out of touch with the needs of the poor. The one who created you also created them. Let's partner with him and care for them.

Lord, I don't want to be blinded by the privileges I have in life and keep a distance between myself and those with less. I humble my heart before you and ask you to enlarge it with your compassionate kindness.

WAIT IN TRUST

O Israel, keep hoping, keep trusting,
and keep waiting on the Lord,
for he is tenderhearted, kind, and forgiving.
He has a thousand ways to set you free!

PSALM 130:7 TPT

Wherever you find yourself today, it is a good day to keep going. Keep hoping, keep trusting, and keep waiting on the Lord. He has not abandoned you or forgotten about you. He oozes with tender kindness toward you. He knows you thoroughly, and he knows just how to help you.

He has a thousand ways to set you free. A thousand! All you need is one, and he has options. If you want breakthrough in your life, you can count on the Lord to bring it. He won't fail you. He is faithful in love and full of all the solutions you need.

Lord, I choose to keep trusting you, even when it is hard. I choose to keep hoping in you, for you are faithful. I choose to keep waiting on you because you always come through.

POWERFUL SPIRIT

God has not given us a spirit of timidity,
but of power and love and discipline.

2 TIMOTHY 1:7 NASB

Timidity isn't just a feeling of being shy. It is a lack of courage and confidence. God has not given us a spirit that leaves us feeling unprepared or lacking resolution. He has given us the spirit of power and love and self-control.

Where there is power, there is a sense of confidence. Where there is love, there is room to try and fail. Where there is discipline, there is the focus and strength to put thought into action. This is what the Spirit of God does for us. He offers us courage, confidence, and grace to try and keep trying. He gives us patience and clarity to keep going, one foot after the other.

Spirit, fill my heart and mind with your love so fear loses its grip. I want to move in confidence and courage, and I need your help to do it.

Good, Good News

The LORD God has put his Spirit in me,
because the LORD has appointed me
to tell the good news to the poor.

ISAIAH 61:1 NCV

The good news of the gospel is for everyone. If it doesn't sound like good news to the poor, the brokenhearted, or those in captivity, it is time to reevaluate what we are sharing. God does not promise us easy lives void of pain. He promises care, breakthrough, and salvation. Those are worth more than our comfort.

Our service to others shouldn't just be to do a job but to share the incomparable love of God. Why would we keep the good news of Christ's kindness to ourselves? Let's spend time refreshing our hearts and minds in the goodness of God's love.

Lord God, fill me up with your love so I have more than enough to offer others, sharing your goodness and faithfulness with those around me.

FOLLOW HIM

"If anyone serves me, he must follow me.
Where I am, there my servant also will be.
If anyone serves me, the Father will honor him."

JOHN 12:26 CSB

Serving Christ isn't just about following a set of religious rules. It is knowing him, relating to him, and following him. This would be a tall order without the help of the Holy Spirit. Thankfully, we have full fellowship with God through Christ, and the Father has given us the company of the Holy Spirit to transform, empower, and teach us. Not to mention the comfort, healing, and miraculous freedom we experience in his presence.

If you want to serve Jesus, take him at his invitation today and follow him. Walk in the ways he walked. Love others, being kind and gracious. Stand on truth and reject duplicity. Read his Word and follow his lead. Invite the Holy Spirit to teach, guide, and correct you. Following Jesus is worth it. There is freedom, revelation, and light in his presence.

Lord Jesus, I choose to follow you. I say yes to your ways and to your leadership.

A TENDER HEART

Instead, be kind to each other, tenderhearted, forgiving one another, just as God through Christ has forgiven you.

EPHESIANS 4:32 NLT

When did society decide that being kind, gentle, and forgiving is weakness? Perhaps the power of love has been underestimated throughout the history of humanity. While brute force and arrogance may intimidate, the power of love is far greater. There is no competition in love. There is no need to prove ourselves. No one is more or less worthy of it.

When we cultivate kindness and choose to stay tenderhearted, it is the stronger path. It is easier to shut down than it is to remain loving when others disappoint, harm, or reject us. Still, the way of God's love is to forgive, to be kind and gracious, to yield our hearts to mercy.

Kind God, your love is stronger than fear or hate. Help me to be kind, tenderhearted, and willing to forgive, especially when others don't.

ALL COMFORT

Praise be to the God and Father of our Lord Jesus Christ, the Father of compassion and the God of all comfort, who comforts us in all our troubles, so that we can comfort those in any trouble with the comfort we ourselves receive from God.

2 CORINTHIANS 1:3-4 NIV

There is comfort in the presence of God. He does not turn away from our pain or weakness. He does not demand that we suffer in silence. He is the God who gets down into the middle of our mess. He meets us in our suffering and pain.

What if, when we saw others in pain and suffering, instead of turning a blind eye in our discomfort, we met them in that space? Comfort doesn't look for quick fixes or pat answers. Compassion is a powerful sensation. When we allow compassion to lead us, we can sit with those in pain and offer comfort without trying to erase the experience.

God of all comfort, help me to resist ignoring or trying to fix other's pain without sitting with them in compassion. Show me the way to be a comfort to others.

CLOTHED IN COMPASSION

Put on then, as God's chosen ones, holy and beloved, compassionate hearts, kindness, humility, meekness, and patience.

COLOSSIANS 3:12 ESV

What does a follower of Christ look like? The Word is clear: it is not through the dogmatic judgment of those who are different. It isn't represented in debates, how sure we are of specific theologies, or the like. A true follower of Christ represents the characteristics of God's love.

There is nothing wrong with seeking the truth, but if we miss the power and place of God's love along the way, we miss the point entirely. Let's put our focus on what we can do as we follow Christ's loving example. We can clothe ourselves in compassion, kindness, humility, gentleness, and patience. Even if we simply choose one to focus on, it is energy well spent.

Lord, help me to stay rooted in what following you really means. Thank you for the opportunities I have to extend kindness, to remain humble, and to practice patience.

Tender Love

The same way a loving father feels toward his children—
that's but a sample of your tender feelings toward us,
your beloved children, who live in awe of you.

Psalm 103:13 TPT

It's so important to know and understand what God is like. He is not impatient or cruel. He isn't controlling or annoyed by us. He is a loving father who feels tenderness, compassion, and hope toward his children.

The more we are convinced of God's love for us, the more confidently we can live with that same love toward others. Even when others reject us, God won't. He is faithful to his Word, and he won't let us down. Let's live out the love of God, offering others the same grace, patience, and kindness we receive. We all fall short of the perfect love of God, but we can try our very best to love others with his generosity.

Father, thank you for your powerful love that fuels my hope, my identity, and fills my own well of love. Let the overflow of your mercy be seen in the way that I choose to treat others.

BE THOUGHTFUL

Rejoice with those who rejoice,
and weep with those who weep.

ROMANS 12:15 NKJV

It is ignorant to show up to a wedding as if it were a funeral. Imagine a person in all black, wiping sad tears from their eyes and showing no signs of happiness at a joyous celebration. It doesn't fit, does it? In the same way, when we are around those who are grieving a deep loss, it is inappropriate for us to try to cheer them up with our own joy.

God knows just what we need in every moment. He comforts us in our grief, even sharing in our sorrow, and he rejoices in our victories. We can all know him in this way, for he has given us access to his presence through fellowship with his Son and Spirit. As he is with us so let us be with others. A little bit of thoughtfulness can go a long way.

Wonderful One, you always know just what to do or say. Help me to be thoughtful in my interactions with others, not wanting to rush them past the significance of what they are feeling.

RENEWAL

Do not be conformed to this world, but be transformed by the renewing of your mind, so that you may prove what the will of God is, that which is good and acceptable and perfect.

ROMANS 12:2 NASB

There is a lot of fighting for our attention and affection these days. If we are not intentional about it, we will give into the despair of the age. What the world values is not the same as the kingdom of Christ. Where wealth, power, and prestige impress many in this world, God isn't influenced one bit.

Instead of blindly adopting the values of those around us, let's allow the Spirit of the Lord to transform us by the renewing of our minds. There is goodness in following the wisdom of God and allowing his Word to penetrate our hearts. We don't need more knowledge; we need wisdom and revelation to renew our minds in the power of Christ.

Perfect One, you are the God of all wisdom. Renew my mind and transform my heart in the power of your love.

OUR HUMBLE KING

"If I, your Lord and Teacher, have washed your feet, you also should wash each other's feet."

JOHN 13:14 NCV

When Jesus washed his disciples' feet, it was no small act. It was both symbolic and a powerful example of what God's love looks like. Jesus took on the job of a servant. It was the lowliest position that washed the dust from a traveler's feet. He was incredibly intentional in this act of service, showing that nothing was beneath him. No act of loving service is beneath us either.

God's love is immensely practical. It does not turn its nose up at washing toilets, bathing the elderly, or picking up trash. It embraces the lowest service with the same attitude as it does the highest. Let's follow the Lord's instruction, showing the incredible love of God through even the most menial tasks.

Lord Jesus, I don't naturally want to serve in some ways. Renew my perspective and help me to choose service, even when it is unappealing. Let me be filled with a heart of love in all I do.

Tenacious Hope

Rejoice in hope; be patient in affliction;
be persistent in prayer.

Romans 12:12 CSB

It's a simple instruction, and yet it can be so hard sometimes. When we choose to rejoice in hope on hard days, it takes courage. When we choose to bear our suffering with patience, it takes higher perspective. When we are persistent in prayer even when we are unbearably busy, it takes intention.

The beautiful caveat to all of this is that we don't do it alone. We have the presence of God with us to help us choose hope in hardship. We have the empowering Spirit of the Lord to give us patience in the midst of our suffering. We have instant access to the Lord through prayer and the fellowship of his Spirit.

Lord, I open my heart before you now and ask for your strength and companionship to help me stay hopeful, patient, and persistent today.

GOD OF MERCY

You, O Lord,
are a God of compassion and mercy,
slow to get angry
and filled with unfailing love and faithfulness.

Psalm 86:15 NLT

The way we become more like the Lord isn't through endless striving. It is in prioritizing our relationship with him. The more we spend time with him, getting to know his true nature, the more we are transformed by his love. It becomes a natural extension to grow in compassion, patience, and faithfulness.

We cannot serve God without knowing him. If we do not know what he is like or what he expects, how can we represent him well? Our God is not quick to anger. He is not indifferent to suffering. He is patient with us. His love is larger than we can imagine. The more we get to know God in his mercy, the more readily we can offer it to others. It all starts and ends with him.

Merciful One, I don't want to get distracted by things that don't matter today. I want to know you more! Reveal your mercy to me in new ways and help me represent your kindness in my life.

HE GETS IT

We do not have a high priest who is unable to empathize with our weaknesses, but we have one who has been tempted in every way, just as we are—yet he did not sin.

HEBREWS 4:15 NIV

Jesus did not live an out-of-touch life. He was not raised in a palace with endless resources at his disposal. He was born in a barn to humble parents. Mary and Joseph weren't anyone special in their society, but to God they were. God loves to use the ordinary to display his power and goodness. This includes you.

Jesus truly understands what life is like. He knew what it was like to go without, to be hungry, and to be sleep-deprived. He knew temptation and hardship. He knew grief and suffering. There isn't a heartbreak we go through in this life that he can't relate to. He sees us, knows us, and loves us as we are, and he shows us the way to keep persevering in love just as he did.

Lord, I'm so glad I have a high priest that empathizes with my weaknesses. Help me, guide me, and give me strength to follow you.

YOUR NEIGHBOR

There is neither Jew nor Greek,
there is neither slave nor free,
there is no male and female,
for you are all one in Christ Jesus.

GALATIANS 3:28 ESV

Scripture says that we are to love our neighbor as we love ourselves. Jesus broke every dividing line that humanity put into place to separate us. In Christ, there is no gender discrimination. There is no power imbalance or class system. There is no ethnic hierarchy. There is only family, belonging, and love.

No one is greater than any other. God loves us each fully and completely, and this is how we are to love one another. Our neighbor isn't the person we choose to love. It is simply the person who is there—no matter who they are. Let's put love on and remove any qualifiers we have for our own indifference. We are all made in the image of God.

Father of all, thank you for the reminder that we are all made in your image. You love me as much as you love anyone, and that includes every person I will ever meet.

MARCH

"Blessed are those who hear the teaching of God and obey it."

LUKE 11:28 NCV

POWERFUL PERSPECTIVE

This means that, contrary to man's perspective, the Lord is not late with his promise to return, as some measure lateness. But rather, his "delay" simply reveals his loving patience toward you, because he does not want any to perish but all to come to repentance.

2 PETER 3:9 TPT

God has not forgotten a single promise he has made. He is not slow in fulfilling them. Though we may grow impatient as God's timeline expands, we can take hope in the goodness of his heart and purposes. His patience and love are on display in all that he does, even when our waiting grows longer than we had hoped.

Jesus promised to return, and he will. It is not for us to know the day or the hour. What matters is how we live our lives as we wait. If we choose to live out his love, helping those around us and being kind, loving, and generous, we reflect his likeness in our lives. These are the things that matter in the end.

God, when I think I know better than you, remind me that I don't see even a fraction of what you do. Help me to remain focused on what truly matters.

LIKE HIM

Gracious is the LORD, and righteous;
Yes, our God is merciful.

PSALM 116:5 NKJV

Serving the Lord, saying yes to him each day, is less about the particulars and more about representing him well. Sure, there will be times when we feel led in a specific direction. Obedience is importance. Still, obedience to him will never require us to move away from his nature.

The Lord is gracious. He is righteous. He is merciful. When we represent him well in our love, we too will be known as gracious. Our integrity will reveal righteousness. Our mercy will point directly to our Father. When we struggle to know just what to do, let's focus our attention more on how we do what we do.

Gracious God, I can get so caught up in the particulars of my life that sometimes I lose sight of the love that undergirds it all. Help me to prioritize my character over everything else.

DON'T FORGET

My whole being, praise the LORD
and do not forget all his kindnesses.

PSALM 103:2 NCV

If we don't give ourselves time to reflect on the goodness of God, we may just forget how wonderful he is. Relationships take effort and intention, and it is no different in our relationship with God. Remembrance is a practice that can add faith, hope, and joy to our hearts. It will bring vibrancy to our lives.

In the Old Testament, many psalms were written as a way to remember what the Lord had done. Stones of remembrance were raised in important places as physical reminders of God's powerful deliverance. How can you build a practice of remembrance in your life so that you stay connected to the wonderful things the Lord has done?

Faithful One, thank you for all you have done for me. I remember your goodness, and I breathe in your peace, hope, and joy today.

IMPORTANCE OF ENDURANCE

We count as blessed those who have endured. You have heard of Job's endurance and have seen the outcome that the Lord brought about—the Lord is compassionate and merciful.

JAMES 5:11 CSB

Endurance is necessary. If we give up easily, we miss out on what is on the other side of perseverance. Not all things in life are worth sticking out, but there are certainly many that are. It is important that we do not give up at the slightest bit of resistance. If we want to grow, we have to be willing to wade through discomfort and trust the Lord even as we struggle to understand.

God is always compassionate and merciful. Those traits aren't up for debate. If we cannot see compassion in our lived reality, let's press in to know him more. Let's ask for his perspective as well as his comfort. Endurance doesn't mean that we don't struggle; it means that we continue to persist in trust as we do.

God, I'm so glad you see things clearly when no one else does. Help me to keep pursuing you, persisting in love and trust, even and especially when it is hard to do so.

FREE FROM CONDEMNATION

There is no condemnation
for those who belong to Christ Jesus.

ROMANS 8:1 NLT

When Christ forgives us, he sets us free from all blame, guilt, and condemnation. He doesn't hold our past against us, and neither should we. There is incredible freedom in his grace and mercy. There are no limits to his love, so let's stretch the boundaries of our expectation to expand in his mercy!

There is a difference between accountability and accusation. Let's be clear on it. Accountability calls people to a standard of honesty, justice, and values, while accusations simply lay blame. It is incredibly important that we take responsibility for our errors, and it's also necessary that we know what we need to let go. God's Spirit of wisdom is there to help us know the difference.

Gracious Jesus, help me to know the difference between being called to account and being condemned. I never want to shrink from the truth. I'm so grateful that in you I have complete freedom from shame.

Tempered by Patience

Time after time he restrained his anger
and did not stir up his full wrath.

PSALM 78:38 NIV

In the world of emotions, we often categorize them as good and bad. Joy feels light, while grief feels heavy. Happiness is praised while anger is avoided. However, the broad spectrum of our emotions reflects the nature of God. While he always does things right and tempered with kindness, we will sometimes get them wrong. This isn't to say we shouldn't try!

Anger is a clue that our boundaries have been crossed, or that we sense an injustice. Scripture says that God restrained his anger instead of stirring it up. He is lavish in mercy—much more than we can imagine. Instead of lashing out in anger, let's step away so we can learn the patience of mercy, while still being kind to ourselves in the process.

Merciful One, I want to grow in temperance, and I know that means being more mindful of my emotions. When I feel anger rising, help me to use it in a productive way.

THE REQUIREMENTS

He has told you, O man, what is good;
and what does the LORD require of you
but to do justice, and to love kindness,
and to walk humbly with your God?

MICAH 6:8 ESV

What are the requirements of following the Lord? They are simple: to do justice, love kindness, and to walk humbly with your God. We are to love kindness, choosing it in our interactions with others, and honoring it when we see it.

As we walk humbly with our God, we allow him to guide us along the path of his love. He corrects us when we step out of his love, forgives us when we repent, and leads us in wisdom. If we will stay open to his correction, we will grow in the values of his kingdom. We don't have to go searching for a better principle to follow today: he has already told us what is good, and what he requires of us.

Lord, thank you for the clarity of your Word and your nature. Help me to uphold justice, acting fairly in all my interactions. Give me strength to choose kindness.

PURE RELIGION

Pure and undefiled religion before God and the Father is this: to visit orphans and widows in their trouble, and to keep oneself unspotted from the world.

JAMES 1:27 NKJV

It is no small thing to keep ourselves unstained from the world, but we can do it as we walk in the love of God. As we follow Christ's ways, saying yes to his compassion and the wisdom of his leadership, we will do as today's verse instructs. Visiting orphans and widows isn't about checking off an obligation but showing up in compassion for those who lack the covering of consistent care. For all of those who have less than we do, it is important that we actively share with a generous heart.

Religion that only looks like going to church services while living for oneself the rest of the week is not what God wants. He wants our surrendered lives, not for selfish reasons, but so that his extravagant love will spread to all the world. Let's spill out with his mercy, visiting those with no one to care for them, and helping those who need it. This is pure religion.

Father, thank you for the power of your love that reaches us all. I partner with your will and ways.

POWERFUL PEACE

"Everything I've taught you is so that the peace which is in me will be in you and will give you great confidence as you rest in me."

JOHN 16:33 TPT

You were not created to strive in angst every day of your life. You were made to know God, to rest in his friendship, and to experience the peace that passes all understanding. You can know the peace of God in every circumstance, for God's presence is with all who surrender their lives to him.

We need peace the most when our hearts are troubled. Whatever sorrows we carry, they don't dictate the presence of God's peace. Philippians 4 says that when you share the details of your life with God, his wonderful peace that transcends human understanding, will guard your heart and mind. Jesus himself is our plentiful portion of peace, and he is near.

Prince of Peace, I need the powerful presence of your peace to guard my heart and mind today. Flood my senses with your presence.

THE GOLDEN RULE

"In everything, therefore, treat people the same way you want them to treat you, for this is the Law and the Prophets."

MATTHEW 7:12 NASB

It doesn't make sense for us to expect more from others than we are willing to offer. In the same way, we set an example of goodness, love, and respect by treating others well. If we want grace and understanding when we mess up, it is good practice to give grace and understanding when others fail.

The golden rule is a simple and powerful way to align our perspectives with the Lord's. If we err on the side of mercy, we will not fail to represent the kindness of God. It is always better to be more loving than to be too rigid in our expectations. We are all human, after all. Let's lead with kindness and remember how it is we want to be treated.

Lord, help me to walk in the ways of your love by remembering to offer grace, kindness, and respect. I want to treat others with generosity and goodness.

RECOUNT HIS GOODNESS

I will recount the favors of the LORD,
the glorious deeds of the LORD,
because of all that the LORD has done for us
and the great kindness he has shown.

ISAIAH 63:7 NCV

The mercy of God is filled with his goodness. There are miracles of his kindness everywhere he touches with his presence. Even if you are in a season of suffering, God's hand is present, and it is full of mercy, grace, and peace.

Sometimes the push we need to keep going is in the remembrance of what matters. God's nature is never changing. He is always loving, always powerful, always near. He is the master restorer, and there isn't a situation or a heartbreak he can't mend or redeem. Let's recount his goodness, remembering his faithfulness to us. He will not change.

Kind Lord, thank you for your goodness toward me. Increase my courage to keep following you in faith. You have my yes today!

CULTIVATE MERCY

Have mercy on those who waver.

JUDE 1:22 CSB

God does not judge us when we waver in doubt. Why is it that we feel the need to do it with others? If instead we cultivate mercy toward one another, we can leave room for the process that others are going through while still showing up in love. We don't have to let fear rule our relationships. Love always makes room, while fear puts up strict parameters.

What would it look like to have curiosity and compassion toward ourselves and others in our doubts? How could that change the dynamic? No one wants to experience doubts, but they can be incredibly helpful and healthy when allowed space to work out. God wasn't afraid of wrestling with those who wavered, and we can trust that he is at work in each heart that seeks him.

Merciful Father, when I don't understand the doubts of others, help me to remember that it is not mine to fix. I want to continue to love them in their process and stand in the truth of your mercy.

LORD OF THE HARVEST

"The harvest is great, but the workers are few. So pray to the Lord who is in charge of the harvest; ask him to send more workers into his fields."

MATTHEW 9:37-38 NLT

There is so much need in this world. People are helpless and confused, without hope, and this is easy to understand when we look at the enormity of the violence, trauma, and need of people around the world. It is not only "out there" but present in our communities too.

Does this mean we should despair? By no means! The Lord is powerful to meet us each where we are. His love is abundant. There is freedom for all in his love. There is an open invitation for salvation. We have only to live out the kindness he has shown us and invite others into the realm of his liberating love.

Jesus, I say yes to you. I want to work in your fields, sharing the power of your love that liberates our souls.

SET APART

"Before I formed you in the womb I knew you,
before you were born I set you apart;
I appointed you as a prophet to the nations."

JEREMIAH 1:5 NIV

You were created with purpose. You were set apart even before you left your mother's womb. There is nothing about you or your life that surprises God. He knows you thoroughly, and he loves you completely.

You can trust that what God calls you to, he leads you in. Will you follow him? He has all the resources you need, and he has solutions for your problems. You will not see the end from the beginning, but he does. You will not know every detail of the path laid out, but you can trust the one who does. He knows the purposes and plans he has for you, and they are for your good.

Creator, I'm so relieved that you know me, love me, and lead me in this life. I am yours, and I choose to follow your lead.

MARCH 15

NEVER-ENDING LOVE

The steadfast love of the LORD never ceases;
his mercies never come to an end;
they are new every morning;
great is your faithfulness.

LAMENTATIONS 3:22-23 ESV

The mercies of God never end. They are new every single morning. That means a fresh start each new day. Wherever you find yourself today, know that God's love reaches you in new measures. It is not stale, and it is not lacking. It is overflowing toward you.

We all need fresh encounters with the love of Christ. We are not meant to live on yesterday's bread. Remember when the Israelites depended on God to feed them in the desert? He sent them manna from heaven new each morning. He does the same in his love toward you. Take and eat the fresh manna of his presence. There is more than enough to meet your needs today.

God, thank you for the provision of your love. I seek you out like the sunflower turns toward the sun. Shine on me, and I will live. You are my light, my life, and my source of strength.

As You Are Able

Every man shall give as he is able, according to the blessing of the Lord your God which He has given you.

Deuteronomy 16:17 NKJV

Each one should give as they are able. The parable of the widow's mite illustrates how God's measurement works. It is not based on the amount we give in and of itself, but of what it costs us. The widow sacrificed more than anyone else though it was but pennies. The Lord does not require us to give more than we are able, but he honors each sacrifice as we grow in generosity.

You may look at your life and think you don't have much to offer. What if the widow had thought the same? Though no one else may take notice of your offering, God does. He sees every act of kindness, every gift of generosity that you offer. Look at what you are able to give and offer it back to the Lord today.

Generous Lord, I don't want to overlook the blessing of giving when I have enough to share. Help me to live a life of open-hearted generosity.

ENCOURAGING HEARTS

Encourage the hearts of your fellow believers and support one another, just as you have already been doing.

1 THESSALONIANS 5:11 TPT

When we seek to encourage the hearts of our brothers and sisters in Christ, we remind each other of the hope we have in him. Encouragement and support go hand-in-hand. When we see each other in our struggles, we don't have to run away from the reality. We get to partner with each other in building each other up in love and hope.

We all have dips in life. We need the encouragement of people who get it to help us along the way. There is no verse in the Bible that tells us to pull ourselves up by the bootstraps and get moving. The way of the kingdom is in partnership and community. Those with higher capacities can help the weak—and be sure of this—we all take turns being the strong as well as the weak. Whether you need encouragement today or can simply be one to offer it to another, don't overlook the power of it.

Lord, thank you for the power of encouragement found in community. Encourage my own heart through others, even as I reach out to support those around me.

RICH FAITH

Listen, my beloved brothers and sisters: did God not choose the poor of this world to be rich in faith and heirs of the kingdom which He promised to those who love Him?

JAMES 2:5 NASB

Faith isn't measured by what we physically own. It is not stored in banks or hidden out of sight. Hebrews 11:1 says, "Faith is the certainty of things hoped for, a proof of things not seen." Through faith Abraham left his homeland not knowing where he was going. He was obedient to God's call.

You don't need anything in this world to measure your faith. There is more than enough available to you. You are an heir of the kingdom of Christ. There is nothing worth more than the love of God, and it is available to all in the same overwhelming measure. Don't disqualify yourself from what God has called you to based on your lack of resources. Be rich in faith and follow him.

Generous God, thank you for your faithfulness. I choose to invest my faith in you.

REMOVE THE CONDITIONS

"Love your enemies, do good to them, and lend to them without hoping to get anything back. Then you will have a great reward, and you will be children of the Most High God, because he is kind even to people who are ungrateful and full of sin."

LUKE 6:35 NCV

Today's verse is not an easy one to follow. There are so many reasons to talk ourselves out of loving those who are hard to get along with, let alone those who harm us. Jesus' love has no conditions, and he asks us to follow in his footsteps. No conditions. Just good-natured grace and kindness.

If we find it hard to follow the Lord's lead, we can always come to him for help. He never withholds his grace from those who ask for it. This includes you and me! If we need a reminder or a reason to treat others with kindness, goodness, and generosity, we have no further to look than to Jesus Christ himself. Let's lay down our resentment and receive the extravagant mercy of God. From his fullness, we have more than enough to offer others—even our enemies.

Merciful Jesus, help me love those who have done me wrong really, truly, and with grace.

BENEFITS OF KINDNESS

A kind man benefits himself,
but a cruel person brings ruin on himself.

PROVERBS 11:17 CSB

Kindness is a trait that honors the bearer as much as it does the recipient. Cruelty is a trait that undermines the perpetrator and their cause; they will be held accountable for their actions. We cannot hide cruelty; it will make itself known. How we act, how we treat others, matters immensely.

The benefits of cultivating kindness are many. When we remove harsh judgment from our interactions with others, we leave room for others to show up as they are. No one is perfect. Where there is grace for our weaknesses, there is room for love to create understanding, forgiveness, and respect.

Kind God, thank you for your merciful heart that offers a fresh start each and every day. Create in me a kind heart as I follow your footsteps.

Never Give Up

Love never gives up, never loses faith, is always hopeful, and endures through every circumstance.

1 Corinthians 13:6-7 NLT

Love never gives up. As we follow the Lord, neither do we. It is not sheer determination that keeps us in the kingdom of Christ. It is the overwhelming power of God's love. It is all that he has already done and offered. We are found in him: found in his love all the days of our lives.

When you say yes to Jesus, you say yes to his love. It is strong enough to cover your failures, not only from your past, but also as you make new ones. Know this: you will never be perfect. God has already perfected you in his love. You can stand unashamed and free from fear in his presence. If you need a reminder to persevere in love, let his presence be your source and your strength.

Lord, your love is the strength of my life. When I fail, you pick me up. When I disappoint myself, you draw me near in mercy and restore my soul.

ABOVE ALL

Above all, love each other deeply,
because love covers over a multitude of sins.

1 PETER 4:8 NIV

Sometimes it can be hard to know what exact things to focus on. As varying voices vie for our attention, we can feel pulled in a hundred directions. The law of love simplifies our spiritual focus. Love above all. Why does love matter so much?

There are many reasons to celebrate in life, and there are also myriad experiences to mourn. It can feel easy to love others when we are in a good place. Our jobs are good, our families stable—you know, the calm seasons of life. However, when the bottom drops out, we need the love of God and others even more. We were created for support and for community. No matter what else we focus on today, let's remember above all to love each other deeply.

Loving Lord, your mercy is steadfast. It does not change with my circumstances. Empower me with your love to love those around me deeply.

LIFEGIVING PURSUIT

Whoever pursues righteousness and kindness
will find life, righteousness, and honor.

PROVERBS 21:21 ESV

It is no insignificant matter to pursue righteousness. It is a path of lifegiving honor. It is like a fountain that fills us with satisfaction. If we want to live the abundant life that Christ offers us, it is found in this pursuit.

The Holy Spirit guides us as we practice lives of holiness. We walk in wisdom's ways and make integrity our aim. We are honest about our limits, remaining humble in love and gracious in our estimation of others. We don't back down from justice, but we do the hard thing when it is the right thing to do. We don't strive for perfection. Instead, we aim to remain teachable, ever-growing in this lifelong pursuit of friendship with God. What grace, life, and abundance is ours as we do.

Lord of life, you are the one I pursue. I will look for ways to grow in your love today.

BUILDERS OF PEOPLE

Let each of us please his neighbor for his good, leading to edification.

ROMANS 15:2 NKJV

Our yes to the Lord begins in the posture of our hearts. It is then revealed in the ways we live out his love in our lives. Serving others for their benefit, encouragement, and good is a practical way to live out our faith. Faith and service work together not in isolation of each other.

James 2 is a helpful reminder that encouraging our neighbor is in fact very practical. If you see someone in need but ignore their physical need, how are you practicing love? Today, when you see a practical way to encourage or please your neighbor, act on it. This will build them up and bolster your own faith.

God, my yes to you includes service to others. Thank you for the reminder to do practical good to others.

CHOOSE TO BLESS

Never retaliate when someone treats you wrongly, nor insult those who insult you, but instead, respond by speaking a blessing over them—because a blessing is what God promised to give you.

1 PETER 3:9 TPT

Have you ever heard the term "operate in the opposite spirit?" It can be a helpful reminder when others curse us to bless them. When someone treats us poorly, we can still choose to treat them kindly. Today's verse is a crash-course in blessing others in all sorts of situations.

It is not a natural reaction to gently respond to someone who is shouting. It is not common to encourage someone who insults us. This is exactly what Scripture says we should do. We get to bless others when they insult us, not because we are weak, afraid, or pitiable, but because the love of God is stronger. A blessing is what God promised to give us, and he does each time we come to him.

Gracious Father, as I encounter harshness in others, may I bless them, operating in the Spirit of your mercy and grace.

KEEP DOING GOOD

Let's not become discouraged in doing good,
for in due time we will reap, if we do not become weary.

GALATIANS 6:9 NASB

Some days are just plain hard. We won't always feel the motivation to be kind, patient, or generous. Some days, we will want to crawl in a hole and stay as far away from others as possible. On these days, let's take God's Word to heart. We can still choose to do good. One off day does not have to dictate how we show up in love.

If your buffer is smaller than usual, take something off your plate. You don't have to try to do all that you would on a good day. Remain rooted in the essentials and let everything else go. Whatever you can do, do it with love. This is what endurance in God's kingdom comes down to—one day at a time.

Good Father, you know me so well, and you aren't surprised by my limitations. What a relief. Help me to scale down on hard days and to remember that it's not giving up when I do.

OUTDO EACH OTHER

Love each other like brothers and sisters.
Give each other more honor than you want for yourselves.

ROMANS 12:10 NCV

We are all built with the desire to succeed. We want to be seen, noticed, accepted, and loved. No one wants to be underestimated or ignored. It is no small thing, then, to be encouraged to give each other more honor than you want for yourselves.

As brothers and sisters in Christ, we are one family. Consider the people you love the most. What do you want for them? What are your wishes for their paths in life? We want the people we love to succeed. We want them to be honored for their gifts. We want them to be loved, cherished, and honored. This is the attitude we can approach each other with. Let's look for ways to outdo one another in honor and respect.

Father, your love knows no limits, and your children are not fighting for your attention. There is no scarcity in your kingdom, only abundance. May I live from that reality.

HOSPITALITY

Share with the saints in their needs;
pursue hospitality.

ROMANS 12:13 CSB

Odds are when you hear the term "hospitality," something or someone comes to mind. If you grew up in the church, you probably already have a specific person who embodies this principle. If not, you might be prone to thinking of the hospitality industry, where creating comfort, welcome, and ease is still a powerful illustrator of this concept.

When we pursue hospitality, it means that we eagerly welcome people into our homes. We openly invite them into our lives. There is a level of familiarity and ease that comes with being in people's homes. We get to see sides of them we wouldn't otherwise. In serving others in love, let's not forget to invite them into our lives, our homes, and offer them the true glimpse of who we are in the process.

Lord, hospitality is a gift, and I don't want to overlook its importance in my relationships with others. Show me who I can be hospitable to in an intentional way today.

ASSURANCE OF INTEGRITY

Good comes to those who lend money generously
and conduct their business fairly.

PSALM 112:5 NLT

It may seem silly to think about running a business fairly as being representative of the kingdom. It's what everyone should do! Still, corruption runs rampant in the world. There are many who care more about their bottom line than about how the people who work for them are treated, compensated, or how their clients or customers feel.

It is good to be generous. Stingy people keep all they have to themselves and expect others to do the same. Generous ones are rewarded for their charity. When we deal with our money with integrity, we have nothing to hide. We also know that the one we rely on is the source of the whole world. He is abundant in all things. We can confidently follow his generous example.

Gracious God, there is no lack in your kingdom. You provide for my needs, and you ask me to trust you with my resources.

GROUNDED IN GENTLENESS

A gentle answer turns away wrath,
but a harsh word stirs up anger.

PROVERBS 15:1 NIV

It takes strength to choose gentleness in response to anger. When we ground ourselves in the love of God, we don't have to go into fight-or-flight mode. The presence of God reminds us that there is space in his grace to offer gentleness. If we simply fight back with the same tone, the fire of anger will only rise.

We cannot control what others will do or say. We can only lay claim to our part—our actions and reactions. When we let go of having to manage others and simply live from a place of grounded grace, we can show up with confidence. Confidence does not have to shout. It can be as soft as a whisper.

God, I don't want to match others' energy when they are upset. Help me to stay rooted and grounded in your love so that I can answer honestly but with gentleness that disarms.

DO NO HARM

Love does no wrong to a neighbor;
therefore love is the fulfilling of the law.

ROMANS 13:10 ESV

Doctors vow to "first do no harm," in their dealings with patients. If we approach our interactions with others in the same way, we actually follow the law of God's love, as laid out in today's Scripture.

We often think of love in terms of what it adds, of what it does to others. However, another way to look at loving others is to consider what it does not do. Love does not harm others. It doesn't actively do wrong. When we aren't sure about whether we are loving in word and deed, it can be helpful to ask ourselves, how does this affect my neighbor? How does it make them feel? Take these questions into your day as you consider what love offers others.

Kind God, when I am rash in my decisions, remind me of today's verse. Lead me into greater love with every interaction, every step, and every choice.

APRIL

"The Son of Man did not come
to be served. He came to serve
others and to give his life
as a ransom for many people."

MARK 10:45 NCV

PROMOTERS OF PEACE

Blessed are the peacemakers,
For they shall be called sons of God.

MATTHEW 5:9 NKJV

Peacemakers sometimes get a bad rap. They are seen as weak in a world that values brute force and strength. Violence is idolized while peace is seen as an unattainable goal. And yet, Jesus lifted peacemakers up. He said that they will be known as children of God.

When we pursue and promote peace, we reflect the likeness of God. Jesus is known as the Prince of Peace. He didn't come to the earth to overthrow governments or to sit on a manmade throne. He subverted every violent expectation and laid down his life in love. Let's be sure that we pursue peace rather than vengeance, for God has called us to unify in love.

Prince of Peace, show me how I can be a promoter of peace in my community, family, and in the world.

KEEP IN MIND

"The way you want others to treat you
is how you should treat everyone else."

LUKE 6:31 TPT

When we measure our actions against Jesus' words, it is clear how we should treat others. The love of God is generous—offensively so. It gives to those who will never repay. It offers compassion to those who don't ask for it. It does good to all, not just to those who also do good.

The love of God does not look for what it can gain, though it does offer us freedom. There are many benefits to treating others the way we want to be treated. And yes, it is disappointing when we are treated poorly. The Lord does so much more than we could ask or imagine. Let's lean on his love and trust him to help us keep choosing kindness, justice, and mercy.

Jesus, may I live from your love today. When I want to rush through an interaction, remind me to come back to this place: how would I want them to treat me?

SERVANT HEART

Have this attitude in yourselves which was also in Christ Jesus, who, as He already existed in the form of God, did not consider equality with God something to be grasped, but emptied Himself by taking the form of a bond-servant and being born in the likeness of men.

PHILIPPIANS 2:5-7 NASB

Jesus' example leaves us no room to question what the posture of our hearts should be before the Lord. Instead of lording his goodness over others, Jesus took on the attitude of a humble servant. There is no room for arrogance, pride, or bullying in the likeness of Christ. If we follow him, we must abandon those attitudes and take on humble love as the cloak we wear.

Life is not easy, but the love of God is full of ease. Where fear restricts, love expands: our understanding, our hope, our peace, our joy. Partnering with God is worth it even when it looks foolish to the world. As we serve others, keeping our hearts humble, we emulate the love of Christ in our lives, and that is no small thing.

Lord, who am I to be full of arrogance, when you remained humble? Help me to stay soft in a hard world. I follow you.

GIVE YOUR BEST

In all the work you are doing, work the best you can. Work as if you were doing it for the Lord, not for people. Remember that you will receive your reward from the Lord, which he promised to his people. You are serving the Lord Christ.

COLOSSIANS 3:23-24 NCV

When you work the best you can, your capacity may look different from day to day. However, your approach to work can remain the same no matter what you do. If you find a coworker or boss hard to handle, framing your work the way today's verse suggests may be just what you need.

Work as if you were doing it for the Lord, not for people. People will frustrate and disappoint, but God will not. He sees what others miss, and he values what others take for granted. If you dedicate your hard work to the Lord, you will remember that it is he who will reward you in the end. Serve him and do the best you can. He requires nothing more of you today.

Lord, you deserve my very best. When I want to give up because of the people around me, remind me that it is not what they think that ultimately matters; it's your perspective that matters most.

THE BEST MODEL

Be imitators of God, as dearly loved children, and walk in love, as Christ also loved us and gave himself for us, a sacrificial and fragrant offering to God.

EPHESIANS 5:1-2 CSB

Jesus is our ultimate example of how to live. As the Son of God, he humbled himself and took on the body of humanity so we could see what God's love looks like in flesh and bones. He is not a far-off, unrelatable deity. He experienced all the weaknesses of the flesh, and yet he didn't sin. He is the King of Glory, and he was a servant to all.

When we don't know how to move forward, let's look to God. We can meditate on the life of Christ, reading his words and fellowshipping with his presence. There is no act of love that Christ did not already do. Let's be imitators of God, and walk in love just as Christ did.

Christ Jesus, your example is the one I always want to follow. May I remain humble before you and remember that you humbled yourself first in love. I choose to walk in your ways.

FRIEND OF GOD

"I no longer call you slaves, because a master doesn't confide in his slaves. Now you are my friends, since I have told you everything the Father told me."

JOHN 15:15 NLT

What does it mean to be a friend of God? Abraham walked in faith, following the lead of the Lord, and it was credited to him as righteousness. He was called a friend of God. Abraham wasn't anyone special, but he was obedient to wisdom. Just as Abraham was chosen before he could choose God, so were you.

God chose you to be his child before you took your first breath or blinked your eyes open to this world. He chose you. The same God who chose you also appointed you to follow him. The fruit of his Spirit will be evident in your life as you walk in his ways and obey his wisdom. You are not a slave but a friend.

Father, when I feel unworthy of your friendship, remind me that it is for relationship with you that I was made. Your love is large, and it washes away my failures and shame.

ALL THINGS

I can do all this through him who gives me strength.

PHILIPPIANS 4:13 NIV

When you are weak, there is one who never falters in strength. When you don't know where to turn, there is one who sees the path clearly and can guide you in your next step. When you are confused, there is one who has perfect wisdom. In Christ, you have fellowship with the one who supplies all your needs, whatever they may be.

When we look at the big picture, we can be overwhelmed by all the demands and needs we see that we aren't able to meet. However, when we look at the next step in front of us, that can be the perspective shift that helps us remember we can do everything necessary through the gracious strength of God with us. We don't have to know how tomorrow will turn out, we have only to do the next right thing.

Provider, thank you for the reminder that I don't have to see every detail or know how it will play out. I partner with your heart, and I ask for your strength.

YOU ARE A WITNESS

"You are my witnesses," declares the LORD,
"and my servant whom I have chosen."

ISAIAH 43:10 ESV

Those of us who follow the Lord are not just servants and friends of the Most High. We are witnesses of his goodness. We are partakers of his mercy. We have tasted and seen that the Lord is good, and his powerful love is the fuel to our testimonies.

We are children of God. We know that God hears our prayers, and he answers them. We have seen how he comes through for those who rely on him. We have been witnesses to his glory, power, and unflinching kindness. His generous grace is our supply. Let's share our perspective with others, giving witness to what the Lord has done, and what we see him doing even now!

Glorious One, may I never hold back the truth of your powerful kindness when I am given the opportunity to share it.

STEWARDS OF MYSTERIES

You must perceive us—not as leaders of factions, but as servants of the Anointed One, those who have been entrusted with God's mysteries. The most important quality of one entrusted with such secrets is that they are faithful and trustworthy.

1 CORINTHIANS 4:1-2 TPT

Faithfulness and trustworthiness are important attributes in any leader. If we cannot trust someone, what they say doesn't matter. If they are not faithful to follow through on their commitments, then their word doesn't hold any weight.

If we want to be trusted with much, we have to be faithful with the little we already have. Nothing is more important than our character. How we live reveals the values we hold dear. When our values align with God's, we have nothing to hide or fear. There are many mysteries of God, but none of them go against his nature.

Lord, may I always remember what is most important in your kingdom. Transform my heart, mind, and life with the power of your values.

Loving Submission

Likewise you younger people, submit yourselves to your elders. Yes, all of you be submissive to one another, and be clothed with humility, for "God resists the proud, But gives grace to the humble."

1 Peter 5:5 NKJV

Submission is not something that some are called to while others remain exempt. In the family of God, we are all called to submit to one another in love. This is where cooperation, compassion, and understanding work together to unify us under Christ.

The world often elevates the proud while overlooking the humble. This is not how the kingdom of God works. God gives grace to the humble and he resists the proud. Cultivating a humble heart, and keeping it that way, is always in our best interest. Let's submit to one another in love. We can be sure that there is grace upon grace for us as we do.

Gracious Father, I sometimes forget the power of staying humble. It is not weakness but strength. Help me to submit to others in kindness and let go of the control I gravitate toward.

PLENTY TO GO AROUND

A generous person will be prosperous,
And one who gives others plenty of water
will himself be given plenty.

PROVERBS 11:25 NASB

We all know people stuck in a scarcity mindset. They fear sharing anything, not knowing what tomorrow will bring. As God's people, we are not called to be stingy but generous. There is more than enough to go around when we are committed to sharing resources with one another.

There are also those who prey on vulnerable people. They bleed their bank accounts dry by offering empty promises they cannot fill. This is not how the kingdom of God works. Generosity is an attitude that starts in our hearts, and we get to choose how we give. It is not manipulated, and it does not control others. When we commit to sharing what we have with others, we reap the benefits of generosity. Love is not a limited resource, so let's not live like it is.

Lord, I know generosity is powerful for those who give and receive. It is reflective of your nature, and I want to be wise and gracious in sharing what I have.

Live Like Jesus

Whoever says that he lives in God
must live as Jesus lived.

1 JOHN 2:6 NCV

The Word of God makes it clear how we should live. In short, we are to live as Jesus lived. Everything else should be held to this standard, even other Scriptures. If we aren't sure how we should treat the beggar on the street, let's look at what Jesus did in those circumstances. If we're not sure how to handle corrupt leaders, we can also look at the example of Jesus.

Jesus lived a life of sacrificial love, but he also stood firmly on the truth. He did not yell at the vulnerable or make those who came to him with seeking hearts feel as if he was too busy or important. He welcomed the little children to him when the adults thought he would be bothered. He talked to the outcast and healed the sick. If we want to live like Jesus, we need to know him, to follow him, and to love like he did.

Lord Jesus, I say yes to your leadership and example.

STILL STANDING

Blessed is the one who endures trials, because when he has stood the test he will receive the crown of life that God has promised to those who love him.

JAMES 1:12 CSB

When you have done all you can, and there is nothing left for you to do, endure. Endurance is the power to withstand the pain of the present moment, trusting it will pass. No feeling lasts forever. When you endure the trials of this life with faith, hope, and love intact, you will be blessed.

There are moments in life that seem unbearable. In these moments, you may need the support of friends, family, or professionals. This is nothing to hide from; this is another way you can endure! When the trial has passed, you will have stood the test not on your own two feet, but by the power of communal support. The presence of God is with you even when no one else is.

Lord, I need the reminder that I am not in this alone. Thank you for the power of your presence that never leaves.

LIVING EXAMPLES

Remember your leaders who taught you the word of God. Think of all the good that has come from their lives, and follow the example of their faith.

HEBREWS 13:7 NLT

While Jesus is our ultimate example, there are also those who live with wisdom, compassion, and integrity that we can learn from in this life. Though they are not perfect, there are good lessons to learn from those who follow the Lord and live out his love in practical, faithful ways.

For all the leaders who fall and fail, there are others who faithfully cling to the mercy and grace of Christ. These are examples to follow: those who humble themselves before God and others. Who is a living example of Christ's compassion that you can honor today?

Lord, thank you for the people in my life that have showed me what your love is like. Their faith fuels my own, and I am encouraged to press on in faith through each season of the soul.

According To Abundance

My God will meet all your needs
according to the riches of his glory in Christ Jesus.

PHILIPPIANS 4:19 NIV

God doesn't have a limit to his resources. He has all that we could imagine, and he doesn't hesitate to help those who rely on him. Let's remember that God lacks no good thing, and we can count on him to meet our needs.

As you pray for provision, do it in accordance with God's abundance. Raise your faith to his faithfulness. Remember what he has already done, and let it fuel your prayers. God is trustworthy, and he won't go back on his Word. Physical provision is important, but even more than that, he has an abundance of love, joy, peace, patience, kindness, hope, and wisdom to offer you. Whatever you need, he has it in spades. Pray and ask him to overwhelm you with his faithfulness once again.

Reliable God, I don't want to forget to ask you for the necessities, as well as the desires of my heart.

SPIRIT HELP

Likewise the Spirit helps us in our weakness. For we do not know what to pray for as we ought, but the Spirit himself intercedes for us with groanings too deep for words.

ROMANS 8:26 ESV

The Spirit helps us in our weakness, and this includes in our inability to know what to pray. There are times in life where we are without words. Nothing seems to fit, and we find ourselves at a loss. Whether due to tragedy, loss, or overwhelming sorrow and suffering, God isn't put off by our silence.

It is so important that we don't leave the flood of feelings in our bodies and try to keep moving through our lives in a normal way. When we are overcome, even without words, this is the time to stop and humble ourselves before the Lord. His Spirit helps us by interceding for us. What a beautiful picture of his loving care for us. As groans escape our grief-stricken bodies, God meets us in the comfort of his presence.

Holy Spirit, intercede for me when I have no words. Meet me in the weakness and suffering and do what only you can do.

To The Point

"When you pray, do not use vain repetitions as the heathen do. For they think that they will be heard for their many words."

MATTHEW 6:7 NKJV

You don't have to string perfect words together in order to be heard by God. You don't have to dress up your requests at all. God loves an honest prayer. Get honest, say what is true, and don't worry about what others would say about it.

When you talk to God like he is a good friend, you don't need to pretend to be anything but yourself. You don't have to explain yourself either. He knows you best—better than you even know yourself. You don't have to impress him. When you pray, it's okay to get straight to the point. So go ahead, pray directly and honestly. You couldn't fool him if you tried.

God, you already know me and see me. I won't beat around the bush, or try to flatter you. Here is my honest prayer...

LISTEN

"Call to Me and I will answer you, and I will tell you great and mighty things, which you do not know."

JEREMIAH 33:3 NASB

Prayer is not just a one-way channel that goes straight to heaven. It is an opening to conversation. Pray, calling to God, and then take time to listen to him. Wait for his answer. He is full of wisdom and revelation to expand your awareness. He brings clarity to your confusion.

In your private prayer practice, don't forget to open the ears of your heart as you listen for the Lord. Come to him, rest in his presence, and wait upon him. He will answer you, telling you great and mighty things. He will bring solutions to your mind, keys of wisdom to take the steps you need to take. The Living Word is alive, and he is speaking even now.

God, I come to you, not only to tell you what's on my heart, but also to hear what is on yours. Speak, Lord. I am listening.

EMBRACE SALVATION

Embrace the power of salvation's full deliverance, like a helmet to protect your thoughts from lies. And take the mighty razor-sharp Spirit-sword of the spoken word of God.

EPHESIANS 6:17-18 TPT

The power of God's salvation is found in Christ. Hiding under the shadow of his presence is like wearing the armor of his kingdom. As we put on the helmet of salvation, our minds are protected in the truth of God's love. As we take up the sword of Scripture, we are able to cut through the debris and get straight to the heart of a matter.

No matter what today brings, you can clothe yourself in Christ. The Holy Spirit is near to you in your need, and he will empower you to walk in the wisdom of the gospel. There is no better day than today than to fully embrace all that God offers you through Christ.

Liberating Lord, I put on the armor of your salvation. Thank you for all that you offer me in your presence. Be my guard as I partner with you.

BOLD REQUESTS

This is the boldness we have in God's presence: that if we ask God for anything that agrees with what he wants, he hears us.

1 JOHN 5:14 NCV

The closer you are to a person, the bolder you can be with them. You probably wouldn't go up to a stranger and demand that they give you their time. With a close friend, though, you could come to them and express your need, and they would gladly take that time with you.

God promises to listen when we call on him from a place of authenticity. We don't have to beg him to listen. He hears us when we cry out to him: the good friend and Father that he is. If we ask him for something and it aligns with his will, he not only hears us, but he answers us. We can be sure of it; he will not leave us in silence or indifference. The more we get to know him, the more we will see this is true.

Father, I want to know you so well that I don't hesitate for a moment at the door of your presence.

GOD'S WILL

Rejoice always, pray constantly, give thanks in everything; for this is God's will for you in Christ Jesus.

1 THESSALONIANS 5:16-18 CSB

God knows what we need. He is a good Father, and he is generous, wise, and kind. When we find ways to rejoice, even in our suffering, praying constantly, and giving thanks in all circumstances, we rest in the will of God.

Why does God want us to pray constantly? So we stay connected to him. Fellowship with God is our gift through Christ. When we look for reasons to rejoice, we open our eyes to God's miraculous mercy as it meets us in the reality of our lives. There is always something to be grateful for. Gratitude shifts our perspective and creates expectations of hope in our hearts. God's will is that we would know him, worship him, and be liberated in his love.

Father, I choose to look for reasons to rejoice today, turning my heart in prayer to you throughout my day. There are so many reasons to be thankful, and I take note of them today.

POWERFUL PRAYER

Don't worry about anything; instead, pray about everything. Tell God what you need, and thank him for all he has done.

PHILIPPIANS 4:6 NLT

Prayer is an open channel of connection between us and God. We don't have to have specific words to pray, or a model to follow, though we certainly can if that's easiest. Jesus taught his disciples how they should pray, and we can always use that as our example.

Fellowship with God is not unattainable. God invites us to come to him anytime and anywhere. There is nothing that stands between us and God; prayer is the way we communicate with him. Don't hesitate to tell the Lord what you need. Don't forget to thank him for all that he has already done; it helps your heart to grow in faith as you do. No matter what is going on, you can pray about it.

Lord Jesus, this is only the beginning of my prayer to you today. I give you all my worries and anxieties, and I come to you with my needs as well as my thanks.

SEEK AND FIND

"Ask and it will be given to you; seek and you will find; knock and the door will be opened to you."

LUKE 11:9 NIV

Whatever you are looking for, you will find. With that in mind, what are you putting your energy into? What things are you seeking? What doors are you knocking on? The Lord promises that when you look for him, you will find him. In all your searching, don't forget to look for him.

God is the source of all life, light, and every good thing. You won't go wrong when you listen to his wisdom. He will never steer you in a bad direction. The fruit of his fellowship is the same as the fruit of his Spirit: love joy, peace, patience, kindness, goodness, faithfulness, gentleness, and self-control. What glorious fruit of knowing God is ours as we seek his face!

Lord, I know that active pursuit produces results. In saying yes to you, I put my energy toward knowing you, hearing you, and following you.

CONFIDENT GRACE

Let us then with confidence draw near to the throne of grace, that we may receive mercy and find grace to help in time of need.

HEBREWS 4:16 ESV

The grace of God gives us confidence to come to him. In his presence, we find compassion. Whether we approach him with repentant hearts, aware and burdened by our failures, or we come to him with the expectation of joy, peace, or greater hope, we are met by love. Even when God corrects us in truth, it is laced with the kindness of his heart. He does not condemn us. His love liberates us, and his mercy covers our flaws.

God is generous in kindness, in grace, in attention. When we approach the throne of his grace, we can be confident of our reception. Whenever we need him, he is there. When we need comfort, it is found in his presence. When we need wisdom, his pure perspective clears the fog of confusion. When we need freedom from our fears, his love grounds us and gives us peace. He has all we need and so much more than we can imagine.

Gracious God, I come to you with confidence that I will be met by love.

FRUIT BEARER

"You did not choose Me, but I chose you and appointed you that you should go and bear fruit, and that your fruit should remain, that whatever you ask the Father in My name He may give you."

JOHN 15:16 NKJV

It's such a beautiful reminder to know that before we knew who Jesus or the Father of creation was, he knew us, chose us, and appointed us as his own. He knows the plans he has for us. He knows the challenges we will face in life, and he provides a pathway through each one with grace, redemption power, and love.

As God's child, he has appointed you to bear fruit. The life-giving fruit that remains is all based in the nature of God. You can't go wrong with setting love as the standard for every interaction. As a bearer of the image of God, your life will bear the fruit of his kingdom as you follow his ways.

Jesus Christ, when I am overwhelmed by all that I cannot do, I remember that you know me and you chose me as your own.

DIRECTED TO THE LORD

Are there any believers in your fellowship suffering great hardship and distress? Encourage them to pray! Are there happy, cheerful ones among you? Encourage them to sing out their praises!

JAMES 5:13 TPT

One way to partner with the Lord is to look for ways to encourage others in hope and connection. When we are going through hard times, the presence of God is accessible. Sometimes we forget though. When a friend encourages us to pray, reaching out to the Lord for help, it can be the reminder we didn't even know we needed.

When we are celebrating happy highs in life, God is still as close as he's ever been. As we turn to him in overflowing praise, we direct our joy in connection to the giver of every good and perfect gift. Through the ups and downs of this life we can know the Lord more, giving him the honest prayers and praises of our hearts. Let's encourage each other to connect to the one who knows us best.

Creator, thank you for the reminder that you are always accessible. May I encourage others to connect to you in the reality of their circumstances, knowing you are near.

LITTLE INTO PLENTY

He took the five loaves and the two fish, and, looking up to heaven, He blessed them and broke them, and gave them to the disciples again and again, to serve the crowd. And they all ate and were satisfied; and the broken pieces which they had left over were picked up, twelve baskets full.

LUKE 9:16-17 NASB

Jesus performed many miracles in the time of his ministry. In fact, John 21:25 reminds us that there is much more than was even recorded. When Jesus took a few loaves and a couple fish into his hands to bless, he knew what the outcome would be. From a small lunch to more than enough to feed thousands of people, the miracle of the multiplied food astounded everyone.

God still takes the little we offer and blesses it. As he does, the effects are multiplied. Why would we hoard our little lunch when we could partner with God and see people nourished by our offering?

Miracle Maker, I offer you my yes, what little I have to give, and trust you to do with it what you will.

AS IN HEAVEN

"Our Father in heaven,
may your name always be kept holy.
May your kingdom come
and what you want be done,
here on earth as it is in heaven."

MATTHEW 6:9-10 NCV

When we pray for God's kingdom to come, bringing his will to the earth as it is in heaven, we align our hearts and prayers with Jesus' own. Sometimes we complicate what the Lord made simple. That can be true as much in our prayer lives as it is in our practical lives.

Instead of following the rabbit trails of our thoughts today, let's simplify our prayers as we direct them to the Lord. Let's pray as Jesus taught us to, joining our yes to his gift of clarity. We don't have anyone to impress, and God is able to answer the needs and desires of our hearts without need for clarification.

Our Father in heaven, may your name always be kept holy. May your kingdom come, and what you want be done here on earth as it is in heaven.

ENLIGHTENED HOPE

I pray that the eyes of your heart may be enlightened so that you may know what is the hope of his calling, what is the wealth of his glorious inheritance in the saints.

EPHESIANS 1:18 CSB

We need the enlightenment of God's perspective to bring clarity and peace to our hearts. There is an abundance of hope in his calling, but if we do not see him clearly, we will miss it.

Paul prayed that the church of Ephesus would know the hope to which they were called, the incredible riches of their glorious inheritance in Christ. That prayer echoes through the centuries and still rings out for every believer. When we follow the wisdom of the Lord, we don't do it with begrudging hearts but with gratitude, knowing the liberty of the love that sets us free to dance, to sing, and to hope.

Glorious Lord, there is no better hope than the hope I have in you. Expand my awareness and enlighten my heart to know the fullness of the hope you promise.

HIS PURPOSES PREVAIL

"It is the same with my word.
I send it out, and it always produces fruit.
It will accomplish all I want it to,
and it will prosper everywhere I send it."

ISAIAH 55:11 NLT

Though life takes unexpected turns, the purposes of God are not foiled. When our worlds seem as though they are falling apart at the seams, the redemptive love of God is still at work in the details, often under the surface of our notice. God's purposes always prevail. Always.

Our timelines are different than the timeline of the Lord. He already has a pathway of breakthrough to guide us through our wilderness seasons; we simply have to follow his lead. We cannot see everything clearly or predict when or how something will work out, but God knows exactly what step to take in every twist and turn of life. He is not discouraged by the things that discourage us, and this should give us great hope. His purposes, his Word, his nature, continue through every generation, including today.

Lord, your ways are higher than mine, and your thoughts are far clearer. I follow you, even when my world turns upside down.

MAY

As each one has received
a special gift, employ it
in serving one another
as good stewards of the
multifaceted grace of God.

1 Peter 4:10 NASB

HUMBLE GREATNESS

"The greatest among you should be like the youngest, and the one who rules like the one who serves."

LUKE 22:26 NIV

When we yield our lives to the Lord, it is not greatness that we are promised. We are promised unending mercy, generous grace, and the power of his presence in our lives. There are many programs out there promising a step-by-step process to success. Everyone has something to sell. But God doesn't sell us a thing. He promises connection, freedom, and salvation.

If we do want to be great in the kingdom of God, we cannot expect to approach it in the same way the world does. It is not through plays of power or a broad platform that reaches thousands. It is through one-on-one connection with the Lord. It is found in obedience. In loving service. In following the example of Jesus, our humble king.

Humble Jesus, I focus my attention on you and on following your lead.

LOVING RESOLUTIONS

The LORD will fulfill his purpose for me;
your steadfast love, O LORD, endures forever.
Do not forsake the work of your hands.

PSALM 138:8 ESV

The Lord will fulfill his purpose for you. What an affirmation to start your day! The unwavering love of God lasts forever. It doesn't recede like the tides. It doesn't evaporate under neglect. It is always overflowing, abundant, and accessible. Always.

Rest in the knowledge that you don't have to earn God's affection. You don't have to beg for his attention or plead with him to help you. Join your heart to his and leave the shame behind. In his love, there is no room for fear of punishment. He is incomparably kind and generous. Trust him when he says he will fulfill his purpose for you. Rest in his love and lean into his fellowship.

Loving Lord, I cannot begin to thank you for the ways you love me so completely. I trust that you will do what I cannot.

ABUNDANT LIFE

"The thief does not come except to steal, and to kill, and to destroy. I have come that they may have life, and that they may have it more abundantly."

JOHN 10:10 NKJV

The purposes of God are to bring life—liberating, abundant life—to all. If we have any other ideas about God, then we need to get in touch with his nature. People have done all sorts of things in the name of God through the centuries, but that does not mean it represents the actual character or purposes of God or his kingdom.

Jesus didn't come to steal, kill, or destroy. If any of our ideas of what Jesus is like or what he wants boils down to destroying others, then we need to realign our understanding of his purposes in the actual Word of God. There is so much life in his love. There is so much freedom and breakthrough in his grace, mercy, and redemption. What hope we have in him!

Jesus, transform my expectations, understanding, and knowledge of who you are in the truth of your nature.

GOOD ADVICE

Your plans will fall apart right in front of you
if you fail to get good advice.
But if you first seek out multiple counselors,
you'll watch your plans succeed.

PROVERBS 15:22 TPT

Seeking out good advice from wise counselors is an act of hopeful wisdom. We can save ourselves a lot of trouble, including unnecessary mistakes, by heeding the advice of those who have walked a similar path.

It is also a good idea to get viewpoints from multiple perspectives. This can help us to see what we may need to focus on. Good advice is usually echoed through multiple counselors. Success in any area of life, including following the ways of the Lord, is found when we keep an open heart, mind, and learn from those around us. Let's remember to include the perspectives of others before we make major decisions, using their advice to inform the best path forward.

Wise God, thank you for the reminder that seeking out good advice is a necessary part of living a wise life.

UNLIKE THIS WORLD

"My kingdom is not of this world. If My kingdom were of this world, My servants would be fighting so that I would not be handed over to the Jews; but as it is, My kingdom is not of this realm."

JOHN 18:36 NASB

Just because something is different than we are used to does not make it wrong. This is as true with the foods and customs of other cultures as it is with the kingdom of Christ and the law of his love.

There are lots of assumptions we grow up with that we realize, through wisdom, maturity, and exposure to truth, are flawed. We get to change our minds as we grow. In fact, it is a sign of wisdom and maturity that when presented with better information, we do change our minds. If we never question our worldview or assumptions, we stay stuck in childlike thinking. As we follow the ways of Christ, we can no longer align ourselves with arrogant ideologies. Let's stay humble before him and open to transforming our understanding under the wisdom of his mercy.

God of justice, I don't want to stay stuck in old patterns of thinking that don't align with your nature, values, or Word. Transform my mindsets in your truth.

YOU'RE SEEN

"Two sparrows cost only a penny, but not even one of them can die without your Father's knowing it."

MATTHEW 10:29 NCV

God doesn't miss anything. If he notices when the smallest animals die, then you can be sure he sees you in your struggles. God knows how many hairs are on your head. Whatever you are going through, you can be sure God sees you.

Whatever you need, God has already provided. Go to him and lay your fears at his feet. He is acquainted with your doubts and your hopes. He cares about you! Let the power of his love envelop you as you give him your worries. Trust him and let his peace that passes all understanding rest on you like a blanket.

Jesus, your love is extravagant; it calms my fears and settles my doubts. I offer you all of my worries today, and I trust you to do what I cannot.

THE NARROW PATH

"Enter through the narrow gate. For the gate is wide and the road broad that leads to destruction, and there are many who go through it. How narrow is the gate and difficult the road that leads to life, and few find it."

MATTHEW 7:13-14 CSB

The gate of God's kingdom isn't narrow because of how few are welcomed, but because of how few actually enter it. The path that leads to life is one of love, and love is hard to choose at all times. The wide, popular path is full of reasons to hold onto vanity, grudges, and indifference. The narrow path of Christ requires our humble submission, laying aside corruption, greed, and judgment.

The narrow path is full of integrity and hope. It is not an easier way to live. It is not more appealing to the masses. It is one of gracious freedom and powerful kindness. If we truly knew the liberation that awaited us in the love of Christ, we wouldn't hesitate to enter through the narrow gate.

Lord Jesus, I know that your path is better than the broad road full of selfish ambition, deceit, and harsh judgments. The power of your mercy liberates me, soul and spirit, and I am free!

EXPERT GUIDE

"I will guide you along the best pathway for your life.
I will advise you and watch over you."

PSALM 32:8 NLT

God, our Creator, shepherd, and Savior, is the best leader there is. He doesn't lose track of his purposes or get sidetracked by the demands of others. He sees everything clearly, and he is able to guide us through the unexpected seasons of life with clarity, kindness, and comfort. Why would we try to wade through on our own, when the God of the universe is ready to guide us along the best path?

We can hide ourselves in the presence of God no matter what happens. He is our shield, our refuge, and our strength. Though there are mysteries too numerous to imagine in our human minds, there are no mysteries to him. He is clear-eyed and sure-footed. Let's follow him, for he is faithful and true.

Faithful Leader, I choose to follow you. I won't hold back from trusting you to lead me in goodness.

PRACTICAL COMPASSION

"Administer true justice; show mercy and compassion to one another. Do not oppress the widow or the fatherless, the foreigner or the poor. Do not plot evil against each other."

ZECHARIAH 7:9-10 NIV

The Word of God could not be clearer that the love of the Lord is as practical as it is powerful. God's justice is without bias. We show mercy and compassion not through empty phrases but through practical care and forgiveness.

We should care for widows and orphans, not exploit them. Let's embrace the Word of God and show love and care for those who are not natives of our land, and those who do not have enough to live in comfort. Let's be generous, as God is generous.

Father of compassion, help me to put your love into practice in every part of my life.

PRIMARY FOCUS

"Seek first the kingdom of God and his righteousness, and all these things will be added to you."

MATTHEW 6:33 ESV

The most important thing we can do today is to seek first the kingdom of God. When we set our hearts before the Lord, and we spend time in his Word and in his presence, we connect with the giver of life. He is the source of all that we need and all that will satisfy. If we want to grow, the best place to water the soil is in the landscape of his presence.

The presence of God grounds us in his love. The pervasive peace of God settles our hearts and minds as we turn toward him just as a sunflower is drenched in the rays that it rotates toward. God is the sun, and we are the flowers who long for the warmth and lifegiving rays of his face.

Righteous One, I turn to you like the plants move toward the light of the sun. I open my heart, my hands, and my life to you today. Shine on me.

SEASONED WITH GRACE

Let your speech always be with grace, seasoned with salt, that you may know how you ought to answer each one.

COLOSSIANS 4:6 NKJV

Grace is like a seasoning that makes everything taste better. When we lace our words with grace, we leave room for compassion, understanding, and mistakes. Perfection is like a harsh statement with no wiggle room. Grace creates space for our mishaps and puts love first.

When we are gracious in the way we talk to others, they will feel safe and seen. Even when they misunderstand where you are coming from, your gracious response can disarm them and help them see that you aren't attacking their identity. Grace is generous and kind, gentle, and honest. As we say yes to God and following his ways, we also say yes to being as gracious with others as he is with us.

Gracious God, I want to be as gracious with the people around me as you are. When I talk to others today, may it be with an open mind, filled with thoughtfulness and kindness.

FIRM FOUNDATION

The Lord Yahweh is always faithful to place you on a firm foundation and guard you from the Evil One.

2 THESSALONIANS 3:3 TPT

There is a lot of shaking happening in the world. Physical shifts, as well as socio-political ones, can rock us to our core. God is faithful to place us and keep us on the firm foundation of his love. While many things may fall away in the storms of life, he never will.

When you stand upon the truth of the Lord and rely on his faithful help, you will know the lifegiving power of his redemption in your life. He is loyal to his love, and he is reliable to follow through on all his promises. Lean into his presence today and follow his leadership. He is more than enough for all that you need.

Faithful One, you are my firm foundation, and I stand upon the strength of your Word.

RECIPROCAL MOVEMENT

Come close to God and He will come close to you.
Cleanse your hands, you sinners;
and purify your hearts, you double-minded.

James 4:8 NASB

When we draw close to God, we can be sure that he draws close to us. He is often closer than we realize. We don't have to yell for his attention. Have you ever called for someone loudly, thinking they were across the house and been surprised by their answer from a few feet away? That is what calling out to God is like. He is already nearer than we know.

When we repent, God forgives us. We don't have to beg him for forgiveness, we simply have to offer our true heart of regret. We purify our hearts by offering them to the Lord. As he liberates us in his love, we are able to live it out in even greater ways.

Lord, I come close to you today. Open my ears and eyes to hear and see where you are already moving in kindness.

Raised Expectations

"God can do anything!"

Luke 1:37 NCV

We have so many limitations in life. Our humanity isn't equipped for endless strength, resources, or capabilities. It can be easy to forget that God has no such restraints. He is able to do absolutely anything. If he created the world, along with everything in it, who are we to say what he can or cannot do?

Let's raise our expectations to the reality of God's power. While he doesn't always intervene in specific ways we hoped, he always works things together for our good. It doesn't mean we shouldn't ask him. Let's look over the history of his faithfulness and what he has done and raise our expectations as we ask for greater things. Let's stretch our imaginations in prayer today.

Great God, there is nothing you cannot do. Help me to remember that when I am discouraged or at a loss. I raise my hope as I pray bigger, bolder prayers.

POWERFUL HONESTY

Putting away lying, speak the truth, each one to his neighbor, because we are members of one another.

EPHESIANS 4:25 CSB

One of the most trustworthy attributes of a person of integrity is their ability to speak the truth. They choose honesty over lying to avoid hard conversations. They choose to say the hard thing when it's the right thing to do. This, combined with genuine compassion and humility, helps to build trust with the people in their lives.

Serving others in love does not mean ignoring important areas of truth. It doesn't mean that we disregard our responsibility to bring up hard conversations. It can be tempting to lie to appease others or to avoid conflict, but it does no one any good. Our responsibility is to tell the truth because that is the loving thing to do.

Lord of truth, I want to be dependable in honesty, for that builds strong bonds of trust when done in care and concern.

SAVED BY GRACE

God saved you by his grace when you believed.
And you can't take credit for this; it is a gift from God.
Salvation is not a reward for the good things we have done,
so none of us can boast about it.

EPHESIANS 2:8-9 NLT

The salvation of our souls is not something we earn. We don't earn our relationship with God either. We don't have to prove ourselves. God's Word says that salvation is a gift from God. It is not something we can hold over others or use to brag about. God's generous love is offered to all in the same measure.

Insecurity may lead us to feeling as if we have to prove our worth or our place in a relationship. We need never feel insecure about God's mercy for us. No one is more or less worthy. We are all in the same boat when it comes to our need. Faith in Christ is an entry point to the freedom and relationship we were created for.

Gracious God, you are the God of my salvation and my hope. I give up trying to impress you and others and instead focus on your love as the fuel to everything in my life.

PRESENT PEACE

"Peace I leave with you; my peace I give you.
I do not give to you as the world gives.
Do not let your hearts be troubled and do not be afraid."

JOHN 14:27 NIV

The peace of God isn't fickle. It isn't available one moment and nowhere to be found the next. It is long-lasting, near, and overwhelmingly good. The peace of God guards our hearts and minds in Christ. It is the atmosphere of God's very presence. We can know what it is to abide in God's peace each and every day.

This isn't to say that our peace won't be tempted. There are many troubles and trials in life. They will cause us to react in fear, but we don't have to stay there. We can take our anxieties, our fears, and our shame to the Lord. He lifts the weight of them with his lavish love and restores our peace.

Good Shepherd, I'm so grateful for your goodness and the powerful rest you offer my heart and mind. When I am troubled, I go to you for a fresh portion of your peace.

LIBERATING TRUTH

"You will know the truth,
and the truth will set you free."

JOHN 8:32 ESV

How do we know the truth? If we hold to Jesus' teaching, following his wisdom and ways, we will be set free by the powerful truth of his message. Jesus said that those who sin are slaves to sin. Since we all fall short of perfection, we know what it is to be bound by harmful habits, ideologies, or actions. They do us no good, and yet, what other option do we have to break free?

This is where our greatest hope comes in. Jesus came to set the sinner free and to liberate the captives from their chains. His powerful mercy covers our sin, removes the need for our perfection, and gives us freedom to walk in the goodness of his ways. There is so much liberty in the powerful truth of Christ!

Lord Jesus, I say yes to following you. You are my freedom and my salvation.

MERCY SONGS

I will sing of Your power;
Yes, I will sing aloud of Your mercy in the morning.

PSALM 59:16 NKJV

Following Jesus isn't just about what we can do for or with him. There is incredible beauty in his friendship. There is power in his fellowship. The Spirit of God empowers us in our weakness and floods us with the palpable love of his presence. We get to know God in the journey of this life.

What does it mean to be a child of God? It gives us a front row seat to his goodness. It opens our eyes to the power of his mercy. He is incredibly personal. He knows us, and he wants us to know him. There isn't a person in this world that needs to stand between us and God. He has knocked down every barrier and brought us into the fullness of his presence through Christ.

God, I sing of your mercy today. You are my guard, and my shelter. I love you!

WONDERFUL REVELATIONS

Open my eyes to see the miracle-wonders
hidden in Scripture.

PSALM 119:18 TPT

There are treasures in the dark seasons of life, and God shines the light of his presence on them as we look to him. His light of truth brings revelation and opens our understanding to the miracle-wonders within Scripture and within our lived experiences.

The truth of God doesn't begin and end on the page. It is in Christ. He is the living Word of God. He is alive and working, and he opens our eyes to the wonderful ways of his nature. There is no shortage of goodness even when it seems hard to find. Let's look for his light as it shines through the cracks, as we would for hidden treasure.

Wonderful One, you are the giver of every good gift. You offer wisdom for my confusion, and clarity for my inability to understand. Open my eyes to see the miracle-wonders hidden in Scripture.

HE WILL RETURN

He who testifies to these things says,
"Yes, I am coming quickly." Amen. Come, Lord Jesus.

REVELATION 22:20 NASB

Jesus promised to return to earth, and he will. Though the waiting may feel like it draws on, our lives are just a breath. We wait in hope, knowing that the one who is faithful will do what he has promised.

How we live in this waiting is important to consider. Jesus already offered us the direction we need. The gospels are full of his wisdom and truth. His law of love is the standard that we are to follow. The Lord is coming, and he won't delay. Our lives are short, and we don't have to live them mindlessly. We can live with intention, surrender, and vision.

Jesus, I believe that you will come again, and you won't delay. Even as I wait, I hope. Whether my life draws to an end, or you return, it does not matter. What matters is how I wait, how I live, and how I love.

NOTHING HIDDEN

"Everything that is hidden will be shown,
and everything that is secret will be made known."

LUKE 12:2 NCV

Nothing remains hidden from the Lord. He sees everything that we try to keep under the notice of others, and he will not let injustice drag on forever. The truth always comes out even if it takes a lifetime to do so. We can trust God to reveal these things.

We cannot keep our motives secret. Corruption reveals itself through the fruit it produces. Abuse will not go unpunished. Love will not go unnoticed either. No one is perfect. We will not stand in ridicule of one another in the courts of our King. There is incredible relief and power in what was in the shadows coming to the light. The presence of God is full of justice, and it is also full of mercy. Let's remember this when we feel fear of exposure. God's kindness corrects us, but it also sets us free.

Lord, I rest in the truth that nothing is a mystery to you.

PATIENT TEACHER

He leads the humble in what is right
and teaches them his way.

PSALM 25:9 CSB

The Lord is patient with us. He is kind to those who come to him. He teaches those who are open and willing to know what is right. He leads them in the truth of his love. It is never too late to humble ourselves before the Lord. We can know the power of his leadership no matter how we have lived up to this point.

God is more than able to restore what we have lost. There isn't a situation he can't turn around, and there isn't a circumstance that he can't use to teach us the power and benefit of his ways. There is always more to learn, so let's humble ourselves before him, remaining open to his leadership and correction.

Teacher, you are full of wisdom, and I want to learn your ways. Lead me in what is right and teach me what matters most to you.

His Timing

Humble yourselves under the mighty power of God, and at the right time he will lift you up in honor.

1 Peter 5:6 NLT

We cannot rush God's timeline, and we can't control exactly when we will meet certain criteria in life. Oh that we could! But that's not how it goes. We must learn to trust God in the waiting periods, and to partner with him in the small ways we can. When we remain humble under God's leadership, we can trust that at the right time he will lift us up.

Instead of trying to rush the timeline, let's focus on what we can do. We can look to the Lord and cultivate a deeper friendship with him. We can be intentional in our relationships, and treat others with kindness, respect, and honor. We can do the small things in our power to do, and we can trust in the faithfulness of God.

Great One, I humble myself before you today. I trust your timing, even when it is hard.

SYMPATHY CONNECTION

All of you, be like-minded, be sympathetic, love one another, be compassionate and humble.

1 PETER 3:8 NIV

It is important in our relationships that we keep our compassion switched on. When we are sympathetic to each other's struggles and circumstances, we take each other's humanity into account. We all have hard days and seasons. It does us no good to refuse to admit the struggles.

When we are connected to each other in love, being compassionate, humble, sympathetic, and like-minded, we know the power of community as it is meant to be. We may not find this in our physical families, but there are friends who can be closer to us than kin. This chosen family is a beautiful picture of God's kingdom. He sets the lonely in families. He is our Father, and we are his children. Let's be sure to cultivate the relationships in our lives and love one another well. It's what we were created for.

Compassionate One, thank you for the community you have given me. Keep me sympathetic and compassionate in my relationships.

BLESSED HARMONY

Live in harmony with one another.
Do not be haughty, but associate with the lowly.
Never be wise in your own sight.

ROMANS 12:16 ESV

It is a beautiful thing to live in harmony with one another. Hurt feelings don't linger long, nor do conflicts. There is no sense of arrogance that separates us from each other. Living in harmony is the epitome of living in God's gracious love, extending kindness and understanding to one another.

When we are intentional in remaining humble, we will not be wise in our own eyes. We leave room to grow, to change our minds and our approach. We remain committed to growing as long as we live. There is room for harmony in the lives of the humble because they make it a priority to change when it is best for everyone to do so.

God of love, in you there is unity and harmony. Your mercy brings us together, and I want to grow in your wisdom, nature, and ways every day of my life.

PUT IT AWAY

Let all bitterness, wrath, anger, clamor, and evil speaking be put away from you, with all malice.

EPHESIANS 4:31 NKJV

The fruit of the Spirit lead to growth and goodness. Bitterness does no one any good. It eats away at the reserve of loving compassion in our hearts and puts our own ideas of justice at the forefront. It is a bitter root that spreads toxic fear.

It is for our good that the Word instructs us to let bitterness go. When we choose to follow in the ways of Christ, saying yes to his love and to his leadership, we give up the need to hold onto such things. Though forgiveness, grace, and peace are not always easy to choose in the moment, they are for our good and the good of others.

Holy Spirit, I choose to put away bitterness, anger, and judgment. I choose your compassion, grace, and kindness, instead.

YIELDED LIFE

My old identity has been co- crucified with Christ and no longer lives. And now the essence of this new life is no longer mine, for the Anointed One lives his life through me—we live in union as one! My new life is empowered by the faith of the Son of God who loves me so much that he gave himself for me, dispensing his life into mine!

GALATIANS 2:20 TPT

Whatever lies in our past, Christ does not hold it against us. When we say yes to him, surrendering our hearts and lives to the leadership of his love, he covers our sin with the power of his cleansing mercy.

Jesus offers us new life in him. And this is no second-rate life! It is full of faith, peace, joy, and love. There is hope, breakthrough, and incredible strength. All the resources of God are offered to us through his gracious Spirit. New life in Christ is full of freedom, joy, and power. It is better than we can imagine.

Lord Jesus, I am yours. My life is yours. Lead me into your lifegiving love.

WEAK THINGS

The insignificant things of the world and the despised God has chosen, the things that are not, so that He may nullify the things that are, so that no human may boast before God.

1 CORINTHIANS 1:28-29 NASB

God uses the weak things of this world to confound the wise in their own eyes. There is no graduate program for following Christ. There is no pedigree. There is only surrender, willingness, and an open heart. It doesn't matter what we have done or not done. Jesus empowers the weak, and he uses the willing.

Where you see weakness, God sees opportunity. This is as true in your own life as it is in the lives of those around you. There isn't a weakness that scares him. He can use the humblest things of this world to bring redemption, hope, and powerful liberation. Let's not write anyone off—including ourselves—as being able to be used by God.

Redeemer, I am weak, but you are strong. I am humble, but you can do all things in the power of your Spirit.

GROWING UP IN CHRIST

Speaking the truth with love,
we will grow up in every way into Christ,
who is the head.

EPHESIANS 4:15 NCV

Many children know how to tell the truth, though they don't know how to do it with tact or compassion. This is to be expected, though we can teach them to grow in discretion as they grow. In later stages of growth, before we reach adulthood, many of us go through a time of pleasing our peers. This causes us to withhold the truth for fear that we may lose our place in our friend group.

When we grow up in Christ, we move beyond the childish ways of simply saying the truth without compassion. We grow out of the need to stay silent for fear of what others may think. We speak the truth in love, for the truth always has a place, and so does compassion.

Jesus, thank you for the reminder that truth spoken in love is powerful and necessary.

PERSUASIVE PATIENCE

A ruler can be persuaded through patience,
and a gentle tongue can break a bone.

PROVERBS 25:15 CSB

Patience is a powerful tool. Leaving space for a person to work out their process rather than jumping in with our initial reaction is important. The more we do it, the more we witness, understand, and grow in trusting the process of patience. Sometimes, simply waiting can allow the person to work out the problem. Other times, it reveals our gracious nature, and they grow in appreciation.

Patience can teach us how to be good listeners. This is a practiced skill. The more we use it, the more accustomed we become to leaving that room. Patience also gives us time to get our own reactions in order. Instead of lashing out in anger, we can regulate ourselves and our tone.

Father, you are more patient than anyone I have known. Teach me by your Spirit to practice patience with the people in my life.

JUNE

God is not unjust so as to
forget your work and the love
which you have shown toward
His name, by having served
and by still serving the saints.

HEBREWS 6:10 NASB

Confident Trust

Do not throw away this confident trust in the Lord.
Remember the great reward it brings you!

Hebrews 10:35 NLT

The Lord is faithful. He is trustworthy. When we are confident of his nature, we rest in the peace of his presence and count on the reliability of his promises. What great reward there is for keeping our hearts tethered to God in hope.

On hard days, our patient trust may be tested. We might want to give up or turn our accusations against God. He can handle our questions and honest prayers. Still, with an open heart of curiosity and trust, we wait on his voice to settle our fears and reassure our hearts. There is power in confidence. If we find ourselves wavering, we have only to go back to the nature of God—his unchanging character.

Lord, you are better than anyone I've known, and I won't give up on you. You never give up on me. I give you my yes again today.

A PRESENT HELP

The LORD is with me; he is my helper.
I look in triumph on my enemies.

PSALM 118:7 NIV

The Lord wasn't only a helper to King David and the other psalmists. He didn't only show up in breakthrough and redemption for the prophets of old. He helps all those who call on him. He is faithful in love, and he rescues those who cry out to him.

God does not run away from any challenge, and we can trust him to empower us to follow him through the storms of this life. There is nothing to fear even when it seems as if there's everything to fear, for the Lord our God is with us. He is our helper, and he won't leave us in our struggles.

Powerful One, there is no problem I face where you are absent. Empower me with the strength of your Spirit and give me the grace I need to endure.

COMMITTED TRUST

Commit your way to the Lord;
trust in him, and he will act.

Psalm 37:5 ESV

When you commit your way to the Lord, you don't have to worry about whether you take the right step or not. As you walk it out, he will direct and redirect you when necessary. The step of faith you take does not need to have the assurance of a guaranteed outcome. Your trust is in the Lord and his nature, not in the exact end you hope will come.

Instead of getting caught up in the details of what you want things to look like, make sure that you prioritize knowing the Lord. The more you know what he is like, the more you will trust him. He is loyal in love, and he won't steer you wrong. When you take a path that leads you into trouble, he will help you through that as well.

Faithful One, I can get so caught up in my own plans that I forget how wonderfully capable you are to do far more than I could even think to ask for. I look to you, my guide, today.

PERFECT LOVE

There is no fear in love; but perfect love casts out fear, because fear involves torment. But he who fears has not been made perfect in love.

1 JOHN 4:18 NKJV

Fear is a poor motivator. Though it can push people into decisions, those will be small and ill-fitting. The love of God is expansive. It is not limiting. It invites us into broader pastures where we can wander, learn, and grow. The perfection of God's love sets us free. Fear seeks to control and limit us.

When faced with the decision to act out of fear or out of love, we can test the fruit. Love may cost us something, but it is deeply resonant and true. It is gracious and kind. It is forgiving. It is not self-seeking. Fear, on the other hand, often rushes us to make decisions we aren't ready for. It may feel like self-protection and safety, but it is so focused on our own comfort that it disconnects from the well-being of others. Perfect love casts out fear.

Lord, I don't want to live from fear or use fear in my relationships. May I be so filled with your liberating love that I can spot the difference between a fear-based reaction and a love-based one.

Wrapped in Love

Yahweh is my strength and my wrap-around shield.
When I fully trust in you, help is on the way.

Psalm 28:7 TPT

God is not only a good leader and glorious savior, he is a present father, a constant friend, and a wrap-around shield. He is a protector and a comforter. There is nothing we need that he doesn't embody perfectly. This is why the psalmists sang. This is why people throughout the ages gave him their praise. This is why we can sing with passionate praise to the one who is trustworthy and true.

Pray, seek, and trust. There is peace for those who wait on God. There is living hope for those who surrender to his love. There is overflowing joy for those who taste and see the goodness of the Lord, and you will taste and see his faithful mercy as it meets you in the details of your life!

Faithful One, I see the evidence of your mercy, and it fills me with hope, joy, and passionate praise!

SPIRIT REMINDERS

"The Helper, the Holy Spirit whom the Father will send in My name, He will teach you all things, and remind you of all that I said to you."

JOHN 14:26 NASB

It is impossible for us to remember all that God has said or done. Thankfully, it is not our job to do so. The Holy Spirit is a teacher, friend, and guide. He reminds us of all that Jesus said, making his Word come alive in our hearts. He offers us the reminders we need at just the right moment.

Have you ever experienced this? Perhaps you found yourself at a loss and in the moment prayed, "Jesus, help me!" How did the Lord come through for you? Whether dropping an idea into your mind, or bringing a person along to help, the answers of the Lord come in both subtle and big ways. Even just a reminder of God's truth can be the bolster we need in the moment. Ask Holy Spirit to teach you and give you timely reminders today.

Holy Spirit, speak to me and teach me the ways of the Lord. I am open.

DEFENDER

The LORD defends those who suffer;
he defends them in times of trouble.

PSALM 9:9 NCV

The Lord doesn't turn away from those who suffer. He defends those who depend on him. He is close in comfort when we are in pain. He comes to our defense when we are in trouble. We can always count on him.

There are times in life when we may be tempted to doubt the Lord's goodness. He doesn't promise us ease of circumstances. A pain-free life is a fantasy, not a proof of faith. Let's remember that the Lord is a defender of the weak. This means that when we are weak, we can rely on his help. And when we are in positions of influence? Let's join his heart by doing the same: defending the suffering and helping those who are troubled.

Defender, you are full of compassion and justice. My yes to you includes a yes to partnering with your heart and ways.

ABIDING TRUTH

"If you remain in me and my words remain in you, ask whatever you want and it will be done for you."

JOHN 15:7 CSB

The power of God's presence dwells with us as we dwell in him. Remaining in God is not passive. It is an active choice. There will be times when we may be tempted to move ahead on our own, charting our own course, leaving the strength and source of God's wisdom behind. This would be to our detriment.

Choosing to remain in the Lord and keeping his words in us is a heart posture. That means, no matter what our lives look like at the moment, we can be remaining in him. Jesus is the living vine, and we are the branches. The source of his love is the lifeforce of our lives. When we abide in him, letting his Word fuel us, we will grow and bear the fruit of his kingdom.

God, you are the source of all that I need, so I choose to remain in you.

HAND THEM OVER

Give all your worries and cares to God,
for he cares about you.

1 PETER 5:7 NLT

There is no shortage of things to worry about in this life. Every day, there is more information that screams for our attention. "Do this!" "Don't do this!" Endless news cycles and warnings pull at our limited capacity and demand we take action to save ourselves from harm. We cannot control what tomorrow brings, but we can trust the one who sees everything clearly.

God cares for us more than anyone else who loves us. He is full of wisdom, and he is full of powerful peace. Jesus invites us to come to him and lay down the burdens of our worries at his feet. We don't have to buckle under their weight. There is lightness to the partnership he offers. He lifts the heavy burdens, and we are left with capacity to trust, to love, and to continue in his peace.

Jesus, I give you my worries and cares today. I partner with you, and I trust your love to cover all that I cannot.

SHIELD OF FAITH

In addition to all this, take up the shield of faith, with which you can extinguish all the flaming arrows of the evil one.

EPHESIANS 6:16 NIV

Flaming arrows are quite the picture of evil. They are darts that don't just aim to harm, but to spread destruction. Faith is like a shield that we can use to extinguish the flaming arrows of the enemy. Faith is confident trust based in the faithful nature and promises of God. Faith can move mountains, but it can also keep destructive forces from overtaking our lives.

Let's put our faith in the trustworthiness of our great God. He is our Savior, our help, and our redeemer. There is nothing he cannot do. Though the earth shakes and dreams shatter, his redemptive love is untouchable. The promises of God are yes and amen, and they cannot be cancelled.

Faithful One, I take up the shield of faith and place all my attention on who you are and what you are able to do.

GENTLE WISDOM

Who is wise and understanding among you? By his good conduct let him show his works in the meekness of wisdom.

JAMES 3:13 ESV

Wisdom and understanding are not proven in the classroom or in the hall of ideas. It is worked out in the reality of our day-to-day lives. Wisdom and understanding are much more practical than we often realize.

Wisdom does not shout at the corner. It consistently speaks the truth in word and deed. Loving action backs up true understanding. The gospel is not to be used to intimidate or control. It is an invitation to freedom, and wisdom understands that. Wisdom is gentle. It is reflected in the integrity of our lives. What we do, how we act, and the values we uphold are the same behind closed doors as they are in front of the masses.

Wise One, I want to follow you, to represent you in Spirit and in truth. I choose consistency.

NEW THINGS

"Do not remember the former things,
Nor consider the things of old.
Behold, I will do a new thing."

ISAIAH 43:18 NKJV

There are times in life when we come up against a dead-end where we thought there was open road. The hard stops in life—death, divorce, job loss, tragedy—they become the markers of before and after. It can be devastating to our expectations and rock us to our core. Still, there is hope. There is new life ahead. There is a way through the wilderness.

We often don't account for the heavy losses in life especially when they come unexpectedly. This does not mean that we have somehow failed though. God is with us in the devastation and the heartbreak. He comforts us in our grief and offers hope in our hurt. While we must process the suffering, there comes a time when God invites us into something new. He will guide you onto pathways of peace, making roads in the wilderness and rivers in the desert.

Redeemer, you never change, even when everything else does. You are my rock and my confidence, and I cling to you.

INCOMPARABLE POWER

Oh, LORD God, you made the skies and the earth with your very great power. There is nothing too hard for you to do.

JEREMIAH 32:17 NCV

Nothing is too hard for God to do. Nothing. Though we struggle to see the good that could come from deep pain and suffering, God turns even the ashes of our disappointment into gardens of his glorious mercy. We cannot rush through the winter seasons, but we can trust that the one who created the earth will usher us into spring at the right time.

When we are waiting for breakthrough, it can be hard to be patient. The Lord offers us comfort and deep stores of his wisdom as we burrow into his presence. He can take what the enemy meant for harm and use it to expand our awareness of his practical love that meets us in every season of the soul.

Marvelous One, it is not too hard for you to bring life out of barren lands, to bring rain to the desert, or to lift me up from the remains of my disappointment. I trust you.

THE GREATEST LOVE

"Greater love has no one than this,
that a person will lay down his life for his friends."

JOHN 15:13 NASB

There is no greater measure of love than the willingness to sacrifice our lives for others. While we often think of this simply in life-or-death matters, there is much more to sacrifice than a one-time act. When we lay down our lives for our friends, we consider their good.

Jesus laid down his life for his friends and for those who considered themselves his enemies. He sacrificed his life not only on the cross but when he came to earth as a baby. He limited himself to the human experience for our good, so we could see, know, and experience the overwhelming love of God. May we love others enough to not have to be completely understood in order to do the right thing.

Lord Jesus, help me to remember that love does not have to be understood by others in order to be acted on. I follow you, and my yes is to you.

HOLD ON

Hold on to loyal love and don't let go,
and be faithful to all that you've been taught.

PROVERBS 3:3 TPT

Every day is a new opportunity to lay hold of the loyal love of God. It is not natural to live in the constant mercy of God and to be gracious, kind, faithful, and true. Our lives can reveal the power of God through the integrity and values we live out. Graciously, love shows itself as strongly in our repentance and redemption as it does in our victories.

Whatever you face today, grab hold of loyal love. Its force is as strong today as it has ever been. You may feel like you have something to prove, but don't get distracted by that pull. Put first things first and follow the simple truth of the gospel. There is power in God's love, and it strengthens you to walk in the ways of Jesus.

God of love, I hold on to your loyal love and I won't let go.

Nothing To Uncover

"I have spoken openly to the world," Jesus answered him. "I have always taught in the synagogue and in the temple, where all the Jews gather, and I haven't spoken anything in secret."

JOHN 18:20 CSB

Jesus was full of integrity. The life he lived away from the eyes of others was built on the same values that the masses saw in his ministry. Jesus didn't hide his teachings from the religious scholars and teachers. He taught openly in the synagogue. What he taught, he openly taught. There was no hiding.

Shame likes to dwell in the shadows. What we keep hidden with shame as its guard threatens to take us down if brought to the light. Our secrets don't always hold this actual power, but that's what shame makes it feel like. The light of God's love, though, liberates us from fear and shame. There is nothing to uncover in a person who lives with integrity, humility, and love as their foundation.

Lord, you have my yes in every area of my life. Nothing is hidden from you, and I bring to you what wants to stay covered.

CREATED AND CALLED

"Do not be afraid, for I have ransomed you.
I have called you by name; you are mine."

ISAIAH 43:1 NLT

There is incredible encouragement in listening to the one who created us from dust. He formed us, putting us together piece by piece. He knows us best, and we don't have to be afraid of his perspective of us. When fear threatens our peace, let's do what today's verse says and listen to the Lord who created us.

There is no fear in God's presence. There is awe and honor. There is love and peace. There is joy and clarity. There is wisdom and grounded truth. There is freedom. The one who formed us also calls us. We belong to him. When we follow him, we don't have to worry about whether we are covered by his love. It is our source, our foundation, and our guiding truth. Do not be afraid, beloved. He has called you by name; you are his.

Creator, you formed me and know me. I will not let fear keep me from you today.

BEFORE YOUR EYES

"Do not be terrified; do not be afraid of them. The LORD your God, who is going before you, will fight for you, as he did for you in Egypt, before your very eyes."

DEUTERONOMY 1:29-30 NIV

There is much that God does under the surface of our understanding. Just like watching a pot come to a boil draws out and we can't sense the subtle changes until the water bubbles, there is much that the Lord does before we see the results of his power at work.

God promises that we will see him work his mercy out before our very eyes. Just because we do not sense it yet does not mean that God is absent or not doing anything. He does what we don't even know to look for. We will see the ripples of his kindness in practical ways. We will see him fight for us. Let's trust him in the in-between spaces of promise and breakthrough.

Lord, you are more powerful and thorough than I can comprehend. I know this is true. I trust you to guide me, to fight for me, and to bring me into breakthrough.

OPPORTUNITY FOR EVERYONE

"Everyone who calls on the name of the Lord will be saved."

ROMANS 10:13 ESV

The love of God isn't limited, and it is also not exclusive. It doesn't matter where we come from or what language we speak. It doesn't matter our customs or styles. The love of God is all encompassing. His salvation is too.

Let's not withhold what God so freely offers. Instead of staying in our comfort, reserving our love and service for those we already know, let's reach outside of our bubbles and serve the stranger and the foreigner. Let's extend the same kindness and grace we offer our friends. Let's let the love of God compel us in compassion and look for ways to practically help those around us who need it.

Savior, may I not remain on an island of my own making when it comes to serving others. Help me to live with walls down and love that builds bridges of connection.

Better Together

A person standing alone can be attacked and defeated,
but two can stand back-to-back and conquer.
Three are even better,
for a triple-braided cord is not easily broken.

Ecclesiastes 4:12 NLT

Depending on the culture we grew up in, the importance of individuality versus community will vary. In many Western cultures, we are taught to value our independence above all things. We praise those who rise from nothing to something, and we value the storylines where it seems like people did it themselves against all odds. The reality, though, however we frame it, is that no one rises on their own. There is always a community of people behind them.

We are better together, stronger and more resourced when we work with others. This is as true in our service as it is in any other area. Instead of going it alone today, let's look for ways to partner with others who are doing the same thing. We are better in community. We were created for it!

Lord, I don't want to depend on my own capabilities all the time. Help me to balance my own strengths and weaknesses with those of others for the glory of your name.

CONSIDER OTHERS

Let nothing be done through selfish ambition or conceit, but in lowliness of mind let each esteem others better than himself.

PHILIPPIANS 2:3 NKJV

It is not too simple to say that love reaches out for the good of others. Selfish ambition and conceit have no place in the kingdom of God. If we act out of self-preservation and to serve our own interests, we can be sure that we value ourselves more than we value others. The love of God is always moving toward others.

Graciously, the love of God meets us right where we are. It floods our hearts and minds. It fuels our own love that then ripples out to others. We must stay humble and consider the humanity of others. This is the way of the kingdom. We partner with God's love to move in kindness, grace, and peace.

Loving Lord, help me to treat others kindly, not for what I get out of that, but for their good.

CONTINUING WORK

I pray with great faith for you, because I'm fully convinced that the One who began this gracious work in you will faithfully continue the process of maturing you until the unveiling of our Lord Jesus Christ!

PHILIPPIANS 1:6 TPT

The work of God is not done in us. As long as we are alive, his mercy moves in us to help us grow, mature, and be more like him. If we think we have reached the pinnacle of what it means to follow him, then we have more humbling of our hearts to do.

The one who started a good work in us is not finished. He is not done with us. As long as we rely on him, he leads us. He teaches us. He molds us. He advises us. His wisdom is always on point. His leadership is always loving even when he corrects us. Take heart that the God of your salvation is the God of your maturity.

Faithful One, I'm so glad you're not done with me. I humble myself before you. Have your way in my heart and life.

Lifegiving Rewards

The reward of humility and the fear of the Lord
Are riches, honor, and life.

Proverbs 22:4 NASB

We may think of the rich and powerful as those who have lives without fault. Beneath the surface, however, there's always something that we don't pick up on. Everyone struggles. Everyone experiences difficulties. Pride and pomp are not the things to aspire to in success. Staying humble is always the way—no matter what we have or don't have. Humble hearts remain teachable, pliable, and rich soil for the seeds of faith to flourish.

If you want riches, honor, and life, Scripture says that the way to find it is through fearing the Lord and staying humble. When we know the Lord, his beautiful character and unchanging nature, we don't quake with terror in his presence. We honor him and stand in awe of his powerful love. It changes everything.

Lord, I honor you with my surrendered heart. Move in me in deep, meaningful ways today. I trust that building on your values is all the confidence I need in life.

JUNE 24

NEVER LOSE HOPE

Jesus used this story to teach his followers
that they should always pray and never lose hope.

LUKE 18:1 NCV

There is always reason to hope. As long as we are breathing, the power of God's redemptive love is at work in our lives. Death cannot stop it, and our struggles can't deter it. Jesus is coming again. We don't have to go searching for the second coming of the Lord. The Spirit makes his home in us, and we will not miss it when he returns.

Prayer is mighty, and it keeps us powerfully connected to God's heart. When the world keeps getting harder to live in, there is strength in the peace of God that passes all understanding. When we are tempted to give up, let's press in to the presence of God in prayer and hold onto hope.

Lord Jesus, I won't stop praying and hoping. When it is hard to hope, come in close with your presence and minister encouragement and gracious strength to my heart.

EVEN HERE

If I go up to heaven, you are there;
if I make my bed in Sheol, you are there.
If I fly on the wings of the dawn
and settle down on the western horizon,
even there your hand will lead me;
your right hand will hold on to me.

PSALM 139:8-10 CSB

No matter where you go, the Lord is there. You can't outrun his presence, and you can't lose his grip on your life. Every time you turn to the Lord, he is near. Every time you cry out for help, he is ready and able to do it.

You might feel as if you're in a mess of your own making; how can God meet you there? The reality is that he meets you wherever you are. Your pain is not too much for him, nor are the details of your problems. He is not overwhelmed by what overwhelms you. Even here, he is near.

Near One, meet me with the power of your love and bring breakthrough as I say yes to you today.

STILL DEVELOPING

Getting wisdom is the wisest thing you can do!
And whatever else you do, develop good judgment.

PROVERBS 4:7 NLT

We are in process, no matter where we find ourselves in this life. This is good news for every person in any stage of faith. There is no one-size-fits-all approach to maturing in the Lord. The details of our lives will look different, but the foundation remains the same. Wisdom is found in fellowship with Christ. Whatever we practically do in this life, developing good judgment will always pay off.

Today, focus on getting wisdom. Are you navigating a transition? There is wisdom to help you through it. Are you trying to repair a relationship? Wisdom will help with that too! There is nothing that wisdom won't support in your life. Lean into the Lord and follow his leading.

Wise God, I need your wisdom for my challenges. I look to you, the author and finisher of my faith.

FASTENED TOGETHER

Over all these virtues put on love,
which binds them all together in perfect unity.

COLOSSIANS 3:14 NIV

Whatever values we live by, love is the covering that encapsulates and pulls them all together. Unity is not possible without gracious understanding. It won't last without the ability to repair and extend forgiveness. Love is the tie that binds us together in Christ Jesus.

As we bear with one another, the way that Scripture encourages us to do, there is grace to be gentle, patience, humble, and kind. And still, above all these things, we can put on the love of God. We don't love based on how others love us. We love based on how God loves us. What a powerful shift this can be in our relationships, communities, and inner worlds!

Lord Jesus, thank you for the power of your love that satisfies, supplies, and covers the error of our ways. You are the one I choose to follow.

HUMBLE RIGHTEOUSNESS

Confess your sins to one another and pray for one another, that you may be healed. The prayer of a righteous person has great power as it is working.

JAMES 5:16 ESV

We are not meant to isolate from each other in our hurt, pain, or confusion. When we make mistakes, we need the support of others. Instead of pushing each other away, let's make confession our practice, and praying for each other our go-to. There is healing in the prayers of the righteous. There is power in the vulnerability of a humble and contrite heart.

Prayer is a powerful avenue to the breakthrough we are looking for in our lives and relationships. We can pray, no matter where we are, reaching our hearts to the King of kings without even moving our lips. Our hearts cry out to God, and he hears. Let's not forget the power of collective prayer and support.

Lord, I will not pretend to be perfect. I need you, and I need community. Thank you for safe people who pray together for breakthrough.

UNDER CONSIDERATION

Think about what I am saying.
The Lord will help you understand all these things.

2 TIMOTHY 2:7 NKJV

When it comes to the wisdom of God's Word and his ways, we can rely on the Holy Spirit to help us understand what may feel confusing. Let's give the wisdom of God—the very practical truth he offers—consideration. The gospel is not complicated; it is simple. The Holy Spirit enlightens our minds to understand what the will of God is.

Take time to meditate on the Word of God, and if you aren't sure as to the deeper meaning, ask God to help you. You aren't expected to know everything. Scripture is a vehicle to know God more. It is a way to ground yourself in the goodness and truth of who God is, how he works, and what he desires.

Wise One, I need your help to understand the values of your kingdom. Holy Spirit, reveal what you want me to know today, and may it spur me on to know you more.

There Is Still Time

There is an appointed time for everything.
And there is a time for every matter under heaven.

ECCLESIASTES 3:1 NASB

Every matter under heaven has its time. Just as the seasons turn, so do the seasons and times of our lives. If you feel like life has passed you by and the best times are behind you, take courage and hope in the truth of God's powerful redemption. There is a time for everything, and you can't miss what the Lord has already prepared for you.

The Lord is with us while we wait. There is a reason that endurance and perseverance are developed in our faith as we journey with the Lord through this life. He is here in the tension and the grace, in the yearning and in the relief. God hasn't lost track of the time, and we can trust him to continue to guide us into his goodness for as long as we live.

Lord, I need your encouragement and the powerful presence of your Spirit with me today. Give me eyes to see your goodness right where I am as I wait for better days.

JULY

"Whoever wants to be first must take last place and be the servant of everyone else."

MARK 9:35 NLT

Reservoirs of Wisdom

Since we first heard about you, we've kept you always in our prayers that you would receive the perfect knowledge of God's pleasure over your lives, making you reservoirs of every kind of wisdom and spiritual understanding.

Colossians 1:9 TPT

We can become reservoirs of God's wisdom and spiritual understanding. As we open ourselves to the leadership of Christ, yielding our hearts to his love, we become learners of his ways. We are the students, and he is our perfect teacher.

Our lives change for the better when we truly understand God's pleasure over our lives. He loves us thoroughly; his mercy becomes our landing place, our fuel for strength, and our best motivation. His love meets us where we are and clears the fog of what could be.

Holy One, I surrender my heart to your leadership today. I open myself up to your great wisdom. I am your vessel. Fill me!

A DEEP KNOWING

We did not receive the spirit of the world,
but we received the Spirit that is from God
so that we can know all that God has given us.

1 CORINTHIANS 2:12 NCV

The spirit of the world is based in fear. The Spirit of God is always moving in expansive love. Fear restricts while love creates space. Fear often motivates in haste while love takes its time and gives grace. We have not been given a spirit that restricts, hurries, or pressures us to know what we do not know. We have been given a Spirit that knows all, gives us permission to choose, and shows us the best way to go.

God is not controlling, though many act like he is. His love is free for all. Salvation is a gift of grace that no one can earn. His love is liberating, setting us free for freedom's sake. He is better than any parent, leader, or friend we have known! What gracious space is ours to take as we step into relationship with the Lord and follow the lead of his love.

Lord, expand my knowledge of all that you are, hold, and release to those you love.

HIGHER STILL

"As heaven is higher than earth,
so my ways are higher than your ways,
and my thoughts than your thoughts."

ISAIAH 55:9 CSB

God really is greater than we can imagine. His ways are better, truer, and purer than our own. He is not biased, and he cannot be controlled or manipulated. No one can fool him. He sees straight through motivations and lies. He sees to the heart of the matter every single time. This is good news for those who are misunderstood.

The perspective of God is clear of any doubt or confusion. He sees everything clearly. Why would we try to work out on our own what God already knows? Let's join our hearts to his and lean on his understanding over our own. He always guides in goodness.

God, when I am overwhelmed by what I do not know, I turn to you. I trust your nature and your perfect understanding to lead me.

STRONG TIES

I want them to be encouraged and knit together by strong ties of love. I want them to have complete confidence that they understand God's mysterious plan, which is Christ himself. In him lie hidden all the treasures of wisdom and knowledge.

COLOSSIANS 2:2-3 NLT

Jesus Christ is the answer to our questions. He is the mysterious plan God set into motion so that we could see, know, and understand what the Father is truly like. Before him, there was confusion around his character. There is now no doubt what God is like. Jesus revealed the nature of God in humanity, in a way that we could understand.

Love is the highest law. It is what we were created from and into, and what we are destined to be found in. God's love is never ending. It goes beyond our comprehension. It is able to do much more than we can imagine. It is our confidence, the source of wisdom, and the solution to every problem we face.

God, I want to take your love seriously. I look to you, Jesus, to find the treasures of heaven's wisdom and knowledge.

HE KNOWS

A person may think their own ways are right,
but the LORD weighs the heart.

PROVERBS 21:2 NIV

All we can do is our best. Even when we do not see any error in our ways, God sees things clearer than we do. This is a relief to those who lean on his leadership. When he corrects us, it is for our good. When he redirects us, we can trust that it is into the better path.

Think back to a time when you thought you knew exactly what you wanted. You worked hard to get it only to realize it wasn't the answer you thought it would be. Even if it was good, it did not solve all your problems. Nothing in life is perfect, including any of us. However, as we trust the Lord to lead us in his perfect wisdom, he transforms us continually by his presence. We don't have to reach for tomorrow because we know the power of his goodness today.

Lord Jesus, you know what you are doing in this world and in my life. As I move, work things out for your kingdom purposes.

DIFFERENT RULES

Though we walk in the flesh,
we are not waging war according to the flesh.

2 CORINTHIANS 10:3 ESV

We are not called to wage war against each other. We are in this world, but we are not meant to live by the standards of it. The law of God's love is higher than the laws of the land, for love does no wrong against its neighbors.

People pick fights over petty things all the time. But this is not how we are meant to live. If we will give our attention to what good we can do in this world, our energy will be directed in the ways of the kingdom of God. We don't wage war; we look for paths of peace. Where others destroy, we bring healing, comfort, and life. It starts with us every time.

Holy One, I choose to follow you no matter how foolish it may look to those who don't understand your love.

REST ASSURED

The LORD is good,
A stronghold in the day of trouble;
And He knows those who trust in Him.

NAHUM 1:7 NKJV

When we are in trouble, the Lord is steadfast. He hasn't changed a bit. He remains good. No matter how we feel about our circumstances, God is a safe place to take shelter.

You are not exempt from God's goodness. You can take refuge in his presence and experience comfort in his loving embrace. He knows your heart. He knows all who trust in him, and you don't have to convince him of a thing. When your inner critic tries to convince you of God's indifference toward you, remember the truth of God's love that overcomes everything that overwhelms you. He is your safe place. Run into the shelter of his presence and find rest there.

Lord, you are my safe place. You have my yes today.

OUR HEALING

It was because of our rebellious deeds that he was pierced and because of our sins that he was crushed. He endured the punishment that made us completely whole, and in his wounding, we found our healing.

ISAIAH 53:5 TPT

In the selfless sacrifice of Christ, we find our healing. Today's Scripture reminds us of this powerful truth. No heartbreak can keep us from the redemptive power of his love. No pain or suffering or loss can keep us from the wholeness he offers us in his fellowship.

Though we may feel like pieces of our former selves when heartbreak hits, the Lord's gracious love holds us together. When we feel like the tight weave of our lives is going loose at the ends, it is into amazing grace that we fall. There is more freedom in his love, more healing for our hurt, than we realize. In our undoing, he makes us whole in him. Instead of letting fear drive us to resist his merciful work, let's allow the natural cycles of death lead to our rebirth in him. There is always redemption. There is always hope. There is always healing.

Healer, I let go of what I can no longer control and trust you to heal me with your powerful love.

WONDERFUL WISDOM

The wisdom from above is first pure, then peace-loving, gentle, reasonable, full of mercy and good fruits, impartial, free of hypocrisy.

JAMES 3:17 NASB

Have you ever wondered how to tell God's wisdom from the world's? It is grounded in truth, in love, in peace, and in good fruit. It is impartial, free from duplicity. It is pure, gentle, and reasonable. It is not overbearing or tricky. It does not promise one thing and then change its mind. It is powerful, and everyone can gain from it.

The wisdom of God isn't tedious. It is wonderful! It is liberating and admirable. It is as valuable to those who don't know the Lord as it is to the family of Christ. There is a reason why the proverbs praise wisdom's virtues.

Wise One, thank you for the reminder of what your wisdom looks like. I say yes to it today!

ACT ON IT

Do what God's teaching says;
when you only listen and do nothing,
you are fooling yourselves.

JAMES 1:22 NCV

Perhaps you have seen today's verse play out in a parent-child dynamic. One can listen and refuse to act, and that means nothing. An adult can encourage or ask a child to do something, and they may agree and then do nothing about it. What good does this do?

In Matthew 21:28-32, Jesus told a story of two sons. The father asked them both to go work in his vineyard. The first son said he wouldn't, then later changed his mind and went. The second son said he would go but didn't. The obedient son was the first. Let's give God our yes by doing what he asks, regardless of how we first respond. It is in the action that obedience happens, not in what we say we will do.

Lord, I don't want to be full of empty yeses. I want my life to show it. Today, I put my effort into action and obedience to your Word.

IMMEASURABLE STRENGTH

Be strengthened by the Lord and by his vast strength.

EPHESIANS 6:10 CSB

We find God's strength through our union with Christ. We can stand in the victory of Christ's resurrection power. His resurrection is not only our hope, but it is the very strength of God at work in our hearts and lives to renew and restore us to himself.

It doesn't matter how unfortunate our situation seems. His strength is as available in this moment as it ever has been. We don't have to prove ourselves or beg for his help. We simply turn to him with our need, and he lavishes us in the empowering grace of his presence. We have all we need, not because we are strong, but because God is!

Victorious One, supernaturally strengthen me in the power of your presence. You are my God, and I turn to you for all that I need.

STRENGTH TO ACT

"Get up, for it is your duty to tell us how to proceed in setting things straight. We are behind you, so be strong and take action."

EZRA 10:4 NLT

It is one thing to know what we ought to do; it is another thing entirely to do it. We can be overwhelmed by the bigger picture of what is required if we feel alone in our efforts. This is where the power of support and the encouragement of community can help motivate and strengthen us.

We don't have to walk this path alone, and we don't have to fill all the needs we see on our own. We do, however, have to do our part. We need to know what we are called to, and we also need the support of others to get there. No one else can do what is ours to do, so let's not wait on the sidelines. If we have a vision that no one else does, we have to take action to get there.

Lord, when I am stuck, not because of lack of vision but because I simply can't get started or moving, remind me of the people who surround me. I won't just sit around today.

EXPRESSIONS OF LOVE

In Christ Jesus neither circumcision nor uncircumcision has any value. The only thing that counts is faith expressing itself through love.

GALATIANS 5:6 NIV

God has broken down every barrier that mankind put into place. Nothing can keep us from his love, and nothing should keep us from loving one another. Faith is expressed in how we serve one another. It is shown through our practical lives: our habits, our interactions, and our service.

If we are in Christ, then we are brothers and sisters with all who are in Christ too. There are no second-class citizens in his kingdom. There aren't any favorites. God's love doesn't discriminate, and it doesn't exclude. There is room for everyone. His capacity is limitless. Let's remember this as we put our love on today and move in faith in practical ways.

Loving Father, it is hard to imagine how expansive your love is. Broaden my understanding and open my eyes to the power of your mercy.

BE BLESSED

"If you know these things,
blessed are you if you do them."

JOHN 13:17 ESV

There is so much blessing in our service. If all we ever did was receive—more knowledge, more resources—we wouldn't know the power of generosity. We have a loving Father who delights in meeting our needs. He also delights when we reach out to help others. The more we mirror his nature, the more fulfilling it is for everyone.

We are blessed if we don't just know the truth and wisdom of God, but we act on it. Jesus is our example to follow. It is through our surrender that the glory of God is manifested in our lives. We are blessed to receive, and we are so very blessed to give. May we be generous and willing servants, friends, and children of God.

Glorious Jesus, there is no excuse for my lack of loving action when I know what to do. I say yes with my life.

EVERLASTING GOD

Before the mountains were brought forth,
Or ever You had formed the earth and the world,
Even from everlasting to everlasting, You are God.

PSALM 90:2 NKJV

When we remember who God is, it can help us to trust his nature, his wisdom, and his power. Our lives are but a breath on a cold day—here one moment and gone the next. But God. He is everlasting.

Just as our lives are a mere blip, so are our circumstances. No experience lasts forever. No suffering or heartache or pain is eternal. And God promises that every tear and trauma will be wiped away in his eternal kingdom. So, what will we do now? How will we live today? It is all we've got, so let's not waste it.

Everlasting God, you are the constant in an ever-changing world. I cling to you today, and I ask for your strength to help me through all the things I face.

CONTINUE TO GROW

Continue to grow and increase in God's grace and intimacy with our Lord and Savior, Jesus Christ. May he receive all the glory both now and until the day eternity begins. Amen!

2 PETER 3:18 TPT

As long as we are walking this earth, there is more for us to learn. There is more grace to experience, and more wisdom to collect. It is never too late to change our minds. It isn't too late to adopt new practices.

As we follow the Lord, we can't predict how he will move in our lives, though we can recognize his nature and mercy at work. He doesn't operate in the same way every time. He doesn't answer prayers in the same way each time either. Let's stop trying to pin God down to our expectations, and instead continue to grow and increase our faith and our fellowship with the Lord Jesus Christ. There is always more room to grow!

Lord, I'm so glad there's more to learn of you and your ways. I press into your presence, and I open my heart to your fellowship today.

RESTORERS

Even if a person is caught in any wrongdoing,
you who are spiritual are to restore such a person
in a spirit of gentleness; each one looking to yourself,
so that you are not tempted as well.

GALATIANS 6:1 NASB

God is the great restorer. He takes broken things and makes something altogether new out of them. The pieces remain, but God's mercy is like the gold that melds us together into wholeness.

None of us is perfect. Gentleness is always the way to lead in trying to restore others back in love and truth. Gentleness does not mean we shirk away from the reality of things. God corrects us with his truth, but he always does it with kindness. He does not yell at us or punish us. He invites us to see our mistakes from his lens, and he lavishes us in love. Let's try to be like him and gently handle mistakes with grace and mercy.

Restorer, there is nothing you can't put back together. When I see someone acting wrongly, help me to wrap the truth in gentleness for the purpose of restoration.

Nourishing Love

"Simon son of John, do you love me more than these?"
He answered, "Yes, Lord, you know that I love you."
Jesus said, "Feed my lambs."

John 21:15 NCV

Jesus loved his disciples. They were his friends. Knowing how much Peter loved him, Jesus tested the lengths of it. This was after Peter denied Jesus. After the shame and guilt that came over him. After the death and resurrection of Christ.

Jesus' heart is for his people. It is for the lambs that need nourishment and care. We, the children of God, are his lambs—the people of his pasture. Jesus asked Peter to take a leadership role in feeding his truth to others. This wasn't a way to stoke his ego, but an invitation to servant leadership: the same as he showed his disciples. Love is meant to be offered to others. Peter knew Jesus well, and he loved him. He was able to show this by serving the early Church.

Lord Jesus, I know that your love nourishes. Out of my love for you, I will offer the grace, patience, peace, joy, self-control, and love you offer.

REVEALING FRUIT

"You'll recognize them by their fruit."

MATTHEW 7:20 CSB

The fruit of our lives reveals what we value. If we claim to know the Lord, but we don't walk in his ways, our heart motivations will show what we truly believe. Jesus didn't say that by a person's words you will know whether they are liars or not; it is through the fruit of their actions.

What does the fruit of a yielded life to Christ look like? It looks like the fruit of the Spirit. It produces love, joy, peace, patience, kindness, goodness, faithfulness, gentleness, and self-control. Stirring up quarrels, being selfish, controlling, jealous, and immoral, these are the many bad fruits that are revealed through the lives of those who don't follow Jesus. Let's not just look at what a person says they believe, but how they actually live.

Holy Spirit, your fruit is good, and it is present in the lives of those who love you and follow your wisdom. I live in your light and ask for your discernment.

THE PRESENT

Whatever you do, do well. For when you go to the grave, there will be no work or planning or knowledge or wisdom.

ECCLESIASTES 9:10 NLT

There is no day like today to do what we already know to do. We don't have to attack every problem or solve every quandary. But there are things that we can do and do well. Whatever we do, let's put our whole hearts into it, and remember that today is all we have to put our energy toward.

Not every day will look highly productive, but it can still be full of mercy, peace, and fellowship with the Lord. There isn't a day that he opts out of helping us as we look to him. His presence is profoundly near. Let's not get lost in what could be tomorrow, but dig in to what is ours here and now to do. And let's do it well.

Mighty God, you do all things well. You guide me into goodness, and I can see the next step that is mine to take today.

UNFATHOMABLE

Great is the LORD and most worthy of praise;
his greatness no one can fathom.

PSALM 145:3 NIV

The Lord is grander than we can imagine. He is mightier than the tallest mountains. He is more astounding than the deepest sea. When we are captivated by the sunset, it is but a glimpse of his glory—and a small one at that!

We can experience awe in all sorts of ways. The way a stranger helps someone in need. The waves crashing over the shore that lulls our senses into meditative peace. An animal, a budding flower, or a turning leaf captivating our imaginations and deepening our sense of appreciation of being a part of this intricate world. Whatever makes you aware of what is bigger than you, go seek those things out today. And when you do, give God praise for the ways he is greater still.

Marvelous One, increase my capacity to know you. I give you praise for your many wonders!

CHART A NEW PATH

Whoever conceals his transgressions will not prosper,
but he who confesses and forsakes them will obtain mercy.

PROVERBS 28:13 ESV

Repentance is necessary for our well-being, and for our freedom. Christ offers us the power of his redemptive mercy that washes us from the guilt of our sin. When we confess our sins, it is not the end of our story. God's forgiveness sets us free and we are able to chart a new path free from those cycles of sin, shame, and compromise.

When we say yes to the Lord, it is not only to receive his mercy. His mercy is powerful and liberating, offering us a new start. Let's forsake the compromise of our past and press on in full fellowship with the Lord who is good and faithful.

Savior, you are my freedom, my gracious God, and my guide. I leave behind the errors of yesterday as I confess and receive your forgiveness.

SLOW TO REACT

Let every man be swift to hear, slow to speak, slow to wrath; for the wrath of man does not produce the righteousness of God.

JAMES 1:19-20 NKJV

When we are quick to speak, to respond in anger and jump to conclusions, others will be cautious around us. This may mean they withhold the necessary truth that would help us grow in grace and love. We should always be quick to listen so we can understand the other person's point of view. If we are too quick to jump in with our own opinion or reaction, we may miss out on what they actually want to communicate.

God is ever so patient with us. He is slow to anger and abounding in love. If we want to be more like him in this, one way to actively practice it is to do what today's verse instructs: be swift to hear, slow to speak. When we listen to understand, we step outside of our own hasty assumptions and seek instead to know the other person's perspective.

Lord, you are patient, loving, and gracious. Oh, how I want to be more like you! I choose to create space in conversations to listen, even when it is uncomfortable for me.

AGELESS VIRTUES

Don't be intimidated by those who are older than you; simply be the example they need to see by being faithful and true in all that you do.

1 TIMOTHY 4:12 TPT

There is no age requirement in the kingdom of heaven. All who come to Christ are welcomed with open arms, from small children to the most mature among us. It is never too early, and it is never too late to follow Christ. The virtues of Christ's kingdom are ageless. We shouldn't be intimidated by others. God is our confidence, and it is his ways that we follow. It is his view of us that matters most.

Obedience sometimes requires stepping outside of our comfort zones. Though older generations may look down on younger ones for their age, what we ought to be looking at is the character of each life. Where there is faithfulness, integrity, and love, there is God's Spirit at work. Let's let go of our biases about age and instead live rightly and unashamedly in the love of Christ.

Jesus, I will not judge others on their age or experience. I put my energy into living for you, the way you ask me to.

BE READY

Remind them to be subject to rulers, to authorities, to be obedient, to be ready for every good deed, to slander no one, not to be contentious, to be gentle, showing every consideration for all people.

TITUS 3:1-2 NASB

In our hyper-independent society, it feels counter-cultural to follow the wisdom of today's verse. What does it look like to follow the authority of the land even when we disagree? Should we not be obedient to the laws, ready to do good whenever we can?

In Christ, we are free from shame, fear, condemnation, and sin. We are not free from living in this world though. Our love is not love when it does not get practical. The fruit of God's Spirit, and the virtues of Christ's kingdom never expire. They are always applicable in any and every circumstance. Let's be ready for every good deed, showing consideration for all people. That is what love looks like in our reality.

Father, yours is the kingdom, and the power, and the glory forever. Who am I to disagree with the way you do things? I align my heart in your love and give up the need to fight for my own rights.

WHY WAIT?

Why wait any longer?
Get up, be baptized, and wash your sins away,
trusting in him to save you.

ACTS 22:16 NCV

There are waiting periods in life that we cannot escape. We cannot control certain outcomes, but we can take the steps we know to move in that direction. Waiting does not mean that we cease to exist. We don't run away to the wilderness for years. We continue to show up.

Today's verse is about self-imposed waiting. Not the kind of waiting God asks us to trust him in. What have you kept pressing pause on for fear of what it would require? What have you been putting off until tomorrow that you can embrace today? If you have been waiting to trust the Lord, there is no better moment to act than right now. If there is something you know he has called you to that you have hesitated on, why not take that leap of faith today?

Lord, I won't hesitate any longer to come close to you and take the step you have cleared ahead of me.

Believe and Live

"I am the resurrection and the life.
The one who believes in me, even if he dies, will live."

John 11:25 CSB

Jesus Christ is the lifegiving Savior that offers redemption for our souls. There is no one else like him. He broke down every barrier that separated us from the Father. In his death, he tore the veil that kept the presence of God from the people. We all have access to God through Christ, both now and forever, because of what he has done.

Thankfully, Jesus didn't stay in the grave. Three days later, he rose from the dead in resurrection life. He is the hope of every nation, the salvation of every soul who comes to him in surrender. His love is stronger than death, and it reaches us even now. There is nothing that can keep us from his presence, including the decay of our mortal bodies. Put your faith in God, for he will revive you in his powerful presence both now and forevermore.

Savior, you have my heart, my soul, my life, and my forever yes.

SPACE FOR GRACE

If I must boast, I would rather boast about the things that show how weak I am.

2 CORINTHIANS 11:30 NLT

God isn't impressed by our resumes. He isn't convinced of our goodness or worth based on what we have accomplished. He knows us through and through. He knows our weakness along with our strength. He sees it all clearly.

There is nothing God cannot do. There is no situation he can't turn around with his redemptive mercy. What is impossible with us is doable for him. Let's stay humble before him and others and remember that our greatest strength is found in his help. Though we may fight this fact on our best days, we embrace it willingly on our worst.

Gracious Father, I don't want to only love and value people based on their strengths. I make room for your grace to move in my heart, my mind, and my relationships.

LIGHT OF LIFE

"I am the light of the world.
Whoever follows me will never walk in darkness,
but will have the light of life."

JOHN 8:12 NIV

When we walk in the light of Christ, there is nothing to hide. There is nothing to run from. There is nothing that can overshadow his love. We don't have to fear anything in his presence. He guides us into goodness around every bend.

Though we cannot escape the trials of life, we can know the constant comfort and power of God's presence. He lights up our lives with glimmers of his mercy. He turns our devastation into pathways of peace. He is the almighty God, and there is no shadow of turning in him. He never leaves or forsakes us. We are safe in the light-filled confidence of his companionship.

Lord Jesus, you radiate light in the darkness and make shadows flee. There is no shame, fear, or sin that can stand your glorious love.

PATIENT UNDERSTANDING

Whoever is slow to anger has great understanding,
but he who has a hasty temper exalts folly.

PROVERBS 14:29 ESV

Throughout life we are tested by situations outside of our control. We may sometimes be caught off-guard and react in a way outside of our normal character. However, if our reactions are often hasty, then we should take some time to ask the deeper reason behind it.

Scripture is clear that God is slow to anger. It doesn't mean that he never gets angry. Being slow to anger also doesn't mean that we never will experience irritation. We may very well get angry at things that are consistently showing up to test us. Persistent patterns of anger mean something else. They may indicate a lack of self-control, or a boundary that we have not enforced. Patient understanding serves us well in our relationships, and in our lives in general. Let's remember to work on being slow to jump to hasty conclusions and instead lead with a desire to understand.

Lord, help me choose your way of wisdom and understanding.

Wisdom's Treasure

Everyone wants gold, but wisdom's worth is far greater.
Silver is sought after,
but a heart of understanding yields
a greater return.

Proverbs 16:16 TPT

It is not a vain pursuit to make a decent living. However, when it is the foundation of all we do, we miss out on the greater treasure available to us. The Lord's wisdom leads to success in life if for no other reason than we walk in the light of goodness and have nothing to regret or fear. The wisdom of God doesn't erode or decay. It is always priceless: worth far more than gold or silver.

When we build our lives upon the foundation of Christ and follow in the wisdom of his ways, we build upon the rock of his incomparable nature. God wants us to thrive. He wants us to know the power of his love, his liberty, and his grace. He has freely given us his wisdom to instruct us. Let's not ignore the importance of wisdom's role in our lives. It is a gift far greater than wealth that is here today and gone tomorrow.

Jesus, you are the embodiment of wisdom. I give my life to know this wisdom in spirit and in truth.

AUGUST

"Anyone who wants to serve me
must follow me, because my
servants must be where I am.
And the Father will honor
anyone who serves me."

JOHN 12:26 NLT

CREATE CONTENTMENT

Let your conduct be without covetousness;
be content with such things as you have.
For He Himself has said,
"I will never leave you nor forsake you."

HEBREWS 13:5 NKJV

Contentment is not something that we have to wait to appear in our hearts. We actually can take an active role in cultivating it. Envy and comparison is a trap that leads us to feeling like we're never enough. We may feel that what we have isn't good enough. But the truth of contentment is that it isn't reserved for tomorrow; it is fostered today.

Gratitude is a powerful tool in helping us nurture contentment in our hearts. When we look at our lives through the lens of thanks, we don't gloss over the beauty and goodness already there. Envy points out what we lack, while gratitude helps us appreciate what we have. The greatest gift we have is the presence of God. That's a good launching point for gratitude today!

God, open my eyes to see the glorious goodness already in my life.

A HIGHER PURSUIT

If you have been raised with Christ,
keep seeking the things that are above,
where Christ is, seated at the right hand of God.

COLOSSIANS 3:1 NASB

In Christ, we put the selfish pursuits of our lives behind us and press on to walk in the ways of his higher kingdom. The values and nature of God are incomparable. There is no higher law than the law of his love, and when we yield to his leadership, our lives begin to reflect his character.

In all that we do, we can reflect the values of God's kingdom. His peace, love, joy, gentleness, hope, and redemption are ours. Let's live like we believe this to be true. We must set our eyes on the things above and not be distracted by the pull of compromise, confusion, or deception. God's wisdom is clear, and walking in his love is simple, though not easy.

Lord, as I lift my eyes above the fray, give me your higher perspective.

EVERYTHING NEW

If anyone belongs to Christ, there is a new creation. The old things have gone; everything is made new!

2 CORINTHIANS 5:17 NCV

The redemptive power of Christ isn't only for us to see and experience; it's for everyone! When Jesus makes us new, he turns our lives around. He transforms us from the inside out, and it is only a matter of time before the people around us see a difference.

All who belong to Christ are made new. The old has gone; the new has come. We are like newborn babies, given a fresh slate in his mercy. What felt impossible before becomes fodder for hope in our hearts as we walk in the confidence of God's love. There is nothing that his restorative love cannot revive. What opportunity we have to continually be transformed in the kind and wise covering of our Father.

Christ Jesus, how grateful I am to be transformed in your presence. Today, have your way in my heart, mind, and soul.

LESSONS IN GOODNESS

Learn to do what is good.
Pursue justice.
Correct the oppressor.
Defend the rights of the fatherless.
Plead the widow's cause.

ISAIAH 1:17 CSB

It is no small thing, no secondary matter, to learn to do what is good. The law of love is lived out in our daily lives. When we pursue justice, we follow the path of God's kingdom. When we correct the oppressor, we call for accountability in the truth and love of our God. When we defend the rights of the fatherless, we pursue the peace that Christ created for all. When we plead the widow's cause, we step in to support, advocate for, and liberate those who have no other options for help.

When we serve others in love, we do what is good. Our lives match our faith, and we walk in the ways of Christ. There is no better way to live than to extend justice, kindness, and support to the vulnerable.

God of justice, may I always choose to side with the vulnerable. I won't turn a blind eye to my own responsibility to actively care for them.

PERFECT IN FAITHFULNESS

He is the Rock; his deeds are perfect.
Everything he does is just and fair.
He is a faithful God who does no wrong;
how just and upright he is!

DEUTERONOMY 32:4 NLT

Everything God does is out of his incomparable nature. His mercy, faithfulness, and justice are not set down one moment and then picked back up again the next. Everything God does, he does in love. He will never change.

God is our firm foundation. He is the solid rock beneath our feet. Even when everything in the world cracks and shifts, he remains steady. When we build our lives upon the Rock, we have nothing to fear. God is faithful. He will never forget a promise. He is persistent, he is powerful, and he is present.

Faithful One, thank you for your powerful presence that never changes and never diminishes. You are the Rock, and I stand upon your faithfulness.

LET GOD HANDLE IT

Do not take revenge, my dear friends,
but leave room for God's wrath, for it is written:
"It is mine to avenge; I will repay," says the Lord.

ROMANS 12:19 NIV

When our hearts are fixated on revenge, we become overwhelmed by it. There is less room for love to lead us. With our hearts and minds focused on Jesus Christ, we let go of the distractions that so incessantly fight for our attention, including the need for retaliation. God is the only perfect judge. We can trust that he will act in truth and justice. He isn't muddled by clouds of self-protection.

Let go and let God handle it. You don't have to fight for your own reputation or defend your character. The truth is always revealed. Keep following the path of God's love, and walk in humility, grace, and kindness before the one who is endlessly humble, gracious, and loving. Revenge will close your heart off, but trusting God and allowing love to move in you will expand it.

Lord, I don't want to give my energy to defending myself or seeking revenge on others. I choose to walk in obedience to your love and trust you.

RETURN

"So you, by the help of your God, return,
hold fast to love and justice,
and wait continually for your God."

HOSEA 12:6 ESV

We don't have to do anything in our own strength. That includes returning to where God beckons us to be. Even when we turn toward him, it is with his help that we take the next step. We have only to turn our attention to him and he is already there with his support and gracious strength to empower us.

Come back to his loyal love as your source. Hold fast to his mercy and hold tightly to his justice. You cannot go wrong with love and justice as your motivation. As you wait on God, which is something you can do continually, you know the power of his presence. He is your Savior, your hope, and your help in all things.

Savior, by your help, I return to the foundation of your ways. I wait, even now, for you.

FRUITS OF LABOR

Do not be deceived, God is not mocked;
for whatever a man sows, that he will also reap.

GALATIANS 6:7 NKJV

We cannot sow seeds of bitterness and expect to reap sweet fruit. What we put our time, intention, and efforts toward, those are the things that will be produced in our lives. God cannot be tricked by false promises. He will not be deceived even when those who have no integrity fool others. We can trust his judgments, and we can also trust that in due time, the fruit of people's lives reveal their intentions.

Jesus himself said that not everyone who claims to know him actually represents him. What is sown in love will always produce good fruit. There are many who use God's Word to oppress others rather than to invite them into the freedom of God's gracious salvation. Let's lead with love, both today and always, for its fruit will not be denied.

Lord, I know that no one can fool you. I choose your ways, and I trust your timing.

HONEST WORK

Life is good for the one who is generous and charitable, conducting affairs with honesty and truth.

PSALM 112:5 TPT

It is best to be honest and truthful in every area of our lives. When we conduct our affairs with integrity, we build a reputation that others can trust. There are no shortcuts to doing things the right way. We simply need to commit to doing what is ours to do well, with generosity, care, and honesty.

Every day, we come into contact with people who have needs that we might be able to help meet. While there are some responsibilities we can't set aside, there is often more that we can do than we offer. Let's look for ways to increase our generosity in the lives we already live. When we open our eyes to see how we can increase our honesty, compassion, and generosity, we will find creative ways to do so.

Perfect One, as I look for ways to serve you and others well, show me little acts of generosity I can do to partner with your heart.

NOURISHING RIGHTEOUSNESS

"Blessed are those who hunger and thirst for righteousness, for they will be satisfied."

MATTHEW 5:6 NASB

As long as we are in this world, we will experience challenges to overcome. Though God is perfect, the world is far from it. But this does not mean there isn't beauty to excavate, or goodness to mine in this life we live.

Jesus said that those who hunger and thirst for righteousness will be filled. We won't be satisfied by the offerings of this world, but by God's own righteousness. Jesus is our righteousness. It is in him that we find complete satisfaction. We don't have to work for it, and we can't erase it with our mistakes. Jesus' gracious sacrifice is what nourishes our souls and brings us into perfect fellowship with the Father.

Righteous One, all who hunger and thirst for you find their satisfaction in your love. I come to you; I yield to you; I rest in you.

RETURN ON INVESTMENT

"Don't judge others, and you will not be judged.
Don't accuse others of being guilty,
and you will not be accused of being guilty.
Forgive, and you will be forgiven."

LUKE 6:37 NCV

The principle that Jesus laid forth in today's verse isn't a new one for most of us. The way we treat others reflects how we expect others to treat us. When we are quick to judge, we experience others' judgments, too. When we refuse to offer grace to others, we are quick to spot it in others, as well.

When we are investing in people, it is important that we nurture the values in ourselves that we want to experience from others. Let's be slow to judge, generous in forgiveness, and leave space to get curious about others' experiences. When we create room for grace, for love, and for understanding, we get that in return.

Lord, I know that it matters how I treat people. Help me to not rush to judgments of others, but rather be curious in compassion, gracious in understanding, and plentiful in forgiveness.

FOUNDATIONAL MATTERS

"Woe to you, scribes and Pharisees... you have neglected the more important matters of the law—justice, mercy, and faithfulness. These things should have been done without neglecting the others."

MATTHEW 23:23 CSB

Jesus rebuked the Jewish religious leaders of his day for neglecting the foundational elements of God's law. While they were sure to give their tithe to the Lord, they did not make sure that their hearts were submitted to God. When we cleanse our hearts and motives, everything else is purified too.

Let's not be like hypocrites that present a standard for others while looking for ways to compromise in our own lives. There is one measure: the measure of Christ. There is one Savior—Christ Jesus. In him, we are purified, forgiven, and set free to build our lives upon his justice, mercy, and faithfulness. Let's start inward today and surrender our hearts to the foundation of our faith.

Lord Jesus, I surrender my heart to you, and I will align my actions with your justice, mercy, and faithfulness.

BUILD ON THE ROCK

"Anyone who listens to my teaching and follows it is wise, like a person who builds a house on solid rock."

MATTHEW 7:24 NLT

It is one thing to listen to others and respect what they say. It is another thing to implement their wisdom in our own lives. Jesus' instructions were not flippant sayings. They reflect the values of the kingdom of God. Jesus revealed what the Father is like and what he wants us to be like in this world.

We build our lives upon the solid rock of Christ when we adopt his ways as our own. We take the wisdom of his Word seriously, not only in the realm of our minds, but in how we interact with others. The one who follows the wisdom of God doesn't start from scratch. They build upon the strong foundation of God's eternal truth. Let's not be like the foolish that hear Christ's wisdom but don't follow it. They are like those who build a house on sand. When the storms of testing come, their house will collapse. But those who adopt the ways of God will stand strong.

Immovable One, you are the way, the truth, and the life, and I follow you.

PERFECTLY GOOD

Good and upright is the LORD;
therefore he instructs sinners in his ways.

PSALM 25:8 NIV

When God is our main focus, we measure everything against his standard. Though it is tempting to be distracted by the bad actions of others—the compromise, the abuse, and the misuse of power—it does not negate the goodness of God. There are many interruptions to pull our attention away from the power of God, so we must be on our guard to redirect our gaze back to him.

When we fix our eyes on Jesus Christ, on his perfect nature and unmatched mercy, we can let everything else fade away. We cannot control what others will do, but we can decide how we will live. Let's decide to keep our eyes focused on his goodness.

God, this I know: you are good, and you are unchanging. I choose to direct my gaze to you today.

UNCOVERING MYSTERIES

He uncovers the deeps out of darkness
and brings deep darkness to light.

JOB 12:22 ESV

Uncovering mysteries and discovering new territory is an exciting venture. Just think of all the unknown elements of the oceans. It might be hard to fathom, but we have only explored a tiny fraction of the seas, even though these waters make up about seventy percent of the earth's surface. Only about twenty percent of the ocean floor has been mapped. This leaves much more mystery than data!

While there are constant innovations and explorations into mysteries happening every day, there is one that sees everything clearly now. Nothing is a mystery to God. He sees what hides from our perceptions, and he uncovers it before us. There isn't anything that God can't light up with his love, and there is certainly no breakthrough too difficult for him.

Wise God, you are full of truth, clarity, and solutions. You are my source, and I trust you to reveal what I am looking for in the light of your love.

OUT OF THE MUCK

He also brought me up out of a horrible pit,
Out of the miry clay,
And set my feet upon a rock,
And established my steps.

PSALM 40:2 NKJV

There are specific moments in life where we find ourselves stuck. We cannot release ourselves from the circumstances we are in. This is when we need the help and support of others. This, especially, is when we turn to the Lord to save us.

God is near to us in our hurt and in our weakness. He does not leave or forsake us. When we are brought down to the pit of despair, he does not leave us to our mess—not even that of our own making! God is able to lift us from the darkest circumstances and set our feet on the rock of his enduring grace. We need never fear, not even when the darkness seems to settle around us. Just a spark of light makes shadows flee, and our God shines as bright as the sun.

Lord, you are the one who sets my feet upon a rock and establishes my steps. When I have nowhere else to turn, you are always there.

PERSISTENT MERCY

The Lord is still waiting to show his favor to you
so he can show you his marvelous love.
He waits to be gracious to you.
He sits on his throne ready to show mercy to you.
For Yahweh is the Lord of justice,
faithful to keep his promises.

ISAIAH 30:18 TPT

God loves to show you his wonderful love. He delights in revealing his kindness toward you. It is present even when you miss it. He lovingly waits to see if you will recognize the fingerprints of his mercy in your life.

Is there an area where you especially need God's mercy to meet you? Turn your attention to the Lord. He patiently waits for you to come to him. He isn't mostly disappointed in you. He is ready to receive you with the delight of his heart. He is ready to show you all the mercy you hope for and even more than you can anticipate.

Faithful One, I come to you as I am, believing that you are good, you are patient, and you are truly loving.

FAITHFUL PROVIDER

He executes justice for the orphan and the widow, and shows His love for the stranger by giving him food and clothing.

DEUTERONOMY 10:18 NASB

God's love is endlessly practical. It is not an idea that we have to hope will reveal itself in real ways in our lives. It is faithful, it is kind, and it is present. God shows us his gracious kindness by taking care of us, and he wants us to take care of others.

There are no unworthy recipients of God's love. He loves the destitute and the outcast as much as he loves our families and friends. Let's join our love to God's by reaching outside of our circles. Let's show our love by feeding and clothing those who are not native to our land, those who are poor and jobless, those who have no hope of covering their needs. This is love: that we care for others no matter who they are.

Jesus, my yes to you includes the willingness to help those who are different from me.

HONORABLE HUMILITY

Pride leads to destruction;
a proud attitude brings ruin.
It is better to be humble and be with those who suffer
than to share stolen property with the proud.

PROVERBS 16:18-19 NCV

Pride shuts us down from helpful feedback. It isolates and restricts us. Humility opens us to different perspectives and gives us opportunities to grow and learn from our mistakes. It is better to be in solidarity with the suffering than to join ourselves with those who care more about their reputation and comfort. Jesus will always be found among the suffering. This is an important thing for us to keep in mind.

A humble heart can take us far in life. It might not look impressive to those who are hungry for power, but it will leave us with nothing to hide and everything to gain. Servant-hearted leadership is the way of Christ, and it is the way we follow in his footsteps.

Lord Jesus, there is no one else quite like you. I reject the pull of pride and embrace your humble attitude to serve others in love.

PERFECTLY JUST

Indeed, it is true that God does not act wickedly
and the Almighty does not pervert justice.

JOB 34:12 CSB

Everything God does, he does rightly. This is almost too much for us to imagine in this fallen world full of disappointment and flaws. God isn't biased, and he's not distracted by his own interests. His love shows us what he is like: patient, kind, and gentle. And still, he is full of truth, and he is perfect in justice.

We cannot fix what is wrong in this world. It is noble to try, but we must not forget that God will do far more than we can. Let's not forget to put our ultimate trust in him. He will make all wrong things right, and he will set every record straight. There is no manipulation, no lie, no deceit of mankind that fools him. He is perfectly just, and he does what is right, true, and good.

Perfect One, the leaders of this world are flawed, but you are not. I won't stop believing you for all that you promised you would do. You are faithful!

Like a Stream

The king's heart is like a stream of water
directed by the LORD;
he guides it wherever he pleases.

PROVERBS 21:1 NLT

When we yield our hearts to the King of kings, he becomes the shepherd of our souls. He leads us through the terrain of this life. Even when we wander, he comes to find us. He rescues us from the traps we fall into, and he brings us back to the pastures of his steady love. We cannot outrun his presence. What a blessed assurance this is to our souls.

When we allow the Holy Spirit to guide us each and every day, our hearts become like a stream of water that he directs. We don't have to try hard to follow his lead. Our surrendered lives reflect the leadership of God, whether we're aware of it in the moment or not.

Good Shepherd, guide my heart with the loving leadership of your presence. I trust you.

AUDIENCE OF ONE

Many seek an audience with a ruler,
but it is from the LORD that one gets justice.

PROVERBS 29:26 NIV

Today's verse is more hopeful than it may seem. The Lord is the one who gives us justice. It is his audience that is more important than any other. The wonderful news about this is that he is available whenever we go to him! Though government offices close and people in power are hard to get a hold of, God is not. He is ever present.

Not only is God available at the exact time that we need him, but he is also the only one who judges perfectly. He is a ready help in times of trouble. He is full of all the strength, hope, and love we need. He has perfect wisdom to transform our perspectives and clarify our confusion. When we are discouraged by the lack of ready help we find around us, let's not forget to go to the one who holds everything together.

God of justice, I come to you with all of my cares, and I ask for your justice to roll.

COMFORTING LEADERSHIP

Even though I walk through
the valley of the shadow of death,
I will fear no evil,
for you are with me;
your rod and your staff,
they comfort me.

PSALM 23:4 ESV

What comfort we have in the fellowship of the Lord. What gracious compassion meets us in our darkest moments. We can't escape the painful parts of life. Following the Lord isn't a get-out-of-suffering free card. The beauty of following the Lord, even in the footsteps of his suffering, is in the peace he offers. It's in the love he gives. It's in the courageous comfort he offers in our pain.

God is our healer. This is true. He is our redeemer. When we go through painful circumstances, instead of questioning where God is in the midst of it, let's turn our attention to his present comfort. We have no reason to despair or fear, for our God never leaves or forsakes us.

Comforter, even when I walk through the darkest times of life, I know you are with me.

WISE WORDS

Open your mouth, judge righteously,
And plead the cause of the poor and needy.

PROVERBS 31:9 NKJV

Today's verse was an encouragement King Lemuel's mother gave him to rule wisely. She taught him to judge others fairly, and to uplift the cause of the vulnerable. What, you may think, does this have to do with you? You may not be a powerful ruler, but you have your own sphere of influence. The principles remain strong and true: speak up for those who are vulnerable in the places where you have a voice.

Don't underestimate your influence. When you hear others degrade the poor, you can speak up on their behalf. When you are able to set the standard of righteous integrity, hold it with the backing of your character. You can use your words in interactions that you already have, speaking truth, accountability, consideration, and kindness.

Wise God, thank you for the reminder that I don't have to be a leader to speak up for those who are overlooked.

REALITY OF LOVE

This is how we have discovered love's reality:
Jesus sacrificed his life for us.
Because of this great love,
we should be willing to lay down our lives for one another.

1 John 3:16 TPT

Love is not a theory. It isn't just a feeling. It is practical and real. It is powerful and liberating. If we cannot see its effects in the fruit of action, then it is not the love of God. Love's reality is ultimately revealed through Jesus' sacrifice.

The great love of Christ is our freedom, and it is also our example. When we are willing to lay down our own rights for the good of others, we follow in Jesus' footsteps. This isn't only shown through the willingness to die, it is also revealed through how we're willing to die to our own privilege, comfort, and desires for the liberation of others. This is the reality of love.

Jesus Christ, your resurrection life is my hope. Sacrifice is not the end. It is the beginning of true freedom and joy.

EMBODIED LOVE

"You shall love the Lord your God with all your heart, and with all your soul, and with all your mind."

MATTHEW 22:37 NASB

Wholehearted love encompasses not only the place we connect to emotions, but it also includes our minds, our beings, and our actions. Love that is true love shows itself through a posture of grace, humility, and intentional kindness.

If you do one thing today, let your aim be to love God with all your heart, soul, and mind. Look for ways to embody the love of God in your practical life. What work can you do as unto the Lord? The love of God is perfect, but you don't have to be perfect in representing it to love the Lord well. Simply do your best until you know better, and then do that. Let love compel you in grace, in understanding, and in connection.

Gracious Lord, I make loving you my ultimate focus today. You are so worthy of my attention, and you transform me as I look to you.

CREATED WITH PURPOSE

You are only human, and human beings have no right to question God. An object should not ask the person who made it, "Why did you make me like this?"

ROMANS 9:20 NCV

The Lord didn't make any mistakes when he made you. You were created with intention, and your being has purpose. The world can make us feel as if we're never enough: we have to look younger, be stronger, get that next certification. The end never comes because the mark always moves.

While it is good and helpful to have a growth mindset in life, when it comes to our inherent value—our identity—there isn't anything more that needs to be done. God not only created us as we are, with our unique quirks and personality traits, but he loves us fully as we are. Instead of asking the Lord why he made us the way we are, let's look for the beauty in our differences.

Maker, I won't fight against how you made me. I accept your love, and I choose to see myself the way you do.

EASE UP

"Many who are first will be last,
and the last first."

MATTHEW 19:30 CSB

When we are focused on becoming the best, we may brush past the important character values built when we actively serve others. There is nothing wrong with being ambitious, but if we let it push out our active love and consideration of others, we need to reevaluate our priorities.

Jesus was the ultimate servant leader. He laid down his very life so all could come to the Father through him. He removed the barriers that sin put up, and he leveled the excuses of the powerful that kept common people at a distance. There is now nothing that separates us from the love of God—nothing! Let's be sure we let love guide us, even in our ambition, making space to slow down and listen to those who need an ear.

Lord, I want to build my life around you and your kingdom values. Thank you for your example.

PERFECT PROMISES

God's way is perfect.
All the LORD's promises prove true.

2 SAMUEL 22:31 NLT

The ways of God are perfect. There is nothing that he doesn't follow through on. We can always count on him to follow through on his promises. He is faithful, and he won't ever stop keeping his Word.

When we are in the fires of testing, it is helpful to remember the promises of God. We can bring them to mind, reminding our hearts of his goodness. Let's look for where the light of his faithfulness has shown through our history. God has not changed. He is a solid rock. Everything he does is wonderful. Everything. He does all things well, and that includes healing, restoring, and leading us in love.

God, you are my firm foundation, and the rock I run to when I am in trouble. Encourage my heart in hope as I remember your faithfulness.

Living Love

If anyone acknowledges that Jesus is the Son of God, God lives in them and they in God. And so we know and rely on the love God has for us. God is love. Whoever lives in love lives in God, and God in them.

1 John 4:15-16 NIV

Jesus is the way, the truth, and the life. He is the Son of God, our living Savior who liberates us from the weight of sin, shame, and fear. We find all that we need in fellowship with Jesus Christ. He leads us onto the path of his lifegiving love, and into the green pastures of his kingdom.

If we truly believe that Jesus Christ is the Son of God, we follow in his footsteps. We adopt the ways of his kingdom as our own. We let go of our excuses and take on love as our covering. We fix our eyes on the forerunner of our faith, and we go where he leads us. There is so much life in his presence. There is so much goodness each and every day to discover in his fellowship.

Lord Jesus, you are the author of my faith, and you lead me in lasting love. Thank you for continual growth in you.

THE FRUIT OF LIGHT

At one time you were darkness, but now you are light in the Lord. Walk as children of light (for the fruit of light is found in all that is good and right and true), and try to discern what is pleasing to the Lord.

EPHESIANS 5:8-10 ESV

In fellowship with the Lord, we are brought from darkness into light. There is no fear, no shame, no lie that can withstand the power of God's glorious love that meets us in our surrendered hearts. Where we feel less than, God's love fills us up and sets us on the foundation of his gracious acceptance. He loves us to life, and we walk in the light of his liberating mercy.

It is good that we actively work to discern what is pleasing to the Lord. And it's no mystery! The values of God's kingdom are all throughout Scripture. The fruit of his Spirit, the power of his justice, and the reality of his compassion display his work in our lives. Whatever is good and right and true, that is the fruit of his light.

Great God, you illuminate the darkness with the purity of your presence. I say yes to you today, and I walk as a child of the light.

September

Above all, fear the Lord
and worship him faithfully
with all your heart;
consider the great things
he has done for you.

1 Samuel 12:24 CSB

DELIVERED

"Call upon Me in the day of trouble;
I will deliver you, and you shall glorify Me."

PSALM 50:15 NKJV

Trouble happens to us all, regardless of character or belief systems. We shouldn't waver or worry when trouble comes. It is yet another opportunity to turn to the Lord and know the power of his presence as it meets us in the details of our lives.

Call upon the Lord in the day of your trouble. He promises to deliver you. You might not know what that deliverance will look like at the outset, but you can trust him to do what he has promised. Humble yourself before the Lord, call to him, and wait on his deliverance. He can do far greater things than you can imagine.

Righteous One, you are the one I call to, not only in trouble, but also in my joy. You are my deliverer.

ENDLESS SUPPLY

He continues to pour out more and more grace upon us.
For it says, "God resists you when you are proud
but continually pours out grace when you are humble."

JAMES 4:6 TPT

There is bountiful grace to meet us in our need. We can never deplete God's stores of grace. He is endlessly generous. Grace is freely given to the humble, but those who put up walls of pride resist what could so easily be theirs if they only admitted their weakness.

When we surrender to God, we humble our hearts before him. We choose his way instead of insisting on our own. As long as we find ourselves in need, there is grace to meet us. There is abundance in the presence of God, and he continually pours it out when we surrender to him.

Gracious God, I humble my heart before you today and admit my weakness and need of you.

Pressing Needs

Our people must also learn to engage in good deeds to meet pressing needs, so that they will not be unproductive.

TITUS 3:14 NASB

The love of God is productive. It doesn't ignore pressing needs, but it pays attention to how it can meet them. We each have a responsibility to live out the love of God in practical ways. Faith, along with active service, reveals the living mercy of God at work within us.

What good deeds have you engaged in lately? If you struggle to pinpoint ways you have done this, take this as an opportunity to look for ways you can engage. Don't let guilt keep you from growing in this. God is patient, and he is gracious. He will help you if you ask him. He will open your eyes to how you can productively partner with his mercy by engaging in good deeds that benefit those around you.

Lord, I look for ways to partner with your love in action today.

WORTH HONORING

You were bought by God for a price.
So honor God with your bodies.

1 Corinthians 6:20 NCV

God's sacrifice was costly, and he counted each of us worth it. He willingly gave all that he could for us to know him, to love him, and to walk in his freedom. Why would we not seek to honor him with our bodies?

As we submit ourselves to the Lord, his living love transforms every part of our lives. We can align the most physical parts of our lives with his kingdom. His values are reflected in everything he does, and we can shoot for the same goal. Let's not neglect the power of God's principles in our bodies, our minds, or our hearts.

God, every part of me was made to reflect you. May you be honored as I submit myself to your kingdom.

QUALIFIED

Brothers and sisters, consider your calling: Not many were wise from a human perspective, not many powerful, not many of noble birth. Instead, God has chosen what is foolish in the world to shame the wise, and God has chosen what is weak in the world to shame the strong.

1 CORINTHIANS 1:26-27 CSB

It doesn't matter where we come from or what credentials we have or lack. The size of our bank accounts or the clothes we wear don't mean a thing to the Lord. God qualifies the weak things of this world as they submit to him. We don't need fancy degrees or introductions from more powerful people to be used by God.

The world is full of standards when it comes to what makes a person valuable. What do they have to offer? This is not how God chooses whom he will use. Our calling in Christ has nothing to do with how we present to others, and it has everything to do with what God says about us. If we will follow him, walking in his wisdom, he partners with us. What a glorious promise!

Wise God, you take my willingness and lead me in wisdom. Thank you.

NO PRETENSE

Don't just pretend to love others. Really love them. Hate what is wrong. Hold tightly to what is good. Love each other with genuine affection, and take delight in honoring each other.

ROMANS 12:9-10 NLT

Love is not an act. It can be an active choice, however. There is a difference between pretending to love others and actively working to love them. We might not always feel loving, but we can create compassion by trying to see from the other perspectives. We can love others even when we don't like them in the moment.

Genuine affection grows over time. It is something that we tend to. When we struggle to love someone, we need the grace of God to help us. If we submit to the love of God, he will grow our capacity to love truly, with genuine affection and honor that brings joy to our hearts.

Lord, your love is deeper than any I've known. I don't want to fake my love for others. Cultivate your true, deep affection in my heart that spills over.

Reason to Celebrate

"We had to celebrate and be glad, because this brother of yours was dead and is alive again; he was lost and is found."

Luke 15:32 NIV

In the parable of the lost son, the brother that never left his father's side felt bitter about the reception his father threw for the prodigal son who had returned. We often focus on the generosity of the father that ran to meet his son, wrapped him up in his robe, and restored him with a large celebration. Let's not forget the response of the father to the older son though.

We lose nothing when a prodigal is restored. It is reason to rejoice! Those of us who never wander have access to all the Father has. We have no need to be jealous of our brothers and sisters when they experience the blessing of God. We should take every opportunity to rejoice when the lost are found and the wandering are brought home.

Gracious God, I don't want to be jealous of the way you work in other's lives. I choose to celebrate in the victories of others even while I wait on my own.

DEEP LISTENING

My son, be attentive to my words;
incline your ear to my sayings.

PROVERBS 4:20 ESV

When our hearts are attentive to the voice of God, we won't miss what he says. We can posture our ears, readying ourselves to hear what he shares. There is so much life in the springs of God's presence. His wisdom and revelation open up our understanding.

God always has something to share with us. Every morning is a new opportunity to come before him with open hearts, welcoming his wisdom and listening for his word. There is lifegiving hope and healing in the words of God. There is direction, clarity, and peace. Whatever we are looking for, whatever we need, God has it to offer. Let's spend time with him at the start of each day, inviting his Spirit to speak as we incline our ears to hear what he says.

God, I posture my heart before you like an open book. I am listening, longing for a fresh word of your present wisdom.

CALM UNDERSTANDING

He who has knowledge spares his words,
And a man of understanding is of a calm spirit.

PROVERBS 17:27 NKJV

Have you ever been around a person who was easily upset? Perhaps you had to choose your words wisely so that you wouldn't offend them or set them off. What you could freely process with others, you are careful to withhold in their presence. They say careless words, and it's hard to get a word in edgewise. This is the opposite kind of person that today's verse speaks about.

The wisdom of God is grounded and calm. It promotes peace, and it does not feel the need to over explain. The presence of God brings calm, understanding, and clarity. It offers us a safe place to land. People of God's wisdom do the same for those around them. We can be powerful pockets of peace for those in need of shelter.

God of wisdom, let me be a place of peace for those who need it, and may I be a fountain of wisdom that knows when to stay silent and when to speak.

VALUED AND HONORED

Recognize the value of every person
and continually show love to every believer.

1 PETER 2:17 TPT

It is no small thing to recognize the value of every person. The world offers us many reasons to dehumanize others, but this is not the way of the kingdom of Christ. No one is perfect, and we will not agree with everyone. Still, this is no reason to dismiss the call to love others no matter how opposed we may be in our lifestyles or belief systems.

Every person is valuable because God made them. He doesn't create some things for love and others for indifference. All are created in, from, and for love. Let's set aside our excuses today and look at the value of the people in front of us. They are made in the image of a wonderful God, and he loves them thoroughly.

Creator, may I never dehumanize the people I disagree with or look for reasons I shouldn't show them love. You love them and that's enough.

BE A FRIEND

"Abraham believed God, and it was credited to him as righteousness," and he was called a friend of God.

JAMES 2:23 NASB

Good friends are trustworthy. They keep their word and follow through on their promises. They admit when they are wrong, and they say they're sorry when they've messed up. They change their ways to honor their friends when they are made aware of harmful actions. They are for each other, and they support one another.

What does it mean to be a friend of God? Abraham believed what God said, stepping out in faith and trusting that he would follow through on his promise. He didn't even know where he was going when he first left his home. We can cultivate trust in our relationship with God by following his wisdom. We stay close to him by doing what we would in any relationship: spending time together, sharing, and listening for another perspective. When we see that we have misrepresented him, we humble ourselves in repentance. What a wonderful friend God is to us. Let's commit to being a good friend to him in return.

Lord, I want to know you as a friend and be known as yours. I step out in faith today.

PRIME EXAMPLE

"I did this as an example
so that you should do as I have done for you."

JOHN 13:15 NCV

What exactly was Jesus talking about in today's verse? It belongs in a passage where Jesus had just finished washing his disciples' feet. He humbled himself by taking the role of a servant. No one is too great to serve others in loving acts, and Jesus wanted to make sure his friends understood this.

This was a task that friends would not volunteer to do for each other. It was a servant's job. Yet, Jesus broke the mold and set the example for what love looks like in relationship. We are not only to serve together, but we are also to serve each other.

Lord Jesus, you set the standard for love in action. Show me ways I can serve others.

COMPLETE JOY

"Until now you have asked for nothing in my name. Ask and you will receive, so that your joy may be complete."

JOHN 16:24 CSB

We are not more noble when we refuse to ask the Lord for anything. Let's take a lesson from the older son in the parable of the prodigal son and remember that we have the resources of our Father right where we are. All we have to do is ask, and he will share what is his with us.

There is more joy waiting for us in the fields of fulfilled dreams. It is good to work hard, but it is also a beautiful partnership that we have in fellowship with the Lord. We don't have to do it all alone. We're not meant to. Let's ask, and we will receive, making our joy overflow and fulfilling our hope with the fruit of God's faithfulness.

Wonderful One, there is no one like you. I won't withhold my prayers or keep myself from asking for your help.

OVERCOME BY LOVE

"Don't sin by letting anger control you.
Don't let the sun go down while you are still angry."

EPHESIANS 4:26 NLT

Take notice of what Scripture says about anger. It doesn't say that you should never feel angry; it is a very common, very potent emotion. It springs up when injustices are committed and boundaries crossed. It can be incredibly helpful in revealing our values as well.

Feeling angry is not a sin. Letting anger control us, moving us to act rashly and cruelly, that is where sin comes in. The longer anger stirs in our hearts, the more apt we are to act on it. We can go to the Lord with all things including our anger. When we just can't seem to let go of it, let's take it to him. His love can soothe the harshest emotion and bring clarity to the fog of confusion.

Lord, you are so full of patience. I don't want bitterness to grow in my heart. May I be overcome by your love, as I bring to you every emotion.

A Kind Welcome

Offer hospitality to one another without grumbling.

1 PETER 4:9 NIV

When we feel put out by others, it's hard to offer them a genuine and kind welcome. Service isn't always convenient. In fact, the sacrifice of serving others in love often requires us to be ready even when we don't feel up to it.

Grumbling adds no good to an interaction or a relationship. Who, after being nagged at, feels better for it? When we are irritable, no one wants to be around us. To be sure, we all have our days when irritation is closer to the surface than others, but we don't have to be bound to it. If we move in love most of the time, being welcoming and kind hosts, serving others in grace, let's not get down on ourselves for a moment of grouchiness. Let's offer a kind welcome whenever we can and put the tension aside to deal with at a time when we are not hosting others.

Lord, I want to be ready to welcome people in season and out. Thank you for the opportunity to serve you.

TRANSFORMATIVE SERVICE

If you pour yourself out for the hungry
and satisfy the desire of the afflicted,
then shall your light rise in the darkness
and your gloom be as the noonday.

ISAIAH 58:10 ESV

Saying yes to the Lord and serving in practical acts of love is not only beneficial for the people who receive it. It is transformative to our souls. When we pour compassion out for the hungry and relieve those in misery, our own gloom lifts. Our light rises like the sun breaking the horizon.

Jesus' example shows us how to live out the love of God. It isn't only for us to receive, though blessedly we do, and it changes it. It is also for us to offer others. When we don't know where to start, let's look for the needs around us. Are there hungry mouths we can feed? Are their grief-stricken people we can comfort? There's always an opportunity to serve. Let's find it today.

Lord, open my eyes to the needs around me, and I will partner with your love to meet them.

RENDER JUSTICE

"Execute judgment and righteousness, and deliver the plundered out of the hand of the oppressor. Do no wrong and do no violence to the stranger, the fatherless, or the widow, nor shed innocent blood in this place."

JEREMIAH 22:3 NKJV

God's justice is not oppressive. It doesn't overwhelm the vulnerable; it sets them free and meets their needs. We are to follow the ways of God by walking in them. There is no excuse for doing wrong to others in the name of his love. There is no excuse for being violent toward foreigners, the fatherless, or widows.

We might not have the power to stop violence from happening, but we can choose how we treat others. Love is gracious, offering help to those who need it. Let's be sure that we treat everyone with kindness and support.

Father, you are loving and kind, protective and strong. May I stand up for the oppressed and support the vulnerable in my community. I choose love.

REMEMBER JESUS

"When you saw me hungry, you fed me.
When you found me thirsty, you gave me drink.
When I had no place to stay, you invited me in."

MATTHEW 25:35 TPT

The most powerful encouragements to serve others are found in the teachings of Christ. When we choose to serve others in love, we do it for the Lord, whether we're aware of it or not. Loving service is found in feeding the hungry, offering drinks to the thirsty, welcoming those without a place to stay into our homes. It is in clothing those whose coverings are threadbare. It is in taking care of the sick and in visiting the imprisoned.

We may not be able to do all these things, but we certainly can do some. When we do, Jesus counts it as if we are doing it for him. We help and honor the Lord by supporting those who are looked upon as the "least of these."

Jesus, I want to see you and honor you in the humble and vulnerable around me. I say yes to loving you through practical service and humble surrender.

EAGER TO SERVE

Never be lazy, but work hard
and serve the Lord enthusiastically.

ROMANS 12:11 NLT

The Holy Spirit fills us with the joy of the Lord. This, in turn, fuels our service. We can stoke the coals of our passion for God by spending time in the presence of the Lord each day. When we prioritize time with him, we will be ready for whatever comes our way.

It is to our credit when we are eager to serve. We grow in grace, in goodness, in faithfulness, in peace, and in joy as we serve the Lord. How different could our lives be if we radiated the Spirit of the Lord, joyfully following his lead? There is so much room to grow in the fruit of his fellowship. Let's give it our all today and let the glorious hope of his goodness burst forth from our surrendered service.

Glorious God, I don't have to serve you—I get to! You have my yes, and it is not a hesitant one.

Turn It Around

Those who are stealing must stop stealing and start working. They should earn an honest living for themselves. Then they will have something to share with those who are poor.

Ephesians 4:28 NCV

There is nothing in our past that Christ can't redeem. Whatever bad habits we have had in our lives, we can turn them around and serve the Lord in truth. We don't stay in the compromise of sin; we leave it behind by the grace of God and put our energy to what is ours to do—the work of honest living.

In the light of Christ, we have full access to his empowering and liberating Spirit. We don't have to circle the table of his goodness for crumbs. We have a seat at the table, and there is more than enough to go around. We fill up, and we generously share what we have with others. Let's leave the shackles of yesterday in the past and move into the freedom of God's liberating love!

Redeemer, I trust that you will turn around the shame of my past and bring fruit from the surrender of my heart.

WHAT YOU HAVE

According to the grace given to us, we have different gifts: If prophecy, use it according to the proportion of one's faith; if service, use it in service; if teaching, in teaching.

ROMANS 12:6-7 CSB

God is a giver of good gifts. Your unique talents and skills are not a mistake. Don't get distracted by the strengths of others and diminish your own. Whatever gift you have, it is yours to develop and use for the glory of the Lord.

It is important to grow in our crafts: the work we are adept at doing. Even the areas we are skilled at but not passionate about can be used to reveal the powerful nature of God. There are spiritual gifts we can develop as well. Let's not neglect our own part. There is only so much strategizing we can do. It is important that we actually do the work! God blesses it as we partner with him.

Good Father, I don't want to be distracted by what I wish were true. My gifts are yours. I will do the work that is mine to do today.

Keep on Loving

Our great desire is that you will keep on loving others as long as life lasts, in order to make certain that what you hope for will come true.

HEBREWS 6:11 NLT

No matter how much we develop in our faith, we will never outgrow the overarching law of God's love. Pride may lead us to think we get to move on from service the more time we put in, but the love of God always compels us in service to one another. As long as life lasts, we are to keep loving others.

Indifference isn't a sign of maturity in the kingdom of Christ. It is a signifier of a lack of love. Love motivates us in perseverance and patience. It moves us toward others even when others isolate and retreat from fellowship. Let's keep on loving others, pressing on toward the hope that we have in Christ. He is the fullness of all we long for, and in him we find the satisfaction that love offers.

Good God, keep me from pride that leads to indifference. I choose to persevere in love as long as life lasts.

ACCESSIBLE WISDOM

I give you sound learning,
so do not forsake my teaching.

PROVERBS 4:2 NIV

The wisdom of God is a benefit to us. The Holy Spirit brings revelation to our minds, enlightening our understanding and planting deep seeds of truth in our hearts. These seeds, under his care, develop into fruit-bearing life. When we remain faithful to God's teaching and leadership, we have no reason to fear failure.

While fresh ideas may invigorate our hearts, ancient truth grounds us in time-tested integrity. There are lifegiving truths already available to us in the fellowship of God's Spirit, and in his Word. Instead of trying to pull ideas out of the air, let's dig up the treasures already under our feet.

Wise God, I don't know why I try to look for answers apart from you when you offer me the wisdom of your ancient truth, lasting love, and persistent presence. I turn to you today for all the wisdom I need.

Take the Opportunity

As we have opportunity, let us do good to everyone, and especially to those who are of the household of faith.

Galatians 6:10 ESV

Every day affords us new opportunities to do good. We get to choose how we treat the people around us. We can set our intentions at the start, harnessing the new beginning of each morning as it dawns. We don't have to depart from our schedule to find opportunities to bless others.

In the body of Christ, we are brothers and sisters. When one suffers, we all feel it. When one rejoices, we take part in that too. When we love others, thinking of their good and our mutual benefit, we won't hesitate to do what we are able to when given the opportunity. It is our offering of service to do good.

Lord, open my eyes to the opportunities hidden within this day to partner with your heart and do good. My heart is yielded to your leadership.

HOLD FAST

You shall walk after the LORD your God and fear Him, and keep His commandments and obey His voice; you shall serve Him and hold fast to Him.

DEUTERONOMY 13:4 NKJV

When we love someone, we honor their perspective and respect their wishes. It is no different in our relationship with God. As we walk after him, we do not chase to catch up. He has bridged the gap that left us separated and brought us in close. We walk hand in hand, and he is our ready support. We are close enough to have a conversation, hearing his heart and sharing our own.

Fellowship with God is a beautiful gift that we have through Christ. We don't have to guess who he is; we get to know him. Relationship with God isn't reserved for some. He welcomes all who come to him through Christ. Jesus is our high priest. No one else needs to be a go-between. Let's press into his presence and spend time with our God, our Savior, our friend.

God, I am overwhelmed at the thought that I can know you as a friend. I choose you, remembering you first chose me.

CONTINUALLY STRENGTHENED

My heart spills over with thanks to God for the way he continually empowers me, and to our Lord Jesus, the Anointed One, who found me trustworthy and who authorized me to be his partner in this ministry.

1 TIMOTHY 1:12 TPT

All the Lord offers us is out of an overflow of love. His heart for us is powerful and true. It is full of compassion, grace, and truth. It is our source of peace, joy, and hope. There is more goodness in knowing him than we have yet tasted. When we remember the beauty of who Christ is, we cannot help but be overcome with gratitude. He really is wonderful!

God's presence is our continual strength. When we face days that seem too hard to bear, his presence is with us. He is near in comfort and close in grace. There is love to center us, wisdom to guide us, and hope to uplift us. Everything we need is in fellowship with him. Let's stir up our gratitude and let our hearts spill over with thanks to the one who never leaves or forsakes us!

Ever Present One, thank you for all that you have already done for and in me. I'm hopeful for all that you will continue to do. I am yours.

MERIT OF SELF-CONTROL

One who is slow to anger is better than the mighty,
And one who rules his spirit, than one who captures a city.

PROVERBS 16:32 NASB

Physical strength is impressive to a point, but one who is strong in spirit is one to be praised. Self-control is listed as a fruit of the Holy Spirit for a reason. It shows self-restraint and the ability to take other's views into consideration. It creates space for peace, understanding, and compassion. Those who are quick to defend themselves rather than taking the time to listen have room to grow in this area.

The importance of self-control is for all. Proverbs says that even a fool is considered wise if he keeps his mouth shut. We are wise when we learn to slow down when we are tempted to snap back hastily. It is not disingenuous to refrain from saying something that would be harmful. It is wisdom that knows when to speak and when to stay silent.

Patient One, I want to grow in self-control and patience. I focus on controlling my reactions and my tongue today, knowing it could bring harm just as quickly as it could encouragement.

KEEP TRUSTING

The LORD saves his servants' lives;
no one who trusts him will be judged guilty.

PSALM 34:22 NCV

We all go through trials and testing. This is no reason to give up hope. It is not a reason to run from the loving wisdom of God. Jesus promised that we would face trials of many kinds, not because he wants that for us, but because it is the reality of living in this world. There is no easy out. The tensions of life cannot be avoided. What will we do when they bear down?

Scripture encourages us to keep hope alive. We are to keep trusting God. He has not left us on our own to fight our battles. His Spirit is our gift and the fullness of God to guide, teach, comfort, and help us. We don't have to worry about whether his faithfulness will prove true. When the pressure builds, his presence is constant. Let's hold on to hope and keep trusting our Savior through the storms of life.

Savior, you are my hope in all seasons of the soul. You will always be faithful to your Word and to your people.

FREE TO SURRENDER

Submit as free people,
not using your freedom as a cover-up for evil,
but as God's slaves.

1 PETER 2:16 CSB

In our freedom, we get to choose how we will live. True liberty does not have restraints. We are not forced to submit to the Lord. We choose whether we will or not.

It is in our best interest to yield our hearts to the one who liberates us in love. He knows what is best, and he guides us in perfect wisdom. Let's not use our freedom as a cover-up to compromise. Let's instead walk in the light of God's kingdom, following his ways and pursuing his nature. As we reflect his fruit in the fields of our lives, he is glorified, and we feast on the riches of his glorious grace. We are free. How will we use that freedom today?

Liberator of my soul, I choose to follow you in my freedom. Not because I have to, but because I want to.

SHARE FREELY

"There will always be some in the land who are poor. That is why I am commanding you to share freely with the poor and with other Israelites in need."

DEUTERONOMY 15:11 NLT

There will always be an opportunity to serve others, sharing generously with those who have less than we do. As long as we are in this world, there will be inequities. The vulnerable are taken advantage of by the powerful, but this does not mean that we turn a cold shoulder or blind eye. We get to be the hands and feet of Jesus by sharing freely with the poor.

The principle of generosity is a kingdom trait. We are generous because God is unyielding in love. He has an unending supply of resources. His well will never run dry, and we can go to him for our own filling, as well as trust him in sharing our resources with others. We have been given much, and we have much to offer those around us. What a cycle of blessing!

Lord, your example is the one I follow in generosity. May I grow in sharing and may it become less like a sacrifice and more like a privilege.

OCTOBER

"Give, and it will be given to you;
a good measure—
pressed down, shaken together,
and running over."

Luke 6:38 csb

DON'T GIVE UP

"As for you, be strong and do not give up,
for your work will be rewarded."

2 CHRONICLES 15:7 NIV

There are some seasons in life where we cannot see the fruit of our labor. Though we work hard, we struggle to see the difference it's making. It's important that we get perspective from the Lord on what we're doing. His Spirit, as well as the counsel of wise friends, can help us to know when we need to pivot and when we need to push through.

If the only reason we're tempted to give up is because we think we should be further ahead than we are, it is a good idea to remember what we are working toward. The really important things in life require perseverance. There will be winter seasons that seem fruitless, but really the work has gone underground. Let's get perspective in the presence of the Lord and seek his wisdom.

Lord, help me to know what can give and what requires perseverance in my life. Help me to prioritize my energy and my focus in these days for this specific season.

FOR SUCH A TIME

"If you keep silent at this time, relief and deliverance will rise for the Jews from another place, but you and your father's house will perish. And who knows whether you have not come to the kingdom for such a time as this?"

ESTHER 4:14 ESV

The story of Esther is a profound picture of what courage, faith, and persistence looks like in relation to our place in the world. Esther quite literally had the ear of the king, able to influence him in rejecting his advisor's plan to persecute the Jews. But she was afraid. The king could also have decided to reject her and punish both her and her family.

We are not in the positions of influence in our lives for no reason. We may not understand how it all works together, but there may come a time when we must decide: will we use the trust we've built to plead for the lives and breakthrough of others, or will we stay silent? It might not be a life-or-death issue, but courage is necessary to speak the truth in the vulnerability of not knowing how it will land. It's still worth it to weigh the cost.

Almighty God, my time is in your hands. Give me strength to know when to take a stand.

MOVED WITH COMPASSION

Jesus, when He came out, saw a great multitude and was moved with compassion for them, because they were like sheep not having a shepherd. So He began to teach them many things.

MARK 6:34 NKJV

All sorts of people came to Jesus looking for answers. Some were looking for healing, others for wisdom, and still others probably didn't know what they were looking for, but they were compelled by Jesus and the miraculous signs and wonders of his ministry.

Jesus was moved with compassion by the multitudes of people that came to see him. He didn't look out with annoyance. He also didn't get overthrown by pride that a crowd had flocked to see him. He saw the hunger in their hearts, and the desire to know the truth and be free. In his compassion, he taught them. What a powerful example. When we are overcome by compassion, let's not stop at meeting a pressing need. Let's take the time to engage and teach what we know.

Lord Jesus, may your compassion well up in my heart and move me to action. I say yes to being compelled by your love.

HEART OF SUBMISSION

Those who are servants, submit to the authority of those who are your masters—not only to those who are kind and gentle but even to those who are hard and difficult.

1 PETER 2:18 TPT

The power of our surrender is not only in our relationship with God. When we are submitted to leadership at our place of work, we don't buck against their plans. We look for ways to help realize what they want to put into practice. While it's easy to submit to those who are understanding and kind, it can be a test of our character to submit to more difficult leaders.

This does not mean we should resist it though. In any place of work or ministry that we find ourselves, we should do our best to be the best workers we can. Let's treat our leaders with the kindness and respect we would like. Let's choose generosity of heart and willingness to do the tasks assigned us. Let's love them well even if we disagree with them.

Lord, I need your help to remain humble under difficult leadership. I pray for breakthrough in their hearts, but I won't compromise my own character in the meantime.

SPEAK UP

Open your mouth for the people who cannot speak,
For the rights of all the unfortunate.

PROVERBS 31:8 NASB

We get to represent Jesus and his goodness in our relationships, as well as in our communities. Picture this: you're chatting with a few people when someone says something derogatory about someone not present, whether an individual or group of people. You don't agree with the remark, but you also struggle to know whether you should say something. Perhaps you feel like you should, but you don't want to upset others.

It's always better to err on the side of loving truth than to stay silent. This is how biases and hatred are left unchecked. Our silence gives them room to grow, and unfortunately it can look like agreement. Let's be people of integrity who speak up for those who cannot.

Lord Jesus, I want to represent you well in what I allow and what I challenge. I choose to stand with you in loving truth and speak up when the opportunity is there.

HE WON'T FORGET

"Can a woman forget the baby she nurses?
Can she feel no kindness
for the child to which she gave birth?
Even if she could forget her children,
I will not forget you."

ISAIAH 49:15 NCV

The Lord isn't just a good father, God is also attentive and caring like a mother. He is the perfect parent. There is so much kindness in his presence, and his love instructs us and teaches us how to relate to others.

When you feel forgotten or looked over by those around you, take heart in the presence of God. He will never forget you. His eyes are on you even now. He sees your struggles and your hope. Knowing he knows you completely, what do you need from him today?

Lord, I don't want to get so caught up in serving you that I forget that I get to know you, just as you know me. I lean in close, desperate for a filling of your gracious love that meets me where I am and boosts my heart in hope.

GENEROUS GIVER

If any of you lacks wisdom, he should ask God—
who gives to all generously and ungrudgingly—
and it will be given to him.

JAMES 1:5 CSB

No matter what you lack in your own resources and strength, God is still filled with abundance. His grace is sufficient to meet every need you have. It is more than enough. Ask God for the wisdom you lack, and he will give you from the generosity of his heart.

We can take on the pressure of needing to perform for the Lord. If only we listen to one more teaching, get one more certification, or meet with one more influential person, we will have what we need to move ahead. Beloved, this is a trap. There will always be more we can do, but we don't have to do any more than go to the Lord. Let that be our starting point. He is more than able to satisfy our needs and desires in the fullness of his presence.

Generous One, I give up the need to do more on my own today, and instead I make my yes a yes to going to you for all the wisdom I need.

EMBRACE CORRECTION

Fear of the LORD is the foundation of true knowledge,
but fools despise wisdom and discipline.

PROVERBS 1:7 NLT

The proud resist correction, while the humble are open to other's insights even if they prove false in the end. When we let either arrogance or insecurity keep us from growing in wisdom, we are the ones that suffer the most from it.

There is no need to pretend we have it all together when we don't. We are all journeying along the path of this life for the first time together. We don't need less accountability; we need the perspective of wise ones who have traveled further than we have. We need the support and encouragement of those around us.

Wise One, thank you for opportunities to grow in grace and in wisdom each day. I follow you, and I listen for your wisdom no matter who it comes through.

UNSEARCHABLE DEPTHS

Oh, the depth of the riches
of the wisdom and knowledge of God!
How unsearchable his judgments,
and his paths beyond tracing out!

ROMANS 11:33 NIV

Though many have spent their lives mining the wisdom of God, none have reached its depths. God's perfect perspective is much higher, purer, and better than our own. It is unclouded by misunderstanding and bias. It sees everything rightly, and we can be sure that when God directs us in wisdom, it is in this same spirit.

We cannot begin to map the paths of God. We can't pinpoint every instance of his miraculous mercy at work in human history. It is beyond our comprehension! And he's still moving today. From eternity's vantage point, wisdom's priceless ways have no beginning and no end. There is more than enough to meet our small (and large) problems and to direct us in truth today.

Lord, I'm so relieved to know that your wisdom has not been exhausted. Bring clarity to my confusion as I come with an open heart today.

Living Word

Let the word of Christ dwell in you richly,
teaching and admonishing one another in all wisdom,
singing psalms and hymns and spiritual songs,
with thankfulness in your hearts to God.

Colossians 3:16 ESV

The Word of God is active. It is not simply words on a page; it is not even just Scripture. It wasn't the Bible that was at the beginning. It was Jesus Christ. His presence is the Word of life that moves in our hearts, dwelling in us.

The Word of God is full of wisdom. We were not brought into the family of God to be slaves to doctrine. We were liberated in Christ's love to know him, to be in relationship with the Father, and to live empowered by his Spirit within us. There is wisdom to teach and encourage one another. There are words given straight from God's perspective to challenge and correct us, as well as build us up in his lifegiving love.

Lord Jesus, I don't want to value a specific theology over who you are. You are the living Word, and I yield to your Spirit in my heart. Teach me, and I will learn your ways.

ONLY A BREATH

Teach us to number our days,
That we may gain a heart of wisdom.

PSALM 90:12 NKJV

The young live as if they will never die. There seems to be no concept of life's brevity. Every day is a gift, and we have no guarantee of how many we get. It is wise to keep the length of our days in mind. None of us knows how long we have in this world. Wisdom keeps this perspective in mind.

Scripture is full of reminders to embrace the day we are given. Joshua 24 says to choose this day whom you will serve. Second Corinthians 6 reminds us that today is the day of salvation. There are many things we put off until tomorrow. Let's be wise in what we embrace today, giving our energy to what serves the greater vision and desires of our hearts and the Lord's purposes.

Great God, your wisdom leads me into greater purpose. Thank you for the clarity of your perspective. No matter how many days I get on this earth, I choose to follow your ways.

PERSPECTIVE SHIFT

The "foolish" things of God have proven to be wiser than human wisdom. And the "feeble" things of God have proven to be far more powerful than any human ability.

1 CORINTHIANS 1:25 TPT

There is nothing in this world that is impossible for God to turn around. He doesn't see people the way we do. He doesn't look at a list of achievements or how impressive someone might seem. He doesn't value people based on their looks or how they might serve him. God's wisdom is wiser than the world's every single time.

This is the reason why Paul embraced his weakness. He knew that his list of impressive traits meant nothing to God. Let's not count ourselves or others out for the kingdom of God, or the power of his purposes, because of what we see as weakness. Just look at Jesus' lineage: it named women and foreigners among kings. Don't disqualify yourself from God using you. He created you and he loves you!

Wise One, I surrender to your leadership in my life, and I take courage in your power. I'm honored to partner with you.

LIGHT AND FREE

If we walk in the Light as He Himself is in the Light,
we have fellowship with one another,
and the blood of Jesus His Son cleanses us from all sin.

1 JOHN 1:7 NASB

When we walk in the light of Christ, there are no differentiators between us. We all belong in the complexity of our unique beings together. Christ sets us free from sin, and we have nothing to hold against each other. The light of Christ is the love of Christ.

If we have more bones to pick with one another than compassion, we need to come closer to the light of Christ. There are no shadows of shame in his presence. There is truth and accountability, but there are no harsh judgments or harboring hostilities. Let's walk in the freedom and light that Christ offers us, as we offer it to others.

Lord, you are the light of life. I choose to walk in you, following your ways.

CONSIDER EACH OTHER

Let us think about each other
and help each other to show love and do good deeds.

HEBREWS 10:24-25 NCV

An important step in showing love to others is knowing what they value. A busy mom might appreciate a night out more than a meal dropped at her doorstep. We are all different, and what one person might choose may be different than our choice.

Thinking about each other is good practice in compassion. Let's be proactive in asking what others would like rather than just assuming we already know. The most effective ways to show love are by listening to those we serve and meeting their specific needs.

Lord, thank you for the reminder that your love is powerfully shown in specific ways. Help me to consider others and ask for their perspective before I jump in to help in a way that might not be needed.

JOYFUL JUSTICE

Justice executed is a joy to the righteous
but a terror to evildoers.

PROVERBS 21:15 CSB

When justice is served, the righteous rejoice. The lovers of God celebrate when truth prevails and accountability is measured. Those who participate in compromising and criminal activities, however, begin to panic.

When we live for love of the Lord and others, justice for the poor, the oppressed, and the overlooked is reason to celebrate. When the powerful get away with criminal acts while the poor are punished for simply trying to survive, we live in an off-kilter society. Though it may seem normal for the world, this is not the way that God's kingdom works. There is justice for the poor and oppressed in Christ's kingdom. There is freedom for the captive. Let's celebrate when justice is served, and let's advocate for it in the meantime.

Righteous One, you can't be bought with money or intimidated by power. I'm so glad that your justice is final and true.

PART OF THE WHOLE

The human body has many parts,
but the many parts make up one whole body.
So it is with the body of Christ.

1 CORINTHIANS 12:12 NLT

You have a part to play in the body of Christ. You weren't meant to blend in and disappear. You were made specifically to be the part you are. Don't let more prominent parts demean your worth. You are important, and the Lord delights in who he created you to be.

The various parts of the body work together for the good of the whole. Our toes can't do what our arms do, and neither are we meant to measure our worth against the abilities of others. An ear is no less valuable than an eye. Instead of comparing ourselves to others today, let's do what we already know to do. Let's be who we are, doing the part that is ours to do. The Lord doesn't value one part of his body over the other, so neither should we.

Christ, thank you for who I am in you. I give up comparing myself to others and embrace who you created me to be.

MUTUAL ENCOURAGEMENT

You and I may be mutually encouraged by each other's faith.

ROMANS 1:12 NIV

There is power in the fellowship of other believers. We can be encouraged, comforted, and strengthened by one another's faith. It is important that we don't forget that God's kingdom is a family. We don't have to do anything alone. The power of Christ's presence is with us, and the gift of encouragement is ours through fellowship with others.

You don't have to wait until the weekend to reach out to a fellow believer for encouragement. In this age of instant access to people around the world, we might get easily distracted, but it is also a tremendous tool for our faith. There is beauty, strength, and love in the mutual encouragement of followers of Christ. Let's press into it by connecting to other believers today.

Father, my yes is yours, and it doesn't happen in isolation. Thank you for the encouragement I find in fellowship with those who love you.

ABUNDANT LOVE

If there is any encouragement in Christ, any comfort from love, any participation in the Spirit, any affection and sympathy, complete my joy by being of the same mind, having the same love, being in full accord and of one mind.

PHILIPPIANS 2:1-2 ESV

Love brings people together, while suspicion and bitterness drive us apart. When our priorities are at odds with love, we will not know the beauty or power of unity. When we put our own comfort above others, never compromising or being willing to share in the pain or perspective of others, we create barriers instead of building bridges.

There is endless comfort and encouragement in Christ. It is the compelling love of Christ that binds us to others in the same kind of mercy. The law of Christ's love encompasses the rest of his kingdom's principles, for all is made complete in it. There is no error in it.

Lord of love, may love guard my mind, my heart, and my attitude today. I choose your love that crosses barriers and takes the hands of others.

PRAYER PARTNERSHIP

These all continued with one accord in prayer and supplication, with the women and Mary the mother of Jesus, and with His brothers.

ACTS 1:14 NKJV

Prayer isn't something we have to do alone. We can connect to prayer anytime, anywhere. What a beautiful invitation and powerful promise this is. We don't have to go to a holy place or be in a sacred building to pray. We can connect with God wherever we are.

Praying together can help unify us. When we don't know what to do, we can seek the wisdom of God together. Group prayer, even if it is only with one other person, can encourage us and remind us that we are not alone. When we have no answers to offer, let's ask if we can pray together, taking the problem to God. He is faithful, and he will meet us with the grace of his presence.

Lord, thank you for the gift of prayer that connects us to you. I won't overlook the opportunity and privilege of praying with others today.

WAY OF LIFE

Delightfully loved ones, if he loved us with such tremendous love, then "loving one another" should be our way of life!

1 JOHN 4:11 TPT

God's love teaches us how to love each other. Far be it from us to measure our love based on the love someone else is willing to give us except when it comes to the author of love himself. The love of God isn't limited. It isn't saved up for special occasions. It is extravagant and overflowing every moment of every day.

As we spend time in the presence of love, let's take that same love to our relationships and circumstances. We already know how we should love because Jesus showed us the way. Where there is hatred disguised as religious fervor, we can see right through it. Where there is bitterness because of disappointment, we choose to extend love anyway. Love is patient, kind, and relentless in the best possible way. As we live for love's sake, we become known by it.

Jesus, who am I to contradict your love? Your love is everything good, everything beautiful and true in this world. I give my life to loving others in the same way you love me.

POWERFUL COMMUNION

Day by day continuing with one mind in the temple, and breaking bread from house to house, they were taking their meals together with gladness and sincerity of heart.

ACTS 2:46 NASB

The power of communion isn't only in the religious act we do in church. The first communion, which Jesus served to his friends, was done over a shared meal. How often do we break bread with other believers, sharing our food and familiarity with one another?

It is good to meet together with those who have the same goal. Knowing the sincerity of fellowship is there, a true desire to know God and to love each other well, is a powerful motivator to meet together more than just on the weekends. We were created for fellowship, and we were made for community. Jesus set the example in this, and the early church followed in his footsteps. Let's look for ways we can do the same.

Lord Jesus, I want my faith in you to reflect in much more than a Sunday service. Connect me with those who want to know you more.

SOMETHING OUT OF NOTHING

I may have the gift of prophecy. I may understand all the secret things of God and have all knowledge, and I may have faith so great I can move mountains. But even with all these things, if I do not have love, then I am nothing.

1 CORINTHIANS 13:2 NCV

Love makes us something. It is God's love that qualifies us. It is through the lens of mercy that he offers us all we need to move, breathe, and have our being. Living with love as our focus, our motivation, and our foundation isn't a wasted effort. It is the only worthwhile endeavor according to the teachings of Christ.

The complexity of our gifts isn't what matters. The offering we give to others, if it lacks love, doesn't mean much at all. God is love. In fellowship with him, we become like love. If we are not transformed by it, reflecting it and offering it to others, then what are we doing? It is worth our pursuit, our attention, and our surrender.

Lord, your love makes me who I am. It is my source and my strength.

LIVING IN HARMONY

How delightfully good
when brothers live together in harmony!

PSALM 133:1 CSB

Is there much better in this life than living at peace? There is beauty and simplicity in the peace of living in harmony with those around us. If we want to live in peace, we have to be willing to compromise and love others well.

There is goodness in dwelling in unity, and it doesn't happen by accident. If we will be cultivators of peace, sowing good fruit in mercy, integrity, and truth, we will experience the power of harmonious living with the close people in our lives. Instead of looking for faults and reasons to quarrel, we offer grace and the ties that unify us.

Lord, thank you for the power of your peace that brings harmony and love. I will look for ways to build bridges instead of walls today.

DAILY ENCOURAGEMENT

Encourage one another daily, as long as it is called "Today," so that none of you may be hardened by sin's deceitfulness.

HEBREWS 3:13 NIV

There is no such thing as too much encouragement. There isn't a limit on the kindness we can show one another. Let's remove the barriers we put up, even the ones in our own minds, to keep us from offering encouragement to the people around us.

Encouragement is a gracious gift we offer to those around us. We all need it. When we are in the presence of someone who builds us up, we leave feeling filled up. Perhaps we didn't even know how low our reserves were getting until they were refilled by the honest encouragement of that friend. Let's be like those people, daily encouraging one another in love, in hope, in peace, in joy, and in truth.

Gracious God, I will be an encourager today, and I ask that you would also send me encouragement for my own needs through others.

GROW IN WISDOM

Fools think their own way is right,
but the wise listen to others.

PROVERBS 12:15 NLT

There is so much wisdom in good counsel. We may have a great idea off the bat, but if we are unwilling to listen to input, we may miss out on helpful perspectives. We don't have to reinvent the wheel. It is better to embrace the clarifying advice of others who have walked the path we are going down than to ignore it.

It is foolish to think that just because we think something, it is the right thing. Our perspectives are limited by our experience. We cannot know everything. This is why we should be hungry to grow in wisdom by listening to others. We can glean understanding and helpful hints from those who have more experience than we do. Let's not hold on to our ideals so tightly that we go down with them. Instead, let's listen to others and grow in wisdom.

Wise God, open my eyes and help me humble my heart, so I can grow in wisdom.

DWELLING OF REFUGE

He who dwells in the shelter of the Most High
will abide in the shadow of the Almighty.
I will say to the LORD, "My refuge and my fortress,
my God, in whom I trust."

PSALM 91:1-2 ESV

God is a ready comfort, a safe place to hide. We can dwell in his shadow, his loving arms surrounding us with the peace of his presence. He is a refuge and fortress, a walled off place of rest and strength.

When we trust the Lord, it doesn't mean that trust is never tested. It doesn't mean that the tendrils of fear won't creep around our hearts. When we are afraid, we can run to him. We can choose to put our faith in him again and again. Call to the Lord in your trouble, and he will answer you, keep you, and honor you. Make the Lord your hiding place, and you will not have to worry.

Most High God, I hide myself in the refuge of your presence. You are my God, and I depend on you.

COURAGEOUS FAITH

We may boldly say:
"The LORD is my helper;
I will not fear.
What can man do to me?"

HEBREWS 13:6 NKJV

What gives us the boldness to declare that the Lord is our helper? Hebrews 13:5 quotes the promise God gave, "I will never leave you nor forsake you." For this reason, we can boldly proclaim that we do not fear even when threats arise.

If God is our confidence, then it doesn't matter what the world does. God, our Creator and Savior, has brought us from the curse of sin and death into the promise of his resurrection life. Even when our bodies fail, his love doesn't. Our souls will know the forever fellowship of his love in the kingdom of Christ. If the world can't touch that, what do we have to fear?

Savior, you are my hope and the strength of my faith. I set my eyes on you and refuse to look away.

LIFELONG DEVOTION

It's not sacrifices that really move your heart.
Burnt offerings, sin offerings—
those aren't what bring you joy.
But when you open my ears and speak to me,
I become your willing servant,
your prisoner of love for life.

PSALM 40:6 TPT

God isn't interested in empty rituals or in displays of our reverence. What God really wants, what he's always wanted, is relationship. He is worthy of our respect and our devotion. He is better to us than we could ever be to ourselves. He is gracious, kind, strong, and wise. There is nothing he cannot do, and he wants us to know him the way that we are known by him.

If we want to move God's heart, it starts by listening to him. Our genuine response, our loving devotion and praise, is only a reflection of the goodness he has to pour out over us. God delights when we take time to hear him, to know his heart and to walk in his ways.

God, may I be moved by your heart today. I take time to listen, not because I have to, but because I get to!

PRESENT STRENGTH

"Have I not commanded you? Be strong and courageous!
Do not be terrified nor dismayed,
for the LORD your God is with you wherever you go."

JOSHUA 1:9 NASB

God's presence is our courage. It is our strength. There isn't a day we are without it. There isn't a trial or trouble where he is not already working out the solution. This world is full of difficult circumstances. We cannot define our lives based on the problems we face. Courage isn't necessary in our comfort zones. It is required when we step out of them.

Whether we are moving into new territory because we want to or because we are forced to, the result is the same: the Lord our God is with us wherever we go. When we are yielded to his leadership, we need never go alone. God is our very present help.

Good God, I trust your presence is with me even now. Empower my heart in your strength and give me courage in your loving embrace.

LIVING STONES

You also are like living stones, so let yourselves be used to build a spiritual temple—to be holy priests who offer spiritual sacrifices to God. He will accept those sacrifices through Jesus Christ.

1 PETER 2:5 NCV

We are living stones in the kingdom of our God. We can resist our part, or we can allow ourselves to be used to build a spiritual temple where God is glorified. We each get to choose our journey: Will we stay humble in the presence of God, growing in his wisdom and his nature, or will we remain resistant and become empty vessels of our own desires?

It is never too late to humble ourselves before the Lord. We don't have to offer him what we think he wants. There are no hoops to jump through. When we come to him with honesty, vulnerability, and openness, he breaks open our perceptions with his love. As living stones in the kingdom of God, we reveal his powerful mercy and living truth to others.

Glorious King, you deserve my adoration and submission. I come to you with openness and a hunger to know you more. Be honored in my life, Lord.

CLEAR SIGNALS

"By this everyone will know that you are my disciples, if you love one another."

JOHN 13:35 CSB

There is no clearer sign that we belong to Christ than through the love we personify. Love is humble and kind; it is generous and compassionate. It believes the best in people, but it doesn't shy away from the truth. It always hopes, always perseveres, and always promotes peace.

What does our love look like? If it doesn't look radical and offensive to those who only know a limited kindness, we have much further to grow in love. Love lays down its life for its friends. It doesn't insist on its own way. There is always room to develop our love. Let's take this opportunity to be intentional in how we love others today.

Jesus Christ, I want to grow in your love. May I know the love that passes all understanding and seek to share it with others.

NOVEMBER

"It is more blessed
to give than to receive."

ACTS 20:35 ESV

HUMBLE YOURSELF

Stop deceiving yourselves.
If you think you are wise by this world's standards,
you need to become a fool to be truly wise.

1 CORINTHIANS 3:18 NLT

We cannot reach the pinnacle of wisdom in this life. As soon as we think we've made it, pride starts to set in. The truth is, even if we had several lifetimes to grow in the wisdom of God, we would never reach the fullness of it. Let's stay humble, admitting our weakness while not neglecting the strength God has given us.

It is always a good idea to humble ourselves before God. Deceit sets in when we think we know all we need to. There is always more to learn, always more to glean from the Lord, and always room to grow in his grace. There is wisdom for those who take humbling themselves seriously. Arrogance has no place in the kingdom of heaven.

Lord, thank you for the reminder of your priorities. I want to be wise by the standards of your kingdom. Teach me, and I will adjust my ways.

ABOVE REPROACH

Live such good lives among the pagans that, though they accuse you of doing wrong, they may see your good deeds and glorify God on the day he visits us.

1 PETER 2:12 NIV

Those who live with integrity have nothing to hide. If we live good lives among those who don't believe in God, there will be nothing to hold against us even when we're falsely accused of doing wrong.

What does it mean to live above reproach? Quite simply, it means that we don't deserve any blame. When we act in goodness, living from love, and abiding by the laws of the land, baseless accusations have nowhere to land. The fruit of a good life is evident to all, no matter what they believe. It really does matter how we live, so let's be intentional in how we do it, both among believers and nonbelievers.

God, I want to glorify you with my lifestyle and actions. May my life be pure and reflective of your mercy and grace.

NO MATTER WHAT

Give thanks in all circumstances;
for this is the will of God in Christ Jesus for you.

1 THESSALONIANS 5:18 ESV

It is God's will that we learn to give thanks in all circumstances. It is not so that we'll deny the reality of our disappointment or pain. It's so that we don't stay in it, sinking into despair. When we admit how hard some things are, but we still move our hearts to thank God for what remains good, and true, and beautiful, we balance the hard with the hope of God's lifegiving presence.

There is no situation so dire that we cannot find a simple reason to give thanks. This is not easy or natural to do. Practices of gratitude help train our hearts and minds to look for the cracks of light that are already there, and it does help us. Not only is this a spiritual principle, science also backs up the benefits of gratitude. The more we look for reasons to be thankful, the more we find.

Lord, thank you for this moment. Thank you for your presence. As I stir up gratitude in my heart, transform my perspective.

CONTINUAL PRAISE

Let us continually offer the sacrifice of praise to God, that is, the fruit of our lips, giving thanks to His name.

HEBREWS 13:15 NKJV

On good days, when all seems to be right in our world, it is easy to praise God. On days when we struggle to see the good, or we cannot escape suffering, praise becomes a sacrifice. Does this mean we should avoid it? By no means! A sacrifice of praise speaks volumes of our surrender to the Lord. Each movement of submission honors him.

Even when we don't have the words to offer, God reads our hearts like an open book. Nothing is hidden from him. Every turn toward him is a bid for his mercy. He sees, he knows, and he rushes to meet us with his kindness.

God, I give you praise on both my best days and my worst. You are unchanging in love, and you are still nearer than I know.

No Restrictions

I'm writing to encourage you to pray with gratitude to God. Pray for all men with all forms of prayers and requests as you intercede with intense passion.

1 Timothy 2:1 TPT

In this season where we focus on building practices of gratitude, there are many ways we can do it. We can incorporate more intentional times of thanking God. As we begin and end each day, we can jot down a few of the simple things we are grateful for. The more we attune our attention to his goodness, the more at peace we become.

There are no restrictions given for what we should pray for. Let's be intentional this week to give time to prayer. Whether through set-aside time in the morning or evening, or just by using a prompt or problem to lift up those around us. There is so much opportunity to connect to the Lord throughout our days, both for our encouragement and for intercession on others' behalf.

Lord, may my prayer life grow as I give intention to it this week.

BEAUTIFUL FRAGRANCE

Thanks be to God, who always leads us in triumph in Christ, and through us reveals the fragrance of the knowledge of Him in every place.

2 CORINTHIANS 2:14 NASB

When we yield our lives to the leadership of God, following in Christ's footsteps and walking in the wisdom of his ways, they become like the fragrance of his glorious presence. Love leaves an impression wherever it goes. Like perfume, it leaves a pleasant aroma in its wake.

Every area of our lives is affected by how we think about things. If our philosophy is to love in action, then our lives will reflect it by what we do. Whatever is true, honorable, right, pure, lovely, and worthy of praise, let's choose those things. As we do, our lives give off the beautiful fragrance of Christ.

Lord Jesus, I want the posture of my heart, the fruit of my thinking, and the actions I live to reflect your truth, your mercy, and your beauty.

DON'T HOLD BACK

Give thanks to the Lord and pray to him.
Tell the nations what he has done.

Psalm 105:1 NCV

As we reflect on the power of God, we come face-to-face with our testimonies. We each have a story to tell. We are witnesses to God's goodness. There are so many reasons to give thanks to the Lord. But let's not stop there. Let's share the power of our testimony with those around us.

The gospel is powerful for all who receive it. Let's not hold back the truth of God's liberating love from those who haven't yet tasted and seen its sweet fruit. If you don't know what to share, look at the life of Christ. What he has done, he still does in the power of his resurrection life and redemptive love.

Faithful One, as I spend time in your presence today, remind me of the power of your mercy in my life.

UNSHAKABLE KINGDOM

Since we are receiving a kingdom that cannot be shaken, let us be thankful. By it, we may serve God acceptably, with reverence and awe,

HEBREWS 12:28 CSB

The kingdom of God cannot be overcome. It won't lose its influence or break apart. The kingdoms of this world rise and fall. Governments shift and change, but the government of our God never changes. He is our ruler, the righteous king, and perfect Prince of Peace. We need never fear his absence.

No matter the shaking we experience in this world, no matter how many leaders come to power or are removed, God's authority never changes. Our foundation is the kingdom of God, not the governments of this world. We plant our faith on the solid rock of God's mercy, knowing his justice will come, and we walk in his ways instead of putting our hope in the world's power.

God, I'm so grateful that your kingdom cannot be overcome or threatened by the ways of this world. I choose your law of love, your truth, and allegiance to your kingdom above all.

COLLECTORS OF WISDOM

Get all the advice and instruction you can,
so you will be wise the rest of your life.

PROVERBS 19:20 NLT

As God's children, we don't have limited resources to draw from. There is abundant wisdom, and it is accessible in many forms. We cannot deny the power of God's Spirit that brings revelation. If we've ever had a thought appear as if out of nowhere, solving a problem, that is the wisdom of God at work. If we've ever received good advice from an expert that brought clarity, that is the power of wisdom as it meets us.

When we are open to learning, we collect advice and instruction, and we implement what fits and leave what doesn't. There is so much that we don't know, and we don't have to struggle through figuring it out on our own. There are others who have already done that and have wisdom to share. How willing are we to listen to the advice of others?

Lord, you are the wisest of all. I trust your Spirit to give me discernment as I collect wisdom and get the training and advice I need.

ABUNDANT FAITH

We ought always to thank God for you, brothers and sisters, and rightly so, because your faith is growing more and more, and the love all of you have for one another is increasing.

2 THESSALONIANS 1:3 NIV

Faith is not static. It expands and contracts, depending on what we are feeding our hearts and minds. The size of our faith, however, doesn't represent how much God loves us. Even a mustard seed of faith, a tiny grain, can move mountains.

Thank God that he knows us well. He sees how eager we are to prove ourselves. Our worth isn't dependent on our faith; and still, God increases our faith as we know him more. Faith and love go hand in hand. We can increase in loving others, just as our faith in God's goodness can grow stronger. There is always more room to grow. Let's not become complacent in our faith or our love.

Faithful One, I am so thankful that each day is a fresh slate in your mercy. Help me to grow more and more in faith.

Continue To Connect

Continue steadfastly in prayer,
being watchful in it with thanksgiving.

Colossians 4:2 ESV

As we position our hearts in prayer, we invite God to meet us. He satisfies our needs and speaks life to our minds, hearts, and lives. There is endless wisdom in his presence. There is clarity for our confusion, and there is peace for our anxiety. There is more than enough every time we turn to him. He is generous in kindness, and he never gets exasperated by how many times we come to him for help.

Let's continue steadfastly in prayer, not because we are desperate and needy, though we may very well be, but because God is a loving Father who always wants to connect with us. There is never a good reason to stay away from him.

Lord, I won't neglect connecting to you in prayer. You are my lifeline, and you are the wisdom that puts the puzzle pieces together.

STEADY HAND

"I, the LORD your God, will hold your right hand,
Saying to you, 'Fear not, I will help you.'"

ISAIAH 41:13 NKJV

Take the steady hand of the Lord as you step into your day. Though you cannot anticipate every challenge that will arise, nothing surprises the Lord. You can trust him to guide you through the tricky weeds as you encounter them. He is more than able to help you no matter the problem.

God's presence is your constant. It is his promised gift to you. He will never abandon you, not even for a moment. He is the God of your challenges, as well as the God of your ease. You can trust his nature in every moment.

Lord my God, here is my hand and my trust. Lead me into this day by your grace and mercy.

ASKED AND ANSWERED

"To You, God of my fathers, I give thanks and praise,
For You have given me wisdom and power;
Even now You have made known to me
what we requested of You,
For You have made known to us the king's matter."

DANIEL 2:23 NASB

God answers the prayers of his people. He did it for Daniel, and he still does it for us today. He gives wisdom to those who ask for it. He offers help to those who need it. He is always ready to help in times of trouble. He is as present with us on our hardest days as he is on our best. We need never fear rejection from him. When we come to him with honest questions, he gives us what we need.

God's solutions are better than our own. He knows the intricacies of the world and our minds. He knows exactly what every heart needs in each moment. What seems impossible with mankind is possible with God. Let's turn to him for the wisdom and strength we need. He never fails.

Glorious God, there is no mystery to you. I ask for wisdom and discernment into problems only you can solve.

MORNING AND EVENING

The Levites also stood every morning and gave thanks and praise to the LORD. They also did this every evening.

1 CHRONICLES 23:30 NCV

When we begin our day with thanks and praise, it sets the tone for the rest of it. When we end our day with the same, it puts perspective on all that has happened, and all that we cannot control. It postures our hearts before the Lord, shifting our perspective to remember the incomparable goodness of God's character.

Even if we only take a few minutes at the beginning and end of each day, it can do wonders to set our hearts in expectation and to settle them in peace. God is worthy of our adoration, our attention, and our submission every moment. When we set aside time to remember who he is, it transforms our mindsets in his faithfulness. It can turn a hard season into one filled with the treasures hidden in darkness, where we collect his goodness.

Lord, every day is the day to thank and praise you. I set my heart on you today, and I will continue to.

PLEASING GOD

It pleases God more when we
demonstrate godliness and justice
than when we merely offer him a sacrifice.

PROVERBS 21:3 TPT

God doesn't want empty offerings. He doesn't care about what looks good on the outside. If we only give to the Lord because of how it appears to others, we miss the point entirely. And we miss out on the goodness we find in following the Lord!

So, what is pleasing to God? To live out his love. When we demonstrate godliness and justice, we align our lifestyles with the values of his kingdom. If our brand of godliness is harsh and judgmental, we miss out on the grace and kindness of God's ways. When we demonstrate God's idea of godliness and justice, it always looks like mercy. Let's keep that in mind as we yield our hearts to him and live out his nature.

God, walking the path of your love isn't easy, but it is worth it. You are worthy of my surrender and my wholehearted love.

GOOD AND PERFECT

Every good and perfect gift is from above,
coming down from the Father of lights,
who does not change like shifting shadows.

JAMES 1:17 CSB

If it reflects the fruit of God's Spirit, it is from the hand of God. It is reflective of his kingdom. We have to readjust our expectations of goodness from being rigid and religious to looking for the fruit of God's love as it meets us in practical ways.

Take some time to consider what is good and perfect in your life. What gifts have brought you goodness, life, and greater understanding? What has produced wisdom, hope, peace, and joy? These are gifts of God, whether or not you considered them to be. God's nature is reflected in his gifts, and he doesn't change. When you spot a good and perfect gift, thank the Lord, and receive it with joy.

Father, you are the best gift giver. I am astounded by your loving care of me, and the ways you surprise me with delight.

JOYFUL REQUESTS

Whenever I pray, I make my requests for all of you with joy, Philemon, because I keep hearing about your faith in the Lord Jesus and your love for all of God's people.

PHILEMON 1:4-5 NLT

When we are thankful for people in our lives, let's not neglect to tell them. Whatever reasons we have to be grateful, let's lean into those and focus on the benefit they bring. As we do, our hearts fill with warmth, gratitude, and affection. This is meant to be shared!

Who are you thankful for? Whose friendship, leadership, or companionship has brought you joy? Thank God for them. Pray that they will be overwhelmed with blessings from on high. And don't forget to also reach out and tell them how thankful you are for them. Be specific, be honest, and be generous.

Jesus, I cannot begin to thank you for the wonderful people I have in my life. What a reflection they are of your many blessings.

EMPOWERED TO EMPOWER

You will be enriched in every way so that you can be generous on every occasion, and through us your generosity will result in thanksgiving to God.

2 CORINTHIANS 9:11 NIV

We are enriched so that we can be generous in sharing what we have with others. We are not offered so much so that we can hoard it for ourselves. Abundance means a deeper well to draw from. It means we have more to offer people who are lacking in those resources.

Generosity is a principle of the kingdom of Christ. We enter into this world with nothing, wholly dependent on those who raise us. All that we have is a gift. Every resource and blessing is a tool that can help us and that we can share with others. Every occasion is an occasion to be generous, as God's Word says. Generosity reflects the abundance of God, his gracious nature, and his powerful love for all.

Lord, I want to be generous, helpful, and an encourager of all who need it. I am enriched to enrich others and empowered to empower others.

VICTORIOUS

Thanks be to God, who gives us the victory
through our Lord Jesus Christ.

1 CORINTHIANS 15:57 ESV

Christ's victory over death is our victory. The finality of death, the curse of sin, was broken when he was resurrected. He is still alive. Our hope, our Savior, and our strength is our forever victory. When death comes for those we love, we grieve, but we don't grieve without hope. We have a higher hope in Christ. His kingdom is eternal, and it is the home of all who give their lives to him.

We live in the space of promise and fulfillment. We will all be changed when Christ returns. Death has lost its victory and its sting because of the triumph of Christ over it. While we wait for the fullness of the promise, our hope does not waver. Christ is alive, and he is our victory. In him, we have confidence, and we will know the power of his victory.

Victorious Jesus, you are my holy hope and my great expectation. When loss is unavoidable, and grief breaks through my comfort, remind me of the hope that is imminent and lasting.

THE FATHER HEARS

Then they took away the stone from the place where the dead man was lying. And Jesus lifted up His eyes and said, "Father, I thank You that You have heard Me."

JOHN 11:41 NKJV

When Jesus prayed for Lazarus to come out of the grave, it was a supernatural act of faith. Everyone was grieving his passing already. Jesus knew, even before Lazarus died, that he would live. Still, he took time to weep with his friends before he prayed. What a kind, compassionate, comforting Savior he is.

When Jesus prayed, he did it out loud so that the people around him could benefit. He prayed, thanking the Father that he heard him. When we pray, we can be sure that the Father hears us, too. It isn't a matter of time or place. Be bold in your prayers today, letting compassion compel you and being confident that the Father hears you.

Father, I thank you that you have heard me today. You are good, powerful, and true, and nothing is impossible for you.

GREAT IS THE LORD

Let all who passionately seek you erupt
with excitement and joy over what you've done!
Let all your devoted lovers rejoice continually in the Savior,
saying, "How great and glorious is our God!"

PSALM 40:16 TPT

Today is a day to give thanks. It's time to declare, "How great and glorious is our God!" Let's actively remember what the Lord has done for us. As we see the miracles of his mercy bursting through the seams of our lives, we will erupt with excitement over what he has done.

God is good, and his nature is evident in the places where his mercy meets us. Where we have experienced breakthrough, there the Lord has brought us into greater freedom. Where we have known comfort, peace, joy, and love, there is the Spirit of God in our midst. Let's offer the Lord our true and grateful praise as we remember the power of his presence at work in our lives.

Lord, you deserve all the gratitude, all the worship, all the heartfelt joy that I can muster. You have been so good to me, and I offer you all my thanks today.

ALL CREATION

Everything created by God is good,
and nothing is to be rejected
if it is received with gratitude.

1 TIMOTHY 4:4 NASB

The Hebrew law means that Jewish people have to keep kosher, eating only what is deemed clean. When Jesus came though, he removed the tedious aspects of the law and instead brought freedom to partake in what the Lord created.

As followers of Christ, we don't have to follow the rigid food rules of Judaism. We also don't have to restrict our diets because of fear. Whatever we receive with gratitude reflects the freedom and goodness of God's creation. Let's give up our judgment of ourselves and others based on religious rote, and embrace what God has so graciously given.

Lord, there is nothing in all of creation that you did not make. Thank you for wisdom in what we put into our bodies, and also thank you for freedom from guilt, shame, and fear.

WHERE WE BELONG

Know that the LORD is God.
He made us, and we belong to him;
we are his people, the sheep he tends.

PSALM 100:3 NCV

We were created by God to know him, and to come alive in the fullness of his fellowship. He made us, and we belong to him. What a powerful truth! We are his people, the sheep he tends. God is a good shepherd, leading and caring for us. His presence is where we belong, for we are his children.

When we remember the powerful goodness of the Lord, convinced of his eternal love and unfailing faithfulness, we run into his presence with joy. We gladly come into his courts with thanksgiving and songs of praise. He is better than we yet know, and still, it is true that we have tasted and seen that the Lord is good.

Good Shepherd, your presence is my home. Thank you for creating me, calling me your own, and caring for me so well. I worship you.

REIGNING PEACE

Let the peace of Christ, to which you were also called in one body, rule your hearts. And be thankful. Let the word of Christ dwell richly among you, in all wisdom teaching and admonishing one another through psalms, hymns, and spiritual songs, singing to God with gratitude in your hearts.

COLOSSIANS 3:15-16 CSB

The power of peace is ours, not only as individuals, but as the body of Christ. As the family of God, we are called to love one another and pursue peace. We can dwell in this lasting harmony, for it is the atmosphere of God's very presence.

If we don't know how to get from tension to peace in our relationships, let's start where Scripture points us today. Christ's teachings direct us in wisdom. As we teach, encourage, and correct one another with compassion, gentleness, and truth, we create pathways where peace can dwell. When we worship the Lord together, we join in unity, adoring and lifting high the name of Jesus Christ, who was, who is, and who is to come.

Lord Jesus, I want to know peace in my relationships and community, and not only in my own heart.

Kingdom Representatives

Whatever you do or say, do it as a representative of the Lord Jesus, giving thanks through him to God the Father.

Colossians 3:17 NLT

The standard for our actions, our words, and our lifestyles isn't the norm of the day. It's not society's measure. It's Jesus Christ. His life, his ministry, his teachings, and his example are ours to follow. When we use Christ as our measure, it doesn't matter how well or poorly others act, we know what we should do.

If instead we only measure our actions based on what others do or don't do, we can easily invite compromise into our lives. The ways of Christ, and his love for mankind, remain pure, kind, peace-loving, and true. There is no wrong motive in his heart. When we align our hearts and lives with his kingdom, we demonstrate his goodness, his compassion, and his power through our surrendered lives.

Lord Jesus, there is no one better than you. I choose to live as a representative of your merciful kingdom.

ENDURING LOVE

Give thanks to the LORD, for he is good.
His love endures forever.

PSALM 136:1 NIV

Today, if all you do is give God thanks, let that be enough. You don't have to grind away at work or make the people around you happy. You can rest in the goodness of God. You can know his peace that passes understanding, his love that endures forever.

Whenever you think of it today, give God thanks. You don't even need a reason! Just saying "thank you" can be like an exhale after holding your breath. Turn your attention to the Lord, even if only for a moment at a time. His love endures forever. That is more than enough reason to keep looking to him. He is good; he is faithful. He is just; he is true. Give thanks to the Lord!

Lord, thank you. Thank you for your love and for your goodness. Thank you for this breath, and this one too. Thank you for holding me, being present, and never leaving.

WONDROUS WORKS

Let them thank the LORD for his steadfast love,
for his wondrous works to the children of man!

PSALM 107:15 ESV

God does all things well. He is not hesitant in helping us when we call out to him. He does not do the bare minimum. He is thorough in gracious strength, and he is complete in winning wisdom. There is nothing that he does not do wonderfully well.

Let's offer God our heartfelt gratitude for all that he has done incredibly well for us. Perhaps we could not see the gracious goodness of his mercy when it first appeared, but with hindsight we see how all the pieces fit together. He is infinitely wiser than we are. He sees every detail we miss, and the bigger picture of it all. Let's trust him with what we are waiting to see come to fruition, for he is still moving.

Faithful God, you are amazing in what you do. Your nature is reflected in your wondrous works.

LACKING NOTHING

Count it all joy when you fall into various trials, knowing that the testing of your faith produces patience. But let patience have its perfect work, that you may be perfect and complete, lacking nothing.

JAMES 1:2-4 NKJV

When we learn to count everything as joy, we cultivate patience in our hearts. Wading through the trials of life doesn't have to be filled with sorrow and despondency. We can know the powerful peace of God that empowers us in joy. Whatever we face, whatever we fall into, God is with us.

Tests of faith are inevitable. When they come, we can persevere in hope, building our patience and keeping the eyes of our faith fixed on Jesus. He is the one who called us, and he keeps us close in the fellowship of the Holy Spirit. When unexpected challenges arise today, let's embrace the opportunity to count it as joy. What a difference it can make when we do.

Gracious God, I won't give up when times are hard. I know that you are with me in the testing and the challenges of life. Grow my faith, even as my patience is strengthened.

RESPONSE OF FAITH

"Not one promise from God is empty of power.
Nothing is impossible with God!"
Then Mary responded, saying, "Yes! I will be a mother for the Lord! As his servant, I accept whatever he has for me. May everything you have told me come to pass."

LUKE 1:37-38 TPT

When the angel announced to Mary that she would carry the Son of God in her womb, she was taken aback at first. But instead of refusing to believe, the encouragement of God's ability and the power of his promises led her to willingly embrace the calling that was hers.

Whatever God has called us to, he equips us to walk in the power of his Spirit. His promises are full of power. Nothing is impossible with him. May we respond as Mary did, accepting what God has for us, and welcoming all that he speaks over our lives. His promise may seem too big, too unbelievable to grasp, and yet the one who promises will, indeed, deliver.

Miracle Maker, your plans and purposes for me are better than any I could come up with on my own. I yield to your leadership, and I say yes to what you have for me.

LOVING LIGHT

Do all things without complaining or arguments; so that you will prove yourselves to be blameless and innocent, children of God above reproach in the midst of a crooked and perverse generation, among whom you appear as lights in the world.

PHILIPPIANS 2:14-15 NASB

Imagine if Jesus walked this earth, complaining about all that he had to do. "Ugh, leave my Father in heaven for these messed up people?" "Why won't they believe who I am? I give up!" Graciously, he willingly, from a heart of love, embraced all that was set before him.

We can learn from Jesus' example. His compassion compelled him in all things. He did not look at the mistakes of mankind and ridicule them. He lovingly taught them what the Father is like. He is still teaching us today. Let's follow his lead and lay aside the grumbling and complaining. Let's give up stoking arguments, and instead humble ourselves in compassion.

Jesus, there is no one better to follow than you. Instead of complaining about what could be, I choose to embrace what is from a heart of love.

DECEMBER

"If I then, your Lord and Teacher,
have washed your feet,
you also ought to wash
one another's feet."

John 13:14 ESV

FREE AS CHILDREN

When the right time came, God sent his Son who was born of a woman and lived under the law. God did this so he could buy freedom for those who were under the law and so we could become his children.

GALATIANS 4:4-5 NCV

At just the right time, God sent his Son to reveal his love. He came to liberate us from sin's grasp so that we could freely come to the Father as his children. What a gracious gift we have in the saving grace of Christ's fellowship.

As free people and children of God, we get to come into his presence boldly. There is generous grace in his presence, and more than enough mercy to meet us. Let's use our freedom to go to God any time of the day, for he is ready and willing to meet us with his full attention.

Gracious Father, I come boldly to your throne of grace for all that I need. You are so patient, kind, and generous with me.

DAWNING LIGHT

The people walking in darkness
have seen a great light;
a light has dawned
on those living in the land of darkness.

ISAIAH 9:2 CSB

Jesus Christ is the light that dispels darkness. When he came to earth, he revealed the disarming and unrivaled love of the Father in flesh and bones. Christ is our lamp; he is living truth, embodied wisdom, and trustworthy hope. There is no shadow that won't light up with his radiant and present love.

Take hope today in the fellowship of light. Christ has already come to earth once, revealing the power of God's liberating mercy. He sits at the right hand of his Father even now, waiting for the fullness of time to mark his return. Graciously, he is not far away from us. God has given us his Holy Spirit to teach, guide, and empower us. The light that dawned remains shining bright today.

Glorious One, shine on the shadows that keep me from walking in the fullness of faith. I trust you.

GIFT OF LIFE

The wages of sin is death,
but the free gift of God is eternal life
through Christ Jesus our Lord.

ROMANS 6:23 NLT

Jesus is our saving grace. He has offered us all the free gift of God—the salvation of our souls. We no longer need to live in fear of death, let alone any harm that could befall us by the hands of others. He is our liberating love, the peace that passes all understanding, and the hope that holds us steady.

Whether we've spent every day turning to Christ, or this is our first time, there is beauty, power, and grace in the fellowship of his presence. When we surrender our hearts to him, we are set free to know him, to love him, and to walk in the ways or his wisdom without shame, fear, or dismay. All who come to the Father through the Son are welcomed with open arms, washed clean of their sins, and given grace to grow in the powerful fruit of God's Spirit.

Savior, I cannot begin to thank you for the love, grace, joy, and peace I have found in you. Wash over me afresh as I come to you.

BRIGHT MORNING STAR

"I, Jesus, have sent my angel to give you this testimony for the churches. I am the Root and the Offspring of David, and the bright Morning Star."

REVELATION 22:16 NIV

Jesus is the bright Morning Star: the light that shines brightly on this world. His radiance never dims, even when the world turns on its axis. Night may fall, but the fire of Christ's radiant presence still burns as hot and bright as ever, even if we see but a reflection of it in the dark sky.

Let's not lose hope in the middle of our night seasons. Morning will dawn, as it always does, bringing relief, clarity, and hope. Jesus remains constant and true. He is always available, and he never turns us away. Let's look for where the glimmers of his light dispel shadows in our lives and in this world.

Lord Jesus, you are the light that all creation is created from. In your light, I come alive.

CLARIFYING PEACE

God is not a God of confusion but of peace.

1 CORINTHIANS 14:33 ESV

God does not work in confusion. He doesn't frustrate us by giving us unsolvable riddles to decipher. His wisdom is simple and profound. His truth is clarifying and practical. God's peace settles our hearts, minds, and bodies, giving us grounded space to feel, think, and experience his living truth.

Fear sows confusion. It pushes us in haste before we can think things through clearly. This is not the way God works. He is not a punisher of his people. He corrects in kindness and leads in gentle truth. He does not shy away from saying the truth; he is not tricky. Even the truth is given with compassion. He is full of peace, hope, and love.

Prince of peace, may I resist the pull of fear when it wants me to move before your wisdom speaks. I choose to slow down and wait for your clarity in the midst of confusion.

ALWAYS REJOICING

Rejoice in the Lord always.
Again I will say, rejoice!

PHILIPPIANS 4:4 NKJV

God's nature is beautiful, unchanging, and powerfully good. When we look to our circumstances for our emotional cues, we put our attention on the ever-changing factors rather than the steadfast one. God remains the same no matter what happens in our world. He is the restorer and Savior of all things. Nothing is out of reach from his powerful redemption.

When we keep our focus on the beauty of our Lord and Savior, we always have reason to rejoice! Think of your favorite person on the earth. When you are around them, life just seems… better. Easier. Lighter. Now, consider that Jesus Christ is a perfect friend, present help, and caring comforter. His presence can make even the darkest night bearable. In light of this, rejoice!

Jesus, you are my friend and my redeemer. I think of all that you have done for me, and I am overwhelmed with gratitude.

VARIED EXPRESSIONS

The fruit produced by the Holy Spirit within you
is divine love in all its varied expressions:
joy that overflows, peace that subdues,
patience that endures, kindness in action,
a life full of virtue, faith that prevails,
gentleness of heart, and strength of spirit.

GALATIANS 5:22-23 TPT

The fruit of God's Spirit are all various expressions of divine love. God is love, and all who live in love abide in him. It makes sense, then, that the fruit of this love is revealed in practical ways.

Read through today's verse again to familiarize yourself with some of these expressions. Pick one or two to intentionally incorporate into your day. You could spend weeks, months, or years honing in on them and still experience the power of its effects in your life. Choose today what you want to nurture in love, and let it be your devotion of worship to the Lord.

Perfect One, may I never grow tired of growing in love, for it isn't simply a feeling or idea. I dedicate my heart and attention to nurturing the seeds of your Spirit in my life.

SPIRITUAL KINGDOM

The kingdom of God is not eating and drinking, but righteousness and peace and joy in the Holy Spirit.

ROMANS 14:17 NASB

Many religious criteria end up as rules and regulations. The Jewish people have the laws of Moses dictating what they can and cannot eat. While there is nothing wrong with keeping the regulations of religious orders, we must not confuse that with our goodness or salvation.

The kingdom of God is not found in what we partake in or abstain from; it is in the power of God's Spirit as it produces the nature of Christ in our lives. We can overcomplicate what God makes simple. Instead of focusing on restrictions, let's turn our attention to what produces righteousness, peace, and joy in God's Spirit.

Holy Spirit, when I am too rigid in my expectations of what God requires, soften my heart in the truth of his love.

GRACE AND TRUTH

Because he was full of grace and truth, from him we all received one gift after another. The law was given through Moses, but grace and truth came through Jesus Christ.

JOHN 1:16-17 NCV

There are endless gifts to receive through Jesus Christ. There is more grace, more mercy, more hope, more joy, more peace for us each and every day. Whatever we need can be fully met in the presence of God.

The truth of Christ is meant to set us free. What grace there is in following his ways! We obey his teachings, and we experience the freedom of his powerful wisdom as it moves through our lives. This is almost too much to grasp. Still, it is our privilege and honor to follow him and to know this liberating grace that connects us to the Father of creation.

Gracious Jesus, I am so glad that you are full of grace and truth, and I can always come to you for more. There is no lack of love in your presence!

God's Likeness

No one has ever seen God.
But God the only Son is very close to the Father,
and he has shown us what God is like.

John 1:18 CSB

While no one has stood face-to-face with the Father and lived to tell about it, Jesus is the reflection of God's nature in a form we can understand. The glory of God is too much for us to stand in our current form, but the gracious nature of Christ is as powerful in its telling of God's radiant character.

We don't have to go searching the world for the goodness of God. We don't even have to go across town to find it. God's goodness, the fullness of his powerful love and permeating peace, is as close as his presence. Thankfully, the Spirit is as close as the air in our lungs. It is the work of the Spirit to reveal what God is like.

Lord Jesus, thank you for coming to earth as a human so that we can see, know, and understand the disarming love of the Father. Reveal the truth of God's nature to my understanding even more today.

HOPE-FILLED

This hope will not lead to disappointment. For we know how dearly God loves us, because he has given us the Holy Spirit to fill our hearts with his love.

ROMANS 5:5 NLT

The hope of God does not leave us wanting. Each of us knows the sting of disappointment in one way or another. Perhaps a relationship didn't work out in the way we expected it. Maybe a job we felt was the right fit chose to go a different direction. Disappointment is part of life, but thankfully it is not something we need fear in our relationship with God.

The hope of God is rooted in his promises. He never lies or changes his mind. The Holy Spirit is our guarantee of God's goodness. He fills our hearts with the tangible love of God so we know from deep within the hope that guides us.

Promise Keeper, you don't shift or change. You are my holy hope. Fill me with the power of your presence to remind me of the goodness you promise.

STRAIGHT ANSWERS

Above all, my brothers and sisters, do not swear—not by heaven or by earth or by anything else. All you need to say is a simple "Yes" or "No." Otherwise you will be condemned.

JAMES 5:12 NIV

There is no need to add "I swear" to anything we promise. In fact, it is a hallmark of those who for one reason or another are unpredictable or untrustworthy in their word. Adding qualifiers only lessens our credibility.

If someone is skeptical of our word, it's not our job to convince them with more words. Our follow-through will speak for itself. We can simply let our yes be yes and our no be no. No need to bind ourselves to an oath we may or may not keep. When we give simple, straight answers, there is no confusion.

Lord, you are honest, true, and I know that your wisdom stands the test of time. Help me to keep my answers simple and straight, letting my actions speak for themselves.

INSEPARABLE

I am sure that neither death nor life, nor angels nor rulers, nor things present nor things to come, nor powers, nor height nor depth, nor anything else in all creation, will be able to separate us from the love of God in Christ Jesus our Lord.

ROMANS 8:38-39 ESV

Paul was convinced that nothing could separate us from the love of God. He wasn't the only one in Scripture that believed or encouraged this. King David said that even darkness could not hide him from God's light. God's presence is full of love, for God himself is love.

No matter what you face today, love is with you. Nothing can separate you from the overwhelming love of the Father! Nothing in the past or in the future, no amount of distance, nothing in all of creation could keep you from the love of Christ. Let that be an encouragement to your heart today.

Loving Lord, thank you for your love that crosses all boundaries and completely overwhelms everything that would keep me from you. I lean into it today.

GRACE-FILLED WORDS

Let no corrupt word proceed out of your mouth,
but what is good for necessary edification,
that it may impart grace to the hearers.

EPHESIANS 4:29 NKJV

How we speak matters. The words we use and the attitude behind them can cause deeper connection or ruptured trust. Let's be sure to wisely and mindfully be gracious in our speech. Let's seek to offer encouragement rather than tear others down with what we say. When we are humble and compassionate, even in speaking the truth, grace abounds.

We can reflect the kindness, truth, and peace of God's wisdom by being careful about the tone and intention of our words. We will not do this perfectly, and that's okay. When we err and see the effects our words have had, we can offer our sincere apology to the one we have hurt. There is grace in this too.

Lord, I don't want to be mindless in the way I speak to others. May I be full of intention, grace, kindness, and encouragement in how I talk.

STEADY PROGRESSION

In the same way you received Jesus our Lord and Messiah by faith, continue your journey of faith, progressing further into your union with him!

COLOSSIANS 2:6 TPT

Every day is a continuation of our journey not only in life, but also in our faith. Each new day is an opportunity to progress further into friendship with the Lord. Our roots grow deep in his loving presence. His life infuses our own with strength, encouragement, and hope. The establishment of our faith is founded first in Christ and all that he offers. It is enriched, growing stronger, as we dedicate ourselves in devotion to knowing, following, and uplifting him in our lives.

Today is a continuation of the days that have gone before. Keep moving in Christ, for he is leading you. Even if you cannot see the changes from day to day, you will look back on your journey with awe as you see the development of your heart, character, and hope when you continue to follow him.

Jesus, thank you for your fellowship. I will keep following you.

REMAIN

"Just as the Father has loved Me, I also have loved you; remain in My love. If you keep My commandments, you will remain in My love; just as I have kept My Father's commandments and remain in His love."

JOHN 15:9-10 NASB

We don't reach a spiritual age where we need to leave the home of our Savior. We don't have to venture off on our own. We find ourselves as he loves us to life in his presence. He goes with us. He walks with us in work, and he stays close with us in our homes. There is no place we go that he is not already there.

We remain in the love of Christ by keeping his commandments. They are not too much for us. They are all based in the law of his love. If all we ever do is follow the loving path, then we keep his commandments. Jesus remained in his Father's love by following his directions. We do the same when we walk in the love of Christ.

Lord, when I cannot do anything else, help me to remember to remain in your love.

IMAGE BEARERS

God created human beings in his image.
In the image of God he created them.
He created them male and female.

GENESIS 1:27 NCV

Every person was created in the image of God. There isn't a person alive that doesn't somehow reflect what he is like. None of us is perfect in our representation, but we each have traits that point to the Father. Let's not devalue others because of their differences. Let's not do that to ourselves either. We were created in love and goodness, and we are worthy of that same love because God said we are.

As we get to know Christ more, spending time in his presence and putting his wisdom into practice, we can reflect the nature of God more. There is transformation in his light. There is beauty in embracing his fellowship and accepting the love he so freely offers us. What freedom is ours as we truly realize how graciously he loves us. We can't earn it, and we never have to!

Creator, I am made in your image. May I see myself and others through the lens of your creative love today.

HOPEFUL EXPECTATION

In this hope we were saved, but hope that is seen is not hope, because who hopes for what he sees? Now if we hope for what we do not see, we eagerly wait for it with patience.

ROMANS 8:24-25 CSB

As long as we are waiting for the Lord, hope is necessary. In truth, as long as we wait for anything in life, hope is strength to our souls. Patience grows in the hopeful expectation of a heart sure that it will receive its promise. Our hope isn't based in the thing we wait on, it's in the nature of the God who promised it in the first place.

God who is unchanging promises that we will not wait in vain for him to come. What he says, he does. In the meantime, our hearts learn to wait with hope and confidence in God's goodness. God is faithful regardless, but our own hearts know peace, endurance, joy, and comfort in the presence of God when we learn to wait in hope.

Lord, thank you for the hope of the fullness of your kingdom. While I wait, encourage my heart in patient and expectant hope.

UNBREAKABLE OATH

God has given both his promise and his oath. These two things are unchangeable because it is impossible for God to lie. Therefore, we who have fled to him for refuge can have great confidence as we hold to the hope that lies before us.

HEBREWS 6:18 NLT

God's oath is the seal of his promise. It is his unbreakable Word. He never takes back a promise, and he doesn't break his Word. His nature, his faithfulness, is the guarantee of his oath. He will not change like the shifting that constantly happens on the earth. He is constant and true, through every generation and season.

We can run to the Lord for refuge at any time. When we find it hard to hope in his Word, let's not let discouragement keep us at a distance. Let's press in to know him more, running into the shelter of his presence. There our confidence grows, and we grab hold of the hope that holds onto us already.

Faithful One, you are the only sure thing in a world full of cheap substitutes. As I run to you today, envelop me in the strength of your presence and encourage my heart in hope.

DEEP ROOTS

I pray that you, being rooted and established in love, may have power, together with all the Lord's holy people, to grasp how wide and long and high and deep is the love of Christ, and to know this love that surpasses knowledge—that you may be filled to the measure of all the fullness of God.

EPHESIANS 3:17-19 NIV

The soil of God's love is full of lifegiving nutrients. It offers the roots our hearts need, not only to grow, but to thrive in the shifting seasons and weather patterns of this world. The love of Christ is strong beyond measure. It cannot be bottled up and sold. It is free to all who come to him.

Don't settle for yesterday's portion when Christ offers you today's bread. You don't have to live off wisdom that met you yesterday but doesn't fill the need you have today. God's love meets you in the fullness of his wisdom. There isn't a need that he won't supply, and there isn't a problem he can't fix. Let your roots grow deeper into his love; there is power in being established in him.

God of love, I have been rooted in the soil of your love, and I soak up what you offer me today.

HEIRS OF THE PROMISE

Being justified by his grace
we might become heirs
according to the hope of eternal life.

TITUS 3:7 ESV

We become members of God's kingdom not by the families we are born into on the earth, but by the gracious justification of Christ's sacrifice. It doesn't matter where we grow up or how little we have. It doesn't matter how well-off we are in the world. The hope of the promise of Christ is for all who come to him.

As heirs of the kingdom of Christ, we share in his inheritance. In Matthew 20, Jesus illustrates the kingdom of heaven through a parable about laborers in a vineyard. The owner went out and hired workers to help him in his vineyard. Though they started at various times, they all received the same generous wage. Christ offers us the same thing through salvation. The Father's generosity offends some, but it is a hallmark of his nature. Let's embrace his promise, and the hope of eternal life offered to all who come to him in the same measure.

Gracious Jesus, I don't want to be offended by your grace. Open my understanding to be generous as you are.

SECURE IN HIM

"My Father, who has given them to Me, is greater than all; and no one is able to snatch them out of My Father's hand. I and My Father are one."

JOHN 10:29-30 NKJV

No one can take away what Christ so graciously offers us. Salvation is not something anyone can take from us. Let's give up the fear that someone or something outside our control could snatch us from the Father's hand. Christ says plainly that no is able to do that.

Confident rest is ours as we realize our security is in God's power and not the power of mankind. God is the only one who can give life to our souls and take that same life away. And we know what he is like! He is gracious, merciful, and just. Let's rest in the security of his love that calls us his own.

Great God, there is no one else like you. Fill me with confident hope, peace, and rest as I find my security in your unfailing nature.

GOD WITH US

The LORD Himself will give you a sign:
Behold, the virgin will conceive and give birth to a son,
and she will name Him Immanuel.

ISAIAH 7:14 NASB

The Father sent Jesus, his Son, so that we would know his overwhelmingly merciful nature. Though many followed God before Jesus came, there was still a misunderstanding of his grace. There was a gap in God's beauty and mankind's understanding of him. Jesus broke every barrier that was between God and man, from the veil that separated God's presence in the temple, to the curse of sin that kept us in bondage.

Jesus came as a humble baby, born into the human experience. He grew in knowledge and character as he matured. By the time Jesus began his ministry in his thirties, he had already been teaching people in the synagogues. Jesus' life, ministry, death, and resurrection have much to teach us. What a powerful Savior we have, and what a humble frame he bore in order to show us the power of God!

Immanuel, thank you for coming to earth to bring us close to the Father. Be glorified in my life as I continually submit to your leadership.

KING OF KINGS

On his robe and on his thigh he had inscribed a name:
King of kings and Lord of lords.

REVELATION 19:16 TPT

Though Jesus was born a baby, he is not still one. As we reflect on the first coming of Christ, let's not forget that he is our victorious Savior—the King of kings and Lord of lords.

Jesus is our humble king, but let's not forget that he is full of authority and power. He is not weak. He is not lacking anything. We can put our full hope in the power of Christ, for he is the one who will rule and reign over his eternal kingdom. He is our confident expectation, our empowering strength, and the giver of life. There is nothing he cannot do. Even while we honor his birth, let's remember who he is now, and who he will always be.

King of kings and Lord of lords, you have all authority in heaven and on earth. I put my whole hope in you. I honor you as the man you were, and the King you are.

BOW DOWN

They came to the house where the child was and saw him with his mother, Mary, and they bowed down and worshiped him. They opened their gifts and gave him treasures of gold, frankincense, and myrrh.

MATTHEW 2:11 NCV

The magi took a long journey to find the Messiah child. They brought him costly gifts to honor him. Today, as we reflect on the miraculous birth of Christ, let's bow down and offer him our worship. He is as worthy of our costly gifts today as he was at first.

There is no better moment to embrace the awe and devotion of our yielded hearts and offer them to the Lord. He is as wonderful today as the moment we first became aware of him. He has not changed a bit. Let's stir up the wonder we felt at first and let that lead us to the feet of our humble King. He is incredible and so worthy to be praised.

Jesus Christ, I humble myself before you, bowing down in reverent worship. What a gift you are to the world. What a gift you are to me! I honor you.

FOREVER THE SAME

Jesus Christ is the same
yesterday, today, and forever.

HEBREWS 13:8 CSB

What does it matter that Jesus is the same if we have never known the power of his presence in our lives? It is important that we receive the gift of grace he so willingly offers. Without offering our hearts to him, we will not follow his lead. Without the revelation of his goodness, we may never offer him our trust.

Jesus came to set the sinner free. He came to heal the sick, raise the dead, and make the brokenhearted whole. There is nothing that he does without the fullness of the Father's love. Even the best people in the world don't come close to the exuberance of his kindness. He is generous, bringing lasting peace, overwhelming hope, and jubilant joy to our hearts. This Jesus, he is the same yesterday, today, and forever.

Wonderful Jesus, your nature is unlike those I encounter on a daily basis. Open my eyes to your glorious goodness, and overwhelm my senses with your marvelous mercy.

CONTINUE TO HONOR HIM

You will be rewarded for this;
your hope will not be disappointed.

PROVERBS 23:18 NLT

When we worship God in holy awe, offering him honor and our submission, we know the living hope that never fades. It fills us with clarity, strength, and joy. It is a bright and shining future that will not dim. God is the bright morning star that lights our path, and we need never venture from his presence.

Let's not give up honoring the Lord in our hearts or our lives. He deserves our surrender and trust every single day. He will never lead us astray. Even the harshest times of our lives will know the powerful redemption of his restorative love. Nothing is wasted in his presence. Take heart and hope as you worship him today. He will lead you on in his unfailing love.

God, I have put my hope and trust in you, and I know you will not disappoint.

GENEROUS FORGIVENESS

"Father, forgive them,
for they do not know what they are doing."

LUKE 23:34 NIV

Jesus not only forgave the people involved with accusing him, he also asked the Father to forgive those who had no idea the weight of their actions. This is an incredible example to follow. It is one thing to offer forgiveness to someone who expresses remorse, but to forgive those who refuse to see the harm of their actions is another thing altogether.

Not only had Jesus forgiven them, but he also advocated for them in his prayers. What if we did the same? When we choose forgiveness, we walk in the ways of Christ. When we pray for them, we follow him even further onto the path of his gracious mercy. Let's join with Jesus' heart and advocate for those who know not what they do in prayer before the Father.

Gracious Lord, help me to forgive others, and to also pray for them.

SPIRIT LEAD

All who are led by the Spirit of God are sons of God.

ROMANS 8:14 ESV

The Spirit of God is not just for some believers. He is for all. When we follow the Holy Spirit's leading, we demonstrate that we are children of God. There are many ways to follow the leading of the Spirit, but it starts in surrendering our hearts to Christ.

The Spirit is the presence of God. He reveals the truth of God, teaches us to walk in his wisdom, and comforts us in our pain. The fellowship of God's Spirit is a priceless gift to all who come to the Father through Christ. There is access today, so let's not delay in pressing in.

Holy Spirit, I'm so thankful for your presence that brings authentic peace, clarifying wisdom, and overwhelming joy to my heart and soul.

HONEST WORSHIP

"God is Spirit, and those who worship Him must worship in spirit and truth."

JOHN 4:24 NKJV

What does it mean to worship the Lord in spirit and truth? In its most simple form, it begins on the inside, where our spirits dwell. It is done with intention and a humble posture of our hearts. Worship that honors the Lord isn't in empty rituals or offerings made out of obligation. God's Spirit meets ours within, and we offer him the overflow of our adoration and awe in that place.

Does it stop there? By no means. It informs what we offer, flowing from the inside out. Let's offer the Lord our honest worship, from the truth of where we are today. He doesn't need us to pretend. He wants our honest connection, and we don't have to fear his reception. He already knows our hearts. Let's honor him by coming to him as we are and offering him what we have right here and now.

Lord, here I am. I offer you my open heart as it is. You are worthy of my worship, no matter how I feel.

INSPIRED

May the Lord Jesus Christ and our Father God, who loved us and in his wonderful grace gave us eternal comfort and a beautiful hope that cannot fail, encourage your hearts and inspire you with strength to always do and speak what is good and beautiful in his eyes.

2 THESSALONIANS 2:16-17 TPT

The Lord loves you more than you can imagine. His wonderful grace offers all the comfort you need in any given moment. The beautiful hope of his promises will never fail.

Take today's verse as a blessing for the year that is about to dawn. Though it may be a simple turning of the calendar page, it is also a chance for a fresh start. It is another year of God's goodness, for his goodness never fails. Be inspired to continue walking in his ways and know the power of doing what is good and beautiful in his eyes.

Lord Jesus, thank you for always going with me into new spaces, times, and seasons. I will follow you into what you have for me, knowing you are good. I say yes to you again.